EIGHT MODERN PLAYS

AUTHORITATIVE TEXTS
BACKGROUNDS
CRITICISM

SECOND EDITION

A NORTON CRITICAL EDITION

EIGHT MODERN PLAYS

AUTHORITATIVE TEXTS OF

THE WILD DUCK · *THREE SISTERS*
CANDIDA · *THE GHOST SONATA*
SIX CHARACTERS IN SEARCH OF AN AUTHOR
LONG DAY'S JOURNEY INTO NIGHT
MOTHER COURAGE AND HER CHILDREN
HAPPY DAYS

BACKGROUNDS AND CRITICISM
SECOND EDITION

Edited by

ANTHONY CAPUTI

CORNELL UNIVERSITY

W · W · NORTON & COMPANY · *New York* · *London*

English translation of *Six Characters in Search of an Author* by Luigi Pirandello
Copyright © 1991 by Anthony Caputi.

Eight Modern Plays is the second edition of *Modern Drama* published by W. W.
Norton & Company, Inc., in 1966.

Printed in the United States of America.

The text of this book is composed in Electra, with the display set in
Bernhard Modern. Composition by PennSet, Inc.
Book design by Antonina Krass.

Library of Congress Cataloging-in-Publication Data
Eight modern plays : authoritative texts, backgrounds, criticism /
edited by Anthony Caputi. — 2nd ed.
p.   cm. — (A Norton critical edition)
1. Drama—19th century. 2. Drama—20th century. I. Caputi,
Anthony Francis, 1924–
PN6112.M534   1991
808.82′034—dc20   89-72171
ISBN 0-393-96015-3
W. W. Norton & Company, Inc., 500 Fifth Avenue, New York, N.Y. 10110
W. W. Norton & Company, Ltd., 10 Coptic Street, London WC1A 1PU
2 3 4 5 6 7 8 9 0

Contents

Foreword

Modern drama, as any list of recent publications will tell you, is an anthologist's heaven. Its wealth of playwrights and plays, its great variety of modes and styles, and its lack of hierarchical categories and time-sanctioned judgments permit excesses of ingenuity and whimsy unknown in other periods of dramatic history. That this should be so is understandable. Even after a full century what continues to be called modern drama is still too much with us for any anthologist to be absolutely certain that this play is not important while that one is, or that this playwright is an innovator of the order of Sophocles while that one is distinctly a third-rate hack. Because it is all so relevant to *us*, and because it is still a living drama whose meaning is obscure because its story is incomplete, we cannot view it as we do, rightly or wrongly, the ages of Pericles or Elizabeth I. With few reliable guidelines and a superabundance of playwrights, critics, theater historians, and amateur experts all hotly disputing the major and minor classifications, we continue to look and to read and to attempt discriminations, conscious that, though our efforts may be tentative, we have no choice but to make them.

Yet a hundred years of study and criticism have not been in vain; they have furnished a number of distinctions and discriminations about the broad movement of modern drama and about the playwrights who have set the outlines of that movement. Slowly but steadily a body of opinion has emerged, which, though it scarcely tells all and predicts almost nothing, has provided a matrix for inquiry and understanding that most scholars and critics accept without protest. The trick for them, and perhaps even more notably for teachers of drama, is to accept and use this way of describing modern drama so that its provisional orderliness illuminates the richness of the subject but does not blind readers and students to its complexity.

It has been my purpose in this collection to do just that: to represent the broad outline of modern drama in the work of those playwrights who, critics and scholars agree, best define it. For each playwright I have tried to choose a play both distinguished in its own right and exemplary of the special contribution made by the playwright on playwriting as he found it. In each case, moreover, I have chosen plays that in my personal experience have proven themselves both accessible and of deep and enduring interest to students. The supporting materials by the playwrights and the essays by diverse hands comprise a mixture of well-known pieces, little-known pieces, and new work; they have been selected to assist, to provoke, to extend, and to enrich the reading of the plays.

Certain of the essays, in fact, declare more explicitly than the plays themselves what has been the second, though no less important principle governing this book. Since no collection of modern plays can avoid being an anthology of documents illustrative of what social critics solemnly call the modern condition, I have deliberately attempted here to present plays and supporting writings that supply material for that study even as they establish the facts of literary and dramatic history. In my opinion, modern drama embodies the peculiar tension, discord, hilarity, and hysteria of the twentieth century with an integrity, or call it all-at-onceness, impossible in its sister genres, for in the unusual fullness of the dramatic image we approach the special quality of contemporary life with a rare immediacy. Certainly among the playwrights represented here several have regularly been accorded major roles in the forging of modern sensibility. It is hoped, in any case, that instructors and students will find in these materials the wherewithal to illuminate both the literary and the cultural achievements of modern drama.

ANTHONY CAPUTI

On Reading Modern Plays

Reading modern plays shares with the reading of plays from any historical period the problem of texts not primarily created to be read. Plays are not, after all, poems or novels: they do not communicate initially and essentially by words, but by actions, by way of actors doing and saying things, a synthesis of visual and auditory resources of which the words are only one. Reading the plays of any period, then, is inevitably a highly creative process by which the reader tries to construct from the verbal text as much as possible of the imagery of actors moving and speaking within a particular theatrical space. Reading modern plays differs from this general activity only to the extent that modern drama works through the languages of dramatic action peculiar to our time.

Of the psychological process by which readers transvalue the words on the page into scenes and series of scenes in the theaters of the mind we know very little. We read, and with the help of imagination and knowledge the images form, breathe, and develop the power to move us. Criticism can be useful to us because it can guide the imagination and supply the knowledge necessary to it, but criticism does not so much explain the creative process of reading as it stimulates it. It is always partial and imperfect because it imposes a critical activity on a creative one; it is valuable to the extent that it assists the reader, by this in some respects false imposition, to a heightened and enriched order of reading.

In reading plays, then, we begin by accepting the premises of criticism: that a play is an ordered whole, a thing constructed to move a beholder in a reasonably circumscribed way. Moreover, the parts of that whole function together, dovetailing into it according to principles that are susceptible to rational analysis. Now these premises are useful, even when accompanied by an awareness that playwrights undoubtedly often work by methods other than rational ones, because only by accepting them can the reader assemble or reassemble the structure of a dramatic action with some assurance that it is a structure and not a chaos. Only in this way can the reader bring to his or her reading a structure and system that will open new avenues of illumination and insight. Having accepted these premises, in any case, the reader is then in a position to read the play as a complex of mutually illuminating artistic decisions, a structure of choices made by the playwright for the purpose of fashioning a particular dramatic action. By moving back and forth from the words or facts of the text to this gradually widening structure of decisions the reader will construct not merely an explanation for the facts, but a line of artistic reasoning that, theoretically, sharpens and enriches his or her perception of the dramatic action. It is futile to point out that the artistic reasoning devolved may have little to do with the actual process by which the playwright designed the work; it has served its purpose if it activates the play and causes it to release its power in a way consistent with the most honest and rigorous thought that the reader can bring to bear.

Reading plays, therefore, can be seen as a process by which the words or facts of the text are converted into animate images, which, in turn, are focused, related to each other, and organized as a totality governed by a pervasive artistic rationale. As a process it is emphatically exploratory: it never exhausts itself, and it always involves a back-and-forth movement between specific questions rooted in fact and controlling rationale. To a large extent it consists of asking proper questions. In *Oedipus Rex* why has Sophocles chosen to conclude his play, not with Oedipus' lamentation after he has gouged out his eyes, but with his scene with his daughters as he prepares to go into exile? In *Hamlet* why has Shakespeare decided to have Ophelia report Hamlet's visit to her bedroom rather than to have them play the scene? In *Long Day's Journey into Night* why has Eugene O'Neill carefully contrived a round robin of colloquies among the members of the Tyrone family? Each of these questions can be formulated in terms of perfectly obvious indications in the verbal text, yet each is at the same time a part of a whole battery of questions that, as they are answered, lead to a progressively fuller conception of what the peculiar nature of this or that dramatic action is.

In the interests of bringing some clarity and system to an activity that can never be pellucid we might identify three distinct kinds or orders of artistic decision in the making of plays. First there is that order of decision that concerns the material out of which the dramatic action is fashioned. Why, it is important to ask, has the playwright chosen to make an action out of this particular story? What is there in its outline, what is there about its characters, what is there about the relationships among its characters that make these materials suitable to his purposes? Why in *Oedipus Rex* the story of Oedipus and not Creon? Why in *Hamlet* the story of a prince who cannot carry out what he sees to be a just revenge? Why in *Three Sisters* the story of three sisters rather than brothers? These are not questions that can be answered in isolation, of course; they must be considered with others and must be related to others. Why does Ophelia have this particular character rather than another? Why in the *Three Sisters* has Chekhov given Andrey this particular combination of strengths and weaknesses and not another? Because these questions concern the basic materials of the play, the substance from which it is formed, the artistic decisions involved might usefully be called substantial decisions.

Somewhat less general and far-reaching is a second order of decision, which concerns the primary shaping of the play. In other words, once the materials or substance have been selected (and it bears repeating that we are constructing a temporal sequence that is useful to the critic-reader but that may have very little to do with the actual composition of the play), what decisions best explain the fundamental shape imposed on these materials? Why has Sophocles chosen to begin his play where he has rather than earlier or later in the story? Why has he represented this scene and reported that one? Why has Shakespeare chosen to treat the events of *Hamlet* in the particular scale and with these proportions? Why has so much time been given to Hamlet's internal debate and, relatively speaking, so little to his love affair with Ophelia? Why in *Henry IV* has Pirandello decided not to reveal Henry's "cure" to the audience until toward the end of act 2? Because these questions probe decisions that we assume conferred a primary shape on the play, because they determined what was to be represented, in what order the various events were to be represented, and in what scale and proportion they were to be represented, the decisions might be called representational decisions.

Finally, there is a third order of decision, which concerns the peculiar focus accorded to a dramatic action. Beyond the decisions that explain why these particular materials have been selected and why they have been shaped to present this basic dramatic image, there is a host of more limited decisions that sharpen particular qualities, highlight particular issues, embolden particular elements, in other words, that focus the action and its peculiar power. Why has Sophocles emphasized blindness in *Oedipus Rex*? Why has Shakespeare encouraged us to compare Hamlet, Laertes, and Fortinbras by putting them in analogous positions? Why has Ibsen entitled his play *The Wild Duck*? This order of decision comprehends all those details of technique that, though they rarely do more than confer a peculiar finish on a play, usually proceed from its fundamental controling intentions. For convenience they might be called focusing decisions, though the term scarcely does justice to their variety.

Taken together, these artistic decisions constitute a structure or system that criticism creates for the purpose of assisting readers in their creation, or more properly re-creation, of the artistic totality of the play. As they read, they probe to construct, isolate to combine, reason to use their imagination the more effectively. In reading plays their aim is to set on the imaginary stage of their minds the most authoritative, most complete version of the dramatic imagery of actors moving and speaking in a particular theatrical space that they can derive form the words on the page.

This way of reading plays, of course, is never quite the same for all plays, and it is notably different for plays from different traditions. Each of the decisions that goes into the making of a play is inevitably conditioned by the special theatrical bias, the special dramatic style, and the special ambience of social, political, and religious values of the historical period in which the play was written. Sophocles could not write a Shakespearean play just as Shakespeare could not write a Sophoclean play: each approached the act of creating for the theater having been formed as a playwright by the physical theaters, the modes of presentation, the theatrical conventions, and the norms of dramatic composition of his time. If readers of plays are to deal fairly with the works of different historical periods, they must incorporate into the creative process of reading as much knowledge as they can recover of the cultural and dramatic history that they honestly feel contributed to the shaping of the play. Their re-creation of the play by way of this always tentative construction of the system of its governing artistic decisions must be filtered through and qualified by this knowledge. Needless to say, the task is always rendered more difficult by gaps in our knowledge: to the extent that we do not know everything about the physical stage in Shakespeare's age, about the style of playing practiced by his actorcolleagues, and about the specific cultural context in which his plays were written and produced—to that extent, it is probably fair to say, we can never know any Shakespearean play definitively. But we do the best we can with the knowledge that the effort is eminently worth making and that printed texts are as close as we are ever likely to come to many of the dramatic masterpieces of our tradition.

Reading modern plays is in many respects a vastly less complicated matter. Although the process of transvaluing the words on the page into the imagery of actors in motion is much the same, we do not have to read deeply in linguistic history to understand the words, in stage history to understand the modes of production, or in cultural history to understand the forces that drive our dramatists. Because the plays derive from our tradition, or from a tradition very close to our own, we come to them with a readiness that we must labor long to duplicate for great plays of the past.

Yet the advantages offered by modern plays must not be exaggerated, for their accessibility is deceptive. To begin with, modern drama embraces tremendous diversity. Unlike their predecessors, modern playwrights range freely over dramatic history, adapting the resources of diverse traditions to their purposes and experimenting with an abandon that makes for unparalleled variety. As readers and theater-goers, we are, unfortunately, ill-prepared for that variety. Typically, we have been introduced to drama by way of films, television plays, and a limited number of experiences in the theater, with the result that we have grown accustomed to plays in the realistic style of Arthur Miller's *All My Sons* or Tennessee Williams's *Night of the Iguana*. Such works present us with relatively familiar actions and worlds and for the most part give little difficulty; moreover, because of them we have been prompted to think, mistakenly, that the realistic mode of presentation is the fundamental language of the theater. It is small wonder, then, that even the most sophisticated readers are frequently bewildered and baffled by that extensive part of modern drama that is nonrealistic, by the radical departures from illusionism to be met in the Surrealists, Expressionists, the dramatists of the Theater of the Absurd, the Performance Theater of the 1960s and 1970s, and the various forms of so-called Post-Modernist theater now. The orientation toward theater that the deeply ingrained tradition of realism encourages us to, with some gains for us, surely, as far as realistic plays go, impedes in us a readiness to deal with that important part of modern drama written in nonrealistic modes.

Moreover, it is possible to argue that our familiarity with realism also entails disadvantages for reading and seeing plays of that kind. Because realism as a way of approaching experience, as a way of looking at the world and thinking about it, is so profoundly embedded in twentieth-century experience, we seldom stop to think that as a movement in art, letters, and, in general, in cultural history, it too was the result of a complicated historical process: it had its beginnings, it had its pioneers, and it underwent various modifications; it was part of that changing fabric of values that steadily conditioned playwrights to formulate new artistic intentions and to search for new solutions to their artistic problems. To see realism and the particular works that derive from it fairly, we must see it with a perspective that familiarity makes difficult for us.

Yet if the problems of reading realistic plays are more deceptive, they are no more difficult than those involved in reading other kinds of modern plays. With every modern play the reader must develop and maintain a perspective on the modern world, on everything that has prompted the playwright to formulate this rather than that artistic purpose, that has led him or her to this rather than that array of artistic decisions. Reading modern plays, accordingly, requires an awareness of the historical process by which our world became what it is, as well as of the manifold shifts in subject matter, forms, and intention by which modern drama became what it is. It requires, in other words, a study as extensive as possible of the history of modern sensibility, of, roughly, the hundred years of moral and psychological crises that have brought us to the last decade of the twentieth century.

Fortunately, modern drama provides abundant evidence for such a study, and, in fact, it is hoped that the plays and essays included in this collection will lend themselves to that purpose. Because of the complexity of the subject, however, no collection of the scope of this one could be adequately illustrative, just as no essay of the scope of the present one could be definitive in its analysis. The intention is to illustrate broadly the principal directions of modern drama and the principal conditions in the modern era that have prompted dramatists to take these directions.

Some time ago John Gassner provided a highly useful distinction for breaking down the multiplicity of forms to be met in modern drama in his *Form and Idea in Modern Theatre*, where he proposed that all roughly contemporary dramatic practice can be generally comprehended under the headings "realism" and "theatricalism." By realism in the theater, of course, he meant that practice of creating or attempting to create illusions of real life on the stage. To understand this important stream in modern theatrical practice, however, we must first see that realism, more broadly considered, was a far-reaching movement in art, politics, religion, and literature that emerged in the last half of the nineteenth century to produce an essentially new, modern way of looking at the world. It might be said, very generally, that with the waning of the closed, orderly world that had been the basis of medieval and much of Renaissance civilization, realism provided a way of conceiving of a new one, more particularly a new way of apprehending and thinking about experience, of making sense of it or of trying to make sense of it.

This distinctive way of approaching the external world can be traced, of course, to many sources, but preeminent among its historical causes was the rise of science and of scientific habits of thought. In the work of Descartes and his fellow pioneers in the seventeenth century the foundations for modern science and for its distinctive approach to truth were laid. Descartes' *Discourse on Method* (1637) is important not only for its emphasis on method, but also for its emphasis on material evidence and the importance of individual experience. After Descartes, again very broadly speaking, truth was to be derived from what was knowable in sensuous terms, both from what could be measured (the material world) and from what could be experienced (the individual life). The result was a new way of relating human beings to their physical surroundings and a new interest in the particular, material world, the consequences of which for traditional beliefs and material and technological developments are too commonplace to rehearse.

By the nineteenth century, of course, the world was quite different from that of Descartes: it was a world with an urban emphasis, with vastly improved technical and industrial means, and with the habit of formulating its problems and of contriving solutions for them in this new way. It is useful to remember that this was the century of Charles Darwin, Karl Marx, Herbert Spencer, and John Stuart Mill, all men prone to look to material fact for their evidence. This was a century, moreover, dominated by that natural son of science, the idea of progress, the belief that physical nature and human nature could be mastered in man's best interests, a belief, it should be added, that at that time, as in our own, was supported by unprecedented changes and apparent improvements in all quarters of life.

The world of letters responded to this movement with most alacrity, not in the theater nor in poetry, but in that form that owes most to this way of approaching experience, the novel. In the theater the progress of realism was slow and discontinuous, and, indeed, the complete story of its emergence in the nineteenth century is too chaotic to tell here. We see signs of its emergence in the popularity of the Well-made Play,

an ingeniously designed dramatic structure that put a premium on prob-
ability of a rather superficial sort, and the sporadic attention to authentic
backgrounds and costumes in scattered productions in England and
France. But all this did little more than prepare the scene for Emile
Zola and the vigorous efforts made toward the end of the century to
produce a revolution in the theater. Zola, already known through his
novels as a champion of that specialized form of realism called naturalism, is chiefly to be credited with articulating the theory of dramatic
realism. In his "Preface" to *Thérèse Raquin* (1873) he claimed that "the
experimental and scientific spirit of the century [would] enter the domain
of the drama," that he had "invented a new formula, namely that there
must be no more formulas." Once Zola had prepared the way, it was
inevitable that an artist from the theater should come forward to take
up his challenge, and one soon did in the improbable figure of an
employee of the Paris Gas Co., André Antoine. With the opening on
March 30, 1887, of Antoine's Théâtre Libre, as Mordecai Gorelik puts
it, "the Baroque ideal of theatrical splendor [went] down forever, having
outlived its usefulness"[1] and the tradition of dramatic realism was put
on a secure footing. Although always a small, experimental theater, the
Théâtre Libre brought realism to the fore and by way of its productions
established its method, encouraged playwrights to practice it and introduced the work of some of them, and prompted the foundation of a
number of similarly dedicated "free" theaters in other European capitals.

The importance of these theaters cannot be too greatly stressed. They
meant the establishment of standards of play-writing and of play production that constitute the nucleus of the realistic tradition in the theater.
At the center of this activity was the purpose to present an objective,
analytic picture of the world, to present a slice of life that candidly
exposed what were confidently taken to be the "facts" of experience. To
carry out this aim, special techniques were devised. The tradition of
elocutionary acting was quickly outmoded by an acting style that emphasized lifelike appearance and behavior, a style most clearly seen in
the work of Constantin Stanislavsky at the Moscow Art Theatre and in
his present-day American disciples, the "Method" actors. The convention of painted scenery and selected properties was replaced by the ideal
of exact reproduction in stage settings: the stage set became an eviron-
ment bearing a meaningful relation to the action it contained. On such
a stage the stage curtain became a fourth wall, an entry to a magic world
of illusion, and the ideal of illusionism—the aim to create and sustain
the illusion that what is being seen is a segment of overseen reality—
became supreme.

Since 1890 dramatic realism has provided the fundamental idiom for
the theater in the West. We have seen it undergo many modifications,
and we have seen it watered down in such a way that illusion has often

1. *New Theatres for Old* (New York, 1957) 79.

been contrived for illusion's sake and the exploratory and critical emphasis of its pioneers has been blurred in favor of a kind of superficial snapshot-taking, as if a snapshot were in itself explanatory. To do justice, then, to the fervor and dedication with which the movement was launched and to its important practitioners, we must keep firmly in view the seriousness of its basic aims and the passion with which its pioneers sought to lay surfaces bare so as to divest fact of its incrustations and penetrate to something on which solid structures could be built.

HENRIK IBSEN (1828–1906) has sometimes been called the Father of Modern Drama probably because he was the first important playwright to realize in practice the profound possibilites of dramatic realism. Yet, though a bias for social criticism is to be found in even his earliest work, it was not until Ibsen left Norway that he entered upon the period of social problem plays in which he perfected the realistic prose form for which he subsequently became famous. These are the plays in which he primarily focused on society and in which he usually found more solidity and honesty in a vigorous individual conscience than in society's rules. This work includes plays like *The League of Youth, Pillars of Society, A Doll's House, Ghosts,* and *An Enemy of the People,* plays that have been called "dramas of retrospective analysis" because they begin in the midst of a crisis and move forward in time while looking back to reconstruct and reinterpret the past in terms of present conditions.

By easy stages this work led Ibsen to an increasing interest in the possibility that perhaps, after all, absolute truth could not be found anywhere, that all truth was relative; and to accommodate this more intricate and elusive subject, he modified the earlier formula to allow for elaborate character analysis. In his next plays, which include *The Wild Duck, Rosmersholm,* and *Hedda Gabler,* he was prompted to an increasing use of metaphoric and symbolistic devices; with them he marked out new possibilities for realistic drama both in his combination of realistic and poetic technique and in the new subjects that he continuously explored. Yet despite his technical penchant toward the end of his career for symbol and metaphor, he remained in a very important sense a realist to the core. His approach to the human condition, his way of assembling evidence, and his assumptions about how it should be regarded and how conclusions should be derived from it, were essentially those of a scientific, critical temperament. He differed from and surpassed those of like temperament chiefly in the rigorous honesty that prompted him to admit that this approach to experience frequently enabled him to raise questions that he could not answer.

In Russia, meantime, ANTON CHEKHOV (1860–1904) was taking the resources of realism in another direction. A doctor by profession, Chekhov won quick success as a writer of short stories, but at first had considerable difficulty as a playwright. His early failures were chiefly the result of the elusive dramatic form he gradually perfected, a form that superficially resembles the work of Ibsen, but that was sufficiently different to require a special style of playing that no company in Russia could provide until the Moscow Art Theatre succeeded with the famous production of *The Sea Gull* in 1898.

Chekhov's plays are certainly nothing if not realistic: what could be truer to life than his depiction of households milling about aimlessly and talking about apparently nothing? But the usual charge that in his plays nothing happens is a misleading exaggeration. Characteristically, Chekhov designed actions in which very little in the way of outward incident is represented, but in which his characters are revealed between the big events of their lives, as they are waiting to go into dinner or while they are sitting around after dinner musing about the past and their wasted youths. Chekhov was difficult for his contemporaries because of this new emphasis: he typically chose to de-emphasize incident in the interests of tracing character and the motions of character through the ebb and flow of trivial conversation. In this way he was able in plays like *Uncle Vanya*, *Three Sisters*, and *The Cherry Orchard* to animate profound strains of vitality in his characters and to throw into relief, not the usual linear development of the action from event to event, but a kind of spatial pattern, inward into the characters rooted in their situation and outward into the implications of the relatively unchanging situation. Moreover, he was able to manage through the imagery of characters doing very little and, though talking a great deal, saying very little a delicate stage-poetry of tremendous power. Although critics might say that in Chekhov's plays nothing happens, none, or at least few, would argue that they are about nothing: somehow he makes the "nothing" of his actions a nothing that has to do with everything.

GEORGE BERNARD SHAW (1856–1950), meanwhile saw still other dramatic possibilities in the program of realism. Although profoundly influenced by Ibsen at the outset, Shaw quickly fashioned from the resources of realism a dramatic form that gave the fullest possible expression to his critical cast of mind and then continued to modify this form during a long life and career. In his early plays, among which are some of his best known, like *Arms and the Man* and *Candida*, he characteristically devised an action that superficially looked like a conventional melodrama, or military romance, or domestic comedy, and then proceeded to undermine it from within in such a way as to upend the traditional assumptions on which the form was based and the traditional attitudes held by most of the characters contained by it. Shaw's aim was to call values into question, to challenge orthodoxies, to explode unexamined assumptions, and in this way to liberate society from obsolescence so that foundations for a new society could be laid. He was frankly didactic, with the artistic consequence that his plays are replete with witty and incisive discussions of issues of all kinds, discussions that gradually grew longer as Shaw grew older until he coined the phrase "the discussion play." But he was always, at bottom, a comic artist, one who saw the limitations of even his most intelligent, most Shavian characters, and the inevitable comedy of the human mind applying itself to the intractable energy of life.

In the work of Shaw, Chekhov, and Ibsen, at any rate, the principal directions of realism were marked out and its principal structural formulae were set forth. Subsequent playwrights in this tradition were to combine, modify, and neglect these precedents in more ways than can be quickly summarized, but they were never—and still are not—entirely free of them. With the work of these pioneers the basic tradition of modern drama was established.

Yet even during the early, most zealous years of the realistic movement, the forces of reaction were already at work. From the beginning certain men of letters and men of the theater had challenged the realist program, and they struck at the very heart of its theory by arguing that the outer world of facts and things, the backgrounds so laboriously recreated, the environments so methodically analyzed, count for nothing. Reality, in their view, was not to be found by studying the material world, but by knowing the inner world, how we feel about the facts, the things and the backgrounds. Mordecai Gorelik has summarized their rebellion in a striking paragraph:

> Do not bring on the stage your carcass of reality. . . . Do not exhibit your vanloads of bricabrac, your butcher shops with real meat, your restaurant walls of cement and tile, your streets paved with real cobblestones. These collections of materials do not tell us the nature of the world; rather they confess your inability to define the nature of the world. If you really wish to give us an illusion of life, you must seize upon the essence of life. Forget the body; give us the soul.[2]

This passage crystallizes the cry of a diverse group of dissenters that from the turn of the century to the present can usefully be gathered under the heading of "theatricalists." The theatricalist movement can be conveniently traced to the production at Paul Fort's Théâtre de l'Art in Paris in 1896 of Alfred Jarry's grotesque play *Ubu-roi*.

Theatricalism in all its historical manifestations, including, among others, Surrealism, Expressionism, and Performance Theater, insists on a radically different use of the theater from that of realism and derives from a vastly different set of assumptions. Its anti-illusionistic bias is tied firmly to the belief that the realists have betrayed the essence of theater by using it to create illusions. By banishing or attempting to banish stage conventions, those shared understandings between performers and spectators by which both accept that a play is a highly artificial and special kind of image of life, the realists have tried to make the theater like life. But the theater is not and should not be like life, the theatricalists insist; it has its own highly specialized and extravagantly colorful and dynamic

2. *New Theatres for Old* 197.

resources, which an exaggerated attention to the certainty of realistic surfaces nullifies.

Much of the initial impulse and fundamental theory for the theatricalists derived from the Symbolist movement in letters at the end of the nineteenth century. Very simply stated, the aim of the Symbolists was to produce in their work analogues to states of being, in poetry, for example, to create verbal analogues to highly complex states of mind and spirit, to use language as sound is used in music to represent a way of feeling about the world. In the theater a key figure in this movement was Richard Wagner (1813–83). Wagner's ambition was to synthesize the arts of poetry, drama, and music in his operas so that the result— the total imagery of music, words, and action—could move an audience to states of feeling and awareness inaccessible by mere reason. The total imagery of Wagner's theater, unified, as it was, by musical principles, was to communicate as only art in its highest reaches can. Translated into theatrical terms, this led to Jean Cocteau's famous distinction between poetry *of* the theater, that poetry which results from an imaginative use of theatrical resources, and poetry *in* the theater, mere verse in the theater.

It was probably inevitable that the leaders of this movement would be, particularly in the early years, scene designers and directors. Building on its premise that the imagery of the theater should make for a peculiar unity, a special language of expression, men like Gordon Craig, Georg Fuchs, and Adolph Appia produced a revolution in scene design, stage lighting, and theater esthetics. Different phases and aspects of the movement go by different names—"the New Stagecraft," "Presentational Staging," "Surrealism," "Expressionism," etc.—but essentially all were governed by the purpose of using theatrical imagery to represent inward conditions. With the theory, moreover, came a new group of theaters: Paul Fort's Théâtre de l'Art was established in 1891, the Munich Artists' Theatre in 1908, and Jacques Copeau's Théâtre du Vieux Colombier in 1913. Russia, where very important work in the realistic mode was being done at the Moscow Art Theatre, saw the most extreme theatricalist experimentation in the work of defectors from that theater.

But developments in theatrical technique alone do not provide a sufficient background for understanding theatricalism any more than they do for understanding realism. The leaders in both movements were deeply interested in the theater, it is true, but they were also interested in the world and in what was happening to the world and themselves. Both theatricalism and realism represent important responses or reactions to the world of the nineteenth century with which the leaders of these respective movements quite consciously saw themselves to be breaking. With the work of Ibsen, Chekhov, Shaw, August Strindberg, and Jarry a new outlook was emerging, a new conception of man, a new idea of his powers and limitations, a new image of his world and of his relations to it.

Basic to this outlook was the profound sense that the past was discontinuous with the present, that an unbridgeable abyss separated modern man from his forbears. Although many of the developments in science and thought that are summoned to account for this abyss had emerged in the nineteenth century, the character and quality of life in that century seem not to have been deeply affected by them. Despite and, indeed, in part because of men like Darwin and Marx, a sovereign optimism was firmly imbedded in much nineteenth-century activity—public, private, and artistic. The Victorians, for example, grandly committed to their high mission in life, still felt that human character was a thing human beings could do something about and that it was the highest of human responsibilites to cultivate it. But as the evidence began to come in to suggest that the millennium was not going to appear as quickly as some had thought it would, as new ideas began to have implications for human beings that no one had foreseen, as institutions of all kinds began to teeter under the pressure of these ideas, as industrialization and urbanization began to produce a variety of inner and outer horrors that no one had predicted, and as society scrambled away from the world it had known and in directions that it realized it knew less and less about, a new insecurity was born. Conditioned in the twentieth century by two world wars, a great depression, and a general intensification of the malaise that has followed from the increasingly dehumanized mechanization of society, this insecurity has compounded until at its worst men have come to feel estranged from all but material values, to feel themselves involved in and even committed to a world they do not understand or want.

Joseph Wood Krutch has argued in *"Modernism" in the Modern Theatre* that the essential effect of all these developments was that man's fate was taken out of his hands. Darwin not only deprived man of his divine birthright; he also posited a view of development and change that made adaptation and not moral will the chief determinant in life. Marx insisted that not only man and other organisms were subject to laws that had nothing to do with man's highest ideals for himself, but institutions and societies as well were so governed—socieities by a law of class warfare that was working itself out whatever men as individuals might wish. Add to this the accumulating findings of the new disciplines of anthropology and sociology, findings that made perfectly clear that men in other places had built societies in quite different ways from ours, and it becomes clear why man became such a dimished creature. Truth had become a relative thing, not an absolute and unchanging reality; at best it was a statement that satisfied an individual or a group at a certain time and in a certain place. Man had become a baffled creature, as Matthew Arnold puts it, "Wandering between two worlds, one dead, / The other powerless to be born."

Of the many convulsions in thought and feeling that led to what is called modernism, however, probably none has had more profound effects on the world of letters and the theater than the new psychology. Traditionally man had been viewed as a fallen but essentially rational creature; each man was presumed to have a distinctive moral character propelled by a moral will that was an expression of that character. But under the onslaughts of the new psychology man gradually became less and less a rational creature and more and more an irrational one, a creature determined by heredity and environment, a bundle of drives, instincts, and nonrational predispositions. One of the consequences of this change was that much that tradition had claimed as evidence of man's greatness and dignity became evidence of personal adjustments or maladjustments. Honor, heroism, cowardice, self-sacrifice, sin, and even love began to be reinterpreted as the peculiar products of particular environments. Perhaps most devastating of all, the traditional concept of character, that belief according to which we all have a reasonably integrated, unique identity with a history and continuity of its own, began to dissolve as the idea grew that man, any man, is substantially an anthology of roles to be played. Beset by an erosive sense of relativity in all things, twentieth-century man capitulated to the sense of estrangement, isolation, fragmentation, and incoherence so readily discovered in contemporary experience.

It is not surprising that playwrights primarily interested in this malaise of spirit should be drawn to theatricalist forms and should be in the fore of theatricalist experimentation. Most of the celebrated "isms" of the twentieth century trace to attempts to discover and represent the quality and character of modern experience and only secondarily to an attempt to comment on it; they break into discrete submovements largely because each emphasizes different clusters of qualities and favors different aspects of that experience. Dadism sought to surprise and disturb by means of ostensibly anarchic combinations of elements, in sculpture, for example, to shock the observer by means of its fur-lined coffeecups and disengaged toilet seats into a kind of defiant integrity of response. More important historically, Surrealism sought to represent the processes of thought and feeling as they are actually experienced in the chaos that is the inner life of modern man—disjointed, grotesque, vaguely nightmarish, and sometimes extremely comic. Both movements were curiously infertile in the theater in that they produced few plays of any consequence, but very important in that they vitalized the theatricalist tradition by marking out more daring, more sensational possibilities than had yet been tried. Expressionism, on the other hand, both influenced theater practice and produced a considerable number of important plays. Originally a term intended as the opposite of Impressionism, it emphasized states of feeling and, as a movement in the theater, took shape in the hands of German writers after the debacle of World War I. Feeling betrayed by civilized ideals—by the social and political rules and customs that suddenly had become obsolete for them, these writers argued that the only reality worth talking about, worth worrying about, worth beginning with in any attempt to build a world was the reality of how they felt; and all they knew for sure was their own terror, disgust, and bewilderment. They developed a mode of dramatic composition and production, accordingly, that communicated as full a sense as possible of their sense of outrage, a cry and a shriek almost always qualified by leftist political implications, and by way of the work of playwrights like Georg Kaiser and Ernst Toller and of directors like Erwin Piscator they soon made their influence felt throughout the world of Western theater.

Actually, much of this work and many of the "isms" that were lovingly articulated and passionately defended had been strangely and brilliantly anticipated by AUGUST STRINDBERG (1849–1912). Strindberg wrote his first plays in the realist mode, and in *The Father* and *Miss Julie* achieved powerful studies of anguish. But the method of dramatic realism was never entirely adequate to his interest in the eternal ambiguity of character and human relationships or to his predilection to render a nigh hallucinatory sense of the world. With *The Dance of Death* and *To Damascus*, accordingly, he developed new dramatic forms, partly symbolic, partly allegorical, partly fantastic—forms that allowed him to represent fragments of character in different incarnations of the same character, to move freely through space and time, to crystalize in dramatic terms the insubstantiality, irrationality, and torment of experience. In these plays and plays like *A Dream Play* and *The Ghost Sonata* he anticipated much that was to become basic to Surrealist and Expressionist theory and practice. Out of the anguish of his personal life, in fact, he succeeded in clarifying possibilities for theatricalism that very few of his followers have been able to realize as fully as he did.

LUIGI PIRANDELLO (1867–1936) was, strictly speaking, neither a realist nor a theatricalist: he wrote plays in both traditions and he excelled in both. Yet perhaps more than any recent playwright he relentlessly searched the personal problems of instability and lostness in modern life. He achieved his first mature representation of what he came to see as the crisis in modern sensibility in *It Is So (If You Think It Is)*, a straightforward realistic play. Thereafter, though he continued to work in realism, he turned more and more frequently to theatricalist methods of his own devising to probe questions of identity, appearance, and reality, and the multiform life of consciousness as it attempts to bring order to a world of fictions. Many have felt that his sense of the chimeric quality of modern experience is most richly and effectively rendered in that group of plays which use the theater as a central metaphor, *Six Characters in Search of an Author*, *Tonight We Improvise*, and *Each in His Own Way*. His *Henry IV* is seen by others as the theater's classic treatment of the instability of character. Altogether, his vision of the modern world as less and less a place with firm reference points and more and more a hall of mirrors has provided the foundation for much of the work that follows him.

In America, which had not lagged far behind Europe in theatrical

developments but where theater was largely derivative through the first
two decades of the twentieth century, the first playwright to respond to
the invitations of realism and theatricalism with work of an important
order was EUGENE O'NEILL (1888–1953). O'Neill's career as a playwright
is a saga of experimentation. After a beginning that featured realistic
forms, he turned to Expressionism in *Emperor Jones* and *The Hairy Ape*
and then to a number of personalized theatricalist forms. But he never
abandoned realism entirely: he returned to it in mid-career in plays like
Desire Under the Elms and then again in such late plays as *Long Day's
Journey into Night* and *A Touch of the Poet*. O'Neill's work as a playwright represents an intensely personal search for coherence in what was
always for him the chaos of twentieth-century experience. Profoundly
influenced by psychoanalytic thought, he typically probed the inner life
of his characters, seeking at levels of only partial consciousness and in
the mysterious bonds and tensions of family life a structure or frame of
reference lacking in the public world. With his decisive emergence and
that of the group of directors, scene designers, actors, and playwrights
who were his contemporaries in the early 1920s, American drama was
at last put on a firm footing, and depths of dramatic energy and imagination were actuated that quickly led to an important dramatic literature.

Since the 1920s both realism and theatricalism have continued to
flourish. In Germany BERTOLT BRECHT (1898–1956) became the chief
theorist and practitioner of a form known as Epic Theater. With his
colleagues he shared with the realists the assumption that human reality
was the sum total of the conditions in which human beings live, but
broke with them on the issue of illusionism. In the same way he shared
the moral outrage of the early Expressionists, but broke with them because they sought to teach through emotion. Brecht insisted that it was
the responsibility of the theater to teach but to teach by engaging the
critical intelligence, by muting what he saw as the narcotics traffic of
emotionalism and prompting a detached, analytic spirit in the beholder.
Over three decades he refined the dramaturgy of Epic Theater in numerous theoretical essays and plays like *Man Is Man*, *The Good Woman
of Setzuan*, and *Mother Courage*. A refugee in America during World
War II, he returned to East Germany in 1949, where he founded the
Berliner Ensemble, a company trained in the special methods and techniques of this variation on theatricalism.

But the decades following World War II saw still further variations
on realism and theatricalism. In the 1950s a remarkable generation of
playwrights appeared who were for a time grouped under the heading
of Theatre of the Absurd. In fact, Eugène Ionesco, Arthur Adamov,
Jean Genet, and Harold Pinter, among others, share certain pessimistic
assumptions about the state of the contemporary world, but they are
notably dissimilar as makers of plays. Where Pinter has modified realism
to the needs of his chilling vision, Ionesco has been nonillusionistic
with a gleeful vengeance. And probably the most important of them,

SAMUEL BECKETT (1906–89), has been still more idiosyncratic. With characters speaking from garbage cans or large jars, or buried to the waist and then to the neck in sand, or reduced, visually, to a mouth fixed in the theater's darkness by an extremely tight spotlight, he has evolved a theatrical minimalism that focuses intently on a single image or metaphor. His chief subject is, like Pirandello's, consciousness and its efforts to hold off chaos, but consciousness limited largely to talking to itself or listening to its own echoes in a resonating void. Works like *Waiting for Godot* and *End Game* declare the conditions of this plight; later plays like *Krapp's Last Tape, Happy Days,* and *Rockabye* treat the voice of consciousness confronting itself.

Many of this brilliant generation are still alive and writing. Yet their example was not sufficient to discourage a still younger generation in the late 1960s and 1970s from developing yet another major departure for theatricalism in that artistic program that has come to be known as Performance Theater. Most notable in America in such groups as The Living Theatre and The Open Theatre, this movement turned away from modernism's emphasis on individual consciousness to celebrate group experience and to explore that experience, not in predetermined texts, but in actions assembled from actors' improvisations and extended discussions. The effort was to reinvigorate drama by returning it to its supposed essentials, the actors, and to exploit the full range of their creativity in epic spectacles with activist political leanings. At its best, in work like The Living Theatre's *Frankenstein* or The Open Theatre's *The Serpent,* it was extremely exciting, and even in its less impressive creations its theory seemed for a time to point to permanent changes in modern theater. Then with the breakup in the 1980s of its leading ensembles it receded quickly to the hinterlands of the avant-garde, not without influence, but without producing the results that its earlier vitality had promised. There it continues in the company of yet newer varieties of theatricalism, which go under the general heading of Post-modern Theater, to fill out the margins around the still vigorous streams of realism and theatricalism.

Thus reading modern plays requires an extraordinary readiness to adjust the imagination to a great many ways of assembling, combining, and animating theatrical resources. Clearly the more one can bring to this act of creative reading of an understanding of the important dramatic idioms to be encountered the closer one will approach the expressive totality that each of these plays is. Unfortunately, the problems of both comprehension and judgment are complicated by the fact that most traditional critical categories and terminologies are of very little help. Before 1850 much of dramatic writing could be usefully referred to such categories as tragedy or comedy; since then, and particularly in the twentieth century, these terms have little utility. Much of our serious dramatic writing cannot be called tragedy, for example, if that term is to have a reasonably precise meaning. In our century serious drama has splintered into a spectrum of forms, some vastly different from others in both method and effect, though all sharing the purpose of dealing with the gravest problems of our time. The readers of modern plays must take these new directions into account for what they are. And the problem is no less complex for comedy. Although a great deal has been written that is loosely called comedy, the term as it applies to works of the past can scarcely comprehend the multiplicity of forms designated by it in our time. All modern drama, it might be argued, is most fairly approached with an openness of outlook that allows the individual work to define its own character and quality.

The Texts of
THE PLAYS

HENRIK IBSEN

The Wild Duck†

Characters

HÅKON WERLE, *businessman, industrialist, etc.*
GREGERS WERLE, *his son*
OLD EKDAL
HJALMAR EKDAL, *his son, a photographer*
GINA EKDAL, HJALMAR's *wife*
HEDVIG, *their fourteen-year-old daughter*
MRS. SØRBY, *housekeeper to* HÅKON WERLE
RELLING, *a doctor*
MOLVIK, *a one-time theological student*
PETTERSEN, HÅKON WERLE's *servant*
GRÅBERG, HÅKON WERLE's *bookkeeper*
JENSEN, *a hired waiter*
A FLABBY GENTLEMAN
A THIN-HAIRED GENTLEMAN
A NEARSIGHTED GENTLEMAN
SIX OTHER GENTLEMEN, HÅKON WERLE's *guests*
SEVERAL HIRED SERVANTS

The first act takes place at the home of HÅKON WERLE; *the four following acts at* HJALMAR EKDAL's.

Act One

At HÅKON WERLE's *house. The study, expensively and comfortably appointed; bookcases and upholstered furniture; in the middle of the room a desk with papers and documents; subdued lighting from lamps with green shades. In the rear, open folding doors with portières drawn back*

† "The Wild Duck" by Henrik Ibsen, translated by Dounia B. Christiani, is reprinted from *The Wild Duck*, Henrik Ibsen, A Norton Critical Edition, translated and edited by Dounia B. Christiani, with the permission of W. W. Norton & Company, Inc. Copyright © 1968 by W. W. Norton & Company, Inc.

reveal a large, elegant drawing room, brilliantly lit by lamps and candelabra. Front right in study, a small baize-covered door to the office wing. Front left, a fireplace with glowing coal fire. Farther back on left wall, double doors to the dining room.

PETTERSEN, WERLE's *servant, in livery, and the hired waiter* JENSEN, *in black, are putting the study in order. In the drawing room, two or three other hired waiters are busy arranging for the guests and lighting more candles. The hum of conversation and the laughter of many voices can be heard from the dining room. Somebody taps his wine glass with a knife to signal he is about to make a speech; silence follows; a toast is proposed; cheers, and again the hum of conversation.*

PETTERSON [*lights a lamp on mantlepiece and sets shade on*]. Say, just listen to them, Jensen. That's the old man on his feet now, making a long toast to Mrs. Sørby.

JENSEN [*moving an armchair forward*]. Do you think it's true, what they're saying—that there's something between them?

PETTERSON. Devil knows.

JENSEN. I guess he must've been quite a guy in his day.

PETTERSON. Could be.

JENSEN. They say he's giving this dinner for his son.

PETTERSON. That's right. His son came home yesterday.

JENSEN. I never even knew old Werle had a son.

PETTERSON. Oh, yes, he's got a son all right. But you can't budge him from the works up at Højdal. He's never once been to town in all the years I've worked in this house.

A HIRED WAITER [*in doorway to drawing room*]. Say, Pettersen, there's an old fellow here . . .

PETTERSON [*grumbling*]. Oh damn. Who'd want to come at this time!

[OLD EKDAL *appears from the right in drawing room. He is dressed in a shabby overcoat with high collar, and woolen mittens. He has a stick and a fur cap in his hand; a parcel wrapped in brown paper under his arm. Wears a dirty reddish-brown wig and has a little gray mustache.*]

PETTERSON [*going toward him*]. Good God! What are you doing here?

EKDAL [*in doorway*]. Absolutely must get into the office, Pettersen.

PETTERSON. The office closed an hour ago, and . . .

EKDAL. They told me that at the gate, old man. But Gråberg's still in there. Be a good sport, Pettersen, and let me slip in through here. [*Points to baize door.*] Been this way before.

PETTERSON. Well, all right then, go ahead. [*Opens door.*] But just be sure you go out the right way. We've got company.

EKDAL. Know that—hm! Thanks, Pettersen, old chap! Good old friend. Thanks. [*Mutters to himself.*] Ass! [*Exit into office.*]

[PETTERSON *shuts door after him.*]

JENSEN. Does he work in the office?

PETTERSON. No, they just give him some copying to do at home when they're rushed. Not that he hasn't been a somebody in his day, old Ekdal.

JENSEN. Yes, he looked like there's something about him.

PETTERSON. Yes, indeed. I want you to know he was once a lieutenant.[1]

JENSEN. Go on—him a lieutenant!

PETTERSON. So help me, he was. But then he switched over to the timber business, or whatever it was. They say he's supposed to have played a dirty low-down trick on Mr. Werle once. The two of them were in on the Højdal works together then, you see. Oh, I know old Ekdal well, I do. Many's the time we've had a bitters and beer together down at Ma Eriksen's place.

JENSEN. Him? He sure can't have much money to throw around?

PETTERSON. Lord, Jensen, no. It's me that stands treat, naturally. Seems to me we owe a little respect to them that's come down in the world.

JENSEN. Oh, so he went bankrupt?

PETTERSON. Worse than that. He was sentenced to hard labor.

JENSEN. Hard labor!

PETTERSON. Anyway, he went to jail . . . [Listening.] Sh! They're getting up from the table now.

[The dining room doors are thrown open from within by two servants. MRS. SØRBY comes out, in conversation with two gentlemen. The rest of the party, among them HÅKON WERLE, follow shortly thereafter. Last come HJALMAR EKDAL and GREGERS WERLE.]

MRS. SØRBY [to the servant, in passing]. Pettersen, will you have the coffee served in the music room, please.

PETTERSON. Very good, Mrs. Sørby.

[She and the two gentlemen exit into drawing room and thence off to right. PETTERSON and JENSEN exit the same way.]

A FLABBY GENTLEMAN [to a THIN-HAIRED ONE]. Whew! What a dinner! That was something to tuck away!

THE THIN-HAIRED GENTLEMAN. Oh, with a little good will it's incredible what one can manage in three hours' time.

THE FLABBY GENTLEMAN. Yes, but afterwards, my dear sir, afterwards!

A THIRD GENTLEMAN. I hear the coffee and liqueurs are being served in the music room.

THE FLABBY GENTLEMAN. Splendid! Then perhaps Mrs. Sørby will play something for us.

THE THIN-HAIRED GENTLEMAN [in an undertone]. As long as Mrs. Sørby doesn't play something on us, one of these days.

---

1. When Pettersen tells the hired servant that old Ekdal was once a lieutenant, the response of the hired servant depends on the fact that the title indicated other than the kind of callow incompetent implied in our term "shavetail" [newly commissioned officer]. Officers of all ranks were generally members of distinguished and well-to-do families, sometimes younger sons who were destined for the army from birth. Understanding this about old Ekdal, we can better appreciate Hjalmar's sense of disgrace in the fallen fortunes of his family and his comments to Gregers about Gina, which imply that he had married beneath himself [Translator's note].

THE FLABBY GENTLEMAN. Oh, Berta wouldn't do that. She isn't the type
  to cast off her old friends.

  [*They laugh and exit into drawing room.*]

WERLE [*in a low, depressed tone*]. I don't think anybody noticed, Gregers.

GREGERS [*looks at him*]. Noticed what?

WERLE. Didn't you notice either?

GREGERS. What was I supposed to notice?

WERLE. We were thirteen at table.

GREGERS. Really? Were there thirteen?

WERLE [*with a glance toward* HJALMAR EKDAL]. As a rule we are always
  twelve. [*To the others.*] In here if you please, Gentlemen!

  [*He and the remaining guests, except* HJALMAR *and* GREGERS, *exit
  rear right.*]

HJALMAR [*who had heard what was said*]. You shouldn't have sent me
  that invitation, Gregers.

GREGERS. What! This party is supposed to be for *me*. And I'm not to
  invite my best, my only friend?

HJALMAR. But I don't think your father approves. I never come to this
  house any other time.

GREGERS. So I hear. But I had to see you and have a talk with you.
  Because I expect to be leaving again soon.—Yes, we two old school
  chums, we've certainly drifted far apart, haven't we. It must be sixteen-
  seventeen years since we saw each other.

HJALMAR. Is it as long as all that?

GREGERS. It is indeed. Well now, how are you getting along? You look
  fine. You've put on weight, you're even a bit stout.

HJALMAR. Hm, stout is hardly the word. But I suppose I do look a bit
  more of a man than I did in the old days.

GREGERS. Yes, you do. Outwardly you don't seem to have suffered much
  harm.

HJALMAR [*in a gloomy voice*]. But inwardly, Gregers! That's a different
  story, believe me. You know, of course, how terribly everything collapsed for me and mine since we last saw each other.

GREGERS [*more softly*]. How are things now with your father?

HJALMAR. Ah, let's not go into that. Naturally, my poor unfortunate
  father makes his home with me. He hasn't anyone else in the world
  to turn to. But look, it's so desperately hard for me to talk about this.—
  tell me instead how you've been, up there at the works.

GREGERS. Delightfully lonely, that's how I've been. Plenty of opportunity
  to think about all sorts of things.—Come over here; let's make ourselves comfortable.

  [*He sits down in an armchair by the fireplace and draws* HJALMAR
  into another beside him.]

HJALMAR [*with sentiment*]. I do want to thank you, all the same, Gregers,
  for asking me to your father's party. Because now I can see you don't
  have anything against me anymore.

GREGERS [*in surprise*]. Whatever gave you the idea I had anything against you?

HJALMAR. Why, you did have, you know, the first few years.

GREGERS. What first few years?

HJALMAR. After the great disaster. And it was only natural that you should. After all, it was only by a hair that your father himself missed being dragged into that . . . oh, that terrible business!

GREGERS. And because of that I'm supposed to have a grudge against you? Whoever gave you that idea?

HJALMAR. I *know* you did, Gregers. Your father told me himself.

GREGERS [*startled*]. My father! Oh, I see. Hm.—Was that the reason I never heard from you afterwards—not a single word?

HJALMAR. Yes.

GREGERS. Not even when you went and became a photographer.

HJALMAR. Your father said it would be better not to write you about anything at all.

GREGERS [*absently*]. Well, well, maybe he was right, at that.—But tell me, Hjalmar—are you pretty well satisfied now with things as they are?

HJALMAR [*with a light sigh*]. Why, yes, on the whole I can't complain, really. At first, as you can imagine, it was all pretty strange. My whole world shot to pieces. But then, so was everything else. That terrible calamity of Father's—the shame and disgrace, Gregers . . .

GREGERS [*shaken*]. I know, I know.

HJALMAR. Of course I couldn't possibly think of continuing my studies. There wasn't a penny left. On the contrary, there were debts—mostly to your father, I believe.

GREGERS. Hm . . .

HJALMAR. Well, so I thought it best to make a clean break, you know—drop my old life and all my connections. It was your father especially who advised me to do that; and since he put himself out to be so helpful to me . . .

GREGERS. My father did?

HJALMAR. Yes, surely you know that? Where could *I* have got the money to learn photography and equip a studio and set up in business? Things like that are expensive, let me tell you.

GREGERS. And my *father* paid for it all?

HJALMAR. Why, of course, didn't you know? I understood him to say he'd written and told you.

GREGERS. Not a word about its being *him*. He must have forgotten. We've never exchanged anything but business letters. So it was my *father* . . . !

HJALMAR. It certainly was. He never wanted it to get around, but it was him, all right. And of course it was also he who put me in a position to get married. Or maybe you didn't know about that either?

GREGERS. No, I certainly did not. [*Clapping him on the arm.*] But my

dear Hjalmar, I can't tell you how delighted I am to hear all this—
and remorseful too. I may have been unjust to my father after all—
on a few points. Because this does reveal a kind heart, doesn't it. It's
as if, in a way, he had a conscience . . .

HJALMAR. A conscience . . . ?

GREGERS. Well, well, whatever you want to call it, then. No, I really
can't tell you how glad I am to hear this about my father.—So you're
a married man, Hjalmar. That's more than I'm ever likely to be.
Well, I trust you are happy in your marriage?

HJALMAR. Yes, indeed I am. She's as capable and fine a wife as any man
could ask for. And she's by no means without culture.

GREGERS [a little surprised]. Why no, I don't suppose she is.

HJALMAR. Life itself is an education, you see. Her daily contact with me
. . . besides which there's a couple of very intelligent fellows we see
regularly. I assure you, you wouldn't know Gina now.

GREGERS. Gina?

HJALMAR. Why yes, don't you remember her name is Gina?

GREGERS. Whose name is Gina? I haven't the faintest idea what . . .

HJALMAR. But don't you remember she was employed here in this house
for a time?

GREGERS [looking at him]. You mean Gina Hansen . . . ?

HJALMAR. Yes, of course I mean Gina Hansen.

GREGERS. . . . who kept house for us the last year of my mother's illness?

HJALMAR. Well of course. But my dear fellow, I know for a fact that
your father wrote and told you I had got married.

GREGERS [who has risen]. Yes, he did that, all right. But not that . . .
[Pacing floor.] Wait a minute—perhaps after all—now that I think
about it. But my father always writes me such short letters. [Sits on
arm of chair.] Listen, Hjalmar, tell me—this is interesting—how did
you happen to meet Gina—your wife, that is?

HJALMAR. Oh, quite simply. Gina didn't stay very long here in this house.
There was so much trouble here at the time, what with your mother's
illness . . . Gina couldn't take all that, so she gave notice and left.
That was the year before your mother died—or maybe it was the
same year.

GREGERS. It was the same year. I was up at the works at the time. But
afterwards?

HJALMAR. Well, Gina went to live with her mother, a Mrs. Hansen, a
most capable and hard-working woman who ran a little eating place.
She also had a room for rent, a really nice, comfortable room.

GREGERS. And you, I suppose, were lucky enough to find it?

HJALMAR. Yes, as a matter of fact it was your father who gave me the
lead. And it was there—you see—that's where I really got to know
Gina.

GREGERS. And so you got engaged?

HJALMAR. Yes. You know how easily young people get to care for each
other—Hm . . .

GREGERS [*rises and walks around*]. Tell me—when you had got engaged—was it then that my father got you to . . . I mean—was it then that you started to take up photography?

HJALMAR. Yes, exactly. Because I did so want to get settled and have a home of my own, the sooner the better. And both your father and I felt that this photography business was the best idea. And Gina thought so too. Oh yes, there was another reason as well. It so happened that Gina had just taken up retouching.

GREGERS. *That* fitted in marvelously well.

HJALMAR [*pleased, rises*]. Yes, didn't it though? It *did* fit in marvelously well, don't you think?

GREGERS. Yes, I must say. Why, my father seems to have been a kind of Providence for you.

HJALMAR [*moved*]. He did not forsake his old friend's son in the hour of need. For he's a man with *heart*, you see.

MRS. SØRBY [*entering arm in arm with* HÅKON WERLE]. Not another word, my dear Mr. Werle. You must not stay in there any longer staring at all those lights. It's not good for you.

WERLE [*letting go her arm and passing his hand over his eyes*]. I rather think you are right.

[PETTERSON *and* JENSEN, *the hired waiter, enter with trays.*]

MRS. SØRBY [*to guests in other room*]. Punch is served, Gentlemen. If anybody wants some he'll have to come in here and get it.

THE FLABBY GENTLEMAN [*walking over to* MRS. SØRBY]. Good heavens, it is true you've abrogated our precious right to smoke?

MRS. SØRBY. Yes, my dear Chamberlain,[2] here in Mr. Werle's private domain it is forbidden.

THE THIN-HAIRED GENTLEMAN. And when did you introduce this harsh restriction into our cigar regulations, Mrs. Sørby?

MRS. SØRBY. After our last dinner, Chamberlain. I'm afraid certain persons allowed themselves to overstep the bounds.

THE THIN-HAIRED GENTLEMAN. And is one not allowed to overstep the bounds just a little, Madame Berta? Not even the least little bit?

MRS. SØRBY. Under no circumstances, Chamberlain Balle.

[*Most of the guests are now assembled in* WERLE's *study; the waiters hand around glasses of punch.*]

WERLE [*to* HJALMAR, *standing over by a table*]. What's that you're so engrossed in, Ekdal?

HJALMAR. It's just an album, Mr. Werle.

THE THIN-HAIRED GENTLEMAN [*drifting about*]. Ah yes, photographs! That's in your line, of course.

THE FLABBY GENTLEMAN [*in an armchair*]. Haven't you brought along any of your own?

HJALMAR. No, I haven't.

---

2. At this period titles of nobility had been abolished in Norway, but the title "chamberlain" (*Kammerherr*) was used to indicate officers of the royal court, in many cases certainly honorary officers [*Translator's note*].

THE FLABBY GENTLEMAN. You should have. It's so good for the digestion, don't you know, to sit and look at pictures.

THE THIN-HAIRED GENTLEMAN. Besides contributing a mite to the general entertainment, you know.

A NEARSIGHTED GENTLEMAN. And all contributions are gratefully accepted.

MRS. SØRBY. The gentlemen mean, when you're invited out, you're expected to work a little for your dinner, Ekdal.

THE FLABBY GENTLEMAN. With a cuisine like this, *that* is an absolute pleasure.

THE THIN-HAIRED GENTLEMAN. Good Lord, if it's a question of the struggle for existence . . .

MRS. SØRBY. You're so right!

[*They continue the conversation, laughing and joking.*]

GREGERS [*quietly*]. You must join in, Hjalmar.

HJALMAR [*with a squirm*]. What am I to talk about?

THE FLABBY GENTLEMAN. Don't you agree, Mr. Werle, that Tokay may be regarded as a relatively healthy wine for the stomach?

WERLE [*by the fireplace*]. I can vouch for the Tokay you had today, at any rate; it is one of the very finest vintages. But of course you must have noticed that yourself.

THE FLABBY GENTLEMAN. Yes, it had a remarkably delicate bouquet.

HJALMAR [*uncertainly*]. Does the vintage make a difference?

THE FLABBY GENTLEMAN [*laughs*]. That's a good one!

WERLE [*smiling*]. There's certainly no point in putting a noble wine in front of *you*.

THE THIN-HAIRED GENTLEMAN. It's the same with Tokay as with photographs, Mr. Ekdal. Both must have sunlight. Or am I mistaken?

HJALMAR. Oh no. In photography, the light is everything.

MRS. SØRBY. Why, it's exactly the same with chamberlains. They also depend on sunshine, as the saying goes—royal sunshine.

THE THIN-HAIRED GENTLEMAN. Ouch! That's a tired old joke.

THE NEARSIGHTED GENTLEMAN. The lady is in great form . . .

THE FLABBY GENTLEMAN. . . . and at our expense, too. [*Wagging his finger.*] Madame Berta! Madame Berta!

MRS. SØRBY. Well, but it *is* perfectly true that vintages can differ enormously. The old vintages are the best.

THE NEARSIGHTED GENTLEMAN. Do you count *me* among the old ones?

MRS. SØRBY. Oh, far from it.

THE THIN-HAIRED GENTLEMAN. Listen to that! But what about *me*, dear Mrs. Sørby?

THE FLABBY GENTLEMAN. Yes, and me! Where do you put us?

MRS. SØRBY. You, among the sweet vintages, Gentlemen.

[*She sips a glass of punch; the chamberlains laugh and flirt with her.*]

WERLE. Mrs. Sørby always finds a way out—when she wants to. But

Gentlemen, you aren't drinking! Pettersen, see to . . . ! Gregers, I think we might take a glass together. [GREGERS *does not move.*] Won't you join us, Ekdal? I didn't get a chance to have a toast with you at table.

[GRÅBERG, *the bookkeeper, looks in at baize door.*]

GRÅBERG. Excuse me, Mr. Werle, but I can't get out.

WERLE. What, have they locked you in again?

GRÅBERG. Yes, and Flakstad's gone home with the keys . . .

WERLE. Well, just come through here, then.

GRÅBERG. But there's somebody else . . .

WERLE. Come on, come on, both of you. Don't be shy.

[GRÅBERG *and* OLD EKDAL *enter from the office.*]

WERLE [*involuntarily*]. What the . . . !

[*Laughter and chatter of guests die down.* HJALMAR *gives a start at the sight of his father, puts down his glass, and turns away toward the fireplace.*]

EKDAL [*does not look up, but makes quick little bows to both sides as he crosses, mumbling*]. Beg pardon. Came the wrong way. Gate's locked . . . gate's locked. Beg pardon.

[*He and* GRÅBERG *go off, rear right.*]

WERLE [*between his teeth*]. Damn that Gråberg!

GREGERS [*staring open-mouthed, to* HJALMAR]. Don't tell me that was . . . !

THE FLABBY GENTLEMAN. What's going on? Who was that?

GREGERS. Oh, nobody. Just the bookkeeper and another man.

THE NEARSIGHTED GENTLEMAN [*to* HJALMAR]. Did you know the man?

HJALMAR. I don't know . . . I didn't notice . . .

THE FLABBY GENTLEMAN [*getting up*]. What the devil's the matter, anyway? [*He walks over to some of the others, who are talking in lowered voices.*]

MRS. SØRBY [*whispers to the servant*]. Slip him something outside, something *really* good.

PETTERSEN [*nods his head*]. I'll do that. [*Goes out.*]

GREGERS [*in a low, shocked voice, to* HJALMAR]. Then it really was he!

HJALMAR. Yes.

GREGERS. And you stood here and denied you knew him!

HJALMAR [*whispers vehemently*]. But how *could* I . . . ?

GREGERS. . . . acknowledge your own father?

HJALMAR [*bitterly*]. Oh, if you were in my place, maybe . . .

[*The conversation among the guests, which has been conducted in low voices, now changes to forced gaiety.*]

THE THIN-HAIRED GENTLEMAN [*approaching* HJALMAR *and* GREGERS *in a friendly manner*]. Ah, are we reminiscing about old student days, Gentlemen? Eh? Don't you smoke, Mr. Ekdal? Can I give you a light? Oh, no, that's right. We are not allowed . . .

HJALMAR. Thank you, I don't smoke.

THE FLABBY GENTLEMAN. Don't you have some nice bit of poetry you could recite for us, Mr. Ekdal? You used to do that so charmingly.

HJALMAR. I'm afraid I can't remember any.

THE FLABBY GENTLEMAN. Oh, what a pity. Well, Balle, what shall we do now?

[*Both men cross and go into the drawing room.*]

HJALMAR [*gloomily*]. Gregers—I'm going! You see, when once a man has felt the crushing blow of fate . . . Say good-bye to your father for me.

GREGERS. Yes, of course. Are you going straight home?

HJALMAR. Yes. Why?

GREGERS. I thought I might drop in later on.

HJALMAR. No, don't do that. Not at my home. My house is a sad place, Gregers—especially after a brilliant banquet like this. We can always meet somewhere in town.

MRS. SØRBY [*has come up to them; in a low voice*]. Are you leaving, Mr. Ekdal?

HJALMAR. Yes.

MRS. SØRBY. Give my best to Gina.

HJALMAR. Thanks.

MRS. SØRBY. And tell her I'll be up to see her one of these days.

HJALMAR. Thanks, I'll do that. [*To* GREGERS.] Don't bother to see me out. I want to slip away unnoticed. [*He crosses room, then into drawing room, and goes off, right.*]

MRS. SØRBY [*softly to the servant, who has returned*]. Well, did you give the old man something?

PETTERSEN. Oh yes; I slipped him a bottle of brandy.

MRS. SØRBY. Oh, you might have thought of something better than that.

PETTERSEN. Not at all, Mrs. Sørby. There's nothing he likes better than brandy.

THE FLABBY GENTLEMAN [*in the doorway, with a sheet of music in his hand*]. What do you say we play something together, Mrs. Sørby?

MRS. SØRBY. Yes, let's do that.

GUESTS. Bravo! Bravo!

[*She and all the guests cross room and go off, right.* GREGERS *remains standing by fireplace.* WERLE *searches for something on the desk and seems to wish* GREGERS *to leave. As* GREGERS *does not move,* WERLE *starts toward the drawing room door.*]

GREGERS. Father, do you have a moment?

WERLE [*stops*]. What is it?

GREGERS. I'd like a word with you.

WERLE. Can't it wait till we're alone?

GREGERS. No, it can't. Because we might very well never be alone.

WERLE [*coming closer*]. And what is that supposed to mean?

[*During the following, the sound of a piano is distantly heard from the music room.*]

GREGERS. How could people here let that family go to the dogs like that?

WERLE. I suppose you mean the Ekdals?

GREGERS. Yes, I mean the Ekdals. After all, Lieutenant Ekdal was once your close friend.

WERLE. Alas, yes—all too close. Years and years I had to smart for it. He's the one I can thank for the fact that my good name and reputation were blemished in a way, mine too.

GREGERS [quietly]. Was he in fact the only guilty one?

WERLE. Who else do you think!

GREGERS. After all, you and he were both in that big timber deal together . . .

WERLE. But was it not Ekdal who drew up the survey map of the area— that fraudulent map? He was the one who did all that illegal felling of timber on State property. In fact, he was in charge of the entire operation up there. I had no idea what Lieutenant Ekdal was up to.

GREGERS. I doubt Lieutenant Ekdal himself knew what he was doing.

WERLE. Maybe so. But the fact remains that he was found guilty and I was acquitted.

GREGERS. Yes, I'm well aware there was no evidence.

WERLE. Acquittal is acquittal. Why do you have to rake up all that miserable old business that turned my hair gray before its time? Is this the sort of stuff you've gone and brooded over all those years up there? I can assure you, Gregers, here in town that whole story was forgotten ages ago—as far as it concerns me.

GREGERS. But what about the poor Ekdals!

WERLE. What exactly do you want me to do for those people? When Ekdal was released he was a broken man, altogether beyond help. There are people in this world who sink to the bottom the minute they get a couple of slugs in them, and they never come up again. You can take my word for it, Gregers, I've put myself out as far as I possibly could, short of encouraging all kinds of talk and suspicion . . .

GREGERS. Suspicion? Oh, I see.

WERLE. I have given Ekdal copying to do for the office, and I pay him far, far more for his work than it is worth . . .

GREGERS [without looking at him]. Hm; I don't doubt that.

WERLE. What's the joke? Don't you think I'm telling you the truth? Naturally, you won't find anything about it in my books. I never enter expenses like that.

GREGERS [with a cold smile]. No, I daresay certain expenses are best not accounted for.

WERLE [starts]. What do you mean by that?

GREGERS [with forced courage]. Did you enter what it cost you to have Hjalmar Ekdal learn photography?

WERLE. I? What do you mean—enter?

GREGERS. I know now it was you who paid for it. And I also know it was you who set him up so cozily.

WERLE. There, and still I'm supposed to have done nothing for the Ekdals! I assure you, those people have certainly put me to enough expense.

GREGERS. Have you entered any of those expenses?

WERLE. Why do you keep asking that?

GREGERS. Oh, I have my reasons. Look, tell me—that time, when you took such a warm interest in your old friend's son—wasn't it exactly when he was about to get married?

WERLE. What the devil—how can I remember, after all these years . . . ?

GREGERS. You wrote me a letter at the time—a business letter, naturally—and in an postscript it said, nothing more, that Hjalmar Ekdal had married a Miss Hansen.

WERLE. That's right. That was her name.

GREGERS. But you neglected to mention that this Miss Hansen was Gina Hansen—our former maid.

WERLE [*with a scornful but forced laugh*]. No, because it certainly never occurred to me that you were particularly interested in our former maid.

GREGERS. I wasn't. But—[*lowers his voice*] there were others in this house who *were*.

WERLE. What do you mean by *that*? [*Flaring up.*] Don't tell me you're referring to *me*!

GREGERS [*quietly but firmly*]. Yes, I'm referring to you.

WERLE. And you dare . . . ! You have the insolence to . . . ! And that ingrate, that, that—photographer! How dare he come here with such accusations!

GREGERS. Hjalmar never said a word about this. I don't think he has the slightest suspicion of anything of the kind.

WERLE. Then where have you got it from? Whoever could have said a thing like that?

GREGERS. My poor, unhappy mother said it. The last time I saw her.

WERLE. Your mother! I might have guessed as much. You and she— you always stuck together. It was she that turned you against me from the start.

GREGERS. No, it was all the things she had to bear, till at last she gave way and went to pieces.

WERLE. Oh, she didn't have anything to bear! No more than plenty of others do, anyway. But there's no way of getting along with morbid, neurotic people—that's a lesson *I* learned, all right. And now here you are, nursing a suspicion like that—mixing up in all kinds of ancient rumors and slander against your own father. Listen here, Gregers, I honestly think that at your age you could find something more useful to do.

GREGERS. Yes, perhaps it is about time.

WERLE. Then maybe you wouldn't take things so seriously as you seem to do now. What's the point in your sitting up there at the works year in year out, slaving away like a common office clerk, refusing to draw a cent more than the standard wage? It's plain silly.

GREGERS. I wish I were so sure about that.

WERLE. Not that I don't understand you. You want to be independent, want to be under no obligation to me. Well, here is your chance to get your independence, to be your own master in everything.

GREGERS. Really? And in what way . . . ?

WERLE. When I wrote you it was urgent that you come to town at once—hm . . .

GREGERS. Yes, what exactly is it you want me for? I have been waiting all day to hear.

WERLE. I propose that you become a partner in the firm.

GREGERS. Me? A partner in your firm?

WERLE. Yes. It needn't mean we'd have to be together all the time. You could take over the business here in town, and I would move up to the works.

GREGERS. *You* would?

WERLE. Well, you see, I don't have the capacity for work that I once had. I've got to go easy on my eyes, Gregers; they've started to get a bit weak.

GREGERS. They've always been that way.

WERLE. Not like now. And besides . . . circumstances might perhaps make it desirable for me to live up there—at any rate for a time.

GREGERS. I never dreamed of anything like that.

WERLE. Look, Gregers—I know we differ on a great many things. But after all, we *are* father and son. Surely we ought to be able to reach some sort of understanding.

GREGERS. To all outward appearances, I take it you mean?

WERLE. Well, even that would be something. Think it over, Gregers. Don't you think it could be done? Eh?

GREGERS [*looks at him coldly*]. There's something behind all this.

WERLE. What do you mean?

GREGERS. There must be something you want to use me for.

WERLE. In a relationship as close as ours surely one can always be of use to the other.

GREGERS. Yes, so they say.

WERLE. I should like to have you home now for a while. I'm a lonely man, Gregers; I've always felt lonely, all my life, but especially now that I'm getting along in years. I need somebody around me.

GREGERS. You've got Mrs. Sørby.

WERLE. Yes, so I have. And she's become just about indispensable to me. She's bright, she's easygoing, she livens up the house—and that I need pretty badly.

GREGERS. Well, then. In that case you've got just what you want.

WERLE. Yes, but I'm afraid it can't last. A woman in this kind of situation can easily have her position misconstrued. For that matter, it doesn't do the man much good either.

GREGERS. Oh, when a man gives such dinner parties as you do, I daresay he can take quite a few risks.

WERLE. Yes, but what about *her*, Gregers? I'm afraid she won't put up with it much longer. And even if she did—even if, out of devotion to me, she ignored the gossip and the aspersions and such . . . ? Do you really feel, Gregers, you with your strong sense of justice . . .

GREGERS [*interrupts him*]. Get to the point. Are you thinking of marrying her?

WERLE. Supposing I were? What then?

GREGERS. Yes, that's what I'm asking, too. What then?

WERLE. Would you be so dead set against it?

GREGERS. No, not at all. By no means.

WERLE. You see, I didn't know if perhaps, out of regard for the memory of your mother . . .

GREGERS. I am not neurotic.

WERLE. Well, whatever you may or may not be, you've taken a great load off my mind. I can't tell you how glad I am that I can count on your support in this matter.

GREGERS [*looks fixedly at him*]. Now I see what you want to use me for.

WERLE. Use you for? What an expression!

GREGERS. Oh, let's not be so particular in our choice of words—not when we are alone, at any rate. [*Short laugh.*] So that's it! That's why I had to make a personal appearance in town, come hell or high water. To put up a show of family life in this house for Mrs. Sørby's sake. Touching little tableau between father and son! *That* would be something new!

WERLE. How dare you talk like that!

GREGERS. When was there ever any family life around here? Never as long as I can remember! But now, all of a sudden, we could use a touch of home-sweet-home. Just think, the fine effect when it can be reported how the son hastened home—on wings of filial piety— to the aging father's wedding feast. *Then* what remains of all the rumors about what the poor dead wife had to put up with? Not a breath. Why, her own son snuffs them out.

WERLE. Gregers—I don't think there's a man on earth you hate as much as me.

GREGERS [*quietly*]. I've seen you too close up.

WERLE. You have seen me through your mother's eyes. [*Drops his voice a little.*] But don't forget that those eyes were—clouded, now and then.

GREGERS [*with trembling voice*]. I know what you're getting at. But who's to blame for Mother's tragic failing? *You*, and all those . . . ! The last of them was that female you palmed off on Hjalmar Ekdal when you yourself no longer . . ugh!

WERLE [*shrugs his shoulders*]. Word for word as though it were your mother talking.

GREGERS [*paying no attention*]. . . . And there he is now, that great trusting, childlike soul, engulfed in treachery—living under the same roof with such a creature. With no idea that what he calls his home is founded on a lie! [*Comes a step closer.*] When I look back upon your long career, it's as if I saw a battlefield strewn at every turn with shattered lives.

WERLE. I almost think the gulf between us is too wide.

GREGERS [*bows stiffly*]. So I have observed. Therefore I'll take my hat and go.

WERLE. Go? Leave the house?

GREGERS. Yes. For now at last I see an objective to live for.

WERLE. What objective is that?

GREGERS. You'd only laugh if I told you.

WERLE. Laughter doesn't come so easily to a lonely man, Gregers.

GREGERS [*pointing to the rear*]. Look, Father—your guests are playing Blind Man's Buff with Mrs. Sørby. Goodnight and good-bye.

[*He goes off, rear right. Laughter and banter are heard from the party, which comes into view in the drawing room.*]

WERLE [*mutters contemptuously after* GREGERS]. Huh! Poor devil. And *he* says he's not neurotic!

Act Two

HJALMAR EKDAL's *studio. The room, which is quite large, is apparently part of an attic. On the right is a pitched roof with a big skylight, half covered by a blue curtain. In the right corner at the rear is the entrance door; downstage on the same side, a door to the living room. On the left there are likewise two doors, with an iron stove between them. In the rear wall, wide double sliding doors. The studio is cheaply but comfortably furnished and arranged. Between the doors on the right and a little out from the wall stand a sofa and table and some chairs; on the table, a lighted lamp with shade; near the stove, an old armchair. Various pieces of photographic equipment here and there about the room. In the rear, left of the sliding doors, a bookcase containing a few books, some boxes and bottles of chemicals, various instruments, tools, and other objects. Photographs and small items such as brushes, paper, and the like are lying on the table.*

GINA EKDAL *is sitting at the table, sewing.* HEDVIG *is sitting on the sofa reading a book, her hands shading her eyes, her thumbs plugging her ears.*

GINA [*after glancing at her several times as if with suppressed anxiety*]. Hedvig!

[HEDVIG *does not hear.*]

GINA [*louder*]. Hedvig!

HEDVIG [*takes away her hands and looks up*]. Yes, Mother?

GINA. Hedvig, darling, you mustn't sit and read so long.

HEDVIG. Oh, please, Mother, can't I read a little more? Just a little!

GINA. No, no. Now you put that book away. Your father doesn't like it; he never reads at night himself.

HEDVIG [*shuts the book*]. No, Father doesn't care much for reading.

GINA [*puts her sewing aside and picks up a pencil and a small notebook from the table*]. Can you remember how much we paid for the butter today?

HEDVIG. It was one crown sixty-five.[3]

GINA. That's right. [*Writes it down.*] The amount of butter we go through in this house! Then there was the sausage and the cheese . . . let me see . . . [*makes a note*] . . . and then the ham . . . hm . . . [*Adding up.*] Yes, that already comes to . . .

HEDVIG. And the beer.

GINA. That's right, of course. [*Notes it down.*] It does mount up. But what can you do.

HEDVIG. But then you and I didn't need anything hot for dinner, since Father was going to be out.

GINA. Yes, that was a help. And besides I did take in eight crowns fifty for the pictures.

HEDVIG. My! As much as that?

GINA. Eight crowns fifty exactly.

[*Silence.* GINA *takes up her sewing again.* HEDVIG *takes paper and pencil and starts to draw, her left hand shading her eyes.*]

HEDVIG. Isn't it nice to think that Father's at a big dinner party at Mr. Werle's?

GINA. You can't say he's at Mr. Werle's, really. It was the son that invited him. [*Short pause.*] We've got nothing to do with old Mr. Werle.

HEDVIG. I can't wait till Father comes home. He promised to ask Mrs. Sørby for something good for me.

GINA. Oh yes, there's plenty of good things in *that* house, all right.

HEDVIG [*still drawing*]. Besides, I am just a bit hungry.

[OLD EKDAL *enters right rear, a bundle of papers under his arm and another parcel in his coat pocket.*]

GINA. How late you are tonight, Grandpa.

EKDAL. They had locked up the office. Had to wait in Gråberg's room. Then I had to go through . . . hm.

3. Statements about the comparative purchasing power are difficult to make accurately, but at the time of the play one American dollar was worth three crowns, seventy-five öre, approximately (one crown = one hundred öre). At that time in America, the New York *Times* could be purchased for two cents daily (three cents on Sundays), and theater tickets ran as high as one dollar and fifty cents. Room and board in a college rooming home was two dollars a week, and first-class steamship passage from New York to Liverpool ranged from sixty to one hundred dollars. In act 4, Hedvig's legacy of one hundred crowns a month was worth less than twenty-seven dollars, but a dollar had considerably more purchasing power than it does today [*Translator's note*].

HEDVIG. Did they give you any more copying to do, Grandfather?

EKDAL. This whole bundle. Just look.

GINA. Well, that's nice.

HEDVIG. And you've got another bundle in your pocket.

EKDAL. What? Nonsense, that isn't anything. [*Stands his walking stick away in the corner.*] This will keep me busy a long time, Gina. [*Draws one of the sliding doors in the rear wall a little to one side.*] Shhh! [*Peeks into the attic a while, then carefully slides the door to.*] Heh-heh! They're sound asleep, the whole lot of 'em. And she has settled in the basket by herself. Heh-heh!

HEDVIG. Are you sure she won't be cold in that basket, Grandfather?

EKDAL. Cold? What an idea! In all that straw? [*Walks toward rear door on left.*] Any matches in my room?

GINA. On the dresser.

[*EKDAL goes into his room.*]

HEDVIG. Isn't it nice Grandfather got all that copying to do.

GINA. Yes, poor old thing. Now he can make himself a little pocket money.

HEDVIG. Besides, he won't be able to sit all morning in that nasty café of Mrs. Eriksen's.

GINA. Yes, that's another thing.

[*A short silence.*]

HEDVIG. Do you think they're still sitting at the table?

GINA. Lord knows. I guess they could be, though.

HEDVIG. Just think, all the delicious things Father must be having! I'm sure he'll be in a good mood when he gets home. Don't you think so, Mother?

GINA. Oh yes. Now, if only we could tell him we got the room rented.

HEDVIG. But we don't need that tonight.

GINA. Oh, it would come in very handy, you know. It's no use to us just standing there empty.

HEDVIG. No, I mean it's not necessary because Father will be in a good mood tonight anyway. It's better to have the news about the room for another time.

GINA [*looks across at her*]. You like having something nice to tell your father when he gets home evenings?

HEDVIG. Certainly, it makes things more cheerful.

GINA [*thinking this over*]. Why yes, I guess there's something in that.

[*OLD EKDAL enters from his room and makes for the door on front left.*]

GINA [*turning half around in her chair*]. Do you want something in the kitchen, Grandpa?

EKDAL. Yes. Don't get up. [*Goes out.*]

GINA. I hope he's not messing with the fire out there! [*Waits a moment.*] Hedvig, go see what he's up to.

[*EKDAL returns with a little mug of steaming water.*]

HEDVIG. Are you getting hot water, Grandfather?

EKDAL. Yes, I am. Need it for something. I've got writing to do, and the ink's gone as thick as mud—hm.

GINA. But you ought to eat your supper first, Grandpa. It's all set out for you.

EKDAL. Can't be bothered with supper, Gina. Terribly busy, I tell you. I don't want anybody coming into my room. Not anybody—hm. [*He goes into his room.* GINA *and* HEDVIG *look at each other.*]

GINA [*in a low voice*]. Where on earth do you suppose he got the money?

HEDVIG. I guess from Gråberg.

GINA. No, impossible. Gråberg always sends the money to me.

HEDVIG. Then he must have got a bottle on credit somewhere.

GINA. Poor old soul. Who'd give *him* anything on credit? [HJALMAR EKDAL, *in topcoat and gray felt hat, enters right.*]

GINA [*throws down her sewing and gets up*]. Why, Hjalmar, you're back .already!

HEDVIG [*simultaneously jumping up*]. Father, what a surprise!

HJALMAR [*lays down his hat*]. Most of them seemed to be leaving.

HEDVIG. So early?

HJALMAR. Well, it was a dinner party, you know. [*About to take off his topcoat.*]

GINA. Let me help you.

HEDVIG. Me too. [*They help him off with his coat.* GINA *hangs it up on the rear wall.*]

HEDVIG. Were there many there, Father?

HJALMAR. Not too many. There were about twelve or fourteen of us at table.

GINA. Did you get to talk to everybody?

HJALMAR. Oh yes, a little. But actually Gregers monopolized me most of the evening.

GINA. Is Gregers as ugly as ever?

HJALMAR. Well, he isn't exactly a beauty. Hasn't the old man come home?

HEDVIG. Yes, Grandfather's in his room writing.

HJALMAR. Did he say anything?

GINA. No, what about?

HJALMAR. He didn't mention anything about . . . ? I thought I heard he'd been to see Gråberg. I think I'll go in and see him a moment.

GINA. No, no, I wouldn't do that . . .

HJALMAR. Why not? Did he say he didn't want to see me?

GINA. I guess he doesn't want *anybody* in there this evening . . .

HEDVIG [*making signs*]. Ahem—ahem!

GINA [*not noticing*]. . . . he's been out and got himself some hot water.

HJALMAR. Aha, is he sitting and . . . ?

GINA. Yes, that's probably it.

HJALMAR. Dear me—my poor old white-haired father!—Well, let him be, let him get what pleasure he can out of life.

[OLD EKDAL, *in dressing gown and with lighted pipe, enters from his room.*]

EKDAL. You back? *Thought* it was you I heard talking.

HJALMAR. I just got in this minute.

EKDAL. Guess you didn't see me, did you?

HJALMAR. No. But they said you'd gone through—so I thought I'd catch up with you.

EKDAL. Hm, good of you, Hjalmar. Who were they, all those people?

HJALMAR. Oh, different ones. There was Chamberlain Flor and Chamberlain Balle and Chamberlain Kaspersen and Chamberlain this-that-and-the-other; I don't know . . .

EKDAL [*nodding his head*]. Hear that, Gina? He's been hobnobbing with nothing but chamberlains.

GINA. Yes, I guess they're mighty high-toned in that house now.

HEDVIG. Did the chamberlains sing, Father? Or give recitations?

HJALMAR. No, they just talked nonsense. They did try to get me to recite something for them, but they couldn't make me.

EKDAL. They couldn't make you, eh?

GINA. Seems to me you could just as well have done it.

HJALMAR. No. One should not be at everybody's beck and call. [*Taking a turn about the room.*] I, at any rate, am not.

EKDAL. No, no. Hjalmar's not that obliging.

HJALMAR. I don't see why *I* should be expected to provide the entertainment the one evening I'm out. Let the others exert themselves. Those fellows do nothing but go from one spread to the next, feasting and drinking day in and day out. Let *them* do something in return for all the good food they get.

GINA. I hope you didn't tell them that?

HJALMAR [*humming*]. Hm . . . hm . . . hm . . . Well, they were told a thing or two.

EKDAL. What, the chamberlains!

HJALMAR. And why not? [*Casually.*] Then we had a little controversy over Tokay.

EKDAL. Tokay, eh? Say, that's a grand wine.

HJALMAR [*pauses*]. It *can* be. But let me tell you, not all vintages are equally fine. It all depends on how much sunshine the grapes have had.

GINA. Why, Hjalmar, if you don't know just about everything!

EKDAL. They started arguing about that?

HJALMAR. They tried to. But then they were given to understand that it's exactly the same with chamberlains. Not all vintages are equally good in their case either—it was pointed out.

GINA. Honest, the things you come up with!

EKDAL. Heh-heh! So they had to put *that* in their pipes and smoke it!

HJALMAR. They got it straight in the face.

EKDAL. Hear that, Gina? He said it straight to the chamberlains' faces.

GINA. Imagine, straight in their face.

HJALMAR. Yes, but I don't want it talked about. You don't repeat this kind of thing. Besides, the whole thing went off in the friendliest possible manner, of course. They were all decent, warm-hearted people—why should I hurt their feelings? No!

EKDAL. Still, straight in the face . . .

HEDVIG [ingratiatingly]. How nice it is to see you all dressed up, Father. You do look nice in a tailcoat.

HJALMAR. Yes, don't you think so? And this one really doesn't fit too badly. It could almost have been made to order for me—a trifle tight in the armholes, maybe . . . Give me a hand, Hedvig. [Takes the tailcoat off.] I'll put on my jacket instead. Where'd you put my jacket, Gina?

GINA. Here it is. [Brings the jacket and helps him on with it.]

HJALMAR. There we are! Now don't forget to let Molvik have the tails back first thing in the morning.

GINA [putting tailcoat aside]. I'll take care of it.

HJALMAR [stretching]. Aaahh, that's more like it. And this type of loose-fitting casual house jacket really suits my style better. Don't you think so, Hedvig?

HEDVIG. Oh yes, Father!

HJALMAR. And if I pull out my tie like this into two flowing ends . . . look! Eh?

HEDVIG. Yes, it goes so well with your mustache and your thick curly hair.

HJALMAR. I wouldn't exactly call my hair curly. Wavy, rather.

HEDVIG. Yes, because the curls are so big.

HJALMAR. Waves, actually.

HEDVIG [after a moment, tugs at his jacket]. Father!

HJALMAR. Well, what is it?

HEDVIG. Oh, you know as well as I.

HJALMAR. Why no, I certainly don't.

HEDVIG [half-laughing, half-whimpering]. Oh yes you do, Daddy! Stop teasing!

HJALMAR. But what is it?

HEDVIG [shaking him]. Come on, give it to me, Daddy. You know, the good things you promised me.

HJALMAR. Oh, dear. Imagine, I completely forgot!

HEDVIG. Now you're just trying to fool me, Daddy! That's not very nice! Where did you hide it?

HJALMAR. No, honest, I really did forget. But wait a minute! I've got something else for you, Hedvig. [Goes across and searches his coat pockets.]

HEDVIG [jumping and clapping her hands]. Oh Mother, Mother!

GINA. See? If you just give him time . . .

HJALMAR [with a sheet of paper]. Look, here it is.

HEDVIG. That? It's just a piece of paper.

HJALMAR. It's the menu, Hedvig, the entire menu. Look, they had it specially printed.

HEDVIG. Haven't you got anything else?

HJALMAR. I forgot the rest, I tell you. But take my word for it, it's no great treat all that fancy stuff. Now, why don't you sit down at the table and read the menu, and later on I'll tell you what the different courses taste like. Here you are, Hedvig.

HEDVIG [*swallowing her tears*]. Thanks.

[*She sits down but does not read.* GINA *makes signs to her, which* HJALMAR *notices.*]

HJALMAR [*pacing the floor*]. It's really incredible the things a family man is expected to keep in mind. And just let him forget the least little thing—right away he gets a lot of sour looks. Oh well, that's another thing you get used to. [*Stops by the stove, where* OLD EKDAL *is sitting.*] Have you looked in there this evening, Father?

EKDAL. You bet I have. She's asleep in her basket.

HJALMAR. No, really? In her basket! She's beginning to get used to it, then.

EKDAL. Sure, I told you she would. But now, you know, there are still one or two other little things . . .

HJALMAR. Improvements, yes.

EKDAL. They've got to be done, you know.

HJALMAR. Yes, let's have a little chat about these improvements, Father. Come over here and we'll sit down on the sofa.

EKDAL. Right! Hm, think I'll just fill my pipe first . . . Got to clean it, too. Hm. [*Goes into his room.*]

GINA [*smiles to* HJALMAR]. Clean his pipe—I'll bet.

HJALMAR. Oh well, Gina, let him be—poor shipwrecked old man.— Yes, those improvements—we'd better get them out of the way tomorrow.

GINA. You won't have time tomorrow, Hjalmar.

HEDVIG [*interrupting*]. Yes he will, Mother!

GINA. Don't forget those prints that need to be retouched. They keep coming around for them.

HJALMAR. What! Those prints again? Don't worry, they'll be ready. Any new orders come in?

GINA. No, worse luck. Tomorrow I've got nothing but that double sitting I told you about.

HJALMAR. Is that all? Well, of course, if one doesn't make an effort . . .

GINA. But what more can I do? I'm advertising in the papers as much as we can afford, seems to me.

HJALMAR. Oh, the papers, the papers—you see for yourself what good *they* are. And I suppose there hasn't been anybody to look at the room, either?

GINA. No, not yet.

HJALMAR. That was only to be expected. If people don't show any initiative, well . . . ! One's got to make a determined effort, Gina!

HEDVIG [*going toward him*]. Couldn't I bring you your flute, Father?

HJALMAR. No, no flute for me. *I* need no pleasures in this world. [*Pacing
about.*] All right, you'll see how I'll get down to work tomorrow, don't
you worry. You can be sure I shall work as long as my strength holds
out . . .

GINA. But, Hjalmar dear, I didn't mean it that way.

HEDVIG. Father, how about a bottle of beer?

HJALMAR. No, certainly not. I don't need anything . . . [*Stops.*] Beer?
Was it beer you said?

HEDVIG [*gaily*]. Yes, Father, nice cold beer.

HJALMAR. Well—if you insist, you might bring in a bottle.

GINA. Yes, do that. That'll be nice and cozy.

> [HEDVIG *runs toward the kitchen door.* HJALMAR, *by the stove, stops
> her, looks at her, takes her face between his hands, and presses her
> to him.*]

HJALMAR. Hedvig! Hedvig!

HEDVIG [*happy and in tears*]. Daddy darling!

HJALMAR. No, don't call me that. There I sat indulging myself at the
rich man's table—sat and gorged myself at the groaning board—and
I couldn't even . . .!

GINA [*seated by the table*]. Oh, don't talk nonsense, Hjalmar.

HJALMAR. No, it's the truth. But you mustn't judge me too harshly. You
know I love you, all the same.

HEDVIG [*throwing her arms around him*]. And we love you too, Daddy—
so much!

HJALMAR. And if I *am* unreasonable once in a while, well—heavens
above—remember I am a man beset by a host of cares. Ah, well!
[*Drying his eyes.*] No beer, no, not at such a moment. Give me my
flute.

> [HEDVIG *runs to the bookcase and fetches it.*]

HJALMAR. Thanks! That's right, yes. With flute in hand and you two at
my side—ah!

> [HEDVIG *sits down at the table beside* GINA. HJALMAR *walks up and
> down and begins a Bohemian folk dance, playing it with vigor but
> in a slow elegiac tempo and with sentimental interpretation.*]

HJALMAR [*breaks off the tune, holds out his left hand to* GINA, *and says
with strong emotion*]. What is this place *is* cramped and shoddy, Gina.
It's still our home. And this I will say: here is my heart's abode.

> [*He starts to play again. Soon after, there is a knock on the hall
> door.*]

GINA [*getting up*]. Shhh, Hjalmar—I think somebody's coming.

HJALMAR [*putting the flute on the shelf*]. Wouldn't you just know!

> [GINA *walks over and opens the door.*]

GREGERS WERLE [*out in the hall*]. I beg your pardon . . .

GINA [*recoiling slightly*]. Oh!

GREGERS. . . . isn't this where Mr. Ekdal the photographer lives?

GINA. Yes, it is.

HJALMAR [*going toward the door*]. Gregers! You came after all? Well, come in then.

GREGERS [*entering*]. I told you I would drop in to see you.

HJALMAR. But tonight . . . ? You left the party?

GREGERS. Both the party and my father's house. —Good evening, Mrs. Ekdal. I don't suppose you recognize me.

GINA. Oh yes. You're not so hard to recognize, Mr. Werle.

GREGERS. No, I resemble my mother, of course. And no doubt you remember her.

HJALMAR. Did I hear you say you left the house?

GREGERS. Yes, I've taken a room at a hotel.

HJALMAR. Really? Well, as long as you're here, take off your coat and sit down.

GREGERS. Thanks. [*Removes his overcoat. He has changed into a plain gray country suit.*]

HJALMAR. Here, on the sofa. Make yourself comfortable.

[GREGERS *sits down on the sofa,* HJALMAR *on a chair by the table.*]

GREGERS. So this is where you keep yourself, Hjalmar. This is your place.

HJALMAR. This is the studio, as you can see . . .

GINA. But it's roomier in here, so this is mostly where we stay.

HJALMAR. We had a nicer place before, but this apartment has one great advantage—there's such a lot of splendid extra space.

GINA. And then we've got a room across the hall that we can rent out.

GREGERS [*to* HJALMAR]. Well, well—so you've got roomers besides.

HJALMAR. No, not yet. It's not so easily done as all that, you know; it calls for initiative. [*To* HEDVIG.] What about that beer?

[HEDVIG *nods and goes out to the kitchen.*]

GREGERS. Your daughter, I take it?

HJALMAR. Yes, that's Hedvig.

GREGERS. Your only child?

HJALMAR. Our only one, yes. She is our greatest joy in the world, and— [*lowers his voice*] she's also our deepest sorrow, Gregers.

GREGERS. What are you saying!

HJALMAR. Yes, Gregers. She's in grave danger of losing her eyesight.

GREGERS. Going blind!

HJALMAR. Yes. So far, there are only the first signs, and things may still be all right for some time yet. But the doctor has warned us. It's inevitable.

GREGERS. But this is a terrible misfortune. How did she get like that?

HJALMAR [*sighs*]. Heredity, most likely.

GREGERS [*with a start*]. Heredity?

GINA. Yes, Hjalmar's mother also had bad eyesight.

HJALMAR. That's what Father says. I can't remember her myself.

GREGERS. Poor child. How does she take it?

HJALMAR. Oh, as you can imagine, we don't have the heart to tell her. She doesn't suspect a thing. Happy and carefree, chirping like a little bird, she is fluttering into life's eternal night. [*Overcome.*] Oh, Gregers, it's heartbreaking for me.

[HEDVIG *enters carrying a tray with beer and glasses, which she sets down on the table.*]

HJALMAR [*stroking her head*]. Thank you, thank you, Hedvig.

[HEDVIG *puts her arms around his neck and whispers in his ear.*]

HJALMAR. No, no sandwiches just now. [*Looks across.*] That is, unless Gregers would care for some?

GREGERS [*declining*]. No, no thanks.

HJALMAR [*with continued pathos*]. Oh well, perhaps you might bring in a few, after all. A crust would be nice, if you happen to have one. Just make sure there's plenty of butter on it.

[HEDVIG *nods delightedly and goes out again to the kitchen.*]

GREGERS [*who has followed her with his eyes*]. She looks strong and healthy enough to me in all other respects.

GINA. Yes, thank God. Otherwise there's nothing the matter with her.

GREGERS. She's going to look like you in time, Mrs. Ekdal. How old might she be now?

GINA. Hedvig's just fourteen; it's her birthday the day after tomorrow.

GREGERS. A big girl for her age.

GINA. Yes, she certainly shot up this last year.

GREGERS. The young ones growing up make us realize how old we ourselves are getting.—How long is it now you've been married?

GINA. We've been married already fifteen years—just about.

GREGERS. Imagine, is it that long!

GINA [*becomes attentive; looks at him*]. Yes, that's what it is, all right.

HJALMAR. Yes, it must be all of that. Fifteen years, give or take a couple of months. [*Changing the subject.*] They must have been long years for you, Gregers, up there at the works.

GREGERS. They seemed long while I was living through them—now, looking back, I hardly know where all that time went.

[OLD EKDAL *enters from his room, without his pipe, but with his old-fashioned lieutenant's cap on his head. His gait is a bit unsteady.*]

EKDAL. All right, Hjalmar, now we can sit down and talk about that . . . hm . . . What was it again?

HJALMAR [*going toward him*]. Father, there's somebody here. Gregers Werle . . . I don't know if you remember him.

EKDAL [*looks at* GREGERS, *who has risen*]. Werle? Is that the son? What does he want with me?

HJALMAR. Nothing. It's me he's come to see.

EKDAL. Oh. So there's nothing the matter?

HJALMAR. No, of course not.

EKDAL [*swinging his arm*]. Not that I care, you know. I'm not scared . . .

GREGERS [*goes up to him*]. I just wanted to bring you greetings from your old hunting grounds, Lieutenant Ekdal.

EKDAL. Hunting grounds?

GREGERS. Yes, up there around the Højdal works.

EKDAL. Oh, up there. Oh yes, I used to know my way around up there at one time.

GREGERS. You were a mighty hunter in those days.

EKDAL. So I was. True enough. You're looking at my officer's cap. I don't ask anybody's permission to wear it here in the house. Just as long as I don't go outside with it . . .

[HEDVIG *brings a plate of open-faced sandwiches, which she sets on the table.*]

HJALMAR. Come sit down now, Father, and have a glass of beer. Help yourself, Gregers.

[EKDAL *mutters and hobbles over to the sofa.* GREGERS *sits down on the chair nearest him,* HJALMAR *on the other side of* GREGERS. GINA *sits a little away from the table, sewing;* HEDVIG *stands beside her father.*]

GREGERS. Do you remember, Lieutenant Ekdal, how Hjalmar and I used to come up and visit you summers and at Christmas?

EKDAL. Did you? No, no, no, that I can't recollect. But I *was* a crack shot, if I do say so myself. Even used to shoot bears. Got nine of 'em, no less.

GREGERS [*looking sympathetically at him*]. And now your hunting days are over.

EKDAL. Oh, I wouldn't say *that*, old chap. Still manage a bit of shooting now and then. Of course, not in the old way. Because the forest, you know . . . the forest, the forest . . . ! [*Drinks.*] Is the forest in good shape up there now?

GREGERS. Not so fine as in your day. There's been a lot of cutting down.

EKDAL. Cutting down? [*Lowers his voice as if afraid.*] That's risky business, that. You don't get away with it. The forest takes revenge.

HJALMAR [*filling his glass*]. Here, Father, have a little more.

GREGERS. How can a man like you—such a lover of the great outdoors—how can you live in the middle of a stuffy city, shut in here by four walls?

EKDAL [*gives a little laugh and glances at* HJALMAR]. Oh, it's not so bad here. Not so bad at all.

GREGERS. But all those things that were once so much a part of you—the cool sweeping breeze, the free life in the forest and on the moors, among birds and beasts . . . ?

EKDAL [*smiling*]. Hjalmar, shall we show it to him?

HJALMAR [*quickly, a little embarrassed*]. No, no, Father. Not tonight.

GREGERS. What does he want to show me?

HJALMAR. Oh, it's only a kind of . . . You can see it another time.

GREGERS [*continues to the old man*]. Well, let me tell you what I had in mind, Lieutenant Ekdal. Why don't you come up to Højdal with me. I'll probably be going back soon. You could easily get some copying to do up there as well. While here you don't have a thing in the world to liven you up or amuse you.

EKDAL [*staring at him in astonishment*]. *Me?* Not a thing in the world to . . . !

GREGERS. Of course, you have Hjalmar. But then he has his own family. And a man like you, who has always been drawn to what is free and untamed . . .

EKDAL [*strikes the table*]. Hjalmar, he's *got* to see it now!

HJALMAR. But, Father, do you really think so? It's dark . . .

EKDAL. Nonsense! It's moonlight. [*Gets up.*] I tell you he's got to see it. Let me pass. Come on and help me, Hjalmar!

HEDVIG. Oh yes, go on, Father!

HJALMAR [*get up*]. Well, all right.

GREGERS [*to* GINA]. What is it?

GINA. Oh, don't expect anything special.

[EKDAL *and* HJALMAR *have gone to the rear wall and each slides one of the double doors aside.* HEDVIG *helps the old man;* GREGERS *remains standing by the sofa;* GINA *sits unconcerned, sewing. Through the open doors can be seen a long, irregular-shaped attic with nooks and crannies and a couple of free-standing chimneys. Bright moonlight falls through skylights on some parts of the attic, while others are in deep shadow.*]

EKDAL [*to* GREGERS]. You're welcome to come right up close.

GREGERS [*goes up to them*]. But what *is* it?

EKDAL. Look and see. Hm.

HJALMAR [*somewhat embarrassed*]. All this belongs to Father, you understand.

GREGERS [*at the door, looking into the attic*]. Why, Lieutenant Ekdal, you keep poultry!

EKDAL. Should hope to say we keep poultry. They're roosting now. But you ought to see this poultry by daylight!

HEDVIG. And then there's . . .

EKDAL. Sh! Sh! Don't say anything yet.

GREGERS. And I see you've got pigeons, too.

EKDAL. Yes indeed, we've got pigeons all right! They have their nesting boxes up under the eaves, they do. Pigeons like to roost high, you see.

HJALMAR. They aren't all of them just ordinary pigeons.

EKDAL. Ordinary! Should say not! We've got tumblers, and a couple of pouters, too. But come over here! Do you see that hutch over there by the wall?

GREGERS. Yes. What do you use that for?

EKDAL. That's where the rabbits sleep at night, old chap.

GREGERS. Oh, so you have rabbits too?

EKDAL. You're damn right we have rabbits! He wants to know if we've got rabbits, Hjalmar! Hm! But now we come to the *real* thing! Now it comes! Move, Hedvig. Come and stand here; that's right! Now, look down there.—Can you see a basket with straw in it?

GREGERS. Why yes. And I see there's a bird sitting in the basket.

EKDAL. Hm—"a bird" . . .

GREGERS. Isn't it a duck?

EKDAL [*offended*]. Well, obviously it's a duck.

HJALMAR. But what *kind* of duck do you suppose it is?

HEDVIG. It's no common ordinary duck . . .

EKDAL. Hush!

GREGERS. And it's not a muscovy duck either.

EKDAL. No, Mr.—Werle, it's not a muscovy duck. It's a wild duck.

GREGERS. What, is it really? A wild duck?

EKDAL. Yessir, that's what it is. That "bird," as you called it—that's the wild duck. Our wild duck, old chap.

HEDVIG. My wild duck. It belongs to me.

GREGERS. And it can really live here in the attic? And thrive?

EKDAL. Of course, you understand, she's got a trough of water to splash around in.

HJALMAR. Fresh water every other day.

GINA [*turning to* HJALMAR]. Hjalmar, please, it's getting freezing cold in here.

EKDAL. Hm, let's shut the door then. Better not to disturb them when they're settled for the night, anyhow. Hedvig, lend a hand.

[HJALMAR *and* HEDVIG *slide the attic door shut.*]

EKDAL. You can take a good look at her some other time. [*Sits down in the armchair by the stove.*] Oh, they're most remarkable, let me tell you, these wild ducks.

GREGERS. But how did you ever catch it, Lieutenant Ekdal?

EKDAL. Wasn't me that caught it. There's a certain man here in town we have to thank for her.

GREGERS [*struck by a thought*]. That man wouldn't happen to be my father, would he?

EKDAL. Oh yes indeed. Precisely your father. Hm.

HJALMAR. Funny you should guess that, Gregers.

GREGERS. Well, you told me before that you owed such a lot to my father, so it occurred to me that . . .

GINA. But we didn't get the duck from Mr. Werle personally . . .

EKDAL. It's Håkon Werle we have to thank for her just the same, Gina. [*To* GREGERS.] He was out in a boat, you see, and took a shot at her. But it happens his sight isn't so good anymore, your father's. Hm. So she was only winged.

GREGERS. I see. She got some shot in her.

HJALMAR. Yes, a few.

HEDVIG. It was in the wing, so she couldn't fly.

GREGERS. So she dived to the bottom, I suppose?

EKDAL [*sleepily, his voice thick*]. Goes without saying. Always do that, wild ducks. Plunge to the bottom—as deep as they can get, old chap—bite themselves fast in the weeds and tangle—and all the other damn mess down there. And never come up again.

GREGERS. But, Lieutenant Ekdal, *your* wild duck did come up again.

EKDAL. He had such an absurdly clever dog, your father . . . And that dog—it dived after and fetched the duck up again.

GREGERS [*turning to* HJALMAR]. And so you brought it here?

HJALMAR. Not right away. First it was taken to your father's house. But it didn't seem to thrive there, so Pettersen was told to do away with it . . .

EKDAL [*half asleep*]. Hm. . . . yes, Pettersen . . . Ass . . .

HJALMAR [*lowering his voice*]. That was how we got it, you see. Father knows Petterson slightly, and when he heard all this about the wild duck, he managed to get it turned over to him.

GREGERS. And now it's thriving perfectly well there in the attic.

HJALMAR. Yes, incredibly well. It's got quite plump. Of course, it's been in there so long now, it's forgotten what real wild life is like. That's the whole secret.

GREGERS. You're probably right, Hjalmar. Just don't ever let it catch sight of sea or sky . . . But I mustn't stay any longer, I think your father's asleep.

HJALMAR. Oh, don't worry about that . . .

GREGERS. But incidentally—didn't you say you had a room for rent— a vacant room?

HJALMAR. Yes, why? Do you happen to know somebody . . . ?

GREGERS. May I have that room?

HJALMAR. You?

GINA. You, Mr. Werle?

GREGERS. May I have the room? I could move in first thing tomorrow morning.

HJALMAR. Sure, with the greatest pleasure . . .

GINA. No, really, Mr. Werle, it's not in the least no room for you.

HJALMAR. Why Gina, how can you say that?

GINA. Well, that room's neither big enough or light enough, and . . .

GREGERS. That doesn't matter too much, Mrs. Ekdal.

HJALMAR. I think it's quite a nice room, myself, and not so badly furnished, either.

GINA. But don't forget those two downstairs.

GREGERS. Who are they?

GINA. Oh, there's one that used to be a private tutor . . .

HJALMAR. That's Molvik. He studied to be a pastor, once.

GINA. . . . And then there's a doctor called Relling.

GREGERS. Relling? I know him slightly; he practiced for a while up at Højdal.

GINA. They're a couple of characters, those two. Out on a binge as often
as not, and then they come home all hours of the night, and they're
not always what you'd call . . .

GREGERS. One soon gets accustomed to things like that. I hope I shall
be like the wild duck . . .

GINA. Hm. I think you'd better sleep on it, all the same.

GREGERS. You certainly don't seems anxious to have me in the house,
Mrs. Ekdal.

GINA. For heaven's sake, whatever gives you *that* idea?

HJALMAR. Yes, Gina, you really are being strange. [*To* GREGERS.] But
tell me, does this mean you'll be staying in town for a while?

GREGERS [*putting on his overcoat*]. Yes, now I think I'll stay.

HJALMAR. But not at your father's? What do you intend to do?

GREGERS. Ah, if only I knew that, Hjalmar—it wouldn't be so bad. But
when you're cursed with a name like Gregers . . . ! "Gregers"—and
then "Werle" on top of that! Have you ever heard anything so ghastly?

HJALMAR. Why, I don't think so at all.

GREGERS. Ugh! Phew! I could spit on a man with a name like that. But
since it's my cross in life to be Gregers Werle—such as I am . . .

HJALMAR [*laughing*]. Ha-ha! Suppose you weren't Gregers Werle, what
would you choose to be?

GREGERS. If I had the choice, I'd like most of all to be a clever dog.

GINA. A dog!

HEDVIG [*involuntarily*]. Oh no!

GREGERS. Yes, a really absurdly clever dog. The kind that goes in after
ducks when they plunge and fasten themselves in the weeds and the
tangle in the mud.

HJALMAR. Honestly now, Gregers—what *are* you talking about.

GREGERS. Oh well, it probably doesn't make much sense. Well then,
first thing tomorrow morning—I'm moving in. [*To* GINA.] I won't be
any trouble to you; I do everything for myself. [*To* HJALMAR.] The rest
we'll talk about tomorrow.—Goodnight, Mrs. Ekdal. [*Nods to*
HEDVIG.] Goodnight.

GINA. Goodnight, Mr. Werle.

HEDVIG. Goodnight.

HJALMAR [*who has lit a candle*]. Wait a minute, I'd better see you down,
it's sure to be dark on the stairs.

[GREGERS *and* HJALMAR *leave by the hall door.*]

GINA [*gazing ahead, her sewing on her lap*]. Wasn't that crazy talk,
wanting to be a dog?

HEDVIG. You know what, Mother—I think he meant something else.

GINA. What else could he mean?

HEDVIG. Oh, I don't know. But it was just as though he meant something
different from what he was saying—the whole time.

GINA. You think so? Well, it sure was queer though.

HJALMAR [*returning*]. The light was still on. [*Blows out candle and puts
it down.*] Ah, at last a man can get a bite to eat. [*Starts on the*

sandwiches.] Well, there you see, Gina—if only you keep your eyes
open . . .

GINA. What do you mean, keep your eyes open?

HJALMAR. Well, wasn't it lucky we finally got the room rented? And then
imagine, to somebody like Gregers—a dear old friend.

GINA. Well, I don't know what to say, myself.

HEDVIG. Oh, Mother, it will be nice, you'll see.

HJALMAR. You *are* funny, you know. First you were so set on getting it
rented, and now you don't like it.

GINA. Well, Hjalmar, if only it had been somebody else. . . . What do
you think Mr. Werle's going to say?

HJALMAR. Old Werle? It's none of his business.

GINA. But can't you see there's something the matter between them
again, since the young one is moving out? You know what those two
are like with each other.

HJALMAR. Yes, that could be, but . . .

GINA. And now maybe Mr. Werle will think you were behind it . . .

HJALMAR. Let him think what he wants! Mr. Werle has done a great
deal for me—God knows, I'm the first to admit it. But that doesn't
mean I've got to be under his thumb all my life.

GINA. But Hjalmar, dear, he could take it out on Grandpa. Suppose he
loses the little money he makes working for Gråberg.

HJALMAR. I almost wish he would! Isn't it rather humiliating for a man
like me to see his poor old white-haired father treated like dirt? But
now the fullness of time is at hand, I feel. [*Helps himself to another
sandwich.*] As sure as I have a mission in life, I shall fulfill it!

HEDVIG. Oh yes, Father, do!

GINA. Shhh! Don't wake him up.

HJALMAR [*in a lower voice*]. I shall fulfill it, I tell you. The day will
come, when . . . That's why it's such a good thing we got the room
rented; it puts me in a more independent position. And independent
is one thing a man with a mission in life has got to be. [*Over by the
armchair, with feeling.*] My poor old white-haired Father . . . Trust
in your Hjalmar! He has broad shoulders—strong shoulders, anyway.
One fine day you'll wake up and . . . [*To* GINA.] Maybe you don't
believe that?

GINA [*getting up*]. Sure, I believe it. But let's see about getting him to
bed first.

HJALMAR. Yes, let's.

[*They carefully lift the old man.*]

Act Three

HJALMAR EKDAL's *studio. It is morning; light is coming through the large
window in the sloping roof; the curtain is drawn back.*

HJALMAR *is sitting at the table, busy retouching a photograph; several more pictures are lying in front of him. After a while,* GINA, *in coat and hat, enters by the hall door; she has a covered basket on her arm.*

HJALMAR. Back already, Gina?

GINA. Oh, yes. I've got no time to waste. [*Puts the basket on a chair and takes off her outdoor things.*]

HJALMAR. Did you look in on Gregers?

GINA. I sure did. And a fine sight it is in there. He certainly fixed the place up the minute he moved in.

HJALMAR. Oh?

GINA. Yes, he wanted to manage for himself, he said. So he decides to light the fire, and what does he do but turn down the damper so the whole room gets filled with smoke. Phew, there's a smell in there like . . .

HJALMAR. Oh dear.

GINA. And that's not the worst of it. Next he wants to put out the fire, so he goes and dumps all the water from the washbasin into the stove, so the whole floor's a stinking mess.

HJALMAR. What a nuisance.

GINA. I got the janitor's wife to clean up after him, the pig, but the place won't be fit to go into again till this afternoon.

HJALMAR. What's he doing with himself meanwhile?

GINA. He's going out for a while, he said.

HJALMAR. I also dropped in on him for a minute—while you were gone.

GINA. So I heard. You've gone and invited him to lunch.

HJALMAR. Just for a little snack, that's all. After all, it's his first day—we can hardly do less. You must have something in the house.

GINA. I'd better see what I can find.

HJALMAR. Make sure there's plenty, though. Because I think Relling and Molvik are also coming up. I happened to run into Relling on the stairs, you see, so of course I had to . . .

GINA. Well, so we've got to have those two besides?

HJALMAR. Good Lord—one more or less, what difference does that make?

OLD EKDAL [*opens his door and looks in*]. I say, Hjalmar . . . [*Notices* GINA.] Never mind.

GINA. Is there something you want, Grandpa?

EKDAL. No, no, it doesn't matter. Hm! [*Goes back inside his room.*]

GINA [*takes the basket*]. Make sure you keep an eye on him, so he don't go out.

HJALMAR. All right, all right, I will.—Say, Gina, a little herring salad would be very nice. Because I suspect Relling and Molvik were out on a binge last night.

GINA. If only they don't barge in before I can . . .

HJALMAR. No, of course they won't. Take your time.

GINA. Well, all right. Meantime you can get a little work done.

HJALMAR. I *am* working, can't you see? I'm working as hard as I can!

GINA. That way you'll get that off your hands, that's all I meant. [*She goes into the kitchen, with the basket.*]

[HJALMAR *sits a while, working on the photograph with a brush, laboring slowly and with distaste.*]

EKDAL [*peeps in, looks around the studio, and says in a low voice*]. You busy, Hjalmar?

HJALMAR. Yes, can't you see I'm sitting here struggling with these pictures?

EKDAL. All right, all right. Goodness' sake, if you're all that busy—hm! [*Goes back inside his room; the door remains open.*]

HJALMAR [*continues working in silence for a while, then puts down his brush and walks over to the door*]. Are *you* busy, Father?

EKDAL [*grumbling, inside his room*]. If you're so busy, then I'm busy too. Hm!

HJALMAR. Oh, all right. [*Returns to his work.*]

EKDAL [*after a while, appears again at his door*]. Hm, look, Hjalmar, I'm not really as busy as all *that*.

HJALMAR. I thought you were writing.

EKDAL. What the hell, that Gråberg can wait a day or two, can't he? I don't suppose it's a matter of life and death.

HJALMAR. Of course not. And besides, you're not a slave.

EKDAL. And then there was this other thing in there . . .

HJALMAR. That's just what I was thinking. Do you want to go in? Shall I open the door for you?

EKDAL. Wouldn't really be such a bad idea.

HJALMAR [*getting up*]. Then we'd have *that* off our hands.

EKDAL. Yes, exactly. It was supposed to be ready first thing tomorrow. It *is* tomorrow, isn't it? Hm?

HJALMAR. Oh, yes, it's tomorrow, all right.

[HJALMAR *and* EKDAL *each pull aside one of the double doors. The morning sun is shining in through the skylights. A few pigeons are flying back and forth; others are cooing on the rafters; from farther back in the attic, now and then, can be heard the clucking of hens.*]

HJALMAR. There, now you can go ahead with it, Father.

EKDAL [*going in*]. Aren't you coming along?

HJALMAR. Well, you know—I rather think . . . [*Sees* GINA *at the kitchen door.*] Who, me? No, I have no time, I've got work to do.—Now, how about this contraption of ours . . .

[*He pulls a cord, and inside the door a curtain comes down. Its lower part consists of a strip of old canvas, its upper part of a piece of fishing net stretched taut. The attic floor is thus no longer visible.*]

HJALMAR [*going across to the table*]. There. Maybe now I can have a few minutes' peace.

GINA. Does he have to go messing around in there again?

HJALMAR. I suppose you'd rather see him running down to Ma Erik-

sen's place? [*Sitting down.*] Do you want something? I thought you
said . . .

GINA. I was only going to ask if you think we could set the table in here.

HJALMAR. Why not? I don't suppose there are any appointments this
early?

GINA. No, I'm only expecting that engaged couple that want to be taken
together.

HJALMAR. Damn! Couldn't they be taken together some other day!

GINA. But, Hjalmar, dear, I especially booked them for this afternoon,
while you're taking your nap.

HJALMAR. Oh, that's all right then. Yes, let's eat in here.

GINA. All right. But there's no rush about setting the table, you can go
on using it for a while yet.

HJALMAR. Well, can't you see I *am* using it for all I'm worth?

GINA. Then you'll be free later on, you see [*Returns to the kitchen.*]
    [*Short pause.*]

EKDAL [*in the attic door, behind the net*]. Hjalmar!

HJALMAR. What?

EKDAL. Afraid we'll have to move the water trough after all.

HJALMAR. Well, that's just what I've been saying all along.

EKDAL. Hm . . . hm . . . hm . . . [*Disappears inside again.*]
    [HJALMAR *works a little while, glances toward the attic, and half
    gets up.* HEDVIG *enters from the kitchen.*]

HJALMAR [*sits down again quickly*]. What is it you want?

HEDVIG. I only wanted to be with you, Father.

HJALMAR [*after a while*]. I have a feeling you're kind of snooping around.
    Were you told to check up on me by any chance?

HEDVIG. No, of course not.

HJALMAR. What's your mother doing out there?

HEDVIG. Oh, she's busy making the herring salad. [*Walks over to the
    table.*] Isn't there some little thing I could help you with, Father?

HJALMAR. No, no. It's best I do it all myself—so long as my strength
    holds out. There's no need, Hedvig; so long as your father manages
    to preserve his health. . . .

HEDVIG. Oh, come on, Daddy, you mustn't say such awful things.
    [*She wanders around a little, stops by the opening to the attic, and
    looks inside.*]

HJALMAR. What's he doing, Hedvig?

HEDVIG. Looks like he's making a new path up to the water trough.

HJALMAR. He'll never manage that by himself, never in the world! And
    here am I, condemned to sit here . . . !

HEDVIG [*going up to him*]. Let me have the brush, Father; I can do it.

HJALMAR. Nonsense; you'll only ruin your eyes.

HEDVIG. No I won't. Come on, give me the brush.

HJALMAR [*getting up*]. Well, it shouldn't take more than a minute or
    two.

HEDVIG. Pooh, take your time. [*Takes the brush.*] There. [*Sits down.*] And here's one I can copy from.

HJALMAR. But don't you dare strain your eyes! You hear? I'm not taking any responsibility; you'll have to take the responsibility yourself. I'm just telling you.

HEDVIG [*retouching*]. Yes, yes, of course I will.

HJALMAR. My, you're good at it, Hedvig. Just for a couple of minutes, you understand.

[*He sneaks past the edge of the curtain into the attic,* HEDVIG *sits at her work.* HJALMAR *and* EKDAL *are heard debating inside.*]

HJALMAR [*appears behind the netting*]. Oh, Hedvig, hand me those pliers on the shelf, will you? And the chisel, please. [*Turns to face into attic.*] Now you'll see, Father. Just give me a chance first to show you what I have in mind. [HEDVIG *fetches the tools he wanted from the shelf and reaches them in to him.*] That's it, thanks. Well, it certainly was a good thing I came.

[*He moves away from the opening. They can be heard carpentering and chatting within.* HEDVIG *stands watching them. Presently there is a knock on the hall door; she does not notice it.* GREGERS WERLE *enters and stands by the door a moment; he is bareheaded and without overcoat.*]

GREGERS. Ahem . . . !

HEDVIG [*turns and goes toward him*]. Good morning. Please, come right in.

GREGERS. Thank you. [*Looks toward the attic.*] Sounds like you've got workmen in the house.

HEDVIG. No, it's only Father and Grandfather. I'll tell them you're here.

GREGERS. No, no, don't do that; I'd rather wait a while. [*Sits down on the sofa.*]

HEDVIG. Everything is in such a mess . . . [*Starting to clear away the photographs.*]

GREGERS. Oh, just leave it. Are those photographs that have to be finished?

HEDVIG. Yes, a little job I'm helping Father with.

GREGERS. Please don't let me disturb you.

HEDVIG. Not a bit.

[*She moves the things back into her reach and settles down to work.* GREGERS *watches her in silence.*]

GREGERS. Did the wild duck sleep well last night?

HEDVIG. Yes, thank you, I think so.

GREGERS [*turning toward the attic*]. It looks quite different by day from what it did last night by moonlight.

HEDVIG. Yes, it can change such a lot. In the morning it looks different than in the afternoon, and when it's raining it looks different from when it's sunny.

GREGERS. Have you noticed that?

HEDVIG. Sure, anybody can see it.

GREGERS. Do you like to stay in there with the wild duck too?

HEDVIG. Yes, whenever I can.

GREGERS. I don't suppose you have much spare time, though. You go to school, of course?

HEDVIG. No, not any more. Father's afraid I'll hurt my eyes reading.

GREGERS. Oh, so he gives you lessons himself, then.

HEDVIG. He promised he would, but he hasn't had the time yet.

GREGERS. But isn't there anybody else to help you a little?

HEDVIG. Well, there's Mr. Molvik. But he isn't always, you know . . . er . . .

GREGERS. You mean he drinks?

HEDVIG. I guess so.

GREGERS. Well, in that case you've got time for all sorts of things. And in there, it must be like a world all its own—I imagine.

HEDVIG. Absolutely all of its own. And there are such a lot of strange things in there.

GREGERS. Really?

HEDVIG. Yes, big cases with books in them, and lots of the books have pictures.

GREGERS. Aha!

HEDVIG. Then there's an old writing desk with drawers and secret compartments, and a big clock with figures that are supposed to pop out on the hour. Only the clock doesn't work any more.

GREGERS. So time has stopped in there—in the wild duck's domain.

HEDVIG. Yes. And then there are old paint-boxes and things like that. And all those books.

GREGERS. And do you ever read the books?

HEDVIG. Oh yes, whenever I get the chance. But most of them are in English, and I can't read that. But then I look at the pictures. There's a great big book called *Harrison's History of London*; it must be a hundred years old, and there's an enormous lot of pictures in it. In front there's a picture of Death with an hourglass, and a girl. I think that's horrible. But then there's all the other pictures of churches and castles and streets and big ships sailing on the sea.

GREGERS. But tell me, where did all those wonderful things come from?

HEDVIG. Oh, an old sea captain used to live here once, and he brought them back with him. They called him "The Flying Dutchman."[4] That's funny, because he wasn't a Dutchman at all.

GREGERS. He wasn't?

HEDVIG. No. But finally he didn't come back, and everything just stayed here.

GREGERS. Tell me something . . . When you sit in there looking at

---

4. A specter-ship or its captain; believed to haunt the waters about the Cape of Good Hope. There are various legends to explain why its captain is condemned to sail around the cape forever and never make port.

pictures, don't you wish you could go abroad and see the real wide world itself?

HEDVIG. Not at all! I want to stay here at home always and help my father and mother.

GREGERS. Retouching photographs?

HEDVIG. Well, not only that. Most of all I'd like to learn how to engrave pictures like the ones in the English books.

GREGERS. Hm. What does your father say to that?

HEDVIG. I don't think Father likes the idea. He's funny about things like that. Imagine, he talks about me learning basket-weaving and braiding straw! I certainly don't think much of that.

GREGERS. No, neither do I.

HEDVIG. Still, he's right when he says that if I'd learned basket-weaving I could have made the new basket for the wild duck.

GREGERS. You could have, true. And of course you'd have been just the right person for the job.

HEDVIG. Because it's *my* wild duck.

GREGERS. Of course it is.

HEDVIG. Oh yes. I own it. But Daddy and Grandfather can borrow it as often as they like.

GREGERS. I see. What do they do with it?

HEDVIG. Oh, they look after it and build things for it, and things like that.

GREGERS. I understand. Because the wild duck must be the most important creature in there.

HEDVIG. Of course, because she's a *real* wild bird. And besides, it's such a pity for her, poor thing. She's got nobody at all to keep her company.

GREGERS. No family, like the rabbits. . . .

HEDVIG. No. The chickens also have plenty of others they grew up together with from the time they were baby chicks. But she's completely cut off from her own kind, poor thing. Everything's so strange about the wild duck, too. Nobody knows her and nobody know where she comes from, either.

GREGERS. And then she has been down in the depths of the sea.

HEDVIG [*glances quickly at him, suppresses a smile, and asks*]. Why do you say "the depths of the sea"?

GREGERS. Why, what *should* I say?

HEDVIG. You could say "the bottom of the sea"—or "the sea bottom."

GREGERS. Can't I just as well say "the depths of the sea"?

HEDVIG. Yes, but it sounds so strange to hear other people say "the depths of the sea."

GREGERS. Why is that? Tell me.

HEDVIG. No, I won't. It's something silly.

GREGERS. Oh, I'm sure it isn't. Come on, tell me why you smiled.

HEDVIG. Well, it's because every time I happen to think about the way it is in there—when it kind of comes in a flash through my mind—

it always seems to me that the whole room and everything in it is called "the depths of the sea." But that's just silly.

GREGERS. I wouldn't say so at all.

HEDVIG. Well, it's only an attic.

GREGERS [*looking intently at her*]. Are you so sure of that?

HEDVIG. [*astonished*]. That it's an attic?

GREGERS. Yes, do you know that for sure?

[HEDVIG *is silent, looking at him open-mouthed.* GINA *enters from the kitchen with a tablecloth and silverware.*]

GREGERS [*getting up*]. I'm afraid I've descended on you too early.

GINA. Oh well, you got to be someplace. Anyhow, everything's just about ready. Clear the table, Hedvig.

[HEDVIG *clears up; she and* GINA *lay the table during the following dialogue.* GREGERS *sits down in the armchair and starts leafing through an album of photographs.*]

GREGERS. I hear you know how to do retouching, Mrs. Ekdal.

GINA [*with a sidelong glance*]. Yes, I know how.

GREGERS. That was indeed most fortunate.

GINA. How do you mean—"fortunate"?

GREGERS. Seeing that Hjalmar became a photographer, I mean.

HEDVIG. Mother knows how to take pictures, too.

GINA. Oh yes, I managed to pick that up, all right.

GREGERS. So perhaps it is really you that carries on the business?

GINA. Well, when Hjalmar hasn't got the time himself . . .

GREGERS. He's very much taken up with his old father, I would imagine.

GINA. Yes. Besides it's no job for a man like Hjalmar, taking pictures of every Tom, Dick and Harry that comes along.

GREGERS. I quite agree. Still, once he's gone in for that line of work, shouldn't he . . .

GINA. Sure, Mr. Werle, you don't imagine Hjalmar is just a common ordinary photographer.

GREGERS. True enough. Nevertheless . . .

[*A shot is fired inside the attic.*]

GREGERS [*jumps up*]. What was that!

GINA. Ugh, they're shooting again!

GREGERS. Do they *shoot* in there?

HEDVIG. They go hunting.

GREGERS. What on earth . . . ! [*Over by the door into the attic.*] Are you hunting, Hjalmar?

HJALMAR [*behind the netting*]. Oh, you're here? I had no idea, I was so busy . . . [*To* HEDVIG.] You might let a person know! [*Enters studio.*]

GREGERS. You go around shooting in the attic?

HJALMAR [*showing him a double-barreled pistol*]. Oh, only with this thing.

GINA. Yes, one of these days you and Grandpa's going to have an accident yet, with that pissle.

HJALMAR [*annoyed*]. I believe I have told you that a firearm such as this is called a pis*tol*.

GINA. Well, I can't see it makes it any safer, whatever you call it.

GREGERS. So you too have taken up hunting, Hjalmar?

HJALMAR. Only a bit of rabbit shooting now and then. Mostly for Father's sake, you understand.

GINA. Ain't men the limit—always got to have *some*thing to detract theirself with.

HJALMAR [*grimly*]. Yes, yes, we always have to distract ourselves with something.

GINA. That's just what I said.

HJALMAR. Hm. Oh well . . . [*To* GREGERS.] Yes, as I was about to say, by a lucky chance the attic is so situated that nobody can hear us shoot. [*Places the pistol on the top shelf.*] Don't touch the pistol, Hedvig! One of the barrels is loaded, remember that.

GREGERS [*looking in through the net*]. You have a hunting rifle too, I see.

HJALMAR. That's Father's old rifle. It's no good anymore, something's gone wrong with the lock. Still, it's fun to have around; we take it apart and clean it once in a while and grease it and put it together again. Of course, it's mostly Father that plays around with that sort of thing.

HEDVIG [*standing by* GREGERS]. Now you can really see the wild duck.

GREGERS. Yes, I was just looking at it. One of her wings droops a bit, it seems to me.

HJALMAR. Well, that's not so strange. After all, she was hit.

GREGERS. And she's dragging one foot slightly. Or am I mistaken?

HJALMAR. Perhaps, just a wee bit.

HEDVIG. Yes, that's the foot the dog got hold of.

HJALMAR. But aside from that there's not a thing the matter with her—which is really remarkable, considering she's got a charge of shot in her and that she's been between the teeth of a dog . . .

GREGERS [*with a glance at* HEDVIG]. . . . and has been in "the depths of the sea"—for so long.

HEDVIG [*smiles*]. Yes.

GINA [*busy at the table*]. My goodness, that blessed wild duck. You sure make a fuss over her.

HJALMAR. Hm.—Lunch ready soon?

GINA. Yes, right away. Hedvig, come give me a hand.

[GINA *and* HEDVIG *go out to the kitchen.*]

HJALMAR [*in an undertone*]. I don't think you'd better stand there watching Father. He doesn't like it.

[GREGERS *moves from attic door.*]

HJALMAR. Maybe I ought to close this door anyhow, before the others get here. [*Clapping his hand to scare the birds.*] Shoo, shoo—beat it! [*Lifting the curtain and pulling the doors together.*] This gadget here is my own invention. It's really quite amusing to have something like this to putter around with and fix up when it gets out of order. Besides which, of course, it's absolutely necessary; Gina doesn't want rabbits and chickens running around in the studio.

GREGERS. No, of course not. And I suppose it's your wife who's in charge here?

HJALMAR. As a rule I leave the routine business to her. That way I can retire to the living room and think about more important things.

GREGERS. What things actually, Hjalmar? Tell me.

HJALMAR. I wonder you didn't ask that sooner. Or maybe you haven't heard about the invention?

GREGERS. Invention? No.

HJALMAR. Really? You haven't? Well, of course, up there in the wilderness . . .

GREGERS. So you've made an invention!

HJALMAR. Not quite *made*, just yet—but I'm busy on it. As you can imagine, when I decided to devote myself to photography it was not merely in order to take pictures of a lot of nobodies . . .

GREGERS. Of course not. Your wife was just saying the same thing.

HJALMAR. I vowed that if I was going to dedicate my powers to this calling, I would raise it so high that it would become both a science and an art. And so I decided to work on this remarkable invention.

GREGERS. What does the invention consist of? What is it going to do?

HJALMAR. Come, come, my dear Gregers, you mustn't ask for details yet. It takes time, you know. Another thing—don't imagine it's vanity that spurs me on. I'm certainly not working for my own sake. Oh no, it is my life's mission that stands before me night and day.

GREGERS. What mission?

HJALMAR. Have you forgotten the silver-haired old man?

GREGERS. Your poor father, yes. But what can you actually do for him?

HJALMAR. I can restore his self-respect by raising the name of Ekdal once again to honor and dignity.

GREGERS. So that is your life's mission.

HJALMAR. Yes, I will rescue the shipwrecked old man. For shipwrecked he was, the moment the storm broke over him. By the time of that terrible investigation he was no longer himself. That pistol there, Gregers—the one we use to shoot rabbits—that has played a role in the tragedy of the House of Ekdal.

GREGERS. The pistol? Really?

HJALMAR. When sentence had been pronounced and he was to be imprisoned—he took that pistol in his hand . . .

GREGERS. He meant to . . . !

HJALMAR. Yes—but didn't dare. Lost his nerve. So broken, so demoralized was he already then. Oh, can you conceive it! He, an army officer, a man who had shot nine bears. He, who was descended from two lieutenant colonels—one after the other, naturally—. Can you conceive it, Gregers?

GREGERS. Yes, very well.

HJALMAR. Not I. Then, once again, the pistol figured in our family
chronicle. When he had put on the gray prison uniform and sat
behind bars . . . Oh, that was a terrible time for me, let me tell you.
I kept the shades down on both my windows. When I peeped out,
there was the sun, shining as usual. I couldn't grasp it. I saw people
walking in the street, laughing and chatting about trivialities. I could
not grasp it. It seemed to me that the whole of existence ought to
come to a standstill, like an eclipse.

GREGERS. That's just how I felt, when my mother died.

HJALMAR. In such an hour did Hjalmar Ekdal point the pistol at his own
breast.

GREGERS. You also thought of . . . !

HJALMAR. Yes.

GREGERS. But you did not fire.

HJALMAR. No. In the decisive moment I won the victory over myself. I
chose to live. And believe me, it takes courage to choose life under
those circumstances.

GREGERS. Well, that depends on how you look at it.

HJALMAR. No, my friend, no doubt about it. But it was all for the best.
Because now I'll soon perfect my invention, and then Dr. Relling
thinks, just as I do, that Father will be allowed to wear his uniform
again. I will demand that as my sole reward.

GREGERS. So it's about wearing the uniform that he . . . ?

HJALMAR. Yes, that's what he yearns and pines for most of all. You have
no idea how my heart bleeds for him. Every time we celebrate some
little family occasion—like Gina's and my wedding anniversary, or
whatever it may be—in trots the old man wearing his uniform of
happier days. But just let him hear so much as a knock on the door—
because he doesn't dare show himself like that in front of strangers,
you see—back into his room he scurries as fast as his old legs will
carry him. Think, Gregers, how heart-rending it is for a son to see
such things!

GREGERS. About how soon do you think the invention will be perfected?

HJALMAR. Good lord, you mustn't ask me for details like dates. An
invention is not a thing entirely under one's control. It's largely a
matter of inspiration—of a sudden insight—and it's next to impossible
to figure out in advance just when that may come.

GREGERS. But you *are* making progress?

HJALMAR. Of course I'm making progress. I grapple every single day with
the invention, I'm filled with it. Every afternoon, right after dinner,
I shut myself in the living room, where I can concentrate in peace.
But I simply must not be rushed; that doesn't do a bit of good. That's
what Relling says, too.

GREGERS. And you don't think all this business in the attic there draws
you away from your work, and distracts you too much?

HJALMAR. No, no, no. Quite the reverse. You mustn't say such things.

After all, I can't go around day in day out everlastingly poring over the same exhausting problems. I must have something to occupy me during the waiting period. The inspiration, the intuition—look, when it's ready to come, it will come, and that's all.

GREGERS. My dear Hjalmar, I almost think there is something of the wild duck in you.

HJALMAR. The wild duck? How do you mean?

GREGERS. You have dived down and bitten yourself fast into the undergrowth.

HJALMAR. Are you by any change alluding to the all but fatal shot that maimed my father—and me as well?

GREGERS. Not exactly. I wouldn't say that you are maimed. But you have landed in a poisonous swamp, Hjalmar; an insidious blight has got hold of you, and you have sunk down to the depths to die in darkness.

HJALMAR. I? Die in darkness! Now look here, Gregers, you'd really better quit talking such nonsense.

GREGERS. Don't worry, I'll get you up again. You see, I too have got a mission in life now. I found it yesterday.

HJALMAR. That's all very well, but just you leave me out of it. I can assure you that—apart from my understandable melancholy, of course—I am as content as any man could wish to be.

GREGERS. The fact that you are content is itself a result of the poison.

HJALMAR. Look, my dear Gregers, will you please cut out all this rot about blight and poison. I am not at all used to that sort of talk; in my house nobody ever talks to me about unpleasant things.

GREGERS. That I can well believe.

HJALMAR. No, because it's not good for me. And there are no swamp vapors here, as you put it. The roof may be low in the poor photographer's home, that I know—and my means are slender. But I am an inventor, man—and a breadwinner as well. That raises me above my humble circumstances . . . Ah, here comes our lunch!

[GINA *and* HEDVIG *enter with bottles of beer, a decanter of schnapps, glasses, and other things for the lunch. At the same time,* RELLING *and* MOLVIK *enter from the hallway, both without hat or overcoat.* MOLVIK *is dressed in black.*]

GINA [*setting things on table*]. Well, here they come right on the dot.

RELLING. Once Molvik got the idea he coud smell herring salad, there was no holding him.—Good morning again, Ekdal.

HJALMAR. Gregers, may I present Mr. Molvik; Dr. . . . that's right, you know Relling, don't you?

GREGERS. Slightly.

RELLING. Oh, it's Mr. Werle junior. Yes indeed, we once had a couple of skirmishes up at the Højdal works. You just moved in?

GREGERS. This morning.

RELLING. Molvik and I live on the floor below, so you're not far from doctor or parson, should you have need of either.

GREGERS. Thanks, it's not unlikely I may—yesterday we were thirteen at table.

HJALMAR. Oh, don't start on that creepy talk again!

RELLING. Relax, Ekdal. You can be damn sure it won't be you.

HJALMAR. I hope not, for my family's sake. Well, come sit down and let's eat, drink, and be merry.

GREGERS. Aren't we going to wait for your father?

HJALMAR. No, he'll have a bite later on in his room. Do sit down!

[*The men sit down at the table, and eat and drink.* GINA *and* HEDVIG *go in and out, waiting on them.*]

RELLING. Molvik really tied one on last night, Mrs. Ekdal.

GINA. Yeah? Again?

RELLING. Didn't you hear him when I brought him home?

GINA. No, I can't say I did.

RELLING. That's good—because last night Molvik really was awful.

GINA. Is it true, Molvik?

MOLVIK. Let us draw a veil over last night's proceedings. Such episodes are totally foreign to my better self.

RELLING [*to* GREGERS]. It comes over him like a sort of possession, so I am obliged to take him out on a binge. Because Mr. Molvik, you see, is dæmonic.

GREGERS. Dæmonic?

RELLING. Molvik is dæmonic, yes.

GREGERS. Hm.

RELLING. And dæmonic natures are not made for the straight and narrow; they've got to kick over the traces once in a while.—Well, so you're still sticking it out up there at those ghastly dark works?

GREGERS. I have till now.

RELLING. Say, did you ever collect on that claim you used to go around with?

GREGERS. Claim? [*Grasps his meaning.*] Oh, that.

HJALMAR. Were you a bill collector, Gregers?

GREGERS. Oh, nonsense.

RELLING. He certainly was. He used to go around to all the workmen's shacks presenting something he called "the claim of the ideal."

GREGERS. I was young in those days.

RELLING. You bet you were. Mighty young. And that claim of the ideal— you never did get it honored as long as I was up there.

GREGERS. Nor afterwards, either.

RELLING. Well, then I imagine you've got the sense by now to knock a little off the bill.

GREGERS. Never—not when I'm dealing with an authentic human being.

HJALMAR. Well, that sounds reasonable enough.—Some butter, Gina.

RELLING. And a slice of pork for Molvik.

MOLVIK. Ugh, not pork!

[*Knocking inside the attic door.*]

HJALMAR. Open up, Hedvig; Father wants to come out.

[HEDVIG *goes and opens the door a little;* OLD EKDAL *enters, carrying a freshly flayed rabbit skin; she closes the door after him.*]

EKDAL. Good morning, Gentlemen! Good hunting today. Bagged a beauty.

HJALMAR. And you went and skinned it without waiting for me!

EKDAL. Salted it down, too. Good tender meat, rabbit. Sweet, too, tastes like sugar. Hearty appetite, Gentlemen! [*Goes into his room.*]

MOLVIK [*rising*]. Excuse me . . . I can't . . . I must get downstairs at once . . .

RELLING. Drink some soda water, man!

MOLVIK [*hurrying*]. Uh . . . uh! [*Exits through the hall door.*]

RELLING [*to* HJALMAR]. Let us drain a glass to the old Nimrod.[5]

HJALMAR [*clinks glasses with him*]. Yes, to the sportsman on the brink of the grave.

RELLING. To the gray-headed . . . [*Drinks.*] By the way—is it gray hair he's got, or is it white?

HJALMAR. Sort of betwixt and between, I'd say. As a matter of fact, not much of either any more.

RELLING. Oh well, life can be good enough under a toupee. Yes, Ekdal, when you come right down to it, you are a lucky man. You have your beautiful goal to strive for . . .

HJALMAR. And I do strive, believe me.

RELLING. And then you've got your excellent wife, waddling so cozily in and out in her felt slippers, swaying her hips and making everything nice and comfortable for you.

HJALMAR. Yes, Gina . . . [*nods to her*] you are a good companion to have on life's journey.

GINA. Oh, don't sit there bisecting me.

RELLING. And then your Hedvig, Ekdal, what?

HJALMAR [*moved*]. The child, yes! First and foremost, the child. Hedvig, come here to me. [*Stroking her hair.*] What day is it tomorrow, eh?

HEDVIG [*shaking him*]. Oh, don't say anything about that, Father.

HJALMAR. It pierces me to the heart to think how little we can do—only a little celebration in the attic . . .

HEDVIG. Oh, but that'll be just lovely!

RELLING. And wait till the marvelous invention comes out, Hedvig!

HJALMAR. Yes indeed—*then* you shall see! Hedvig, I am resolved to secure your future. You shall want for nothing as long as you live. For you, I shall demand . . . something or other. That will be the poor inventor's sole reward.

HEDVIG [*whispers, her arms around his neck*]. Oh you dear, dear Daddy!

5. Nimrod is described in Genesis 10.9 as "a mighty hunter before the Lord" [*Translator's note*].

RELLING [*to* GREGERS]. Well, now, don't you think it's nice, for a change, to sit at a well-laid table in a happy family circle?

HJALMAR. Yes, I really appreciate these meal-times.

GREGERS. I, for my part, do not thrive in swamp vapors.

RELLING. Swamp vapors?

HJALMAR. Oh, don't start on *that* again!

GINA. God knows there's no swamp vapors around here, Mr. Werle. I air the house out every blessed day.

GREGERS [*leaving the table*]. The stench I have in mind, you can hardly air out.

HJALMAR. Stench!

GINA. Yes, Hjalmar, how do you like that!

RELLING. Pardon me—I don't suppose it could be yourself that brought the stink with you from the pits up north?

GREGERS. It's just like you to call what I bring to this house a stink.

RELLING [*goes up to him*]. Listen here, Mr. Werle junior, I have a strong suspicion you are still carrying around that "claim of the ideal" un-abridged in your back pocket.

GREGERS. I carry it in my heart.

RELLING. Well wherever the hell you carry it, I advise you not to play bill collector here as long as *I'm* around.

GREGERS. And suppose I do?

RELLING. You'll be sent head first down the stairs. Now you know.

HJALMAR [*rising*]. No, Relling, really . . . !

GREGERS. Go ahead, throw me out . . .

GINA [*interposing*]. You can't do that, Relling. But I must say, Mr. Werle, you've got a nerve to talk to *me* about smells, after the mess you made with your stove.

[*There is a knock on the hall door.*]

HEDVIG. Mother, somebody's knocking.

HJALMAR. Darn! Now all we need is customers barging in.

GINA. I'll go . . . [*Goes and opens the door; gives a start; draws back.*] Oh! What the . . . !

[HÅKON WERLE, *in a fur coat, takes a step into the room.*]

WERLE. I beg your pardon, but I believe my son is staying here.

GINA [*gulping*]. Yes.

HJALMAR [*coming forward*]. Sir, won't you do us the honor to . . . ?

WERLE. Thanks, I just want a word with my son.

GREGERS. Yes, what is it? Here I am.

WERLE. I wish to talk with you in your room.

GREGERS. In my room—all right . . . [*About to go.*]

GINA. God, no. It's not fit in there for . . .

WERLE. Very well, out in the hall, then. I want to talk to you in private.

HJALMAR. You can do it right here, Mr. Werle. Relling, come into the living room.

[HJALMAR *and* RELLING *exit right.* GINA *takes* HEDVIG *off with her to the kitchen.*]

GREGERS [*after a brief pause*]. Well, now we are alone.

WERLE. You let drop certain remarks last night . . . And in view of the fact that you've gone and moved in with the Ekdals, I can only assume that you have something or other in mind against me.

GREGERS. I intend to open Hjalmar Ekdal's eyes. He must see his position for what it is—that's all.

WERLE. Is that the objective in life you spoke of yesterday?

GREGERS. Yes. You have left me no other.

WERLE. Is it I, then, who twisted your mind, Gregers?

GREGERS. You've twisted my whole life. I'm not thinking of all that concerning Mother . . . But it's you I have to thank that I am forever driven and tormented by a guilty conscience.

WERLE. Aha, your conscience! So that's your trouble.

GREGERS. I should have stood up to you that time the trap was laid for Lieutenant Ekdal. I should have warned him—for I suspected well enough how it was all going to end.

WERLE. Yes, in that case you certainly ought to have spoken out.

GREGERS. I didn't dare. That's what a frightened coward I was. I was so unspeakably afraid of you—not only then but long after.

WERLE. You've got over that fear now, it appears.

GREGERS. Yes, fortunately. The crime committed against old Ekdal, both by myself and by—others—that can never be redeemed. But Hjalmar I can still rescue from all the lies and deceit that threaten to destroy him.

WERLE. Do you think you'll be doing him a favor?

GREGERS. I *know* it.

WERLE. I suppose you think our good photographer is the kind of man to thank you for such a friendly service?

GREGERS. Yes! He certainly is.

WERLE. Hm . . . we'll see.

GREGERS. And besides . . . if I am to go on living, I must find some cure for my sick conscience.

WERLE. It will never be well. Your conscience has been sickly right from childhood. It is a legacy from your mother, Gregers—the only thing she ever left you.

GREGERS [*with a contemptuous half-smile*]. So you still haven't swallowed your disappointment that she didn't bring you the dowry you counted on?

WERLE. Let us keep to the point.—Are you quite resolved to set young Ekdal on what you assume to be the right track?

GREGERS. Yes, quite resolved.

WERLE. Well, in that case I could have saved myself the trouble of coming up here. Then I suppose it's no use asking you to come back home?

GREGERS. No.

WERLE. And you won't join the firm, either?

GREGERS. No.

WERLE. Very well. But since I intend to marry again, your share of my estate will be turned over to you at once.[6]

GREGERS [*quickly*]. No, I don't want that.

WERLE. You don't want it?

GREGERS. No, I don't dare. My conscience won't let me.

WERLE [*after a pause*]. Are you going up to the works again?

GREGERS. No, I consider myself released from your service.

WERLE. But what are you going to do?

GREGERS. Accomplish my mission. That's all.

WERLE. All right, but afterwards? What are you going to live on?

GREGERS. I've put aside a little of my salary.

WERLE. Yes, but how long will *that* last!

GREGERS. I think it will last out my time.

WERLE. What's that supposed to mean?

GREGERS. I'm answering no more questions.

WERLE. Good-bye, then, Gregers.

GREGERS. Good-bye.

[HÅKON WERLE *goes.*]

HJALMAR [*peeping in*]. Has he gone?

GREGERS. Yes.

[HJALMAR *and* RELLING *enter; also* GINA *and* HEDVIG, *from the kitchen.*]

RELLING. Well, that fixed *that* lunch.

GREGERS. Put on your things, Hjalmar. You're coming with me for a long walk.

HJALMAR. Gladly. What did your father want? Anything to do with me?

GREGERS. Just come. We must have a little talk. I'll go get my coat. [*Goes out by the hall door.*]

GINA. You shouldn't go with him, Hjalmar.

RELLING. No, don't you do it, old man. Stay where you are.

HJALMAR [*getting his coat and hat*]. What! When an old friend feels the need to open his heart to me in private . . . !

RELLING. But damn it!—can't you see the fellow is mad, cracked, off his rocker!

GINA. There, what did I tell you? His mother used to get these here fits and conniptions too.

HJALMAR. All the more reason he needs a friend's watchful eye. [*To* GINA.] Be sure and have dinner ready on time. So long. [*Goes out by the hall door.*]

RELLING. What a calamity that fellow didn't go straight to hell down one of the Højdal pits.

GINA. Good God!—what makes you say that?

RELLING [*muttering*]. Oh, I have my reasons.

GINA. Do you think young Werle is really crazy?

6. As a widower, the elder Werle could not remarry without securing some part of his estate to surviving children of his previous marriage [*Translator's note*].

RELLING. No, worse luck; he's no more crazy than most. But there's one bug he certainly has got in his system.

GINA. What's the matter with him, anyway?

RELLING. Well, I'll tell you, Mrs. Ekdal. He's got a severe case of inflamed integrity.

GINA. Inflamed integrity?

HEDVIG. Is that a kind of disease?

RELLING. Oh yes. It's a national disease. But it only breaks out sporadically. [*Nods to* GINA.] Thanks for lunch!

[*He goes out by the hall door.*]

GINA [*pacing the floor, disturbed*]. Ugh, that Gregers Werle—he always *was* a queer fish.

HEDVIG [*standing by the table and looking searchingly at her*]. I think this is all so strange.

Act Four

HJALMAR EKDAL's *studio. Photographs have apparently just been taken; a camera covered with a cloth, a stand, two chairs, a console, and other portrait materials are set out in the middle of the room. Afternoon light; the sun is about to set; after a while it begins to get dark.*

GINA *is standing at the open hall door with a dark slide and a wet photographic plate in her hand. She is speaking to somebody outside.*

GINA. Yes, positively. When I make a promise, I keep it. The first dozen will be ready on Monday.—Good-bye now, good-bye!

[*Footsteps can be heard going down the stairs.* GINA *shuts the door, puts the plate in the slide, and inserts the slide in the covered camera.*]

HEDVIG [*entering from the kitchen*]. Did they leave?

GINA [*tidying up*]. Yes, thank goodness. I finally got rid of them.

HEDVIG. Can you understand why Father isn't back yet?

GINA. You're sure he's not down at Relling's?

HEDVIG. No, he's not there. I just went down the back stairs and asked.

GINA. And his dinner standing there getting cold.

HEDVIG. Imagine! And Father's always so punctual about dinner.

GINA. Well, he'll be here soon, don't worry.

HEDVIG. Oh, I wish he'd come. Everything seems so strange.

GINA [*calls out*]. There he is!

[HJALMAR EKDAL *comes in through the hall door*].

HEDVIG [*up to him*]. Father! We've been waiting and waiting for you!

GINA [*glancing across*]. You sure have been out a long time, Hjalmar.

HJALMAR [*without looking at her*]. I suppose I have, yes.

[*He takes off his overcoat.* GINA *and* HEDVIG *try to help him; he waves them aside.*]

GINA. Maybe you ate someplace with Werle?

HJALMAR [*hanging up his coat*]. No.

GINA [*going toward the kitchen door*]. Then I'll go get your dinner.

HJALMAR. No, never mind. I don't want anything now.

HEDVIG [*coming closer*]. Aren't you feeling well, Father?

HJALMAR. Feeling well? Oh yes, tolerably. We had a tiring walk together, Gregers and I.

GINA. You shouldn't do that, Hjalmar, you're not used to it.

HJALMAR. Hm. There are lots of things a man must get used to in this world. [*Paces up and down.*] Did anybody come while I was out?

GINA. Only the engaged couple.

HJALMAR. No new orders?

GINA. No, not today.

HEDVIG. There'll be some tomorrow, Father, you'll see.

HJALMAR. I hope you're right, because tomorrow I mean to get down to work in real earnest.

HEDVIG. Tomorrow! Don't you remember what day it is tomorrow?

HJALMAR. Oh, that's right . . . Well, the day after tomorrow, then. From now on I intend to do everything myself; I want to do all the work entirely on my own.

GINA. What on earth for, Hjalmar? You'd only make your life a misery. I can still manage the photography; you go on with the invention.

HEDVIG. And what about the wild duck—and all the chickens and rabbits . . .

HJALMAR. Don't talk to me about that junk! I'm never setting foot in that attic again.

HEDVIG. But Father, you promised me there'd be a party tomorrow . . .

HJALMAR. Hm, that's right. Well, starting the day after tomorrow, then. That damn wild duck, I'd like to wring its neck!

HEDVIG [*cries out*]. The wild duck!

GINA. Well, I never!

HEDVIG [*shaking him*]. But Father, it's *my* wild duck!

HJALMAR. That's the only thing that stops me. I haven't the heart—for your sake, Hedvig, I haven't got the heart. But deep down I feel I ought to do it. I ought not tolerate under my roof any creature that has been in that man's hands.

GINA. Goodness sake, just because Grandpa got it off that good-for-nothing Pettersen . . .

HJALMAR [*walking up and down*]. There are certain demands . . . what shall I call them? Let us say—demands of the ideal—certain claims that a man cannot disregard without peril to his soul.

HEDVIG [*following him about*]. But think, the wild duck—that poor wild duck!

HJALMAR [*halts*]. I *told* you I'll spare it—for your sake. Not a hair of its head shall be . . . hm. As I said, I shall spare it. I have more important things to think about now. But now you ought to go for a little walk, Hedvig; the twilight is just right for you.

HEDVIG. I don't care to go out now.

HJALMAR. Yes, go on. Seems to me you're blinking your eyes a lot. It's not good for you, all these fumes in here. The air is close under this roof.

HEDVIG. Well, all right, I'll run down the kitchen way and walk around a little. My hat and coat . . . ? That's right, they're in my room. Father—promise you won't do anything to the wild duck while I'm gone.

HJALMAR. Not a feather of its head shall be touched. [*Presses her to him.*] You and I, Hedvig—we two . . . ! Well, run along now.

[HEDVIG *nods to her parents and goes out through the kitchen.*]

HJALMAR [*walks up and down without looking up*]. Gina.

GINA. Yes?

HJALMAR. As of tomorrow . . . or, let us say as of the day after tomorrow—I wish to keep the household accounts myself.

GINA. You want to keep the accounts also?

HJALMAR. Yes, keep track of what we take in, at any rate.

GINA. Oh, God help us, *that's* soon done.

HJALMAR. I wonder. It seems to me you make the money go a remarkably long way. [*Halts and looks at her.*] How do you do it?

GINA. That's because Hedvig and I need so little.

HJALMAR. Is it true that Father is highly paid for the copying he does for Mr. Werle?

GINA. I don't know if it's all that high. I don't know what the rates are for things like that.

HJALMAR. Well, roughly what *does* he get? I want to know.

GINA. It differs. I guess it come to about what he costs us, and a little pocket money.

HJALMAR. What he *costs* us! You never told me that before!

GINA. No, how could I. It made you so happy to think he got everything from you.

HJALMAR. And in fact it comes from Mr. Werle!

GINA. Oh, don't worry. He can afford it.

HJALMAR. Light me the lamp!

GINA [*lighting the lamp*]. Besides, how can we tell if it actually comes from him; it could easily be Gråberg . . .

HJALMAR. Why do you suddenly drag Gråberg into this?

GINA. Well, I don't know, I just thought . . .

HJALMAR. Hm!

GINA. Anyway, it wasn't me that got Grandpa the copying to do. You know yourself it was Berta, the time she took service there.

HJALMAR. It seems to me your voice is trembling.

GINA [*putting the shade on the lamp*]. Is it?

HJALMAR. And your hands are shaking. Aren't they?

GINA [*firmly*]. Say it straight out, Hjalmar. What's he gone and told you about me?

HJALMAR. Is it true—*can* it be true—that there was something between you and Mr. Werle while you were working in his house?

GINA. It's not true. Not then, there wasn't. He was after me all right, that I will say. And the Missus thought there was something going on, and she made such a fuss and a hullaballoo about it and went for me tooth and nail. She sure did.—So I quit.

HJALMAR. But then, afterwards . . . !

GINA. Well, *you* know, I went home. And my mother . . . she wasn't exactly as straight as you thought she was, Hjalmar. Anyway, she got after me about this, that, and the other. Because by that time Werle was a widower.

HJALMAR. All right! And then?

GINA. Well, I guess you might as well know it. He wouldn't give up till he had his way.

HJALMAR [*striking his hands together*]. And this is the mother of my child! How could you keep a thing like that from me!

GINA. Yes, I know it was wrong. I should've told you long ago, I guess.

HJALMAR. Right at the *start* you should have told me—then I'd have known the sort of woman you were.

GINA. But would you have married me, just the same?

HJALMAR. What do *you* think?

GINA. There you are, that's why I didn't dare tell you at the time. You know how much I'd come to care for you. So how could I go and make my own life a misery?

HJALMAR [*pacing about*]. And this is my Hedvig's mother! And to realize that everything I lay my eyes on . . . [*kicks a chair*] . . . my entire home . . . I owe to a favored predecessor! Oh, that old lecher!

GINA. Do your regret the fourteen-fifteen years we've had together?

HJALMAR [*fronting her*]. Tell me, have you not—every day, every hour—regretted this web of deceit you've spun around me, like a spider? Answer me! Have you really gone around here and not suffered agonies of remorse and shame?

GINA. Bless you, Hjalmar, I've had enough to think about just running the house and everything . . .

HJALMAR. You mean you never even give a thought to your past?

GINA. No, God knows I'd just about forgotten that old business.

HJALMAR. Oh, this dull, apathetic calm! That's what I find so outrageous. Imagine—not even a twinge of remorse!

GINA. But just tell me, Hjalmar—what would've become of you, if you hadn't had a wife like me?

HJALMAR. Like you!

GINA. Well, you've got to admit I've always been kind of more practical and with my feet on the ground than you. Well, of course I *am* a couple of years older.

HJALMAR. What would have become of me!

GINA. Because you weren't exactly living right when you first met me; you can't deny that.

HJALMAR. Is that what you call not living right? Oh, what would you know about a man's feelings when he falls into grief and despair—especially a man of my fiery temperament.

GINA. All right, all right, have it your way. Anyhow, I don't want to make no song and dance about it. Because you certainly turned out to be a real good man, once you got your own home and family. And now we'd got things so nice and comfortable here, and Hedvig and me was just thinking that soon we could spend a little on ourselves in the way of food and clothes.

HJALMAR. In this swamp of deceit, yes.

GINA. Oh, why did that nasty creature have to come poking his nose in here for!

HJALMAR. I, too, thought our home a happy one. What a delusion! And now where am I to find the inner force I need in order to bring forth my invention? Perhaps it will die with me. And then it will have been your past, Gina, that killed it.

GINA [about to weep]. Please, Hjalmar, you mustn't say a thing like that. When all my days I only tried to make everything the best for you!

HJALMAR. I ask you—what happens now to the breadwinner's dream? As I would lie there on the sofa, pondering the invention, I suspected full well that it would drain the last drop of my strength. Well I knew that the dayI held the patent in my hands, that day would mark my—final hour. And so it was my dream that you would be left the well-do-do widow of the late inventor.

GINA [drying her tears]. Hjalmar, don't talk like that. God forbid I should ever live to see the day I'm left a widow!

HJALMAR. Oh well, what's the difference. It's all over now, anyway. All over!

[GREGERS WERLE cautiously opens the hall door and looks in.]

GREGERS. May I come in?

HJALMAR. Yes, come in.

GREGERS [advances, his face radiant with joy, and reaches out his hands to them]. Well, you two dear people . . . ! [Looks from the one to the other and whispers to HJALMAR.] You haven't done it yet?

HJALMAR [aloud]. It is done.

GREGERS. It is?

HJALMAR. I have lived through the bitterest hour of my life.

GREGERS. But also, I trust, the most sublime.

HJALMAR. Anyway, for the time being it's done and over with.

GINA. God forgive you, Mr. Werle.

GREGERS [in great amazement]. But I don't understand this.

HJALMAR. What don't you understand?

GREGERS. So great an accounting—an accounting that a whole new way of life is to be founded on—a way of life, a partnership in truth, free of all deception . . .

HJALMAR. Yes, yes, I know. I know all that.

GREGERS. I was absolutely confident that when I came through that door I would be met by a radiance of transfiguration shining from the faces of both husband and wife. And all I see is this dull, heavy, gloomy . . .

GINA. Is that it. [*Takes the shade off the lamp.*]

GREGERS. You're not trying to understand me, Mrs. Ekdal. Well, well, I suppose you'll need time . . . But *you*, now, Hjalmar? Surely *you* must feel exalted by this great reckoning.

HJALMAR. Yes, naturally I do. That is—in a kind of way.

GREGERS. For surely nothing in the world can compare to finding forgiveness in one's heart for one who has erred, and raising her up to you with love.

HJALMAR. Do you think a man so easily gets over the bitter cup I just drained?

GREGERS. No, not an ordinary man, perhaps. But a man like *you* . . . !

HJALMAR. All right, I know, I know. But don't push me, Gregers. It takes time.

GREGERS. There is much of the wild duck in you, Hjalmar.

[RELLING *has entered by the hall door.*]

RELLING. What's this? Are we back to the wild duck again?

HJALMAR. Yes. The damaged trophy of Mr. Werle's sport.

RELLING. Werle senior? Is it him you're talking about?

HJALMAR. Him and . . . the rest of us.

RELLING [*to* GREGERS, *under his breath*]. Damn you to hell!

HJALMAR. What's that you're saying?

RELLING. I was expressing the fervent wish that this quack here would take himself off where he belongs. If he stays around here much longer, he's quite capable of messing you both up.

GREGERS. These two are not going to be "messed up," Mr. Relling. I need not speak for Hjalmar. Him we know. But she too must surely have, deep down inside, something worthy of trust, something of integrity . . .

GINA [*on the point of tears*]. Then why couldn't you leave me be like I was.

RELLING [*to* GREGERS]. Would it be impertinent to ask what it is exactly you want in this house?

GREGERS. I want to lay the foundation for a true marriage.

RELLING. So you don't think the Ekdals' marriage is good enough as it is?

GREGERS. It's probably as good a marriage as most, I regret to say. But a true marriage it has yet to become.

HJALMAR. You never did have an eye for the claim of the ideal, Relling.

RELLING. Nonsense, my boy!—Begging your pardon, Mr. Werle, but how many—at a rough guess—how many true marriages have you seen in your life?

GREGERS. Hardly a single one.

RELLING. Neither have I.

GREGERS. But I *have* seen innumerable marriages of the opposite sort. And I had occasion to observe at close quarters the havoc such a marriage can wreak on both partners.

HJALMAR. A man's whole moral foundation can crumble under his feet; that's the terrible thing.

RELLING. Well, of couse I've never been exactly married myself, so I can't judge about that. But this I do know, that the child is part of a marriage too. And you had better leave the child in peace.

HJALMAR. Oh—Hedvig! My poor Hedvig!

RELLING. Yes, see to it you keep Hedvig out of this. You two are grown people. In God's name, go ahead and muck up your own affairs to your heart's content. But I'm warning you—go easy with Hedvig, or you may end by doing her serious injury.

HJALMAR. Injury!

RELLING. Yes, or else she might do heself one—and maybe not only to herself.

GINA. How can you tell a thing like that, Relling?

HJALMAR. There's no immediate danger to her eyes, is there?

RELLING. This has nothing to do with her eyes. But Hedvig is at a difficult age. There's no telling *what* wild ideas she can get into her head.

GINA. Say, that's right! Lately she's started to fool around in such a peculiar way with the stove out in the kitchen. "Playing house on fire," she calls it. Sometimes I'm scared she *will* burn down the house.

RELLING. There you are; I knew it.

GREGERS [*to* RELLING]. But how do you explain a thing like that?

RELLING [*sullenly*]. Puberty, man.

HJALMAR. As long as the child has me! As long as I'm above the ground . . . !

[*There is a knock on the door.*]

GINA. Shhh, Hjalmar, there's somebody outside. [*Calls.*] Come in!

[*Enter* MRS. SØRBY, *in outdoor clothes.*]

MRS. SØRBY. Good evening!

GINA [*going toward her*]. Why, Berta, it's *you*!

MRS. SØRBY. It certainly is. Have I come at an inconvenient time?

HJALMAR. Gracious, no—a messenger from that house . . .

MRS. SØRBY [*to* GINA]. To tell the truth I hoped I wouldn't find your menfolk at home this time of day. So I dropped in to have a little chat with you and say good-bye.

GINA. Oh? Why? Are you going away?

MRS. SØRBY. Yes, tomorrow early—up to Højdal. Mr. Werle left this afternoon. [*Casually, to* GREGERS.] He sends his regards.

GINA. Imagine!

HJALMAR. So Mr. Werle has left? And you're following him?

MRS. SØRBY. Yes, Ekdal, what do you say to that?

HJALMAR. I say—beware!

GREGERS. Let me explain. My father is marrying Mrs. Sørby.

HJALMAR. Marrying her!

GINA. Oh, Berta—finally!

RELLING [*his voice trembling slightly*]. Surely this can't be true?

MRS. SØRBY. Yes, my dear Relling, it's quite true.

RELLING. You are going to get married again?

MRS. SØRBY. It looks like it. Werle has got a special license, and we're going to have a quiet wedding up at the works.

GREGERS. Then I suppose I must wish you joy, like a good stepson.

MRS. SØRBY. Thank you, if you really mean it. I do hope it will lead to happiness for both Werle and myself.

RELLING. You have every reason for hope. Mr. Werle never gets drunk— at least not to my knowledge. And I doubt he's in the habit of beating his wives, either, like the late lamented horse-doctor.

MRS. SØRBY. Oh, come now, let Sørby rest in peace. He had his good points too.

RELLING. Mr. Werle has better ones, I'm sure.

MRS. SØRBY. At any rate he didn't go and throw away the best that was in him. The man who does that must take the consequences.

RELLING. Tonight I will go out with Molvik.

MRS. SØRBY. Don't do that, Relling. Don't—for my sake.

RELLING. Can't be helped. [*To* HJALMAR.] Come along too, if you like.

GINA. No, thanks. Hjalmar don't go on such disserpations.

HJALMAR [*angrily, in an undertone*]. Oh, be still!

RELLING. Good-bye, Mrs.—Werle. [*Exit through hall door.*]

GREGERS [*to* MRS. SØRBY]. It appears that you and Dr. Relling are rather intimately acquainted.

MRS. SØRBY. Yes, we've known each other a good many years. As a matter of fact, at one time something or other might have even come of it.

GREGERS. It was certainly lucky for you it didn't.

MRS. SØRBY. You may well say that. But I have always been careful not to act on impulse. After all, a woman can't afford to throw herself away.

GREGERS. Aren't you the least bit afraid I might drop a hint to my father about this old friendship?

MRS. SØRBY. You may be quite sure I told him myself.

GREGERS. Oh?

MRS. SØRBY. Your father knows every last thing that anyone could possibly say about me with any truth. I've told him everything of that kind. It was the first thing I did when I realized what he had in mind.

GREGERS. Then I'd say you are exceptionally frank.

MRS. SØRBY. I have always been frank. For us women it's the best policy.

HJALMAR. What do you say to that, Gina?

GINA. Oh, us women can't all be the same. Some's made one way and some another.

MRS. SØRBY. Well, Gina, I do think it's best to go about things as I did.

And Werle hasn't kept back anything about himself, either. You know, that's mainly what brought us together. With me he can sit and talk as openly as a child. He never got a chance to do that before. Imagine, a healthy, vigorous man like him, listening all his youth and the best years of his life to nothing but hell-fire sermons. And many a time sermons about completely imaginary offenses—to judge by what I've heard.

GINA. That's God's truth, all right.

GREGERS. If you ladies are going to embark on that topic, you'll have to excuse me.

MRS. SØRBY. There's no need to go on that account. I won't say another word. But I wanted you to know that I haven't hushed up a thing or done anything underhanded. People may say I'm making quite a catch—and so I am, in a way. But still, I don't think I'm getting any more than I'm giving. I will never let him down. And I can look after him and help him as nobody else can, now that he'll soon be helpless.

HJALMAR. Soon be helpless?

GREGERS [to MRS. SØRBY]. All right, all right, don't talk about it here.

MRS. SØRBY. It's no use trying to hide it any more, much as he'd like to. He's going blind.

HJALMAR [struck]. Going blind? But how extraordinary. He too?

GINA. Well, lots of people do.

MRS. SØRBY. And you can imagine what that means for a businessman. Well, I'll try to use my eyes for him as best I can. But now I really must be going, I've got a thousand things to do.—Oh yes, Ekdal, I was to tell you that if there's anything at all Mr. Werle can do for you, just get in touch with Gråberg.

GREGERS. That offer you may be sure Hjalmar Ekdal will decline with thanks.

MRS. SØRBY. Really? I didn't have the impression in the past . . .

GINA. No, Berta, Hjalmar don't need anything more from Mr. Werle.

HJALMAR [slowly and with emphasis]. Will you pay my respects to your intended husband and tell him that in the very near future I propose to call on Gråberg . . .

GREGERS. What! You want to do that!

HJALMAR. . . . to call on Gråberg, I repeat, and demand an account of what I owe his employer. I will pay that debt of honor . . . Ha-ha-ha, "debt of honor," that's a good joke! But enough of that. I will pay it all, with five percent interest.

GINA. But Hjalmar, dear, God knows we haven't got the money for that.

HJALMAR. Will you inform your intended that I am working indefatigably on my invention. Tell him that what sustains me in that exhausting labor is the wish to free myself from a painful burden of debt. This is my motive for the invention. The entire proceeds shall be used to release me from my pecuniary obligations to your future spouse.

MRS. SØRBY. Something has happened in this house.

HJALMAR. Yes, so it has.

MRS. SØRBY. Well, good-bye then. I still had something I wanted to talk to you about, Gina, but it will have to wait for another time. Good-bye.

[HJALMAR *and* GREGERS *bow silently;* GINA *follows* MRS. SØRBY *to the door.*]

HJALMAR. Not a step beyond the threshold, Gina!

[MRS. SØRBY *leaves;* GINA *shuts the door after her.*]

HJALMAR. There, Gregers; now I've got that load of debt off my mind.

GREGERS. Soon, anyway.

HJALMAR. I believe my attitude may be called correct.

GREGERS. You are the man I always took you for.

HJALMAR. In certain cases it is impossible to disregard the claim of the ideal. As provider for my family, naturally I'm bound to writhe and groan. Believe me, it's no joke for a man without private means to pay off a debt of many years' standing—a debt over which, so to speak, the dust of oblivion had already settled. But never mind. My human dignity also demands its rights.

GREGERS [*laying his hand on his shoulder*]. Dear Hjalmar—wasn't it a good thing that I came?

HJALMAR. Yes.

GREGERS. Getting your whole situation clarified—wasn't that a good thing?

HJALMAR [*a bit impatiently*]. Yes, of course it was. But there's one thing that outrages my sense of justice.

GREGERS. And what is that?

HJALMAR. It's this, that . . . Well, I don't know if I ought to speak so freely about your father.

GREGERS. Don't hesitate in the least on *my* account.

HJALMAR. Well, then. Can't you see . . . I think it's absolutely outrageous, to realize it turns out that it's not I but *he* who will achieve the true marriage.

GREGERS. How can you say such a thing!

HJALMAR. Because it's so. Aren't your father and Mrs. Sørby entering upon a marriage built on full confidence, built on complete and unconditional frankness on both sides? They sweep nothing under the carpet, nothing is hushed up between them. There has been declared between them, if I may so put it, mutual forgiveness of sin.

GREGERS. All right, what about it?

HJALMAR. Well—then it's all *there*. You said yourself this was the difficulty in founding the true marriage.

GREGERS. But Hjalmar, that's entirely different. Surely you're not going to compare either yourself or her with those two . . . ? Oh, *you* know what I mean.

HJALMAR. All the same, I can't get over the fact that there's something in all this that offends my sense of justice. Why, it looks exactly as if there were no divine Providence in the world.

GINA. For God's sake, Hjalmar, don't talk like that.

GREGERS. Hm; let's not get involved in those questions.

HJALMAR. Though on the other hand, I think I'm beginning to make out the hand of fate after all. He *is* going blind.

GINA. Oh, maybe it's not so certain.

HJALMAR. There's no doubt about it. At least we *ought* not to doubt it, because precisely in that fact lies the proof of just retribution. He blinded the eyes of a trusting fellow being once.

GREGERS. Alas, he has blinded many.

HJALMAR. And now comes Nemesis, mysterious and inexorable, and demands the man's own eyes.[7]

GINA. Don't say such awful things! It scares me.

HJALMAR. It profits a man to immerse himself, once in a while, in the dark side of existence.

[HEDVIG, *in her hat and coat, comes in through the hall door, happy and breathless.*]

GINA. Are you back already?

HEDVIG. Yes, I didn't feel like walking any more. It was lucky, too, because I just met somebody outside the house.

HJALMAR. That Mrs. Sørby, I suppose.

HEDVIG. Yes.

HJALMAR [*pacing the floor*]. I hope you have seen her for the last time.

[*Silence.* HEDVIG *looks timidly from one to the other as though trying to gauge their mood.*]

HEDVIG [*approaching* HJALMAR, *ingratiatingly*]. Daddy . . . ?

HJALMAR. Well—what is it, Hedvig?

HEDVIG. Mrs. Sørby brought something for me.

HJALMAR [*halts*]. For you?

HEDVIG. Yes. It's something for tomorrow.

GINA. Berta always brings some little thing for your birthday.

HJALMAR. What is it?

HEDVIG. No, you're not supposed to find out yet. Mother is to bring it to me in bed first thing in the morning.

HJALMAR. All these intrigues; all these secrets . . . !

HEDVIG [*hastily*]. Oh, you can see it if you want. It's a big letter. [*Takes the letter out of her coat pocket.*]

HJALMAR. A letter too?

HEDVIG. The letter is all there is. The other thing is coming later on, I guess. But imagine—a letter! I never got a letter before. And it says "Miss"[8] on the outside. [*Reads.*] "Miss Hedvig Ekdal." Imagine— that's me!

HJALMAR. Let me see that letter.

7. Nemesis was the Greek goddess of revenge, and the term is used still, as here, for providential retribution [*Translator's note*].
8. The term "Miss" (*Frøken*), which Hedvig is pleased to find before her name on the letter containing the deed of gift, implied not only that she was growing up but also a certain amount of social status, as the same term implies in the title of Strindberg's *Fröken Julie* (variously translated "Miss Julie" or "Lady Julia") [*Translator's note*].

HEDVIG [*handing it to him*]. There, you see?

HJALMAR. It's Mr. Werle's handwriting.

GINA. Are you sure, Hjalmar?

HJALMAR. See for yourself.

GINA. What would *I* know about it?

HJALMAR. Hedvig, may I open the letter—and read it?

HEDVIG. Yes, of course you may, if you want to.

GINA. Not tonight, Hjalmar. You know it's meant for tomorrow.

HEDVIG [*in a low voice*]. Oh, why not let him read it! It's bound to be something nice, then he'll be glad and everything will be all right again.

HJALMAR. I may open it, then?

HEDVIG. Yes, please do, Father. It will be fun to find out what it is.

HJALMAR. Very well. [*Opens the letter, reads it, and appears bewildered.*] What *is* this . . . ?

GINA. Why, what does it say?

HEDVIG. Please, Father—tell us!

HJALMAR. Be quiet. [*Reads it through again. He has turned pale, but speaks with control.*] It's a bequest, Hedvig, a deed of gift.

HEDVIG: Really? What do I get?

HJALMAR. Read it yourself.

[HEDVIG *goes over to the lamp and reads.*]

HJALMAR [*in an undertone, clenching his fists*]. The eyes! The eyes— and now this letter!

HEDVIG [*interrupts her reading*]. Yes, but it looks to me like it's Grandfather who's getting it.

HJALMAR [*takes the letter from her*]. You, Gina—can you understand this?

GINA. I don't know the first thing about it. Why don't you just *tell* me?

HJALMAR. Mr. Werle writes to Hedvig that her old grandfather need not trouble himself any more about the copying but that from now on he can draw a hundred crowns every month from the office . . .

GREGERS. Aha!

HEDVIG. A hundred crowns, Mother! I read that part.

GINA. That will be nice for Grandpa.

HJALMAR. . . . one hundred crowns, for as long as he needs it—naturally that means till he passes on.

GINA. Well, that's him provided for, poor old soul.

HJALMAR. But then it comes. You didn't read far enough, Hedvig. Afterwards, the gift passes to you.

HEDVIG. To me? All of it?

HJALMAR. You are assured the same amount for the rest of your life, he writes. Do you hear that, Gina?

GINA. Yes, I hear.

HEDVIG. Imagine—all the money I'm going to get! [*Shaking him.*] Father, Father, aren't you glad?

HJALMAR [*disengages himself from her*]. Glad! [*Walking about.*] Oh, what vistas, what perspectives open up before me! It's Hedvig—*she's* the one he's providing for so amply!

GINA. Naturally. She's the one with the birthday . . .

HEDVIG. Oh, but you'll get it anyway, Father! Don't you know I'll give it all to you and Mother?

HJALMAR. To your mother, yes! There we have it.

GREGERS. Hjalmar, this is a trap that's being set for you.

HJALMAR. Another trap, you think?

GREGERS. When he was here this morning, he said: "Hjalmar Ekdal is not the man you think he is."

HJALMAR. Not the man . . . !

GREGERS. "Just wait, you'll see," he said.

HJALMAR. See that I would let myself be bought off with a bribe . . . !

HEDVIG. Mother, what *is* this all about?

GINA. Go and take off your things.

[HEDVIG, *about to cry, goes out by the kitchen door.*]

GREGERS. Yes, Hjalmar, now we see who is right—he or I.

HJALMAR [*slowly tears the letter in two and lays the pieces on the table*]. Here is my answer.

GREGERS. Just as I thought.

HJALMAR [*goes over to* GINA, *who is standing by the stove, and speaks in a low voice*]. Now, I want the whole truth. If everything was over between you and him when you—"got to care" for me, as you call it—why did he arrange things so we could afford to get married?

GINA. I guess he thought he'd be able to come and go here as he liked.

HJALMAR. Only that? Wasn't he afraid of a certain possibility?

GINA. I don't know what you mean.

HJALMAR. I want to know if—your child has the right to live under my roof.

GINA [*drawing herself up, her eyes flashing*]. You ask me that!

HJALMAR. I want a straight answer. Is Hedvig mine—or . . . Well?

GINA [*looks at him with cold defiance*]. I don't know.

HJALMAR [*quavering*]. You don't know!

GINA. How should I know? A woman like me . . .

HJALMAR [*quietly, turning away from her*]. Then I have nothing more to do in this house.

GREGERS. Think well what you're doing, Hjalmar!

HJALMAR [*putting on his overcoat*]. There's nothing to think about, for a man like me.

GREGERS. On the contrary, there's everything in the world to think about. You three must stay together if you are to win through to the sublime spirit of sacrifice and forgiveness.

HJALMAR. I don't *want* to! Never! Never! My hat! [*Takes his hat.*] My house lies in ruins about me. [*Bursts into tears.*] Gregers, I have no child!

HEDVIG [*who has opened the kitchen door*]. What are you saying! [*Up to him.*] Father! Father!

GINA. *Now* look what you did!

HJALMAR. Don't come near me, Hedvig. Get away from me. I can't bear to look at you. Oh, those eyes . . . ! Good-bye. [*He makes for the door.*]

HEDVIG [*clinging to him, cries out*]. No! No! Don't leave me!

GINA [*shouts*]. Look at the child, Hjalmar! Look at the child!

HJALMAR. I won't! I can't! I must get out—away from all this. [*He tears himelf loose from* HEDVIG *and goes.*]

HEDVIG [*despair in her eyes*]. He's leaving us, Mother! He's leaving us! He'll never come back any more!

GINA. Don't you cry, Hedvig. Your father's coming back, you'll see.

HEDVIG [*throws herself sobbing on the sofa*]. No, no, he's never coming back to us again.

GREGERS. You do believe I meant it all for the best, Mrs. Ekdal?

GINA. Yes, I imagine you did. But God forgive you all the same.

HEDVIG [*on the sofa*]. Oh, I just want to die! What did I do to him! Mother, you've got to get him home again!

GINA. Yes, yes, yes. Just calm down and I'll go out and look for him. [*Putting on her coat.*] Maybe he's gone down to Relling. But you mustn't lie there bawling like that. Promise?

HEDVIG [*sobbing convulsively*]. All right, I'll stop. If only Father comes back.

GREGERS [*to* GINA, *who is about to leave*]. Wouldn't it perhaps be better if you first let him go through his ordeal?

GINA. Oh, he can do that after. First of all we have to get the child quieted down. [*Goes out by hall door.*]

HEDVIG [*sitting up, drying her tears*]. Now you've got to tell me what's the matter. Why doesn't my father want me any more?

GREGERS. You're not to ask that till you're all grown up.

HEDVIG [*with little catches in her breath*]. But I can't go on feeling so awful all the time till I'm grown up—I know what it is. Maybe I'm not really Father's child.

GREGERS [*uneasily*]. How could that be?

HEDVIG. Mother could have found me somewhere. And now maybe Father got to know about it. I've read about things like that.

GREGERS. Well, even in that case . . .

HEDVIG. You'd think he could care for me just the same. Even more, almost. After all, we got the wild duck as a present too, and look how much I love her.

GREGERS [*glad to change the subject*]. Yes, that's right, the wild duck. Let's talk a little about the wild duck, Hedvig.

HEDVIG. That poor wild duck. He can't stand the sight of her either, any more. Imagine, he wanted to wring her neck!

GREGERS. Oh, he wouldn't do that.

HEDVIG. No, but he *said* it. And I think it's an awful thing to say, because I pray for the wild duck every night, that she should be safe from death and everything bad.

GREGERS [*looking at her*]. Do you say your prayers every night?

HEDVIG. Oh yes.

GREGERS. Who taught you that?

HEDVIG. Myself. One time when Father was terribly sick and had leeches on his neck, and he said he was lying at death's door.

GREGERS. Really?

HEDVIG. So I prayed for him when I went to bed. And I've kept it up ever since.

GREGERS. And now you pray for the wild duck too?

HEDVIG. I thought I'd better include her, because she was so sick in the beginning.

GREGERS. Do you also say your prayers in the morning?

HEDVIG. Of course not.

GREGERS. Why *not* in the morning, as well?

HEDVIG. Why, it's light in the morning, so what's there to be afraid of.

GREGERS. And that wild duck you love so much, your father wanted to wring its neck . . .

HEDVIG. No, he said he *ought* to do it, but that he would spare her for my sake. That was nice of him.

GREGERS [*drawing closer to her*]. But supposing now that you of your own free will sacrificed the wild duck for *his* sake?

HEDVIG [*rising*]. The wild duck!

GREGERS. Supposing you were ready to sacrifice for him the most precious thing you have in the world?

HEDVIG. Do you think that would help?

GREGERS. Try it, Hedvig.

HEDVIG [*softly, with eyes shining*]. Yes—I will.

GREGERS. Have you will power enough for that, do you think?

HEDVIG. I'll ask Grandfather to shoot her for me.

GREGERS. Yes, do that. But not a word about this to your mother!

HEDVIG. Why not?

GREGERS. She doesn't understand us.

HEDVIG. The wild duck . . . ? I'll do it in the morning!

   [GINA *enters by the hall door.*]

HEDVIG [*up to her*]. Did you find him, Mother?

GINA. No, but I heard he'd been down to Relling and gone out with him.

GREGERS. Are you sure?

GINA. Yes, the janitor's wife said so. Molvik went with them too, she said.

GREGERS. At a time like this, when his soul so desperately needs to struggle in solitude . . . !

GINA [*taking off her coat*]. Yes, men sure are something. God only knows where Relling dragged him off to. I ran across to Ma Eriksen's, but they're not there.

HEDVIG [*fighting back her tears*]. What if he never comes back!

GREGERS. *He'll* come back. I shall get word to him in the morning, and then you'll *see* how he comes back. You can count on that. Sleep well, Hedvig. Goodnight. [*Goes out by hall door.*]

HEDVIG [*throws her arms around* GINA's *neck, sobbing*]. Mother! Mother!

GINA [*patting her back, sighing*]. Ah, yes. Relling knew what he was talking about, all right. This is what you get when these here maniacs get after you with their "claim of the ordeal."

Act Five

HJALMAR EKDAL's *studio in the cold gray light of morning. There is wet snow on the big panes of the skylight.*

GINA, *aproned and carrying a broom and dust cloth, enters from the kitchen and goes toward the living room door. At the same moment,* HEDVIG *rushes in from the hall.*

GINA [*stops*]. Well?

HEDVIG. Yes, Mother, I think he is down at Relling's . . .

GINA. What did I tell you!

HEDVIG. . . . because the janitor's wife said she heard Relling bring home two others when he came back last night.

GINA. I thought as much.

HEDVIG. But what good does it do, if he won't come up to us.

GINA. Well, at least I can go down and talk to him.

[OLD EKDAL, *in dressing gown and slippers and smoking his pipe, appears at the door of his room.*]

EKDAL. Say, Hjalmar . . . Isn't Hjalmar home?

GINA. No, he's gone out.

EKDAL. So early? In this blizzard? All right, suit yourself, I can do the morning tour without you.

[*He slides the attic door open.* HEDVIG *helps him. He goes in, and she closes the door after him.*]

HEDVIG [*in a low voice*]. Mother, just think, when poor Grandfather finds out that Father wants to leave us.

GINA. Silly! Grandpa mustn't hear anything about it. What a godsend he wasn't home yesterday in all that hullaballoo.

HEDVIG. Yes, but . . .

[GREGERS *enters through the hall door.*]

GREGERS. Well? Any trace of him?

GINA. He's downstairs at Relling's, from what I hear.

GREGERS. At Relling's! Has he really been out with those two?

GINA. Looks like it.

GREGERS. How *could* he—just when he desperately needed to be alone and really pull himself together . . . !

GINA. You can say *that* again.

[RELLING *enters from the hall.*]

HEDVIG [*up to him*]. Is Father with you?

GINA [*at the same time*]. Is he there?

RELLING. Yes, he's there all right.

HEDVIG. And you never told us!

RELLING. I know, I'm a bea-east. But first I had to look after that other bea-east, the dæmonic one, I mean. And then I dropped off into such a heavy sleep that . . .

GINA. What's Hjalmar got to say today?

RELLING. Not a thing.

HEDVIG. Isn't he talking at all?

RELLING. Not a blessed word.

GREGERS. Ah, no. I understand that so well.

GINA. What's he doing with himself then?

RELLING. He's lying on the sofa, snoring.

GINA. Oh? Yes, Hjalmar snores something terrific.

HEDVIG. He's asleep? Can he sleep now?

RELLING. Looks damn well like it.

GREGERS. It's understandable, after the spiritual upheaval he's been through . . .

GINA. And him not used to gallivantin' nights, either.

HEDVIG. Maybe it's a good thing he's getting some sleep, Mother.

GINA. That's what I'm thinking too. But in that case we'd better not wake him up too soon. Thanks a lot, Relling. Well, first I'll get the house cleaned and straightened up, and then . . . Come and help me, Hedvig.

[GINA *and* HEDVIG *go into the living room.*]

GREGERS [*turns to* RELLING]. How would you describe the spiritual turmoil going on in Hjalmar Ekdal?

RELLING. I'm damned if I've noticed any spiritual turmoil in him.

GREGERS. What! At such a turning point, when his whole life has acquired a new foundation . . . ! How can you imagine that with a character like Hjalmar's . . . ?

RELLING. Character! *Him?* If he ever had a tendency to anything as abnormal as you mean by "character," I assure you it was cleared out of him root and branch while he was still a boy.

GREGERS. That would indeed be strange—considering the tender upbringing he enjoyed.

RELLING. By those two crackpot, hysterical maiden aunts of his, you mean?

GREGERS. Let me tell you, *there* were women who never lost sight of the claim of the ideal .. . all right, now I suppose you'll start being funny again.

RELLING. No, I'm not in the mood. Besides, I know what I'm talking about, he has certainly spouted enough rhetoric about those "twin soul-mothers" of his. Personally, I don't think he has much to thank them for. Ekdal's misfortune is that in his own little circle he has always been taken for a shining light . . .

GREGERS. And you don't think he is? Deep down inside, I mean.

RELLING. I never noticed anything of the kind. That his father thought so—that doesn't mean a thing. The old Lieutenant always *was* a bit simple.

GREGERS. He's always been a man with the innocence of a child. That's what you don't understand.

RELLING. All right, all right. But then when our dear sweet Hjalmar managed to get into the University—after a fashion—right away he became the light of the future for his fellow students too. Of course, he was good-looking, the rascal—pink and white—just the type the girls falls for. And as he had that easy sentimentality and that appealing something in his voice, and a pretty knack for declaiming other people's poetry and other people's ideas . . .

GREGERS [*indignantly*]. Is it Hjalmar Ekdal you're talking about like this?

RELLING. Yes, with your permission. For that's what he looks like inside, this idol you are groveling to.

GREGERS. I hardly think I'm as blind as all that.

RELLING. Well, you're not far from it. You see, you are a sick man, too.

GREGERS. There you are right.

RELLING. Yes indeed. Yours is a complicated case. First there's this pesky fever of integrity you suffer from. And then, what's even worse, you're forever going around in a delirium of adoration—forever butting in where you don't belong, looking for something to admire.

GREGERS. Well, I certainly won't find anything of the sort where I do belong.

RELLING. The trouble is, you're so shockingly mistaken about those fabulous beings you dream up around you. Here you are at it again, coming to a tenement with your claim of the ideal. Nobody in this house is solvent.

GREGERS. If that's all you think of Hjalmar Ekdal, how can you take pleasure in being everlastingly in his company?

RELLING. Good Lord, I'm supposed to be a doctor of sorts, though I'm ashamed to say it. The least I can do is look after the sick I live in the same house with.

GREGERS. Really! Is Hjalmar Ekdal sick too?

RELLING. Pretty nearly everybody is sick, I'm afraid.

GREGERS. And what treatment are you giving Hjalmar?

RELLING. The usual. I see to it that his life-lie is kept going.

GREGERS. Life—lie? Did I hear you right . . . ?

RELLING. That's right, I said life-lie. You see, the life-lie is the stimulating principle.

GREGERS. May I ask what life-lie you're injecting into Hjalmar?

RELLING. Sorry, I don't betray professional secrets to quacks. You'd be in a position to mess him up even worse than you have. But the method is tried and true. I've used it on Molvik as well. Him I made "dæmonic"—that's *his* shot in the arm.

GREGERS. Then he's *not* dæmonic?

RELLING. What the devil does it mean, to be dæmonic? It's just some nonsense I hit on to keep life in him. If I hadn't done that, the poor harmless slob would have succumbed to self-contempt and despair years ago. Same with the old Lieutenant. Though he managed to find his treatment by himself.

GREGERS. Lieutenant Ekdal? What about him?

RELLING. Well, what do *you* think? He, the great bear-hunter, stalking rabbits in that dark attic. And there's not a happier sportsman alive than that old man when he's playing around in there with all that rubbish. The four or five dried-up Christmas trees he saved up, to him they're the same as the whole great living Højdal forest. The rooster and chickens, why, they're wild fowl in the treetops; and the rabbits bumping around underfoot, they are bears he grapples with, the lusty old Nimrod.

GREGERS. Poor, unfortunate old Lieutenant Ekdal—yes. He has certainly had to renounce the ideals of his youth.

RELLING. While I think of it, Mr. Werle junior—don't use this fancy word "ideals." We have a perfectly good plain one: lies.

GREGERS. Are you trying to say the two things are related?

RELLING. Yes, about like typhus and typhoid fever.

GREGERS. Dr. Relling, I won't give up till I have rescued Hjalmar from your clutches!

RELLING. So much the worse for him. Take away the life-lie from the average person, and you take his happiness along with it. [*To* HEDVIG, *who enters from the living room.*] Well, little duck-mother, I'll go down and see if Papa is still lying there pondering on that remarkable invention. [*Goes out by the hall door.*]

GREGERS [*approaching* HEDVIG]. I can see by your look that it's not yet accomplished.

HEDVIG. What? Oh, about the wild duck. No.

GREGERS. Your courage failed you, I suppose, when it came to the point.

HEDVIG. No, it's not that. But when I woke up this morning and re-membered what we had talked about, it seemed so queer.

GREGERS. Queer?

HEDVIG. Yes, I don't know . . . Last night, right when you said it, I thought there was something so lovely about the idea; but after I slept and it all came back to me again, it didn't seem like anything much.

GREGERS. Ah no, you could hardly be expected to grow up in this house without being the worse for it in some way.

HEDVIG. I don't care anything about that. If only my father would come back . . .

GREGERS. Ah, had your eyes but been opened to what really makes life worthwhile—had you the true, joyful, courageous spirit of sacrifice, then you would see how fast he'd come back to you—But I still have faith in you, Hedvig. [*He goes out through hall door.*]

[HEDVIG *wanders about the room. She is about to go into the kitchen, when there is a knocking from within the attic.* HEDVIG *goes and opens the door a little way.* OLD EKDAL *comes out; she pushes the door to again.*]

EKDAL. Hm, not much fun going for your morning walk by yourself.

HEDVIG. Wouldn't you like to go hunting, Grandfather?

EKDAL. It's not hunting weather today. So *dark*. You can hardly see in front of you.

HEDVIG. Don't you ever feel like shooting something besides rabbits?

EKDAL. Why, aren't the rabbits good enough, maybe?

HEDVIG. Yes, but how about the wild duck?

EKDAL. Ho, ho, so you're scared I'll go and shoot your wild duck? Never in the world, child. Never.

HEDVIG. No, I guess you couldn't. It's supposed to be very hard to shoot wild ducks.

EKDAL. Couldn't I? Should hope to say I could.

HEDVIG. How would you go about it, Grandfather?—I don't mean with *my* wild duck, but with some other one.

EKDAL. Would aim to get the shot in just below the breast, you know. That's the surest. And then you've got to shoot *against* the lie of the feathers, see, not *with*.

HEDVIG. Do they die then, Grandfather?

EKDAL. Damn right they die—if you shoot 'em properly. Well, got to go and spruce up. Hm . . . you know why . . . hm. [*Goes into his room.*]

[HEDVIG *waits a moment, glances toward the living room door, goes to the bookcase, and, standing on tiptoe, takes the double-barreled pistol down off the shelf and looks at it.* GINA, *with broom and dust cloth, enters from the living room.* HEDVIG *hastily puts back the pistol, without* GINA *noticing.*]

GINA. Don't go fooling with your father's things, Hedvig.

HEDVIG [*moving away from the bookcase*]. I only wanted to straighten up a little.

GINA. Why don't you go in the kitchen and see if the coffee is still hot, I'm taking a tray down to him when I go.

[HEDVIG *goes out.* GINA *begins to clear the studio. Presently the hall door is hesitantly opened, and* HJALMAR EKDAL *looks in. He has his overcoat on, but no hat. He looks unwashed and unkempt; his eyes are sleepy and dull.*]

GINA [*stops in the midst of sweeping and looks at him*]. Bless me, HJALMAR—are you back after all?

HJALMAR [*enters, answers in a dull voice*]. I come—only to depart at once.

GINA. Yes, yes, I imagine. But, gosh sakes! Don't you look a sight!

HJALMAR. A sight?

GINA. And just look at your good winter coat! Well, that's had it.

HEDVIG [*at the kitchen door*]. Mother, do you want me . . . [*Sees* HJALMAR, *gives a shout of joy and runs toward him.*] Father! Father!

HJALMAR [*turns aside and waves her away*]. Go away! Go away! [*To* GINA.] Get her away from me, I tell you!

GINA [*in a low voice*]. Go in the living room, Hedvig.

[HEDVIG *goes in silently.*]

HJALMAR [*busy, pulling out the table drawer*]. I must have my books with me. Where are my books?

GINA. What books?

HJALMAR. My scientific works, naturally—the technical journals I use for my invention.

GINA [*looking in the bookcase*]. Is it these here that there's no covers on?

HJALMAR. Yes, of course.

GINA [*puts a pile of unbound volumes on the table*]. Shouldn't I get Hedvig to cut the pages for you?

HJALMAR. Nobody needs to cut pages for me.

[*Short silence.*]

GINA. So you've made up your mind to leave us, Hjalmar?

HJALMAR [*rummaging among the books*]. That goes without saying, I should think.

GINA. All right.

HJALMAR [*vehemently*]. You expect me to stay around here and have a knife twisted in my heart every minute of the day?

GINA. God forgive you for thinking I could be that bad.

HJALMAR. Prove to me . . . !

GINA. Seems to me *you're* the one that's got something to prove.

HJALMAR. With a past like yours? There are certain claims . . . I am tempted to call them claims of the ideal . . .

GINA. And what about Grandpa? What's to become of *him*, poor old thing?

HJALMAR. I know my duty. The helpless old man comes with me. I must go into town and make the necessary arrangements . . . Hm . . . [*Hesitantly.*] Has anybody found my hat on the stairs?

GINA. No. Did you lose your hat?

HJALMAR. Of course I had it on when I came back last night, there's no doubt about that. But now I can't find it.

GINA. Gosh sakes, wherever did you go with them two rowdies?

HJALMAR. Oh, don't bother me with trivialities. Do you think I'm in a mood to remember datails.

GINA. I only hope you didn't catch a cold, Hjalmar. [*Goes into kitchen.*]

HJALMAR [*talking angrily to himself in a low voice as he empties the drawer*]. You're a scoundrel, Relling!—A villain is what you are! You rotten traitor!—If I could just get somebody to murder you!

[*He puts some old letters to one side, finds the torn gift document of the day before, picks it up and looks at the pieces. As* GINA *enters, he quickly puts them down again.*]

GINA [*setting a laden coffee tray on the table*]. Here's a drop of something hot, in case you'd like it. And some cold cuts.

HJALMAR [*glances at the tray*]. Cold cuts? Never again, under this roof! True, I've taken no solid nourishment for nearly twenty-four hours, but never mind.—My notes! The beginning of my memoirs! Where have you put my diary and all my important papers? [*Opens the door to the living room, but draws back.*] There she is again!

GINA. For God's sake, Hjalmar, the child's got to be *some*place.

HJALMAR. Get out.

[*He stands back.* HEDVIG, *terrified, comes into the studio.*]

HJALMAR [*his hand on the doorknob, to* GINA]. As I spend these last moments in what was once my home, I wish to be spared the presence of intruders . . . [*Goes into the living room.*]

HEDVIG [*darting towards her mother, asks in a low and trembling voice*]. Does he mean me?

GINA. Stay in the kitchen, Hedvig. Or no—better go to your own room. [*To* HJALMAR, *as she goes in to him.*] Wait a minute, Hjalmar, don't mess up the whole bureau. I know where everything is.

HEDVIG [*stands motionless for a moment, in terror and confusion, biting her lips to keep from crying. Then she clenches her hands convulsively and says softly*]. The wild duck!

[*She steals across and takes the pistol from the shelf, opens the attic door a little, slips in and pulls it shut after her.* HJALMAR *and* GINA *begin arguing in the living room.*]

HJALMAR [*appears with some notebooks and a pile of old sheets of paper, which he puts on the table*]. Oh, what good will the valise do! There are a thousand things I've got to drag along with me.

GINA [*follows with the valise*]. Well, leave the rest for the time being, just take a clean shirt and some underwear.

HJALMAR. Phew! All these exhausting preparations! [*Takes off his overcoat and throws it on the sofa.*]

GINA. Meantime your coffee's standing there getting cold.

HJALMAR. Hm. [*Without thinking, he takes a mouthful, and then another.*]

GINA [*dusting the backs of the chairs*]. Your worst job will be finding another attic big enough for the rabbits.

HJALMAR. What! Am I expected to drag along all those rabbits too?

GINA. Well, Grandpa can't do without his rabbits, you know that.

HJALMAR. He'll just have to get used to it. There are more important things in life than rabbits that I have to give up.

GINA [*dusting the bookcase*]. Should I put your flute in the bag for you?

HJALMAR. No. No flute for me. But give me the pistol.

GINA. You want to take that old gun with you?

HJALMAR. Yes. My loaded pistol.

GINA [*looking for it*]. It's gone. He must have taken it in with him.

HJALMAR. Is he in the attic?

GINA. Sure he's in the attic.

HJALMAR. Hm. Poor lonely old man. [*He eats an open-face sandwich, finishes his cup of coffee.*]

GINA. If only we hadn't rented out the room, you could've moved in there.

HJALMAR. And stay under the same roof as . . . ! Never! Never!

GINA. But couldn't you move into the living room for a day or two? There you could have everything all to yourself.

HJALMAR. Never, within these walls!

GINA. Well, how about moving in with Relling and Molvik, then?

HJALMAR. Don't mention their names to me! I get sick just thinking about them. Oh no, I must out into the storm and the snowdrifts— go from house to house seeking shelter for my father and myself.

GINA. But Hjalmar, you haven't got a hat! You lost your hat, remember?

HJALMAR. Oh, that despicable pair, those depraved villains! A hat must be procured. [*Takes another sandwich.*] Arrangements must be made. After all, I don't propose to catch my death of cold. [*Looks for something on the tray.*]

GINA. What are you looking for?

HJALMAR. Butter.

GINA. In a minute. [*Goes into the kitchen.*]

HJALMAR [*calls after her*]. Oh, don't bother. Dry bread is good enough for me.

GINA [*bringing a butter dish*]. Here you are. It's fresh churned, they told me.

[*She pours him another cup of coffee. He sits down on the sofa, spreads more butter on his bread, eats and drinks in silence for a while.*]

HJALMAR. Could I, without being interfered with by anyone—and I mean *anyone*—stay in the living room a day or two, do you suppose?

GINA. Sure you could, if you wanted.

HJALMAR. Because I don't see much likelihood of moving all of Father's things in such a rush.

GINA. And another thing, too. First you'll have to tell him you're not going to live with us others no more.

HJALMAR [*pushes his cup away*]. That too, yes. To have to go into all these complicated matters all over again . . . I must consider ways and means. I must have breathing space. I can't take on all these burdens in a single day.

GINA. No, and in such rotten weather, too.

HJALMAR [*moving Werle's letter*]. I see this paper is still lying around.

GINA. Yes, I didn't touch it.

HJALMAR. Not that that scrap of paper concerns me . . .

GINA. Well, *I* certainly don't intend to use it.

HJALMAR. . . . still, I don't suppose we should just let it get destroyed. In all the confusion while I'm moving out it could easily . . .

GINA. I'll take care of it, Hjalmar.

HJALMAR. After all, the letter belongs to Father in the first place; it's his business whether he wants to make use of it or not.

GINA [*sighing*]. Yes, poor old Father . . .

HJALMAR. Just to be on the safe side . . . Where will I find some paste?

GINA [*goes to the bookshelf*]. Here's the paste.

HJALMAR. And a brush?

GINA. The brush is here too. [*Brings him the things.*]

HJALMAR [*picks up a pair of scissors*]. Just a strip of paper along the back . . . [*Cutting and pasting.*] Far be it from me to lay hands on somebody else's property—least of all a penniless old man's. —Well, or on—the other person's, either . . . There we are. Let it stay there a while. And when it's dry—remove it. I don't wish to lay eyes on that document again. Ever!

[GREGERS WERLE *enters from the hall.*]

GREGERS [*a little surprised*]. What—you sitting here, Hjalmar?

HJALMAR [*gets up quickly*]. I sank down from sheer exhaustion.

GREGERS. I see you've had breakfast, though.

HJALMAR. The body, too, makes claims on us occasionally.

GREGERS. What have you decided to do?

HJALMAR. For a man like myself there is but one way open. I am in the process of gathering together my most important possessions. But you realize it takes time.

GINA [*a bit impatient*]. Well, do I get the room ready for you, or do I pack the bag?

HJALMAR [*after an irritated glance at* GREGERS]. Pack—and get the room ready.

GINA [*takes the valise*]. All right. I'll put in the shirt and the other things, then. [*Goes into the living room and shuts the door behind her.*]

GREGERS [*after a short pause*]. I never dreamed it would end like this. Is it really necssary for you to leave house and home?

HJALMAR [*paces restlessly up and down*]. What do you expect me to do?—I'm not made for unhappiness, Gregers. I must have things nice and secure and peaceful around me.

GREGERS. But *can't* you stay? Just try. To my mind you now have a firm foundation to build on—so start all over again. And remember, you have your invention to live for, besides.

HJALMAR. Oh, don't talk about the invention. It may be a long way off yet.

GREGERS. Really?

HJALMAR. For God's sake, what do you expect me to invent, anyway? They've already invented just about everything. It gets to be more difficult every day . . .

GREGERS. After all the work you've put into it . . . !

HJALMAR. It was that dissolute Relling who got me into it.

GREGERS. Relling?

HJALMAR. Yes, he was the one who first called attention to my talent for making some marvelous invention or other in photography.

GREGERS. Aha! . . . It was Relling!

HJALMAR. Oh, what deep satisfaction I got out of that thing. Not so much the invention itself, but because Hedvig believed in it—believed with all the faith and fervor of a child . . . that is, like a fool I went around imagining she believed in it.

GREGERS. Can you really think that Hedvig deceived you!

HJALMAR. I'm ready to think anything now. It's Hedvig that stands in the way. She'll end up shutting the sun out of my life forever.

GREGERS. Hedvig! You mean Hedvig! How could *she* do anything like that?

HJALMAR [*without answering*]. It's beyond words, how I loved that child. Beyond words, how happy I was every time I came home to my humble rooms and she would run to greet me, with her sweet blinking eyes. Oh, credulous fool that I was! I loved her so unutterably—and so I persuaded myself of the fiction that she loved me the same.

GREGERS,. Are you saying it wasn't true?

HJALMAR. How can I tell? Gina I can't get a word out of. And anyway she has absolutely no conception of the principles involved in the situation. But I do feel the need to unburden myself to you, Gregers. It's this terrible doubt . . . Maybe Hedvig never really loved me at all.

GREGERS. You may yet have proof that she did. [*Listening.*] What's that? The wild duck's cry?

HJALMAR. She's quacking. Father's in there.

GREGERS. Is he! [*Joy lights up his face.*] I tell you, you may yet have proof that your poor misunderstood Hedvig loves you!

HJALMAR. Oh, what proof can she give me! I don't dare believe in any assurance from *that* quarter.

GREGERS. Surely Hedvig is incapable of deception.

HJALMAR. Oh, Gregers, that's just what isn't so certain. Who knows what Gina and that Mrs. Sørby have sat here whispering and tittle-tattling about? And nothing escapes Hedvig, believe me. It could even be that the birthday gift wasn't such a surprise. As a matter of fact, I thought I noticed something of the kind.

GREGERS. What on earth has got into you!

HJALMAR. My eyes have been opened. Just you watch—you'll see, the gift is only a beginning. Mrs. Sørby always did have a great liking for Hedvig, and now of couse she's in a position to do whatever she wants for the child. They can take her away from me any time they like.

GREGERS. Hedvig would never leave you. Never.

HJALMAR. Don't be too sure. With them standing and beckoning to her with full hand? And I who have loved her so unutterably . . . ! I, whose greatest joy it would have been to take her gently by the hand and lead her, as one leads a child that's afraid of the dark through a great empty room!—I feel it now with painful certainty—the poor photographer in his attic apartment never really meant anything to her. She was just shrewd enough to play along with him till the time was ripe.

GREGERS. Hjalmar, you don't believe that yourself.

HJALMAR. The terrible thing is just that I don't know what to believe— that I can *never* know. But do you really doubt that I'm right? Hoho, my dear Gregers, you count too much on the claim of the ideal! Just let the others come with overflowing hands and call to the child: Leave him; life awaits you here with us . . .

GREGERS [*quickly*]. Yes, what then, do you think?

HJALMAR. If I asked her then: Hedvig, are you willing to turn your back on life for me? [*Laughs scornfully.*] Thanks a lot—you'd soon hear the answer I'd get!

[*A pistol shot is heard from within the attic.*]

GREGERS [*shouts with joy*]. Hjalmar!

HJALMAR. Damn! He *would* have to go hunting now!

GINA [*entering*]. Ugh, Hjalmar, it sounds like the old man's banging away in there by himself.

HJALMAR. I'll go have a look . . .

GREGERS [*quicky, excitedly*]. Wait! Do you know what that was?

HJALMAR. Of course I know.

GREGERS. No, you don't. But *I* know. That was the proof!

HJALMAR. What proof?

GREGERS. It was a child's act of sacrifice. She's got your father to shoot the wild duck.

HJALMAR. Shoot the wild duck!

GINA. Imagine . . . !

HJALMAR. Whatever for?

GREGERS. She wanted to sacrifice to you the most precious thing she had in the world. Because then, she thought, you would be sure to love her again.

HJALMAR [*softly, with emotion*]. Oh, that child!

GINA. The things she'll think of!

GREGERS. All she wanted was to have your love again, Hjalmar. She felt she couldn't live without it.

GINA [*fighting back her tears*]. There you see, Hjalmar.

HJALMAR. Gina, where is she?

GINA [*sniffling*]. Poor little thing, sitting out in the kitchen, I guess.

HJALMAR [*crosses, and throws open the kitchen door*]. Hedvig—come! Come to me! [*Looks around.*] No, she's not in here.

GINA. Then she must be in her little room. [HJALMAR *walks out.*]

HJALMAR [*offstage*]. No, she's not here either. [*Re-enters the studio.*] She must have gone out.

GINA. Well, you wouldn't let her stay anyplace in the house.

HJALMAR. Oh, if only she'd come home soon—so I can tell her . . . Everything will be all right now, Gregers. Now I really believe we can start life over again.

GREGERS [*quietly*]. I knew it. Redemption would come through the child.

[OLD EKDAL *appears at the door of his room. He is in full uniform, and is busy trying to buckle on his saber.*]

HJALMAR [*astonished*]. Father! You *there*?

GINA. You were shooting in your *room*?

EKDAL [*approaches indignantly*]. So, now you go hunting without me, do you, HJALMAR?

HJALMAR [*tense, bewildered*]. You mean it wasn't you that fired the shot in the attic?

EKDAL Me? Hm!

GREGERS [*calls out to* HJALMAR]. She has shot the wild duck herself!

HJALMAR. What *is* all this? [*Rushes to the attic door, tears it open, looks in, and screams.*] Hedvig!

GINA [*running to the door*]. My God, what is it?

HJALMAR [*going inside*]. She's lying on the floor!

GREGERS. Hedvig? On the floor? [*Follows* HJALMAR *in.*]

GINA [*at the same time*]. Hedvig! [*Enters the attic.*] No! No! No!

EKDAL. Ho-ho, so *she's* taken to hunting too, now.

[HJALMAR, GINA, *and* GREGERS *carry* HEDVIG *into the studio. Her right hand hangs down, the fingers still gripping the pistol.*]

HJALMAR [*dazed*]. The pistol went off. She's been hit. Call for help! Help!

GINA [*runs out into the hall and shouts down*]. Relling! Relling! Dr. Relling, come up here quick!

[HJALMAR *and* GREGERS *lay* GINA *down on the sofa.*]

EKDAL [*quietly*]. The forest's revenge.

HJALMAR [*on his knees beside* HEDVIG.] She'll come to, right away. She's coming to—yes, yes,yes.

GINA [*having returned*]. Where is she she hit? I can't see a thing . . .

[RELLING *hurries in, followed closely by* MOLVIK. *The latter is without vest or collar, and his jacket is unbuttoned.*]

RELLING. What's going on here?

GINA. They say Hedvig shot herself.

HJALMAR. Come here and help!

RELLING. Shot herself! [*He pushes the table aside and starts to examine her.*]

HJALMAR [*still kneeling, looking anxiously up at him*]. Surely it can't be serious? What, Relling? She's hardly bleeding at all. Surely it can't be serious?

RELLING. How did this happen?

HJALMAR. Oh, how do I know . . .

GINA. She wanted to shoot the wild duck.

RELLING. The wild duck?

HJALMAR. The pistol must have gone off by itself.

RELLING. Hm. Indeed.

EKDAL. The forest's revenge. Still, I'm not afraid. [*Goes into the attic and shuts himself in.*]

HJALMAR. Well, Relling . . . why don't you *say* something?

RELLING. The bullet entered the chest.

HJALMAR. Yes, but she's coming to!

RELLING. Can't you see? Hedvig is dead.

GINA [*bursts into tears*]. Oh, my baby! My baby!

GREGERS [*huskily*]. In the depths of the sea . . .

HJALMAR [*springing up*]. No, no, she's *got* to live! Oh dear God, Relling— just for a moment—just long enough so I can tell her how unutterably I loved her the whole time!

RELLING. The heart's been hit. Internal hemorrhage. She died instantly.

HJALMAR. And I drove her away from me like an animal! And in terror she crept into the attic and died for love of me. [*Sobbing.*] Never to be able to make up for it! Never to be able to tell her . . . ! [*Clenches his hands and cries to heaven.*] Oh, Thou above . . . ! If Thou *art* there! Why hast Thou done this thing to me . . .

GINA. Hush, hush, you mustn't carry on like this. I guess maybe we didn't have the right to keep her.

MOLVIK. The child is not dead. She but sleeps.

RELLING. Nonsense.

HJALMAR [*quiets down, goes over to the sofa, folds his arms, and looks at* HEDVIG]. There she lies, so stiff and still.

RELLING [*trying to free the pistol*]. It's so tight, so tight.

GINA. No, no, Relling, don't hurt her fingers. Leave the gun be.

HJALMAR. She shall take it with her.

GINA. Yes, let her. But the child's not going to lie out here for a show. She'll go into her own little room, that's what. Give me a hand, Hjalmar.

[HJALMAR *and* GINA *take* HEDVIG *between them.*]

HJALMAR [*as they carry her out*]. Oh, Gina, Gina, can you bear this!

GINA. We'll have to help each other. Now she's as much yours as mine.

MOLVIK [*stretching forth his arms and mumbling*]. Praised be the name of the Lord. Dust unto dust . . . dust unto dust . . .

RELLING [*whispers*]. Shut up, man! You're drunk.

[HJALMAR *and* GINA *carry the body out by the kitchen door.* RELLING *shuts it after them.* MOLVIK *slinks out into the hall.*]

RELLING [*crosses to* GREGERS]. No one will ever persuade me that this was an accident.

GREGERS [*who has stood horror-stricken, twitching convulsively*]. Who can say how this terrible thing happened.

RELLING. There were powder burns on her dress. She must have pressed the muzzle right against her chest and fired.

GREGERS. Hedvig has not died in vain. Did you see how this sorrow brought out all the nobility in him?

RELLING. Most people become noble when they stand in the presence of death. But how long do you think this glory of his will last?

GREGERS. Surely it will last and flourish for the rest of his life!

RELLING. Before the year is out little Hedvig will be nothing more to him than a theme for pretty declamations.

GREGERS. You dare say that about Hjalmar Ekdal!

RELLING. We'll talk about it again when the first grass has withered on her grave. *Then* listen to the vomit about "the child untimely torn from its father's breast," *then* watch him wallow in sentimentality and self-admiration and self-pity. Just you wait!

GREGERS. If *you* are right, and *I* am wrong, then life's not worth living.

RELLING. Oh, life wouldn't be too bad if it weren't for these blessed bill collectors who come pestering us poor folk with their claims of the ideal.

GREGERS [*staring into space*]. In that case, I'm glad my destiny is what it is.

RELLING. And may I ask—what *is* your destiny?

GREGERS [*on the point of leaving*]. To be the thirteenth man at the table.

RELLING. The devil it is.

ANTON CHEKHOV

Three Sisters†

Characters in the Play

PROZOROV, *Andrey Serghyeevich*
NATASHA *(Natalia Ivanovna), his fiancée, afterwards his wife*
OLGA *(Olga Serghyeevna, Olia)* ⎫
MASHA *(Maria Serghyeevna)* ⎬ *his sisters*
IRENA *(Irena Serghyeevna)* ⎭
KOOLYGHIN, *Fiodor Ilyich, master at the High School for boys, husband of Masha*
VERSHININ, *Alexandr Ignatyevich, Lieutenant-Colonel, Battery Commander*
TOOZENBACH, *Nikolai Lvovich, Baron, Lieutenant in the Army*
SOLIONY, *Vassily Vassilich, Captain*
CHEBUTYKIN, *Ivan Romanych, Army Doctor*
FEDOTIK, *Aleksey Petrovich, Second Lieutenant*
RODÈ, *Vladimir Karlovich, Second Lieutenant*
FERAPONT *(Ferapont Spiridonych), an old porter from the County Office*
ANFISA, *the Prozorovs' former nurse, an old woman of 80*

The action takes place in a country town

Act One

A drawing-room in the Prozorovs' house; it is separated from a large ballroom[1] *at the back by a row of columns. It is midday; there is cheerful sunshine outside. In the ballroom the table is being laid for lunch.* OLGA, *wearing the regulation dark-blue dress of a secondary school mistress, is correcting her pupils' work, standing or walking about as she does so.*

† From PLAYS by Anton Chekhov, translated by Elisaveta Fen (Penguin Classics, 1951), copyright © Elisaveta Fen, 1951. Reproduced by permission of Penguin Books, Ltd. After this translation was made, an important manuscript text of the play was found in Moscow in 1953; A. R. Vladimirskaya has studied it, and Ronald Hingley has reproduced her findings in Appendix III of *The*

Oxford Chekhov (London, 1964), III, 307–12. In my notes I have represented the more significant of the variant readings; I follow Hingley in referring to the text as the Moscow manuscript.
1. A large room, sparsely furnished, used for receptions and dances in Russian houses [*Translator's note*].

MASHA, *in a black dress, is sitting reading a book, her hat on her lap.* IRENA, *in white, stands lost in thought.*

OLGA. It's exactly a year ago that Father died, isn't it? This very day, the fifth of May—your Saint's day, Irena. I remember it was very cold and it was snowing. I felt then as if I should never survive his death; and you had fainted and were lying quite still, as if you were dead. And now—a year's gone by, and we talk about it so easily. You're wearing white, and your face is positively radiant. . . .
[*A clock strikes twelve.*]
The clock struck twelve then, too. [*A pause.*] I remember when Father was being taken to the cemetery there was a military band, and a salute with rifle fire. That was because he was a general, in command of a brigade. And yet there weren't many people at the funeral. Of course, it was raining hard, raining and snowing.

IRENA. Need we bring up all these memories?
[*Baron* TOOZENBACH, CHEBUTYKIN *and* SOLIONY *appear behind the columns by the table in the ballroom.*]

OLGA. It's so warm to-day that we can keep the windows wide open, and yet there aren't any leaves showing on the birch trees. Father was made a brigadier eleven years ago, and then he left Moscow and took us with him. I remember so well how everything in Moscow was in blossom by now, everything was soaked in sunlight and warmth. Eleven years have gone by, yet I remember everything about it, as if we'd only left yesterday. Oh, Heavens! When I woke up this morning and saw this flood of sunshine, all this spring sunshine, I felt so moved and so happy! I felt such a longing to get back home to Moscow!

CHEBUTYKIN [*to* TOOZENBACH]. The devil you have!

TOOZENBACH. It's nonsense, I agree.

MASHA [*absorbed in her book, whistles a tune under her breath*].

OLGA. Masha, do stop whistling! How can you? [*A pause.*] I suppose I must get this continual headache because I have to go to school every day and go on teaching right into the evening. I seem to have the thoughts of someone quite old. Honestly, I've been feeling as if my strength and youth were running out of me drop by drop, day after day. Day after day, all these four years that I've been working at the school. . . . I just have one longing and it seems to grow stronger and stronger. . . .

IRENA. If only we could go back to Moscow! Sell the house, finish with our life here, and go back to Moscow.

OLGA. Yes, Moscow! As soon as we possibly can.
[CHEBUTYKIN *and* TOOZENBACH *laugh.*]

IRENA. I suppose Andrey will soon get a professorship. He isn't likely to go on living here. The only problem is our poor Masha.

OLGA. Masha can come and stay the whole summer with us every year in Moscow.

MASHA [*whistles a tune under her breath*].

IRENA. Everything will settle itself, with God's help. [*Looks through the window.*] What lovely weather it is to-day! Really, I don't know why there's such joy in my heart. I remembered this morning that it was my Saint's day,[2] and suddenly I felt so happy, and I thought of the time when we were children, and Mother was still alive. And then such wonderful thoughts came to me, such wonderful stirring thoughts!

OLGA. You're so lovely to-day, you really do look most attractive. Masha looks pretty to-day, too. Andrey could be good-looking, but he's grown so stout. It doesn't suit him. As for me, I've just aged and grown a lot thinner. I suppose it's through getting so irritated with the girls at school. But to-day I'm at home, I'm free, and my headache's gone, and I feel much younger than I did yesterday. I'm only twenty-eight, after all. . . . I suppose everything that God wills must be right and good, but I can't help thinking sometimes that if I'd got married and stayed at home, it would have been a better thing for me. [*A pause.*] I would have been very fond of my husband.

TOOZENBACH [*to* SOLIONY]. Really, you talk such a lot of nonsense, I'm tired of listening to you. [*Comes into the drawing-room.*] I forgot to tell you: Vershinin, our new battery commander, is going to call on you to-day. [*Sits down by the piano.*]

OLGA. I'm very glad to hear it.

IRENA. Is he old?

TOOZENBACH. No, not particularly. Forty, forty-five at the most. [*Plays quietly.*] He seems a nice fellow. Certainly not a fool. His only weakness is that he talks too much.

IRENA. Is he interesting?

TOOZENBACH. He's all right, only he's got a wife, a mother-in-law and two little girls. What's more, she's his second wife. He calls on everybody and tells them that he's got a wife and two little girls. He'll tell you about it, too. I'm sure of that. His wife seems to be a bit soft in the head. She wears a long plait like a girl, she is always philosophizing and talking in high-flown language, and then she often tries to commit suicide, apparently just to annoy her husband. I would have run away from a wife like that years ago, but he puts up with it, and just grumbles about it.

SOLIONY [*enters the drawing-room with* CHEBUTYKIN]. Now I can only lift sixty pounds with one hand, but with two I can lift two hundred pounds, or even two hundred and forty. So I conclude from that that two men are not just twice as strong as one, but three times as strong, if not more.

CHEBUTYKIN [*reads the paper as he comes in*]. Here's a recipe for falling hair . . . two ounces of naphthaline, half-a-bottle of methyllated spirit . . . dissolve and apply once a day. . . . [*Writes it down in a notebook.*] Must make a note of it. [*To* SOLIONY.] Well, as I was trying to explain

2. The feast day of the saint after whom she was named; a day celebrated like a birthday in many European countries.

to you, you cork the bottle and pass a glass tube through the cork. Then you take a pinch of ordinary powdered alum, and . . .

IRENA. Ivan Romanych, dear Ivan Romanych!

CHEBUTYKIN. What is it, my child, what is it?

IRENA. Tell me, why is it I'm so happy to-day? Just as if I were sailing along in a boat with big white sails, and above me the wide, blue sky, and in the sky great white birds floating around?

CHEBUTYKIN [kisses both her hands, tenderly]. My little white bird!

IRENA. You know, when I woke up this morning, and after I'd got up and washed, I suddenly felt as if everything in the world had become clear to me, and I knew the way I ought to live. I know it all now, my dear Ivan Romanych. Man must work by the sweat of his brow whatever his class, and that should make up the whole meaning and purpose of his life and happiness and contentment. Oh, how good it must be to be a workman, getting up with the sun and breaking stones by the roadside—or a shepherd—or a schoolmaster teaching the children—or an engine-driver on the railway. Good Heavens! it's better to be a mere ox or horse, and work, than the sort of young woman who wakes up at twelve, and drinks her coffee in bed, and then takes two hours dressing. . . . How dreadful! You know how you long for a cool drink in hot weather? Well, that's the way I long for work. And if I don't get up early from now on and really work, you can refuse to be friends with me any more, Ivan Romanych.

CHEBUTYKIN [tenderly]. So I will, so I will. . . .

OLGA. Father taught us to get up at seven o'clock and so Irena always wakes up at seven—but then she stays in bed till at least nine, thinking about something or other. And with such a serious expression on her face, too! [Laughs.]

IRENA. You think it's strange when I look serious because you always think of me as a little girl. I'm twenty, you know!

TOOZENBACH. All this longing for work. . . . Heavens! how well I can understand it! I've never done a stroke of work in my life. I was born in Petersburg, an unfriendly, idle city—born into a family where work and worries were simply unknown. I remember a valet pulling off my boots for me when I came home from the cadet school. . . . I grumbled at the way he did it, and my mother looked on in admiration. She was quite surprised when other people looked at me in any other way. I was so carefully protected from work! But I doubt whether they succeeded in protecting me for good and all—yes, I doubt it very much! The time's come: there's a terrific thunder-cloud advancing upon us, a mighty storm is coming to freshen us up! Yes, it's coming all right, it's quite near already, and it's going to blow away all this idleness and indifference, and prejudice against work, this rot of boredom that our society is suffering from. I'm going to work, and in twenty-five or thirty years' time every man and woman will be working. Every one of us!

CHEBUTYKIN. I'm not going to work.

TOOZENBACH. You don't count.

SOLIONY. In twenty-five years' time you won't be alive, thank goodness. In a couple of years you'll die from a stroke—or I'll lose my temper with you and put a bullet in your head, my good fellow. [*Takes a scent bottle from his pocket and sprinkles the scent over his chest and hands.*]

CHEBUTYKIN [*laughs*]. It's quite true that I never have done any work. Not a stroke since I left the university. I haven't even read a book, only newspapers. [*Takes another newspaper out of his pocket.*] For instance, here. . . . I know from the paper that there was a person called Dobroliubov, but what he wrote about I've not the faintest idea. . . . God alone knows. . . .

[*Someone knocks on the floor from downstairs.*]

There! They're calling me to come down: there's someone come to see me. I'll be back in a moment. . . . [*Goes out hurriedly, stroking his beard.*]

IRENA. He's up to one of his little games.

TOOZENBACH. Yes. He looked very solemn as he left. He's obviously going to give you a present.

IRENA. I do dislike that sort of thing. . . .

OLGA. Yes, isn't it dreadful? He's always doing something silly.

MASHA. 'A green oak grows by a curving shore, And round that oak hangs a golden chain'[3] . . . [*Gets up as she sings under her breath.*]

OLGA. You're sad to-day, Masha.

MASHA [*puts on her hat, singing*].

OLGA. Where are you going?

MASHA. Home.

IRENA. What a strange thing to do.

TOOZENBACH. What! Going away from your sister's party?

MASHA. What does it matter? I'll be back this evening. Good-bye, my darling. [*Kisses* IRENA.] And once again—I wish you all the happiness in the world. In the old days when Father was alive we used to have thirty or forty officers at our parties. What gay parties we had! and to-day—what have we got to-day? A man and a half, and the place is as quiet as a tomb. I'm going home. I'm depressed to-day, I'm sad, so don't listen to me. [*Laughs through her tears.*] We'll have a talk later, but good-bye for now, my dear. I'll go somewhere or other. . . .

IRENA [*displeased*]. Really, you are a . . .

---

3. Masha three times quotes these lines from the prologue to N. Pushkin's *Ruslan and Ludmilla* (1820), here, at the end of the act, and at the end of act 4. The full passage goes as follows:

A green oak on a curved seashore,
Upon that oak a golden chain,

And on that chain a learned cat,
Who walks in circles night and day.
On walking right, he sings a song,
On walking left, he tells a tale.

OLGA [*tearfully*]. I understand you, Masha.

SOLIONY. If a man starts philosophizing, you call that philosophy, or possibly just sophistry, but if a woman or a couple of women start philosophizing you call that . . . what would you call it, now? Ask me another!

MASHA. What are you talking about? You are a disconcerting person!

SOLIONY. Nothing.

'He had no time to say "Oh, oh!"
Before that bear had struck him low' . . .[4]

[*A pause.*]

MASHA [*to* OLGA, *crossly*]. Do stop snivelling!

[*Enter* ANFISA *and* FERAPONT, *the latter carrying a large cake.*]

ANFISA. Come along, my dear, this way. Come in, your boots are quite clean. [*To* IRENA.] A cake from Protopopov, at the Council Office.

IRENA. Thank you. Tell him I'm very grateful to him. [*Takes the cake.*]

FERAPONT. What's that?

IRENA [*louder*]. Tell him I sent my thanks.

OLGA. Nanny, will you give him a piece of cake? Go along, Ferapont, they'll give you some cake.

FERAPONT. What's that?

ANFISA. Come along with me, Ferapont Spiridonych, my dear. Come along. [*Goes out with* FERAPONT.]

MASHA. I don't like that Protopopov fellow, Mihail Potapych, or Ivanych, or whatever it is. It's best not to invite him here.

IRENA. I haven't invited him.

MASHA. Thank goodness.

[*Enter* CHEBUTYKIN, *followed by a soldier carrying a silver samovar. Murmurs of astonishment and displeasure.*]

OLGA [*covering her face with her hands*]. A samovar! But this is dreadful![5]

[*Goes through to the ballroom and stands by the table.*]

IRENA. My dear Ivan Romanych, what are you thinking about?

TOOZENBACH [*laughs*]. Didn't I tell you?

MASHA. Ivan Romanych, you really ought to be ashamed of yourself!

CHEBUTYKIN. My dear, sweet girls, I've no one in the world but you. You're dearer to me than anything in the world! I'm nearly sixty, I'm an old man, a lonely, utterly unimportant old man. The only thing that's worth anything in me is my love for you, and if it weren't for you, really I would have been dead long ago. [*To* IRENA.] My dear, my sweet little girl, haven't I known you since the very day you were born? Didn't I carry you about in my arms? . . . didn't I love your dear mother?

IRENA. But why do you get such expensive presents?

CHEBUTYKIN [*tearfully and crossly*]. Expensive presents! . . . Get along

4. From I.A. Krylov's fable *The Peasant and the Laborer*.

5. "Dreadful" because in Russia a silver samovar is the traditional gift for a twenty-fifth wedding anniversary.

with you! [*To the orderly.*] Put the samovar over there. [*Mimics* IRENA.] Expensive presents!

[*The orderly takes the samovar to the ballroom.*]

ANFISA [*crosses the drawing-room*]. My dears, there's a strange colonel just arrived. He's taken off his coat and he's coming up now. Irenushka, do be nice and polite to him, won't you? [*In the doorway.*] And it's high time we had lunch, too. . . . Oh, dear! [*Goes out.*]

TOOZENBACH. It's Vershinin, I suppose.

[*Enter* VERSHININ.]

TOOZENBACH. Lieutenant-Colonel Vershinin!

VERSHININ [*to* MASHA *and* IRENA]. Allow me to introduce myself—Lieutenant-Colonel Vershinin. I'm so glad, so very glad to be here at last. How you've changed! Dear, dear, how you've changed!

IRENA. Please, do sit down. We're very pleased to see you, I'm sure.

VERSHININ [*gaily*]. I'm so glad to see you, so glad! But there were three of you, weren't there?—three sisters. I remember there were three little girls. I don't remember their faces, but I knew your father, Colonel Prozorov, and I remember he had three little girls. Oh, yes, I saw them myself. I remember them quite well. How time flies! Dear, dear, how it flies!

TOOZENBACH. Alexandr Ignatyevich comes from Moscow.

IRENA. From Moscow? You come from Moscow?

VERSHININ. Yes, from Moscow. Your father was a battery commander there, and I was an officer in the same brigade. [*To* MASHA.] I seem to remember your face a little.

MASHA. I don't remember you at all.

IRENA. Olia, Olia! [*Calls towards the ballroom.*] Olia, do come!

[OLGA *enters from the ballroom.*]

IRENA. It seems that Lieutenant-Colonel Vershinin comes from Moscow.

VERSHININ. You must be Olga Serghyeevna, the eldest. And you are Maria. . . . And you are Irena, the youngest. . . .

OLGA. You come from Moscow?

VERSHININ. Yes. I studied in Moscow and entered the service there. I stayed there quite a long time, but then I was put in charge of a battery here—so I moved out here, you see. I don't really remember you, you know, I only remember that there were three sisters. I remember your father, though, I remember him very well. All I need to do is to close my eyes and I can see him standing there as if he were alive. I used to visit you in Moscow.

OLGA. I thought I remembered everybody, and yet . . .

VERSHININ. My Christian names are Alexandr Ignatyevich.

IRENA. Alexandr Ignatyevich, and you come from Moscow! Well, what a surprise!

OLGA. We're going to live there, you know.

IRENA. We hope to be there by the autumn. It's our home town, we were born there. . . . In Staraya Basmannaya Street.

[*Both laugh happily.*]

MASHA. Fancy meeting a fellow townsman so unexpectedly! [*Eagerly.*] I remember now. Do you remember, Olga, there was someone they used to call 'the lovesick Major'? You were a Lieutenant then, weren't you, and you were in love with someone or other, and everyone used to tease you about it. They called you 'Major' for some reason or other.

VERSHININ [*laughs*]. That's it, that's it. . . . 'The lovesick Major', that's what they called me.

MASHA. In those days you only had a moustache. . . . Oh, dear, how much older you look! [*Tearfully.*] How much older!

VERSHININ. Yes, I was still a young man in the days when they called me 'the lovesick Major'. I was in love then. It's different now.

OLGA. But you haven't got a single grey hair! You've aged, yes, but you're certainly not an old man.

VERSHININ. Nevertheless, I'm turned forty-two. Is it long since you left Moscow?

IRENA. Eleven years. Now what are you crying for, Masha, you funny girl? . . . [*Tearfully.*] You'll make me cry, too.

MASHA. I'm not crying. What was the street you lived in?

VERSHININ. In the Staraya Basmannaya.

OLGA. We did, too.

VERSHININ. At one time I lived in the Niemietzkaya Street. I used to walk from there to the Krasny Barracks, and I remember there was such a gloomy bridge I had to cross. I used to hear the noise of the water rushing under it. I remember how lonely and sad I felt there. [*A pause.*] But what a magnificently wide river you have here! It's a marvellous river!

OLGA. Yes, but this is a cold place. It's cold here, and there are too many mosquitoes.

VERSHININ. Really? I should have said you had a really good healthy climate here, a real Russian climate. Forest, river . . . birch-trees, too. The dear, unpretentious birch-trees—I love them more than any of the other trees. It's nice living here. But there's one rather strange thing, the station is fifteen miles from the town. And no one knows why.

SOLIONY. I know why it is.

[*Everyone looks at him.*]

Because if the station were nearer, it wouldn't be so far away, and as it is so far away, it can't be nearer.

[*An awkward silence.*]

TOOZENBACH. You like your little joke, Vassily Vassilich.

OLGA. I'm sure I remember you now. I know I do.

VERSHININ. I knew your mother.

CHEBUTYKIN. She was a good woman, God bless her memory!

IRENA. Mamma was buried in Moscow.

OLGA. At the convent of Novo-Dievichye.[6]

MASHA. You know, I'm even beginning to forget what she looked like. I suppose people will lose all memory of us in just the same way. We'll be forgotten.

VERSHININ. Yes, we shall all be forgotten. Such is our fate, and we can't do anything about it. And all the things that seem serious, important and full of meaning to us now will be forgotten one day—or anyway they won't seem important any more.

[A pause.]

It's strange to think that we're utterly unable to tell what will be regarded as great and important in the future and what will be thought of as just paltry and ridiculous. Didn't the great discoveries of Copernicus[7]—or of Columbus, if you like—appear useless and un-important to begin with?—whereas some rubbish, written up by an eccentric fool, was regarded as a revelation of great truth? It may well be that in time to come the life we live to-day will seem strange and uncomfortable and stupid and not too clean, either, and perhaps even wicked. . . .[8]

TOOZENBACH. Who can tell? It's just as possible that future generations will think that we lived our lives on a very high plane and remember us with respect. After all, we no longer have tortures and public executions and invasions, though there's still a great deal of suffering!

SOLIONY [in a high-pitched voice as if calling to chickens]. Cluck, cluck, cluck! There's nothing our good Baron loves as much as a nice bit of philosophizing.

TOOZENBACH. Vassily Vassilich, will you kindly leave me alone? [Moves to another chair.] It's becoming tiresome.

SOLIONY [as before]. Cluck, cluck, cluck! . . .

TOOZENBACH [to VERSHININ]. The suffering that we see around us—and there's so much of it—itself proves that our society has at least achieved a level or morality which is higher. . . .

VERSHININ. Yes, yes, of course.

CHEBUTYKIN. You said just now, Baron, that our age will be called great; but people are small all the same. . . . [Gets up.] Look how small I am.

[A violin is played off stage.]

MASHA. That's Andrey playing the violin; he's our brother, you know.

IRENA. We've got quite a clever brother. . . . We're expecting him to be a professor. Papa was a military man, but Andrey chose an academic career.

OLGA. We've been teasing him to-day. We think he's in love, just a little.

---

6. The new monastery of the Virgin, the most famous in Moscow.
7. Nicolaus Copernicus (1473–1547) postulated the astronomical system that argues that the sun is the center of our solar system. It provided the basis for modern astronomy.
8. The Moscow ms. has "and it's perhaps even terribly wicked."

IRENA. With a girl who lives down here. She'll be calling in to-day most likely.

MASHA. The way she dresses herself is awful! It's not that her clothes are just ugly and old-fashioned, they're simply pathetic. She'll put on some weird-looking, bright yellow skirt with a crude sort of fringe affair, and then a red blouse to go with it. And her cheeks look as though they've been scrubbed, they're so shiny! Andrey's not in love with her—I can't believe it; after all, he has got some taste. I think he's just playing the fool, just to annoy us. I heard yesterday that she's going to get married to Protopopov, the chairman of the local council. I thought it was an excellent idea. [*Calls through the side door.*] Andrey, come here, will you? Just for a moment, dear.

[*Enter* ANDREY.]

OLGA. This is my brother, Andrey Serghyeevich.

VERSHININ. Vershinin.

ANDREY. Prozorov. [*Wipes the perspiration from his face*]. I believe you've been appointed battery commander here?

OLGA. What do you think, dear? Alexandr Ignatyevich comes from Moscow.

ANDREY. Do you, really? Congratulations! You'll get no peace from my sisters now.

VERSHININ. I'm afraid your sisters must be getting tired of me already.

IRENA. Just look, Andrey gave me this little picture frame to-day. [*Shows him the frame.*] He made it himself.

VERSHININ [*looks at the frame, not knowing what to say*]. Yes, it's . . . it's very nice indeed. . . .

IRENA. Do you see that little frame over the piano? He made that one, too.

[ANDREY *waves his hand impatiently and walks off.*]

OLGA. He's awfully clever, and he plays the violin, and he makes all sorts of things, too. In fact, he's very gifted all round. Andrey, please, don't go. He's got such a bad habit—always going off like this. Come here!

[MASHA *and* IRENA *take him by the arms and lead him back, laughing.*]

MASHA. Now just you come here!

ANDREY. Do leave me alone, please do!

MASHA. You are a silly! They used to call Alexandr Ignatyevich 'the lovesick Major', and he didn't get annoyed.

VERSHININ. Not in the least.

MASHA. I feel like calling you a 'lovesick fiddler'.

IRENA. Or a 'lovesick professor'.

OLGA. He's fallen in love! Our Andriusha's in love!

IRENA [*clapping her hands*]. Three cheers for Andriusha! Andriusha's in love!

CHEBUTYKIN [*comes up behind* ANDREY *and puts his arms round his waist*].

'Nature created us for love alone.' . . . [*Laughs loudly, still holding his paper in his hand.*]

ANDREY. That's enough of it, that's enough. . . . [*Wipes his face.*] I couldn't get to sleep all night, and I'm not feeling too grand just now. I read till four o'clock, and then I went to bed, but nothing happened. I kept thinking about one thing and another . . . and it gets light so early; the sun just pours into my room. I'd like to translate a book from the English while I'm here during the summer.

VERSHININ. You read English, then?

ANDREY. Yes. My father—God bless his memory—used to simply wear us out with learning. It sounds silly, I know, but I must confess that since he died I've begun to grow stout, as if I'd been physically relieved of the strain. I've grown quite stout in a year. Yes, thanks to Father, my sisters and I know French and German and English, and Irena here knows Italian, too. But what an effort it all cost us!

MASHA. Knowing three languages in a town like this is an unnecessary luxury. In fact, not even a luxury, but just a sort of useless encumbrance . . . it's rather like having a sixth finger on your hand. We know a lot of stuff that's just useless.

VERSHININ. Really! [*Laughs.*] You know a lot of stuff that's useless! It seems to me that there's no place on earth, however dull and depressing it may be, where intelligence and education can be useless. Let us suppose that among the hundred thousand people in this town, all of them, no doubt, very backward and uncultured, there are just three people like yourselves. Obviously, you can't hope to triumph over all the mass of ignorance around you; as your life goes by, you'll have to keep giving in little by little until you get lost in the crowd, in the hundred thousand. Life will swallow you up, but you'll not quite disappear, you'll make some impression on it. After you've gone, perhaps six more people like you will turn up, then twelve, and so on, until in the end most people will have become like you. So in two or three hundred years life on this old earth of ours will have become marvellously beautiful. Man longs for a life like that, and if it isn't here yet, he must imagine it, wait for it, dream about it, prepare for it, he must know and see more than his father and his grandfather did. [*Laughs.*] And you're complaining because you know a lot of stuff that's useless.

MASHA [*takes off her hat*]. I'll be staying to lunch.

IRENA [*with a sigh*]. Really, someone should have written all that down. [ANDREY *has left the room, unnoticed.*]

TOOZENBACH. You say that in time to come life will be marvellously beautiful. That's probably true. But in order to share in it now, at a distance so to speak, we must prepare for it and work for it.

VERSHININ [*gets up*]. Yes. . . . What a lot of flowers you've got here! [*Looks round.*] And what a marvellous house! I do envy you! All my life I seem to have been pigging it in small flats, with two chairs and a sofa and a stove which always smokes. It's the flowers that I've missed in my life, flowers like these! . . . [*Rubs his hands.*] Oh, well, never mind!

TOOZENBACH. Yes, we must work. I suppose you're thinking I'm a sentimental German. But I assure you I'm not—I'm Russian. I don't speak a word of German. My father was brought up in the Greek Orthodox faith. [*A pause.*]

VERSHININ [*walks up and down the room*]. You know, I often wonder what it would be like if you could start your life over again—deliberately, I mean, consciously. . . . Suppose you could put aside the life you'd lived already, as though it was just a sort of rough draft, and then start another one like a fair copy. If that happened, I think the thing you'd want most of all would be not to repeat yourself. You'd try at least to create a new environment for yourself, a flat like this one, for instance, with some flowers and plenty of light. . . . I have a wife, you know, and two little girls; and my wife's not very well, and all that. . . . Well, if I had to start my life all over again, I wouldn't marry. . . . No, no!

[*Enter* KOOLYGHIN, *in the uniform of a teacher.*]

KOOLYGHIN [*approaches* IRENA]. Congratulations, dear sister—from the bottom of my heart, congratulations on your Saint's day. I wish you good health and everything a girl of your age ought to have! And allow me to present you with this little book. . . . [*Hands her a book.*] It's the history of our school covering the whole fifty years of its existence. I wrote it myself. Quite a trifle, of course—I wrote it in my spare time when I had nothing better to do—but I hope you'll read it nevertheless. Good morning to you all! [*To* VERSHININ.] Allow me to introduce myself. Koolyghin's the name; I'm a master of the secondary school here. And a town councillor. [*To* IRENA.] You'll find a list in the book of all the pupils who have completed their studies at our school during the last fifty years. *Feci quod potui, faciant meliora potentes.*[9] [*Kisses* MASHA.]

IRENA. But you gave me this book last Easter!

KOOLYGHIN [*laughs*]. Did I really? In that case, give it me back—or no, better give it to the Colonel. Please do take it, Colonel. Maybe you'll read it some time when you've nothing better to do.

VERSHININ. Thank you very much. [*Prepares to leave.*] I'm so very glad to have made your acquaintance. . . .

OLGA. You aren't going, are you? . . . Really, you mustn't.

IRENA. But you'll stay and have lunch with us! Please do.

OLGA. Please do.

VERSHININ [*bows*]. I see I've intruded on your Saint's day party. I didn't know. Forgive me for not offering you my congratulations.

[*Goes into the ballroom with* OLGA.]

9. "I did what I could, let those who are more able do better."

KOOLYGHIN. To-day is Sunday, my friends, a day of rest; let us rest and enjoy it, each according to his age and position in life! We shall have to roll up the carpets and put them away till the winter. . . . We must remember to put some naphthaline on them, or Persian powder. . . . The Romans enjoyed good health because they knew how to work *and* how to rest. They had *mens sana in corpore sano*.[1] Their life had a definite shape, a form. . . . The director of the school says that the most important thing about life is form. . . . A thing that loses its form is finished—that's just as true of our ordinary, everyday lives. [*Takes* MASHA *by the waist and laughs.*] Masha loves me. My wife loves me. Yes, and the curtains will have to be put away with the carpets, too. . . . I'm cheerful to-day, I'm in quite excellent spirits. . . . Masha, we're invited to the director's at four o'clock to-day. A country walk has been arranged for the teachers and their families.

MASHA. I'm not going.

KOOLYGHIN [*distressed*]. Masha, darling, why not?

MASHA. I'll tell you later. . . . [*Crossly.*] All right, I'll come, only leave me alone now. . . . [*Walks off.*]

KOOLYGHIN. And after the walk we shall all spend the evening at the director's house. In spite of weak health, that man is certainly sparing no pains to be sociable. A first-rate, thoroughly enlightened man! A most excellent person! After the conference yesterday he said to me: 'I'm tired, Fiodor Ilyich. I'm tired!' [*Looks at the clock, then at his watch.*] Your clock is seven minutes fast. Yes, 'I'm tired,' he said.

[*The sound of the violin is heard off stage.*]

OLGA. Will you all come and sit down, please! Lunch is ready. There's a pie.

KOOLYGHIN. Ah, Olga, my dear girl! Last night I worked up to eleven o'clock, and I felt tired, but to-day I'm quite happy. [*Goes to the table in the ballroom.*] My dear Olga!

CHEBUTYKIN [*puts the newspaper in his pocket and combs his beard*]. A pie? Excellent!

MASHA [*sternly to* CHEBUTYKIN]. Remember, you mustn't take anything to drink to-day. Do you hear? It's bad for you.

CHEBUTYKIN. Never mind. I've got over that weakness long ago! I haven't done any heavy drinking for two years. [*Impatiently.*] Anyway, my dear, what does it matter?

MASHA. All the same, don't you dare to drink anything. Mind you don't now! [*Crossly, but taking care that her husband does not hear.*] So now I've got to spend another of these damnably boring evenings at the director's!

TOOZENBACH. I wouldn't go if I were you, and that's that.

CHEBUTYKIN. Don't you go, my dear.

MASHA. Don't go, indeed! Oh, what a damnable life! It's intolerable. . . . [*Goes into the ballroom.*]

1. "A sound mind in a sound body."

CHEBUTYKIN [*follows her*]. Well, well! . . .

SOLIONY [*as he passes* TOOZENBACH *on the way to the ballroom*]. Cluck, cluck, cluck!

TOOZENBACH. Do stop it, Vassily Vassilich. I've really had enough of it. . . .

SOLIONY. Cluck, cluck, cluck! . . .

KOOLYGHIN [*gaily*]. Your health, Colonel! I'm a schoolmaster . . . and I'm quite one of the family here, as it were. I'm Masha's husband. She's got a sweet nature, such a very sweet nature!

VERSHININ. I think I'll have a little of this dark vodka. [*Drinks.*] Your health! [*To* OLGA.] I do feel so happy with you people!

[*Only* IRENA *and* TOOZENBACH *remain in the drawing-room.*]

MASHA. Masha's a bit out of humour to-day. You know, she got married when she was eighteen, and then her husband seemed the cleverest man in the world to her. It's different now. He's the kindest of men, but not the cleverest.

OLGA [*impatiently*]. Andrey, will you please come?

ANDREY [*off stage*]. Just coming. [*Enters and goes to the table.*]

TOOZENBACH. What are you thinking about?

IRENA. Oh, nothing special. You know, I don't like this man Soliony, I'm quite afraid of him. Whenever he opens his mouth he says something silly.

TOOZENBACH. He's a strange fellow. I'm sorry for him, even though he irritates me. In fact, I feel more sorry for him than irritated. I think he's shy. When he's alone with me, he can be quite sensible and friendly, but in company he's offensive and bullying. Don't go over there just yet, let them get settled down at the table. Let me stay beside you for a bit. Tell me what you're thinking about. [*A pause.*] You're twenty . . . and I'm not thirty yet myself. What years and years we still have ahead of us, a whole long succession of years, all full of my love for you! . . .

IRENA. Don't talk to me about love, Nikolai Lvovich.

TOOZENBACH [*not listening*]. Oh, I long so passionately for life, I long to work and strive so much, and all this longing is somehow mingled with my love for you, Irena. And just because you happen to be beautiful, life appears beautiful to me! What are you thinking about?

IRENA. You say that life is beautiful. Maybe it is—but what if it only seems to be beautiful? Our lives, I mean the lives of us three sisters, haven't been beautiful up to now. The truth is that life has been stifling us, like weeds in a garden. I'm afraid I'm crying. . . . So unnecessary. . . . [*Quickly dries her eyes and smiles.*] We must work, work! The reason we feel depressed and take such a gloomy view of life is that we've never known what it is to make a real effort. We're the children of parents who despised work. . . .

[*Enter* NATALIA IVANOVNA. *She is wearing a pink dress with a green belt.*]

NATASHA. They've gone in to lunch already. . . . I'm late. . . . [*Glances

at herself in a mirror, adjusts her dress.] My hair seems to be all right.
. . . [*Catches sight of* IRENA.] My dear Irena Serghyeevna, congratulations! [*Gives her a vigorous and prolonged kiss.*] You've got
such a lot of visitors. . . . I feel quite shy. . . . How do you do,
Baron?

OLGA [*enters the drawing-room*]. Oh, there you are, Natalia Ivanovna!
How are you, my dear?

[*They kiss each other.*]

NATASHA. Congratulations! You've such a lot of people here, I feel
dreadfully shy. . . .

OLGA. It's all right, they're all old friends. [*Alarmed, dropping her voice.*]
You've got a green belt on! My dear, that's surely a mistake!

NATASHA. Why, is it a bad omen, or what?

OLGA. No, but it just doesn't go with your dress . . . it looks so
strange. . . .

NATASHA [*tearfully*]. Really? But it isn't really green, you know, it's a
sort of dull colour. . . . [*Follows* OLGA *to the ballroom.*]

[*All are now seated at the table; the drawing-room is empty.*]

KOOLYGHIN. Irena, you know, I do wish you'd find yourself a good
husband. In my view it's high time you got married.

CHEBUTYKIN. You ought to get yourself a nice little husband, too, Natalia
Ivanovna.

KOOLYGHIN. Natalia Ivanovna already has a husband in view.

MASHA [*strikes her plate with her fork*].[2] A glass of wine for me, please!
Three cheers for our jolly old life! We keep our end up, we do!

KOOLYGHIN. Masha, you won't get more than five out of ten for good
conduct!

VERSHININ. I say, this liqueur's very nice. What is it made of?

SOLIONY. Black beetles!

IRENA. Ugh! ugh! How disgusting!

OLGA. We're having roast turkey for dinner to-night, and then apple tart.
Thank goodness, I'll be here all day to-day . . . this evening, too.
You must all come this evening.

VERSHININ. May I come in the evening, too?

IRENA. Yes, please do.

NATASHA. They don't stand on ceremony here.

CHEBUTYKIN. 'Nature created us for love alone.' . . . [*Laughs.*]

ANDREY [*crossly*]. Will you stop it, please? Aren't you tired of it yet?

[FEDOTIK *and* RODÈ *come in with a large basket of flowers.*]

FEDOTIK. Just look here, they're having lunch already!

RODÈ [*in a loud voice*]. Having their lunch? So they are, they're having
lunch already.

FEDOTIK. Wait half a minute. [*Takes a snapshot.*] One! Just one minute
more! . . . [*Takes another snapshot.*] Two! All over now.

---

2. This piece of business is omitted in the Moscow ms.

[*They pick up the basket and go into the ballroom where they are greeted uproariously.*]

RODÈ [*loudly*]. Congratulations, Irena Serghyeevna! I wish you all the best, everything you'd wish for yourself! Gorgeous weather to-day, absolutely marvellous. I've been out walking the whole morning with the boys. You do know that I teach gym at the high school, don't you? . . .

FEDOTIK. You may move now, Irena Serghyeevna, that is, if you want to. [*Takes a snapshot.*] You do look attractive to-day. [*Takes a top out of his pocket.*] By the way, look at this top. It's got a wonderful hum.

IRENA. What a sweet little thing!

MASHA. 'A green oak grows by a curving shore. And round that oak hangs a golden chain.' . . . A green chain around that oak. . . . [*Peevishly.*] Why do I keep on saying that? Those lines have been worrying me all day long!

KOOLYGHIN. Do you know, we're thirteen at table?

RODÈ [*loudly*]. You don't really believe in these old superstitions, do you? [*Laughter.*]

KOOLYGHIN. When thirteen people sit down to table, it means that some of them are in love. Is it you, by any chance, Ivan Romanych?

CHEBUTYKIN. Oh, I'm just an old sinner. . . . But what I can't make out is why Natalia Ivanovna looks so embarrassed.

[*Loud laughter.* NATASHA *runs out into the drawing-room,* ANDREY *follows her.*]

ANDREY. Please, Natasha, don't take any notice of them! Stop . . . wait a moment. . . . Please!

NATASHA. I feel so ashamed. . . . I don't know what's the matter with me, and they're all laughing at me. It's awful of me to leave the table like that, but I couldn't help it. . . . I just couldn't. . . . [*Covers her face with her hands.*]

ANDREY. My dear girl, please, please don't get upset. Honestly, they don't mean any harm, they're just teasing. My dear, sweet girl, they're really good-natured folks, they all are, and they're fond of us both. Come over to the window, they can't see us there. . . . [*Looks round.*]

NATASHA. You see, I'm not used to being with a lot of people.

ANDREY. Oh, how young you are, Natasha, how wonderfully, beautifully young! My dear, sweet girl, don't get so upset! Do believe me, believe me. . . . I'm so happy, so full of love, of joy. . . . No, they can't see us here! They can't see us! How did I come to love you, when was it? . . . I don't understand anything. My precious, my sweet, my innocent girl, please—I want you to marry me! I love you, I love you as I've never loved anybody. . . . [*Kisses her.*]

[*Enter two officers and, seeing* NATASHA *and* ANDREY *kissing, stand and stare in amazement.*]

CURTAIN

Act Two

The scene is the same as in Act I
It is eight o'clock in the evening. The faint sound of an accordion is heard coming from the street.
The stage is unlit. Enter NATALIA IVANOVNA *in a dressing-gown, carrying a candle. She crosses the stage and stops by the door leading to* ANDREY'S *room.*

NATASHA. What are you doing, Andriusha? Reading? It's all right, I only wanted to know. . . . [*Goes to another door, opens it, looks inside and shuts it again.*] No one's left a light anywhere. . . .

ANDREY [*enters with a book in his hand*]. What is it, Natasha?

NATASHA. I was just going round to see if anyone had left a light anywhere. It's carnival week, and the servants are so excited about it . . . anything might happen! You've got to watch them. Last night about twelve o'clock I happened to go into the dining-room, and—would you believe it?—there was a candle alight on the table. I've not found out who lit it. [*Puts the candle down.*] What time is it?

ANDREY [*glances at his watch*]. Quarter past eight.

NATASHA. And Olga and Irena still out. They aren't back from work yet, poor things! Olga's still at some teachers' conference, and Irena's at the post office. [*Sighs.*] This morning I said to Irena: 'Do take care of yourself, my dear.' But she won't listen. Did you say it was a quarter past eight? I'm afraid Bobik is not at all well. Why does he get so cold? Yesterday he had a temperature, but to-day he feels quite cold when you touch him. . . . I'm so afraid!

ANDREY. It's all right, Natasha. The boy's well enough.

NATASHA. Still, I think he ought to have a special diet. I'm so anxious about him. By the way, they tell me that some carnival party's supposed to be coming here soon after nine. I'd rather they didn't come, Andriusha.

ANDREY. Well, I really don't know what I can do. They've been asked to come.

NATASHA. This morning the dear little fellow woke up and looked at me, and then suddenly he smiled. He recognized me, you see. 'Good morning, Bobik,' I said, 'good morning, darling precious!' And then he laughed. Babies understand everything, you know, they understand us perfectly well. Anyway, Andriusha, I'll tell the servants not to let that carnival party in.

ANDREY [*irresolutely*]. Well . . . it's really for my sisters to decide, isn't it? It's their house, after all.

NATASHA. Yes, it's their house as well. I'll tell them, too. . . . They're so kind. . . . [*Walks off.*] I've ordered sour milk for supper. The doctor says you ought to eat nothing but sour milk, or you'll never get any thinner. [*Stops.*] Bobik feels so cold. I'm afraid his room is too cold for him. He ought to move into a warmer room, at least until the warm weather comes. Irena's room, for instance—that's just a perfect room for a baby; it's dry, and it gets the sun all day long. We must tell her: perhaps she'd share Olga's room for a bit. . . . In any case, she's never at home during the day, she only sleeps there. . . . [*A pause.*] Andriusha, why don't you say anything?

ANDREY. I was just day-dreaming. . . . There's nothing to say, any-way. . . .

NATASHA. Well. . . . What was it I was going to tell you? Oh, yes! Ferapont from the Council Office wants to see you about something.

ANDREY [*yawns*]. Tell him to come up.

[NATASHA *goes out.* ANDREY, *bending over the candle which she has left behind, begins to read his book. Enter* FERAPONT *in an old shabby overcoat, his collar turned up, his ears muffled in a scarf.*]

ANDREY. Hullo, old chap! What did you want to see me about?

FERAPONT. The chairman's sent you the register and a letter or some-thing. Here they are. [*Hands him the book and the letter.*]

ANDREY. Thanks. That's all right. Incidentally, why have you come so late? It's gone eight already.

FERAPONT. What's that?

ANDREY [*raising his voice*]. I said, why have you come so late? It's gone eight already.

FERAPONT. That's right. It was still daylight when I came first, but they wouldn't let me see you. The master's engaged, they said. Well, if you're engaged, you're engaged. I'm not in a hurry. [*Thinking that* ANDREY *has said something.*] What's that?

ANDREY. Nothing. [*Turns over the pages of the register.*] To-morrow's Friday, there's no meeting, but I'll go to the office just the same . . . do some work. I'm so bored at home! . . . [*A pause.*] Yes, my dear old fellow, how things do change, what a fraud life is! So strange! To-day I picked up this book, just out of boredom, because I hadn't anything to do. It's a copy of some lectures I attended at the University. . . . Good Heavens! Just think—I'm secretary of the local council now, and Protopopov's chairman, and the most I can ever hope for is to become a member of the council myself! I—a member of the local council! I, who dream every night that I'm a professor in Moscow University, a famous academician, the pride of all Russia!

FERAPONT. I'm sorry, I can't tell you. I don't hear very well.

ANDREY. If you could hear properly I don't think I'd be talking to you like this. I must talk to someone, but my wife doesn't seem to un-derstand me, and as for my sisters . . . I'm afraid of them for some reason or other, I'm afraid of them laughing at me and pulling my leg. . . . I don't drink and I don't like going to pubs, but my word! how I'd enjoy an hour or so at Tyestov's, or the Great Moscow Restaurant! Yes, my dear fellow, I would indeed!

FERAPONT. The other day at the office a contractor was telling me about some business men who were eating pancakes in Moscow. One of them ate forty pancakes and died. It was either forty or fifty, I can't remember exactly.

ANDREY. You can sit in some huge restaurant in Moscow without knowing anyone, and no one knowing you; yet somehow you don't feel that you don't belong there. . . . Whereas here you know everybody, and everybody knows you, and yet you don't feel you belong here, you feel you don't belong at all. . . . You're lonely and you feel a stranger.

FERAPONT. What's that? [A *pause.*] It was the same man that told me—of course, he may have been lying—he said that there's an enormous rope stretched right across Moscow.

ANDREY. Whatever for?

FERAPONT. I'm sorry, I can't tell you. That's what he said.

ANDREY. What nonsense! [*Reads the book.*] Have you ever been to Moscow?

FERAPONT [*after a pause*]. No. It wasn't God's wish. [A *pause.*] Shall I go now?

ANDREY. Yes, you may go. Good-bye.

[FERAPONT *goes out.*]

Good-bye. [*Reading.*] Come in the morning to take some letters. . . . You can go now. [A *pause.*] He's gone.

[A *bell rings.*]

Yes, that's how it is. . . . [*Stretches and slowly goes to his room.*]

[*Singing is heard off stage; a nurse is putting a baby to sleep. Enter* MASHA *and* VERSHININ. *While they talk together, a maid lights a lamp and candles in the ballroom.*]

MASHA. I don't know. [A *pause.*] I don't know. Habit's very important, of course. For instance, after Father died, for a long time we couldn't get accustomed to the idea that we hadn't any orderlies to wait on us. But, habit apart, I think it's quite right what I was saying. Perhaps it's different in other places, but in this town the military certainly do seem to be the nicest and most generous and best-mannered people.

VERSHININ. I'm thirsty. I could do with a nice glass of tea.

MASHA [*glances at her watch*]. They'll bring it in presently. You see, they married me off when I was eighteen. I was afraid of my husband because he was a school-master, and I had only just left school myself. He seemed terribly learned then, very clever and important. Now it's quite different, unfortunately.

VERSHININ. Yes. . . . I see. . . .

MASHA. I don't say anything against my husband—I'm used to him now—but there are such a lot of vulgar and unpleasant and offensive people among the other civilians. Vulgarity upsets me, it makes me feel insulted, I actually suffer when I meet someone who lacks refinement and gentle manners, and courtesy. When I'm with the other teachers, my husband's friends, I just suffer.

VERSHININ. Yes, of course. But I should have thought that in a town like this the civilians and the army people were equally uninteresting. There's nothing to choose between them. If you talk to any educated person here, civilian or military, he'll generally tell you that he's just worn out. It's either his wife, or his house, or his estate, or his horse, or something. . . . We Russians are capable of such elevated thoughts—then why do we have such low ideals in practical life? Why is it, why?

MASHA. Why?

VERSHININ. Yes, why does his wife wear him out, why do his children wear him out? And what about *him* wearing out his wife and children?

MASHA. You're a bit low-spirited to-day, aren't you?

VERSHININ. Perhaps. I haven't had any dinner to-day. I've had nothing to eat since morning. One of my daughters is a bit off colour, and when the children are ill, I get so worried. I feel utterly conscience-stricken at having given them a mother like theirs. Oh, if only you could have seen her this morning! What a despicable woman! We started quarrelling at seven o'clock, and at nine I just walked out and slammed the door. [*A pause.*] I never talk about these things in the ordinary way. It's a strange thing, but you're the only person I feel I dare complain to. [*Kisses her hand.*] Don't be angry with me. I've nobody, nobody but you. . . . [*A pause.*]

MASHA. What a noise the wind's making in the stove! Just before Father died the wind howled in the chimney just like that.

VERSHININ. Are you superstitious?

MASHA. Yes.

VERSHININ. How strange. [*Kisses her hand.*] You really are a wonderful creature, a marvellous creature! Wonderful, marvellous! It's quite dark here, but I can see your eyes shining.

MASHA [*moves to another chair*]. There's more light over here.

VERSHININ. I love you, I love you, I love you. . . . I love your eyes, I love your movements. . . . I dream about them. A wonderful, marvellous being!

MASHA [*laughing softly*]. When you talk to me like that, somehow I can't help laughing, although I'm afraid at the same time. Don't say it again, please. [*Half-audibly.*] Well, no . . . go on. I don't mind. . . . [*Covers her face with her hands.*] I don't mind. . . . Someone's coming. . . . Let's talk about something else. . . .

[*Enter* IRENA *and* TOOZENBACH *through the ballroom.*]

TOOZENBACH. I have a triple-barrelled name—Baron Toozenbach-Krone-Alschauer—but actually I'm a Russian. I was baptized in the Greek-Orthodox faith, just like yourself. I haven't really got any German characteristics, except maybe the obstinate patient way I keep on pestering you. Look how I bring you home every evening.

IRENA. How tired I am!

TOOZENBACH. And I'll go on fetching you from the post office and bringing you home every evening for the next twenty years—unless you send me away. . . . [*Noticing* MASHA *and* VERSHININ, *with pleasure.*] Oh it's you! How are you?

IRENA. Well, here I am, home at last! [*To* MASHA.] A woman came into the post office just before I left. She wanted to send a wire to her brother in Saratov to tell him her son had just died, but she couldn't remember the address. So we had to send the wire without an address, just to Saratov. She was crying and I was rude to her, for no reason at all. 'I've no time to waste,' I told her. So stupid of me. We're having the carnival crowd to-day, aren't we?

MASHA. Yes.

IRENA [*sits down*]. How nice it is to rest! I am tired!

TOOZENBACH [*smiling*]. When you come back from work, you look so young, so pathetic, somehow. . . . [*A pause.*]

IRENA. I'm tired. No, I don't like working at the post office, I don't like it at all.

MASHA. You've got thinner. . . . [*Whistles.*] You look younger, too, and your face looks quite boyish.

TOOZENBACH. It's the way she does her hair.

IRENA. I must look for another job. This one doesn't suit me. It hasn't got what I always longed for and dreamed about. It's the sort of work you do without inspiration, without even thinking.

[*Someone knocks at the floor from below.*]

That's the Doctor knocking. [*To* TOOZENBACH.] Will you answer him, dear? . . . I can't. . . . I'm so tired.

TOOZENBACH [*knocks on the floor*].

IRENA. He'll be up in a moment. We must do something about all this. Andrey and the Doctor went to the club last night and lost at cards again. They say Andrey lost two hundred roubles.

MASHA [*with indifference*]. Well, what are we to do about it?

IRENA. He lost a fortnight ago, and he lost in December, too. I wish to goodness he'd lose everything we've got, and soon, too, and then perhaps we'd move out of this place. Good Heavens, I dream of Moscow every night. Sometimes I feel as if I were going mad. [*Laughs.*] We're going to Moscow in June. How many months are there till June? . . . February, March, April, May . . . nearly half-a-year!

MASHA. We must take care that Natasha doesn't get to know about him losing at cards.

IRENA. I don't think she cares.

[*Enter* CHEBUTYKIN. *He has been resting on his bed since dinner and has only just got up. He combs his beard, then sits down at the table and takes out a newspaper.*]

MASHA. There he is. Has he paid his rent yet?

IRENA [*laughs*]. No. Not a penny for the last eight months. I suppose he's forgotten.

MASHA [*laughs*]. How solemn he looks sitting there!

[*They all laugh. A pause.*]

IRENA. Why don't you say something, Alexandr Ignatyevich?

VERSHININ. I don't know. I'm just longing for some tea. I'd give my life for a glass of tea! I've had nothing to eat since morning. . . .

CHEBUTYKIN. Irena Serghyeevna!

IRENA. What is it?

CHEBUTYKIN. Please come here. *Venez ici!*

[IRENA *goes over to him and sits down at the table.*]

I can't do without you.

[IRENA *lays out the cards for a game of patience.*]

VERSHININ. Well, if we can't have any tea, let's do a bit of philosophizing, anyway.

TOOZENBACH. Yes, let's. What about?

VERSHININ. What about? Well . . . let's try to imagine what life will be like after we're dead, say in two or three hundred years.

TOOZENBACH. All right, then. . . . After we're dead, people will fly about in balloons, the cut of their coats will be different, the sixth sense will be discovered, and possibly even developed and used, for all I know. . . . But I believe life itself will remain the same; it will still be difficult and full of mystery and full of happiness. And in a thousand years' time people will still be sighing and complaining: 'How hard this business of living is'!—and yet they'll still be scared of death and unwilling to die, just as they are now.

VERSHININ [*after a moment's thought*]. Well, you know . . . how shall I put it? I think everything in the world is bound to change gradually— in fact, it's changing before our very eyes. In two or three hundred years, or maybe a thousand years—it doesn't matter how long ex- actly—life will be different. It will be happy. Of course, we shan't be able to enjoy that future life, but all the same, what we're living for now is to create it, we work and . . . yes, we suffer in order to create it. That's the goal of our life, and you might say that's the only happiness we shall ever achieve.

MASHA [*laughs quietly*].

TOOZENBACH. Why are you laughing?

MASHA. I don't know. I've been laughing all day to-day.

VERSHININ [*to* TOOZENBACH]. I went to the same cadet school as you did but I never went on to the Military Academy. I read a great deal, of course, but I never know what books I ought to choose, and probably I read a lot of stuff that's not worth anything. But the longer I live the more I seem to long for knowledge. My hair's going grey and I'm getting on in years, and yet how little I know, how little! All the same, I think I do know one thing which is not only true but also most important. I'm sure of it. Oh, if only I could convince you that there's not going to be any happiness for our own generation, that there mustn't be and won't be. . . . We've just got to work and work. All the happiness is reserved for our descendants, our remote descendants.

[*A pause.*] Anyway, if I'm not to be happy, then at least my children's children will be.

[FEDOTIK *and* RODÈ *enter the ballroom; they sit down and sing quietly, one of them playing on a guitar.*]

TOOZENBACH. So you won't even allow us to dream of happiness! But what if I *am* happy?

VERSHININ. You're not.

TOOZENBACH [*flinging up his hands and laughing*]. We don't understand one another, that's obvious. How can I convince you?

MASHA [*laughs quietly*].

TOOZENBACH [*holds up a finger to her*]. Show a finger to her and she'll laugh! [*To* VERSHININ.] And life will be just the same as ever not merely in a couple of hundred years' time, but in a million years. Life doesn't change, it always goes on the same; it follows its own laws, which don't concern us, which we can't discover anyway. Think of the birds that migrate in the autumn, the cranes, for instance: they just fly on and on. It doesn't matter what sort of thoughts they've got in their heads, great thoughts or little thoughts, they just fly on and on, not knowing where or why. And they'll go on flying no matter how many philosophers they happen to have flying with them. Let them philosophize as much as they like, as long as they go on flying.

MASHA. Isn't there some meaning?

TOOZENBACH. Meaning? . . . Look out there, it's snowing. What's the meaning of that? [*A pause.*]

MASHA. I think a human being has got to have some faith, or at least he's got to seek faith. Otherwise his life will be empty, empty. . . . How can you live and not know why the cranes fly, why children are born, why the stars shine in the sky! . . . You must either know why you live, or else . . . nothing matters . . . everything's just wild grass. . . . [*A pause.*]

VERSHININ. All the same, I'm sorry my youth's over.

MASHA. 'It's a bore to be alive in this world, friends,' that's what Gogol[3] says.

TOOZENBACH. And I feel like saying: it's hopeless arguing with you, friends! I give you up.

CHEBUTYKIN [*reads out of the paper*]. Balsac's marriage took place at Berdichev.[4]

IRENA [*sings softly to herself*].

CHEBUTYKIN. Must write this down in my notebook. [*Writes.*] Balsac's marriage took place at Berdichev. [*Reads on.*]

IRENA [*playing patience, pensively*]. Balsac's marriage took place at Berdichev.

TOOZENBACH. Well, I've thrown in my hand. Did you know that I'd sent in my resignation, Maria Serghyeevna?

3. Russian novelist and playwright (1809–52).
4. A town in Western Russia well known for its almost exclusively Jewish population [*Translator's note*].

MASHA. Yes, I heard about it. I don't see anything good in it, either. I don't like civilians.

TOOZENBACH. Never mind. [*Gets up.*] What sort of a soldier do I make, anyway? I'm not even good-looking. Well, what does it matter? I'll work. I'd like to do such a hard day's work that when I came home in the evening I'd fall on my bed exhausted and go to sleep at once. [*Goes to the ballroom.*] I should think working men sleep well at nights!

FEDOTIK [*to* IRENA]. I've got you some coloured crayons at Pyzhikov's, in Moscow Street. And this little penknife, too. . . .

IRENA. You still treat me as if I were a little girl. I wish you'd remember I'm grown up now. [*Takes the crayons and the penknife, joyfully.*] They're awfully nice!

FEDOTIK. Look, I bought a knife for myself, too. You see, it's got another blade here, and then another . . . this thing's for cleaning your ears, and these are nail-scissors, and this is for cleaning your nails. . . .

RODÈ [*in a loud voice*]. Doctor, how old are you?

CHEBUTYKIN. I? Thirty-two.

[*Laughter.*]

FEDOTIK. I'll show you another kind of patience. [*Sets out the cards.*]

[*The samovar is brought in, and* ANFISA *attends to it. Shortly afterwards* NATASHA *comes in and begins to fuss around the table.*]

SOLIONY [*enters, bows to the company and sits down at the table*].

VERSHININ. What a wind, though!

MASHA. Yes. I'm tired of winter. I've almost forgotten what summer is like.

IRENA [*playing patience*]. It's coming out. We'll get to Moscow!

FEDOTIK. No, it's not coming out. You see, the eight has to go on the two of spades. [*Laughs.*] That means you won't go to Moscow.

CHEBUTYKIN [*reads the paper*]. Tzitzikar.[5] Smallpox is raging. . . .

ANFISA [*goes up to* MASHA]. Masha, the tea's ready, dear. [*To* VERSHININ.] Will you please come to the table, your Excellency? Forgive me, your name's slipped my memory. . . .

MASHA. Bring it here, Nanny. I'm not coming over there.

IRENA. Nanny!

ANFISA. Comi-ing!

NATASHA [*to* SOLIONY]. You know, even tiny babies understand what we say perfectly well! 'Good morning, Bobik,' I said to him only to-day, 'Good morning, my precious!'—and then he looked at me in such a special sort of way. You may say it's only a mother's imagination, but it isn't, I do assure you. No, no! He really is an extraordinary child!

SOLIONY. If that child were mine, I'd cook him up in a frying pan and eat him. [*Picks up his glass, goes into the drawing-room and sits down in a corner.*]

---

5. A resort town famed for its beauty.

NATASHA [*covers her face with her hands*]. What a rude, ill-mannered person!

MASHA. People who don't even notice whether it's summer or winter are lucky! I think I'd be indifferent to the weather if I were living in Moscow.

VERSHININ. I've just been reading the diary of some French cabinet minister—he wrote it in prison. He got sent to prison in connection with the Panama affair. He writes with such a passionate delight about the birds he can see through the prison window—the birds he never even noticed when he was a cabinet minister. Of course, now he's released he won't notice them any more. . . . And in the same way, you won't notice Moscow once you live there again. We're not happy and we can't be happy: we only want happiness.

TOOZENBACH [*picks up a box from the table*]. I say, where are all the chocolates?

IRENA. Soliony's eaten them.

TOOZENBACH. All of them?

ANFISA [*serving* VERSHININ *with tea*]. Here's a letter for you, Sir.

VERSHININ. For me? [*Takes the letter.*] From my daughter. [*Reads it.*] Yes, of course. . . . Forgive me, Maria Serghyeevna, I'll just leave quietly. I won't have any tea. [*Gets up, agitated.*] Always the same thing. . . .

MASHA. What is it? Secret?

VERSHININ [*in a low voice*]. My wife's taken poison again. I must go. I'll get away without them seeing me. All this is so dreadfully unpleasant. [*Kisses* MASHA's *hand.*] My dear, good, sweet girl. . . . I'll go out this way, quietly. . . . [*Goes out.*]

ANFISA. Where's he off to? And I've just brought him some tea! What a queer fellow!

MASHA [*flaring up*]. Leave me alone! Why do you keep worrying me? Why don't you leave me in peace? [*Goes to the table, cup in hand.*] I'm sick and tired of you, silly old woman!

ANFISA. Why. . . . I didn't mean to offend you, dear.

ANDREY'S VOICE [*off stage*]. Anfisa!

ANFISA [*mimics him*]. Anfisa! Sitting there in his den! . . . [*Goes out.*]

MASHA [*by the table in the ballroom, crossly*]. Do let me sit down somewhere! [*Jumbles up the cards laid out on the table.*] You take up the whole table with your cards! Why don't you get on with your tea?

IRENA. How bad-tempered you are, Masha!

MASHA. Well, if I'm bad-tempered, don't talk to me, then. Don't touch me.

CHEBUTYKIN [*laughs*]. Don't touch her! . . . Take care you don't touch her!

MASHA. You may be sixty, but you're always gabbling some damn nonsense or other, just like a child. . . .

NATASHA [*sighs*]. My dear Masha, need you use such expressions? You

know, with your good looks you'd be thought so charming, even by
the best people—yes, I honestly mean it—if only you wouldn't use
these expressions of yours! Je vous prie, pardonnez moi, Marie, mais
vous avez des manières un peu grossières.[6]

TOOZENBACH [*with suppressed laughter*]. Pass me. . . . I say, will you
please pass me. . . . Is that cognac over there, or what? . . .

NATASHA. Il parait que mon Bobik déjà ne dort pas.[7] . . . I think he's
awake. He's not been too well to-day. I must go and see him . . .
excuse me. [*Goes out.*]

IRENA. I say, where has Alexandr Ignatyevich gone to?

MASHA. He's gone home. His wife's done something queer again.

TOOZENBACH [*goes over to* SOLIONY *with a decanter of cognac*]. You always
sit alone brooding over something or other—though what it's all about
nobody knows. Well, let's make it up. Let's have a cognac together.
[*They drink.*] I suppose I'll have to play the piano all night to-night—
a lot of rubbishy tunes, of course. . . . Never mind!

SOLIONY. Why did you say 'let's make it up'? We haven't quarrelled.

TOOZENBACH. You always give me the feeling that there's something
wrong between us. You're a strange character, no doubt about it.

SOLIONY [*recites*]. 'I am strange, but who's not so? Don't be angry,
Aleko!"[8]

TOOZENBACH. What's Aleko got to do with it? . . . [*A pause.*]

SOLIONY. When I'm alone with somebody I'm all right, I'm just like
other people. But in company, I get depressed and shy, and . . . I
talk all sorts of nonsense. All the same, I'm a good deal more honest
and well-intentioned than plenty of others. I can prove I am.

TOOZENBACH. You often make me angry because you keep on pestering
me when we're in company—but all the same, I do like you for some
reason. . . . I'm going to get drunk to-night, whatever happens! Let's
have another drink!

SOLIONY. Yes, let's [*A pause.*] I've never had anything against you personally, Baron. But my temperament's rather like Lermontov's.[9] [*In
a low voice.*] I even look a little like Lermontov, I've been told. . . .
[*Takes a scent bottle from his pocket and sprinkles some scent on his
hands.*]

TOOZENBACH. I have sent in my resignation! Finished! I've been considering it for five years, and now I've made up my mind at last. I'm
going to work.

SOLIONY [*recites.*] 'Don't be angry, Aleko. . . . Away, away with all your
dreams!'

[*During the conversation* ANDREY *enters quietly with a book in his
hand and sits down by the candle.*]

6. "I beg you, pardon me, Marie, but your manners are a bit coarse."
7. "It seems that my Bobik already isn't asleep."
As unidiomatic in French as in English.
8. From M. J. Lermontov's poem *The Gypsies*.

9. Russian poet (1814–41). In his comments on
the play Chekhov was firm on the point that Soliony does not really resemble Lermontov. The
resemblance exists only in his mind.

TOOZENBACH. I'm going to work!

CHEBUTYKIN [*comes into the drawing-room with* IRENA]. And the food they treated me to was the genuine Caucasian stuff; onion soup, followed by chehartma—that's a meat dish, you know.

SOLIONY. Cheremsha isn't meat at all; it's a plant, something like an onion.

CHEBUTYKIN. No-o, my dear friend. Chehartma isn't an onion, it's roast mutton.

SOLIONY. I tell you cheremsha is a kind of onion.

CHEBUTYKIN. Well, why should I argue about it with you? You've never been to the Caucasus and you've never tasted chehartma.

SOLIONY. I haven't tasted it because I can't stand the smell of it. Cheremsha stinks just like garlic.

ANDREY [*imploringly*]. Do stop it, friends! Please stop it!

TOOZENBACH. When's the carnival crowd coming along?

IRENA. They promised to be here by nine—that means any moment now.

TOOZENBACH [*embraces* ANDREY *and sings*]. 'Ah, my beautiful porch, my lovely new porch, my . . .¹

ANDREY [*dances and sings*]. 'My new porch all made of maple-wood. . . .'

CHEBUTYKIN [*dances*]. 'With fancy carving over the door. . . .'
    [*Laughter.*]

TOOZENBACH [*kisses* ANDREY]. Let's have a drink, the devil take it! Andriusha, let's drink to eternal friendship. I'll come with you when you go back to Moscow University.

SOLIONY. Which university? There are two universities in Moscow.

ANDREY. There's only one.

SOLIONY. I tell you there are two.

ANDREY. Never mind, make it three. The more the merrier.

SOLIONY. There are two universities in Moscow.
    [*Murmurs of protest and cries of 'Hush!'*]
    There are two universities in Moscow, an old one and a new one. But if you don't want to listen to what I'm saying, if my conversation irritates you, I can keep silent. In fact I can go to another room. . . .
    [*Goes out through one of the doors.*]

TOOZENBACH. Bravo, bravo! [*Laughs.*] Let's get started, my friends, I'll play for you. What a funny creature that Soliony is! . . . [*Sits down at the piano and plays a waltz.*]

MASHA [*dances alone*]. The Baron is drunk, the Baron is drunk, the Baron is drunk. . . .
    [*Enter* NATASHA.]

NATASHA [*to* CHEBUTYKIN]. Ivan Romanych! [*Speaks to him, then goes out quietly.* CHEBUTYKIN *touches* TOOZENBACH *on the shoulder and whispers to him.*]

---

1. A traditional Russian dance-song [*Translator's note*].

IRENA. What is it?

CHEBUTYKIN. It's time we were going. Good-night.

IRENA. But really. . . . What about the carnival party?

ANDREY [embarrassed]. The carnival party's not coming. You see, my dear, Natasha says that Bobik isn't very well, and so . . . Anyway, I don't know . . . and I certainly don't care. . . .

IRENA [shrugs her shoulders]. Bobik's not very well! . . .

MASHA. Never mind, we'll keep our end up! If they turn us out, out we must go! [To IRENA.] It isn't Bobik who's not well, it's her. . . . There! . . . [Taps her forehead with her finger.] Petty little bourgeois housewife! [ANDREY goes to his room on the right. CHEBUTYKIN follows him. The guests say good-bye in the ballroom.]

FEDOTIK. What a pity! I'd been hoping to spend the evening here, but of course, if the baby's ill. . . . I'll bring him some toys tomorrow.

RODÈ [in a loud voice]. I had a good long sleep after lunch to-day on purpose, I thought I'd be dancing all night. I mean to say, it's only just nine o'clock.

MASHA. Let's go outside and talk it over. We can decide what to do then. [Voices are heard saying 'Good-bye! God bless you!' and TOOZENBACH is heard laughing gaily. Everyone goes out. ANFISA and a maid clear the table and put out the lights. The nurse sings to the baby off-stage. Enter ANDREY, wearing an overcoat and hat, followed by CHEBUTYKIN. They move quietly.]

CHEBUTYKIN. I've never found time to get married, somehow . . . partly because my life's just flashed past me like lightning, and partly because I was always madly in love with your mother and she was married. . . .

ANDREY. One shouldn't marry. One shouldn't marry because it's so boring.

CHEBUTYKIN. That may be so, but what about loneliness? You can philosophize as much as you like, dear boy, but loneliness is a dreadful thing. Although, really . . . well, it doesn't matter a damn, of course! . . .

ANDREY. Let's get along quickly.

CHEBUTYKIN. What's the hurry? There's plenty of time.

ANDREY. I'm afraid my wife may try to stop me.

CHEBUTYKIN. Ah!

ANDREY. I won't play cards to-night, I'll just sit and watch. I'm not feeling too well. . . . What ought I to do for this breathlessness, Ivan Romanych?

CHEBUTYKIN. Why ask me, dear boy? I can't remember—I simply don't know.

ANDREY. Let's go through the kitchen. [They go out. A bell rings. The ring is repeated, then voices and laughter are heard.]

IRENA [coming in]. What's that?

ANFISA [in a whisper]. The carnival party.

[*The bell rings again.*]

IRENA. Tell them there's no one at home, Nanny. Apologize to them. [ANFISA *goes out.* IRENA *walks up and down the room, lost in thought. She seems agitated. Enter* SOLIONY.]

SOLIONY [*puzzled*]. There's no one here. . . . Where is everybody?

IRENA. They've gone home.

SOLIONY. How strange! Then you're alone here?

IRENA. Yes, alone. [*A pause.*] Well . . . good-night.

SOLIONY. I know I behaved tactlessly just now, I lost control of myself. But you're different from the others, you stand out high above them— you're pure, you can see where the truth lies. . . . You're the only person in the world who can possibly understand me. I love you. . . . I love you with a deep, infinite . . .

IRENA. Do please go away. Good-night!

SOLIONY. I can't live without you. [*Follows her.*] Oh, it's such a delight just to look at you! [*With tears.*] Oh, my happiness! Your glorious, marvellous, entrancing eyes—eyes like no other woman's I've ever seen. . . .

IRENA [*coldly*]. Please stop it, Vassily Vassilich!

SOLIONY. I've never spoken to you of my love before . . . it makes me feel as if I were living on a different planet. . . . [*Rubs his forehead.*] Never mind! I can't force you to love me, obviously. But I don't intend to have any rivals—successful rivals, I mean. . . . No, no! I swear to you by everything I hold sacred that if there's anyone else, I'll kill him. Oh, how wonderful you are!

[*Enter* NATASHA *carrying a candle.*]

NATASHA [*pokes her head into one room, then into another, but passes the door leading to her husband's room*]. Andrey's reading in there. Better let him read. Forgive me, Vassily Vassilich, I didn't know you were here. I'm afraid I'm not properly dressed.

SOLIONY. I don't care. Good-bye. [*Goes out.*]

NATASHA. You must be tired, my poor dear girl. [*Kisses* IRENA.] You ought to go to bed earlier.

IRENA. Is Bobik asleep?

NATASHA. Yes, he's asleep. But he's not sleeping peacefully. By the way, my dear, I've been meaning to speak to you for some time but there's always been something . . . either you're not here, or I'm too busy. . . . You see, I think that Bobik's nursery is so cold and damp. . . . And your room is just ideal for a baby. Darling, do you think you could move into Olga's room?

IRENA [*not understanding her*]. Where to?

[*The sound of bells is heard outside, as a 'troika' is driven up to the house.*]

NATASHA. You can share a room with Olia for the time being, and Bobik can have your room. He is such a darling! This morning I said to him: 'Bobik, you're my very own! My very own!' And he just gazed at me with his dear little eyes.

[*The door bell rings.*]

That must be Olga. How late she is!

[*A maid comes up to* NATASHA *and whispers in her ear.*]

NATASHA. Protopopov! What a funny fellow! Protopopov's come to ask me to go for a drive with him. In a troika! [*Laughs.*] Aren't these men strange creatures! . . .

[*The door bell rings again.*]

Someone's ringing. Shall I go for a short drive? Just for a quarter of an hour? [*To the maid.*] Tell him I'll be down in a minute.

[*The door bell rings.*]

That's the bell again. I suppose it's Olga. [*Goes out.*]

[*The maid runs out;* IRENA *sits lost in thought. Enter* KOOLYGHIN *and* OLGA, *followed by* VERSHININ.]

KOOLYGHIN. Well! What's the meaning of this? You said you were going to have a party.

VERSHININ. It's a strange thing. I left here about half an hour ago, and they were expecting a carnival party then.

IRENA. They've all gone.

KOOLYGHIN. Masha's gone, too? Where has she gone to? And why is Protopopov waiting outside in a troika? Who's he waiting for?

IRENA. Please don't ask me questions. I'm tired.

KOOLYGHIN. You . . . spoilt child!

OLGA. The conference has only just ended. I'm quite worn out. The headmistress is ill and I'm deputizing for her. My head's aching, oh, my head, my head. . . . [*Sits down.*] Andrey lost two hundred roubles at cards last night. The whole town's talking about it. . . .

KOOLYGHIN. Yes, the conference exhausted me, too. [*Sits down.*]

VERSHININ. So now my wife's taken it into her head to try to frighten me. She tried to poison herself. However, everything's all right now, so I can relax, thank goodness. . . . So we've got to go away? Well, good-night to you, all the best. Fiodor Illych, would you care to come along with me somewhere or other? I can't stay at home tonight, I really can't. . . . Do come!

KOOLYGHIN. I'm tired. I don't think I'll come. [*Gets up.*] I'm tired. Has my wife gone home?

IRENA. I think so.

KOOLYGHIN [*kisses* IRENA's *hand*]. Good-night. We can rest to-morrow and the day after to-morrow, two whole days! Well, I wish you all the best. [*Going out.*] How I long for some tea! I reckoned on spending the evening in congenial company, but—o, *fallacem hominum spem!*[2] Always use the accusative case in exclamations.

VERSHININ. Well, it looks as if I'll have to go somewhere by myself. [*Goes out with* KOOLYGHIN, *whistling.*]

OLGA. My head aches, oh, my head. . . . Andrey lost at cards . . . the whole town's talking. . . . I'll go and lie down. [*Going out.*] Tomorrow

2. "Oh, the futile hopes of men."

I'm free. Heavens, what a joy! To-morrow I'm free, and the day after to-morrow I'm free. . . . My head's aching, oh, my poor head. . . .

IRENA [*alone*]. They've all gone. No one's left.

[*Someone is playing an accordion in the street. The nurse sings in the next room.*]

NATASHA [*crosses the ballroom, wearing a fur coat and a cap. She is followed by the maid*]. I'll be back in half an hour. I'm just going for a little drive. [*Goes out.*]

IRENA [*alone, with intense longing*]. Moscow! Moscow! Moscow!

CURTAIN

Act Three

A *bedroom now shared by* OLGA *and* IRENA. *There are two beds, one on the right, the other on the left, each screened off from the centre of the room. It is past two o'clock in the morning. Off-stage the alarm is being sounded on account of a fire which has been raging for some time.*[3] *The inmates of the house have not yet been to bed.* MASHA *is lying on a couch, dressed, as usual, in black.* OLGA *and* ANFISA *come in.*

ANFISA. Now they're sitting down there, under the stairs. . . . I keep telling them to come upstairs, that they shouldn't sit down there, but they just cry. 'We don't know where our Papa is,' they say, 'perhaps he's got burned in the fire.' What an idea! And there are people in the yard, too . . . half-dressed. . . .

OLGA [*takes a dress out of a wardrobe*]. Take this grey frock, Nanny. . . . And this one. . . . This blouse, too. . . . And this skirt. Oh, Heavens! what is happening! Apparently the whole of the Kirsanovsky Street's been burnt down. . . . Take this . . . and this, too. . . .

[*Throws the clothes into* ANFISA'S *arms.*]

The poor Vershinins had a fright. Their house only just escaped being burnt down. They'll have to spend the night here . . . we musn't let them go home. Poor Fedotik's lost everything, he's got nothing left . . . .

ANFISA. I'd better call Feropont Oliushka, I can't carry all this.

OLGA [*rings*]. No one takes any notice when I ring. [*Calls through the door.*] Is anyone there? Will someone come up, please!

[*A window, red with the glow of the fire, can be seen through the open door. The sound of a passing fire engine is heard.*]

How dreadful it all is! And how tired of it I am!

[*Enter* FERAPONT.]

Take this downstairs please. . . . The Kolotilin girls are sitting under the stairs . . . give it to them. And this, too. . . .

---

3. Chekhov insisted that act 3 was to be very quiet, that all the noise was to be in the distance. He himself directed the sound effects.

FERAPONT. Very good, Madam. Moscow was burned down in 1812 just the same. Mercy on us! . . . Yes, the French were surprised all right.

OLGA. Go along now, take this down.

FERAPONT. Very good. [*Goes out.*]

OLGA. Give it all away, Nanny dear. We won't keep anything, give it all away. . . . I'm so tired, I can hardly keep on my feet. We mustn't let the Vershinins go home. The little girls can sleep in the drawing-room, and Alexandr Ignatyevich can share the downstairs room with the Baron. Fedotik can go in with the Baron, too, or maybe he'd better sleep in the ballroom. The doctor's gone and got drunk—you'd think he'd done it on purpose; he's so hopelessly drunk that we can't let anyone go into his room. Vershinin's wife will have to go into the drawing-room too.

ANFISA [*wearily*]. Don't send me away, Oliushka, darling! Don't send me away!

OLGA. What nonsense you're talking, Nanny! No one's sending you away.

ANFISA [*leans her head against* OLGA's *breast*]. My dearest girl! I do work, you know, I work as hard as I can. . . . I suppose now I'm getting weaker, I'll be told to go. But where can I go? Where? I'm eighty years old. I'm over eighty-one!

OLGA. You sit down for a while, Nanny. . . . You're tired, you poor dear. . . . [*Makes her sit down.*] Just rest a bit. You've turned quite pale.

[*Enter* NATASHA.]

NATASHA. They're saying we ought to start a subscription in aid of the victims of the fire. You know—form a society or something for the purpose. Well, why not? It's an excellent idea! In any case it's up to us to help the poor as best we can. Bobik and Sofochka are fast asleep as if nothing had happened. We've got such a crowd of people in the house; the place seems full of people whichever way you turn. There's 'flu about in the town. . . . I'm so afraid the children might catch it.

OLGA [*without listening to her*]. You can't see the fire from this room; it's quiet in here.

NATASHA. Yes. . . . I suppose my hair is all over the place. [*Stands in front of the mirror.*] They say I've got stouter, but it's not true! I'm not a bit stouter. Masha's asleep . . . she's tired, poor girl. . . . [*To* ANFISA, *coldly.*] How dare you sit down in my presence? Get up! Get out of here!

[ANFISA *goes out. A pause.*]

I can't understand why you keep that old woman in the house.

OLGA [*taken aback*]. Forgive me for saying it, but I can't understand how you . . .

NATASHA. She's quite useless here. She's just a peasant woman, her right place is in the country. You're spoiling her. I do like order in the home. I don't like having useless people about. [*Strokes* OLGA's *cheek.*]

You're tired, my poor dear! Our headmistress is tired! You know, when my Sofochka grows up and goes to school, I'll be frightened of you.

OLGA. I'm not going to be a headmistress.

NATASHA. You'll be asked to, Olechka. It's settled.

OLGA. I'll refuse. I couldn't do it. . . . I wouldn't be strong enough. [*Drinks water.*] You spoke so harshly to Nanny just now. . . . You must forgive me for saying so, but I just can't stand that sort of thing . . . it made me feel quite faint. . . .

NATASHA [*agitated*]. Forgive me, Olia, forgive me. I didn't mean to upset you.

[MASHA *gets up, picks up a pillow and goes out in a huff.*]

OLGA. Please try to understand me, dear. . . . It may be that we've been brought up in a peculiar way, but anyway I just can't bear it. When people are treated like that, it gets me down, I feel quite ill. . . . I simply get unnerved. . . .

NATASHA. Forgive me, dear, forgive me! . . . [*Kisses her.*]

OLGA. Any cruel or tactless remark, even the slightest discourtesy, upsets me. . . .

NATASHA. It's quite true, I know I often say things which would be better left unsaid—but you must agree with me, dear, that she'd be better in the country somewhere.

OLGA. She's been with us for thirty years.

NATASHA. But she can't do any work now, can she? Either I don't understand you, or you don't want to understand me. She can't work, she just sleeps or sits about.

OLGA. Well, let her sit about.

NATASHA [*In surprise*]. What do you mean, let her sit about! Surely she is a servant! [*Tearfully.*] No, I don't understand you, Olia! I have a nurse for the children and a wet nurse and we share a maid and a cook. Whatever do we want this old woman for? What for?

[*The alarm is sounded again.*]

OLGA. I've aged ten years to-night.

NATASHA. We must sort things out, Olia.[4] You're working at your school, and I'm working at home. You're teaching and I'm running the house. And when I say anything about the servants, I know what I'm talking about. . . . That old thief, that old witch must get out of this house to-morrow! . . . [*Stamps her feet.*] How dare you vex me so? How dare you? [*Recovering her self-control.*] Really, if you don't move downstairs, we'll always be quarrelling. This is quite dreadful!

[*Enter* KOOLYGHIN.]

KOOLYGHIN. Where's Masha? It's time we went home. They say the fire's getting less fierce. [*Stretches.*] Only one block got burnt down, but to begin with it looked as if the whole town was going to be set on fire

---

4. Moscow ms.: "We must sort things out once and for all, Olia."

by that wind. [*Sits down.*] I'm so tired, Olechka, my dear. You know, I've often thought that if I hadn't married Masha, I'd have married you, Olechka. You're so kind. I'm worn out. [*Listens.*]

OLGA. What is it?

KOOLYGHIN. The doctor's got drunk just as if he'd done it on purpose. Hopelessly drunk. . . . As if he'd done it on purpose. [*Gets up.*] I think he's coming up here. . . .Can you hear him? Yes, he's coming up.[*Laughs.*] What a fellow, really! . . . I'm going to hide myself. [*Goes to the wardrobe and stands between it and the wall.*] What a scoundrel!

OLGA. He's been off drinking for two years, and now suddenly he goes and gets drunk. . . .

[*Walks with* NATASHA *towards the back of the room.*]

[CHEBUTYKIN *enters; walking firmly and soberly he crosses the room, stops, looks round, then goes to the wash-stand and begins to wash his hands.*]

CHEBUTYKIN [*glumly*]. The devil take them all . . . all the lot of them! They think I can treat anything just because I'm a doctor, but I know positively nothing at all. I've forgotten everything I used to know. I remember nothing, positively nothing.

[OLGA *and* NATASHA *leave the room without his noticing.*]

The devil take them! Last Wednesday I attended a woman at Zasyp. She died, and it's all my fault that she did die. Yes. . . . I used to know a thing or two twenty-five years ago, but now I don't remember anything. Not a thing! Perhaps I'm not a man at all, but I just imagine that I've got hands and feet and a head. Perhaps I don't exist at all, and I only imagine that I'm walking about and eating and sleeping. [*Weeps.*] Oh, if only I could simply stop existing! [*Stops crying, glumly.*] God knows. . . . The other day they were talking about Shakespeare and Voltaire at the club. . . . I haven't read either, never read a single line of either, but I tried to make out by my expression that I had. The others did the same. How petty it all is! How despicable! And then suddenly I thought of the woman I killed on Wednesday. It all came back to me, and I felt such a swine, so sick of myself that I went and got drunk. . . .

[*Enter* IRENA, VERSHININ *and* TOOZENBACH. TOOZENBACH *is wearing a fashionable new civilian suit.*]

IRENA. Let's sit down here for a while. No one will come in here.

VERSHININ. The whole town would have been burnt down but for the soldiers. They're a fine lot of fellows! [*Rubs his hands with pleasure.*] Excellent fellows! Yes, they're a fine lot!

KOOLYGHIN [*approaches them*]. What's the time?

TOOZENBACH. It's gone three. It's beginning to get light.

IRENA. Everyone's sitting in the ballroom and nobody thinks of leaving. That man Soliony there, too. . . . [*To* CHEBUTYKIN.] You ought to go to bed, Doctor.

CHEBUTYKIN. I'm all right. . . . Thanks. . . . [*Combs his beard.*]

KOOLYGHIN [*laughs*]. Half seas over,[5] Ivan Romanych! [*Slaps him on the shoulder.*] You're a fine one! *In vino veritas,*[6] as they used to say in Rome.

TOOZENBACH. Everyone keeps asking me to arrange a concert in aid of the victims of the fire.

IRENA. Well, who'd you get to perform in it?

TOOZENBACH. It could be done if we wanted to. Maria Serghyeevna plays the piano wonderfully well, in my opinion.

KOOLYGHIN. Yes, wonderfully well!

IRENA. She's forgotten how to. She hasn't played for three years. . . . Or maybe it's four.

TOOZENBACH. Nobody undertands music in this town, not a single person. But I do—I really do—and I assure you quite definitely that Maria Serghyeevna plays magnificently. She's almost a genius for it.

KOOLYGHIN. You're right, Baron. I'm very fond of Masha. She's such a nice girl.

TOOZENBACH. Fancy being able to play so exquisitely, and yet having nobody, nobody at all, to appreciate it!

KOOLYGHIN [*sighs*]. Yes. . . . But would it be quite proper for her to play in a concert? [*A pause.*] I don't know anything about these matters, my friends. Perhaps it'll be perfectly all right. But you know, although our director is a good man, a very good man indeed, and most intelligent, I know that he does hold certain views. . . . Of course, this doesn't really concern him, but I'll have a word with him about it, all the same, if you like.

CHEBUTYKIN [*picks up a china clock and examines it*].

VERSHININ. I've got my clothes in such a mess helping to put out the fire, I must look like nothing on earth. [*A pause.*] I believe they were saying yesterday that our brigade might be transferred to somewhere a long way away. Some said it was to be Poland, and some said it was Cheeta, in Siberia.

TOOZENBACH. I heard that, too. Well, the town will seem quite deserted.

IRENA. We'll go away, too!

CHEBUTYKIN [*drops the clock and breaks it*]. Smashed to smithereens!

[*A pause. Everyone looks upset and embarrassed.*]

KOOLYGHIN [*picks up the pieces*]. Fancy breaking such a valuable thing! Ah, Ivan Romanych, Ivan Romanych! You'll get a bad mark for that!

IRENA. It was my mother's clock.

CHEBUTYKIN. Well, supposing it was. If it was your mother's, then it was your mother's. Perhaps I didn't smash it. Perhaps it only appears that I did. Perhaps it only appears to us that we exist, whereas in reality we don't exist at all. I don't know anything, no one knows anything. [*Stops at the door.*] Why are you staring at me? Natasha's

---

5. Britishism meaning "almost drunk."   6. "In wine there is truth."

having a nice little affair with Protopopov, and you don't see it. You sit here seeing nothing, and meanwhile Natasha's having a nice little affair with Protopopov. . . . [*Sings.*] Would you like a date?[7] . . . [*Goes out.*]

VERSHININ. So. . . . [*Laughs.*] How odd it all is, really! [*A pause.*] When the fire started, I ran home as fast as I could. When I got near, I could see that our house was all right and out of danger, but the two little girls were standing there, in the doorway in their night clothes. Their mother wasn't there. People were rushing about, horses, dogs . . . and in the kiddies' faces I saw a frightened, anxious, appealing look, I don't know what! . . . My heart sank when I saw their faces. My God, I thought, what will these children have to go through in the course of their poor lives? And they may live a long time, too! I picked them up and ran back here with them, and all the time I was running, I was thinking the same thing: what will they have to go through?

[*The alarm is sounded. A pause.*]

When I got here, my wife was here already . . . angry, shouting!

[*Enter* MASHA *carrying a pillow; she sits down on the couch.*]

VERSHININ. And when my little girls were standing in the doorway with nothing on but their night clothes, and the street was red with the glow of the fire and full of terrifying noises, it struck me that the same sort of thing used to happen years ago, when armies used to make sudden raids on towns, and plunder them and set them on fire. . . . Anyway, is there any essential difference between things as they were and as they are now? And before very long, say, in another two or three hundred years, people may be looking at our present life just as we look at the past now, with horror and scorn. Our own times may seem uncouth to them, boring and frightfully uncomfortable and strange. . . . Oh, what a great life it'll be then, what a life! [*Laughs.*] Forgive me, I'm philosophizing my head off again . . . but may I go on, please? I'm bursting to philosophize just at the moment. I'm in the mood for it. [*A pause.*] You seem as if you've all gone to sleep. As I was saying: what a great life it will be in the future! Just try to imagine it. . . . At the present time there are only three people of your intellectual calibre in the whole of this town, but future generations will be more productive of people like you. They'll go on producing more and more of the same sort until at last the time will come when everything will be just as you'd wish it yourselves. People will live their lives in your way, and then even you may be outmoded, and a new lot will come along who will be even better than you are. . . . [*Laughs.*] I'm in quite a special mood to-day. I feel full of a tremendous urge to live. . . . [*Sings.*]

'To Love all ages are in fee,

---

7. Chekhov identified this as a line from a contemporary operetta the name of which he could not recall.

The passion's good for you and me.' . . .[8] [*Laughs.*]

MASHA [*sings*]. Tara-tara-tara. . . .

VERSHININ. Tum-tum. . . .

MASHA. Tara-tara . . .

VERSHININ. Tum-tum, tum-tum. . . . [*Laughs.*]

[*Enter* FEDOTIK.]

FEDOTIK [*dancing about*]. Burnt, burnt! Everything I've got burnt! [*All laugh.*]

IRENA. It's hardly a joking matter. Has everything really been burnt?

FEDOTIK [*laughs*]. Everything, completely. I've got nothing left. My guitar's burnt, my photographs are burnt, all my letters are burnt. Even the little note-book I was going to give you has been burnt.

[*Enter* SOLIONY.]

IRENA. No, please go away, Vassily Vassilich. You can't come in here.

SOLIONY. Can't I? Why can the Baron come in here if I can't?

VERSHININ. We really must go, all of us. What's the fire doing?

SOLIONY. It's dying down, they say. Well, I must say it's a peculiar thing that the Baron can come in here, and I can't. [*Takes a scent bottle from his pocket and sprinkles himself with scent.*]

VERSHININ. Tara-tara.

MASHA. Tum-tum, tum-tum.

VERSHININ [*laughs, to* SOLIONY]. Let's go to the ballroom.

SOLIONY. Very well, we'll make a note of this. 'I hardly need to make my moral yet more clear: That might be teasing geese, I fear!'[9] [*Looks at* TOOZENBACH.] Cluck, cluck, cluck!

[*Goes out with* VERSHININ *and* FEDOTIK.]

IRENA. That Soliony has smoked the room out. . . . [*Puzzled.*] The Baron's asleep. Baron! Baron!

TOOZENBACH [*waking out of his doze*]. I must be tired. The brick-works. . . . No, I'm not talking in my sleep. I really do intend to go to the brick-works and start working there quite soon. I've had a talk with the manager. [*To* IRENA, *tenderly.*] You are so pale, so beautiful, so fascinating. . . . Your pallor seems to light up the darkness around you, as if it were luminous, somehow. . . . You're sad, you're dissatisfied with the life you have to live. . . . Oh, come away with me, let's go away and work together!

MASHA. Nikolai Lvovich, I wish you'd go away.

TOOZENBACH [*laughs*]. Oh, you're here, are you? I didn't see you. [*Kisses* IRENA's *hand.*] Good-bye, I'm going. You know, as I look at you now, I keep thinking of the day—it was a long time ago, your Saint's day—when you talked to us about the joy of work. . . .You were so gay and high-spirited then. . . . And what a happy life I saw ahead of me! Where is it all now? [*Kisses her hand.*] There are tears in your

8. From P. I. Tchaikovsky's operatic version of Pushkin's *Eugene Onegin*.

9. From I. A. Krylov's fable *Geese* [*Translator's note*].

eyes. You should go to bed, it's beginning to get light . . . it's almost morning. . . . Oh, if only I could give my life for you!

MASHA. Nikolai Lvovich, please go away! Really now. . . .

TOOZENBACH. I'm going. [*Goes out.*]

MASHA [*lies down*]. Are you asleep, Fiodor?

KOOLYGHIN. Eh?

MASHA. Why don't you go home?

KOOLYGHIN. My darling Masha, my sweet, my precious Masha. . . .

IRENA. She's tired. Let her rest a while, Fyedia.

KOOLYGHIN. I'll go in a moment. My wife, my dear, good wife. . . . How I love you! . . . only you!

MASHA [*crossly*]. *Amo, amas, amat, amamus, amatis, amant!*[1]

KOOLYGHIN [*laughs*]. Really, she's an amazing woman!—I've been married to you for seven years, but I feel as if we were only married yesterday. Yes, on my word of honour, I do! You really are amazing! Oh, I'm so happy, happy, happy!

MASHA. And I'm so bored, bored, bored! [*Sits up.*] I can't get it out of my head. . . . It's simply disgusting. It's like having a nail driven into my head. No, I can't keep silent about it any more. It's about Andrey. . . . He's actually mortgaged this house to a bank, and his wife's got hold of all the money—and yet the house doesn't belong to him, it belongs to all four of us! Surely, he must realize that, if he's got any honesty.

KOOLYGHIN. Why bring all this up, Masha? Why bother about it now? Andriusha owes money all around. . . . Leave him alone.

MASHA. Anyway, it's disgusting. [*Lies down.*]

KOOLYGHIN. Well, we aren't poor, Masha. I've got work, I teach at the country school, I give private lessons in my spare time. . . .I'm just a plain, honest man. . . . *Omnia mea mecum porto,*[2] as they say.

MASHA. I don't ask for anything, but I'm just disgusted by injustice. [*A pause.*] Why don't you go home, Fiodor?

KOOLYGHIN [*kisses her*]. You're tired. Just rest here for a while. . . . I'll go home and wait for you. . . . Go to sleep. [*Goes to the door.*] I'm happy, happy, happy! [*Goes out.*]

IRENA. The truth is that Andrey is getting to be shallow-minded. He's ageing and since he's been living with that woman he's lost all the inspiration he used to have! Not long ago he was working for a professorship, and yet yesterday he boasted of having at last been elected a member of the County Council. Fancy him a member, with Protopopov as chairman! They say the whole town's laughing at him, he's the only one who doesn't know anything or see anything. And now, you see, everyone's at the fire, while he's just sitting in his room, not taking the slightest notice of it. Just playing his violin. [*Agitated.*]

---

1. She conjugates the verb "to love."   2. "Everything I have I carry with me."

Oh, how dreadful it is, how dreadful, how dreadful! I can't bear it any longer, I can't, I really can't! . . .

[*Enter* OLGA. *She starts arranging things on her bedside table.*]

IRENA [*sobs loudly*]. You must turn me out of here! Turn me out; I can't stand it any more!

OLGA [*alarmed*]. What is it? What is it, darling?

IRENA [*sobbing*]. Where. . . . Where has it all gone to? Where is it? Oh, God! I've forgotten. . . . I've forgotten everything . . . there's nothing but a muddle in my head. . . . I don't remember what the Italian for 'window' is, or for 'ceiling'. . . . Every day I'm forgetting more and more, and life's slipping by, and it will never, never come back. . . . We shall never go to Moscow. . . . I can see that we shall never go. . . .

OLGA. Don't, my dear, don't. . . .

IRENA [*trying to control herself*]. Oh, I'm so miserable! . . . I can't work, I won't work! I've had enough of it, enough! . . . First I worked on the telegraph, now I'm in the County Council office, and I hate and despise everything they give me to do there. . . . I'm twenty-three years old, I've been working all this time, and I feel as if my brain's dried up. I know I've got thinner and uglier and older, and I find no kind of satisfaction in anything, none at all. And the time's passing . . . and I feel as if I'm moving away from any hope of a genuine, fine life, I'm moving further and further away and sinking into a kind of abyss. I feel in despair, and I don't know why I'm still alive, why I haven't killed myself. . . .

OLGA. Don't cry, my dear child, don't cry. . . . It hurts me.

IRENA. I'm not crying any more. That's enough of it. Look, I'm not crying now. Enough of it, enough! . . .

OLGA. Darling, let me tell you something. . . . I just want to speak as your sister, as your friend. . . . That is, if you want my advice. . . . Why don't you marry the Baron?

IRENA [*weeps quietly*].

OLGA. After all, you do respect him, you think a lot of him. . . . It's true, he's not good-looking, but he's such a decent, clean-minded sort of man. . . . After all, one doesn't marry for love, but to fulfil a duty. At least, I think so, and I'd marry even if I weren't in love. I'd marry anyone that proposed to me, as long as he was a decent man. I'd even marry an old man.

IRENA. I've been waiting all this time, imagining that we'd be moving to Moscow, and I'd meet the man I'm meant for there. I've dreamt about him and I've loved him in my dreams. . . . But it's all turned out to be nonsense . . . nonsense. . . .

OLGA [*embracing her*]. My darling sweetheart, I understand everything perfectly. When the Baron resigned his commission and came to see us in his civilian clothes, I thought he looked so plain that I actually started to cry. . . . He asked me why I was crying. . . . How could

I tell him? But, of course, if it were God's will that he should marry
you, I'd feel perfectly happy about it. That's quite a different matter,
quite different!

[NATASHA, *carrying a candle, comes out of the door on the right,
crosses the stage and goes out through the door on the left without
saying anything.*]

MASHA [*sits up*]. She goes about looking as if she'd started the fire.

OLGA. You're silly, Masha. You're the stupidest person in our family.
Forgive me for saying so.

[*A pause.*]

MASHA. My dear sisters, I've got something to confess to you. I must get
some relief, I feel the need of it in my heart. I'll confess it to you two
alone, and then never again, never to anybody! I'll tell you in a
minute. [*In a low voice.*] It's a secret, but you'll have to know everything. I can't keep silent any more. [*A pause.*] I'm in love, in love.
. . . I love that man. . . . You saw him here just now. . . . Well,
what's the good? . . . I love Vershinin. . . .

OLGA [*goes behind her screen*]. Don't say it. I don't want to hear it.

MASHA. Well, what's to be done? [*Holding her head.*] I thought he was
queer at first, then I started to pity him . . . then I began to love him
. . . love everything about him—his voice, his talk, his misfortunes,
his two little girls. . . .

OLGA. Nevertheless, I don't want to hear it. You can say any nonsense
you like, I'm not listening.

MASHA. Oh, you're stupid, Olia![3] If I love him, well—that's my fate!
That's my destiny. . . . He loves me, too. It's all rather frightening,
isn't it? Not a good thing, is it?

[*Takes* IRENA *by the hand and draws her to her.*]

Oh, my dear! . . . How are we going to live through the rest of our
lives? What's going to become of us? When you read a novel, everything in it seems so old and obvious, but when you fall in love yourself,
you suddenly discover that you don't really know anything, and you've
got to make your own decisions. . . . My dear sisters, my dear sisters!
. . . I've confessed it all to you, and now I'll keep quiet. . . . I'll be
like that madman in the story by Gogol—silence . . . silence! . . .

[*Enter* ANDREY *followed by* FERAPONT.]

ANDREY [*crossly*]. What do you want? I don't understand you.

FERAPONT [*stopping in the doorway, impatiently*]. I've asked you about
ten times already, Andrey Serghyeevich.

ANDREY. In the first place, you're not to call me Andrey Serghyeevich—
call me 'Your Honour'.

FERAPONT. The firemen are asking Your Honour if they may drive
through your garden to get to the river. They've been going a long
way round all this time—it's a terrible business!

---

3. Moscow ms.: "Oh, you're funny, Olia."

ANDREY. All right. Tell them it's all right.

[FERAPONT *goes out.*]

They keep on plaguing me. Where's Olga?

[OLGA *comes from behind the screen.*]

I wanted to see you. Will you give me the key to the cupboard? I've lost mine. You know the key I mean, the small one you've got. . . .

[OLGA *silently hands him the key.* IRENA *goes behind the screen on her side of the room.*]

ANDREY. What a terrific fire! It's going down through. That Ferapont annoyed me, the devil take him! Silly thing he made me say. . . . Telling him to call me 'Your Honour'! . . . [*A pause.*] Why don't you say anything, Olia? [*A pause.*] It's about time you stopped this nonsense . . . sulking like this for no reason whatever. . . . You here, Masha? And Irena's here, too. That's excellent! We can talk it over then, frankly and once for all. What have you got against me? What is it?

OLGA. Drop it now, Andriusha. Let's talk it over to-morrow. [*Agitated.*] What a dreadful night!

ANDREY [*in great embarrassment*]. Don't get upset. I'm asking you quite calmly, what have you got against me? Tell me frankly.

VERSHININ'S VOICE [*off stage*]. Tum-tum-tum!

MASHA [*in a loud voice, getting up*]. Tara-tara-tara! [*To* OLGA.] Good-bye, Olia, God bless you! [*Goes behind the screen and kisses* IRENA.] Sleep well. . . . Good-bye, Andrey, I should leave them now, they're tired . . . talk it over to-morrow. . . . [*Goes out.*]

OLGA. Really, Andriusha, let's leave it till to-morrow. . . . [*Goes behind the screen on her side of the room.*] It's time to go to bed.

ANDREY. I only want to say one thing, then I'll go. In a moment. . . . First of all, you've got something against my wife, against Natasha. I've always been conscious of it from the day we got married. Natasha is a fine woman, she's honest and straightforward and high-principled. . . . That's my opinion. I love and respect my wife. You understand that I respect her, and I expect others to respect her, too. I repeat: she's an honest, high-principled woman, and all your grievances against her—if you don't mind my saying so—are just imagination, and nothing more. . . . [*A pause.*] Secondly, you seem to be annoyed with me for not making myself a professor, and not doing any academic work. But I'm working in the Council Office, I'm a member of the County Council, and I feel my service there is just as fine and valuable as any academic work I might do. I'm a member of the County Council, and if you want to know, I'm proud of it! [*A pause.*] Thirdly . . . there's something else I must tell you. . . . I know I mortgaged the house without asking your permission. . . . That was wrong, I admit it, and I ask you to forgive me. . . . I was driven to it by my debts. . . . I'm in debt for about thirty-five thousand roubles. I don't play cards any more, I've given it up long ago. . . . The only thing

I can say to justify myself is that you girls get an annuity, while I don't get anything . . . no income, I mean. . . . [A *pause*.]

KOOLYGHIN [*calling through the door*]. Is Masha there? She's not there? [*Alarmed*.] Where can she be then? It's very strange. . . . [*Goes away*.]

ANDREY. So you won't listen? Natasha is a good, honest woman, I tell you. [*Walks up and down the stage, then stops*.] When I married her, I thought we were going to be happy, I thought we should all be happy. . . . But . . . oh, my God! . . . [*Weeps*.] My dear sisters, my dear, good sisters, don't believe what I've been saying, don't believe it. . . . [*Goes out*.]

KOOLYGHIN [*through the door, agitated*]. Where's Masha? Isn't Masha here? Extraordinary! [*Goes away*.]

[*The alarm is heard again. The stage is empty*.]

IRENA [*speaking from behind the screen*]. Olia! Who's that knocking on the floor?

OLGA. It's the doctor, Ivan Romanych. He's drunk.

IRENA. It's been one thing after another all night. [*A pause*.] Olia! [*Peeps out from behind the screen*.] Have you heard? The troops are being moved from the district . . . they're being sent somewhere a long way off.

OLGA. That's only a rumour.

IRENA. We'll be left quite alone then. . . . Olia!

OLGA. Well?

IRENA. Olia, darling, I do respect the Baron. . . . I think a lot of him, he's a very good man. . . . I'll marry him, Olia, I'll agree to marry him, if only we can go to Moscow! Let's go, please do let's go! There's nowhere in all the world like Moscow. Let's go, Olia! Let's go!

CURTAIN

Act Four

The old garden belonging to the Prozorovs' house. A river is seen at the end of a long avenue of fir-trees, and on the far bank of the river a forest. On the right of the stage there is a verandah with a table on which champagne bottles and glasses have been left. It is midday. From time to time people from the street pass through the garden to get to the river. Five or six soldiers march through quickly.

CHEBUTYKIN, *radiating a mood of benevolence which does not leave him throughout the act, is sitting in a chair in the garden. He is wearing his army cap and is holding a walking stick, as if ready to be called away at any moment.* KOOLYGHIN, *with a decoration round his neck and with his moustache shaved off,* TOOZENBACH *and* IRENA *are standing on the verandah saying good-bye to* FEDOTIK *and* RODÈ, *who are coming down the steps. Both officers are in marching uniform.*

TOOZENBACH [*embracing* FEDOTIK]. You're a good fellow, Fedotik; we've been good friends! [*Embraces* RODÈ.] Once more, then. . . . Good-bye, my dear friends!

IRENA. Au revoir!

FEDOTIK. It's not 'au revoir'. It's good-bye. We shall never meet again.

KOOLYGHIN. Who knows? [*Wipes his eyes, smiling.*] There! you've made me cry.

IRENA. We'll meet some time.

FEDOTIK. Perhaps in ten or fifteen years' time. But then we'll hardly know one another. . . . We shall just meet and say: 'How are you?' coldly. . . . [*Takes a snapshot.*] Wait a moment. . . . Just one more, for the last time.

RODÈ [*embraces* TOOZENBACH]. We're not likely to meet again. . . . [*Kisses* IRENA's *hand.*] Thank you for everything . . . everything!

FEDOTIK [*annoyed*]. Do just wait a second!

TOOZENBACH. We'll meet again if we're fated to meet. Do write to us. Be sure to write.

RODÈ [*glancing round the garden*]. Good-bye, trees! [*Shouts.*] Heigh-ho! [*A pause.*] Good-bye, echo!

KOOLYGHIN. I wouldn't be surprised if you got married out there, in Poland. . . . You'll get a Polish wife, and she'll put her arms round you and say: Kohane![4] [*Laughs.*]

FEDOTIK [*glances at his watch*]. There's less than an hour to go. Soliony is the only one from our battery who's going down the river on the barge. All the others are marching with the division. Three batteries are leaving to-day by road and three more to-morrow—then the town will be quite peaceful.

TOOZENBACH. Yes, and dreadfully dull, too.

RODÈ. By the way, where's Maria Serghyeevna?

KOOLYGHIN. She's somewhere in the garden.

FEDOTIK. We must say good-bye to her.

RODÈ. Good-bye. I really must go, or I'll burst into tears.

[*Quickly embraces* TOOZENBACH *and* KOOLYGHIN, *kisses* IRENA's *hand.*]

Life's been very pleasant here. . . .

FEDOTIK [*to* KOOLYGHIN]. Here's something for a souvenir for you—a note-book with a pencil. . . . We'll go down to the river through here. [*They go off, glancing back.*]

RODÈ [*shouts*]. Heigh-ho!

KOOLYGHIN [*shouts*]. Good-bye!

[*At the back of the stage* FEDOTIK *and* RODÈ *meet* MASHA, *and say good-bye to her; she goes off with them.*]

IRENA. They've gone. . . . [*Sits down on the bottom step of the verandah.*]

CHEBUTYKIN. They forgot to say good-bye to me.

---

4. A Polish word meaning "beloved" [*Translator's note*].

IRENA. Well, what about you?

CHEBUTYKIN. That's true, I forgot, too. Never mind, I'll be seeing them again quite soon. I'll be leaving to-morrow. Yes . . . only one more day. And then, in a year's time I'll be retiring. I'll come back here and finish the rest of my life near you. There's just one more year to go and then I get my pension. . . . [Puts a newspaper in his pocket and takes out another.] I'll come back here and lead a reformed life. I'll be a nice, quiet, well-behaved little man.

IRENA. Yes, it's really time you reformed, my dear friend. You ought to live a different sort of life, somehow.

CHEBUTYKIN. Yes. . . . I think so, too. [Sings quietly.] Tarara-boom-di-ay. . . . I'm sitting on a tomb-di-ay. . . .

KOOLYGHIN. Ivan Romanych is incorrigible! Incorrigible!

CHEBUTYKIN. Yes, you ought to have taken me in hand. You'd have reformed me!

IRENA. Fiodor's shaved his moustache off. I can't bear to look at him.

KOOLYGHIN. Why not?

CHEBUTYKIN. If I could just tell you what your face looks like now—but I daren't.

KOOLYGHIN. Well! Such are the conventions of life! Modus vivendi,[5] you know. The director shaved his moustache off, so I shaved mine off when they gave me an inspectorship. No one likes it, but personally I'm quite indifferent. I'm content. Whether I've got a moustache or not, it's all the same to me. [Sits down.]

ANDREY [passes across the back of the stage pushing a pram with a child asleep in it].

IRENA. Ivan Romanych, my dear friend, I'm awfully worried about something. You were out in the town garden last night—tell me what happened there?

CHEBUTYKIN. What happened? Nothing. Just a trifling thing. [Reads his paper.] It doesn't matter anyway.

KOOLYGHIN. They say that Soliony and the Baron met in the town garden outside the theatre last night and . . .

TOOZENBACH. Don't, please! What's the good? . . . [Waves his hand at him deprecatingly and goes into the house.]

KOOLYGHIN. It was outside the theatre. . . . Soliony started badgering the Baron, and he lost patience and said something that offended him.

CHEBUTYKIN. I don't know anything about it. It's all nonsense.

KOOLYGHIN. A school-master once wrote 'nonsense' in Russian over a pupil's essay, and the pupil puzzled over it, thinking it was a Latin word. [Laughs.] Frightfully funny, you know! They say that Soliony's in love with Irena and that he got to hate the Baron more and more. . . . Well, that's understandable. Irena's a very nice girl. She's a bit

5. "Manner of living."

like Masha, she tends to get wrapped up in her own thoughts. [*To* IRENA.] But your disposition is more easy-going than Masha's. And yet Masha has a very nice disposition, too. I love her, I love my Masha.

[*From the back of the stage comes a shout: 'Heigh-ho!'*]

IRENA [*starts*]. Anything seems to startle me to-day. [*A pause.*] I've got everything ready, too. I'm sending my luggage off after lunch. The Baron and I are going to get married to-morrow, and directly afterwards we're moving to the brick-works, and the day after to-morrow I'm starting work at the school. So our new life will begin, God willing! When I was sitting for my teacher's diploma, I suddenly started crying for sheer joy, with a sort of feeling of blessedness. . . . [*A pause.*] The carrier will be coming for my luggage in a minute. . . .

KOOLYGHIN. That's all very well, but somehow I can't feel that it's meant to be serious. All ideas and theories, but nothing really serious. Anyway, I wish you luck from the bottom of my heart.

CHEBUTYKIN [*moved*]. My dearest girl, my precious child! You've gone on so far ahead of me, I'll never catch you up now. I've got left behind like a bird which has grown too old and can't keep up with the rest of the flock. Fly away, my dears, fly away, and God be with you! [*A pause.*] It's a pity you've shaved your moustache off, Fiodor Illyich.

KOOLYGHIN. Don't keep on about it, please! [*Sighs.*] Well, the soldiers will be leaving to-day, and everything will go back to what it was before. Anyway, whatever they say, Masha is a good, loyal wife. Yes, I love her dearly and I'm thankful for what God has given me. Fate treats people so differently. For instance, there's an excise clerk here called Kozyrev. He was at school with me and he was expelled in his fifth year because he just couldn't grasp the *ut consecutivum*.[6] He's dreadfully hard up now, and in bad health, too, and whenever I meet him, I just say to him: 'Hullo, *ut consecutivum*!' 'Yes', he replies, 'that's just the trouble—*consecutivum*' . . . and he starts coughing. Whereas I—I've been lucky all my life. I'm happy, I've actually been awarded the order of Saint Stanislav, second class—and now I'm teaching the children the same old *ut consecutivum*. Of course, I'm clever, cleverer than plenty of other people, but happiness does not consist of merely being clever. . . .

[*In the house someone plays 'The Maiden's Prayer'.*]

IRENA. To-morrow night I shan't have to listen to the 'Maiden's Prayer'. I shan't have to meet Protopopov. . . . [*A pause.*] By the way, he's in the sitting-room. He's come again.

KOOLYGHIN. Hasn't our headmistress arrived yet?

IRENA. No, we've sent for her. If you only knew how difficult it is for me to live here by myself, without Olia! She lives at the school now; she's the headmistress and she's busy the whole day. And I'm here alone, bored, with nothing to do, and I hate the very room I live in.

6. "And so it follows."

So I've just made up my mind—if I'm really not going to be able to live in Moscow, that's that. It's my fate, that's all. Nothing can be done about it. It's God's will, everything that happens, and that's the truth. Nikolai Lvovich proposed to me. . . . Well, I thought it over, and I made up my mind. He's such a nice man, it's really extraordinary how nice he is. . . . And then suddenly I felt as though my soul had grown wings, I felt more cheerful and so relieved somehow that I wanted to work again. Just to start work! . . . Only something happened yesterday, and now I feel as though something mysterious is hanging over me. . . .

CHEBUTYKIN. Nonsense!

NATASHA [*speaking through the window*]. Our headmistress!

KOOLYGHIN. Our headmistress has arrived! Let's go indoors.

[*Goes indoors with* IRENA.]

CHEBUTYKIN [*reads his paper and sings quietly to himself*]. Tarara-boom-di-ay. . . . I'm sitting on a tomb-di-ay. . . .

[MASHA *walks up to him;* ANDREY *passes across the back of the stage pushing the pram.*]

MASHA. You look very comfortable sitting here. . . .

CHEBUTYKIN. Well, why not? Anything happening?

MASHA [*sits down*]. No, nothing. [*A pause.*] Tell me something. Were you in love with my mother?

CHEBUTYKIN. Yes, very much in love.

MASHA. Did she love you?

CHEBUTYKIN [*after a pause*]. I can't remember now.

MASHA. Is my man here? Our cook Marfa always used to call her policeman 'my man'. Is he here?

CHEBUTYKIN. Not yet.

MASHA. When you have to take your happiness in snatches, in little bits, as I do, and then lose it, as I've lost it, you gradually get hardened and bad-tempered. [*Points at her breast.*] Something's boiling over inside me, here. [*Looking at* ANDREY, *who again crosses the stage with the pram.*] There's Andrey, our dear brother. . . . All our hopes are gone. It's the same as when thousands of people haul a huge bell up into a tower. Untold labour and money is spent on it, and then suddenly it falls and gets smashed. Suddenly, without rhyme or reason. It was the same with Andrey. . . .

ANDREY. When are they going to settle down in the house? They're making such a row.

CHEBUTYKIN. They will soon. [*Looks at his watch.*] This is an old-fashioned watch: it strikes. . . . [*Winds his watch which then strikes.*] The first, second and fifth batteries will be leaving punctually at one o'clock. [*A pause.*] And I shall leave to-morrow.

ANDREY. For good?

CHEBUTYKIN. I don't know. I may return in about a year. Although, God knows . . . it's all the same . . .

[*The sounds of a harp and a violin are heard.*]

ANDREY. The town will seem quite empty. Life will be snuffed out like a candle. [*A pause.*] Something happened yesterday outside the theatre; everybody's talking about it. I'm the only one that doesn't seem to know about it.

CHEBUTYKIN. It was nothing. A lot of nonsense. Soliony started badgering the Baron, or something. The Baron lost his temper and insulted him, and in the end Soliony had to challenge him to a duel. [*Looks at his watch.*] I think it's time to go. . . . At half-past twelve, in the forest over there, on the other side of the river. . . . Bang-bang! [*Laughs.*] Soliony imagines he's like Lermontov. He actually writes poems. But, joking apart, this is his third duel.

MASHA. Whose third duel?

CHEBUTYKIN. Soliony's.

MASHA. What about the Baron?

CHEBUTYKIN. Well, what about him? [*A pause.*]

MASHA. My thoughts are all in a muddle. . . . But what I mean to say is that they shouldn't be allowed to fight. He might wound the Baron or even kill him.

CHEBUTYKIN. The Baron's a good enough fellow, but what does it really matter if there's one Baron more or less in the world? Well, let it be! It's all the same.

> [*The shouts of 'Ah-oo!' and 'Heigh-ho!' are heard from beyond the garden.*]

That's Skvortsov, the second, shouting from the boat. He can wait.

ANDREY. I think it's simply immoral to fight a duel, or even to be present at one as a doctor.

CHEBUTYKIN. That's only how it seems. . . . We don't exist, nothing exists, it only seems to us that we do. . . . And what difference does it make?

MASHA. Talk, talk, nothing but talk all day long! . . . [*Starts to go.*] Having to live in this awful climate with the snow threatening to fall at any moment, and then on the top of it having to listen to all this sort of talk. . . . [*Stops.*] I won't go into the house, I can't bear going in there. . . . Will you let me know when Vershinin comes? . . . [*Walks off along the avenue.*] Look, the birds are beginning to fly away already! [*Looks up.*] Swans or geese. . . . Dear birds, happy birds. . . . [*Goes off.*]

ANDREY. Our house will seem quite deserted. The officers will go, you'll go, my sister will get married, and I'll be left alone in the house.

CHEBUTYKIN. What about your wife?

> [*Enter FERAPONT with some papers.*]

ANDREY. My wife is my wife. She's a good, decent sort of woman . . . she's really very kind, too, but there's something about her which pulls her down to the level of an animal . . . a sort of mean, blind, thick-skinned animal—anyway, not a human being. I'm telling you this as a friend, the only person I can talk openly to. I love Natasha, it's true. But at times she appears to me so utterly vulgar, that I feel quite bewildered by it, and then I can't understand why, for what reasons I love her—or, anyway, did love her. . . .

CHEBUTYKIN [*gets up*]. Well, dear boy, I'm going away to-morrow and it may be we shall never see each other again. So I'll give you a bit of advice. Put on your hat, take a walking stick, and go away. . . . Go away, and don't ever look back. And the further you go, the better.

[SOLIONY *passes across the back of the stage accompanied by two officers. Seeing* CHEBUTYKIN, *he turns towards him, while the officers walk on.*]

SOLIONY. It's time, Doctor. Half past twelve already. [*Shakes hands with* ANDREY.]

CHEBUTYKIN. In a moment. Oh, I'm tired of you all. [*To* ANDREY.] Andriusha, if anyone asks for me, tell them I'll be back presently. [*Sighs.*] Oh-ho-ho!

SOLIONY. 'He had no time to say "Oh, oh!"
       Before that bear had struck him low.' . . .
[*Walks off with him.*] What are you groaning about, old man?

CHEBUTYKIN. Oh, well!

SOLIONY. How do you feel?

CHEBUTYKIN [*crossly*]. Like a last year's bird's-nest.

SOLIONY. You needn't be so agitated about it, old boy. I shan't indulge in anything much, I'll just scorch his wings a little, like a woodcock's. [*Takes out a scent bottle and sprinkles scent over his hands.*] I've used up a whole bottle to-day, but my hands still smell. They smell like a corpse. [*A pause.*] Yes. . . . Do you remember that poem of Lermontov's?
       'And he, rebellious, seeks a storm,
       As if in storms there were tranquillity.' . . .

CHEBUTYKIN. Yes.
       'He had no time to say "Oh, oh!"
       Before that bear had struck him low.'
[*Goes out with* SOLIONY.]
[*Shouts of* 'Heigh-ho!' 'Ah-oo!' *are heard. Enter* ANDREY *and* FERAPONT.]

FERAPONT. Will you sign these papers, please?

ANDREY [*with irritation*]. Leave me alone! Leave me alone, for Heaven's sake. [*Goes off with the pram.*]

FERAPONT. Well, what am I supposed to do with the papers then? They are meant to be signed, aren't they? [*Goes to back of stage.*]
[*Enter* IRENA *and* TOOZENBACH, *the latter wearing a straw hat.* KOOLYGHIN *crosses the stage, calling:* 'Ah-oo! Masha! Ah-oo!']

TOOZENBACH. I think he's the only person in the whole town who's glad that the army is leaving.

IRENA. That's quite understandable, really. [*A pause.*] The town will look quite empty.

TOOZENBACH. My dear, I'll be back in a moment.

IRENA. Where are you going?

TOOZENBACH. I must slip back to the town, and then . . . I want to see some of my colleagues off.

IRENA. It's not true. . . . Nikolai, why are you so absent-minded today? [*A pause.*] What happened outside the theatre last night?

TOOZENBACH [*with a movement of impatience*]. I'll be back in an hour. . . . I'll be back with you again. [*Kisses her hands.*] My treasure! . . . [*Gazes into her eyes.*] It's five years since I first began to love you, and still I can't get used to it, and you seem more beautiful every day. What wonderful, lovely hair! What marvellous eyes! I'll take you away to-morrow. We'll work, we'll be rich, my dreams will come to life again. And you'll be happy! But—there's only one 'but', only one—you don't love me!

IRENA. I can't help that! I'll be your wife, I'll be loyal and obedient to you, but I can't love you. . . . What's to be done? [*Weeps.*] I've never loved anyone in my life. Oh, I've had such dreams about being in love! I've been dreaming about it for ever so long, day and night . . . but somehow my soul seems like an expensive piano which someone has locked up and the key's got lost. [*A pause.*] Your eyes are so restless.

TOOZENBACH. I was awake all night. Not that there's anything to be afraid of in my life, nothing threatening. . . . Only the thought of that lost key torments me and keeps me awake. Say something to me. . . . [*A pause.*] Say something![7]

IRENA. What? What am I to say? What?

TOOZENBACH. Anything.

IRENA. Don't, my dear, don't. . . . [*A pause.*]

TOOZENBACH. Such trifles, such silly little things sometimes become so important suddenly, for no apparent reason! You laugh at them, just as you always have done, you still regard them as trifles, and yet you suddenly find they're in control, and you haven't the power to stop them. But don't let us talk about all that! Really, I feel quite elated. I feel as if I was seeing those fir-trees and maples and birches for the first time in my life. They all seem to be looking at me with a sort of inquisitive look and waiting for something. What beautiful trees— and how beautiful, when you think of it, life ought to be with trees like these!

[*Shouts of 'Ah-oo! Heigh-ho!' are heard.*]

I must go, it's time. . . . Look at that dead tree, it's all dried-up, but it's still swaying in the wind along with the others. And in the same way, it seems to me that, if I die, I shall still have a share in life

---

7. The Moscow ms. adds these lines:

IRENA. But what? What? Everything around us is so mysterious, the old trees stand there so silently. [*Lays her head on his chest.*]

TOOZENBACH. Say something to me.

somehow or other. Goodbye, my dear. . . . [*Kisses her hands.*] Your papers, the ones you gave me, are on my desk, under the calendar.

IRENA. I'm coming with you.

TOOZENBACH [*alarmed*]. No, no! [*Goes off quickly, then stops in the avenue.*] Irena!

IRENA. What?

TOOZENBACH [*not knowing what to say*]. I didn't have any coffee this morning. Will you tell them to get some ready for me? [*Goes off quickly.*]

[IRENA *stands, lost in thought, then goes to the back of the stage and sits down on a swing. Enter* ANDREY *with the pram;* FERAPONT *appears.*]

FERAPONT. Andrey Serghyeech, the papers aren't mine, you know, they're the office papers. I didn't make them up.

ANDREY. Oh, where has all my past life gone to?—the time when I was young and gay and clever, when I used to have fine dreams and great thoughts, and the present and the future were bright with hope? Why do we become so dull and commonplace and uninteresting almost before we've begun to live? Why do we get lazy, indifferent, useless, unhappy? . . . This town's been in existence for two hundred years; a hundred thousand people live in it, but there's not one who's any different from all the others! There's never been a scholar or an artist or a saint in this place, never a single man sufficiently outstanding to make you feel passionately that you wanted to emulate him. People here do nothing but eat, drink and sleep. . . . Then they die and some more take their places, and they eat, drink and sleep, too—and just to introduce a bit of variety into their lives, so as to avoid getting completely stupid with boredom, they indulge in their disgusting gossip and vodka and gambling and law-suits. The wives deceive their husbands, and the husbands lie to their wives, and pretend they don't see anything and don't hear anything. . . . And all this overwhelming vulgarity and pettiness crushes the children and puts out any spark they might have in them, so that they, too, become miserable, half-dead creatures, just like one another and just like their parents! . . . [*To* FERAPONT, *crossly.*] What do you want?

FERAPONT. What? Here are the papers to sign.

ANDREY. What a nuisance you are!

FERAPONT [*hands him the papers.*] The porter at the finance department told me just now . . . he said last winter they had two hundred degrees of frost in Petersburg.

ANDREY. I hate the life I live at present, but oh! the sense of elation when I think of the future! Then I feel so light-hearted, such a sense of release! I seem to see light ahead, light and freedom. I see myself free, and my children, too—free from idleness, free from *kvass*,[8] free

8. A thin sour beer made from rye or barley.

from eternal meals of goose and cabbage, free from after-dinner naps, free from all this degrading parasitism! . . .

FERAPONT. They say two thousand people were frozen to death. They say everyone was scared stiff. It was either in Petersburg or in Moscow, I can't remember exactly.

ANDREY [*with sudden emotion, tenderly*]. My dear sisters, my dear good sisters! [*Tearfully.*] Masha, my dear sister! . . .

NATASHA [*through the window*]. Who's that talking so loudly there? Is that you, Andriusha? You'll wake Sofochka. *Il ne faut pas faire du bruit, la Sophie est dormie déjà. Vous êtes un ours.*[9] [*Getting angry.*] If you want to talk, give the pram to someone else. Ferapont, take the pram from the master.

FERAPONT. Yes, Madam. [*Takes the pram.*]

ANDREY [*shamefacedly*]. I was talking quietly.

NATASHA [*in the window, caressing her small son*]. Bobik! Naughty Bobik! Aren't you a naughty boy!

ANDREY [*glancing through the papers*]. All right, I'll go through them and sign them if they need it. You can take them back to the office later. [*Goes into the house, reading the papers.*]

[*FERAPONT wheels the pram into the garden.*]

NATASHA [*in the window*]. What's Mummy's name, Bobik? You darling! And who's that lady? Auntie Olia. Say: 'Hullo, Auntie Olia.'

[*Two street musicians, a man and a girl, enter and begin to play on a violin and a harp;* VERSHININ, OLGA *and* ANFISA *come out of the house and listen in silence for a few moments; then* IRENA *approaches them.*]

OLGA. Our garden's like a public road; everybody goes through it. Nanny, give something to the musicians.

ANFISA [*giving them money*]. Go along now, God bless you, good people!

[*The musicians bow and go away.*]

Poor, homeless folk! Whoever would go dragging round the streets playing tunes if he had enough to eat? [*To* IRENA.] How are you, Irenushka? [*Kisses her.*] Ah, my child, what a life I'm having! Such comfort! In a large flat at the school with Oliushka—and no rent to pay, either! The Lord's been kind to me in my old age. I've never had such a comfortable time in my life, old sinner that I am! A big flat, and no rent to pay, and a whole room to myself, with my own bed. All free. Sometimes when I wake up in the night I begin to think, and then—Oh, Lord! Oh, Holy Mother of God!—there's no one happier in the world than me!

VERSHININ [*glances at his watch*]. We shall be starting in a moment, Olga Serghyeevna. It's time I went. [*A pause.*] I wish you all the happiness in the world . . . everything. . . . Where's Maria Serghyeevna?

---

9. "You must not make any noise, Sophie is asleep already. You're a bear."

IRENA. She's somewhere in the garden. I'll go and look for her.

VERSHININ. That's kind of you. I really must hurry.

ANFISA. I'll come and help to look for her. [*Calls out.*] Mashenka, ah-oo!

[*Goes with* IRENA *towards the far end of the garden.*]
Ah-oo! Ah-oo!

VERSHININ. Everything comes to an end. Well, here we are—and now it's going to be 'good-bye'. [*Looks at his watch.*] The city gave us a sort of farewell lunch. There was champagne, and the mayor made a speech, and I ate and listened, but in spirit I was with you here. . . . [*Glances round the garden.*] I've grown so . . . so accustomed to you.

OLGA. Shall we meet again some day, I wonder?

VERSHININ. Most likely not! [*A pause.*] My wife and the two little girls will be staying on here for a month or two. Please, if anything happens, if they need anything. . . .

OLGA. Yes, yes, of course. You needn't worry about that. [*A pause.*] To-morrow there won't be a single officer or soldier in the town. . . . All that will be just a memory, and, of course, a new life will begin for us here. . . . [*A pause.*] Nothing ever happens as we'd like it to. I didn't want to be a headmistress, and yet now I am one. It means we shan't be going to live in Moscow. . . .

VERSHININ. Well. . . . Thank you for everything. Forgive me if ever I've done anything. . . . I've talked a lot too much, far too much. . . . Forgive me for that, don't think too unkindly of me.

OLGA [*wipes her eyes*]. Now . . . why is Masha so long coming?

VERSHININ. What else can I tell you now it's time to say 'good-bye'? What shall I philosophize about now? . . . [*Laughs.*] Yes, life is difficult. It seems quite hopeless for a lot of us, just a kind of impasse. . . . And yet you must admit that it is gradually getting easier and brighter, and it's clear that the time isn't far off when the light will spread everywhere. [*Looks at his watch.*] Time, it's time for me to go. . . . In the old days the human race was always making war, its entire existence was taken up with campaigns, advances, retreats, victories. . . . But now all that's out of date, and in its place there's a huge vacuum, clamouring to be filled. Humanity is passionately seeking something to fill it with and, of course, it will find something some day. Oh! If only it would happen soon! [*A pause.*] If only we could educate the industrious people and make the educated people industrious. . . . [*Looks at his watch.*] I really must go. . . .

OLGA. Here she comes!

[*Enter* MASHA.]

VERSHININ. I've come to say good-bye. . . .

[OLGA *walks off and stands a little to one side so as not to interfere with their leave-taking.*]

MASHA [*looking into his face*]. Good-bye! . . . [*A long kiss.*]

OLGA. That'll do, that'll do.

MASHA [*sobs loudly*].

VERSHININ. Write to me. . . . Don't forget me! Let me go . . . it's time. Olga Serghyeevna, please take her away . . . I must go . . . I'm late already. . . . [*Deeply moved, kisses* OLGA's *hands, then embraces* MASHA *once again, and goes out quickly.*]

OLGA. That'll do, Masha! Don't, my dear, don't. . . .

[*Enter* KOOLYGHIN.]

KOOLYGHIN [*embarrassed*]. Never mind, let her cry, let her. . . . My dear Masha, my dear, sweet Masha. . . . You're my wife, and I'm happy in spite of everything. . . . I'm not complaining, I've no reproach to make—not a single one. . . . Olga here is my witness. . . . We'll start our life over again in the same old way, and you won't hear a word from me . . . not a hint. . . .

MASHA [*suppressing her sobs*]. 'A green oak grows by a curving shore, And round that oak hangs a golden chain.' . . . 'A golden chain round that oak.' . . . Oh, I'm going mad. . . . By a curving shore . . . a green oak. . . .

OLGA. Calm yourself, Masha, calm yourself. . . . Give her some water.

MASHA. I'm not crying any more. . . .

KOOLYGHIN. She's not crying any more . . . she's a good girl.

[*The hollow sound of a gun-shot is heard in the distance.*]

MASHA. 'A green oak grows by a curving shore. And round that oak hangs a golden chain.' . . . A green cat[1] . . . a green oak . . . I've got it all mixed up. . . . [*Drinks water.*] My life's messed up. . . . I don't want anything now. . . . I'll calm down in a moment. . . . It doesn't matter. . . . What *is* 'the curving shore'? Why does it keep coming into my head all the time? My thoughts are all mixed up.

[*Enter* IRENA.]

OLGA. Calm down, Masha. That's right . . . good girl! . . . Let's go indoors.

MASHA [*irritably*]. I'm not going in there! [*Sobs, but immediately checks herself.*] I don't go into that house now, and I'm not going to. . . .

IRENA. Let's sit down together for a moment, and not talk about anything. I'm going away to-morrow, you know. . . . [*A pause.*]

KOOLYGHIN. Yesterday I took away a false beard and a moustache from a boy in the third form. I've got them here. [*Puts them on.*] Do I look like our German teacher? . . . [*Laughs.*] I do, don't I? The boys are funny.

MASHA. It's true, you do look like that German of yours.

---

1. She mixes this green cat up with the "learned cat" of the next line of the passage:

> And on that chain a learned cat,
> Who walks in circles night and day.

On walking right, he sings a song, On walking left, he tells a tale.

On this point see Sandra Manderson and Donald M. Fiene, "Chekhov's *Three Sisters*," *Explicator* 36 (1978) 2: 22–23.

OLGA [*laughs*]. Yes, he does.

    [MASHA *cries.*]

IRENA. That's enough, Masha!

KOOLYGHIN. Very much like him, I think!

    [*Enter* NATASHA.]

NATASHA [*to the maid*]. What? Oh, yes. Mr. Protopopov is going to keep an eye on Sofochka, and Andrey Serghyeevich is going to take Bobik out in the pram. What a lot of work these children make! . . . [*To* IRENA.] Irena, you're really leaving to-morrow? What a pity! Do stay just another week, won't you?

    [*Catching sight of* KOOLYGHIN, *shrieks; he laughs and takes off the false beard and moustache.*]

Get away with you! How you scared me! [*To* IRENA.] I've grown so accustomed to you being here. . . . You mustn't think it's going to be easy for me to be without you. I'll get Andrey and his old violin to move into your room: he can saw away at it as much as he likes there. And then we'll move Sofochka into his room. She's such a wonderful child, really! Such a lovely little girl! This morning she looked at me with such a sweet expression, and then she said: 'Mamma!'

KOOLYGHIN. It's quite true, she is a beautiful child.

NATASHA. So to-morrow I'll be alone here. [*Sighs.*] I'll have this fir-tree avenue cut down first, then that maple tree over there. It looks so awful in the evenings.[2] . . . [*To* IRENA.] My dear, that belt you're wearing doesn't suit you at all. Not at all good taste. You want something brighter to go with that dress. . . . I'll tell them to put flowers all round here, lots of flowers, so that we get plenty of scent from them. . . . [*Sternly.*] Why is there a fork lying on this seat? [*Going into the house, to the maid.*] Why is that fork left on the seat there? [*Shouts.*] Don't answer me back!

KOOLYGHIN. There she goes again!

    [*A band plays a military march off-stage; all listen.*]

OLGA. They're going.

    [*Enter* CHEBUTYKIN.]

MASHA. The soldiers are going. Well. . . . Happy journey to them! [*To her husband.*] We must go home. . . . Where's my hat and cape? . . .

KOOLYGHIN. I took them indoors. I'll bring them at once.

OLGA. Yes, we can go home now. It's time.

CHEBUTYKIN. Olga Serghyeevna!

OLGA. What is it? [*A pause.*] What?

CHEBUTYKIN. Nothing. . . . I don't know quite how to tell you. . . .

    [*Whispers into her ear.*]

OLGA [*frightened*]. It can't be true!

---

2. Moscow ms.: "It is so frightful and looks so awful in the evenings."

CHEBUTYKIN. Yes . . . a bad business. . . . I'm so tired . . . quite worn out. . . . I don't want to say another word. . . . [*With annoyance.*] Anyway, nothing matters! . . .

MASHA. What's happened?

OLGA [*puts her arms round* IRENA]. What a dreadful day! . . . I don't know how to tell you, dear. . . .

IRENA. What is it? Tell me quickly, what is it? For Heaven's sake! . . . [*Cries.*]

CHEBUTYKIN. The Baron's just been killed in a duel.

IRENA [*cries quietly*]. I knew it, I knew it. . . .

CHEBUTYKIN [*goes to the back of the stage and sits down*]. I'm tired. . . . [*Takes a newspaper out of his pocket.*] Let them cry for a bit. . . . [*Sings quietly to himself.*] Tarara-boom-di-ay, I'm sitting on a tomb-di-ay. . . . What difference does it make? . . .

[*The three sisters stand huddled together.*]

MASHA. Oh, listen to that band! They're leaving us . . . one of them's gone for good . . . for ever! We're left alone . . . to start our lives all over again. We must go on living . . . we must go on living. . . .

IRENA [*puts her head on* OLGA's *breast*]. Some day people will know why such things happen, and what the purpose of all this suffering is. . . . Then there won't be any more riddles. . . . Meanwhile we must go on living . . . and working. Yes, we must just go on working! To-morrow I'll go away alone and teach in a school somewhere; I'll give my life to people who need it. . . . It's autumn now, winter will soon be here, and the snow will cover everything . . . but I'll go on working and working! . . .

OLGA [*puts her arms round both her sisters*]. How cheerfully and jauntily that band's playing—really I feel as if I wanted to live! Merciful God! The years will pass, and we shall all be gone for good and quite forgotten. . . . Our faces and our voices will be forgotten and people won't even know that there were once three of us here. . . . But our sufferings may mean happiness for the people who come after us. . . . There'll be a time when peace and happiness reign in the world, and then we shall be remembered kindly and blessed. No, my dear sisters, life isn't finished for us yet! We're going to live! The band is playing so cheerfully and joyfully—maybe, if we wait a little longer, we shall find out why we live, why we suffer. . . . Oh, if we only knew, if only we knew!

[*The music grows fainter and fainter.* KOOLYGHIN, *smiling happily, brings out the hat and the cape.* ANDREY *enters; he is pushing the pram with* BOBIK *sitting in it.*]

CHEBUTYKIN [*sings quietly to himself*]. Tarara-boom-di-ay. . . . I'm sitting on a tomb-di-ay. . . . [*Reads the paper.*] What does it matter? Nothing matters!

OLGA. If only we knew, if only we knew! . . .

CURTAIN

GEORGE BERNARD SHAW

Candida†

Act One

A *fine morning in October 1894 in the north east quarter of London, a vast district miles away from the London of Mayfair and St. James's, and much less narrow, squalid, fetid and airless in its slums. It is strong in unfashionable middle class life: wide-streeted; myriad-populated; well served with ugly iron urinals, Radical clubs, and tram lines carrying a perpetual stream of yellow cars; enjoying in its main thoroughfares the luxury of grass-grown "front gardens" untrodden by the foot of man save as to the path from the gate to the hall door; blighted by a callously endured monotony of miles and miles of unlovely brick houses, black iron railings, stony pavements, slated roofs, and respectably ill dressed or disreputably worse dressed people, quite accustomed to the place, and mostly plodding uninterestedly about somebody else's work. The little energy and eagerness that crop up shew themselves in cockney cupidity and business "push." Even the policemen and the chapels are not infrequent enough to break the monotony. The sun is shining cheerfully: there is no fog; and though the smoke effectually prevents anything, whether faces and hands or bricks and mortar, from looking fresh and clean, it is not hanging heavily enough to trouble a Londoner.*

This desert of unattractiveness has its oasis. Near the outer end of the Hackney Road is a park of 217 acres, fenced in, not by railings, but by a wooden paling, and containg plenty of greensward, trees, a lake for bathers, flower beds which are triumphs of the admired cockney art of carpet gardening, and a sandpit, originally imported from the seaside for the delight of children, but speedily deserted on its becoming a natural vermin preserve for all the petty fauna of Kingsland, Hackney, and Hoxton. A bandstand, an unfurnished forum for religious, anti-religious, and political orators, cricket pitches, a gymnasium, and an old fashioned stone kiosk are among its attractions. Wherever the prospect is bounded by trees or rising green grounds, it is a pleasant place. Where the ground stretches flat to the grey palings, with bricks and mortar, sky signs, crowded chimneys and smoke beyond, the prospect makes it desolate and sordid.

The best view of Victoria Park is commanded by the front window of St. Dominic's Parsonage, from which not a brick is visible. The parsonage is semi-detached, with a front garden and a porch. Visitors go up the flight of steps to the porch: tradespeople and members of the family go down by a door under the steps to the basement, with a breakfast room, used for all meals, in front, and the kitchen at the back. Upstairs, on the level of the hall door, is the drawingroom, with its large plate glass window looking out on the park. In this, the only sitting room that can be spared from the children and the family meals, the parson, the REVEREND JAMES MAVOR MORELL, does his work. he is sitting in a strong round backed revolving chair at the end of a long table, which stands across the window, so that he can cheer himself with a view of the park over his left shoulder. At the opposite end of the table, adjoining it, is a little table only half as wide as the other, with a typewriter on it. His typist is sitting at this machine, with her back to the window. The large table is littered with pamphlets, journals, letters, nests of drawers, an office diary, postage scales and the like. A spare chair for visitors having business with the parson is in the middle, turned to his end. Within reach of his hand is a stationery case, and a photograph in a frame. The wall behind him is fitted with bookshelves, on which an adept eye can measure the parson's casuistry and divinity by Maurice's Theological Essays and a complete set of Browning's poems, and the reformer's politics by a yellow backed Progress and Poverty, Fabian Essays, A Dream of John Ball, Marx's Capital, and half a dozen other literary landmarks in Socialism. Facing him on the other side of the room, near the typewriter, is the door. Further down opposite the fireplace, a bookcase stands on a cellaret, with a sofa near it. There is a generous fire burning; and the hearth, with a comfortable armchair and a black japanned flower-painted coal scuttle at one side, a miniature chair for children on the other, a varnished wooden mantelpiece, with neatly moulded shelves, tiny bits of mirror let into the panels, a travelling clock in a leather case (the inevitable wedding present), and on the wall above a large autotype of the chief figure in Titian's Assumption of the Virgin, is very inviting. Altogether the room is the room of a good housekeeper, vanquished, as far as the table is concerned, by an untidy man, but elsewhere mistress of the situation. The furniture, in its ornamental aspect, betrays the style of the advertised "drawingroom suite" of the pushing suburban furniture dealer; but there is nothing useless or pretentious in the room, money being too scarce in the house of an east end parson to be wasted on snobbish trimmings.

The REVEREND JAMES MAVOR MORELL is a Christian Socialist clergyman of the Church of England, and an active member of the Guild of St Matthew and the Christian Social Union. A vigorous, genial, popular man of forty, robust and goodlooking, full of energy, with pleasant, *hearty, considerate manners, and a sound unaffected voice, which he uses with the clean athletic articulation of a practised orator, and with a wide range and perfect command of expression. He is a first rate clergyman, able to say what he likes to whom he likes, to lecture people without setting himself up against them, to impose his authority on them without humiliating them, and, on occasion, to interfere in their business without impertinence. His well-spring of enthusiasm and sympathetic emotion has never run dry for a moment: he still eats and sleeps heartily enough to win the daily battle between exhaustion and recuperation triumphantly. Withal, a great baby, pardonably vain of his powers and unconsciously pleased with himself. He has a healthy complexion: good forehead, with the brows somewhat blunt, and the eyes bright and eager, mouth resolute but not particularly well cut, and a substantial nose, with the mobile spreading nostrils of the dramatic orator, void, like all his features, of subtlety.*

The typist, MISS PROSERPINE GARNETT, *is a brisk little woman of about 30, of the lower middle class, neatly but cheaply dressed in a black merino skirt and a blouse, notably pert and quick of speech, and not very civil in her manner, but sensitive and affectionate. She is clattering away busily at her machine whilst Morell opens the last of his morning's letters. He realizes its contents with a comic groan of despair.*

PROSERPINE. Another lecture?

MORELL. Yes. The Hoxton Freedom Group want me to address them on Sunday morning. [*He lays great emphasis on Sunday, this being the unreasonable part of the business.*] What are they?

PROSERPINE. Communist Anarchists, I think.

MORELL. Just like Anarchists not to know that they cant have a parson on Sunday! Tell them to come to church if they want to hear me: it will do them good. Say I can come on Mondays and Thursdays only. Have you the diary there?

PROSERPINE [*taking up the diary*]. Yes.

MORELL. Have I any lecture on for next Monday?

PROSERPINE [*referring to diary*]. Tower Hamlets Radical Club.

MORELL. Well, Thursday then?

PROSERPINE. English Land Restoration League.

MORELL. What next?

PROSERPINE. Guild of St Matthew on Monday. Independent Labor Party, Greenwich Branch, on Thursday. Monday, Social-Democratic Federation, Mile End Branch. Thursday, first Confirmation class. [*Impatiently.*] Oh, I'd better tell them you cant come. Theyre only half a dozen ignorant and conceited costermongers[1] without five shillings between them.

MORELL [*amused*]. Ah; but you see theyre near relatives of mine.

---

1. A street-vendor of fruits and vegetables.

PROSERPINE [*staring at him*]. Relatives of yours!

MORELL. Yes: we have the same father—in Heaven.

PROSERPINE [*relieved*]. Oh, is that all?

MORELL [*with a sadness which is a luxury to a man whose voice expresses it so finely*]. Ah, you dont believe it. Everybody says it: nobody believes it: nobody. [*Briskly, getting back to business.*] Well, well! Come, Miss Proserpine: cant you find a date for the costers? What about the 25th? That was vacant the day before yesterday.

PROSERPINE [*referring to diary*]. Engaged. The Fabian Society.[2]

MORELL. Bother the Fabian Society! Is the 28th gone too?

PROSERPINE. City dinner. Youre invited to dine with the Founders' Company.

MORELL. Thatll do: I'll go to the Hoxton Group of Freedom instead.

[*She enters the engagement in silence, with implacable disparagement of the Hoxton Anarchists in every line of her face.* MORELL *bursts open the cover of a copy of* The Church Reformer, *which has come by post, and glances through Mr Stewart Headlam's*[3] *leader and the Guild of St Matthew news. These proceedings are presently enlivened by the appearance of* MORELL's *curate, the* REVEREND ALEXANDER MILL, *a young gentleman gathered by* MORELL *from the nearest University settlement, whither he had come from Oxford to give the east end of London the benefit of his university training. He is a conceitedly well intentioned, enthusiastic, immature novice, with nothing positively unbearable about him except a habit of speaking with his lips carefully closed a full half inch from each corner for the sake of a finicking articulation and a set of university vowels, this being his chief means so far of bringing his Oxford refinement (as he calls his habits) to bear on Hackney vulgarity.* MORELL, *whom he has won over by a doglike devotion, looks up indulgently from* The Church Reformer, *and remarks*]

Well, Lexy? Late again, as usual!

LEXY. I'm afraid so. I wish I could get up in the morning.

MORELL [*exulting in his own energy*]. Ha! Ha! [*Whimsically.*] Watch and pray, Lexy: watch and pray.

LEXY. I know. [*Rising wittily to the occasion.*] But how can I watch and pray when I am asleep? Isnt that so, Miss Prossy? [*He makes for the warmth of the fire.*]

PROSERPINE [*sharply*]. Miss Garnett, if you please.

LEXY. I beg your pardon. Miss Garnett.

PROSERPINE. Youve got to do all the work today.

LEXY [*on the hearth*]. Why?

PROSERPINE. Never mind why. It will do you good to earn your supper before you eat it, for once in a way, as I do. Come! dont dawdle. You should have been off on your rounds half an hour ago.

---

2. The socialist society to which Shaw belonged and for which he was a leading lecturer.
3. Stewart Duckworth Headlam (1847–1924), a progressive clergyman and prolific writer on socialism and religion.

LEXY [*perplexed*]. Is she in earnest, Morell?

MORELL [*in the highest spirits: his eyes dancing*]. Yes. I am going to dawdle today.

LEXY. You! You dont know how.

MORELL [*rising*]. Ha! ha! Dont I? I'm going to have this morning all to myself. My wife's coming back: she's due here at 11.45.

LEXY [*surprised*]. Coming back already! with the children? I thought they were to stay to the end of the month.

MORELL. So they are: she's only coming up for two days, to get some flannel things for Jimmy, and to see how we're getting on without her.

LEXY [*anxiously*]. But, my dear Morell, if what Jimmy and Fluffy had was scarlatina, do you think it wise—

MORELL. Scarlatina! Rubbish! it was German measles. I brought it into the house myself from the Pycroft Street school. A parson is like a doctor, my boy: he must face infection as a soldier must face bullets.

[*He claps* LEXY *manfully on the shoulders.*]

Catch the measles if you can, Lexy: she'll nurse you; and what a piece of luck that will be for you! Eh?

LEXY [*smiling uneasily*]. It's so hard to understand you about Mrs Morell—.

MORELL [*tenderly*]. Ah, my boy, get married: get married to a good woman; and then youll understand. Thats a foretaste of what will be best in the Kingdom of Heaven we are trying to establish on earth. That will cure you of dawdling. An honest man feels that he must pay Heaven for every hour of happiness with a good spell of hard unselfish work to make others happy. We have no more right to consume happiness without producing it than to consume wealth without producing it. Get a wife like my Candida; and youll always be in arrear with your repayment.

[*He pats* LEXY *affectionately and moves to leave the room.*]

LEXY. Oh, wait a bit: I forgot.

[MORELL *halts and turns with the door knob in his hand.*]

Your father-in-law is coming round to see you.

[MORELL, *surprised and not pleased, shuts the door again, with a complete change of manner.*]

MORELL. Mr Burgess?

LEXY. Yes. I passed him in the park, arguing with somebody. He asked me to let you know that he was coming.

MORELL [*half incredulous*]. But he hasnt called here for three years. Are you sure, Lexy? Youre not joking, are you?

LEXY [*earnestly*]. No sir, really.

MORELL [*thoughtfully*]. Hm! Time for him to take another look at Candida before she grows out of his knowledge. [*He resigns himself to the inevitable, and goes out.*]

[LEXY *looks after him with beaming worship.* MISS GARNETT, *not being able to shake* LEXY, *relieves her feelings by worrying the typewriter.*]

LEXY. What a good man! What a thorough loving soul he is! [*He takes* MORELL's *place at the table, making himself very comfortable as he takes out a cigaret.*]

PROSERPINE [*impatiently, pulling the letter she has been working at off the typewriter and folding it*]. Oh, a man ought to be able to be fond of his wife without making a fool of himself about her.

LEXY [*shocked*]. Oh, Miss Prossy!

PROSERPINE [*snatching at the stationery case for an envelope, in which she encloses the letter as she speaks*]. Candida here, and Candida there, and Candida everywhere! [*She licks the envelope.*] It's enough to drive anyone out of their senses [*thumping the envelope to make it stick*] to hear a woman raved about in that absurd manner merely because she's got good hair and a tolerable figure.

LEXY [*with reproachful gravity*]. I think her extremely beautiful, Miss Garnett. [*He takes the photograph up; looks at it; and adds, with even greater impressiveness.*] Extremely beautiful. How fine her eyes are!

PROSERPINE. Her eyes are not a bit better than mine: now!

[*He puts down the photograph and stares austerely at her.*]

And you know very well you think me dowdy and second rate enough.

LEXY [*rising majestically*]. Heaven forbid that I should think of any of God's creatures in such a way! [*He moves stiffly away from her across the room to the neighborhood of the bookcase.*]

PROSERPINE [*sarcastically*]. Thank you. Thats very nice and comforting.

LEXY [*saddened by her depravity*]. I had no idea you had any feeling against Mrs Morell.

PROSERPINE [*indignantly*]. I have no feeling against her. She's very nice, very good-hearted: I'm very fond of her, and can appreciate her real qualities far better than any man can.

[*He shakes his head sadly. She rises and comes at him with intense pepperiness.*]

You dont believe me? You think I'm jealous? Oh, what a knowledge of the human heart you have, Mr Lexy Mill! How well you know the weaknesses of Woman, dont you? It must be so nice to be a man and have a fine penetrating intellect instead of mere emotions like us, and to know that the reason we dont share your amorous delusions is that we're all jealous of one another! [*She abandons him with a toss of her shoulders, and crosses to the fire to warm her hands.*]

LEXY. Ah, if you women only had the same clue to Man's strength that you have to his weakness, Miss Prossy, there would be no Woman Question.

PROSERPINE [*over her shoulder, as she stoops, holding her hands to the blaze*]. Where did you hear Morell say that? You didnt invent it yourself: youre not clever enough.

LEXY. Thats quite true. I am not ashamed of owing him that, as I owe him so many other spiritual truths. He said it at the annual conference of the Women's Liberal Federation. Allow me to add that though they didnt appreciate it, I, a mere man, did. [*He turns to the bookcase again, hoping that this may leave her crushed.*]

PROSERPINE [*putting her hair straight at a panel of mirror in the mantelpiece*]. Well, when you talk to me, give me your own ideas, such as they are, and not his. You never cut a poorer figure than when you are trying to imitate him.

LEXY [*stung*]. I try to follow his example, not to imitate him.

PROSERPINE [*coming at him again on her way back to her work*]. Yes, you do: you imitate him. Why do you tuck your umbrella under your left arm instead of carrying it in your hand like anyone else? Why do you walk with your chin stuck out before you, hurrying along with that eager look in your eyes? you! who never get up before half past nine in the morning. Why do you say "knoaledge" in church, though you always say "knolledge" in private conversation! Bah! do you think I dont know? [*She goes back to the typewriter.*] Here! come and set about your work: weve wasted enough time for one morning. Here's a copy of the diary for today. [*She hands him a memorandum.*]

LEXY [*deeply offended*]. Thank you.

[*He takes it and stands at the table with his back to her, reading it. She begins to transcribe her shorthand notes on the typewriter without troubling herself about his feelings.*

The door opens; and MR BURGESS *enters unannounced. He is a man of sixty, made coarse and sordid by the compulsory selfishness of petty commerce, and later on softened into sluggish bumptiousness by overfeeding and commercial success. A vulgar ignorant guzzling man, offensive and contemptuous to people whose labor is cheap, respectful to wealth and rank, and quite sincere and without rancor or envy in both attitudes. The world has offered him no decently paid work except that of a sweater; and he has become, in consequence, somewhat hoggish. But he has no suspicion of this himself, and honestly regards his commercial prosperity as the inevitable and socially wholesome triumph of the ability, industry, shrewdness, and experience in business of a man who in private is easygoing, affectionate, and humorously convivial to a fault. Corporeally he is podgy, with a snoutish nose in the centre of a flat square face, a dust colored beard with a patch of grey in the centre under his chin, and small watery blue eyes with a plaintively sentimental expression, which he transfers easily to his voice by his habit of pompously intoning his sentences.*]

BURGESS [*stopping on the threshold, and looking round*]. They told me Mr Morell was here.

PROSERPINE [*rising*]. I'll fetch him for you.

BURGESS [*staring disappointedly at her*]. Youre not the same young lady as hused to typewrite for him?

PROSERPINE. No.

BURGESS [*grumbling on his way to the hearthrug*]. No: she was younger.

[MISS GARNETT *stares at him; then goes out, slamming the door.*]
Startin on your rounds, Mr Mill?

LEXY [*folding his memorandum and pocketing it*]. Yes: I must be off
presently.

BURGESS [*momentously*]. Dont let me detain you, Mr Mill. What I come
about is private between me and Mr Morell.

LEXY [*huffily*]. I have no intention of intruding, I am sure, Mr Burgess.
Good morning.

BURGESS [*patronizingly*]. Oh, good morning to you.

[MORELL *returns as* LEXY *is making for the door.*]

MORELL [*to* LEXY]. Off to work?

LEXY. Yes, sir.

MORELL. Take my silk handkerchief and wrap your throat up. Theres a
cold wind. Away with you.

[LEXY, *more than consoled for* BURGESS's *rudeness, brightens up and
goes out.*]

BURGESS. Spoilin your korates as usu'l, James. Good mornin. When I
pay a man, an' 'is livin depens on me, I keep him in 'is place.

MORELL [*rather shortly*]. I always keep my curates in their places as my
helpers and comrades. If you get as much work out of your clerks and
warehousemen as I do out of my curates, you must be getting rich
pretty fast. Will you take your old chair.

[*He points with curt authority to the armchair beside the fireplace;
then takes the spare chair from the table and sits down at an unfamiliar distance from his visitor.*]

BURGESS [*without moving*]. Just the same as hever, James!

MORELL. When you last called—it was about three years ago, I think—
you said the same thing a little more frankly. Your exact words then
were "Just as big a fool as ever, James!"

BURGESS [*soothingly*]. Well, praps I did; but [*with conciliatory cheerfulness*] I meant no hoffence by it. A clorgyman is privileged to be a bit
of a fool, you know: it's ony becomin in 'is profession that he should.
Anyhow, I come here, not to rake up hold differences, but to let
bygones be bygones. [*Suddenly becoming very solemn, and approaching* MORELL.] James: three yeas ago, you done me a hil turn. You
done me hout of a contrac; and when I gev you arsh words in my
natral disappointment, you turned my daughrter again me. Well, Ive
come to hact the part of a Kerischin. [*Offering his hand.*] I forgive
you, James.

MORELL [*starting up*]. Confound your impudence!

BURGESS [*retreating, with almost lachrymose deprecation of this treatment*]. Is that becomin language for a clorgyman, James? And you
so particlar, too!

MORELL [*hotly*]. No, sir: it is not becoming language for a clergyman. I used the wrong word. I should have said damn your impudence: thats what St Paul or any honest priest would have said to you. Do you think I have forgotten that tender of yours for the contract to supply clothing to the workhouse?

BURGESS [*in a paroxysm of public spirit*]. I hacted in the hinterest of the ratepayers, James. It was the lowest tender: you carnt deny that.

MORELL. Yes, the lowest, because you paid worse wages than any other employer—starvation wages—aye, worse than starvation wages—to the women who made the clothing. Your wages would have driven them to the streets to keep body and soul together. [*Getting angrier and angrier.*] Those women were my parishioners. I shamed the Guardians out of accepting your tender: I shamed the ratepayers out of letting them do it: I shamed everybody but you. [*Boiling over.*] How dare you, sir, come here and offer to forgive me, and talk about your daughter, and—

BURGESS. Heasy, James! heasy! heasy! Dont git hinto a fluster about nothink. Ive howned I was wrong.

MORELL. Have you? I didnt hear you.

BURGESS. Of course I did. I hown it now. Come: I harsk your pardon for the letter I wrote you. Is that enough?

MORELL [*snapping his fingers*]. Thats nothing. Have you raised the wages?

BURGESS [*triumphantly*]. Yes.

MORELL. What!

BURGESS [*unctuously*]. Ive turned a moddle hemployer. I dont hemploy no women now: theyre all sacked; and the work is done by machinery. Not a man 'as less than sixpence a *hour*; and the skilled ands gits the Trade Union rate. [*Proudly.*] What ave you to say to me now?

MORELL [*overwhelmed*]. Is it possible! Well, theres more joy in heaven over one sinner that repenteth!—

[*Going to* BURGESS *with an explosion of apologetic cordiality.*]

My dear Burgess: how splendid of you! I most heartily beg your pardon for my hard thoughts.

[*Grasping his hand.*]

And now, dont you feel the better for the change? Come! confess! youre happier. You look happier.

BURGESS [*ruefully*]. Well, praps I do. I spose I must, since you notice it. At all events, I git my contrax assepted by the County Council. [*Savagely.*] They dussent ave nothink to do with me unless I paid fair wages: curse em for a parcel o meddlin fools!

MORELL [*dropping his hand, utterly discouraged*]. So that was why you raised the wages! [*He sits down moodily.*]

BURGESS [*severely, in spreading, mountingtones*]. Woy helse should I do it? What does it lead to but drink and huppishness in workin men? [*He seats himself magisterially in the easy chair.*] It's hall very well for you, James: it gits you hinto the papers and makes a great man of you; but you never think of the arm you do, puttin money into the pockets of workin men that they dunno ow to spend, and takin it from people that might be makin a good huse on it.

MORELL [*with a heavy sigh, speaking with cold politeness*]. What is your business with me this morning? I shall not pretend to believe that you are here merely out of family sentiment.

BURGESS [*obstinately*]. Yes I ham: just family sentiment and nothink helse.

MORELL [*with weary calm*]. I dont believe you.

BURGESS [*rising threateningly*]. Dont say that to me again, James Mavor Morell.

MORELL [*unmoved*]. I'll say it just as often as may be necessary to convince you that it's true. I dont believe you.

BURGESS [*collapsing into an abyss of wounded feeling*]. Oh, well, if youre detormined to be hunfriendly, I spose I'd better go.

[*He moves reluctantly towards the doors.* MORELL *makes no sign. He lingers.*]

I didnt hexpect to find a hunforgivin spirit in you, James.

[MORELL *still not responding, he takes a few more reluctant steps doorwards. Then he comes back, whining.*]

We huseter git on well enough, spite of our different hopinions. Woy are you so changed to me? I give you my word I come here in peeorr [pure] frenliness, not wishin to be hon bad terms with my hown daughrter's usban. Come, James: be a Kerishchin, and shake ands.

[*He puts his hand sentimentally on* MORELL'*s shoulder.*]

MORELL [*looking up at him thoughtfully*]. Look here, Burgess. Do you want to be as welcome here as you were before you lost that contract?

BURGESS. I do, James. I do—honest.

MORELL. Then why dont you behave as you did then?

BURGESS [*cautiously removing his hand*]. Ow d'y' mean?

MORELL. I'll tell you. You thought me a young fool then.

BURGESS [*coaxingly*]. No I didnt, James. I—

MORELL [*cutting him short*]. Yes, you did. And I thought you an old scoundrel.

BURGESS [*most vehemently deprecating this gross self-accusation on* MORELL'*s part*]. No you didnt, James. Now you do yourself a hinjustice.

MORELL. Yes I did. Well, that did not prevent our getting on very well together. God made you what I call a scoundrel as He made me what you call a fool.

[*The effect of this observation on* BURGESS *is to remove the keystone of his moral arch. He becomes bodily weak, and, with his eyes fixed on* MORELL *in a helpless stare, puts out his hand apprehensively to balance himself, as if the floor had suddenly sloped under him.* MORELL *proceeds, in the same tone of quiet conviction.*]

It was not for me to quarrel with His handiwork in the one case more than in the other. So long as you come here honestly as a self-respecting, thorough, convinced scoundrel, justifying your scoundrelism and proud of it, you are welcome. But [*and now* MORELL's *tone becomes formidable; and he rises and strikes the back of the chair for greater emphasis*] I wont have you here snivelling about being a model employer and a converted man when youre only an apostate with your coat turned for the sake of a County Council contract. [*He nods at him to enforce the point; then goes to the hearth-rug, where he takes up a comfortably commanding position with his back to the fire, and continues.*] No: I like a man to be true to himself, even in wickedness. Come now: either take your hat and go; or else sit down and give me a good scoundrelly reason for wanting to be friends with me.

[BURGESS, *whose emotions have subsided sufficiently to be expressed by a dazed grin, is relieved by this concrete proposition. He ponders it for a moment, and then, slowly and very modestly, sits down in the chair* MORELL *has just left.*]

Thats right. Now out with it.

BURGESS [*chuckling in spite of himself*]. Well, you orr a queer bird, James, and no mistake. But [*almost enthusiastically*] one carnt elp likin you: besides, as I said afore, of course one dont take hall a clorgyman says seriously, or the world couldnt go on. Could it now? [*He composes himself for graver discourse, and, turning his eyes on* MORELL, *proceeds with dull seriousness.*] Well, I dont mind tellin you, since it's your wish we should be free with one another, that I did think you a bit of a fool once; but I'm beginnin to think that praps I was be'ind the times a bit.

MORELL [*exultant*]. Aha! Youre finding that out at last, are you?

BURGESS [*portentously*]. Yes: times 'as changed mor'n I could a believed. Five yorr [year] ago, no sensible man would a thought o takin hup with your hidears. I hused to wonder you was let preach at all. Why, I know a clorgyman what 'as bin kep hout of his job for yorrs by the Bishop o London, although the pore feller's not a bit more religious than you are. But today, if hennyone was to horffer to bet me a thousan poud that youll hend by bein a bishop yourself, I dussent take the bet. [*Very impressively.*] You and your crew are gittin hinfluential: I can see that. Theyll ave to give you somethink someday, if it's honly to stop your mouth. You ad the right instinc arter all, James: the line you took is the payin line in the long run for a man o your sort.

MORELL [*offering his hand with thorough decision*]. Shake hands, Burgess. Now youre talking honestly. I dont think theyll make me a bishop; but if they do, I'll introduce you to the biggest jobbers I can get to come to my dinner parties.

BURGESS [*who has risen with a sheepish grin and accepted the hand of friendship*]. You will ave your joke, James. Our quarrel's made up now, ain it?

A WOMAN'S VOICE. Say yes, James.

> [*Startled, they turn quickly and find that* CANDIDA *has just come in, and is looking at them with an amused maternal indulgence which is her characteristic expression. She is a woman of 33, well built, well nourished, likely, one guesses, to become matronly later on, but now quite at her best, with the double charm of youth and motherhood. Her ways are those of a woman who has found that she can always manage people by engaging their affection, and who does so frankly and instinctively without the smallest scruple. So far, she is like any other pretty woman who is just clever enough to make the most of her sexual attractions for trivially selfish ends; but* CANDIDA's *serene brow, courageous eyes, and well set mouth and chin signify largeness of mind and dignity of character to ennoble her cunning in the affections. A wise-hearted observer, looking at her, would at once guess that whoever had placed the Virgin of the Assumption over her hearth did so because he fancied some spiritual resemblance between them, and yet would not suspect either her husband or herself of any such idea, or indeed of any concern with the art of Titian.*
>
> *Just now she is in bonnet and mantle, carrying a strapped rug with her umbrella stuck through it, a handbag, and a supply of illustrated papers.*]

MORELL [*shocked at his remissness*]. Candida! Why—[*He looks at his watch, and is horrified to find it so late.*] My darling! [*Hurrying to her and seizing the rug strap, pouring forth his remorseful regrets all the time.*] I intended to meet you at the train. I let the time slip. [*Flinging the rug on the sofa.*] I was so engrossed by—[*returning to her*]—I forgot—oh! [*He embraces her with penitent emotion.*]

BURGESS [*a little shamefaced and doubtful of his reception*]. How orr you, Candy?

> [*She, still in* MORELL's *arms, offers him her cheek, which he kisses.*]

James and me is come to a nunnerstannin. A honorable unnerstannin. Ain we, James?

MORELL [*impetuously*]. Oh bother your understanding! Youve kept me late for Candida. [*With compassionate fervor.*] My poor love: how did you manage about the luggage? How—

CANDIDA [*stopping him and disengaging herself*]. There! there! there! I wasnt alone. Eugene has been down with us; and we travelled together.

MORELL [*pleased*]. Eugene!

CANDIDA. Yes: he's struggling with my luggage, poor boy. Go out, dear, at once; or he'll pay for the cab; and I dont want that.

> [MORELL *hurries out.* CANDIDA *puts down her handbag; then takes off her mantle and bonnet and puts them on the sofa with the rug, chatting meanwhile.*]

Well, papa: how are you getting on at home?

BURGESS. The ouse aint worth livin in since you left it, Candy. I wish youd come round and give the gurl a talkin to. Who's this Eugene thats come with you?

CANDIDA. Oh, Eugene's one of James discoveries. He found him sleeping on the Embankment last June. Havnt you noticed our new picture [*pointing to the Virgin*]? He gave us that.

BURGESS [*incredulously*]. Garn! D'you mean to tell me—your hown father!—that cab touts or such like, orf the Embankment, buys pictures like that? [*Severely.*] Dont deceive me, Candy: it's a 'Igh Church picture; and James chose it hisself.

CANDIDA. Guess again. Eugene isnt a cab tout.

BURGESS. Then what is he? [*Sarcastically.*] A nobleman, I spose.

CANDIDA [*nodding delightedly*]. Yes. His uncle's a peer! A real live earl.

BURGESS [*not daring to believe such good news*]. No!

CANDIDA. Yes. He had a seven day bill for £55 in his pocket when James found him on the Embankment. He thought he couldnt get any money for it until the seven days were up; and he was too shy to ask for credit. Oh, he's a dear boy! We are very fond of him.

BURGESS [*pretending to belittle the aristocracy, but with his eyes gleaming*]. Hm! I thort you wouldnt git a hearl's nevvy visitin in Victawriar Pawrk unless he were a bit of a flat. [*Looking again at the picture.*] Of course I dont old with that picture, Candy; but still it's a 'igh class fust rate work of ort: I can see that. Be sure you hintrodooce me to im, Candy. [*He looks at his watch anxiously.*] I can ony stay about two minutes.

[MORELL *comes back with* EUGENE, *whom* BURGESS *contemplates moist-eyed with enthusiasm. He is a strange, shy youth of eighteen, slight, effeminate, with a delicate childish voice, and a hunted tormented expression and shrinking manner that shew the painful sensitiveness of very swift and acute apprehensiveness in youth, before the character has grown to its full strength. Miserably irresolute, he does not know where to stand or what to do. He is afraid of* BURGESS, *and would run away into solitude if he dared; but the very intensity with which he feels a perfectly commonplace position comes from excessive nervous force; and his nostrils, mouth, and eyes betray a fiercely petulant wilfulness, as to the bent of which his brow, already lined with pity, is reassuring. He is so uncommon as to be almost unearthly; and to prosaic people there is something noxious in this unearthliness, just as to poetic people there is something angelic in it. His dress is anarchic. He wears an old blue serge jacket, unbuttoned, over a woollen lawn tennis shirt, with a silk handkerchief for a cravat, trousers matching the jacket, and brown canvas shoes. In these garments he has apparently lain in the heather and waded through the waters; and there is no evidence of his having ever brushed them.*

As he catches sight of a stranger on entering, he stops, and edges along the wall on the opposite side of the room.]

MORELL [*as he enters*]. Come along: you can spare us quarter of an hour at all events. This is my father-in-law. Mr Burgess—Mr Marchbanks.

MARCHBANKS [*nervously backing against the bookcase*]. Glad to meet you, sir.

BURGESS [*crossing to him with great heartiness, whilst* MORELL *joins* CANDIDA *at the fire*]. Glad to meet you, I'm shore, Mr Morchbanks. [*Forcing him to shake hands.*] Ow do you find yoreself this weather? Ope you aint lettin James put no foolish ideas into your ed?

MARCHBANKS. Foolish ideas? Oh, you mean Socialism? No.

BURGESS. Thats right. [*Again looking at his watch.*] Well, I must go now: theres no elp for it. Yore not comin my way, orr you, Mr Morchbanks?

MARCHBANKS. Which way is that?

BURGESS. Victawriar Pawrk Station. Theres a city train at 12.25.

MORELL. Nonsense. Eugene will stay to lunch with us, I expect.

MARCHBANKS [*anxiously excusing himself*]. No—I—I—

BURGESS. Well, well, I shornt press you: I bet youd rather lunch with Candy. Some night, I ope, youll come and dine with me at my club, the Freeman Founders in Nortn Folgit. Come: say you will!

MARCHBANKS. Thank you, Mr Burgess. Where is Norton Folgate? Down in Surrey, isnt it?

[BURGESS, *inexpressibly tickled, begins to splutter with laughter.*]

CANDIDA [*coming to the rescue*]. Youll lose your train, papa, if you dont go at once. Come back in the afternoon and tell Mr Marchbanks where to find the club.

BURGESS [*roaring with glee*]. Down in Surrey! Har, har! thats not a bad one. Well, I never met a man as didnt know Nortn Folgit afore. [*Abashed at his own noisiness.*] Goodbye, Mr Morchbanks: I know yore too ighbred to take my pleasantry in bad part. [*He again offers his hand.*]

MARCHBANKS [*taking it with a nervous jerk*]. Not at all.

BURGESS. Bye, bye, Candy. I'll look in again later on. So long, James.

MORELL. Must you go?

BURGESS. Dont stir. [*He goes out with unabated heartiness.*]

MORELL. Oh, I'll see you off. [*He follows him.*]

[EUGENE *stares after them apprehensively, holding his breath until* BURGESS *disappears.*]

CANDIDA [*laughing*]. Well, Eugene?

[*He turns with a start, and comes eagerly towards her, but stops irresolutely as he meets her amused look.*]

What do you think of my father?

MARCHBANKS. I—I hardly know him yet. He seems to be a very nice old gentleman.

CANDIDA [*with gentle irony*]. And youll go to the Freeman Founders to dine with him, wont you?

MARCHBANKS [*miserably, taking it quite seriously*]. Yes, if it will please you.

CANDIDA [*touched*]. Do you know, you are a very nice boy, Eugene, with all your queerness. If you had laughed at my father I shouldnt have minded; but I like you ever so much better for being nice to him.

MARCHBANKS. Ought I to have laughed? I noticed that he said something funny; but I am so ill at ease with strangers; and I never can see a joke. I'm very sorry. [*He sits down on the sofa, his elbows on his knees and his temples between his fists, with an expression of hopeless suffering.*]

CANDIDA [*bustling him goodnaturedly*]. Oh come! You great baby, you! You are worse than usual this morning. Why were you so melancholy as we came along in the cab?

MARCHBANKS. Oh, that was nothing. I was wondering how much I ought to give the cabman. I know it's utterly silly; but you dont know how dreaful such things are to me—how I shrink from having to deal with strange people. [*Quickly and reassuringly.*] But it's all right. He beamed all over and touched his hat when Morell gave him two shillings. I was on the point of offering him ten.

[MORELL *comes back with a few letters and newspapers which have come by the midday post.*]

CANDIDA. Oh, James dear, he was going to give the cabman ten shillings! ten shillings for a three minutes drive! Oh dear!

MORELL [*at the table, glancing through the letters*]. Never mind her, Marchbanks. The overpaying instinct is a generous one: better than the underpaying instinct, and not so common.

MARCHBANKS [*relapsing into dejection*]. No: cowardice, incompetence. Mrs Morell's quite right.

CANDIDA. Of course she is. [*She takes up her hand-bag.*] And now I must leave you to James for the present. I suppose you are too much of a poet to know the state a woman finds her house in when she's been away for three weeks. Give me my rug.

[EUGENE *takes the strapped rug from the couch, and gives it to her. She takes it in her left hand, having the bag in her right.*]

Now hang my cloak across my arm.

[*He obeys.*]

Now my hat.

[*He puts it into the hand which has the bag.*]

Now open the door for me.

[*He hurries before her and opens the door.*]

Thanks.

[*She goes out; and* MARCHBANKS *shuts the door.*]

MORELL [*still busy at the table*]. Youll stay to lunch, Marchbanks, of course.

MARCHBANKS [*scared*]. I musnt. [*He glances quickly at* MORELL, *but at once avoids his frank look, and adds, with obvious disingenuousness*] I mean I cant.

MORELL. You mean you wont.

MARCHBANKS [*earnestly*]. No: I should like to, indeed. Thank you very
much. But—but—

MORELL. But—but—but—but—Bosh! If youd like to stay, stay. If youre
shy, go and take a turn in the park and write poetry until half past
one; and then come in and have a good feed.

MARCHBANKS. Thank you, I should like that very much. But I really
mustnt. The truth is, Mrs Morell told me not to. She said she didnt
think youd ask me to stay to lunch, but that I was to remember, if
you did, that you didnt really want me to. [*Plaintively.*] She said I'd
understand; but I dont. Please dont tell her I told you.

MORELL [*drolly*]. Oh, is that all? Wont my suggestion that you should
take a turn in the park meet the difficulty?

MARCHBANKS. How?

MORELL [*exploding good-humoredly*]. Why, you duffer—

[*But this boisterousness jars himself as well as* EUGENE. *He checks
himself.*]

No: I wont put it in that way.

[*He comes to* EUGENE *with affectionate seriousness.*]

My dear lad: in a happy marriage like ours, there is something very
sacred in the return of the wife to her home.

[MARCHBANKS *looks quickly at him, half anticipating his meaning.*]
An old friend or a truly noble and sympathetic soul is not in the way
on such occasions; but a chance visitor is.

[*The hunted horror-stricken expression comes out with sudden viv-
idness in* EUGENE's *face as he understands.* MORELL, *occupied with
his own thoughts, goes on without noticing this.*]

Candida thought I would rather not have you here; but she was wrong.
I'm very fond of you, my boy; and I should like you to see for yourself
what a happy thing it is to be married as I am.

MARCHBANKS. Happy! Your marriage! You think that! You believe that!

MORELL [*buoyantly*]. I know it, my lad. Larochefoucauld[4] said that there
are convenient marriages but no delightful ones. You dont know the
comfort of seeing through and through a thundering liar and rotten
cynic like that fellow. Ha! ha! Now, off with you to the park, and
write your poem. Half past one, sharp, mind: we never wait for
anybody.

MARCHBANKS [*wildly*]. No: stop: you shant. I'll force it into the light.

MORELL [*puzzled*]. Eh? Force what?

MARCHBANKS. I must speak to you. There is something that must be
settled between us.

MORELL [*with a whimsical glance at his watch*]. Now?

MARCHBANKS [*passionately*]. Now. Before you leave this room. [*He retreats a few steps, and stands as if to bar* MORELL's *way to the door.*]

MORELL [*without moving, and gravely, perceiving now that there is some-*

---

4. François, duc de La Rochefoucauld (1613–80), a French writer and moral philosopher. His *Maxims*
(1665) express the pessimistic conviction that self-interest is the master human passion.

thing serious the matter]. I'm not going to leave it, my dear boy: I thought you were.

[EUGENE, *baffled by his firm tone, turns his back on him, writhing with anger.* MORELL *goes to him and puts his hand on his shoulder strongly and kindly, disregarding his attempt to shake it off.*]

Come: sit down quietly; and tell me what it is. And remember: we are friends, and need not fear that either of us will be anything but patient and kind to the other, whatever we may have to say.

MARCHBANKS [*twisting himself round on him*]. Oh, I am not forgetting myself: I am only [*covering his face desperately with his hands*] full of horror. [*Then, dropping his hands, and thrusting his face forward fiercely at* MORELL, *he goes on threateningly.*] You shall see whether this is a time for patience and kindness.

[MORELL, *firm as a rock, looks indulgently at him.*]

Dont look at me in that self-complacent way. You think yourself stronger than I am; but I shall stagger you if you have a heart in your breast.

MORELL [*powerfully confident*]. Stagger me, my boy. Out with it.

MARCHBANKS. First—

MORELL. First?

MARCHBANKS. I love your wife.

[MORELL *recoils, and, after staring at him for a moment in utter amazement, bursts into uncontrollable laughter.* EUGENE *is taken aback, but not disconcerted; and he soon becomes indignant and contemptuous.*]

MORELL [*sitting down to have his laugh out*]. Why, my dear child, of course you do. Everybody loves her: they cant help it. I like it. But [*looking up jocosely at him*] I say, Eugene: do you think yours is a case to be talked about? Youre under twenty: she's over thirty. Doesnt it look rather too like a case of calf love?

MARCHBANKS [*vehemently*]. You dare say that of her! You think that way of the love she inspires! It is an insult to her!

MORELL [*rising quickly, in an altered tone*]. To her! Eugene: take care. I have been patient. I hope to remain patient. But there are some things I wont allow. Dont force me to shew you the indulgence I should shew to a child. Be a man.

MARCHBANKS [*with a gesture as if sweeping something behind him*]. Oh, let us put aside all that cant. It horrifies me when I think of the doses of it she has had to endure in all the weary years during which you have selfishly and blindly sacrificed her to minister to your self-sufficiency: you! [*turning on him*] who have not one thought—one sense—in common with her.

MORELL [*philosophically*]. She seems to bear it pretty well. [*Looking him straight in the face.*] Eugene, my boy: you are making a fool of yourself: a very great fool of yourself. Theres a piece of wholesome plain speaking for you. [*He knocks in the lesson with a nod in his old way, and posts himself on the hearthrug, holding his hands behind him to warm them.*]

MARCHBANKS. Oh, do you think I dont know all that? Do you think that the things people make fools of themselves about are any less real and true than the things they behave sensibly about?

[MORELL's *gaze wavers for the first time. He forgets to warm his hands, and stands listening, startled and thoughtful.*]

They are more true: they are the only things that are true. You are very calm and sensible and moderate with me because you can see that I am a fool about your wife; just as no doubt that old man who was here just now is very wise over your Socialism, because he sees that you are a fool about it.

[MORELL's *perplexity deepens markedly.* EUGENE *follows up his advantage, plying him fiercely with questions.*]

Does that prove you wrong? Does your complacent superiority to me prove that I am wrong?

MORELL. Marchbanks: some devil is putting these words into your mouth. It is easy—terribly easy—to shake a man's faith in himself. To take advantage of that to break a man's spirit is devil's work. Take care of what you are doing. Take care.

MARCHBANKS [*ruthlessly*]. I know. I'm doing it on purpose. I told you I should stagger you.

[*They confront one another threateningly for a moment. Then* MORELL *recovers his dignity.*]

MORELL [*with noble tenderness*]. Eugene: listen to me. Some day, I hope and trust, you will be a happy man like me.

[EUGENE *chafes intolerably, repudiating the worth of his happiness.* MORELL, *deeply insulted, controls himself with fine forbearance, and continues steadily, with great artistic beauty of delivery.*]

You will be married; and you will be working with all your might and valor to make every spot on earth as happy as your own home. You will be one of the makers of the Kingdon of Heaven on earth; and—who knows?—you may be a master builder where I am only a humble journeyman; for dont think, my boy, that I cannot see in you, young as you are, promise of higher powers than I can ever pretend to. I well know that it is in the poet that the holy spirit of man—the god within him—is most godlike. It should make you tremble to think of that—to think that the heavy burthen and great gift of a poet may be laid upon you.

MARCHBANKS [*unimpressed and remorseless, his boyish crudity of assertion telling sharply against* MORELL's *oratory*]. It does not make me tremble. It is the want of it in others that makes me tremble.

MORELL [*redoubling his force of style under the stimulus of his genuine feeling and* EUGENE's *obduracy*]. Then help to kindle it in them—in me—not to extinguish it. In the future, when you are as happy as I am, I will be your true brother in the faith. I will help you to believe that God has given us a world that nothing but our own folly keeps from being a paradise. I will help you to believe that every stroke of your work is sowing happiness for the great harvest that all—even the humblest—shall one day reap. And last, but trust me, not least, I will help you to believe that your wife loves you and is happy in her home. We need such help, Marchbanks: we need it greatly and always. There are so many things to make us doubt, if once we let our understanding be troubled. Even at home, we sit as if in camp, encompassed by a hostile army of doubts. Will you play the traitor and let them in on me?

MARCHBANKS [*looking round wildly*]. Is it like this for her here always? A woman, with a great soul, craving for reality, truth, freedom; and being fed on metaphors, sermons, stale perorations, mere rhetoric. Do you think a woman's soul can live on your talent for preaching?

MORELL [*stung*]. Marchbanks: you make it hard for me to control myself. My talent is like yours insofar as it has any real worth at all. It is the gift of finding words for divine truth.

MARCHBANKS [*impetuously*]. It's the gift of the gab, nothing more and nothing less. What has your knack of fine talking to do with the truth, any more than playing the organ has? Ive never been in your church; but Ive been to your political meetings; and Ive seen you do whats called rousing the meeting to enthusiasm: that is, you excited them until they behaved exactly as if they were drunk. And their wives looked on and saw what fools they were. Oh, it's an old story: youll find it in the Bible. I imagine King David, in his fits of enthusiasm, was very like you. [*Stabbing him with the words.*] "But his wife despised him in her heart."

MORELL [*wrathfully*]. Leave my house. Do you hear? [*He advances on him threateningly.*]

MARCHBANKS [*shrinking back against the couch*]. Let me alone. Dont touch me.

> [MORELL *grasps him powerfully by the lappell of his coat: he cowers down on the sofa and screams passionately.*]

Stop, Morell: if you strike me, I'll kill myself: I wont bear it. [*Almost in hysterics.*] Let me go. Take your hand away.

MORELL [*with slow emphatic scorn*]. You little snivelling cowardly whelp. [*He releases him.*] Go, before you frighten yourself into a fit.

MARCHBANKS [*on the sofa, gasping, but relieved by the withdrawal of* MORELL'*s hand*]. I'm not afraid of you: it's you who are afraid of me.

MORELL [*quietly, as he stands over him*]. It looks like it, doesnt it?

MARCHBANKS [*with petulant vehemence*]. Yes, it does.

> [MORELL *turns away contemptuously.* EUGENE *scrambles to his feet and follows him.*]

You think because I shrink from being brutally handled—because [*with tears in his voice*] I can do nothing but cry with rage when I am met with violence—because I cant lift a heavy trunk down from the top of a cab like you—because I cant fight you for your wife as a drunken navvy would: all that makes you think I'm afraid of you. But youre wrong. If I havnt got what you call British pluck, I havnt British cowardice either: I'm not afraid of a clergyman's ideas. I'll fight your ideas. I'll rescue her from her slavery to them. I'll pit my own ideas against them. You are driving me out of the house because you darent let her choose between your ideas and mine. You are afraid to let me see her again.

[MORELL, *angered, turns suddenly on him. He flies to the door in involuntary dread.*]

Let me alone, I say. I'm going.

MORELL [*with cold scorn*]. Wait a moment: I am not going to touch you: dont be afraid. When my wife comes back she will want to know why you have gone. And when she finds that you are never going to cross our threshold again, she will want to have that explained too. Now I dont wish to distress her by telling her that you have behaved like a blackguard.

MARCHBANKS [*coming back with renewed vehemence*]. You shall. You must. If you give any explanation but the true one, you are a liar and a coward. Tell her what I said; and how you were strong and manly, and shook me as a terrier shakes a rat; and how I shrank and was terrified; and how you called me a snivelling little whelp and put me out of the house. If you dont tell her, I will: I'll write it to her.

MORELL [*puzzled*]. Why do you want her to know this?

MARCHBANKS [*with lyric rapture*]. Because she will understand me, and know that I understand her. If you keep back one word of it from her—if you are not ready to lay the truth at her feet as I am—then you will know to the end of your days that she really belongs to me and not to you. Goodbye. [*Going.*]

MORELL [*terribly disquieted*]. Stop: I will not tell her.

MARCHBANKS [*turning near the door*]. Either the truth or a lie you must tell her, if I go.

MORELL [*temporizing*]. Marchbanks: it is sometimes justifiable—

MARCHBANKS [*cutting him short*]. I know: to lie. It will be useless. Goodbye, Mr Clergyman.

[*As he turns finally to the door, it opens and* CANDIDA *enters in her housekeeping dress.*]

CANDIDA. Are you going, Eugene? [*Looking more observantly at him.*] Well, dear me, just look at you, going out into the street in that state! You are a poet, certainly. Look at him, James!

[*She takes him by the coat, and brings him forward, shewing him to* MORELL.]

Look at his collar! look at his tie! look at his hair! One would think somebody had been throttling you.

[EUGENE *instinctively tries to look round at* MORELL; *but she pulls him back.*]

Here! Stand still.

[*She buttons his collar; ties his neckerchief in a bow; and arranges his hair.*]

There! Now you look so nice that I think youd better stay to lunch after all, though I told you you musnt. It will be ready in half an hour.

[*She puts a final touch to the bow. He kisses her hand.*]

Dont be silly.

MARCHBANKS. I want to stay, of course; unless the reverend gentleman your husband has anything to advance to the contrary.

CANDIDA. Shall he stay, James, if he promises to be a good boy and help me to lay the table?

MORELL [*shortly*]. Oh yes, certainly: he had better. [*He goes to the table and pretends to busy himself with his papers there.*]

MARCHBANKS [*offering his arm to* CANDIDA]. Come and lay the table.

[*She takes it. They go to the door together. As they pass out he adds*]

I am the happiest of mortals.

MORELL. So was I—an hour ago.

Act Two

The same day later in the afternoon. The same room. The chair for visitors has been replaced at the table. MARCHBANKS, *alone and idle, is trying to find out how the typewriter works. Hearing someone at the door, he steals guiltily away to the window and pretends to be absorbed in the view.* MISS GARNETT, *carrying the notebook in which she takes down* MORELL'*s letters in shorthand from his dictation, sits down at the typewriter and sets to work transcribing them, much too busy to notice* EUGENE. *When she begins the second line she stops and stares at the machine. Something wrong evidently.*

PROSERPINE. Bother! Youve been meddling with my typewriter, Mr Marchbanks; and theres not the least use in your trying to look as if you hadnt.

MARCHBANKS [*timidly*]. I'm very sorry, Miss Garnett. I only tried to make it write. [*Plaintively.*] But it wouldnt.

PROSERPINE. Well, youve altered the spacing.

MARCHBANKS [*earnestly*]. I assure you I didnt. I didnt indeed. I only turned a little wheel. It gave a sort of click.

PROSERPINE. Oh, now I understand. [*She restores the spacing, talking volubly all the time.*] I suppose you thought it was a sort of barrel-organ. Nothing to do but turn the handle, and it would write a beautiful love letter for you straight off, eh?

MARCHBANKS [*seriously*]. I suppose a machine could be made to write love letters. Theyre all the same, arnt they?

PROSERPINE [*somewhat indignantly: any such discussion, except by way of pleasantry, being outside her code of manners*]. How do I know? Why do you ask me?

MARCHBANKS. I beg your pardon. I thought clever people—people who can do business and write letters and that sort of thing—always had to have love affairs to keep them from going mad.

PROSERPINE [*rising, outraged*]. Mr Marchbanks! [*She looks severely at him, and marches majestically to the bookcase.*]

MARCHBANKS [*approaching her humbly*]. I hope I havnt offended you. Perhaps I shouldnt have alluded to your love affairs.

PROSERPINE [*plucking a blue book from the shelf and turning sharply on him*]. I havnt any love affairs. How dare you say such a thing? The idea!

[*She tucks the book under her arm, and is flouncing back to her machine when he addresses her with awakened interest and sympathy.*]

MARCHBANKS. Really! Oh, then you are shy, like me.

PROSERPINE. Certainly I am not shy. What do you mean?

MARCHBANKS [*secretly*]. You must be: that is the reason there are so few love affairs in the world. We all go about longing for love: it is the first need of our natures, the first prayer of our hearts; but we dare not utter our longing: we are too shy. [*Very earnestly.*] Oh, Miss Garnett, what would you not give to be without fear, without shame—

PROSERPINE [*scandalized*]. Well, upon my word!

MARCHBANKS [*with petulant impatience*]. Ah, dont say those stupid things to me: they dont deceive me: what use are they? Why are you afraid to be your real self with me? I am just like you.

PROSERPINE. Like me! Pray are you flattering me or flattering yourself? I dont feel quite sure which. [*She again tries to get back to her work.*]

MARCHBANKS [*stopping her mysteriously*]. Hush! I go about in search of love; and I find it in unmeasured stores in the bosoms of others. But when I try to ask for it, this horrible shyness strangles me; and I stand dumb, or worse than dumb, saying meaningless things: foolish lies. And I see the affection I am longing for given to dogs and cats and pet birds, because they come and ask for it. [*Almost whispering.*] It must be asked for: it is like a ghost: it cannot speak unless it is first spoken to. [*At his usual pitch, but with deep melancholy.*] All the love in the world is longing to speak; only it dare not, because it is shy! shy! shy! That is the world's tragedy. [*With a deep sigh he sits in the visitors' chair and buries his face in his hands.*]

PROSERPINE [*amazed, but keeping her wits about her: her point of honor in encounters with strange young men*]. Wicked people get over that shyness occasionally, dont they?

MARCHBANKS [*scrambling up almost fiercely*]. Wicked people means people who have no love: therefore they have no shame. They have the power to ask love because they dont need it: they have the power to offer it because they have none to give. [*He collapses into his seat, and adds, mournfully*] But we, who have love, and long to mingle it with the love of others: we cannot utter a word. [*Timidly.*] You find that, dont you?

PROSERPINE. Look here: if you dont stop talking like this, I'll leave the room, Mr Marchbanks: I really will. It's not proper.

[*She resumes her seat at the typewriter, opening the blue book and preparing to copy a passage from it.*]

MARCHBANKS [*hopelessly*]. Nothing thats worth saying is proper. [*He rises, and wanders about the room in his lost way.*] I cant understand you, Miss Garnett. What am I to talk about?

PROSERPINE [*snubbing him*]. Talk about indifferent things. Talk about the weather.

MARCHBANKS. Would you talk about indifferent things if a child were by, crying bitterly with hunger?

PROSERPINE. I suppose not.

MARCHBANKS. Well: *I* cant talk about indifferent things with my heart crying out bitterly in its hunger.

PROSERPINE. Then hold your tongue.

MARCHBANKS. Yes: that is what it always comes to. We hold our tongues. Does that stop the cry of your heart? for it does cry: doesn't it? It must, if you have a heart.

PROSERPINE [*suddenly rising with her hand pressed on her heart*]. Oh, it's no use trying to work while you talk like that. [*She leaves her little table and sits on the sofa. Her feelings are keenly stirred.*] It's no business of yours whether my heart cries or not; but I have a mind to tell you, for all that.

MARCHBANKS. You neednt. I know already that it must.

PROSERPINE. But mind! if you ever say I said so, I'll deny it.

MARCHBANKS [*compassionately*]. Yes, I know. And so you havnt the courage to tell him?

PROSERPINE [*bouncing up*]. Him! Who?

MARCHBANKS. Whoever he is. The man you love. It might be anybody. The curate, Mr Mill, perhaps.

PROSERPINE [*with disdain*]. Mr Mill!!! A fine man to break my heart about, indeed! I'd rather have you than Mr Mill.

MARCHBANKS [*recoiling*]. No, really: I'm very sorry; but you mustnt think of that. I—

PROSERPINE [*testily, going to the fire-place and standing at it with her back to him*]. Oh, dont be frightened: it's not you. It's not any one particular person.

MARCHBANKS. I know. You feel that you could love anybody that offered—

PROSERPINE [*turning, exasperated*]. Anybody that offered! No, I do not. What do you take me for?

MARCHBANKS [*discouraged*]. No use. You wont make me real answers:

only those things that everybody says. [*He strays to the sofa and sits down disconsolately.*]

PROSERPINE [*nettled at what she takes it to be a disparagement of her manners by an aristocrat*]. Oh well, if you want original conversation, youd better go and talk to yourself.

MARCHBANKS. That is what all poets do: they talk to themselves out loud; and the world overhears them. But it's horribly lonely not to hear someone else talk sometimes.

PROSERPINE. Wait until Mr Morell comes. He'll talk to you.

[MARCHBANKS *shudders.*]

Oh, you neednt make wry faces over him: he can talk better than you. [*With temper.*] He'd talk your little head off.

[*She is going back angrily to her place, when he, suddenly enlightened, springs up and stops her.*]

MARCHBANKS. Ah! I understand now.

PROSERPINE [*reddening*]. What do you understand?

MARCHBANKS. Your secret. Tell me: is it really and truly possible for a woman to love him?

PROSERPINE [*as if this were beyond all bounds*]. Well!!

MARCHBANKS [*passionately*]. No: answer me. I want to know: I must know. *I* cant understand it. I can see nothing in him but words, pious resolutions, what people call goodness. You cant love that.

PROSERPINE [*attempting to snub him by an air of cool propriety*]. I simply dont know what youre talking about. I dont understand you.

MARCHBANKS [*vehemently*]. You do. You lie.

PROSERPINE. Oh!

MARCHBANKS. You do understand; and you know. [*Determined to have an answer.*] Is it possible for a woman to love him?

PROSERPINE [*looking him straight in the face*]. Yes.

[*He covers his face with his hands.*]

Whatever is the matter with you!

[*He takes down his hands. Frightened at the tragic mask presented to her, she hurries past him at the utmost possible distance, keeping her eyes on his face until he turns from her and goes to the child's chair beside the hearth, where he sits in the deepest dejection. As she approaches the door, it opens and* BURGESS *enters. Seeing him, she ejaculates*]

Praise heaven! here's somebody

[*and feels safe enough to resume her place at her table. She puts a fresh sheet of paper into the typewriter as* BURGESS *crosses to* EUGENE].

BURGESS [*bent on taking care of the distinguished visitor*]. Well: so this is the way they leave you to yoreself, Mr Morchbanks. Ive come to keep you company.

[MARCHBANKS *looks up at him in consternation, which is quite lost on him.*]

James is receivin a deppitation in the dinin room; and Candy is hupstairs heducating of a young stitcher gurl she's hinterested in.

[*Consolingly.*] You must fine it lonesome here with no one but the typist to talk to. [*He pulls round the easy chair, and sits down.*]

PROSERPINE [*highly incensed*]. He'll be all right now that he has the advantage of your polished conversation: thats one comfort, anyhow. [*She begins to typewrite with clattering asperity.*]

BURGESS [*amazed at her audacity*]. Hi was not addressin myself to you, young woman, that I'm awerr of.

PROSERPINE. Did you ever see worse manners, Mr Marchbanks?

BURGESS [*with pompous severity*]. Mr Morchbanks is a gentleman, and knows his place, which is more than some people do.

PROSERPINE [*fretfully*]. It's well you and I are not ladies and gentlemen: I'd talk to you pretty straight if Mr Marchbanks wasnt here. [*She pulls the letter out of the machine so crossly that it tears.*] There! now I've spoiled this letter! have to be done all over again! Oh, I cant contain myself: silly old fathead!

BURGESS [*rising, breathless with indignation*]. Ho! I'm a silly ole fat'ead, am I? Ho, indeed [*gasping*]! Hall right, my gurl! Hall right. You just wait till I tell that to yore hemployer. Youll see. I'll teach you: see if I dont.

PROSERPINE [*conscious of having gone too far*]. I—

BURGESS [*cutting her short*]. No: youve done it now. No huse a-talkin to me. I'll let you know who I am.

[PROSERPINE *shifts her paper carriage with a defiant bang, and disdainfully goes on with her work.*]

Dont you take no notice of her, Mr Morchbanks. She's beneath it. [*He loftily sits down again.*]

MARCHBANKS [*miserably nervous and disconcerted*]. Hadnt we better change the subject? I—I dont think Miss Garnett meant anything.

PROSERPINE [*with intense conviction*]. Oh, didnt I though, just!

BURGESS. I wouldnt demean myself to take notice on her.

[An electric bell rings twice.]

PROSERPINE [*gathering up her note-book and papers*]. Thats for me. [*She hurries out.*]

BURGESS [*calling after her*]. Oh, we can spare you. [*Somewhat relieved by the triumph of having the last word, and yet half inclined to try to improve on it, he looks after her for a moment; then subsides into his seat by* EUGENE, *and addresses him very confidentially.*] Now we're alone, Mr Morchbanks, let me give you a friendly int that I wouldnt give to heverybody. Ow long ave you known my son-in-law James ere?

MARCHBANKS. I dont know. I never can remember dates. A few months, perhaps.

BURGESS. Ever notice hennythink queer about him?

MARCHBANKS. I dont think so.

BURGESS [*impressively*]. No more you wouldnt. Thats the danger on it. Well, he's mad.

MARCHBANKS. Mad!

BURGESS. Mad as a Morch 'are. You take notice on him and youll see.

MARCHBANKS [*uneasily*]. But surely that is only because his opinions—

BURGESS [*touching him on the knee with his forefinger, and pressing it to hold his attention*]. Thats the same what I hused to think, Mr Morchbanks. Hi thought long enough that it was only his opinions; though, mind you, hopinions becomes vurry serious things when people takes to hactin on em as e does. But thats not what I go on.
[*He looks round to make sure that they are alone, and bends over to* EUGENE'*s ear.*]
What do you think he sez to me this mornin in this very room?

MARCHBANKS. What!

BURGESS. He sez to me—this is as sure as we're settin here now—he sez "I'm a fool," he sez; "and yore a scounderl." Me a scounderl, mind you! And then shook ands with me on it, as if it was to my credit! Do you mean to tell me as that man's sane?

MORELL [*outside, calling to* PROSERPINE *as he opens the door*]. Get all their names and addresses, Miss Garnett.

PROSERPINE [*in the distance*]. Yes, Mr Morell.
[MORELL *comes in, with the deputation's documents in his hands.*]

BURGESS [*aside to* MARCHBANKS]. Yorr he iss. Just you keep your heye on im and see. [*Rising momentously.*] I'm sorry, James, to ave to make a complaint to you. I dont want to do it; but I feel I oughter, as a matter o right and dooty.

MORELL. Whats the matter?

BURGESS. Mr Morchbanks will bear me hout: he was a witness. [*Very solemnly.*] Yore young woman so far forgot herself as to call me a silly ole fat'ead.

MORELL [*with tremendous heartiness*]. Oh, now, isnt that exactly like Prossy? She's so frank: she cant contain herself! Poor Prossy! Ha! ha!

BURGESS [*trembling with rage*]. And do you hexpec me to put up with it from the like of er?

MORELL. Pooh, nonsense! you cant take any notice of it. Never mind.
[*He goes to the cellaret*[5] *and puts the papers into one of the drawers.*]

BURGESS. Oh, Hi dont mind. Hi'm above it. But is it right? thats what I want to know. Is it right?

MORELL. Thats a question for the Church, not for the laity. Has it done you any harm? thats the question for you, eh? Of course it hasnt. Think no more of it. [*He dismisses the subject by going to his place at the table and setting to work at his correspondence.*]

BURGESS [*aside to Marchbanks*]. What did I tell you? Mad as a atter.
[*He goes to the table and asks, with the sickly civility of a hungry man.*] When's dinner, James?

MORELL. Not for a couple of hours yet.

---

5. A small cabinet.

BURGESS [*with plaintive resignation*]. Gimme a nice book to read over the fire, will you, James: thur's a good chap.

MORELL. What sort of book? A good one?

BURGESS [*with almost a yell of remonstrance*]. Nah-oo! Summat pleasant, just to pass the time.

[MORELL *takes an illustrated paper from the table and offers it. He accepts it humbly.*]

Thank yer, James. [*He goes back to the big chair at the fire, and sits there at his ease, reading.*]

MORELL [*as he writes*]. Candida will come to entertain you presently. She has got rid of her pupil. She is filling the lamps.

MARCHBANKS [*starting up in the wildest consternation*]. But that will soil her hands. I cant bear that, Morell: it's a shame. I'll go and fill them. [*He makes for the door.*]

MORELL. Youd better not.

[MARCHBANKS *stops irresolutely.*]

She'd only set you to clean my boots, to save me the trouble of doing it myself in the morning.

BURGESS [*with grave disapproval*]. Dont you keep a servant now, James?

MORELL. Yes; but she isnt a slave; and the house looks as if I kept three. That means that everyone has to lend a hand. It's not a bad plan: Prossy and I can talk business after breakfast while we're washing up. Washing up's no trouble when there are two people to do it.

MARCHBANKS [*tormentedly*]. Do you think every woman is as coarse-grained as Miss Garnett?

BURGESS [*emphatically*]. Thats quite right, Mr Morchbanks: thats quite right. She is corsegrained.

MORELL [*quietly and significantly*]. Marchbanks!

MARCHBANKS. Yes?

MORELL. How many servants does your father keep?

MARCHBANKS [*pettishly*]. Oh, I dont know. [*He moves to the sofa, as if to get as far as possible from* MORELL's *questioning, and sits down in great agony of spirit, thinking of the paraffin.*][6]

MORELL [*very gravely*]. So many that you dont know! [*More aggressively.*] When theres anything coarse-grained to be done, you just ring the bell and throw it on to somebody else, eh?

MARCHBANKS. Oh, dont torture me. You dont even ring the bell. But your wife's beautiful fingers are dabbling in paraffin oil while you sit here comfortably preaching about it: everlasting preaching! preaching! words! words! words!

BURGESS [*intensely appreciating his retort*]. Har, har! Dcvil a better! [*Radiantly.*] Ad you there, James, straight.

[CANDIDA *comes in, well aproned, with a reading lamp trimmed,*

6. Britishism for kerosene.

filled, and ready for lighting. She places it on the table near MORELL, *ready for use.*]

CANDIDA [*brushing her finger tips together with a slight twitch of her nose*]. If you stay with us, Eugene, I think I will hand over the lamps to you.

MARCHBANKS. I will stay on condition that you hand over all the rough work to me.

CANDIDA. Thats very gallant; but I think I should like to see how you do it first. [*Turning to* MORELL.] James: youve not been looking after the house properly.

MORELL. What have I done—or not done—my love?

CANDIDA [*with serious vexation*]. My own particular pet scrubbing brush has been used for blackleading.

[*A heartbreaking wail bursts from* MARCHBANKS. BURGESS *looks round, amazed.* CANDIDA *hurries to the sofa.*]

Whats the matter? Are you ill, Eugene?

MARCHBANKS. No: not ill. Only horror! horror! horror! [*He bows his head on his hands.*]

BURGESS [*shocked*]. What! Got the orrors, Mr Morchbanks! Oh, thats bad, at your age. You must leave it off grajally.

CANDIDA [*reassured*]. Nonsense, papa! It's only poetic horror, isnt it, Eugene [*petting him*]?

BURGESS [*abashed*]. Oh, poetic orror, is it? I beg your pordon, I'm shore. [*He turns to the fire again, deprecating his hasty conclusion.*]

CANDIDA. What is it, Eugene? the scrubbing brush?

[*He shudders.*]

Well, there! never mind.

[*She sits down beside him.*]

Wouldnt you like to present me with a nice new one, with an ivory back inlaid with mother-of-pearl?

MARCHBANKS [*softly and musically, but sadly and longingly*]. No, not a scrubbing brush, but a boat: a tiny shallop to sail away in, far from the world, where the marble floors are washed by the rain and dried by the sun; where the south wind dusts the beautiful green and purple carpets. Or a chariot! to carry us up into the sky, where the lamps are stars, and dont need to be filled with paraffin oil every day.

MORELL [*harshly*]. And where there is nothing to do but to be idle, selfish, and useless.

CANDIDA [*jarred*]. Oh, James! how could you spoil it all?

MARCHBANKS [*firing up*]. Yes, to be idle, selfish, and useless: that is, to be beautiful and free and happy: hasnt every man desired that with all his soul for the woman he loves? Thats my ideal: whats yours, and that of all the dreadful people who live in these hideous rows of houses? Sermons and scrubbing brushes! With you to preach the sermon and your wife to scrub.

CANDIDA [*quaintly*]. He cleans the boots, Eugene. You will have to clean them to-morrow for saying that about him.

MARCHBANKS. Oh, dont talk about boots! Your feet should be beautiful on the mountains.

CANDIDA. My feet would not be beautiful on the Hackney Road without boots.

BURGESS [*scandalized*]. Come, Candy! dont be vulgar. Mr Morchbanks aint accustomed to it. Youre givin him the orrors again. I mean the poetic ones.

[MORELL *is silent. Apparently he is busy with his letters: really he is puzzling with misgiving over his new and alarming experience that the surer he is of his moral thrusts, the more swiftly and effectively* EUGENE *parries them. To find himself beginning to fear a man whom he does not respect afflicts him bitterly.*

MISS GARNETT *comes in with a telegram.*]

PROSERPINE [*handing the telegram to* MORELL]. Reply paid. The boy's waiting. [*To* CANDIDA, *coming back to her machine and sitting down.*] Maria is ready for you now in the kitchen, Mrs Morell.

[*Candida rises.*]

The onions have come.

MARCHBANKS [*convulsively*]. Onions!

CANDIDA. Yes, onions. Not even Spanish ones: nasty little red onions. You shall help me to slice them. Come along.

[*She catches him by the wrist and runs out, pulling him after her.* BURGESS *rises in consternation, and stands aghast on the hearth-rug, staring after them.*]

BURGESS. Candy didnt oughter andle a hearl's nevvy like that. It's goin too fur with it. Lookee ere, James: do e often git taken queer like that?

MORELL [*shortly, writing a telegram*]. I dont know.

BURGESS [*sentimentally*]. He talks very pretty. I awlus had a turn for a bit of poetry. Candy takes arter me that-a-way. Huseter make me tell er fairy stories when she was ony a little kiddy not that igh. [*Indicating a stature of two feet or thereabouts.*]

MORELL [*preoccupied*]. Ah, indeed. [*He blots the telegram and goes out.*]

PROSERPINE. Used you to make the fairy stories up out of your own head?

[BURGESS, *not deigning to reply, strikes an attitude of the haughtiest disdain on the hearth-rug.*]

PROSERPINE [*calmly*]. I should never have supposed you had it in you. By the way, I'd better warn you, since youve taken such a fancy to Mr Marchbanks. He's mad.

BURGESS. Mad! What! Im too!!

PROSERPINE. Mad as a March hare. He did frighten me, I can tell you, just before you came in that time. Havent you noticed the queer things he says?

BURGESS. So thats what the poetic orrors means. Blame me if it didnt come into my ed once or twyst that he was a bit horff 'is chump! [*He crosses the room to the door, lifting up his voice as he goes.*] Well, this is a pretty sort of asylum for a man to be in, with no one but you to take care of him!

PROSERPINE [*as he passes her*]. Yes, what a dreadful thing it would be if anything happened to you!

BURGESS [*loftily*]. Dont you haddress no remarks to me. Tell your hemployer that Ive gone into the gorden for a smoke.

PROSERPINE [*mocking*]. Oh!

[*Before* BURGESS *can retort,* MORELL *comes back.*]

BURGESS [*sentimentally*]. Goin for a turn in the gording to smoke, James.

MORELL [*brusquely*]. Oh, all right, all right.

[BURGESS *goes out pathetically in the character of a weary old man.* MORELL *stands at the table, turning over his papers, and adding, across to* PROSERPINE, *half humorously, half absently.*]

Well, Miss Prossy, why have you been calling my father-in-law names?

PROSERPINE [*blushing fiery red, and looking quickly up at him, half scared, half reproachful*]. I—[*She bursts into tears.*]

MORELL [*with tender gaiety, leaning across the table towards her, and consoling her*]. Oh, come! come! come! Never mind, Pross: he is a silly old fathead, isnt he?

[*With an explosive sob, she makes a dash at the door, and vanishes, banging it.* MORELL, *shaking his head resignedly, sighs, and goes wearily to his chair, where he sits down and sets to work, looking old and careworn.*

CANDIDA *comes in. She has finished her household work and taken off the apron. She at once notices his dejected appearance, and posts herself quietly at the visitors' chair, looking down at him attentively. She says nothing.*]

MORELL [*looking up, but with his pen raised ready to resume his work*]. Well? Where is Eugene?

CANDIDA. Washing his hands in the scullery under the tap. He will make an excellent cook if he can only get over his dread of Maria.

MORELL [*shortly*]. Ha! No doubt. [*He begins writing again.*]

CANDIDA [*going nearer, and putting her hand down softly on his to stop him as she says*]. Come here, dear. Let me look at you.

[*He drops his pen and yields himself to her disposal. She makes him rise, and brings him a little away from the table, looking at him critically all the time.*]

Turn your face to the light.

[*She places him facing the window.*]

My boy is not looking well. Has he been overworking?

MORELL. Nothing more than usual.

CANDIDA. He looks very pale, and grey, and wrinkled, and old.

[*His melancholy deepens; and she attacks it with wilful gaiety.*]

Here: [*pulling him towards the easy chair*] youve done enough writing for to-day. Leave Prossy to finish it. Come and talk to me.

MORELL. But—

CANDIDA [*insisting*]. Yes, I must be talked to.

[*She makes him sit down, and seats herself on the carpet beside his knee.*]

Now [*patting his hand*] youre beginning to look better already. Why must you go out every night lecturing and talking? I hardly have one evening a week with you. Of course what you say is all very true; but it does no good: they dont mind what you say to them one little bit. They think they agree with you; but whats the use of their agreeing with you if they go and do just the opposite of what you tell them the moment your back is turned? Look at our congregation at St Dominic's! Why do they come to hear you talking about Christianity every Sunday? Why, just because theyve been so full of business and money-making for six days that they want to forget all about it and have a rest on the seventh; so that they can go back fresh and make money harder than ever! You positively help them at it instead of hindering them.

MORELL [*with energetic seriousness*]. You know very well, Candida, that I often blow them up soundly for that. And if there is nothing in their churchgoing but rest and diversion, why dont they try something more amusing? more self-indulgent? There must be some good in the fact that they prefer St Dominic's to worse places on Sundays.

CANDIDA. Oh, the worse places arnt open; and even if they were, they darent be seen going to them. Besides, James dear, you preach so splendidly that it's as good as a play for them. Why do you think the women are so enthusiastic?

MORELL [*shocked*]. Candida!

CANDIDA. Oh, I know. You silly boy: you think it's your Socialism and your religion; but if it were that, theyd do what you tell them instead of only coming to look at you. They all have Prossy's complaint.

MORELL. Prossy's complaint! What do you mean, Candida?

CANDIDA. Yes, Prossy, and all the other secretaries you ever had. Why does Prossy condescend to wash up the things, and to peel potatoes and abase herself in all manner of ways for six shillings a week less than she used to get in a city office? She's in love with you, James: thats the reason. Theyre all in love with you. And you are in love with preaching because you do it so beautifully. And you think it's all enthusiasm for the kingdom of Heaven on earth; and so do they. You dear silly!

MORELL. Candida: what dreadful! what soul-destroying cynicism! Are you jesting? Or—can it be?—are you jealous?

CANDIDA [*with curious thoughtfulness*]. Yes, I feel a little jealous sometimes.

MORELL [*incredulously*]. Of Prossy?

CANDIDA [*laughing*]. No, no, no, no. Not jealous of anybody. Jealous for somebody else, who is not loved as he ought to be.

MORELL. Me?

CANDIDA. You! Why, youre spoiled with love and worship: you get far more than is good for you. No: I mean Eugene.

MORELL [*startled*]. Eugene!

CANDIDA. It seems unfair that all the love should go to you, and none to him; although he needs it so much more than you do.

[*A convulsive movement shakes him in spite of himself.*]

Whats the matter? Am I worrying you?

MORELL [*hastily*]. Not at all. [*Looking at her with troubled intensity.*] You know that I have perfect confidence in you, Candida.

CANDIDA. You vain thing! Are you sure of your irresistible attractions?

MORELL. Candida; you are shocking me. I never thought of my attractions. I thought of your goodness, of your purity. That is what I confide in.

CANDIDA. What a nasty uncomfortable thing to say to me! Oh, you are a clergyman, James: a thorough clergyman!

MORELL [*turning away from her, heart-stricken*]. So Eugene says.

CANDIDA [*with lively interest, leaning over to him with her arms on his knee*]. Eugene's always right. He's a wonderful boy: I have grown fonder and fonder of him all the time I was away. Do you know, James, that though he has not the least suspicion of it himself, he is ready to fall madly in love with me?

MORELL [*grimly*]. Oh, he has no suspicion of it himself, hasnt he?

CANDIDA. Not a bit. [*She takes her arms from his knee, and turns thoughtfully, sinking into a more restful attitude with her hands in her lap.*] Some day he will know: when he is grown up and experienced, like you. And he will know that I must have known. I wonder what he will think of me then.

MORELL. No evil, Candida. I hope and trust, no evil.

CANDIDA [*dubiously*]. That will depend.

MORELL [*bewildered*]. Depend!

CANDIDA [*looking at him*]. Yes: it will depend on what happens to him. [*He looks vacantly at her.*] Dont you see? It will depend on how he comes to learn what love really is. I mean on the sort of woman who will teach it to him.

MORELL [*quite at a loss*]. Yes. No. I dont know what you mean.

CANDIDA [*explaining*]. If he learns it from a good woman, then it will be all right: he will forgive me.

MORELL. Forgive?

CANDIDA. But suppose he learns it from a bad woman, as so many men do, especially poetic men, who imagine all women are angels! Suppose he only discovers the value of love when he has thrown it away and degraded himself in his ignorance! Will he forgive me then, do you think?

MORELL. Forgive you for what?

CANDIDA [*realizing how stupid he is, and a little disappointed, though quite tenderly so*]. Dont you understand?

[*He shakes his head. She turns to him again, so as to explain with the fondest intimacy*].

I mean, will he forgive me for not teaching him myself? For abandoning him to the bad women for the sake of my goodness, of my purity, as you call it? Ah, James, how little you understand me, to talk of your confidence in my goodness and purity! I would give them both to poor Eugene as willingly as I would give my shawl to a beggar dying of cold, if there were nothing else to restrain me. Put your trust in my love for you, James; for if that went, I should care very little for your sermons: mere phrases that you cheat yourself and others with every day. [*She is about to rise.*]

MORELL. His words!

CANDIDA [*checking herself quickly in the act of getting up*]. Whose words?

MORELL. Eugene's.

CANDIDA [*delighted*]. He is always right. He understands you; he understands me; he understands Prossy; and you, darling, you understand nothing.

[*She laughs, and kisses him to console him. He recoils as if stabbed, and springs up.*]

MORELL. How can you bear to do that when—Oh, Candida [*with anguish in his voice*] I had rather you had plunged a grappling iron into my heart than given me that kiss.

CANDIDA [*amazed*]. My dear: whats the matter?

MORELL [*frantically waving her off*]. Dont touch me.

CANDIDA. James!!!

[*They are interrupted by the entrance of* MARCHBANKS *with* BURGESS, *who stop near the door, staring.*]

MARCHBANKS. Is anything the matter?

MORELL [*deadly white, putting an iron constraint on himself*]. Nothing but this: that either you were right this morning, or Candida is mad.

BURGESS [*in loudest protest*]. What! Candy mad too! Oh, come! come! come! [*He crosses the room to the fireplace, protesting as he goes, and knocks the ashes out of his pipe on the bars*].

[MORELL *sits down at his table desperately, leaning forward to hide his face, and interlacing his fingers rigidly to keep them steady.*]

CANDIDA [*to* MORELL, *relieved and laughing*]. Oh, youre only shocked! Is that all? How conventional all you unconventional people are! [*She sits gaily on the arm of the chair.*]

BURGESS. Come: be'ave yourself, Candy. Whatll Mr Morchbanks think of you?

CANDIDA. This comes of James teaching me to think for myself, and never to hold back out of fear of what other people may think of me. It works beautifully as long as I think the same things as he does. But now! because I have just thought something different! look at him! Just look! [*She points to* MORELL, *greatly amused.*]

[EUGENE *looks, and instantly presses his hand on his heart, as if some pain had shot through it. He sits down on the sofa like a man witnessing a tragedy.*]

BURGESS [*on the hearthrug*]. Well, James, you certnly haint as himpressive lookin as usu'l.

MORELL [*with a laugh which is half a sob*]. I suppose not. I beg all your pardons: I was not conscious of making a fuss. [*Pulling himself together.*] Well, well, well, well, well! [*He sets to work at his papers again with resolute cheerfulness.*]

CANDIDA [*going to the sofa and sitting beside* MARCHBANKS, *still in a bantering humor*]. Well, Eugene: why are you so sad? Did the onions make you cry?

MARCHBANKS [*aside to her*]. It is your cruelty. I hate cruelty. It is a horrible thing to see one person make another suffer.

CANDIDA [*petting him ironically*]. Poor boy! have I been cruel? Did I make it slice nasty little red onions?

MARCHBANKS [*earnestly*]. Oh, stop, stop: I dont mean myself. You have made him suffer frightfully. I feel his pain in my own heart. I know that it is not your fault: it is something that must happen; but dont make light of it. I shudder when you torture him and laugh.

CANDIDA [*incredulously*]. *I* torture James! Nonsense, Eugene: how you exaggerate! Silly! [*She rises and goes to the table, a little troubled.*] Dont work any more, dear. Come and talk to us.

MORELL [*affectionately but bitterly*]. Ah no: *I* cant talk. I can only preach.

CANDIDA [*caressing his hand*]. Well, come and preach.

BURGESS [*strongly remonstrating*]. Aw no, Candy, 'Ang it all!

[LEXY MILL *comes in, anxious and important.*]

LEXY [*hastening to shake hands with* CANDIDA]. How do you do, Mrs Morell? So glad to see you back again.

CANDIDA. Thank you, Lexy. You know Eugene, dont you?

LEXY. Oh yes. How do you do, Marchbanks?

MARCHBANKS. Quite well, thanks.

LEXY [*to* MORELL]. Ive just come from the Guild of St Matthew. They are in the greatest consternation about your telegram.

CANDIDA. What did you telegraph about, James?

LEXY [*to* CANDIDA]. He was to have spoken for them tonight. Theyve taken the large hall in Mare Street and spent a lot of money on posters. Morell's telegram was to say he couldnt come. It came on them like a thunderbolt.

CANDIDA [*surprised, and beginning to suspect something wrong*]. Given up an engagement to speak!

BURGESS. Fust time in his life, I'll bet. Ain it, Candy?

LEXY [*to* MORELL]. They decided to send an urgent telegram to you asking whether you could not change your mind. Have you received it?

MORELL [*with restrained impatience*]. Yes, yes: I got it.

LEXY. It was reply paid.

MORELL. Yes, I know. I answered it. I cant go.

CANDIDA. But why, James?

MORELL [*almost fiercely*]. Because I dont choose. These people forget that I am a man: they think I am talking machine to be turned on for their pleasure every evening of my life. May I not have one night at home, with my wife, and my friends?

[*They are all amazed at this outburst, except* EUGENE. *His expression remains unchanged.*]

CANDIDA. Oh, James, you musnt mind what I said about that. And if you dont go youll have an attack of bad conscience to-morrow.

LEXY [*intimidated, but urgent*]. I know, of course, that they make the most unreasonable demands on you. But they have been telegraphing all over the place for another speaker; and they can get nobody but the President of the Agnostic League.

MORELL [*promptly*]. Well, an excellent man. What better do they want?

LEXY. But he always insists so powerfully on the divorce of Socialism from Christianity. He will undo all the good we have been doing. Of course you know best; but—[*He shrugs his shoulders and wanders to the hearth beside* BURGESS.]

CANDIDA [*coaxingly*]. Oh, do go, James. We'll all go.

BURGESS [*grumblingly*]. Look 'ere, Candy! I say! Let's stay at home by the fire, comfortable. He wont need to be more'n a couple-o-hour away.

CANDIDA. Youll be just as comfortable at the meeting. We'll all sit on the platform and be great people.

EUGENE [*terrified*]. Oh please dont let us go on the platform. No: everyone will stare at us: I couldnt. I'll sit at the back of the room.

CANDIDA. Dont be afraid. Theyll be too busy looking at James to notice you.

MORELL. Prossy's complaint, Candida! Eh?

CANDIDA [*gaily*]. Yes: Prossy's complaint.

BURGESS [*mystified*]. Prossy's complaint! What are you talkin about, James?

MORELL [*not heeding him, rises; goes to the door; and holds it open, calling in a commanding tone*]. Miss Garnett.

PROSERPINE [*in the distance*]. Yes, Mr Morell. Coming.

[*They all wait, except* BURGESS, *who turns stealthily to* LEXY.]

BURGESS. Listen ere, Mr Mill. Whats Prossy's complaint? Whats wrong with er?

LEXY [*confidentially*]. Well, I dont exactly know; but she spoke very strangely to me this morning. I'm afraid she's a little out of her mind sometimes.

BURGESS [*overwhelmed*]. Why, it must be catchin! Four in the same ouse!

PROSERPINE [*appearing on the threshold*]. What is it, Mr Morell?

MORELL. Telegraph to the Guild of St Matthew that I am coming.

PROSERPINE [*surprised*]. Dont they expect you?

MORELL [*peremptorily*]. Do as I tell you.

> [PROSERPINE, *frightened, sits down at her typewriter, and obeys.*
> MORELL, *now unaccountably resolute and forceful, goes across to*
> BURGESS. CANDIDA *watches his movements with growing wonder and*
> *misgiving.*]

MORELL. Burgess: you dont want to come.

BURGESS. Oh, dont put it like that, James. It's only that it aint Sunday, you know.

MORELL. I'm sorry. I thought you might like to be introduced to the chairman. He's on the Works Committee of the County Council, and has some influence in the matter of contracts.

> [BURGESS *wakes up at once.*]

Youll come?

BURGESS [*with enthusiasm*]. Cawrse I'll come, James. Aint it awlus a pleasure to ear you!

MORELL [*turning to* PROSSY]. I shall want you to take some notes at the meeting, Miss Garnett, if you have no other engagement.

> [*She nods, afraid to speak.*]

You are coming, Lexy, I suppose?

LEXY. Certainly.

CANDIDA. We're all coming, James.

MORELL. No: you are not coming; and Eugene is not coming. You will stay here and entertain him—to celebrate your return home.

> [EUGENE *rises, breathless.*]

CANDIDA. But, James—

MORELL [*authoritatively*]. I insist. You do not want to come; and he does not want to come.

> [CANDIDA *is about to protest.*]

Oh, dont concern yourselves: I shall have plenty of people without you: your chairs will be wanted by unconverted people who have never heard me before.

CANDIDA [*troubled*]. Eugene: wouldnt you like to come?

MORELL. I should be afraid to let myself go before Eugene: he is so critical of sermons. [*Looking at him.*] He knows I am afraid of him: he told me as much this morning. Well, I shall shew him how much afraid I am by leaving him here in your custody, Candida.

MARCHBANKS [*to himself, with vivid feeling*]. Thats brave. Thats beautiful.

CANDIDA [*with anxious misgiving*]. But—but— Is anything the matter, James? [*Greatly troubled.*] I cant understand—

MORELL [*taking her tenderly in his arms and kissing her on the forehead*]. Ah, I thought it was *I* who couldnt understand, dear.

Act Three

Past ten in the evening. The curtains are drawn, and the lamps lighted.
The typewriter is in its case: the large table has been cleared and tidied:
everything indicates that the day's work is over.

Candida and Marchbanks are sitting by the fire. The reading lamp is
on the mantelshelf above Marchbanks, who is in the small chair, reading
aloud. A little pile of manuscripts and a couple of volumes of poetry are
on the carpet beside him. Candida is in the easy chair. The poker, a light
brass one, is upright in her hand. Leaning back and looking intently at
the point of it, with her feet stretched towards the blaze, she is in a waking
dream, miles away from her surroundings and completely oblivious of
EUGENE.

MARCHBANKS [*breaking off in his recitation*]. Every poet that ever lived
has put that thought into a sonnet. He must: he cant help it.
   [*He looks to her for assent, and notices her absorption in the poker.*]
Havnt you been listening?
   [*No response.*]
Mrs Morell!
CANDIDA [*starting*]. Eh?
MARCHBANKS. Havnt you been listening?
CANDIDA [*with a guilty excess of politeness*]. Oh yes. It's very nice. Go
on, Eugene. I'm longing to hear what happens to the angel.
MARCHBANKS [*letting the manuscript drop from his hand to the floor*]. I
beg your pardon for boring you.
CANDIDA. But you are not boring me, I assure you. Please go on. Do,
Eugene.
MARCHBANKS. I finished the poem about the angel quarter of an hour
ago. Ive read you several things since.
CANDIDA [*remorsefully*]. I'm so sorry, Eugene. I think the poker must
have hypnotized me. [*She puts it down.*]
MARCHBANKS. It made me horribly uneasy.
CANDIDA. Why didnt you tell me? I'd have put it down at once.
MARCHBANKS. I was afraid of making you uneasy too. It looked as if
it were a weapon. If I were a hero of old I should have laid my
drawn sword between us. If Morell had come in he would have
thought you had taken up the poker because there was no sword
between us.
CANDIDA [*wondering*]. What? [*With a puzzled glance at him.*] I cant
quite follow that. Those sonnets of yours have perfectly addled me.
Why should there be a sword between us?
MARCHBANKS [*evasively*]. Oh, never mind. [*He stoops to pick up the
manuscript.*]
CANDIDA. Put that down again, Eugene. There are limits to my appetite

for poetry: even your poetry. Youve been reading to me for more than two hours, ever since James went out. I want to talk.

MARCHBANKS [*rising, scared*]. No: I mustnt talk. [*He looks round him in his lost way, and adds, suddenly*] I think I'll go out and take a walk in the park. [*He makes for the door.*]

CANDIDA. Nonsense: it's closed long ago. Come and sit down on the hearth-rug, and talk moonshine as you usually do. I want to be amused. Dont you want to?

MARCHBANKS [*half in terror, half enraptured*]. Yes.

CANDIDA. Then come along. [*She moves her chair back a little to make room.*]

[*He hesitates; then timidly stretches himself on the hearth-rug, face upwards, and throws back his head across her knees, looking up at her.*]

MARCHBANKS. Oh, Ive been so miserable all the evening, because I was doing right. Now I'm doing wrong; and I'm happy.

CANDIDA [*tenderly amused at him*]. Yes: I'm sure you feel a great grown-up wicked deceiver. Quite proud of yourself, arnt you?

MARCHBANKS [*raising his head quickly and turning a little to look round at her*]. Take care. I'm ever so much older than you, if you only knew. [*He turns quite over on his knees, with his hands clasped and his arms on her lap, and speaks with growing impulse, his blood beginning to stir.*] May I say some wicked things to you?

CANDIDA [*without the least fear or coldness, and with perfect respect for his passion, but with a touch of her wise-hearted maternal humor*]. No. But you may say anything you really and truly feel. Anything at all, no matter what it is. I am not afraid, so long as it is your real self that speaks, and not a mere attitude: a gallant attitude, or a wicked attitude, or even a poetic attitude. I put you on your honor and truth. Now say whatever you want to.

MARCHBANKS [*the eager expression vanishing utterly from his lips and nostrils as his eyes light up with pathetic spirituality*]. Oh, now I cant say anything: all the words I know belong to some attitude or other— all except one.

CANDIDA. What one is that?

MARCHBANKS [*softly, losing himself in the music of the name*]. Candida, Candida, Candida, Candida, Candida. I must say that now, because you have put me on my honor and truth; and I never think or feel Mrs Morell: it is always Candida.

CANDIDA. Of course. And what have you to say to Candida?

MARCHBANKS. Nothing but to repeat your name a thousand times. Dont you feel that every time is a prayer to you?

CANDIDA. Doesnt it make you happy to be able to pray?

MARCHBANKS. Yes, very happy.

CANDIDA. Well, that happiness is the answer to your prayer. Do you want anything more?

MARCHBANKS. No: I have come into heaven, where want is unknown.

[MORELL *comes in. He halts on the threshold, and takes in the scene at a glance.*]

MORELL [*grave and self-contained*]. I hope I dont disturb you.

[CANDIDA *starts up violently, but without the smallest embarrassment, laughing at herself.* EUGENE, *capsized by her sudden movement, recovers himself without rising, and sits on the rug hugging his ankles, also quite unembarrassed.*]

CANDIDA. Oh, James, how you startled me! I was so taken up with Eugene that I didnt hear your latchkey. How did the meeting go off? Did you speak well?

MORELL. I have never spoken better in my life.

CANDIDA. That was first rate! How much was the collection?

MORELL. I forgot to ask.

CANDIDA [*to* EUGENE]. He must have spoken splendidly, or he would never have forgotten that. [*To* MORELL.] Where are all the others?

MORELL. They left long before I could get away: I thought I should never escape. I believe they are having supper somewhere.

CANDIDA [*in her domestic business tone*]. Oh, in that case, Maria may go to bed. I'll tell her. [*She goes out to the kitchen.*]

MORELL [*looking sternly down at* MARCHBANKS]. Well?

MARCHBANKS [*squatting grotesquely on the hearth-rug, and actually at ease with* MORELL: *even impishly humorous*]. Well?

MORELL. Have you anything to tell me?

MARCHBANKS. Only that I have been making a fool of myself here in private whilst you have been making a fool of yourself in public.

MORELL. Hardly in the same way, I think.

MARCHBANKS [*eagerly, scrambling up*]. The very, very very same way. I have been playing the Good Man. Just like you. When you began your heroics about leaving me here with Candida—

MORELL [*involuntarily*]. Candida!

MARCHBANKS. Oh yes: Ive got that far. But dont be afraid. Heroics are infectious: I caught the disease from you. I swore not to say a word in your absence that I would not have said a month ago in your presence.

MORELL. Did you keep your oath?

MARCHBANKS [*suddenly perching himself on the back of the easy chair*]. It kept itself somehow until about ten minutes ago. Up to that moment I went on desperately reading to her—reading my own poems—anybody's poems—to stave off a conversation. I was standing outside the gate of Heaven, and refusing to go in. Oh, you cant think how heroic it was, and how uncomfortable! Then—

MORELL [*steadily controlling his suspense*]. Then?

MARCHBANKS [*prosaically slipping down into a quite ordinary attitude on the seat of the chair*]. Then she couldnt bear being read to any longer.

MORELL. And you approached the gate of Heaven at last?

MARCHBANKS. Yes.

MORELL. Well? [*Fiercely.*] Speak, man: have you no feeling for me?

MARCHBANKS [*softly and musically*]. Then she became an angel; and there was a flaming sword that turned every way, so that I couldnt go in; for I saw that that gate was really the gate of Hell.

MORELL [*triumphantly*]. She repulsed you!

MARCHBANKS [*rising in wild scorn*]. No, you fool: if she had done that I should never have seen that I was in Heaven already. Repulsed me! You think that would have saved us! virtuous indignation! Oh, you are not worthy to live in the same world with her. [*He turns away contemptuously to the other side of the room.*]

MORELL [*who has watched him quietly without changing his place*]. Do you think you make yourself more worthy by reviling me, Eugene?

MARCHBANKS. Here endeth the thousand and first lesson. Morell: I dont think much of your preaching after all: I believe I could do it better myself. The man I want to meet is the man that Candida married.

MORELL. The man that—? Do you mean me?

MARCHBANKS. I dont mean the Reverend James Mavor Morell, moralist and windbag. I mean the real man that the Reverend James must have hidden somewhere inside his black coat: the man that Candida loved. You cant make a woman like Candida love you by merely buttoning your collar at the back instead of in front.

MORELL [*boldly and steadily*]. When Candida promised to marry me, I was the same moralist and windbag you now see. I wore my black coat; and my collar was buttoned behind instead of in front. Do you think she would have loved me any the better for being insincere in my profession?

MARCHBANKS [*on the sofa, hugging his ankles*]. Oh, she forgave you, just as she forgives me for being a coward, and a weakling, and what you call a snivelling little whelp and all the rest of it. [*Dreamily.*] A woman like that has divine insight: she loves our souls, and not our follies and vanities and illusions, nor our collars and coats, nor any other of the rags and tatters we are rolled up in. [*He reflects on this for an instant; then turns intently to question* MORELL.] What I want to know is how you got past the flaming sword that stopped me.

MORELL. Perhaps because I was not interrupted at the end of ten minutes.

MARCHBANKS [*taken aback*]. What!

MORELL. Man can climb to the highest summits; but he cannot dwell there long.

MARCHBANKS [*springing up*]. It's false: there can he dwell for ever, and there only. It's in the other moments that he can find no rest, no sense of the silent glory of life. Where would you have me spend my moments, if not on the summits?

MORELL. In the scullery, slicing onions and filling lamps.

MARCHBANKS. Or in the pulpit, scrubbing cheap earthenware souls?

MORELL. Yes, that too. It was there that I earned my golden moment, and the right, in that moment, to ask her to love me. *I* did not take the moment on credit; nor did I use it to steal another man's happiness.

MARCHBANKS [*rather disgustedly, trotting back towards the fireplace*]. I have no doubt you conducted the transaction as honestly as if you were buying a pound of cheese.[*He stops on the brink of the hearth-rug, and adds, thoughtfully, to himself, with his back turned to* MORELL.] *I* could only go to her as a beggar.

MORELL [*starting*]. A beggar dying of cold! asking for her shawl!

MARCHBANKS [*turning, surprised*]. Thank you for touching up my poetry. Yes, if you like: a beggar dying of cold, asking for her shawl.

MORELL [*excitedly*]. And she refused. Shall I tell you why she refused? I can tell you, on her own authority. It was because of—

MARCHBANKS. She didnt refuse.

MORELL. Not!

MARCHBANKS. She offered me all I chose to ask for: her shawl, her wings, the wreath of stars on her head, the lilies in her hand, the crescent moon beneath her feet—

MORELL [*seizing him*]. Out with the truth, man: my wife is my wife: I want no more of your poetic fripperies. I know well that if I have lost her love and you have gained it, no law will bind her.

MARCHBANKS [*quaintly, without fear or resistance*]. Catch me by the shirt collar, Morell: she will arrange it for me afterwards as she did this morning. [*With quiet rapture.*] I shall feel her hands touch me.

MORELL. You young imp, do you know how dangerous it is to say that to me? Or [*with a sudden misgiving*] has something made you brave?

MARCHBANKS. I'm not afraid now. I disliked you before: that was why I shrank from your touch. But I saw today—when she tortured you—that you love her. Since then I have been your friend: you may strangle me if you like.

MORELL [*releasing him*]. Eugene: if that is not a heartless lie—if you have a spark of human feeling left in you—will you tell me what has happened during my absence?

MARCHBANKS. What happened! Why, the flaming sword

[MORELL *stamps with impatience.*]

—Well, in plain prose, I loved her so exquisitely that I wanted nothing more than the happiness of being in such love. And before I had time to come down from the highest summits, you came in.

MORELL [*suffering deeply*]. So it is still unsettled. Still the misery of doubt.

MARCHBANKS. Misery! I am the happiest of men. I desire nothing now but her happiness. [*In a passion of sentiment.*] Oh, Morell, let us both give her up. Why should she have to choose between a wretched little nervous disease like me, and a pig-headed parson like you? Let us go on a pilgrimage, you to the east and I to the west, in search of a worthy lover for her: some beautiful archangel with purple wings—

MORELL. Some fiddlestick! Oh, if she is mad enough to leave me for you, who will protect her? who will help her? who will work for her? who will be a father to her children? [*He sits down distractedly on the sofa, with his elbows on his knees and his head propped on his clenched fists.*]

MARCHBANKS [*snapping his fingers wildly*]. She does not ask those silly questions. It is she who wants somebody to protect, to help, to work for: somebody to give her children to protect, to help and to work for. Some grown up man who has become as a little child again. Oh, you fool, you fool, you triple fool! I am the man, Morell: I am the man. [*He dances about excitedly, crying*] You dont understand what a woman is. Send for her, Morell: send for her and let her choose between—

[*The door opens and* CANDIDA *enters. He stops as if petrified*].

CANDIDA [*amazed, on the threshold*]. What on earth are you at, Eugene?

MARCHBANKS [*oddly*]. James and I are having a preaching match; and he is getting the worst of it.

[CANDIDA *looks quickly round at* MORELL. *Seeing that he is distressed, she hurries down to him, greatly vexed.*]

CANDIDA. You have been annoying him. Now I wont have it, Eugene: do you hear? [*She puts her hand on* MORELL's *shoulder, and quite forgets her wifely tact in her anger.*] My boy shall not be worried: I will protect him.

MORELL [*rising proudly*]. Protect!

CANDIDA [*not heeding him: to* EUGENE]. What have you been saying?

MARCHBANKS [*appalled*]. Nothing. I—

CANDIDA. Eugene! Nothing?

MARCHBANKS [*piteously*]. I mean—I—I'm very sorry. I wont do it again: indeed I wont. I'll let him alone.

MORELL [*indignantly, with an aggressive movement towards* EUGENE]. Let me alone! You young—

CANDIDA [*stopping him*]. Sh!—no: let me deal with him, James.

MARCHBANKS. Oh, youre not angry with me, are you?

CANDIDA [*severely*]. Yes I am: very angry. I have a good mind to pack you out of the house.

MORELL [*taken aback by* CANDIDA's *vigor, and by no means relishing the position of being rescued by her from another man*]. Gently, Candida, gently. I am able to take care of myself.

CANDIDA [*petting him*]. Yes, dear: of course you are. But you mustnt be annoyed and made miserable.

MARCHBANKS [*almost in tears, turning to the door*]. I'll go.

CANDIDA. Oh, you neednt go: I cant turn you out at this time of night. [*Vehemently.*] Shame on you! For shame!

MARCHBANKS [*desperately*]. But what have I done?

CANDIDA. I know what you have done: as well as if I had been here all the time. Oh, it was unworthy! You are like a child: you cannot hold your tongue.

MARCHBANKS. I would die ten times over sooner than give you a moment's pain.

CANDIDA [*with infinite contempt for this puerility*]. Much good your dying would do me!

MORELL. Candida, my dear: this altercation is hardly quite seemly. It is a matter between two men; and I am the right person to settle it.

CANDIDA. Two men! Do you call that a man? [*To* EUGENE.] You bad boy!

MARCHBANKS [*gathering a whimsically affectionate courage from the scolding*]. If I am to be scolded like a boy, I must make a boy's excuse. He began it. And he's bigger than I am.

CANDIDA [*losing confidence a little as her concern for* MORELL'*s dignity takes the alarm*]. That cant be true. [*To* MORELL.] You didnt begin it, James, did you?

MORELL [*contemptuously*]. No.

MARCHBANKS [*indignant*]. Oh!

MORELL [*to* EUGENE]. You began it: this morning.

[CANDIDA, *instantly connecting this with his mysterious allusion in the afternoon to something told him by* EUGENE *in the morning, looks at him with quick suspicion.* MORELL *proceeds, with the emphasis of offended superiority.*]

But your other point is true. I am certainly the bigger of the two, and, I hope, the stronger, Candida. So you had better leave the matter in my hands.

CANDIDA [*again soothing him*]. Yes, dear; but—[*troubled*] I dont understand about this morning.

MORELL [*gently snubbing her*]. You need not understand, my dear.

CANDIDA. But James, I [*the street bell rings*]—Oh bother! Here they all come. [*She goes out to let them in.*]

MARCHBANKS [*running to* MORELL]. Oh, Morell, isnt it dreadful? She's angry with us: she hates me. What shall I do?

MORELL [*with quaint desperation, walking up and down the middle of the room*]. Eugene: my head is spinning round. I shall begin to laugh presently.

MARCHBANKS [*following him anxiously*]. No, no: she'll think Ive thrown you into hysterics. Dont laugh.

[*Boisterous voices and laughter are heard approaching.* LEXY MILL, *his eyes sparkling, and his bearing denoting unwonted elevation of spirit, enters with* BURGESS, *who is greasy and self-complacent, but has all his wits about him.* MISS GARNETT, *with her smartest hat and jacket on, follows them; but though her eyes are brighter than before, she is evidently a prey to misgiving. She places herself with her back to her typewriting table, with one hand on it to steady herself, passing the other across her forehead as if she were a little tired and giddy.* MARCHBANKS *relapses into shyness and edges away into the corner near the window, where Morell's books are.*]

LEXY [*exhilarated*]. Morell: I must congratulate you. [*Grasping his hand.*] What a noble, splendid, inspired address you gave us! You surpassed yourself.

BURGESS. So you did, James. It fair kep me awake to the lars' word. Didnt it, Miss Gornett?

PROSERPINE [*worriedly*]. Oh, I wasnt minding you: I was trying to make notes. [*She takes out her note-book, and looks at her stenography, which nearly makes her cry.*]

MORELL. Did I go too fast, Pross?

PROSERPINE. Much too fast. You know I cant do more than ninety words a minute. [*She relieves her feelings by throwing her note-book angrily beside her machine, ready for use next morning.*]

MORELL [*soothingly*]. Oh well, well, never mind, never mind, never mind. Have you all had supper?

LEXY. Mr Burgess has been kind enough to give us a really splendid supper at the Belgrave.

BURGESS [*with effusive magnanimity*]. Dont mention it, Mr Mill. [*Modestly.*] Youre arty welcome to my little treat.

PROSERPINE. We had champagne. I never tasted it before. I feel quite giddy.

MORELL [*surprised*]. A champagne supper! That was very handsome. Was it my eloquence that produced all this extravagance?

LEXY [*rhetorically*]. Your eloquence, and Mr Burgess's goodness of heart. [*With a fresh burst of exhilaration.*] And what a very fine fellow the chairman is, Morell! He came to supper with us.

MORELL [*with long drawn significance, looking at* BURGESS]. O-o-o-h! the chairman. Now I understand.

[BURGESS *covers with a deprecatory cough a lively satisfaction with his own diplomatic cunning.* LEXY *folds his arms and leans against the head of the sofa in a high-spirited attitude after nearly losing his balance.* CANDIDA *comes in with glasses, lemons, and a jug of hot water on a tray.*]

CANDIDA. Who will have some lemonade? You know our rules: total abstinence. [*She puts the tray on the table, and takes up the lemon squeezer, looking enquiringly round at them.*]

MORELL. No use, dear. Theyve all had champagne. Pross has broken her pledge.

CANDIDA [*to* PROSERPINE]. You dont mean to say youve been drinking champagne!

PROSERPINE [*stubbornly*]. Yes I do. I'm only a beer teetotaller, not a champagne teetotaller. I dont like beer. Are there any letters for me to answer, Mr Morell?

MORELL. No more to-night.

PROSERPINE. Very well. Goodnight, everybody.

LEXY [*gallantly*]. Had I not better see you home, Miss Garnett?

PROSERPINE. No thank you. I shant trust myself with anybody tonight.

I wish I hadnt taken any of that stuff. [*She takes uncertain aim at the door; dashes at it; and barely escapes without disaster.*]

BURGESS [*indignantly*]. Stuff indeed! That gurl dunno what champagne is! Pommery and Greeno at twelve and six a bottle. She took two glasses amost straight horff.

MORELL [*anxious about her*]. Go and look after her, Lexy.

LEXY [*alarmed*]. But if she should really be— Suppose she began to sing in the street, or anything of that sort.

MORELL. Just so: she may. Thats why youd better see her safely home.

CANDIDA. Do, Lexy: theres a good fellow. [*She shakes his hand and pushes him gently to the door.*]

LEXY. It's evidently my duty to go. I hope it may not be necessary. Goodnight, Mrs Morell. [*To the rest.*] Goodnight.

[*He goes.* CANDIDA *shuts the door.*]

BURGESS. He was gushin with hextra piety hisself arter two sips. People carnt drink like they huster. [*Bustling across to the hearth.*] Well, James: it's time to lock up. Mr Morchbanks: shall I ave the pleasure of your company for a bit o the way ome?

MARCHBANKS [*affrightedly*]. Yes: I'd better go.

[*He hurries towards the door; but* CANDIDA *places herself before it, barring his way.*]

CANDIDA [*with quiet authority*]. You sit down. Youre not going yet.

MARCHBANKS [*quailing*]. No: I—I didnt mean to. [*He sits down abjectly on the sofa.*]

CANDIDA. Mr Marchbanks will stay the night with us, papa.

BURGESS. Oh well, I'll say goodnight. So long, James.

[*He shakes hands with* MORELL, *and goes over to* EUGENE.]

Make em give you a nightlight by your bed, Mr Morchbanks: itll comfort you if you wake up in the night with a touch of that complaint of yores. Goodnight.

MARCHBANKS. Thank you: I will. Goodnight, Mr Burgess.

[*They shake hands.* BURGESS *goes to the door.*]

CANDIDA [*intercepting* MORELL, *who is following* BURGESS]. Stay here, dear: I'll put on papa's coat for him.

[*She goes out with* BURGESS.]

MARCHBANKS [*rising and stealing over to* MORELL]. Morell: theres going to be a terrible scene. Arnt you afraid?

MORELL. Not in the least.

MARCHBANKS. I never envied you your courage before. [*He puts his hand appealingly on* MORELL'*s forearm.*] Stand by me, wont you?

MORELL [*casting him off resolutely*]. Each for himself, Eugene. She must choose between us now.

[CANDIDA *returns.* EUGENE *creeps back to the sofa like a guilty schoolboy.*]

CANDIDA [*between them, addressing* EUGENE]. Are you sorry?

MARCHBANKS [*earnestly*]. Yes. Heartbroken.

CANDIDA. Well then, you are forgiven. Now go off to bed like a good little boy: I want to talk to James about you.

MARCHBANKS [*rising in great consternation*]. Oh, I cant do that, Morell. I must be here. I'll not go away. Tell her.

CANDIDA [*her suspicions confirmed*]. Tell me what?

[*His eyes avoid hers furtively. She turns and mutely transfers the question to* MORELL.]

MORELL [*bracing himself for the catastrophe*]. I have nothing to tell her, except [*here his voice deepens to a measured and mournful tenderness*] that she is my greatest treasure on earth—if she is really mine.

CANDIDA [*coldly, offended by his yielding to his orator's instinct and treating her as if she were the audience at the Guild of St Matthew*]. I am sure Eugene can say no less, if that is all.

MARCHBANKS [*discouraged*]. Morell: she's laughing at us.

MORELL [*with a quick touch of temper*]. There is nothing to laugh at. Are you laughing at us, Candida?

CANDIDA [*with quiet anger*]. Eugene is very quick-witted, James. I hope I am going to laugh; but I am not sure that I am not going to be very angry.

[*She goes to the fireplace, and stands there leaning with her arms on the mantlepiece, and her foot on the fender, whilst* EUGENE *steals to* MORELL *and plucks him by the sleeve.*]

MARCHBANKS [*whispering*]. Stop, Morell. Dont let us say anything.

MORELL [*pushing* EUGENE *away without deigning to look at him*]. I hope you dont mean that as a threat, Candida.

CANDIDA [*with emphatic warning*]. Take care, James. Eugene: I asked you to go. Are you going?

MORELL [*putting his foot down*]. He shall not go. I wish him to remain.

MARCHBANKS. I'll go. I'll do whatever you want. [*He turns to the door.*]

CANDIDA. Stop! [*He obeys.*] Didnt you hear James say he wished you to stay? James is master here. Dont you know that?

MARCHBANKS [*flushing with a young poet's rage against tyranny*]. By what right is he master?

CANDIDA [*quietly*]. Tell him, James.

MORELL [*taken aback*]. My dear: I dont know of any right that makes me master. I assert no such right.

CANDIDA [*with infinite reproach*]. You dont know! Oh, James! James! [*To* EUGENE, *musingly.*] I wonder do you understand, Eugene!

[*He shakes his head helplessly, not daring to look at her.*]

No: youre too young. Well, I give you leave to stay: to stay and learn. [*She comes away from the hearth and places herself between them.*] Now, James! whats the matter? Come: tell me.

MARCHBANKS [*whispering tremulously across to him*]. Dont.

CANDIDA. Come. Out with it!

MORELL [*slowly*]. I meant to prepare your mind carefully, Candida, so as to prevent misunderstanding.

CANDIDA. Yes, dear: I am sure you did. But never mind: I shant misunderstand.

MORELL. Well—er— [*He hesitates, unable to find the long explanation which he supposed to be available.*]

CANDIDA. Well?

MORELL [*blurting it out baldly*]. Eugene declares that you are in love with him.

MARCHBANKS [*frantically*]. No, no, no, no, never. I did not, Mrs Morell: it's not true. I said I loved you. I said I understood you, and that he couldnt. And it was not after what passed there before the fire that I spoke: it was not, on my word. It was this morning.

CANDIDA [*enlightened*]. This morning!

MARCHBANKS. Yes. [*He looks at her, pleading for credence, and then adds simply.*] That was what was the matter with my collar.

CANDIDA. Your collar? [*Suddenly taking in his meaning she turns to MORELL, shocked.*] Oh, James: did you—[*she stops*]?

MORELL [*ashamed*]. You know, Candida, that I have a temper to struggle with. And he said [*shuddering*] that you despised me in your heart.

CANDIDA [*turning quickly on EUGENE*]. Did you say that?

MARCHBANKS [*terrified*]. No.

CANDIDA [*almost fiercely*]. Then James has just told me a falsehood. Is that what you mean?

MARCHBANKS. No, no: I—I—[*desperately*] it was David's wife. And it wasnt at home: it was when she saw him dancing before all the people.

MORELL [*taking the cue with a debater's adroitness*]. Dancing before all the people, Candida; and thinking he was moving their hearts by his mission when they were only suffering from—Prossy's complaint. [*She is about to protest: he raises his hand to silence her.*] Dont try to look indignant, Candida—

CANDIDA. Try!

MORELL [*continuing*]. Eugene was right. As you told me a few hours after, he is always right. He said nothing that you did not say far better yourself. He is the poet, who sees everything; and I am the poor parson, who understands nothing.

CANDIDA [*remorsefully*]. Do you mind what is said by a foolish boy, because I said something like it in jest?

MORELL. That foolish boy can speak with the inspiration of a child and the cunning of a serpent. He has claimed that you belong to him and not to me; and, rightly or wrongly, I have come to fear that it may be true. I will not go about tortured with doubts and suspicions. I will not live with you and keep a secret from you. I will not suffer the intolerable degradation of jealousy. We have agreed—he and I— that you shall choose between us now. I await your decision.

CANDIDA [*slowly recoiling a step, her heart hardened by his rhetoric in spite of the sincere feeling behind it*]. Oh! I am to choose, am I? I suppose it is quite settled that I must belong to one or the other.

MORELL [*firmly*]. Quite. You must choose definitely.

MARCHBANKS [*anxiously*]. Morell: you dont understand. She means that she belongs to herself.

CANDIDA [*turning on him*]. I mean that, and a good deal more, Master Eugene, as you will both find out presently. And pray, my lords and masters, what have you to offer for my choice? I am up for auction, it seems. What do you bid, James?

MORELL [*reproachfully*]. Cand— [*He breaks down: his eyes and throat fill with tears: the orator becomes a wounded animal.*] I cant speak—

CANDIDA [*impulsively going to him*]. Ah, dearest—

MARCHBANKS [*in wild alarm*]. Stop: it's not fair. You musnt shew her that you suffer, Morell. I am on the rack too; but I am not crying.

MORELL [*rallying all his forces*]. Yes: you are right. It is not for pity that I am bidding.

[*He disengages himself from* CANDIDA.]

CANDIDA [*retreating, chilled*]. I beg your pardon, James: I did not mean to touch you. I am waiting to hear your bid.

MORELL [*with proud humility*]. I have nothing to offer you but my strength for your defence, my honesty for your surety, my ability and industry for your livelihood, and my authority and position for your dignity. That is all it becomes a man to offer to a woman.

CANDIDA [*quite quietly*]. And you, Eugene? What do you offer?

MARCHBANKS. My weakness. My desolation. My heart's need.

CANDIDA [*impressed*]. Thats a good bid, Eugene. Now I know how to make my choice.

[*She pauses and looks curiously from one to the other, as if weighing them.* MORELL, *whose lofty confidence has changed into heartbreaking dread at* EUGENE's *bid, loses all power of concealing his anxiety.* EUGENE, *strung to the highest tension, does not move a muscle.*]

MORELL [*in a suffocated voice: the appeal bursting from the depths of his anguish*]. Candida!

MARCHBANKS [*aside, in a flash of contempt*]. Coward!

CANDIDA [*significantly*]. I give myself to the weaker of the two.

[EUGENE *divines her meaning at once: his face whitens like steel in a furnace.*]

MORELL [*bowing his head with the calm of collapse*]. I accept your sentence, Candida.

CANDIDA. Do you understand, Eugene?

MARCHBANKS. Oh, I feel I'm lost. He cannot bear the burden.

MORELL [*incredulously, raising his head and voice with comic abruptness*]. Do you mean me, Candida?

CANDIDA [*smiling a little*]. Let us sit and talk comfortably over it like three friends. [*To* MORELL.] Sit down, dear.

[MORELL, *quite lost, takes the chair from the fireside: the children's chair.*]

Bring me that chair, Eugene.

[*She indicates the easy chair. He fetches it silently, even with some-thing like cold strength, and places it next* MORELL, *a little behind him. She sits down. He takes the visitor's chair himself, and sits, inscrutable. When they are all settled she begins, throwing a spell of quietness on them by her calm, sane, tender tone.*]

You remember what you told me about yourself, Eugene: how nobody has cared for you since your old nurse died: how those clever fashionable sisters and successful brothers of yours were your mother's and father's pets: how miserable you were at Eton: how your father is trying to starve you into returning to Oxford: how you have had to live without comfort or welcome or refuge: always lonely, and nearly always disliked and misunderstood, poor boy!

MARCHBANKS [*faithful to the nobility of his lot*]. I had my books. I had Nature. And at last I met you.

CANDIDA. Never mind that just at present. Now I want you to look at this other boy here: my boy! spoiled from his cradle. We go once a fortnight to see his parents. You should come with us, Eugene, to see the pictures of the hero of that household. James as a baby! the most wonderful of all babies. James holding his first school prize, won at the ripe age of eight! James as the captain of his eleven! James in his first frock coat! James under all sorts of glorious circumstances! You know how strong he is (I hope he didnt hurt you): how clever he is: how happy. [*With deepening gravity.*] Ask James's mother and his three sisters what it cost to save James the trouble of doing anything but be strong and clever and happy. Ask me what it costs to be James's mother and three sisters and wife and mother to his children all in one. Ask Prossy and Maria how troublesome the house is even when we have no visitors to help us to slice the onions. Ask the tradesmen who want to worry James and spoil his beautiful sermons who it is that puts them off. When there is money to give, he gives it: when there is money to refuse, I refuse it. I build a castle of comfort and indulgence and love for him, and stand sentinel always to keep little vulgar cares out. I make him master here, though he does not know it, and could not tell you a moment ago how it came to be so. [*With sweet irony.*] And when he thought I might go away with you, his only anxiety was—what should become of me! And to tempt me to stay he offered me [*leaning forward to stroke his hair caressingly at each phrase*] his strength for my defence! his industry for my livelihood! his dignity for my position! his—[*relenting*] ah, I am mixing up your beautiful cadences and spoiling them, am I not, darling?

[*She lays her cheek fondly against his.*]

MORELL [*quite overcome, kneeling beside her chair and embracing her with boyish ingenuousness*]. It's all true, every word. What I am you have made me with the labor of your hands and the love of your heart. You are my wife, my mother, my sisters: you are the sum of all loving care to me.

CANDIDA [*in his arms, smiling, to* EUGENE]. Am I your mother and sisters to you, Eugene?

MARCHBANKS [*rising with a fierce gesture of disgust*]. Ah, never. Out, then, into the night with me!

CANDIDA [*rising quickly*]. You are not going like that, Eugene?

MARCHBANKS [*with the ring of a man's voice—no longer a boy's—in the words*]. I know the hour when it strikes. I am impatient to do what must be done.

MORELL [*who has also risen*]. Candida: dont let him do anything rash.

CANDIDA [*confident, smiling at* EUGENE]. Oh, there is no fear. He has learnt to live without happiness.

MARCHBANKS. I no longer desire happiness: life is nobler than that. Parson James: I give you my happiness with both hands: I love you because you have filled the heart of the woman I loved. Goodbye. [*He goes towards the door.*]

CANDIDA. One last word.

[*He stops, but without turning to her. She goes to him.*]

How old are you, Eugene?

MARCHBANKS. As old as the world now. This morning I was eighteen.

CANDIDA. Eighteen! Will you, for my sake, make a little poem out of the two sentences I am going to say to you? And will you promise to repeat it to yourself whenever you think of me?

MARCHBANKS [*without moving*]. Say the sentences.

CANDIDA. When I am thirty, she will be forty-five. When I am sixty, she will be seventy-five.

MARCHBANKS [*turning to her*]. In a hundred years, we shall be the same age. But I have a better secret than that in my heart. Let me go now. The night outside grows impatient.

CANDIDA. Goodbye.

[*She takes his face in her hands; and as he divines her intention and falls on his knees, she kisses his forehead. Then he flies out into the night. She turns to* MORELL, *holding out her arms to him.*]

Ah, James!

They embrace. But they do not know the secret in the poet's heart.

AUGUST STRINDBERG

The Ghost Sonata†

Characters

THE OLD MAN
THE STUDENT
THE MILKMAID, *a vision*
THE CARETAKER'S WIFE
THE DEAD MAN, *a Consul*
THE DARK LADY, *daughter to the* CARETAKER'S WIFE *by the* DEAD MAN
THE COLONEL
THE MUMMY, *wife to the* COLONEL
THE "COLONEL'S DAUGHTER", *in reality the* OLD MAN'S *daughter*
THE NOBLEMAN, *known as* BARON SKANSKORG, *engaged to the* CARETAKER'S
    DAUGHTER
JOHANSSON, *servant to the* OLD MAN
BENGTSSON, *footman to the* COLONEL
THE FIANCÉE, *a white-haired old lady, formerly engaged to the* OLD MAN
THE COOK
A MAIDSERVANT
BEGGARS

*The ground floor and first floor of a fashionable house. Only a corner of
it is visible. The ground floor ends in a circular drawing-room, the first
floor in a balcony with a flagstaff.*

*As the blinds are raised in the drawing-room they reveal through the
open windows a white marble statue of a young woman, surrounded by
palms which are bathed in bright sunlight. In the window to the left
stand vases of hyacinths, blue, white and pink.*

† From *The Plays of Strindberg*, Volume I, by
August Strindberg, translated by Michael Meyer.
Copyright © 1964 by Michael Meyer. Reprinted
by permission of Random House, Inc. and David
Higham Associates Limited. Strindberg insisted
that the play be called not *The Spook Sonata*, but
The Ghost Sonata after his favorite Beethoven sonata, 17, opus 31, number 2, "The Tempest,"
which he himself called "the Ghost Sonata." He
suggested, though he did not use, the subtitle
"Kama-loka," a name the Theosophists gave to a
dream world where people wandered before they
achieved peace in death. (For this note and many
that follow, I am indebted to August Strindberg,
The Chamber Plays, trans. Evert Sprinchorn, Seabury Quinn, Jr., and Kenneth Petersen [Minne-
apolis, 1962] xxii–xxxiv. 225–28.)

Over the railing of the balcony, at the corner of the first floor, hangs a blue silk eiderdown, with two white pillows. The windows to the left are draped with white sheets. It is a clear Sunday morning.

Downstage, in front of the house, is a green bench. Downstage right, a public fountain. To the left is a pillar, with posters pasted round it.

Upstage left is the front entrance to the house. Through it we can see the staircase, which is of white marble, with banisters of mahogany and brass. On the pavement outside, laurels in tubs stand on either side of the door.

The corner of the house which contains the round drawing-room also looks on to a side street which leads upstage.

To the left of the entrance, on the ground floor, is a window with a mirror outside it set at an angle.

As the curtain rises, the bells of several churches can be heard pealing in the distance.

[*The doors of the house are open. A* WOMAN *dressed in dark clothes is standing motionless on the staircase. The* CARETAKER'S WIFE *is cleaning the front step; then she polishes the brass on the front door, and waters the laurels.*

In a wheel chair by the pillar, the OLD MAN[1] *sits reading the paper. He has white hair, a white beard, and spectacles.*

The MILKMAID *enters from the left, carrying bottles in a wire basket. She is in summer clothes, with brown shoes, black stockings and a white cap. She takes off the cap and hangs it on the fountain, wipes the sweat from her forehead, drinks from the cup, washes her hands and arranges her hair, using the water as a mirror.*

A steamship's bell rings, and the bass notes of an organ in a nearby church intermittently pierce the silence.

After a few moments of this silence, when the MILKMAID *has finished her toilet, the* STUDENT *enters from the left, sleepless and unshaven. He goes straight to the fountain.*]

[*Pause.*]

STUDENT. May I have the cup?

[THE MILKMAID *hugs the cup to her.*]

You've finished with it, haven't you?

[THE MILKMAID *looks at him frightened.*]

OLD MAN [*to himself*]. Who's he talking to? I can't see anyone. Is he mad? [*He continues to watch them in great amazement.*]

---

1. This character may owe something to a Stockholm merchant whose showy philanthropy annoyed Strindberg. It has also been suggested that the figure has a mythic antecedent in the biblical Jacob, who was a patriarch as well. The main points of contact are that the OLD MAN, Jacob Hummel, is also associated with a well and is also lame; he also has a wife who is put aside, also has a single daughter, also gained his birthright unfairly, and also had advance knowledge of the coming of a redeemer. For a detailed study of these and other parallels, see Stephen C. Bandy, "Strindberg's Biblical Sources for *The Ghost Sonata*" *Scandinavian Studies* 40 (1968): 200–209.

STUDENT. What are you staring at? Am I so repulsive? Oh, I see. I haven't slept all night, so of course you think I've been dissipating. [*She still stares at him with the same expression.*] Drinking punch, hm? Does my breath smell of punch? [*Her expression remains unchanged.*] I haven't shaved—oh, I know. Give me a drink of water, girl—I've earned it. [*Pause.*] Oh, very well. I suppose I'll have to tell you. I've been bandaging wounds all night, and tending the injured; I was there when the house collapsed yesterday evening. Now you know.

    [THE MILKMAID *rinses the cup and gives him a drink.*]
Thank you.

    [THE MILKMAID *does not move.*]
[*Slowly.*] Will you do me a service? [*Pause.*] It's like this. My eyes are swollen, as you can see, but I daren't touch them with my hands because I've been fingering open wounds and dead bodies. Will you take this handkerchief, moisten it in the clean water and bathe my eyes? Will you do that? Will you be my Good Samaritan?[2]

    [*She hesitates, but does as he asks.*]
Thank you, dear friend.

    [*Takes out his purse. She makes a gesture of refusal.*]
Oh—forgive me for being so thoughtless—I'm not really awake——

OLD MAN [*to the* STUDENT]. Pardon my addressing you, but did I hear you say you witnessed that accident last night? I've just been reading about it in the paper——

STUDENT. Oh, have they got hold of it already?

OLD MAN. Yes, the whole story's here. And your photograph; but they regret they were unable to discover the name of the brilliant young student who——

STUDENT [*looks at the paper*]. Really? That's me! Well, well.

OLD MAN. Whom were you talking to just now?

STUDENT. Didn't you see her?

    [*Pause.*]

OLD MAN. Would it be impertinent of me to ask—to be allowed the honour of knowing—your name?

STUDENT. What'd be the point? I don't want any publicity; once you become famous people start saying foul things about you. Depreciation's become a fine art nowadays. Anyway, I'm not looking for any reward——

OLD MAN. You are rich?

STUDENT. Quite the contrary. I'm ab-absolutely penniless.

OLD MAN. Wait a moment! I seem to know that voice. When I was young I had a friend who couldn't say absinthe, he always said ab-absinthe. He's the only person I've ever come across with that par-

---

2. A possible allusion to the woman of Samaria who gave Christ water to drink (John 4.7.30).

ticular stammer. And now you! I wonder if you could possibly be any relation to a wholesale merchant of the name of Arkenholz?[3]

STUDENT. He was my father.

OLD MAN. The ways of fate are strange. I saw you once, when you were a little child—under very painful circumstances——

STUDENT. Yes. I'm said to have been born into this world in the home of a bankrupt.

OLD MAN. Precisely.

STUDENT. Perhaps I may ask your name?

OLD MAN. My name is Hummel.

STUDENT. Are *you*——? Yes—now I remember——

OLD MAN. You've often heard my name mentioned by your family?

STUDENT. Yes.

OLD MAN. Mentioned, I dare say, with a certain—distaste?

[THE STUDENT *is silent.*]

Oh, yes—I can imagine! I've no doubt they told you it was I who ruined your father? People who ruin themselves by idiotic speculation always swear they've been ruined by the one man they failed to fool. [*Pause.*] The truth of the matter is that your father swindled me out of seventeen thousand crowns—a sum which at the time represented my entire savings.

STUDENT. It's strange how a story can exist in two such different versions.

OLD MAN. You think I'm not telling you the truth.

STUDENT. What else am I to think? My father never lied?

OLD MAN. True, true. One's own father never lies. But I am a father, too; so——

STUDENT. What are you trying to tell me?

OLD MAN. I saved your father from complete destitution, and he rewarded me with hatred—the dreadful hatred of a man tied to another by the knot of gratitude. He taught his family to spit on my name.

STUDENT. Perhaps you made him ungrateful by poisoning your charity with unnecessary humiliations?

OLD MAN. All charity is humiliating, my dear sir.

STUDENT. What do you want from me?

OLD MAN. Oh, not money. If you would just perform one or two trivial services for me, I shall think myself well repaid. I am, as you see, a cripple. Some say it is my own fault, others blame my parents. I prefer to believe that life itself is to blame; she's a cunning snarer; sidestep one pit and you walk straight into the next. Be that as it may, I cannot run up stairs or pull bell-ropes, and therefore I say to you: "Please help me."

STUDENT. What can I do?

---

3. The STUDENT's name, "Arkenholz," meaning "wood of the ark," suggests a religious hero, someone who saves others. The name could also allude to Johan Arckenholtz, a Swedish mystic who flour- ished in the time of Emanuel Swedenborg (1688– 1772), the mystic thinker who exerted a profound influence on Strindberg.

OLD MAN. First of all, push my chair so that I can read these posters. I want to see what they're playing tonight at the theatre——

STUDENT [*pushes the wheel chair*]. Haven't you a servant?

OLD MAN. Yes, but he's gone on an errand. He'll be back soon. So you're a medical student, are you?

STUDENT. No, I'm studying languages. I haven't really decided yet what I'm going to be——

OLD MAN. Ah-ha! Are you any good at arithmetic?

STUDENT. I know a little.

OLD MAN. Good! Would you like a job?

STUDENT. Yes. Why not?

OLD MAN. Excellent! [*Reads one of the posters.*] They're giving a matinée this afternoon of *The Valkyrie*.[4] The Colonel'll be there with his daughter. He always sits at the end of the sixth row. I'll put you beside them. Go into that telephone kiosk, will you, and book a ticket for seat number 82 in the sixth row?

STUDENT. You want me to go to the opera this afternoon?

OLD MAN. Yes. Just do as I tell you and you'll be well rewarded. I want you to be happy, to find wealth and honour. By tomorrow your gallant deeds of rescue will be in every mouth, and your name will have a considerable market value——

STUDENT [*goes towards the telephone kiosk*]. This is a strange adventure.

OLD MAN. Are you a gambler?

STUDENT. Yes. That's my tragedy.

OLD MAN. It shall be your fortune. Go along and do your telephoning. [*He reads his newspaper. The* WOMAN *dressed in dark clothes has come out on to the pavement and is talking to the* CARETAKER'S WIFE. *The* OLD MAN *listens, but the audience cannot hear what they say. The* STUDENT *returns.*]

OLD MAN. Have you done it?

STUDENT. Yes.

OLD MAN. You see that house?

STUDENT. Yes. I've noticed it before. I was walking past it yesterday, as the sun was shining in its windows. I thought of all the beauty and luxury there must be inside, and said to my companion: "If only one had an apartment there, four floors up, with a beautiful young wife, two pretty children and a private income of 20,000 crowns a year."

OLD MAN. You said that, did you, did you indeed? Well, now; I love this house, too——

STUDENT. You speculate in houses?

OLD MAN. Mm—yes. But not the way you mean——

STUDENT. You know the people who live there?

OLD MAN. Every one of them. When you live to be as old as I am, you

---

4. An opera by Richard Wagner, written in 1854–56. The several references to it suggest parallels between the STUDENT and Siegfried as well as between Brünnhilde and the DAUGHTER, who is dressed in a riding habit and wearing boots when we first see her and whom the STUDENT tries to free.

know everyone, who their fathers were and their forefathers, and you find you're related to all of them in some way or other. I'm eighty; but no-one knows me; not really—I'm interested in people's destinies——

[*The blind in the round drawing-room is raised. The* COLONEL *is seen within, dressed in mufti. After looking at the thermometer, he turns back into the room and stops in front of the marble statue.*]

OLD MAN. Look, there's the Colonel. You'll be sitting next to him this afternoon——

STUDENT. Is that—the Colonel? I don't understand what any of this means—it's like a fairy tale——

OLD MAN. My whole life is a book of fairy tales, my dear sir; and although each tale is different, a single thread links them, there is a *leitmotif* that recurs continually——

STUDENT. Whom does the marble statue represent?

OLD MAN. His wife, of course.

STUDENT. Was she so beautiful?

OLD MAN. Mm—yes. Yes.

STUDENT. Tell me.

OLD MAN. Ah, my dear boy, we must not judge our fellow mortals. If I were to tell you that he struck her, that she left him, that she came back to him, and re-married him, and that she now sits in there in the shape of a mummy, worshipping her own statue, you would think I was mad.

STUDENT. I don't understand.

OLD MAN. I didn't suppose you would. Then we have the hyacinth window. That's where his daughter lives. She's out riding, but she'll be home soon——

STUDENT. Who is the dark lady talking to the caretaker's wife?

OLD MAN. Well, that's a bit complicated. It's to do with the dead man upstairs—up there, where you can see the white sheets——

STUDENT. Who was he?

OLD MAN. A human being, like us; but vain—vain. If you were a Sunday child, in a few minutes you would see him come out through the door to look at the consulate flag flying at half-mast. He was a consul, and loved crowns and lions, plumed hats and coloured ribbons——

STUDENT. Sunday child, you said. They say I was born on a Sunday——

OLD MAN. You don't say! Were you really? I might have guessed it from the colour of your eyes. Then you can see what others cannot see. Have you noticed that?

STUDENT. I don't know what other people can see, but sometimes— well, I'd rather not talk about it.

OLD MAN. I knew it. Come on, you can tell me. I understand about these things——

STUDENT. Well—yesterday, for example, I felt myself drawn to that quite ordinary little street in which, in a few minutes, a house was to collapse. I walked down it and stopped in front of the building—I'd never seen it before. Then I noticed a crack in the wall and heard the floorboards snapping. I ran forward and snatched hold of a child who was walking close by the wall. The next moment, the house collapsed. I was safe. But in my arms, where I thought I was holding the child, there was nothing.[5]

OLD MAN. Extraordinary. I guessed as much. But tell me something. Why were you gesticulating like that at the fountain just now? And why were you talking to yourself?

STUDENT. Didn't you see the milkmaid?

OLD MAN [recoils]. Milkmaid?

STUDENT. Yes, the one who gave me the cup?

OLD MAN. Ah-ha? So that's how it is? Well, I can't see, but I can——
[A white-haired woman sits down by the window beside the angled mirror.]

OLD MAN. Look at that old woman in the window. You see her? Good. She was my fiancée once—sixty years ago. I was twenty. Don't be afraid, she doesn't recognise me. We see each other every day, but I don't feel anything, though we once vowed to be eternally true to each other. Eternally.

STUDENT. How little your generation understood of life. We don't talk to our girls like that nowadays.

OLD MAN. Forgive us, my boy, we knew no better. But can you see that this old woman was once young and beautiful?

STUDENT. No. Yes, she has an attractive glance. Though—I can't see her eyes——
[The CARETAKER'S WIFE comes out with a basket and scatters pine twigs.][6]

OLD MAN. Ah, yes. The caretaker's wife. The dark lady over there is her daughter, by the dead man. That's how her husband got the job as caretaker. But the dark lady has a lover; a nobleman, with great expectations. He's getting divorced from his wife—she's giving him a fine house so as to be rid of him. This noble lover is son-in-law to the dead man—you can see his bedclothes being aired up there on the balcony. Complicated, isn't it?

STUDENT. Confoundedly complicated.

OLD MAN. Yes; it's a complicated house, inside and out. Yet it looks quite ordinary, doesn't it?

STUDENT. But who was the dead man, then?

OLD MAN. You asked me just now, and I told you. If you could see round the corner to the back entrance, you'd see a crowd of paupers whom he used to help. When he felt inclined——

5. A possible allusion to Buddha, who also tried to save people from the decaying old house that was the world of sensuality and religious ignorance ("The Parable of the Burning House").
6. A custom in Sweden when someone has died [Translator's note].

STUDENT. He was a kind man, then?

OLD MAN. Sometimes.

STUDENT. Not always?

OLD MAN. No. People are like that. Now, my dear sir, move my chair a little so that it gets the sun. I'm so horribly cold; when one can't move, the blood stiffens. I'm going to die soon, I know that, but there are one or two things I've got to do before I go. Take my hand, feel how cold I am.

STUDENT [*recoils*]. It's horrible!

OLD MAN. Don't leave me. I'm tired, I'm lonely, but I haven't always been like this, you know. I've an interminably long life behind me— oh, interminably long. I've made people unhappy, and people have made me unhappy—I suppose the one cancels out the other—but before I die I want to see you happy. Our destinies are wedded— through your father—and in other ways, too.

STUDENT. Let go of my hand, you're draining my strength, you're freez-ing me.[7] What do you want?

OLD MAN. Be patient. You will see and understand. Here comes the young lady.

STUDENT. The Colonel's daughter?

OLD MAN. Yes! His daughter! Look at her! Did you ever see such a masterpiece?

STUDENT. She's like the marble statue in there.

OLD MAN. That's her mother.

STUDENT. Yes—you're right! I never saw such a woman—of woman born. Happy the man who leads her to the altar and to his home!

OLD MAN. Ah—you see it, then? Not everyone appreciates her beauty. Good, good; it is written so.

[*The* DAUGHTER *enters from the left in a fashionable English riding habit, with breeches, and walks slowly, without looking at anyone, to the door. She pauses, and says a few words to the* CARETAKER'S WIFE; *then she enters the house. The* STUDENT *puts his hand to his eyes.*]

OLD MAN. Are you crying?

STUDENT. When one stands face to face with the unattainable, what else can one do but despair?

OLD MAN. I can open doors, and human hearts, if only I can find a hand to perform my will. Serve me, and you will win her.

STUDENT. Is this a pact? Must I sell my soul?

OLD MAN. Sell nothing! Listen. All my life I have taken; now I have a longing to give. To give! But no one will take anything from me. I am rich, very rich, but I have no heirs—only a rascal, who plagues the life out of me. Be a son to me, be my heir while I am still alive, enjoy life so that I can watch you enjoy it—if only from a distance.

7. The first instance of vampirism in the play.

STUDENT. What must I do?

OLD MAN. First, go and listen to *The Valkyrie*.[8]

STUDENT. I've agreed to that. What else?

OLD MAN. Tonight you shall sit in there, in the round drawing-room.

STUDENT. How shall I get in there?

OLD MAN. Through *The Valkyrie*!

STUDENT. Why have you chosen me as your medium? Did you know me before?

OLD MAN. Yes, of course. I've had my eye on you for a long time. But look up there, now—on the balcony! The maid's hoisting the flag to half mast for the consul. Now she's turning the bedclothes. You see the blue eiderdown? That was made for two to sleep under. Now it serves for one.

[*The* DAUGHTER, *who has changed her clothes, enters and waters the hyacinths in the window.*]

That's my little girl—look at her, look! She's talking to the flowers— isn't she like a blue hyacinth herself? She's giving them drink—just plain water, but they turn it into colour and perfume. Here comes the Colonel with his newspaper. He's showing her the paragraph about the accident. Now he's pointing at your photograph! She's interested; she's reading of your bravery. It's clouding over, what if it should rain? I'll be in a fine pickle stuck here if Johansson doesn't get back soon.

[*It clouds over and becomes dark. The* OLD LADY *at the mirror shuts her window.*]

Now my fiancée's shutting her window . . . seventy-nine . . . that mirror's the only one she uses, because she can't see herself in it, only the outside world, and that from two angles—but the world can see her, she hasn't thought of that. She's a beautiful old lady, though. . . .

[*The* DEAD MAN, *in his winding-sheet, emerges from the door.*]

STUDENT. God Almighty, what do I see now?

OLD MAN. What do you see?

STUDENT. Can't you see? There—in the doorway! The dead man?

OLD MAN. I see nothing. But I was expecting this. Tell me.

STUDENT. He's going out into the street. [*Pause.*] Now he's turning his head and looking at the flag.

OLD MAN. What did I tell you? Next he'll count the wreaths and read the names on the cards. Woe to those whose names he cannot find!

STUDENT. Now he's going round the corner——

OLD MAN. He's going to count the beggars at the back door. It always looks good to have the poor at one's funeral. "Accompanied to his grave by the blessings of the people." Yes, he won't have my blessing, though. Between ourselves, he was a dreadful scoundrel——

8. In *The Valkyrie* Wotan seeks to redeem himself from a life of greed and exploitation by arranging the encounter of Siegfried and Brünnhilde. Their love is to undo the curse of the Ring of Gold.

STUDENT. But charitable——

OLD MAN. A charitable scoundrel, whose only dream in life was to have a beautiful funeral. When he felt that the end was near, he fleeced the estate of 50,000 crowns. Now his daughter's living with another woman's husband, worrying whether she'll get her inheritance. He can hear everything we say, the rogue, and serve him right! Ah, here's Johansson.

[JOHANSSON *enters from the left.*]

OLD MAN. Well, what news?

[JOHANSSON *speaks inaudibly.*]

Not at home? Fool! Anything on the telegraph? Nothing. Go on. Six o'clock this evening? That's good. Special edition? With his full name? Arkenholz . . . student . . . born . . . parents . . . Excellent! Oh, I think it's starting to rain. What did he say? I see, I see. . . . Didn't want to . . . ? Well he must. . . . Here comes the noble lover. Push me round the corner, Johansson, I want to hear what the beggars are saying. Arkenholz, wait for me here; you understand? Hurry, hurry!

[JOHANSSON *pushes the wheel-chair round the corner. The* STUDENT *remains where he is, watching the* DAUGHTER, *who is now raking the earth in the flowerpots.*]

NOBLEMAN [*in mourning, addresses the* DARK LADY, *who has come out on to the pavement*]. Well, what can we do about it? We'll just have to wait.

LADY. I cannot wait.

NOBLEMAN. Is that so? Better leave town, then.

DARK LADY. I don't want to do that.

NOBLEMAN. Come over here, or they'll hear what we're saying.

[*They go over by the pillar and continue their conversation inaudibly.*]

JOHANSSON [*enters from the right and addresses the* STUDENT]. The master says please not to forget the other matter.

STUDENT. Does your master own this house?

JOHANSSON. Yes.

STUDENT. Tell me—who is he?

JOHANSSON. Ah! He's a lot of things—and he *has* been everything.

STUDENT. Is he sane?

JOHANSSON. Depends what you mean by that. All his life he says he's been looking for a Sunday child. Might not be true, of course.

STUDENT. What does he want? Is he a miser?

JOHANSSON. He wants power. All day he drives round in his chariot like the great god Thor.[9] He looks at houses, knocks them down, opens up streets, builds over public squares—and he breaks into houses, too, creeps in through windows, mucks around with people's destinies, kills his enemies, and never forgives. But would you believe it, sir,

---

9. The strongest and bravest of the Norse gods.

this little cripple used to be a Don Juan once. Always lost his women in the end, though.

STUDENT. Oh, why was that?

JOHANSSON. Well, he's crafty, you see. Got them to leave him once he'd tired of them. Now he's become a horse-thief—only he don't steal horses, he steals human beings. All sorts of ways. Me, now for example. He literally stole me from out of the hands of justice. I'd committed a—hm—little blunder, and he was the only one who knew about it. Well, instead of putting me inside he made me his slave. Which I do just for my food, which ain't the best——

STUDENT. What does he want to do in this house?

JOHANSSON. Ah, that I wouldn't like to say. It's all very complicated.

STUDENT. I think I'm getting out of this.

JOHANSSON. Look, the young lady's dropped her bracelet through the window.

[The DAUGHTER has dropped her bracelet through the open window. The STUDENT goes slowly forward, picks it up and hands it to her. She thanks him stiffly. The STUDENT goes back to JOHANSSON.]

JOHANSSON. Mm, so you're thinking of going? That's not so easy, once he's got his net over your head. He's afraid of nothing between earth and heaven—oh, yes, one thing. Or rather, one person——

STUDENT. Wait a moment. I think I know.

JOHANSSON. How can you?

STUDENT. I can guess. Is it—a little milkmaid?

JOHANSSON. He always turns his face away when he meets a milkcart. And he talks in his sleep—says he was once in Hamburg——

STUDENT. Can one believe that man?

JOHANSSON. You can believe him all right. Whatever he says.

STUDENT. What's he doing round the corner now?

JOHANSSON. Listening to the beggars. Drops a word—picks each brick out, grain by grain, till the house collapses. Figuratively speaking, of course. I'm an educated man, you know. Used to be a bookseller—once. You going now?

STUDENT. I don't want to seem ungrateful. This man saved my father once, and now he's only asking a small service of me in return——

JOHANSSON. What's that?

STUDENT. He wants me to go and see *The Valkyrie*.

JOHANSSON. Can't understand that. But he's always thinking up new ideas. Look, now he's talking to the policeman. He always keeps in with the police—uses them, implicates them in his affairs, ties their hands with false hopes and promises, and all the time pumps them for information. You'll see—before the night's over he'll have nosed his way into that round room.

STUDENT. What does he want there? What is there between him and the Colonel?

JOHANSSON. Ah—I could make a guess, but I ain't sure. You'll see for yourself when you get there.

STUDENT. I shall never be admitted there.

JOHANSSON. That depends on you. Go to *The Valkyrie*——

STUDENT. You mean, then I might——?

JOHANSSON. If that's what he's told you to do. Look at him now, riding in his war chariot! Look at the beggars drawing him in triumph! They won't get a penny for their pains—just a nod to remind them they'll get a blow-out at his funeral.

OLD MAN [*enters, standing in his wheel-chair, drawn by a beggar and followed by others*]. Hail to the noble youth who, at the peril of his own life, saved many lives in yesterday's disaster. Hail, Arkenholz!

[*The* BEGGARS *take off their caps, but do not cheer. The* DAUGHTER *waves her handkerchief at her window. The* COLONEL *stares out through his window. The* OLD WOMAN *stands up at her window. The* MAID *on the balcony hoists the flag to the top of the mast.*]

OLD MAN. Clap your hands, fellow citizens! It is Sunday, but the ass at the well and the ear in the field absolve us by their toil. Although I am not a Sunday child, yet I possess the gift of prophecy, and also the gift of healing. I once summoned a drowning girl back to life. It was in Hamburg—one Sunday morning—as it might be now——

[*The* MILKMAID *enters, seen only by the* STUDENT *and the* OLD MAN. *She stretches up her arms like a drowning person, and stares fixedly at the* OLD MAN.]

OLD MAN [*sits down and cringes in terror*]. Johansson, take me away! Quickly! Arkenholz, do not forget *The Valkyrie!*

STUDENT. What does all this mean?

JOHANSSON. We shall see. We shall see.

Inside the round drawing-room. Upstage, a cylindrical, white-tiled stove, with mirrors in it. A pendulum clock; candelabra. On the right is an entrance hall, with a perspective of a green room containing mahogany furniture. On the left stands the statue, shadowed by palms. There is a curtain that can be drawn to conceal it. Upstage left is the door to the hyacinth room, where the DAUGHTER *sits, reading. The* COLONEL's *back is visible as he sits writing in the green room.*

[BENGTSSON, *the* COLONEL's *footman, enters from the hall dressed in livery, with* JOHANSSON, *who is wearing tails and a white cravat.*]

BENGTSSON. Right, then. You do the serving, and I'll take their clothes. Ever done this kind of thing before?

JOHANSSON. I spend all day pushing his chariot, as you know, but I sometimes serve at parties of an evening. It's always been my dream to enter this house. Queer bunch, aren't they?

BENGTSSON. Uh-huh. Bit out of the ordinary.

JOHANSSON. Musical evening, or what?

BENGTSSON. No—just the usual spook supper. That's what we call it.

They sit round drinking tea, none of them utters a word—unless maybe the Colonel talks on his own. They nibble little cakes, all together. Sounds like rats in an attic.

JOHANSSON. Why do you call it the spook supper?

BENGTSSON. Well, they look like spooks. They've been doing this for twenty years, always the same bunch saying the same things, or keeping their traps shut for fear of making fools of themselves.

JOHANSSON. Hasn't he a wife here, too?

BENGTSSON. Yes, but she's mad. Sits in a cupboard, because her eyes can't stand the light. In here. [*Points to a door concealed[1] in the wall.*]

JOHANSSON. In there?

BENGTSSON. Yes. I told you they're a bit out of the ordinary.

JOHANSSON. What does she look like?

BENGTSSON. Like a mummy. Care to see her? [*Opens the concealed door.*] Look, there she is.

JOHANSSON. Jesus Chr——!

MUMMY [*in the voice of a small child*]. Why are you opening the door? Haven't I said it's to be kept shut!

BENGTSSON [*talking baby-talk*]. Now, now, now, now. Little girlie must be good, and she'll get a sweetie. Pretty Poll!

MUMMY [*speaks like a parrot*]. Pretty Poll! Is Jacob there? Funny man.

BENGTSSON. She thinks she's a parrot. Could be she is. [*To* MUMMY.] Now then, Polly, whistle for us.

[*The* MUMMY *whistles.*]

JOHANSSON. I've seen a good deal in my time, but never the likes of this.

BENGTSSON. Well, you know, when a house gets old it starts to decay, and when people sit for years in the same room torturing each other, they go off their nut. Madam here, now—quiet, Polly!—this mummy's been sitting here for forty years. Same husband, same furniture, same relatives, same friends. [*Shuts the door on the* MUMMY *again.*] As to what's gone on in this house—well, I shouldn't like to commit myself. See this statue? That's her when she was young.

JOHANSSON. My God! *This*—the mummy?

BENGTSSON. Yes. Enough to make you cry, isn't it? And that's not all. Somehow or other—imagination, maybe—she's become just like a parrot in all sorts of little ways. Can't stand cripples, for example. Or invalids. Can't even bear the sight of her own daughter, because she's ill——

JOHANSSON. The young lady? Is she ill?

BENGTSSON. Didn't you know?

JOHANSSON. No. What about the Colonel? What sort of a man's he?

BENGTSSON. You'll see.

JOHANSSON [*looks at the statue*]. It's horrible. How old is—Madam—now?

BENGTSSON. No-one knows. They say that when she was thirty-five she

---

1. Actually a wallpapered door, quite common in Swedish houses in the nineteenth century.

looked nineteen, and got the Colonel to believe she was. In this very
house. Know what that black Japanese screen's for, over by the chaise
longue? That's called the death screen. They put it out when someone's going to die—like in a hospital——

JOHANSSON. What a horrible house! And that young student was pining
his heart out to get in here, as though it was Paradise——

BENGTSSON. What student? Oh, him. The one who's coming this evening. The Colonel and his daughter met him at the opera. They both
fell for him. Hm! Now it's my turn to ask you a question. Who's—
er—behind him? That old boy in the wheel chair?

JOHANSSON. Yes. Yes. He coming too?

BENGTSSON. He hasn't been invited.

JOHANSSON. He'll come uninvited. If need be.

[*The* OLD MAN *appears in the entrance lobby, wearing a long, black
frock-coat and top hat. He edges silently forward on his crutches
and listens.*]

BENGTSSON. Real old robber, I've heard.

JOHANSSON. One of the worst.

BENGTSSON. Looks like Old Nick himself.

JOHANSSON. He's a magician, too. He can pass through closed
doors——

OLD MAN [*on them, seizes* JOHANSSON *by the ear*]. Villain! Beware! [*To*
BENGTSSON.] Tell the Colonel I have arrived.

BENGTSSON. But he's expecting guests——

OLD MAN. I know. But he's been half-expecting me; if not exactly looking
forward to it.

BENGTSSON. Oh, I see. What name shall I say? Mr. Hummel?

OLD MAN. Yes.

[BENGTSSON *goes through the lobby to the green room, the door of
which is then closed.*]

OLD MAN [*to* JOHANSSON]. Clear out.

[JOHANSSON *hesitates.*]

Clear out!

[JOHANSSON *goes out into the hall. The* OLD MAN *looks round the
room; stops amazed in front of the statue.*]

OLD MAN. Amelia! It's she! Yes! It's she! [*Wanders round the room,
fingering things; arranges his wig in front of the mirror; goes back to
the statue.*]

MUMMY [*from the cupboard*]. Pretty Poll!

OLD MAN [*starts*]. What was that? Is there a parrot in the room? But I
don't see one.

MUMMY. Is Jacob there?

OLD MAN. It's a ghost!

MUMMY. Jacob!

OLD MAN. I'm frightened! So this is the kind of thing they've been
concealing! [*Looks at a painting, his back towards the cupboard.*]
That's him! Him!

MUMMY [*comes up behind the* OLD MAN *and tweaks his wig*]. Funny Man! Is it Funny Man?

OLD MAN [*jumps into the air*]. God Almighty! Who is it?

MUMMY [*in an ordinary human voice*]. Is it Jacob?

OLD MAN. My name *is* Jacob——

MUMMY [*with emotion*]. And my name is Amelia.

OLD MAN. No, no, no! Oh, Lord Jesus——

MUMMY. This is how I look now. Yes. And I used to look like that. One lives and learns. I stay in the cupboard mostly, to avoid seeing people—and being seen. What are you looking for in here, Jacob?

OLD MAN. My child. Our child.

MUMMY. She's sitting over there.

OLD MAN. Where?

MUMMY. There. In the hyacinth room.

OLD MAN [*looks at the* DAUGHTER]. Yes—it's she! [*Pause.*] What does her father say? I mean—the Colonel—your husband——

MUMMY. I lost my temper with him once, and told him everything——

OLD MAN. Yes?

MUMMY. He didn't believe me. He just replied: "That's what all wives say when they want to murder their husbands." It was a beastly thing to do. His life's a lie too, though. Even his pedigree. Sometimes I look at the List of Nobility and think of myself: "She's got a false birth certificate, like a little kitchen slut. People get sent to prison for that."

OLD MAN. Lots of people lie about their birth. You did once—to me——

MUMMY. My mother made me. I wasn't to blame. But the crime which you and I committed—you were to blame for that.

OLD MAN. No it was your husband's fault; he stole my sweetheart from me. I was born like that—I can't forgive until I've punished. To me, that's a command, a duty—I still feel so.

MUMMY. What are you looking for in this house? What do you want? How did you get in? Is it my daughter—? If you touch her, you shall die.

OLD MAN. I only wish her well.

MUMMY. But you must spare her father. I mean, my husband——

OLD MAN. No!

MUMMY. Then you shall die. In this room, behind that screen——

OLD MAN. That may be. But once I have fastened my teeth into someone, I cannot let go.

MUMMY. You want her to marry the student. Why? He's nothing. No money——

OLD MAN. I shall make him rich.

MUMMY. Were you invited for this evening?

OLD MAN. No. But I shall invite myself to this ghost supper.

MUMMY. Do you know who's coming?

OLD MAN. Not for sure.

MUMMY. The baron—the one who lives upstairs—the son-in-law of the man who was buried this afternoon——

OLD MAN. Oh, the one who's getting divorced so that he can marry the caretaker's daughter! He was once your lover.

MUMMY. And the woman to whom you were once betrothed—and whom my husband seduced——

OLD MAN. A pretty bunch!

MUMMY. Oh, God! If we could die! If we could only die!

OLD MAN. Why do you all keep on meeting?

MUMMY. Our crimes bind us; our secrets, and our guilt. We have tried to break away many times. But we always come back.

OLD MAN. I think I hear the Colonel.

MUMMY. I'll go in to Adèle, then. [*Pause.*] Jacob, mind what you do. Spare him. [*Pause. She goes.*]

[*The* COLONEL *enters, cold and reserved.*]

COLONEL. Please be seated.

[*The* OLD MAN *sits, slowly. Pause. The* COLONEL *looks at him.*] You wrote this letter?

OLD MAN. Yes.

COLONEL. Your name is Hummel?

OLD MAN. Yes [*Pause.*]

COLONEL. I know you have purchased all my notes of hand, and that I am therefore in your power. What do you want?

OLD MAN. Payment. In some form.

COLONEL. What form?

OLD MAN: Something quite simple. Let's not talk about money. I merely ask that you tolerate me in your house, as your guest.

COLONEL. If so trifling a service can be of use to you——

OLD MAN. Thank you.

COLONEL. What else?

OLD MAN. Dismiss Bengtsson.

COLONEL. But why should I do that? My trusted servant, who has been with me all his life—who wears his country's medal for loyal and faithful service? Why should I dismiss him?

OLD MAN. He possesses these virtures only in your imagination. He is not the man he appears to be.

COLONEL. Who is?

OLD MAN [*recoils*]. True. But Bengtsson must go.

COLONEL. Are you going to decide what happens in my own home?

OLD MAN. Yes. I own everything you see here. Furniture, curtains, china, linen. Other things, too.

COLONEL. What other things?

OLD MAN. Everything. Everything you see. It is all mine.

COLONEL. Very well. All that is yours. But my patent of nobility and my good name—they at least are still mine.

OLD MAN. No. Not even those. [*Pause.*] You're not a nobleman.

COLONEL. How dare you?

OLD MAN [*takes out a paper*]. If you read this letter from the College of Heralds you will see that the family whose name you bear has been extinct for a hundred years.

COLONEL [*reads*]. I—have heard rumours to this effect, it is true—But I inherited the title from my father——[*Reads.*] No. It is true. You are right. I am not a nobleman. Even that is taken from me. I can no longer wear this ring. Take it. It belongs to you.

OLD MAN [*puts on the ring*]. Good. Now let's continue. You're not a Colonel either.

COLONEL. Not a Colonel?

OLD MAN. No. Because of your name you were commissioned colonel in the American Volunteers, but since the Cuban War and the re-organization of the American Army all such commissions have been cancelled.

COLONEL. Is that true?

OLD MAN [*puts his hand towards his pocket*]. Would you like to read about it?

COLONEL. No—there's no need. Who are you, that you claim the right to sit there and strip me like this?

OLD MAN. You'll find out. Talking of stripping—I suppose you do know who you really are?

COLONEL. You have the effrontery——!

OLD MAN. Take off your wig and look at yourself in the glass; take out your teeth, shave off your moustaches; get Bengtsson to unlace your corset. Perhaps then a certain footman may recognise himself; who used to sponge food from a certain cook in a certain kitchen——

[*The* COLONEL *reaches towards the bell on the table.*]

OLD MAN [*stops him*]. Don't touch that bell. Don't call for Bengtsson. If you do, I shall have him arrested. Your guests are arriving. Keep calm, now; we'll go on playing our old parts for a little longer.

COLONEL. Who are you? I seem to recognise the expression in your eyes—and voice——

OLD MAN. Ask no more. Be silent, and obey.

STUDENT [*enters and bows to the* COLONEL]. Sir!

COLONEL. Welcome, young man. Your noble conduct in this great disaster has made your name a household word, and I count it an honour to be permitted to receive you in my home——

STUDENT. Colonel—my humble origins—your famous name—your noble heritage——

COLONEL. Hm—may I present—Mr. Arkenholz, Mr. Hummel. Will you be so good as to go in and introduce yourself to the ladies? I have a little business to finish with Mr. Hummel.

[*The* STUDENT *is shown into the hyacinth room, where he remains visible, engaged in shy conversation with the* DAUGHTER.]

COLONEL. A superb young man—musician—singer—poet—If only he

were of noble stock—my peer genealogically—I wouldn't set my face against having him as a—hm, yes——

OLD MAN. As a what?

COLONEL. My daughter——

OLD MAN. *Your* daughter? Talking of her, why does she always sit in there?

COLONEL. She feels a compulsion to sit in the hyacinth room when she isn't out of doors. It's a quirk she has——Ah, here comes Mademoiselle Beata von Holsteinkrona—a charming old lady—tremendously wealthy—a great benefactress——

OLD MAN [*to himself*]. My true love!

  [*The* FIANCÉE *curtsies and sits. The* NOBLEMAN, *a secretive figure dressed in mourning, enters and sits.*]

COLONEL. Baron Skanskorg——

OLD MAN [*aside, without getting up*]. I think he's the fellow who stole those jewels. [*To the* COLONEL.] Let out the mummy, and the party'll be complete.

COLONEL [*at the doorway to the hyacinth room*]. Polly!

MUMMY [*enters*]. Funny man!

COLONEL. Shall we have the young people in, too?

OLD MAN. No. Not the young. Let them be spared.

  [*They all sit in a dumb circle.*]

COLONEL. Shall we take tea?

OLD MAN. Why? None of us likes tea. Why pretend we do?

  [*Pause.*]

COLONEL. Shall we talk, then?

OLD MAN [*slowly and with pauses*]. About the weather, which we know? Ask after each other's health? We know that, too. I prefer silence. Then one can hear thoughts, and see the past. Silence hides nothing. Words conceal. I read the other day that differences of language arose through the need of primitive peoples to keep their tribal secrets private. Languages are cyphers; it's only a question of finding the key; but secrets can be exposed without the key, especially when it's a question of proving one's parentage. Legal proof is another matter, of course; a couple of false witnesses can furnish that—provided their testimonies agree. But in cases such as the one I have in mind, there are no witnesses, for nature has endowed man with a sense of shame which seeks to hide that which should be hid. Nevertheless, the time sometimes comes when that which is most secret must be revealed, when the mask is stripped from the deceiver's face, when the identity of the criminal is exposed.

  [*Pause. They all look at each other in silence.*]

What a silence!

  [*Long silence.*]

Here, for example, in this respectable house, this exquisite home, where beauty, culture and wealth are united——

  [*Long silence.*]

We who sit here, we know what we are—hm?—I don't need to underline that. And you all know me, though you pretend you don't. In that room sits my daughter—yes, *mine!* You know that, too. She has lost the desire to live—she doesn't know why—this air foul with crime and treachery and falsehood has withered her. I have tried to find her a friend through whom she may discover light and warmth— the light and the warmth that a noble action engenders.

[*Long silence.*]

That was why I came to this house; to burn out the weeds, expose the crimes, balance the ledger, so that these young people may start life afresh in this home which I have given them.

[*Long silence.*]

Now I give you leave to depart in peace, each of you in your turn. Anyone who stays I shall have arrested.

[*Long silence.*]

Listen to the clock ticking, the clock of death on the wall. Do you hear what she's saying? " 'Tis time—'tis time." In a little while, she will strike, and your time will be up; then you may depart, but not till then. But before she strikes, she whispers this threat. Listen! She's warning you! "The clock—can—strike." I too, can strike! [*He strikes the table with his crutch.*] You hear?

MUMMY [*goes over to the clock and stops the pendulum. Then she says clearly and earnestly*]. But I can halt time. I can wipe out the past, undo what has been done. Not with bribes, not with threats; but through suffering and contrition. [*Goes over to the* OLD MAN.] We are weak and pitiable creatures; we know that. We have erred, and sinned, like all mortals. We are not what we seem, for our true selves live, within us, condemning our failings. But that you, Jacob Hummel, sit here wearing your false name and judge us, proves you worse than us, wretched as we are. You are not what you seem any more than we are. You are a robber of souls, for you robbed me of mine with your false promises; you murdered the consul they buried today, you strangled him with your notes of hand; and now you have stolen the student's soul for a feigned debt of his father, who never owed you a penny.

[*The* OLD MAN *has tried to rise and interrupt her, but has fallen back in his chair, and shrunk small. During what follows, he shrinks smaller and smaller.*]

MUMMY. But there is a black spot in your life. I don't know the full truth about it; but I can guess. And I fancy Bengtsson knows. [*Rings the bell on the table.*]

OLD MAN. No! Not Bengtsson! Not him!

MUMMY. Ah! Then he does know. [*Rings again.*]

[*The little* MILKMAID *appears in the door leading from the hall, unseen by anyone except the* OLD MAN, *who cringes in terror. The* MILKMAID *disappears as* BENGTSSON *enters.*]

MUMMY. Bentgsson, do you know this man?

BENGTSSON. Yes; I know him, and he knows me. Life has its ups and downs; he has served in my house, as I now serve in this one. He hung around my cook for two years. So that he could get away by three o'clock, we had to have dinner ready by two; and then we had to make do with the warmed-up remains of what he'd left. He drank the juice from the meat, too, so that we had to eke out what was left with water. He sat there like a vampire sucking all the goodness out of our home, and left us skeletons; then, when we called the cook a thief, he had us put in prison. Later, I met this man in Hamburg, under another name. He'd become a usurer—another kind of blood-sucker; besides which, he was accused of having lured a young girl out on the ice to drown her, because she'd been witness to a crime he was afraid might get discovered——

MUMMY [*puts her hand over the* OLD MAN's *face*]. You see yourself. Now give me your notes of hand. And the deeds of the house.

[JOHANSSON *appears in the door leading to the hall, and watches the scene with interest, realising it means his release from slavery. The* OLD MAN *takes out a bundle of papers and throws them on the table.*]

MUMMY [*strokes the* OLD MAN's *back*]. Pretty parrot. Jacob? Jacob?

OLD MAN [*in a parrot's voice*]. Jacob's here! Cacadora! Dora![2]

MUMMY. Can the clock strike?

OLD MAN [*clucks*]. The clock can strike. [*Imitates a cuckoo clock.*] Cuc-koo, cuc-koo, cuc-koo.

MUMMY [*opens the cupboard door*]. Now the clock has struck. Get up and go into the cupboard where I have sat for twenty years, mourning our folly. In it there hangs a rope. Let it remind you of the rope with which you strangled the Consul upstairs, and thought to strangle your benefactor. Go!

[*The* OLD MAN *goes into the cupboard. The* MUMMY *shuts the door.*]

Bengtsson! Put out the screen. The death screen.

[BENGTSSON *puts the screen in front of the door.*]

It is accomplished. May God have mercy on his soul.

ALL. Amen.

[*Long silence.*]

[*In the hyacinth room, the* DAUGHTER *becomes visible. She plays on a harp as the student sings.*]

SONG [*preceded by a prelude*].

I saw the sun.[3]

I seemed to see the Hidden One.

Man reaps as he sows.

The doer of good shall receive blessing.

Answer not with evil what was done in anger.

---

2. According to Strindberg, gray parrots with red tails were often called Jacob because their cry sounded like "Jacob."
3. From "The Song of the Sun" from the Icelan-

dic *Elder Edda* (10–13 centuries A.D.). The song deals with a deceased father's speech to his son concerning the moment of release from life.

Repay with goodness him thou hast robbed.
He who hath done no wrong hath nought to fear.
Innocence is goodness.

*A room somewhat bizarrely decorated in Oriental style. Hyacinths[4] of
all colours, everywhere. On the top of the tiled stove sits a large statue
of Buddha, with a flat root on his knees. Out of it rises the stalk of an
Ascalon flower, with its globe of white, star-shaped petals.*

*Upstage right a door leads out to the round drawing room, where the
COLONEL and the MUMMY sit silent, doing nothing. Part of the death
screen is also visible. On the left, a door leads out to the kitchen and
pantry.*

[*The STUDENT and the DAUGHTER are at the table, she seated at her
harp, he standing.*]

DAUGHTER. Sing for my flowers.

STUDENT. Is the hyacinth your flower?

DAUGHTER. It is my only flower. You love the hyacinth, too?

STUDENT. Above all other flowers. I love its slim figure, which rises erect
and virginal from its roots, rests on water, and sinks its pure, white
tendrils in the colourless stream. I love its colours; the white of snow
and innocence, the honey-gold of sweetness, the rose-pink of youth,
the scarlet of maturity; but above all the blue—the blue of deep eyes,
of dew, of steadfastness. I love them all, more than gold or pearls. I
have loved hyacinths ever since I was a child. I have worshipped
them, because they embody everything I lack. And yet——

DAUGHTER. Yes.

STUDENT. My love is unrequited, for these beautiful flowers hate me.

DAUGHTER. Why do you say that?

STUDENT. Their perfume, strong and clean with the first zephyrs of
spring, which have passed over melting snow, confuses my senses,
deafens me, blinds me, drives me from my room, shoots me with
poisoned arrows which sadden my heart and set my head aflame.
Don't you know the legend of this flower?[5]

DAUGHTER. Tell me.

STUDENT. First, I will tell you its meaning. The root, resting on the
water or buried in the soil, is the earth. The stalk shoots up, straight

<hr>

4. For Strindberg hyacinths were the perfect
expression of surface beauty, immensely attractive
but empty. Strindberg wrote:

> The hyacinth is beautiful to look at, per-
> fectly beautiful; and perhaps it is even
> capable of perceiving something like
> pain and pleasure. But without self-con-
> sciousness, reason, and free will there is
> no possibility for a soul to develop, and

to be without a soul is virtually to be
dead—at least to those of us who are
alive.

(This translation appears in *The Chamber Plays*,
trans. Evert Sprinchorn, Seabury Quinn, Jr., and
Kenneth Petersen [Minneapolis, 1962] xxxiii.)

5. In the myth the beautiful youth Hyacinthus is
killed accidently by his lover, Apollo.

as the axis of the world, and on the top of it rest the star-flowers with their six-headed petals.

DAUGHTER. Stars over the earth! How beautiful! Where did you find that vision, how did you see it?

STUDENT. Where? In your eyes. It is an image of the world. Buddha sits with the earth on his knees, brooding over it, watching it grow outwards and upwards, transforming itself into a heaven. This unhappy earth shall become a heaven! It is that that Buddha awaits.

DAUGHTER. Yes—now I see it! Is not the snow-flower starred with six points like the hyacinth lily?

STUDENT. Yes. Snow-flowers are falling stars——

DAUGHTER. And the snowdrop is a snow-star, risen from the snow.

STUDENT. But Sirius, the largest and most beautiful of the stars of the firmament in its gold and red, is the narcissus with its gold and red cup and its six white petals——

DAUGHTER. Have you seen the Ascalon flower?

STUDENT. Yes—yes, I have. It carries its blooms in a sphere like the sphere of heaven, strewn with white flowers.

DAUGHTER. Yes! Ah, God—how wonderful! Who first imagined this vision?

STUDENT. You.

DAUGHTER. You.

STUDENT. You and I together. We have given birth to a vision. We are wed.

DAUGHTER. Not yet.

STUDENT. What remains?

DAUGHTER. The waiting, the trials, the patience.

STUDENT. Good! Try me. [*Pause.*] Tell me—why do your parents sit so silently in there, never saying a word?

DAUGHTER. They have nothing to say to each other, for neither will believe what the other says. My father once said: "What is the point of our talking? We cannot deceive each other."

STUDENT. How horrible.

DAUGHTER. Here comes the cook. Look at her! How big and fat she is!

STUDENT. What does she want?

DAUGHTER. She wants to ask me about dinner. I look after the house while my mother is ill——

STUDENT. Must we bother about what happens in the kitchen?

DAUGHTER. We have to eat. Look at the cook—I can't look at her——

STUDENT. Who is this ogress?

DAUGHTER. One of the Hummels—that breed of vampires. She is devouring us——

STUDENT. Why don't you dismiss her?

DAUGHTER. She won't go. We have no control over her. She is our punishment for our sins. Can't you see? We are wasting away. We are being consumed.

STUDENT. Doesn't she give you any food?

DAUGHTER. Oh, yes. She cooks us many dishes, but there is no nourishment in them. She boils the meat till it is nothing but sinews and water, while she herself drinks the juice from it. When she roasts she cooks the meat till the goodness is gone; she drinks the gravy and the blood. Everything she touches loses its moisture, as though her eyes sucked it dry. She drinks the coffee and leaves us the dregs, she drinks the wine from the bottles and fills them with water——

STUDENT. Drive her out of the house!

DAUGHTER. We can't.

STUDENT. Why not?

DAUGHTER. We don't know. She won't go. No one has any control over her. She has drained the strength from us.

STUDENT. Can I send her away?

DAUGHTER. No. It is ordained. She must stay with us. She asks what we will have for dinner. I reply. She objects. And in the end, she does as she pleases.

STUDENT. Let her decide the meals, then.

DAUGHTER. She will not.

STUDENT. This is a strange house. It is bewitched.

DAUGHTER. Yes. Ah! She turned away when she saw you!

COOK [*in the doorway*]. No, that wasn't why. [*Grins, showing her teeth.*]

STUDENT. Get out!

COOK. When I feel like it. [*Pause.*] Now I feel like it. [*Goes.*]

DAUGHTER. Never mind. You must learn patience. She is one of the trials we have to endure in this house. We have a maid, too. We have to dust everywhere after her.

STUDENT. My head reels. *Cor in aethere.*[6] Sing to me!

DAUGHTER. Wait!

STUDENT. Sing to me!

DAUGHTER. Be patient. This room is called the room of trial. It is beautiful to look at, but consists only of imperfections——

STUDENT. Incredible. But we must turn a blind eye to them. It is beautiful, but a little cold. Why don't you have a fire lit?

DAUGHTER. Because it smokes.

STUDENT. Can't you have the chimney cleaned?

DAUGHTER. That doesn't help. You see that desk?

STUDENT. It's very beautiful.

DAUGHTER. But it won't stand straight. Each day I put a cork disc under its leg, but the maid takes it away when she dusts, and I have to cut a new one. Every morning the pen is clogged with ink, and the inkwell too. I have to wash them after she's gone, every day of my life. [*Pause.*] What's the worst thing you know?

STUDENT. Counting laundry. Ugh!

6. "Heart in the clouds."

DAUGHTER. That's what I have to do. Ugh!

STUDENT. What else?

DAUGHTER. To be woken in the middle of the night, and have to get up to fasten the window-catch, because the maid's forgotten to.

STUDENT. What else?

DAUGHTER. To climb up a ladder and mend the cord of the damper on the stove, when she's wrenched it loose.

STUDENT. What else?

DAUGHTER. To clean up after her, and dust behind her, and light the fire after her—she only puts in the wood. To open the damper, dry the glasses, re-lay the table, uncork the bottles, open the windows to air the rooms, re-make my bed, clean the water carafe when it grows green with slime, buy matches and soap, which we're always out of, dry the lamps and trim the wicks so that they won't smoke—I have to fill them myself so that they won't go out when we have guests——

STUDENT. Sing to me!

DAUGHTER. Wait! First the toil, the toil of holding the dirt of life at bay.

STUDENT. But you're rich. Why don't you keep two maids?

DAUGHTER. It wouldn't help, even if we had three. Life is hard—sometimes I grow tired. Imagine if there were a nursery as well!

STUDENT. The greatest joy of all——

DAUGHTER. The most expensive. Is life worth so much trouble?

STUDENT. It depends what one wants in return. I would shrink from nothing to win your hand.

DAUGHTER. Don't talk like that. You can never win me.

STUDENT. Why not?

DAUGHTER. You mustn't ask.

[Pause.]

STUDENT. You dropped your bracelet out of the window.

DAUGHTER. Because my hand has grown so thin——

[Pause. The COOK appears, with a Japanese bottle in her hand.]

DAUGHTER. It's she who is devouring me. Devouring us all.

STUDENT. What's she got in her hand?

DAUGHTER. The colorite bottle with the scorpion lettering. It contains soya,[7] to make water into stock. We use it instead of gravy, and to cook cabbage in, and to make turtle soup——

STUDENT. Get out!

COOK. You drain the goodness out of us, and we drain it from you. We take the blood and give you back the water—with the colorite. This is colorite. I'm going now, but I'm staying in this house as long as I want. [Goes.]

STUDENT. Why does Bengtsson wear a medal?

DAUGHTER. For faithful service.

STUDENT. Has he no faults?

---

7. A derivative of soy beans.

DAUGHTER. Yes, very great ones. But you don't get medals for them.
[*They both laugh.*]

STUDENT. You have many secrets in this house.

DAUGHTER. Like everyone else. Let us keep ours.
[*Pause.*]

STUDENT. Do you love honesty?

DAUGHTER. Yes. Quite.

STUDENT. Sometimes I'm seized with a passionate desire to say everything I think; but I know that if people were really honest the world would come to an end. [*Pause.*] The other day I was at a funeral. In the church. It was very impressive, very beautiful.

DAUGHTER. Was it Hummel's?

STUDENT. Yes. My benefactor. At the head of the coffin stood an old friend of the dead man, holding the funeral mace. The priest impressed me deeply by his dignified bearing and his moving sermon. I wept. We all wept. Afterwards we went to a hotel. There I learned that the man with the mace had been in love with the dead man's son. [*The DAUGHTER looks at him, not understanding.*] And that the dead man had borrowed money from his son's admirer. [*Pause.*] And the next day the priest was arrested for stealing from the church funds. Pretty, isn't it?

DAUGHTER. Horrible.
[*Pause.*]

STUDENT. Do you know what I'm thinking? About you?

DAUGHTER. Don't tell me. If you do, I shall die.

STUDENT. I must, or I shall die.

DAUGHTER. In madhouses, people say everything they think.

STUDENT. I know. My father died in a madhouse.

DAUGHTER. Was he sick?

STUDENT. No. He was perfectly well; just mad. He only showed it once; I'll tell you how. He was surrounded, as we all are, by a circle of— associates; he called them friends, the word was shorter and more convenient. They were a gang of scoundrels, of course; most people are. But he had to have someone to talk to, he couldn't bear to be alone. One doesn't ordinarily tell people what one thinks of them, and neither did he. He knew they were false and treacherous; but he was a wise man, and had been well brought up, so he was always polite to everyone. But one day he gave a great party. It was in the evening; he was tired after his day's work, and tired with the strain of listening to his guests and exchanging spiteful gossip with them.
[*The DAUGHTER shudders.*]
Well, he rapped on the table for silence, and stood up with his glass to make a speech. Then the safety-catch flew off, and as he talked he stripped the company naked, flinging their hypocrisy in their faces. Then he sat down exhausted on the middle of the table, and told them all to go to hell.

DAUGHTER. Oh!

STUDENT. I was there, and I shall never forget what happened next. My mother hit him, he hit her, the guests rushed for the door—and Father was taken to the madhouse, where he died. [*Pause.*] Water which has remained stationary and silent for too long becomes rotten. It's the same with this house. Something has rotted here, too. And when I saw you walk through the door for the first time, I thought it was Paradise. I stood there one Sunday morning, and gazed in through the windows. I saw a Colonel who was not a Colonel, I found a noble benefactor who turned out to be a crook, and had to hang himself, I saw a mummy that was not a mummy, and a maid. . . . Where is virginity to be found? Or beauty? Only in flowers and trees . . . and in my head when I am dressed in my Sunday clothes. Where are faith and honour to be found? In fairy tales and games that children play. Where can I find anything that will fulfil its promise? Only in my imagination. Your flowers have poisoned me, and I have poisoned you in return. I asked you to be my wife and share my home, we wrote poems, we sang and played. And then the cook came in. *Sursum corda!*[8] Try once more to strike fire and purple from your golden harp! Try, I beg you! I command you—on my knees. Then I shall do it myself. [*Takes the harp, but no sound comes from the strings.*] It is deaf and dumb. Why should the most beautiful flowers be the most poisonous? It is a curse that hangs over all creation, all life. Why would you not be my bride? Because the source of life is poisoned in you. Now I can feel that vampire in the kitchen beginning to suck my blood—perhaps she's a Lamia who lives on the blood of children— it's always in the kitchen that children's hearts are nipped, if it hasn't already happened in the bedroom. There are poisons which blind and poisons which open the eyes. I must have been born with the second kind in my veins, because I can't see beauty in ugliness or call evil good—I can't! Jesus Christ descended into hell when he wandered through this madhouse, this brothel, this morgue which we call earth. The madmen killed him when he tried to set them free, and released a robber instead; the robber always gets the sympathy. Alas for us all, alas! O Saviour of the World, save us! We are dying.

[*The* DAUGHTER *has crumpled in her chair. She rings.* BENGTSSON *enters.*]

DAUGHTER. Bring the screen. Quickly! I am dying.

BENGTSSON *comes back with the screen, which he opens and places in front of the* DAUGHTER.]

STUDENT. The deliverer cometh. Welcome, Thou pale and gentle One. And you, beautiful, unhappy, innocent creature, who must suffer for the guilt of others, sleep! Sleep dreamlessly, and when you wake again may you be greeted by a sun that will not burn, in a home without dust, by friends ignorant of dishonour, by a love that knows no im-

8. "Lift up your hearts." The opening words of the preface to the Mass.

perfections. O wise and gentle Buddha, who sitteth waiting for a heaven to rise up out of the earth, grant us patience in our time of trial, and grant us purity of will, that thy hopes may be fulfilled.

[*The harp's strings begin to whisper. The room becomes filled with a white light.*]

SONG.

I saw the sun.

I seemed to see the Hidden One.

Man reaps as he sows.

The doer of good shall receive blessing.

Answer not with evil what was done in anger.

Repay with goodness him thou hast robbed.

He who hath done no wrong hath nought to fear.

Innocence is goodness.

[*A moaning is heard from behind the screen.*]

STUDENT. Unhappy child, born into this world of delusion, guilt, suffering and death, this world that is for ever changing, for ever erring, for ever in pain! The Lord of Heaven be merciful to you on your journey.

[*The room disappears. Böcklin's painting of the* Island of the Dead[9] *appears in the background. Soft music, calm and gently melancholy, is heard from the island outside.*]

9. In Strindberg's Intimate Theatre a copy of Arnold Böcklin's *Island of the Dead* had been hung on one side of the proscenium, with one of his *Island of Life* on the other. In a letter to his German publisher, Emil Schering (April 7, 1907), Strindberg suggested that the following passage from Apocalypse 21.4 might appear on the picture: "And he shall wipe away every tear from their eyes; and death shall be no more; neither shall there be mourning, nor crying, nor pain, any more: the first things are passed away" (quoted in *The Chamber Plays* 228).

LUIGI PIRANDELLO

Six Characters in Search of an Author†

The Characters in the Play-within-the-Play

THE FATHER
THE MOTHER
THE STEPDAUGHTER
THE SON
THE BOY ⎫
THE LITTLE GIRL ⎬ *they do not speak*
MADAME PACE, *who appears when invoked*

The Members of the Company

THE DIRECTOR
THE LEADING ACTRESS
THE LEADING ACTOR
THE SUPPORTING ACTRESS
THE INGENUE
THE YOUNG LEADING MAN
OTHER ACTORS AND ACTRESSES
THE STAGE MANAGER
THE PROMPTER
THE PROPERTY MAN
THE STAGE TECHNICIAN
THE DIRECTOR'S SECRETARY
THE DOORMAN
BACKSTAGE WORKERS

† © Anthony Caputi. This translation is based on a revised text of *Six Characters in Search of an Author*, by Luigi Pirandello, published in 1925 by Bemporad, Florence. The original text of *Six Characters in Search of an Author*, copyright by Luigi Pirandello, was renewed in 1950 in the names of Stefano, Fausto, and Lietta Pirandello. Translated by permission of the publisher, Dutton, an imprint of New American Library, a division of Penguin Books, USA, the 1925 text has since then been accepted as the definitive version of the play. This translation is printed here for the first time.

It is daytime; the scene is the stage of a theater.

N.B. *The play has no acts or scenes. The performance will be interrupted a first time, without the curtain's being lowered, when the* DIRECTOR *and the* FATHER *retire to work out the scenario and the* ACTORS *leave the stage, and a second time when by mistake the* STAGE TECHNICIAN *lowers the curtain.*

[Act One]

As the spectators come in, they will find the curtain raised and the stage as it is during the day, without flats or scenery, empty and rather dark. From the beginning they should have the impression of a performance that has not been prepared.

Two small stairways, one at the right and the other at the left, facilitate going from the stage to the auditorium.

On the stage the small, dome-shaped hood that screens the PROMPTER *has been moved to the side of his well in the stage floor.*

At the side, on the apron, there is a small table and an armchair, the back toward the audience, for the DIRECTOR.

Two further tables, one larger than the other, with several chairs, are set at random on the apron to be ready as they are needed for the rehearsal. Still other chairs are scattered about for the ACTORS, *and at the back of the stage, to one side, almost out of sight, there is a piano.*

When the lights in the auditorium are down, the STAGE TECHNICIAN, *in blue coveralls and with a satchel hanging from his belt, enters from the wings and takes a few boards from a corner at the rear. These he arranges on the apron, and, kneeling, he begins to nail them. At the sounds of the hammer the* STAGE MANAGER *comes from the door leading to the dressing rooms.*

STAGE MANAGER. What are you doing?

STAGE TECHNICIAN. Doing? I'm nailing.

STAGE MANAGER. Now? [*He looks at his watch.*] It's 10:30 already. The Director will be here any minute for the rehearsal.

STAGE TECHNICIAN. Hey, look, I've got to have time for my work too!

STAGE MANAGER. You'll have it. But not now.

STAGE TECHNICIAN. When then?

STAGE MANAGER. When we're not rehearsing. Come on, now, get all this out of here so I can arrange the scene for the second act of *The Game of Parts.*

[*The* STAGE TECHNICIAN, *grumbling under his breath, gathers up the boards and goes off. In the meantime the* ACTORS, *both men and women, begin to come in from the wings, first one, then another, then two together, altogether nine or ten, as many as are needed for the rehearsal of Pirandello's play* The Game of Parts *scheduled for this day. They greet the* STAGE MANAGER *and each other as they enter. Some go to their dressing rooms; others, including the* PROMPTER, *who has the play text in a roll under his arm, wait on the stage for the* DIRECTOR *to arrive and start the rehearsal. While waiting, some sitting with their legs crossed and others standing, they exchange a few words. One lights a cigarette; one complains about the role he has been assigned; one reads quite loudly for the benefit of the others a news item from a theatrical newspaper. It will be fitting if both the* ACTRESSES *and the* ACTORS *are dressed in rather bright, cheerful clothes and if this first improvised scene is very lively while being entirely natural. At some point one of the* ACTORS *might sit at the piano and begin playing a dance tune, and the youngest among them might dance.*]

STAGE MANAGER. [*clapping his hands to call them to order*]. Come now, come on! Stop that! Here's the Director.

[*The music and dancing cease on the spot, and the* ACTORS *turn and look toward the auditorium where the* DIRECTOR *appears. Wearing a derby hat and with a cane under his arm and a large cigar in his mouth, he passes down the aisle and, to greetings from the* ACTORS, *comes up one of the small stairways to the stage. His* SECRETARY *hands him his mail: a couple of newspapers and a playtext in a wrapper.*]

DIRECTOR. Any letters?

SECRETARY. None. This is all there is.

DIRECTOR [*handing him the playtext*]. Take it to my dressing room. [*Then, looking around and turning to the* STAGE MANAGER] You can't see anything here. Please, give us a little light.

STAGE MANAGER. Right away.

[*He goes to give the order. A few moments later the right side of the stage, where the* ACTORS *are, is flooded in brilliant white light. In the meantime the* PROMPTER *has taken his place in the well, lit the lamp, and spread out the text in front of him.*]

DIRECTOR [*clapping his hands*]. Come on, come on, let's begin. [*To the* STAGE MANAGER.] Is anyone missing?

STAGE MANAGER. Our Leading Lady.

DIRECTOR. As usual. [*He looks at his watch.*] We're ten minutes late already. Make a note of it, please. We've got to teach her to be on time for rehearsals.

[*He has not finished saying this when from the rear of the auditorium the voice of the* LEADING ACTRESS *is heard.*]

LEADING ACTRESS. No. No. Please. Here I am! Here I am! [*Dressed all in white, she wears a large, flamboyant hat and has a pretty little dog in her arms. She runs down the aisle and hurries up one of the small stairways.*]

DIRECTOR. You make a point of making us wait.

LEADING ACTRESS. I'm sorry. I looked everywhere for a taxi. But now I see you haven't even begun. And I don't come on right away. [*Then, calling the* STAGE MANAGER *by name and handing him the dog*] Please, put him in my dressing room.

DIRECTOR. [*grumbling*]. That's all we needed. As if there weren't enough dogs around here. [*He claps his hands again and turns to the* PROMPTER.] Come on now, come on—the second act of *The Game of Parts*. [*Sitting in his chair.*] Pay attention, everybody. Who's on stage?

[*The* ACTORS *and* ACTRESSES *clear the apron and go to sit at the side except for the three who are about to start the rehearsal and the* LEADING ACTRESS, *who, without paying any attention to the* DIREC- TOR'S *question, seats herself at one of the two tables.*]

DIRECTOR [*to the* LEADING ACTRESS]. You're on stage now?

LEADING ACTRESS. Me? No.

DIRECTOR [*annoyed*]. Well, get up then, for God's sake!

[*The* LEADING ACTRESS *gets up and goes to sit with the other* ACTORS, *who have already distanced themselves.*]

DIRECTOR [*to the* PROMPTER]. Begin. Begin.

PROMPTER [*reading from the text*]. "In the house of Leone Gala. A strange combination of both living room and study."

DIRECTOR [*turning to the* STAGE MANAGER]. Set up the red room.

STAGE MANAGER [*taking notes on a sheet of paper*]. The red one. Fine.

PROMPTER [*continuing to read from the text*]. "A table set for dining and a desk with books and papers. Shelves full of books and glass-doored cupboards containing fine china and utensils. An exit on the left to the kitchen. The main entrance is to the right."

DIRECTOR [*getting up and pointing*]. O.K., pay attention now. The main entrance is that way. The kitchen that way. [*Turning to the actor who plays the part of Socrates.*] You'll come in and go out this way. [*To the* STAGE MANAGER.] Put the interior door at the rear there, and put up some curtains. [*He sits again.*]

STAGE MANAGER [*taking notes*]. Got it.

PROMPTER [*reading, as above*]. "First scene. Leone Gala, Guido Ven- anzi, Filippo known as Socrates." [*To the* DIRECTOR.] Should I read the stage directions too?

DIRECTOR. Yes. Yes. I've told you a hundred times!

PROMPTER [*reading, as above*]. "As the curtain goes up, Leone Gala, in a chef's hat and apron, is intently whipping an egg with a wooden mixing spoon. Filippo, also dressed like a cook, is doing the same. Guido Venanzi, seated, watches and listens."

LEADING ACTOR [*to the* DIRECTOR]. Excuse me. Do I have to wear this chef's hat?

DIRECTOR [*irritated*]. Of course! If that's what the text says! [*He points to the text.*]

LEADING ACTOR. But it's ridiculous.

DIRECTOR [*leaping to his feet, angry*]. "Ridiculous," you say. What do
you want from me if France isn't sending us anything good just now
and we have to do plays by Pirandello? Three cheers for whoever
understands them! They're made expressly to irritate everyone—actors, critics, and the public!

[*The* ACTORS *laugh. Then he, getting up and going close to the*
LEADING ACTOR, *bellows*]

The chef's hat, you'll wear it! And you'll beat the eggs! And don't
think that beating these eggs is all you have to think about. Don't kid
yourself. You've still got to act the shell of the eggs you're beating.

[*The* ACTORS *start laughing again and begin making jesting comments to each other.*]

Quiet! And pay attention when I explain! [*Turning again to the* LEAD-
ING ACTOR.] That's right, the shell: or, as we ought to say, the empty
form of reason, without the fullness of instinct, which is blind. You
are reason and your wife is instinct in a game of assigned roles in
which whoever plays his part is intentionally a puppet of himself.
Understand?

LEADING ACTOR [*opening his arms*]. No.

DIRECTOR [*going back to his place*]. And neither do I! But let's get on
with it, then you can congratulate me when it's over. [*Confidentially.*]
Please, face three quarters front. If you don't, what with the abstruse-
ness of the dialogue and your not being heard, everything will be lost.
[*Clapping his hands again.*] All right now. Look sharp now. Let's go.

PROMPTER. Excuse me, but is it all right if I pull the hood over me?
There's a bit of a draught here.

DIRECTOR. Yes, yes. Go ahead.

[*In the meantime the* DOORMAN *has come into the auditorium and
he comes down the aisle. As he nears the stage, he announces to the*
DIRECTOR *the arrival of six characters, who, by now in the auditorium as well, begin to follow him looking lost and perplexed.*

*Whoever wishes to undertake a production of this play should use
every device available to set the six characters off from the actors of
the company. The placement of the two groups when the characters
go up onto the stage, as already indicated in the stage directions,
will of course help, as will different colorations by way of special
lights. But the most suitable and effective device will be the use of
special masks for the characters, masks made of materials that will
not wilt from perspiration and yet be light-weight for the performers
who wear them. They should be cut and shaped so as to leave the
eyes, the nostrils, and the mouth free.*

*All this should sharpen the underlying meaning of the play. The
characters should not in fact seem like phantasms, but like created
realities, unchanging constructions of the imagination and therefore
more substantial and real than the unstable naturalness of the
actors. The masks should help give the impression of faces fashioned*

by art, each fixed in the expression of its fundamental emotion, whether it be remorse for the FATHER, *vindictiveness for the* STEPDAUGHTER, *disdain for the* SON, *or acute grief for the* MOTHER. *She could have fixed wax tears in the swellings around her eyes and down her cheeks such as we see in sculptured and painted images of the* Mater Dolorosa *in churches. And let their clothes, too, be of a special material and style, without extravagance, with stiff pleats and of an almost statuary mass, altogether of a kind not made of material that could be purchased or cut and sewn in a tailor shop.*

The FATHER *is in his fifties, going bald but not yet so, with light brown hair and thick mustaches that curl around his still young mouth, a mouth that often breaks into an uncertain and empty smile. He is pale—notably his ample forehead, and his eyes are blue, very bright and keen. He is dressed in light trousers and a dark jacket. At times he speaks almost mellifluously; at others he is given to bitter, severe outbursts.*

The MOTHER *seems broken and crushed by an intolerable weight of shame and dejection. Wearing a heavy widow's veil, she is dressed humbly in black, and when she raises her veil, she reveals not a face torn by suffering, but one that looks set in wax. She always keeps her eyes down.*

The STEPDAUGHTER, *eighteen years old, is bold, almost impudent. Beautiful, she too is dressed in mourning, but with a showy elegance. She is contemptuous of the air of timidity, distress, and lostness of her younger brother, a dreary child of fourteen, also dressed in black; but she shows a lively tenderness for her little sister, a child of about four dressed in white with a black sash at her waist.*

The SON, *twenty-two years old and tall, seems by turns almost frozen in a studied contempt for the* FATHER *and a sullen indifference for the* MOTHER; *he wears a light blue overcoat and a long green scarf around his neck.*]

DOORMAN [*his hat in his hand*]. Excuse me, sir.

DIRECTOR [*explosively and rudely*]. What is it now?

DOORMAN [*timidly*]. Some people are asking to see you.

[*The* DIRECTOR *and the* ACTORS *turn in astonishment to look into the auditorium.*]

DIRECTOR [*furious again*]. But I'm rehearsing! You know perfectly well that during rehearsal no one is allowed in here. [*Turning himself around.*] Who are you people? What do you want?

FATHER [*coming forward to one of the two stairways, followed by the others*]. We're here in search of an author.

DIRECTOR [*angry and amazed*]. For an author? What author?

FATHER. For any author, sir.

DIRECTOR. But there's no author here; we're not rehearsing a new play.

STEPDAUGHTER [*with cheerful vivacity as she quickly comes up the stairs*].

So much the better, then. So much the better. We can be your new play.

AN ACTOR [amid comments and laughter from the others]. Did you hear that?

FATHER [following the STEPDAUGHTER to the stage]. Yes, but if there's no author . . . [To the DIRECTOR.] Unless you'd be willing to be him . . .

[The BOY and the MOTHER, holding the CHILD by the hand, come up the first steps of the stairway and stop. The SON remains below, peevish.]

DIRECTOR. Are you trying to be funny?

FATHER. Not at all, sir. On the contrary. We are bringing you a powerful drama.

STEPDAUGHTER. We could make this your lucky day.

DIRECTOR. Will you please do me a favor and go away; we don't have time to lose with crazies.

FATHER [hurt but elegantly in hand]. Sir, you know perfectly well that life is infinitely crazy; its absurdities don't even need to seem plausible because they're true.

DIRECTOR. What the devil are you talking about?

FATHER. I'm saying that there is something crazy about doing what life does not do, that is, making its absurdities seem plausible so that they then appear to be true. And if that's crazy, let me point out, it's what you do all the time.

[The ACTORS stir, annoyed.]

DIRECTOR [rising and looking him up and down]. So you think that ours is a profession of madmen?

FATHER. Well, to make appear true what isn't—on no compulsion, as a game . . . Isn't it your business to give life to characters who've been dreamed up?

DIRECTOR [quickly, becoming the spokesman for the rising indignation of his ACTORS]. I do hope you understand, my dear sir, that acting is a noble profession. If nowadays our playwrights give us stupid plays and puppets to act instead of men, be aware that we also take pride in having given life—here, on these very boards—to immortal works!

[The ACTORS, satisfied, applaud him.]

FATHER [bursting into this, heatedly]. That's right! Very good! You've given life to living beings, beings more alive than those who breathe and wear clothes! Less real, perhaps, but truer! We agree with each other perfectly.

[The ACTORS look at each other, dumbfounded.]

DIRECTOR. But how? If you were just saying . . .

FATHER. But no, please. I said that because you said you didn't have time for crazies. In fact no one knows better than you that nature makes use of the imagination to carry its creative work—this work that could be called crazy—forward, ever higher.

DIRECTOR. All right. All right. But what are you trying to conclude from all this?

FATHER. Nothing. Merely to show that one can be born into life in many forms, as a tree or a stone, as water or a butterfly . . . or a woman. And one can even be born as a character in a play.

DIRECTOR [with feigned ironic astonishment]. And you, as well as these people with you, were born characters?

FATHER. Precisely. And alive, as you see.

[The DIRECTOR and the ACTORS burst out laughing.]

FATHER [hurt]. I'm sorry you find this funny because, as I've said, we carry within us a painful drama, as you might guess from this woman veiled in black.

[Saying this, he extends his hand to the MOTHER to help her up the last steps and, continuing to hold her hand, leads her with a kind of tragic solemnity to the other side of the stage where suddenly an unearthly light comes on. The CHILD and the BOY follow the MOTHER, then the SON, who will keep to himself, in the rear, then the STEPDAUGHTER, who also sets herself off, on the apron, leaning against the proscenium. The ACTORS, at first stunned then moved to admiration at this development, break into applause, as if for an entertainment offered to them.]

DIRECTOR [at first lost for words, then angry]. Enough of this now! Be quiet! [Then, turning to the CHARACTERS] And you, go! Clear out of here! [To the STAGE MANAGER.] For God's sake, get them out of here!

STAGE MANAGER [coming forward, but then stopping as if held by a strange fear]. Please leave now. Let's go.

FATHER [to the DIRECTOR]. But no, look here, we . . .

DIRECTOR. After all, we've got work to do!

LEADING ACTOR. It's not right to make fools of . . .

FATHER [coming forward, determined]. I'm astonished! Why don't you believe me? Aren't you by now accustomed to seeing characters in a script spring to life, face to face? Is it because he [he points to the PROMPTER] has no text for us?

STEPDAUGHTER [approaching the DIRECTOR, smiling and ingratiating]. You'll see, we are six really terribly interesting characters. Even if we have been side-tracked.

FATHER [brushing her aside]. Yes, "side-tracked." That's good. [To the DIRECTOR, in a rush.] In the sense that the author who brought us into being, alive in his mind, wouldn't or couldn't put us materially into a work of art. And that was a crime, sir, because whoever has the good luck to be born a living character is superior even to death. He cannot die. The man, the writer, the instrument of creation—he will die; but his creation does not die. And to live forever this creation doesn't even need extraordinary gifts or need to do wonderful things.

Who was Sancho Panza?[1] Who was Don Abbondio?[2] And yet they live forever because they were living seeds that had the good luck to find a fertile soil, an imagination that knew how to raise and nourish them, to make them live forever.

DIRECTOR. All this is fine. But what do you people want here?

FATHER. We want to live!

DIRECTOR [*ironically*]. Forever?

FATHER. No, sir; but at least for a moment, in them.

AN ACTOR. Just listen to that, will you?

LEADING ACTRESS. They want to live in us.

YOUNG LEADING MAN [*indicating the* STEPDAUGHTER]. That's all right with me, if this one comes to me.

FATHER. But look here! The play has to be made. [*To the* DIRECTOR.] Yet if you are willing, and your actors are willing, we can arrange it quickly among ourselves.

DIRECTOR [*annoyed*]. What is this "arrange"? We don't give concerts here, with arrangements. We perform dramas and comedies!

FATHER. All right. We've come here precisely for that, to you.

DIRECTOR. And where's the text?

FATHER. It's in us.

[*The actors laugh.*]

The drama is in us; it is us. And we're impatient to play it; a passion drives us to it.

STEPDAUGHTER [*sneering, impudent, with treacherous charm*]. My passion . . . for him.

[*She indicates the* FATHER *and makes a pretense of embracing him, but then breaks into coarse laughter.*]

FATHER [*with sudden anger*]. You stay where you are, for now. And please don't laugh like that!

STEPDAUGHTER. No? In that case permit me, *mesdames et messieurs*: although I've been an orphan barely two months, please observe how I sing and dance. [*She begins to sing with wicked playfulness the first stanza of "Prends garde à Tchou-Thin-Tchou" by Dave Stamper, arranged as a fox-trot or slow one-step by Francis Salabert. She dances as she sings.*]

Les chinois sont un peuple malin,
De Shangai à Pekin,
Ils ont mis des écriteaux partout:
Prenez-garde à Tchou-Thin-Tchou![3]

[*While she sings and dances, the* ACTORS, *and especially the young ones, move toward her, as if drawn by a strange fascination, and*

1. Don Quixote's servant in Miguel de Cervantes' classic *The History of Don Quixote de la Mancha* (1605–15).
2. A comic priest in Alessandro Manzoni's novel *The Betrothed* (1825–26).
3. "The Chinese are a cunning lot, / From Shanghai to Peking, / They've put up placards everywhere: / Beware of Tchou-Thin-Tchou."

*raise their hands just enough to seem about to take hold of her. She
eludes them; when they applaud and the DIRECTOR reproves her, she
becomes distant and prepossessed.*]

THE ACTORS AND ACTRESSES [*laughing and applauding*]. Bravo! Well
done! Very good!

DIRECTOR [*angry*]. Quiet! What is this, a cabaret-concert?

[*Taking the FATHER a little apart, dismayed.*]

Tell me, is she mad?

FATHER. Mad? No. It's worse than that.

STEPDAUGHTER [*going quickly to the DIRECTOR*]. Worse! Yes, worse! And
still worse than that! Listen, please. Let us put this play on, right
away, so that you can see that at a certain moment I—when this
darling here

[*She takes the CHILD, who has been next to the MOTHER, by the hand
and leads her to the DIRECTOR*]

—you see how pretty she is?

[*She picks her up and kisses her.*]

Darling. Darling.

[*She puts the CHILD down, moved, almost against her will.*]

Well, when this darling here, when God takes her, suddenly, from
this poor mother, and this little idiot

[*Taking hold of the BOY by the sleeve, she jerks him forward*]

does the worst of the worst things imaginable, like the half-wit he is

[*she pushes him back toward the MOTHER*]

—then you'll see me take off. Yes, my dear sir, I'll be off! Gone!
And I can't wait, believe me, I can't wait! Because after what happened
between him and me—oh, very intimate— [*she indicates the FATHER
with a horrible wink*] I can't stay with them, to watch this mother's
suffering at the hands of that clown there. [*She indicates the SON.*]
Look at him! Just look at him! Indifferent and cold, because he's the
legitimate son, him; full of contempt for me, and for him, [*she indicates the BOY*] and for the baby, because we're bastards. Do you
understand? Bastards. [*She goes to the MOTHER and embraces her.*]
And this poor mother, the mother of us all, he refuses to recognize
as his mother. He looks down on her—him!—as the mother of bastards. Vile! [*She says all this rapidly, with great agitation, and when
she gets to "vile," having raised her voice sharply on "bastards," she
speaks the word quietly, almost spitting it out.*]

MOTHER [*with great anguish, to the DIRECTOR*]. In the name of these
two children, I beg of you . . . [*She grows faint and seems about to
fall.*] Oh, my God.

FATHER [*moving quickly to support her, as do almost all the ACTORS,
stunned and bewildered*]. Please, a chair, a chair for this poor widow.

THE ACTORS [*hurrying*]. But it's really true then? She's really fainting.

DIRECTOR. A chair here, quickly!

[*One of the ACTORS gets a chair; the others gather around, concerned.*

The MOTHER, *seated, tries to stop the* FATHER *as he raises the veil covering her face.*]

FATHER. Look at her, ladies and gentlemen, look at her!

MOTHER. No, in the name of God, stop it!

FATHER. Let them see you. [*He raises the veil.*]

MOTHER [*getting up and covering her face with her hands, despondent*]. Sir, I beg you to stop him. Don't let him do this. For me it's horrible.

DIRECTOR [*perplexed*]. I don't understand any of you. What is the situation here? [*To the* FATHER.] Is this woman your wife?

FATHER. Yes, sir, my wife.

DIRECTOR. Then how come she's a widow if you're alive?

[*The* ACTORS *relieve their astonishment by breaking into loud laughter.*]

FATHER [*hurt and irritated*]. Don't laugh! Don't laugh like that, for God's sake! Her drama turns precisely on that point. She had another man, a lover who ought to be here.

MOTHER [*with a cry*]. No! No!

STEPDAUGHTER. He's the lucky one: he's dead. Two months ago, as I told you. We're still in mourning, as you can see.

FATHER. But, look, though he's dead, that's not the reason he's not here. He's not here because . . . Well, look at her, sir, please, it's all there. Her drama could not turn on her having two lovers: she's not made that way; she hardly felt anything for them beyond, perhaps, a little gratitude (and that not for me, but for the other one). No, she's not that kind of woman. She's a mother. And her drama—powerful, very powerful—consists entirely in these four children by the two men she's had.

MOTHER. Me? That I've had? Do you dare to say I had them, as if I had wanted them? He did it. He pushed me on the other one. He forced me to go away with him.

STEPDAUGHTER [*in a burst, indignant*]. That's not true!

MOTHER [*stunned*]. What do you mean it's not true?

STEPDAUGHTER. It's not true! It's not true!

MOTHER. And what can you know about it?

STEPDAUGHTER. It's not true! [*To the* DIRECTOR.] Don't believe it. Do you know why she says it? For that one there. [*She points to the* SON.] She wastes away, she tortures herself for neglecting him, and she tries to make him understand that if she abandoned him when he was two, it was because he [*she indicates the* FATHER] made her.

MOTHER [*heatedly*]. He forced me. He forced me. As God is my witness! [*To the* DIRECTOR.] Ask him about it. [*She indicates her husband.*] Ask him if it's not true. Make him say it! She [*she indicates the* STEPDAUGHTER] couldn't know anything about it.

STEPDAUGHTER. I know that with my father, as long as he lived, you were always at peace and happy. You can't deny it.

MOTHER. I don't deny it. No . . .

STEPDAUGHTER. Always affectionate and attentive to you. [*To the* BOY, *angrily.*] It's true, isn't it! Tell them! Why don't you speak, you little fool?

MOTHER. Leave the poor boy alone. Why do you want to make me seem ungrateful, child? I don't want to offend your father. I'm simply saying it wasn't my fault and it wasn't for my pleasure that I left his house and my son.

FATHER. It's true. It was me.

[*Pause.*]

LEADING ACTOR [*to the company*]. What a spectacle!

LEADING ACTRESS. And we're the audience this time.

YOUNG LEADING MAN. For a change.

DIRECTOR [*who is beginning to be interested*]. We're listening. We're listening. [*Saying this, he goes down one of the stairways into the auditorium and stands facing the stage as if to get a spectator's view of the scene.*]

SON [*without moving, cold, unruffled, ironic*]. Right. And now you'll hear a pretty piece of philosophy. Now he'll tell you about the demon of experiment.

FATHER. You're a stupid cynic, and I've said so a hundred times. [*To the* DIRECTOR *in the auditorium.*] He makes fun of me because of this expression I use to defend myself.

SON. Expressions!

FATHER. Yes, expressions! Words! Aren't they a solace for all of us? When we're face to face with a fact that can't be explained, or an evil that eats us up, isn't it a help to find a word that may say nothing but that brings relief?

STEPDAUGHTER. They even help remorse. In fact, especially remorse.

FATHER. Remorse? That's not true. I've never relieved remorse with words alone.

STEPDAUGHTER. Of course a little money helps too. Oh, yes, you can get relief with a little money. Like the hundred lire he was going to pay me, ladies and gentlemen!

[*A wave of horror among the* ACTORS.]

SON [*with contempt for the* STEPDAUGHTER]. This is vile!

STEPDAUGHTER. Vile? There they were in a light blue envelope on a little mahogany table at the back of Madame Pace's shop. You know Madame Pace, sir. She's one of those madames who behind the sham of selling *robes et manteaux*[4] attracts poor girls of good family to her workshop.

SON. And with that money she has bought the right to tyrannize over all of us, with the hundred lire he was going to pay but that—and note this carefully—he fortunately had no reason to pay.

STEPDAUGHTER. But it was a near thing. [*She bursts into laughter.*]

4. "Dresses and coats."

MOTHER [*protesting*]. Shame, child! Shame!

STEPDAUGHTER. Shame? This is my revenge! I'm trembling, sir, trembling to live it, that scene. The room . . . here the showcase with the capes, there the daybed, the mirror, a screen, and by the window that mahogany table with the light blue envelope and the hundred lire. I see it. I could almost pick it up. But you gentlemen are going to have to turn away, because I'm practically nude. I don't blush anymore. I leave the blushing to him. [*She indicates the* FATHER.] Ah he was pale, very pale indeed, just then. [*To the* DIRECTOR.] Believe me, sir.

DIRECTOR. I can't make this out at all!

FATHER. Of course. Set upon from all sides like this. Insist on a little order, sir. Let me tell you how it was, and pay no attention to all the abuse she's trying to heap on me. With such ferocity. Without any attempt to explain.

STEPDAUGHTER. This is no place to tell stories. Here they don't tell stories.

FATHER. But I'm not telling a story. I want to explain.

STEPDAUGHTER. Sure. Wonderful. In your own way.

[*At this point the* DIRECTOR *comes back to the stage to re-establish order.*]

FATHER. But all the trouble is there, in words. We all have within us a world of things, each of us our own special world made of these things. Now how can we understand each other if I use words for these things that have meanings and values particular to my special world, while whoever hears my words relates them to meanings and values particular to his special world? We think we understand each other, but we never do. Look: my pity, all my pity for this woman, [*he indicates the* MOTHER] she sees as the most ferocious cruelty.

MOTHER. You drove me away!

FATHER. Do you hear? "Drove" her. She really believes I drove her away.

MOTHER. You have the words. I don't. But believe me, sir, after he married me—who knows why (I was a poor, simple woman) . . .

FATHER. But that was precisely it: I married you for your simplicity, which I loved, believing . . .

[*He stops when she gestures her disbelief, then seeing that he'll never get her to understand him, he opens his arms and turns again to the* DIRECTOR.]

No. You see? She says no. Terrifying, my dear sir, it's terrifying, believe me, this mental deafness. [*He taps his forehead.*] Feeling she has, yes, for her children. But a deafness, a deafness of mind that will drive you crazy.

STEPDAUGHTER. Yes. Now make him tell you what a lot of good his intelligence has done for us.

FATHER. If we could only foresee the harm that can come from the good we think we're doing!

[*At this point the* LEADING ACTRESS, *who has been growing furious watching the* LEADING ACTOR *flirt with the* STEPDAUGHTER, *comes forward and asks the* DIRECTOR]

LEADING ACTRESS. Excuse me, but are we going to continue the rehearsal?

DIRECTOR. Of course. Of course. But let me listen now.

YOUNG LEADING MAN. This is quite original.

INGENUE. Fascinating.

LEADING ACTRESS. For people interested in this sort of thing. [*She looks meaningfully at the* LEADING ACTOR.]

DIRECTOR [*to the* FATHER]. But you must explain yourself clearly. [*He sits.*]

FATHER. Very well. It was like this: I had a man working for me, a secretary, a poor man who was wholly devoted, and he found a soulmate in her [*he indicates the* MOTHER] and she in him. There wasn't a hint of wrongdoing, mind you—good, simple, like her, incapable not only of doing wrong, but of thinking it.

STEPDAUGHTER. So *he* thought it for them, and *he* did it.

FATHER. That's not true. I meant to do them good, and, yes, I admit it, to do myself good too. I had reached a point where I couldn't say a word to either of them without seeing them exchange knowing looks and one search the expression of the other for help on how to interpret me and to keep me from getting angry. You can imagine that that was enough to keep me in a constant rage, an intolerable state of exasperation.

DIRECTOR. And why didn't you send him away, this secretary?

FATHER. Very good! In fact, I did send him away. But then I had to watch this poor woman drag around the house as if she were lost, like some stray animal you take home out of pity.

MOTHER. Eh! Naturally.

FATHER [*turning on her suddenly, in anticipation*]. The son, right?

MOTHER. He had already taken my son from me!

FATHER. But not out of cruelty! So he could grow up healthy and strong, in contact with the earth!

STEPDAUGHTER [*pointing to the* SON, *ironically*]. So we see.

FATHER [*quickly*]. And that's my fault too, I suppose, that he's turned out like this? I sent him to a wet nurse in the country, a peasant woman, because his mother didn't seem strong enough, even if she was of simple stock. I did it for the same reason I had married her. A foolish reason, perhaps, but there you are. I've always had a cursed yearning for a certain solid moral sanity.

[*The* STEPDAUGHTER *again breaks into a noisy laugh.*]

Make her stop! This is unbearable!

DIRECTOR. Stop it! Let me hear him out, for God's sake!

[*In a flash, once again, at the* DIRECTOR's *rebuke she seems under a spell, distanced, the laughter still half-formed on her lips. Again the* DIRECTOR *goes down from the stage to gather an impression of the scene.*]

FATHER. I couldn't keep her with me any longer. [*He indicates the* MOTHER.] But, believe me, not so much out of irritation, or boredom—the suffocating boredom—as out of the suffering, the painful anguish I felt for her.

MOTHER. And he sent me away!

FATHER. Well provided with everything, to the other man, ladies and gentlemen, so she could be free of me.

MOTHER. And he could be free too!

FATHER. Yes. Me too. I admit it. And from that a great wrong has come. I meant well when I did it . . . and I did it more for her than for me. I swear it. [*He folds his arms and turns again to the* MOTHER.] Did I ever lose sight of you?—tell them—did I ever let you out of my sight? Until all at once he took you to another town, without my knowing it, because he became foolishly alarmed by my interest, a pure interest, believe me, sir, without the least ulterior motive. I watched her raise her new family with the tenderest concern. Even she'll tell you. [*He indicates the* STEPDAUGHTER.]

STEPDAUGHTER. Oh yes, and more! I was a little doll, you realize, with pigtails down my shoulders and underwear longer than my skirt, a doll, and I used to see him waiting at the entrance when I came out of school. He came to see how I was coming along.

FATHER. This is perverse! Abominable!

STEPDAUGHTER. Really? And why?

FATHER. Abominable! Abominable! [*With great excitement, to the* DIRECTOR, *explaining.*] With her gone, sir, my house seemed empty. She was my torment, but her presence filled it for me. Alone, I wandered through the rooms like a trapped fly. This one here, [*he indicates the* SON] raised elsewhere—I don't know—when he came home, he didn't seem mine any more. Without a mother there to bring us together, he grew up without any connection with me, either intellectual or emotional, on his own. And then (it's strange but true) I became curious about her little family. And little by little I was drawn to them, this issue of what I had done. The very thought of her began to fill the emptiness around me. I needed, really needed, to believe she was at peace, happy, busy with the simple duties of living, fortunate to be at a safe distance from the complicated torments of my spirit. And to assure myself that this was so, I used to go to see the child coming out of school.

STEPDAUGHTER. That's right. He used to follow me, and smile at me, and, when I got home, he'd wave to me, like this. I used to stare at him, annoyed. I didn't know who he was. I told my mother about him, and she must have guessed right off it was him.

[*The* MOTHER *nods yes.*]

At first she didn't want to send me to school any more, for several days. And when I went again, there he was at the door again—ridiculous—with a big package. He came up to me, he caressed me, and he took from the package a lovely large straw hat with a little garland of tiny May roses. For me.

DIRECTOR. But all this is only a loose narrative, dear people.

SON [disdainful]. Of course. Literature! Literature!

FATHER. What do you mean "literature"? This is life, sir! Passion!

DIRECTOR. That may be. But it isn't theatrical.

FATHER. I agree, sir. All this is background. I'm not suggesting that this be staged. As you see, in fact, she [indicating the STEPDAUGHTER] is no longer that little girl with pigtails down her shoulders—

STEPDAUGHTER. —and underwear showing below her skirt.

FATHER. The drama comes now, sir. New, complex.

STEPDAUGHTER [coming forward somberly, fierce]. As soon as my father was dead . . .

FATHER [quickly, to drown her out]. . . . They were destitute. And so they came back here, without letting me know. All her foolishness. [He indicates the MOTHER.] It's true she hardly knows how to write. But she could have had her daughter, or that boy, write to me that they were hard up.

MOTHER. Tell me, sir, how was I supposed to guess he felt this way?

FATHER. That's precisely your failing: you've never understood my feelings.

MOTHER. After so many years of separation, and all that had happened . . .

FATHER. And is it my fault if that wonderful man took you away? [He turns again to the DIRECTOR.] As I told you, it happened overnight . . . because he had found some kind of job or other. It was impossible to trace them, and then, over some years, my interest inevitably waned. The drama erupted, unexpected and violent, on their return, when I, unfortunately, driven by the needs of my flesh, still keen . . . Ah, the wretchedness, the wretchedness, truly, of a man alone who despises squalid liaisons, not yet old enough to do without women, and not young enough to be able, normally and without embarrassment, to look for one. Did I say "wretchedness"? It's worse than that. A horror! A horror! Because no woman will give him love. And when you've understood that . . . I suppose you ought to do without. But no. Each of us, for the eyes of others, dresses himself in a certain dignity, while at the same time we all know perfectly well what's going on in our intimate selves. Unspeakable. And we yield, we give in to temptation, and then immediately afterwards straighten up again—God help us—to recompose as quickly as possible this dignity of ours, complete and undamaged, like a monument over a pit, burying and hiding even from our eyes every sign and memory of our shame. It's the same with everybody. But it takes courage to admit these things.

STEPDAUGHTER. But the courage to do them, everybody's got that.

FATHER. Everybody. Though always in secret. And for that reason it
takes still more courage to admit them. Let just one person admit
these things, and bang, he's tarred with the brush of cynic. Yet it's
not true: he's like everyone else, better in fact, better because he's not
afraid to use his mind and to expose the red rawness of shame, there,
in his human bestiality, where the eyes never look so as not to see it.
Look at women—how does a woman behave? She looks at us, pro-
vocative and inviting. You take her in your arms. Then as soon as
she's held, she closes her eyes. In that gesture she symbolizes her
mission; it says to the man: "Be blind like me!"

STEPDAUGHTER. And when she stops closing them? When she no longer
needs to conceal the rawness of her shame, and instead sees, now
dry-eyed and indifferent, the shame of the man who, as devoid of
love as she, has refused to see it. Eh, how disgusting, then, all this
philosophy that discovers the beast and then tries to redeem it . . . I
can't listen to it. When anyone tries to simplify life—by reducing it
to the level of beasts, for example—and he throws out all the human
encumbrances of aspiration, innocence, all sense of the ideal, duty,
decency, and shame, nothing is more contemptible and nauseous
than his remorse. Crocodile tears!

DIRECTOR. Let's get to the point, my friends, let's get to the point! This
is just a lot of talk.

FATHER. All right. But a fact is like a sack: when it's empty, it won't
stand up. To make it stand up, we've got to put reason and feeling
into it to give it body. I couldn't possibly know about the death of
that man, or their return here in poverty, or that she, to provide for
her children, [he indicates the MOTHER] would find work as a seam-
stress, or that she'd find it with Madame Pace!

STEPDAUGHTER. A modiste of the most elegant sort, if you really want
to know, gentlemen. On the surface she serves the best clientele, but
she has arranged things that these fashionable ladies serve her in turn,
and without prejudice to the other ladies, who also serve her and who
are not so special.

MOTHER. Believe me, sir, it never entered my mind that that witch gave
me work because she had her eyes on my daughter . . .

STEPDAUGHTER. Poor Mama. Do you know what she used to do, that
one, when I brought back the work Mama had finished? She'd show
me how Mama had ruined it, and then she'd reduce the pay. And
she did that again and again. In the end I was the one who paid while
this poor dear believed she was sacrificing herself for me and those
two there, sewing into the night for Madame Pace.

[Movement and exclamations of dismay among the ACTORS.]

DIRECTOR [quickly]. And there, one day, you met . . .

STEPDAUGHTER [indicating the FATHER]. Him. Yes sir, him. An old
customer. You'll see what a scene that will make! Superb!

FATHER. With her coming in, the Mother—

STEPDAUGHTER [*quickly, maliciously*]. —almost in time—

FATHER [*screaming*]. No, in time! In time! Because, luckily, I recognized her in time. And then I take them all home with me. Try to imagine the situation, mine and hers, now that we know each other: she as you see her now and me unable to look her in the face.

STEPDAUGHTER. Ridiculous! How is it possible for me to pretend, after all this, to be a proper young lady, virtuous and well brought up, in sympathy with his cursed yearning for "a solid moral sanity"?

FATHER. For me the drama is precisely in that, in my consciousness that I, that each of us, in fact, believes himself to be one person, when that's not true. Each of us is many persons, many, depending on all the possibilities for being within us. For this man we're one person, for that one another. We're multiple. Yet we live with the illusion that we're the same for everyone—always the same person in everything we do. It's not true! We see this very clearly in those desperately unfortunate things we sometimes do. All at once we feel caught and hauled aloft, suspended. What I'm trying to say is that we see then that that one act is not all of us, that only a part of us is present in it, and that therefore it's a dreadful injustice to judge us by that act alone, to keep us hanging there, in pillory, for a whole lifetime, as if our life were summed up in that act. Now can you understand the treachery of this girl? She surprised me in a place—in an act—where we ought never to have existed for each other. And now she wants to impose that reality on me—a reality that I would never have dreamed of assuming toward her—because of this fleeting, shameful moment in my life. This I feel above all. And as you'll see, from this the drama derives tremendous value. Then there's the situation of the others. There's his . . . [*He indicates the* SON.]

SON [*shrugging contemptuously*]. Leave me alone! I have nothing to do with this.

FATHER. What do you mean you have nothing to do with it?

SON. Just that. And I don't want to have anything to do with it. You know perfectly well I don't belong with the rest of you.

STEPDAUGHTER. We're vulgar. He's refined. You may have noticed, sir, how whenever I look at him—with the contempt he deserves, of course—he lowers his eyes. Because he knows the wrong he's done me.

SON [*barely glancing at her*]. Me?

STEPDAUGHTER. You! You! I owe to you, dear boy, that I went on the streets!

[*Movement and expressions of horror among the* ACTORS.]

You denied us—admit it!—I won't say the intimacy of your home, but that courtesy that makes guests feel welcome. We were intruders who invaded your "legitimacy." Sir, I would like you to see certain little scenes we played, he and I. He says I ran roughshod over everyone. But, don't you see, it was really because of his attitude that I took advantage of what had happened to gain access to his house, with my mother, who is also his mother. He calls that "vile," but I came in as the lady of the house!

SON [*slowly coming forward*]. It's easy for them to make me look bad. But imagine what it's like for a son who one fine day, as he sits quietly at home, sees a young woman show up, arrogant, her head high. She asks for his father, whom she has to tell God knows what, and then he sees her come back, still with the same manner, this time with the child there. And finally he sees her treat his father—who knows why—in a strange, brusque way, asking for money in a tone suggesting he had to give it to her because it was his duty.

FATHER. But in fact it is my duty, because of your mother.

SON. And how should I know that? When have I ever seen her? When have I ever heard you speak of her? I saw her appear, one day, with her [*he indicates the* STEPDAUGHTER] and that boy and the child. They tell me, "By the way, she's your mother too, you know." Gradually, I gather from her behavior [*again he indicates the* STEPDAUGHTER] why, suddenly like that, they've moved in. Frankly, sir, I'd rather not try to express what I feel and think. I might just possibly whisper it, and I won't even do that, not even to myself. That's why, as you see, I can't lend myself to any of this. I tell you, sir, I'm an unrealized character dramatically. I'm ill at ease in their company. Let them leave me alone!

FATHER. But wait a minute. It's just because you're like this . . .

SON [*infuriated*]. And what would you know about how I am? When did you ever pay any attention to me?

FATHER. I admit it. I admit it. And isn't that a situation too? This aloofness of yours, so cruel for me and for your mother, who, once in the house, sees you almost for the first time, grown up as you are, and she doesn't know you though she knows you're her son . . . [*Indicating the* MOTHER *to the* DIRECTOR.] There she is! Look at her! She's crying!

STEPDAUGHTER [*angry, stamping her foot*]. Like an idiot!

FATHER [*pointing to the* STEPDAUGHTER]. And she can't stand him, you know [*Turning and referring to the* SON.] He says he has nothing to do with it, yet he's practically the hub of the whole action. Look at that little boy, always next to his mother, bewildered and ashamed . . . He's like that because of him! It's possible his situation is the most painful of all: he feels left out, more than the others; he feels a painful humiliation, poor boy, for having been taken in like this, out of charity. [*Confidentially.*] He's like his father. Humble. He doesn't speak.

DIRECTOR. He's not especially goodlooking. You can't imagine what a nuisance boys are on the stage.

FATHER. Oh, he eliminates that nuisance quickly. The child, too—in fact she's the first to go.

DIRECTOR. Wonderful. Yes. I tell you, all this interests me, it interests me a lot. I can feel, I feel there's material here for a good play.

STEPDAUGHTER [*trying to insinuate herself*]. With a character like me!

FATHER [*pushing her away, concerned about the DIRECTOR's decision*]. Be quiet, you!

DIRECTOR [*continuing without paying attention to the interruption*]. New, yes . . .

FATHER. Absolutely new, sir.

DIRECTOR. It took a lot of nerve, nonetheless, to throw it at me like that . . .

FATHER. It's understandable, sir, born as we are for the stage . . .

DIRECTOR. Are you amateur actors?

FATHER. No. I said "born for the stage" in that . . .

DIRECTOR. Come on, you must have acted!

FATHER. But no. Only the role in life that each of us assigns himself or that's assigned to us by others. In me, as it happens, passion always becomes, all by itself when I'm excited—as in everyone—a little theatrical . . .

DIRECTOR. Oh, come on, come on! You do understand that without an author . . . Of course I could send you to someone . . .

FATHER. But no. Look, you be the author.

DIRECTOR. Me? What do you mean?

FATHER. You. Yes, you. Why not?

DIRECTOR. Because I've never been an author.

FATHER. Well, why couldn't you be one now? There's nothing to it. Everybody does it. And your job will be made much simpler by the fact that we're here, all of us, living, before your eyes.

DIRECTOR. But that's not enough.

FATHER. Why not? Seeing us live our drama . . .

DIRECTOR. Maybe so. But someone still has to write it.

FATHER. No. Someone has only to write it down, if even that, having us right here, living it, scene by scene. It will be enough to sketch it out in advance, quickly, just an outline, and then rehearse.

DIRECTOR [*going back up on the stage*]. Hm. I'm almost, almost tempted. For the hell of it. I could actually try . . .

FATHER. Of course. You'll see what scenes will emerge! I can note them down for you right now.

DIRECTOR. It tempts me, it tempts me. All right, let's try it. Come with me to my office. [*Turning to the ACTORS.*] You take a break for a few minutes, but don't wander away. In fifteen, twenty minutes, be back here. [*To the FATHER.*] Let's go. Let's try. Maybe something extraordinary will come out of it . . .

FATHER. I'm sure of it. They'd better come too, don't you think? [*He indicates the CHARACTERS.*]

DIRECTOR. Yes. Come on. Come on. [*He starts off, but then turns again to the ACTORS.*] Please! Be punctual. In a quarter of an hour.

[*The* DIRECTOR *and the six* CHARACTERS *cross the stage and go off. The* ACTORS *remain, stunned, looking at each other.*]

LEADING ACTOR. Is he serious? What does he want to do?

YOUNG LEADING MAN. It's lunacy pure and simple.

A THIRD ACTOR. Does he want us to improvise a play, on the spur of the moment?

YOUNG LEADING MAN. That's right. Like the actors in *commedia dell'arte.*[5]

LEADING ACTRESS. If he thinks I'm going to lend myself to that kind of joke . . .

INGENUE. And neither will I!

A FOURTH ACTOR. I'd like to know who those people are. [*He alludes to the* CHARACTERS.]

THIRD ACTOR. Who do you imagine? They're either crazy or up to some scheme.

YOUNG LEADING MAN. And he takes them seriously!

INGENUE. Vanity. Now he sees himself as an author . . .

LEADING ACTOR. But this is unheard of. If the theater has come to this . . .

A FIFTH ACTOR. I find it amusing.

THIRD ACTOR. Well, after all, we've yet to see what comes out of it.

[*Then, talking among themselves, the* ACTORS *leave the stage, some going by the door at the rear, some through the wings to their dressing rooms.*

The curtain remains up. The performance will be suspended for twenty minutes.]

[Act Two]

The theater buzzer announces that the performance is about to continue.

The ACTORS, *the* STAGE MANAGER, *the* STAGE TECHNICIAN, *the* PROMPTER, *and the* PROPERTY MAN *come from the wings, the door at the rear, and the auditorium as the* DIRECTOR *and the six* CHARACTERS *come from his office.*

The lights in the auditorium go out, and the stage lights come on as before.

DIRECTOR. Come, come, ladies and gentlemen. Are we all here? Pay attention now. Let's begin. Technician!

STAGE TECHNICIAN. Here.

DIRECTOR. Set up the scene in the private room. Two flats for the sides and another with a door for the rear. Quickly, please!

[*The* STAGE TECHNICIAN *hurries about these tasks, and, while the*

---

5. The phrase describes professional theatrical troupes of the late sixteenth, seventeenth, and eighteenth centuries in Italy in which each of the actors specialized in one of a largely fixed set of characters; the troupe then improvised the plays it performed from mere outlines of the action, or scenarios.

DIRECTOR *is conferring with the* STAGE MANAGER, *the* PROPERTY MAN, *the* PROMPTER, *and the* ACTORS, *he arranges a simulation of the scene called for: two side flats and a rear flat with a door, all with wallpaper in pink and gold stripes.*]

DIRECTOR [*to the* PROPERTY MAN]. You might see if there's a sofa-bed in the storeroom.

PROPERTY MAN. There is, there's that green one.

STEPDAUGHTER. No. Green won't do. It was yellow, flowered, plush, very large. And very accommodating.

PROPERTY MAN. Hmm. There's nothing like that.

DIRECTOR. It doesn't matter. Bring out what you have.

STEPDAUGHTER. What do you mean it doesn't matter? This is the notorious couch of Madame Pace!

DIRECTOR. We're only rehearsing now. Please, don't interfere. [*To the* STAGE MANAGER.] See if there isn't a glass show-case, something long and low.

STEPDAUGHTER. And the little table, the little mahogany table for the pale blue envelope!

STAGE MANAGER [*to the* DIRECTOR]. There's that little one, with gold trim.

DIRECTOR. Good. Use it.

FATHER. And a mirror.

STEPDAUGHTER. And a screen. By all means a screen. Otherwise how can I manage?

STAGE MANAGER. All right. We've got a lot of screens. Don't worry about it.

DIRECTOR [*to the* STEPDAUGHTER]. Then some clothes trees, isn't that right?

STEPDAUGHTER. Yes, lots of them, lots of them.

DIRECTOR [*to the* STAGE MANAGER]. See how many there are and have them brought it.

STAGE MANAGER. I'll take care of it.

[*The* STAGE MANAGER *also hurries to carry out these orders, and, while the* DIRECTOR *continues to speak with the* PROMPTER *and then with the* CHARACTERS *and the* ACTORS, *he will have the items brought in and will arrange them as seems to him most suitable.*]

DIRECTOR [*to the* PROMPTER]. You, meantime, take your place. Look, this is the outline of the scenes, act by act. [*He hands him some sheets of paper.*] But now I'm going to have to ask you to do something rather extraordinary.

PROMPTER. Take it down in shorthand?

DIRECTOR [*pleasantly surprised*]. Ah, wonderful! Do you know shorthand?

PROMPTER. I may not know how to prompt, but shorthand . . .

DIRECTOR. Better and better. [*Turning to a* STAGEHAND.] Go fetch some paper from my office, a lot of it, all you can find.

[*The* STAGEHAND *hurries off and returns shortly with a large sheaf of paper which he hands to the* PROMPTER.]

DIRECTOR [*continuing to the* PROMPTER]. You follow the scenes as they're presented and try to get the lines down, at least the most important. [*Then, turning to the* ACTORS] Let's clear the stage, ladies and gentlemen. Here, you go over there. [*He points to a location at the side.*] And be very attentive!

LEADING ACTRESS. But, excuse me, we . . .

DIRECTOR [*anticipating her*]. You won't have to improvise. Don't worry.

LEADING ACTOR. What *are* we to do?

DIRECTOR. Nothing. For the moment just listen and watch. Later everyone will have a written part. For now, as best we can, we'll have a rehearsal. They're going to do it. [*He indicates the* CHARACTERS.]

FATHER [*bewildered amid the confusion on stage*]. We? Excuse me, but what do you mean a rehearsal?

DIRECTOR. A rehearsal. A rehearsal for them. [*He indicates the* ACTORS.]

FATHER. But if we are the characters . . .

DIRECTOR. All right, you're the characters, if you say so. But here, my dear sir, characters don't perform. Here actors perform. The characters are there, in the text [*he points to the* PROMPTER's *well.*] —when there is a text.

FATHER. Exactly. And since there isn't one and you have the good luck to have the characters here in front of you, alive . . .

DIRECTOR. Oh splendid! You want to do it all yourselves? To act, to appear before the public?

FATHER. Yes, just as we are.

DIRECTOR. I guarantee you'd make a stunning spectacle!

LEADING ACTOR. And what's the point of our being here then?

DIRECTOR. I hope you don't delude yourself that you know anything at all about acting. You'll make me laugh.

[*The* ACTORS *begin to laugh.*]

There, you see, they're all laughing. [*Recalling what he was about.*] But, yes, to my business. I've got to assign the parts, but that should be easy because they practically assign themselves. [*To the* SUPPORTING ACTRESS.] You, Madame, the Mother. [*To the* FATHER.] We'll have to find a name for her.

FATHER. Amalia.

DIRECTOR. But that's your wife's name. We wouldn't want to use her real name.

FATHER. And why not, since it *is* her real name . . . ? Ah, yes, if this woman is going to be . . . [*With a small gesture he indicates the* SUPPORTING ACTRESS.] I see her [*he indicates the* MOTHER.] as Amalia. But do as you like . . . [*Becoming more confused*]. I don't know what to tell you. Already my own words—I don't know—begin to sound false. They have a different ring altogether.

DIRECTOR. Don't worry about it, don't worry. We'll be responsible for getting the right ring. And as for her name, if you want, let it be "Amalia"—she's Amalia. Or we'll find another. For now we'll assign the characters like this: [*To the* YOUNG LEADING MAN.] You the Son. [*To the* LEADING ACTRESS.] You, of course, the Stepdaughter.

STEPDAUGHTER [*amused*]. What? Me? That woman? [*She bursts into laughter.*]

DIRECTOR [*irritated*]. And what's so funny?

LEADING ACTRESS [*indignant*]. No one has ever dared laugh at me! I insist on being treated with respect or I'm leaving.

STEPDAUGHTER. No, please, I'm not laughing at you.

DIRECTOR. You ought to feel honored to be played by . . .

LEADING ACTRESS [*interrupting, with disdain*]. "That woman!"

STEPDAUGHTER. But I wasn't thinking of you. Believe me. I meant myself, because I can't see anything of myself in you. That's all. I don't know, you aren't—you don't resemble me at all.

FATHER. Exactly! That's right! Look, sir, our way of expressing ourselves . . .

DIRECTOR. What are you talking about, your way of expressing yourselves? Do you think you have your way of expressing yourselves locked inside you? Not at all!

FATHER. What are you saying? That we don't have our own way of expressing ourselves?

DIRECTOR. Not at all! Here your way of expressing yourselves becomes material which the actors give new body and shape, voice and gesture to. These same actors, I might point out to you, have very effectively given expression to much more exalted material than yours. If your little drama makes it on the stage, the credit, believe me, will go entirely to my actors.

FATHER. I wouldn't dream of contradicting you, sir. But you must understand that seeing them is very hard on us since we are as you see us, with our bodies and our faces . . .

DIRECTOR [*interrupting, impatient*]. But we'll take care of that with make-up—with make-up, dear sir, as far as the face is concerned.

FATHER. All right. But the voice, the gestures . . .

DIRECTOR. Look now, after all! Here, on stage, as yourselves, you can't exist! Here an actor represents you and that's all there is to it!

FATHER. I understand. And now perhaps I also see why our author, who saw us alive, as we are, didn't want to put us on the stage. I don't want to offend your actors, heaven help me. But I think that to see myself acted now . . . by whom I don't know . . .

LEADING ACTOR [*rising with lofty dignity and coming toward him, followed by the giddy young* ACTRESSES]. By me, if you've no objection.

FATHER [*humbly, very evenly*]. Most honored, dear sir. [*He bows.*] Still, I think that however much this gentleman tries, with the best will in the world and all his art, to take me into himself . . . [*He is momentarily at a loss for words.*]

LEADING ACTOR. Finish. Say what you want to say.

   [*Laughter from the* ACTRESSES.]

FATHER. Well, I must say, his performance will be—even if he does his best with make-up to look like me—I must say, given his height . . .

   [*all the* ACTORS *laugh*]

it will hardly be a representation of me, as I really am. Instead, he'll be as he interprets me, as he finds me—if he finds me—and not as I feel myself to be within myself. And it seems to me that anyone who is called upon to form an opinion about us should take this into account.

DIRECTOR. Now you're worrying about the critics! While I'm still waiting to get started! Let them say what they like. And let's us think about putting on this play—if that's possible! [*Standing apart and looking around.*] Come on, now. Is the stage set? [*To the* ACTORS *and the* CHARACTERS.] Stand back there! Stand back! Let me see! [*He goes down into the auditorium.*] Let's not lose any more time! [*To the* STEPDAUGHTER.] Does the set seem all right to you?

STEPDAUGHTER. Not really. I can't say I find myself here.

DIRECTOR. Oh, come now! You can't imagine we're going to build the room you knew, as it was, at the back of Madame Pace's shop! [*To the* FATHER.] You told me a little room with flowered wallpaper.

FATHER. That's right. White.

DIRECTOR. Well, this isn't white; it's got stripes. But it doesn't matter. As for the furniture, more or less, it seems to me we're all right. That little table, move it a little forward there.

   [*The* STAGEHANDS *move the table.*]

[*To the* PROPERTY MAN.] You try to find an envelope, light blue if possible, and give it to this gentleman. [*He indicates the* FATHER.]

PROPERTY MAN. An envelope for letters?

DIRECTOR *and* FATHER. For letters! For letters!

PROPERTY MAN. Right away. [*He goes out.*]

DIRECTOR. Let's go. Let's go. The first scene is with the young lady.

   [*The* LEADING ACTRESS *comes forward.*]

No, wait. Her. I said the young lady. [*He indicates the* STEPDAUGHTER.] You stand and watch . . .

STEPDAUGHTER [*overlapping, quickly*]. . . . how I'll live it!

LEADING ACTRESS [*annoyed*]. And don't think I won't know how to live it! Once I get into it!

DIRECTOR [*his hands at his head*]. Ladies and gentlemen, please! No more talk! All right. The first scene is the young lady's with Madame Pace. Oh! [*Lost, he looks around and goes back up on the stage.*] And this Madame Pace? Where is she?

FATHER. She's not with us.

DIRECTOR. Well, what do we do now?

FATHER. But she's alive; she's alive too.

DIRECTOR. That's fine. But where?

FATHER. Well . . . Look, let me explain. [*Turning to the* ACTRESSES.]
   If these ladies will be so kind as to lend me their hats for a moment.

THE ACTRESSES [*half-surprised and half-laughing in chorus*].
   What?
   Our hats?
   What did he say?
   Why?
   Listen to this!

DIRECTOR. What do you want with their hats?
      [*The* ACTORS *laugh.*]

FATHER. Nothing, really. To hang them on these clothes trees for
   a moment. And if someone would be so good as to take off her
   coat?

THE ACTORS [*still laughing*]. A coat too.
And what then?
He must be mad.

A FEW OF THE ACTRESSES [*still bemused*]. But why?
Only the coat?

FATHER. To hang it here for a moment . . . Please. As a favor to me.
   Will you?

THE ACTRESSES [*as they take off their hats and one of them supplies a
   coat, they continue to laugh and hang their contributions on the clothes
   trees*].
Well, why not?
There you are.
But, seriously, what a joke!
Are we putting them up for sale?

FATHER. Precisely, Miss, like that, as if for sale.

DIRECTOR. Would you please tell me what you're trying to do?

FATHER. It's like this: perhaps, with the stage set a little more suitably
   for her, maybe, drawn by her stock in trade—who knows—maybe
   she'll come among us . . . [*He directs their gaze to the door at the
   rear of the stage.*] Look now! Look!

      [*The door at the rear opens and* MADAME PACE *enters, takes a few
      steps, and stops. She's a grim old battleaxe, very fat, with a garish,
      carrot-colored wig and a bright red rose at her ear, Spanish style.
      Heavily made-up, she is dressed with the ludicrous elegance of a
      showy red silk dress; she holds a feather fan in one hand and a lit
      cigarette in the other, slightly raised. At her appearance the* ACTORS
      and the DIRECTOR *bolt from the stage with terrified cries, scurrying
      down the stairways and giving every sign of fleeing up the aisle. The*
      STEPDAUGHTER, *meanwhile, hurries to her, humble, as one might
      to an employer.*]

STEPDAUGHTER [*moving rapidly*]. Here she is! Here she is!

FATHER [*pleased with himself*]. It's her! What did I tell you? There she
   is!

DIRECTOR [*overcoming his initial shock and indignant*]. What kind of
trick is this?

LEADING ACTOR [*This speech and the following come one on top of each
other*]. What is this, after all?

YOUNG LEADING MAN. Where did she come from?

INGENUE. They've been holding her in reserve!

LEADING ACTRESS. This is a trick from some magic act!

FATHER [*overriding the protests*]. Please! Why do you want to spoil this
marvel in the name of a vulgar, factual truth? Here we see a reality
that's teased, shaped, and called into life by the scene itself, and that
has a better right to live here than you do because it's very much truer
than you are. Now which of you actresses will play Madame Pace?
Well, this *is* Madame Pace! Surely you have to admit that the actress
who plays her will be less true than she is. There she is in person!
See how my daughter recognized her and went straight to her! Now
watch, now you'll see the scene.

[*Hesitantly, the* DIRECTOR *and the* ACTORS *come back onto the stage.*
But the scene between the STEPDAUGHTER *and* MADAME PACE *has*
already begun during the protests by the ACTORS *and the* FATHER'S
explanation. They're speaking in whispers, in a way that's natural
enough but impossible on the stage. And when the ACTORS, *called*
to attention by the FATHER, *turn to watch, they see that* MADAME
PACE *has just put her hand under the* STEPDAUGHTER'S *chin to make*
her look up, but they cannot hear what is said. They listen intently
for a moment, then they give up.]

DIRECTOR. Well?

LEADING ACTOR. What's she saying?

LEADING ACTRESS. You can't hear anything.

YOUNG LEADING MAN. Louder! Louder!

STEPDAUGHTER [*leaving* MADAME PACE, *who breaks into a priceless smile,*
she comes down to the group of actors]. "Louder?" Oh, sure. What
do you mean "louder?" These aren't things you can speak about
loudly! I spoke out about them a moment ago to shame him [*she*
indicates the FATHER] and have my revenge. But with Madame Pace
it's another matter, ladies and gentlemen. There's the danger of prison.

DIRECTOR. That's great! So that's it! Well here, my dear, you have to
make yourself heard! Yet even we can't hear you, up on the stage!
Think of the problem for an audience in the threater! You have to
make the scene carry. Besides, we won't be here as we are now: you
can speak right up. You simply pretend you're alone, in the room at
the back of the shop, and no one can hear you.

[*Smiling impishly, the* STEPDAUGHTER *very prettily gestures no with*
her finger.]

DIRECTOR. What do you mean no?

STEPDAUGHTER [*sottovoce, mysterious*]. Someone else will hear if she
[*she indicates* MADAME PACE] speaks up.

DIRECTOR [*nervously*]. You mean someone else is going to pop out?

[*The* ACTORS *get ready to run from the stage again.*]

FATHER. No, sir. She's referring to me. I have to be here, there behind the door, waiting. And Madame knows it. So, with your permission, I'll go so I'll be ready.

DIRECTOR [*stopping him*]. No. Wait. We have to respect the demands of the threater here. Before you get set for your part . . .

STEPDAUGHTER [*interrupting him*]. Oh come on now! Get on with it! I'm dying to live it, I tell you, to live this scene! If he wants to go ahead with it, I'm more than ready.

DIRECTOR [*forcefully*]. But first we've got to show the scene between you and her, [*he indicates* MADAME PACE] so it can be understood. Do you understand?

STEPDAUGHTER. Good Lord! She merely told me what you already know: that Mama's sewing has been badly done again and the material's ruined. If she's going to continue to help us in our difficulties, I have to bear with her.

MADAME PACE [*coming forward with an air of importance*]. Eh, bien, señor. I no desiderar profitto. Yo no profitto from the señorita . . .

DIRECTOR [*alarmed*]. What? Is that the way she speaks?

[*All the* ACTORS *break into loud laughter.*]

STEPDAUGHTER [*laughing as well*]. Yes, sir, that's the way she speaks: half Spanish, half Italian, in a funny hodge-podge.

MADAME PACE. Ah, no mi seem cortesia make comico da me when I speak Italiano, señor.

DIRECTOR. But of course! You're right! Speak like that, just like that, Madame. It couldn't be better if only to give a little comic relief to the coarseness of the situation. Speak like that! It'll be marvellous!

STEPDAUGHTER. Marvellous! And why not? Hearing certain proposals made in a language like that, well, how can you resist? It sounds like a joke. You have to laugh when you hear there's a "señor anziano" who wants to amuse himself "con mi." Isn't that so, Madame?

MADAME PACE. A little anziano, sì, un poco, bella mia. But better per te porque even if no please you, ha mucha prudencia.

MOTHER [*rushing forward amid the shock and consternation of the* ACTORS, *who have not been paying attention to her, she throws herself on* MADAME PACE *as the* ACTORS *try with smiles to restrain her, tears off her wig, and throws it to the floor*]. Witch! Witch! My little girl!

STEPDAUGHTER [*rushing to hold her back*]. No Mama, no! Please!

FATHER [*rushing to her as well*]. Be calm! Be calm, now! Come sit down.

MOTHER. Take her out of my sight!

STEPDAUGHTER [*to the* DIRECTOR, *who has also come over*]. My mother can't possibly stay here.

FATHER [*to the* DIRECTOR *as well*]. They can't be in the same place. That's why, you see, when we came in, that one wasn't with us. When they're together, you understand, everything's revealed at once, inevitably.

DIRECTOR. It doesn't matter. It doesn't matter. For the moment it's only a first sketch. Every little bit helps, so that I can pull together, even like this, all the various elements. [*Turning again to the* MOTHER *and leading her back to her place.*] Come now, Madame. Be calm. Just be calm. Sit down again.

[*Meanwhile the* STEPDAUGHTER *goes again to center stage and addresses* MADAME PACE.]

STEPDAUGHTER. Go on with it, Madame, go on.

MADAME PACE [*offended*]. Ah no, muchas gracias. Aquì I no do nada con tu madre presente.

STEPDAUGHTER. Oh, come on. Bring on this "señor anziano" so he can amuse himelf "con mi." [*Turning on the others imperiously.*] At last, we can play it, this scene! Let's get on with it! [*To* MADAME PACE.] You can go.

MADAME PACE. Certo, me voy, me voy—seguramente!

[*She goes out, furious, snatching up her wig and glaring fiercely at the* ACTORS, *who, laughing mockingly, applaud her.*]

STEPDAUGHTER [*to the* FATHER]. Now you make your entrance. No, there's no reason for you to go out and come back. Come here. Imagine you've already come in. Now I'm standing here with my eyes down, modestly. Come on, speak up! Say "Good afternoon, Miss" in that special tone of voice, as if you've just come in from outside.

DIRECTOR [*he has gone down into the auditorium again*]. Listen to her, will you! Hey, who's the Director here, you or me? [*To the* FATHER, *who looks on lost and perplexed.*] Yes, go on, do it. Go upstage but don't go off, and then come back.

[*The* FATHER *does this, bewildered. He is very pale, but he quickly enters into the reality of his created life, smiling as he approaches the rear of the stage like someone wholly unaware of the drama about to sweep over him. The* ACTORS *are instantly attentive as the scene begins.*]

DIRECTOR [*whispering rapidly to the* PROMPTER *in his well*]. And you, on your toes, ready to write now!

The Scene

FATHER [*coming forward, in a new tone of voice*]. "Good afternoon, Miss."

STEPDAUGHTER [*her head down, she speaks as if trying to conceal her disgust*]. "Good afternoon."

FATHER [*he glances beneath the brim of her hat, which almost hides her face, and sees that she is very young. Partly out of fear, partly out of fear that he will compromise himself in a risky adventure, he stammers, almost to himself*]. "Ah! . . . —But . . . look, this wouldn't be your first time . . . that you're here? Would it?"

STEPDAUGHTER [*as before*]. "No, sir."

FATHER. "You've been here before?"

[*The* STEPDAUGHTER *nods yes.*]

"More than once?" [*He waits a moment for her reply, and again studies her face beneath the brim of her hat. He smiles and then goes on.*] "Well, then . . . there's no need to be so . . . Permit me to take your hat."

STEPDAUGHTER [*quickly, to stop him, unable to conceal her disgust*]. "No, I'll take it off myself."

[*She does so, shaking with emotion. Meanwhile, the* MOTHER, *the* SON, *and the two smaller children pressed against her form a group across from the* ACTORS. *She follows the scene on tenterhooks, registering in turn pain, disdain, anxiety, and horror at the words and gestures of the* FATHER *and* STEPDAUGHTER. *Part of the time she covers her face with her hands, at other times she sobs.*]

MOTHER. Oh my God! My God!

FATHER [*he does not move for a moment, as if turned to stone; then he resumes his former tone*]. "Here, give it to me. I'll put it down for you." [*He takes the hat.*] "But a charming, pretty little head like yours should really have a more stylish hat. Would you like to help me choose one from among those that Madame is offering? No?"

INGENUE [*interrupting*]. Be careful there. Those are our hats.

DIRECTOR [*flying into a fury*]. For God's sake, shut up! Spare us your wit! We're working on this scene! [*Turning again to the* STEP-DAUGHTER.] Begin again please, Miss.

STEPDAUGHTER [*continuing*]. "No thank you, sir."

FATHER. "Come on, don't say no. You must accept it. I'll take it amiss . . . Look, there are some lovely ones. And this way we'll make Madame happy. She puts them out here on purpose."

STEPDAUGHTER. "No, sir. Look, I couldn't possibly wear it."

FATHER. "You mean because of what they'd say at home, if you came in with a new hat? Really! Don't you know how to handle that? Shall I tell you what to say?"

STEPDAUGHTER [*highly agitated, about to explode*]. "That's not the reason! I wouldn't be able to wear it because I'm . . . as you see. By now you should have noticed!" [*Indicating the black dress.*]

FATHER. "You're in mourning. Of course. Yes, I see now. Please forgive me. Believe me, I'm terribly sorry."

STEPDAUGHTER [*pulling herself together in an attempt to overcome her contempt and revulsion*]. "Stop, please. Don't say any more. It's my place to thank you and not yours to feel ashamed or upset. Please pay no attention to what I said. For me too, you understand—I really should forget" [*she forces herself to smile and then goes on*] "that I'm dressed like this."

DIRECTOR [*interrupting, he speaks to the* PROMPTER *as he comes back up on stage*]. Hold it. Just a minute. Do't take down that last line. Leave it. [*Turning to the* FATHER *and the* STEPDAUGHTER.] It's going very well, very well. [*Then to the* FATHER *alone.*] Then she'll go on as we worked it out. [*To the* ACTORS.] Pretty good that scene with the hat, don't you think?

STEPDAUGHTER. But the best part is coming now. Why aren't we going on?

DIRECTOR. Be patient a moment. [*Turning to the* ACTORS.] Of course it will have to be handled with a lighter touch—

LEADING ACTOR. —yes, with nimbleness—

LEADING ACTRESS. Of course. It won't be difficult. [*To the* LEADING ACTOR.] Shall we try it now?

LEADING ACTOR. It's all right with me. I'll get ready for my entrance. [*He goes out to be ready to re-enter from the door at the rear.*]

DIRECTOR [*to the* LEADING ACTRESS]. All right, then. Listen. The scene between you and Madame Pace has finished—I'll see about writing it. You are standing . . . No, where are you going?

LEADING ACTRESS. Wait a minute. I'll put my hat on. [*She crosses to take her hat from a clothes tree.*]

DIRECTOR. Ah, yes. Very good. Now you're standing here, with your head down.

STEPDAUGHTER [*amused*]. But she's not dressed in black.

LEADING ACTRESS. I *will* be dressed in black, and much more tellingly than you!

DIRECTOR [*to the* STEPDAUGHTER]. Be quiet, please. Just stand and watch. You may learn something. [*Clapping his hands.*] Let's go now. Let's go. With his entrance.

[*He goes down from the stage again to get perspective on the scene. The door at the rear opens, and the* LEADING ACTOR *comes forward with the breezy, roguish air of an aging gallant. From his first words the scene as the* ACTORS *play it seems another thing, yet without the least suggestion of burlesque. It seems, somehow, simplified and cleansed of grit. Of course the* STEPDAUGHTER *and* FATHER *cannot recognize themselves in the* LEADING ACTRESS *and* ACTOR, *and as they hear them speak their words, they register their surprise, astonishment, anguish, etc., in a variety of gestures, smiles, protests, etc., as will be seen presently. From the* PROMPTER's *box the* PROMPTER's *voice can be clearly heard prompting each line.*]

LEADING ACTOR. "Good afternoon, Miss."

FATHER [*immediately, unable to restrain himself*]. Oh, no!

[*Seeing the* LEADING ACTOR *enter as he does, the* STEPDAUGHTER *breaks into laughter.*]

DIRECTOR [*angry*]. Be quiet! And you, once and for all, stop laughing! We'll never get anywhere this way!

STEPDAUGHTER [*coming to the apron*]. Excuse me, but it's only natural. This lady [*she indicates the* LEADING ACTRESS] is taking my part, right enough; but since she's supposed to be me, I can assure her that if I heard someone say "Good afternoon" like that, in that tone, I'd burst out laughing—just as I did.

FATHER. That's right . . . The manner, the tone . . .

DIRECTOR. That's enough about manner and tone! Will you please get out of the way and let me watch the rehearsal?

LEADING ACTOR [*coming forward*]. Look, if I'm supposed to play an old man who comes to a house of ill-fame . . .

DIRECTOR. Of course, pay no attention, for God's sake! Please go on. It's going splendidly. [*Waiting for the* ACTOR *to go on.*] Well?

LEADING ACTOR. "Good afternoon, Miss."

LEADING ACTRESS. "Good afternoon."

LEADING ACTOR [*imitating the* FATHER's *business of glancing under the brim of her hat and then registering, very distinctly, first his kindness and then his fear*]. "Ah! . . .—But . . . look, this wouldn't be your first time . . . that you're here? Is it?"

FATHER [*correcting him automatically*]. Not "Is it." "Would it." "Would it."

DIRECTOR. Say "Would it"—as a question.

LEADING ACTOR [*pointing to the* PROMPTER]. I heard "Is it."

DIRECTOR. All right. They're both the same, "would it" or "is it." Go on now. Go on. [*He goes back up on the stage, and himself runs quickly through the business up to the* FATHER's *entrance.*] "Good afternoon, Miss."

LEADING ACTRESS. "Good afternoon."

DIRECTOR. "Ah! . . .—But . . . look," [*turning to the* LEADING ACTOR *to show him how he glimpses the* LEADING ACTRESS *under the brim of her hat*] Surprise . . . fear and kindness . . . [*Then, starting again, he turns to he* LEADING ACTRESS.] "This wouldn't be your first time . . . that you're here? Would it?" [*Again he turns to the* LEADING ACTOR, *now with a questioning look.*] Do I make myself clear? [*To the* LEADING ACTRESS.] And then you say: "No, sir." [*Again to the* LEADING ACTOR.] How can I be clearer than that? It wants suppleness. [*Again he goes down into the auditorium.*]

LEADING ACTRESS. "No, sir . . ."

LEADING ACTOR. "You've been here before? More than once?"

DIRECTOR. Good Lord, no. Hold the second line until she [*he indicates the* LEADING ACTRESS] nods yes. "You've been here before?"

[*The* LEADING ACTRESS *raises her head a little, half-closing her eyes as if out of pain and disgust, and then when the* DIRECTOR *says "Down," she lets her head sink twice.*]

STEPDAUGHTER [*involuntarily*]. My God! [*She quickly puts her hand over her mouth to stifle her laughter.*]

DIRECTOR [*turning*]. What's wrong?

STEPDAUGHTER [*quickly*]. Nothing, nothing.

DIRECTOR [*to the* LEADING ACTOR]. It's your cue. Go on.

LEADING ACTOR. "More than once? Well, then . . . there's no need to be so . . . Permit me to take your hat."

[*He says this last line with a tone and gesture that force the*

STEPDAUGHTER, *her hands still over her mouth, to burst into laughter despite her efforts. She laughs noisily through her fingers.*]

LEADING ACTRESS [*turning, indignant*]. No! I'm not going to stay here to be laughed at by that creature!

LEADING ACTOR. And neither am I! Let's call the whole thing off!

DIRECTOR [*to the* STEPDAUGHTER, *screaming*]. Once and for all, will you stop it? Keep quiet!

STEPDAUGHTER. Yes. I'm very sorry. Very sorry.

DIRECTOR. You're rude and ill-bred, that's what you are. You go too far.

FATHER [*trying to intervene*]. Yes, it's true. It's true. But be generous.

DIRECTOR [*coming back up on the stage*]. What do you want me to be generous about? Her behavior is indecent!

FATHER. That's right. But believe me, all this does seem strange—

DIRECTOR. . . . Strange? What do you mean "strange"? How strange?

FATHER. Dear sir, I admire your actors. That gentleman there [*he indicates the* LEADING ACTOR] and the young lady, [*he indicates the* LEADING ACTRESS] but certainly . . . well, they're not us.

DIRECTOR. Of course! How could they be you? They're actors!

FATHER. Exactly. They're actors. And they play our parts well, both of them. But for us, believe me, we hardly recognize what they're doing. It tries to be like us, but it isn't.

DIRECTOR. What do you mean it isn't? What is it like then?

FATHER. Something that . . . it becomes theirs. It's not ours any longer.

DIRECTOR. But that's inevitable! I've already told you that!

FATHER. Yes, I know. I understand . . .—

DIRECTOR. —Well, then, that's all there is to it! [*He turns again to the* ACTORS.] That means that *we'll* handle the rehearsals, as it should be. I've always found it a curse to rehearse with the author present. They're never satisfied! [*Turning again to the* FATHER *and the* STEPDAUGHTER.] Come on, let's begin again. And let's see if you can keep from laughing.

STEPDAUGHTER. I won't laugh any more. I promise. My best part is just coming up. You'll see.

DIRECTOR. Now, when you say: "Please pay no attention to what I said. For me too, you understand—" [*turning to the* FATHER] you should break in quickly: "I understand, yes, I understand . . ." and then immediately ask—

STEPDAUGHTER [*interrupting*]. Wait a minute. What does he ask?

DIRECTOR. —the reason for your mourning.

STEPDAUGHTER. Oh, no. Not at all. Look, when I tell him that I shouldn't fret about being dressed like this, do you know what he says? "All right, then, let's take it off, let's take this dress off right now!"

DIRECTOR. Great! Better and better! That *would* bring the house down!

STEPDAUGHTER. But it's the truth.

DIRECTOR. Oh, come off it—what truth? Spare me! This is theater! The truth, yes, but up to a certain point!

STEPDAUGHTER. What do you want, then, if you don't mind?

DIRECTOR. You'll see. You'll see. Leave it to me now!

STEPDAUGHTER. No, I won't. I know what you want to do. From my nausea, from everything that makes me what I am, like this, one reason more brutal and more vile than the other, you want to serve up a little sentimental cream puff, with him asking me why I'm in mourning and me answering, in tears, that my father died two months ago. Oh, no. That won't do! He must say what he really said: "All right, then, let's take it off, let's take this dress off right now!" And I with my heart still full of two month's mourning, I went over there— do you see?—behind that screen, and with these fingers trembling with shame and disgust I unhooked the dress and the brassiere . . .

DIRECTOR [digging his fingers into his hair]. For God's sake! What are you saying?

STEPDAUGHTER. The truth! The truth!

DIRECTOR. Of course. I don't deny it. It probably is the truth . . . and I understand, believe me, all your horror, Miss. But you must understand, too, that all this is impossible on the stage!

STEPDAUGHTER. Impossible? Well, then, thanks for everything, I'm leaving.

DIRECTOR. But wait. Listen . . .

STEPDAUGHTER. I'm leaving! I'll have nothing more to do with it! The two of you, when you were in there, worked out what is possible on the stage. I see that now, and thanks. He's eager to get to the part [affecting the FATHER's manner] where he plays his spiritual torments. But I want to play my drama! Mine!

DIRECTOR [annoyed, shrugging his shoulders impatiently]. Ah, there we have it, don't we? Your drama! But there's not only yours, you know. There's also the drama of the others. His drama, [he indicates the FATHER] your mother's drama. We can't have one character dominating everything, overwhelming the others, taking over the stage. We have to balance everything in a harmonious picture and then represent what is representable. I know perfectly well that everyone has an interior life and that he wants to give expression to it. But what's difficult is precisely that: to know how to bring out only that part of it that's necessary, in relation to the others, and yet by means of that small part to convey a sense of all the life that remains within. Oh, wouldn't it be lovely if each character in a nice little monologue, or—with no apologies at all—in a lecture, could serve up to the audience all that's boiling within him? [In a good-humored, conciliatory tone.] You must discipline yourself, Miss. Believe me, in your own best interests. Because you can easily make a bad impression, I warn you, with all this fury torn to shreds, this exasperated disgust, especially when you yourself, I'm sorry, have admitted that you had been with others, before him, at Madama Pace's, more than once.

STEPDAUGHTER [*lowering her head; after a pause in which she pulls herself together, in a new, deeper tone*]. It's true. But you know all those others, for me, were him.

DIRECTOR [*not understanding*]. How do you mean, the others? What are you saying?

STEPDAUGHTER. For anyone who has gone wrong, isn't the person who caused the first lapse responsible for everything. For me he's that person, and it all goes back to even before I was born. Look at him; see if it's not true.

DIRECTOR. All right. And does this burden of remorse seem nothing to you. Give him a chance to show it!

STEPDAUGHTER. But how, if you don't mind my asking? How can he show all his "noble" remorse, all his "moral" torment, if you're going to spare him the horror of one fine day finding in his arms, after having invited her to take off her mourning clothes, the little girl he used to watch coming out of school, that same little girl who's now a whore?

[*She says these last words with a voice quivering with emotion. Hearing her speak like this, the* MOTHER, *overcome by a rush of anguish which she expresses first in stifled sobs, at last breaks into unrestrained weeping. Everyone is deeply moved. A long pause.*]

STEPDAUGHTER [*as soon as the* MOTHER *shows signs of coming under control, speaking gravely and firmly*]. We're here among ourselves now, and the public knows nothing of us. Tomorrow you'll present this play about us, which you'll believe in, having arranged it in your own way. But do you want to see the real drama? To see it explode into life, as it really happened?

DIRECTOR. Of course, I'd like nothing better, so that I can use from it as much as possible.

STEPDAUGHTER. Then make my mother leave.

MOTHER [*rising from her chair, her soft weeping becoming a cry*]. No, no! Don't allow it, sir! Don't allow it!

DIRECTOR. But it's only so I can see how it was.

MOTHER. I can't bear it! I can't bear it!

DIRECTOR. But if it's all happened before? After all. I don't understand.

MOTHER. No. It's happening now! It's happening all the time! I'm not pretending this anguish. I'm alive here and now, always, feeling every moment of my suffering, constantly, and it keeps renewing itself, in the present. These two children here, you haven't heard them speak, have you? That's because they can't speak anymore! They keep hanging on me, all the time, to keep the pain alive in me. For themselves they no longer exist—no longer exist! And this one [*she indicates the* STEPDAUGHTER], she fled, she ran away from me and got lost! Lost! If she's here now, it's for the same reason, for that alone, to renew in me constantly, constantly, constantly, to keep alive and present the pain I've suffered on her account.

FATHER [*solemnly*]. The eternal moment. As I tried to tell you, sir. She [*he indicates the* STEPDAUGHTER] she's here to hold me, to fix me, to keep me hooked and suspended, forever in pillory, in that one fugitive, shameful moment of my life. She can't let go, and you, sir, you can't save me from it.

DIRECTOR. Yes. But I'm not saying we won't present it. On the contrary, it will form the core of the whole first act, up to the point where she arrives and surprises you—[*He indicates the* MOTHER.]

FATHER. That's good. Because that's my punishment, sir; all our passion must culminate in her final scream. [*Again indicating the* MOTHER.]

STEPDAUGHTER. It's still ringing in my ears. It drove me mad, that scream! —You can have me acted as you wish, sir—it doesn't matter. Even dressed. As long as my arms—only my arms—are bare. So that, look, standing like this,

[*she goes to the* FATHER *and puts her head on his chest*]

with my head resting like this, and my arms like this around his neck, I see here, in my arm, a vein throbbing. And then as if only that living vein disgusts me, I shut my eyes, like this, and bury my head in his chest. [*Turning to the* MOTHER.] Scream! Scream, Mama! [*She buries her head in the* FATHER's *chest and with her shoulders hunched as if to fend off the scream, she goes on in a voice of stifled pain.*] Scream the way you screamed then!

MOTHER [*hurling herself on them to separate them*]. No, my darling! My darling daughter! [*And after having separated her from him*] You brute! Brute! She's my daughter! Don't you see she's my daughter?

DIRECTOR [*retreating at the scream, down to the footlights, amid the dismay of the* ACTORS]. Wonderful! Yes, wonderful! And then the curtain.

FATHER [*hurrying to him, convulsed*]. That's it, because it actually happened like that!

DIRECTOR [*full of admiration, conclusively*]. Yes, right here. No doubt about it. Curtain. Curtain.

[*At the* DIRECTOR's *calls for curtain, the* STAGE TECHNICIAN *lowers it, catching the* DIRECTOR *and the* FATHER *standing in front of it.*]

DIRECTOR [*looking to heaven, his arms raised*]. The fools! I say curtain meaning that the act should finish here, and he actually lowers the curtain! [*To the* FATHER, *raising the hem of the curtain to pass upstage.*] But that's wonderful! Wonderful! A marvellous effect! It must finish like that. I guarantee it, I guarantee the power of this first act. [*He goes in with the* FATHER.]

[Act Three]

When the curtain goes up, we see that the STAGEHANDS *have taken down the scenery used in the previous act and in its place brought out a small garden fountain.*

On one side of the stage the ACTORS *are seated in a row, on the other the* CHARACTERS. *The* DIRECTOR *stands in the middle of the stage with his fist clenched over his mouth, thinking.*

DIRECTOR [*after a brief pause, shrugging his shoulders*]. All right, then, let's go ahead with the second act. If you'll leave everything to me, as we agreed, it'll be fine.

STEPDAUGHTER. We go to live in his house. [*She indicates the* FATHER.] Despite his objections. [*She indicates the* SON.]

DIRECTOR [*impatient*]. That's right, but let me take care of it, will you?

STEPDAUGHTER. Just so his opposition is clear.

MOTHER [*shaking her head in her corner*]. For all the good that's come of it . . .

STEPDAUGHTER [*turning on her quickly*]. That doesn't matter! The more we're hurt, the more he can feel remorse!

DIRECTOR [*impatient*]. I know. I know. And all this will be taken into account, after all. Don't worry!

MOTHER [*pleading*]. But treat it so that it's clear, please, to set my mind at rest, that I tried everything to—

STEPDAUGHTER [*interrupting spitefully, and completing her sentence*]. — to pacify me, to persuade me not to take this wretch down a peg. [*To the* DIRECTOR.] Go on, do as she asks, make her happy, because it's true, she did try hard. While I took the greatest pleasure in what I was doing. Even now you can see: the more submissive she is, the more he's aloof—absent! I can't imagine what she gets out of it!

DIRECTOR. Do you think we can start the second act now?

STEPDAUGHTER. I won't say another word. But you'll see that you can't play all of it in the garden, as you'd like to.

DIRECTOR. Why not?

STEPDAUGHTER. Because he [*she indicates the* SON *again*] always stays shut up in his room, by himself! And then all the parts concerning that bewildered devil of a boy there happen in the house. As I told you.

DIRECTOR. All right. At the same time you realize we can't keep putting up signs indicating the locale, or change the set three or four times in one act.

LEADING ACTOR. They used to do it, once upon a time . . .

DIRECTOR. Sure! When the public was as simple as that baby over there!

LEADING ACTRESS. And illusions were easier to create!

FATHER [*getting up quickly*]. Illusions? For God's sake, don't talk about illusions! Please don't even mention the word: it's particularly painful for us.

DIRECTOR [*stunned*]. And why is that, if you please?

FATHER. It's just painful! Painful! You should understand that!

DIRECTOR. And what should we call it, then? This illusion that we create here, for the audience—

LEADING ACTOR. —with our acting—

DIRECTOR. —this illusion of a reality?

FATHER. I understand you, sir. But perhaps you can't understand us. Forgive me. Because—here, you see—here for you and your actors— all this is only—and rightly so—it's only a game.

LEADING ACTRESS [*interrupting, indignant*]. What do you mean a game? We're scarcely children, after all. Our work is serious.

FATHER. I'm not saying it isn't. And, in fact, what I mean is the game of your art, which should convey—as he says—a perfect illusion of reality.

DIRECTOR. Exactly.

FATHER. Now, try to keep in mind that we, as we are here, [he indicates summarily the other five CHARACTERS] we have no reality outside this illusion.

DIRECTOR [*stunned, then looking at his actors, who are also helpless with amazement*]. And what does that mean?

FATHER [*with a faint smile, after having looked at them briefly*]. But of course, ladies and gentlemen. What other reality exists for us? What for you is an illusion, something to be fabricated, is for us, instead, our only reality. [*Brief pause. He comes forward a few steps toward the* DIRECTOR *and then goes on.*] And that's true not only for us, you know. Think about it carefully. [*He looks in the* DIRECTOR's *eyes.*] Can you tell me who you are? [*He keeps his finger pointed at the* DIRECTOR.]

DIRECTOR [*upset, but with half a smile*]. What do you mean, who am I? —I'm me!

FATHER. And what if I said that isn't true, because you're me?

DIRECTOR. I'd tell you you're crazy.

[*The* ACTORS *laugh.*]

FATHER. They're quite right to laugh, because here everything's a game. [*To the* DIRECTOR.] That's why you can point out to me that as part of the game that gentleman there, [*he indicates the* LEADING ACTOR] who is himself, has to be me, while, at the same time, I am myself, the man you see here. You see, I've caught you.

[*The* ACTORS *begin to laugh again.*]

DIRECTOR [*annoyed*]. But we heard all this a little while ago! Are we going to go through it all again?

FATHER. No. In fact, that isn't what I wanted to say. Actually, I'm trying to offer you a way out of this game [*looking at the* LEADING ACTRESS, *as if anticipating her*] of art! Yes, art! The game you reguarly play here with your actors. And again I ask you seriously, who are you?

DIRECTOR [*turning to the* ACTORS *with amazement and irritation*]. You've got a lot of nerve! Someone who tells us he's a character asks me who I am!

FATHER [*with dignity but no trace of annoyance*]. A character, dear sir, can always ask a man who he is. Because a character truly has a life of his own, one stamped by his own specific traits, traits which always declare he's "somebody." While a man—I'm not speaking of you now—a man, so-to-speak in general, can be "nobody."

DIRECTOR. All right. But now you're asking me, the head man! I'm the Director! Do you understand that?

FATHER [*very softly, with something like honeyed humility*]. I ask, sir, only to learn if you see yourself now, really, to be the same as you were once, if, given the perspective of time, with all you know now about the illusions of that time, all the things within you and around you, as they seemed then—and as they were, yes, real for you? Well, thinking back on those illusions, long since discarded, all those things which no longer seem what in fact they *were* then, don't you think that tomorrow, not merely the floorboards of this stage, but what you are feeling now as well, your reality for today, in fact the very earth beneath your feet, might also seem an illusion?

DIRECTOR [*having difficulty following him, a bit dazed by the elusive argument*]. So? And what do you conclude from that?

FATHER. Nothing, dear sir. Only to make you see that if we [*he indicates again the* CHARACTERS *and himself*] have no reality outside illusion, then you too have reason to mistrust your reality. Because what you are breathing and touching today—like yesterday's reality—is sure to seem an illusion tomorrow.

DIRECTOR [*deciding to make fun of him*]. Very good! But you're saying too that in this play you're putting on you're more real than I am.

FATHER [*intensely serious*]. That is certainly true.

DIRECTOR. Really?

FATHER. I was sure you realized that from the beginning.

DIRECTOR. More real than I am?

FATHER. If your reality can change from today to tomorrow . . .

DIRECTOR. But we all know it can change, for God's sake! It's always changing, like everybody else's!

FATHER [*emphatically*]. But ours doesn't change! Don't you see? That's the difference between us. Ours doesn't change. It can't change, it can't be something else, never, because it's fixed—like this—this is it!—forever. It's terrible, this unchanging reality. It should make you shudder to come near us.

DIRECTOR [*struck by a thought, he quickly moves squarely in front of the* FATHER]. Yet I'd like to know this: whoever saw a character step out of his role and start lecturing about it, and make suggestions about it, and explain it, the way you're doing? When? Can you tell me? I've never seen it happen!

FATHER. You've not seen it because authors usually conceal the labor that goes into their creations. When characters are alive, actually living in the presence of their author, he faithfully reproduces their words and actions. The characters suggest them to him, and it's important that he wants them to be as the characters say they should be—there's trouble if he doesn't! When a character is born, he instantly acquires a being so independent—even from his creator—that it's easy to see him in a great many situations that the author never even thought of. He can even take on, sometimes, a meaning that the author never dreamed of giving him.

DIRECTOR. I know that!

FATHER. Well, then, why are you so amazed at us? Consider what a disaster it is for a character to be created by an author's imagination and then to be denied life. Then tell me that this same character, abandoned like this, alive but without a life, isn't right to do what we're doing now, here, in your presence, after having spent ages, ages, believe me, with him, persuading him, pushing him, first me, then her, [*he indicates the* STEPDAUGHTER] then her poor mother . . .

STEPDAUGHTER [*coming forward, lost in a reverie*]. It's true. Me too, to prevail on him, so many times, in the gloom of his study, just at dusk. He'd be sitting there, sunk in his armchair, with the light off. The shadows filled the room; the darkness seethed with our presence. We had come to try to persuade him . . . [*As if she sees herself in the study. She's annoyed at the presence of the* ACTORS.] All of you clear out! Please leave us alone! Mama here with her son—me with the little girl—that boy there always alone—and then me with him [*she indicates the* FATHER] —and then me alone, alone . . . —in the shadows. [*All of a sudden she turns as if in her vision of herself, gleaming in the shadows and alive, she wants to seize herself.*] Oh, what a life! What scenes, what scenes we proposed to him! I tried to persuade him—even more than the others!

FATHER. That's so! And maybe it was because of you he did nothing, because you were so insistent, because of your ridiculous lack of control!

STEPDAUGHTER. Not at all! Didn't he himself make me that way? [*She goes to the* DIRECTOR *to speak to him in confidence.*] I think it's more likely that he was depressed about the theater, even despised it as the public saw it and wanted it . . .

DIRECTOR. Let's get on with it, let's get going, for God's sake! Let's get to the point, my friends!

STEPDAUGHTER. I'm sorry, but it seems to me that, with our moving into his house [*she indicates the* FATHER] there's already too much action. You said we couldn't put up signs announcing new locales or change sets every five minutes.

DIRECTOR. Of course! That's true! We have to combine things, group them together in a tight unified action. What you want to do is out of the question—to first see your little brother coming home from school and then wandering through the house like a shadow, hiding behind doors and hatching a scheme. What did you say this did to him?

STEPDAUGHTER. Drained him. Dried him up.

DIRECTOR. Have it your way. You said you could only tell that from his eyes, right?

STEPDAUGHTER. That's right! Look at him! [*She points to him next to the* MOTHER.]

DIRECTOR. You're terrific! And then at the same time you would like the little girl to be playing in her little world, in the garden. One in the house, the other in the garden! Come on now!

STEPDAUGHTER. Yes, in the sun, happy! That's my only pleasure, her joy, her delight, in that garden, far from the misery and squalor of the miserable room where the four of us slept—her with me. With me—just think of it!—me with my vile body next to hers, and with her hugging me tight in her little arms, so tender and innocent. As soon as she saw me, in the garden, she'd run and take me by the hand. She didn't care for the big flowers; she ran around looking for the tee-tiny ones, because she wanted to show them to me. So happy! So happy!

[*Saying this, wracked by the memory, she gives a long, despairing cry and beats her head on her arms lying limply on the table. Everyone is deeply moved. The* DIRECTOR *goes to her with almost fatherly concern and speaks gently to her.*]

DIRECTOR. We'll do the garden scene, we'll do the garden scene. Don't fret about it. And you'll see, you'll be pleased. We'll group the scenes around that. [*He calls a* STAGEHAND.] Look, lower a few branches of tree for me! Two small cypresses just here, in front of the fountain.

[*We see two cypresses descend from the flies. The* STAGE TECHNICIAN *hurries up to nail their bases in place.*]

[*To the* STEPDAUGHTER.] This will do for now, just to give you the idea. [*He again calls the* STAGEHAND.] Now give me a little something for sky!

STAGEHAND [*from above*]. What do you want?

DIRECTOR. A little sky. A backcloth that comes down here, behind the fountain.

[*We see a white cloth descend from the flies.*]

Not white. I said sky. This doesn't give us anything. But leave it, I'll take care of it. [*Calling.*] Hey, electrician! Take down the lights and give me a little atmosphere . . . a kind of lunar atmosphere . . . blue from the instruments and blue on the cloth—and use the reflector! That's it! That'll do.

[*In keeping with these orders, a mysterious lunar light floods the scene, a light so distinctive that it induces the* ACTORS *to speak and move as if it were a moonlit evening in a garden.*]

[*To the* STEPDAUGHTER.] There. You see? And now instead of the boy's hiding behind doors in the house, he can move about the garden and hide behind these trees. But you do realize it'll be hard to find a little girl that young to play the scene with you, where she shows you the flowers. [*Turning to the* BOY.] Come here you, come here. Let's see how this works.

[*But the* BOY *doesn't move.*]

Come on, come over here!

[*Then, pulling him forward and trying to make him hold his head up, to no avail.*]

Ah, really! This is a nuisance, the boy too . . . But what's wrong? Good God, he's going to have to say something, after all . . .

[*He moves close to him and puts a hand on his shoulder, then leads him behind one of the trees.*]

Come on, come. A bit more. Let me see! Hide here . . . That's it . . . Try showing your head just a little, to spy . . .

[*He moves to one side to see the effect. As the* BOY *executes this action, the* ACTORS *are transfixed.*]

Ah, very good . . . excellent . . . [*Turning to the* STEPDAUGHTER.] As I was about to say, if the little girl, now, were to catch him spying like that and would run over to him: he could say something.

STEPDAUGHTER [*getting to her feet*]. Don't expect him to speak as long as that one's here. [*She indicates the* SON.] You'll have to send him away first.

SON [*heading toward one of the small stairways*]. At your service! Delighted! Nothing will please me more!

DIRECTOR [*quickly holding him back*]. No! Where are you going? Wait!

[*The* MOTHER *gets up, distraught, upset at the thought that he's actually leaving, and instinctively she raises her arms as if to restrain him, though she doesn't move from her place.*]

SON [*at the footlights, to the* DIRECTOR, *who is holding him*]. In fact, I have really nothing to do here. Let me go, please! Let me go!

DIRECTOR. What do you mean you have nothing to do?

STEPDAUGHTER [*serenely, ironically*]. But you don't have to hold him. He's not going anywhere.

FATHER. He has to play the terrible scene in the garden, with his mother.

SON [*quickly, determined and angry*]. I'm not going to play anything! I've said so from the beginning! [*To the* DIRECTOR.] Let me go!

STEPDAUGHTER [*going to the* DIRECTOR]. If you don't mind, sir.

[*She makes him release his hold on the* SON.]

Let him go. [*Then, turning on the* SON *as quickly as the* DIRECTOR *has let him go*] All right now, get out!

[*The* SON *stays where he is, straining for the stairs, but, as if held by an occult force, unable to move. Then, amid the stupor and dismay of the* ACTORS, *he moves slowly along the edge of the apron toward the second stairway, yet there too he stops and strains but cannot descend. The* STEPDAUGHTER, *who has followed him with her eyes, as if daring him, breaks into laughter.*]

—He can't, see? He can't do it! He's got to stay here, chained to us! There's no escape! And since I'm the one who finally takes off, after what must happen has happened, and I do it because I hate him and can't stand the sight of him—well, if I'm still here now and somehow I'm managing to put up with him—why in heaven should he go?

After all, he has to stay, afterwards, with his precious father, and his
mother there, who then has no children except him . . . [*Turning to
the* MOTHER.] Come on, Mama. Come. [*Turning back to the* DIRECTOR
and pointing to her.] You see? She got up, she got up to hold him
back . . . [*To the* MOTHER, *moving her as if by magic.*] Come on.
Come on. [*Then, to the* DIRECTOR.] Imagine what it must be like for
her to reveal to your actors what she's feeling. But the pressure to be
near him is so great that—look at her—you see? Now she's ready to
live her scene!

> [*The* MOTHER *has in fact approached the* SON, *and, as soon as the*
> STEPDAUGHTER *finishes, she opens her arms as a gesture that she's
> ready.*]

SON [*quickly*]. But not me! No! Not me! If I can't go, then I'll stay here.
But I repeat: I won't perform anything!

FATHER [*to the* DIRECTOR, *trembling*]. You can make him!

SON. No one can make me!

FATHER. I'll make you!

STEPDAUGHTER. Wait! Wait! First the baby has to go to the fountain!

> [*She hurries to the* LITTLE GIRL, *kneels down in front of her, and
> takes her face in her hands.*]

My poor darling, you look so lost, with those beautiful eyes. Who
knows what all this seems like to you? We're on a stage, sweetheart.
And what's a stage? Well, don't you see? It's a place where they play
and are serious about it. Here they put on plays. And right now we're
putting on a play. Really and truly. You too . . .

> [*She embraces her, pulling her to her breast and rocking her gently.*]

Oh my darling, my darling, what a horrible part you have to play!
What terrible things they've thought up for you! The garden, the
fountain . . . Oh, it's a make-believe fountain, of course. The trouble
is, sweetheart, it's all make-believe here. But maybe for you, a little
girl, a make-believe fountain is better than a real one, so you can
play in it, eh? No: for the others it's a game, but not for you, unfortunately. You're real, darling, and you play for real in a real fountain,
beautiful, large, green, with bamboo palms casting shadows over it.
You watch your reflection in the water, and lots of baby ducks are
swimming there, breaking up the shadows. You want to catch one of
the baby ducks . . . [*With a cry that frightens everyone.*] No, Rosetta,
no! Mama's not watching you! Because of that pig of a son! I'm going
mad . . . And that one there . . .

> [*She leaves the* LITTLE GIRL *and grabs the* BOY.]

What are you doing here, always mooning around like a beggar? It'll
be your fault too if the baby drowns, with this stupid way of yours.
As if I didn't pay for all of us when I got us in here!

> [*She seizes his arm to force his hand out of his pocket.*]

What have you got there? What are you hiding? Out with it! Show
me that hand!

> [*She pulls his hand from the pocket, and to everyone's horror he's

holding a revolver. She looks at him for a moment, as if she has satisfied herself about something, then says darkly]

Huh! Where, how did you get it?

[*And when the* BOY, *frightened, his eyes still bewildered and vacant, does not reply*]

Idiot! If I were you, instead of killing myself I'd kill one of them, or both of them, both father and son!

[*She pushes him behind the cypress where he had been hiding, then she takes the* LITTLE GIRL *and lowers her into the fountain, laying her down so that she cannot be seen. At last she sinks down there, her face in her arms against the edge of the fountain.*]

DIRECTOR. Very good! [*Turning to the* SON.] And at the same time . . .

SON [*contemptuously*]. What do you mean "at the same time"? That can't be! There was no scene here between her and me! [*He indicates the* MOTHER.] Let her tell you herself how it was.

[*Meanwhile, the* SUPPORTING ACTRESS *and the* YOUNG LEADING MAN *have stepped away from the group of* ACTORS. *She has gone up to the* MOTHER *and she's studying her carefully, and he to the* SON, *as if in preparation for acting their roles.*]

MOTHER. It's true, sir. I went to his room.

SON. To my room! Understand? Not in the garden!

DIRECTOR. But that's not important. We have to re-group the scenes, as I said.

SON [*becoming aware of the* YOUNG LEADING MAN]. What do you want?

YOUNG LEADING MAN. Nothing. I'm just watching.

SON [*turning away; then to the* SUPPORTING ACTRESS]. Ah, and here *you* are! Getting ready to play her part? [*He indicates the* MOTHER.]

DIRECTOR. Precisely. Precisely. And you should be grateful, it seems to me, for their application.

SON. Naturally! Thanks. But you still don't understand that you can't do this play. You haven't the faintest idea of what we are; the best your actors can do is to study us, from outside. Do you really think it's possible for someone to live in a mirror image of himself? Especially when the image is frozen, or, even worse, a grotesque distortion in which we can't recognize ourselves?

FATHER. That's right. That's right. I agree about that.

DIRECTOR [*to the* YOUNG LEADING MAN *and the* SUPPORTING ACTRESS]. All right. Go back with the others.

SON. It's no use. I won't do a thing.

DIRECTOR. Be quiet now and let me hear what your mother has to say. [*To the* MOTHER.] All right. You went to his room.

MOTHER. Yes, to his room. I couldn't bear it any longer. I wanted to tell him everything, to pour out my heart to him, all my torment. But as soon as he saw me—

SON. —There was no scene. I left. I left to avoid a scene. Because I don't make scenes! Understand?

MOTHER. That's true. That's the way it was. Like that.

DIRECTOR. But now we have to create that scene between you. It's indispensable.

MOTHER. As for me, I'm ready. It might even give me the chance to speak to him for a moment, to tell him what's in my heart.

FATHER [*moving close to the* SON, *intense*]. You'll do it! For your mother! For your mother!

SON [*more determined than ever*]. I won't do anything!

FATHER [*taking hold of his jacket and shaking him*]. By God, do as I say! Do as I say! Don't you hear how she's speaking to you? What kind of son are you?

SON [*seizing him in turn*]. No. No. That's enough, once and for all!
    [*General confusion. The* MOTHER, *terrified, tries to intervene and separate them.*]

MOTHER. For the love of God! Please!

FATHER [*without letting go*]. Listen to me! Listen!

SON [*he continues to struggle with him until at last, to everyone's horror, he throws him to the floor near the stairway*]. What's come over you? Have you gone mad? Have you lost all self-respect that you want to show everyone your disgrace, and ours? I'll have nothing to do with it! Nothing! And that's what our author wanted: he didn't want to put us on the stage!

DIRECTOR. But after all is said and done you've come here.

SON [*pointing to the* FATHER]. Him! Not me!

DIRECTOR. And aren't you here too?

SON. He wanted to come, dragging all of us with him! Then he went in there with you to patch together not only what really happened but, as if that weren't enough, what never happened!

DIRECTOR. Well, you tell me then, at least tell me what really happened. Tell it to me. You left your room. Without saying anything?

SON [*after a moment's hesitation*]. Without saying anything. Because I didn't want to make a scene.

DIRECTOR [*urging him on*]. Well, and then? What did you do?

SON [*amid spellbound anguish on all sides he takes a few steps across the stage*]. Nothing . . . Crossing the garden . . . [*He stops, absorbed and depressed.*]

DIRECTOR [*still urging him on, impressed by his reluctance*]. Well? Crossing the garden?

SON [*exasperated, hiding his face in his arms*]. Why do you want to make me say it? It's horrible.
    [*The* MOTHER *is visibly shaking with stifled sobs; she's looking toward the fountain.*]

DIRECTOR [*catching sight of her look, he turns to the* SON *and with growing apprehension, softly*]. The little girl?

SON [*looking straight ahead, into the auditorium*]. There, in the fountain . . .

FATHER [*still on the floor, pointing to the* MOTHER, *pityingly*]. And she was following him!

DIRECTOR [*anxiously, to the* SON]. And then what did you do?

SON [*slowly, continuing to look straight ahead*]. I ran, I hurried to pull her out . . . But then I stopped, dead in my tracks, because behind that tree I saw something that froze me: the boy was standing there, stock still, with the eyes of a mad creature, looking at his little sister drowned in the fountain.

> [*The* STEPDAUGHTER, *still bent over the fountain so as to conceal the* LITTLE GIRL, *sobs out of control, like an echo from the deep.*]
> [*A pause.*]

I started to go nearer, and then . . .

> [*Behind the tree where the* SON *has been hiding there's the sound of a shot.*]

MOTHER [*with a piercing cry she and the* SON *and the* ACTORS *amid complete confusion run to the place*]. My son! Oh, my son! [*And then against the turmoil and disconnected cries of the others.*] Help! Help!

DIRECTOR [*amidst the screams, trying to make his way through the others, as the* SON *is raised up and carried behind the white backcloth*]. Is he wounded? Is he really wounded?

> [*Everyone, except the* DIRECTOR *and the* FATHER, *still on the floor near the stairway, has by now disappeared behind the backcloth for the sky, and we hear them there talking anxiously for a few moments. Then the* ACTORS *come back around both sides of the cloth.*]

LEADING ACTRESS [*coming from the right, deeply moved*]. He's dead! The poor boy! He's dead! How horrible!

LEADING ACTOR [*coming from the left, laughing*]. What do you mean "dead"? It's all a fiction. Make-believe. Don't you believe it!

OTHER ACTORS FROM THE RIGHT. Fiction? It's real! Real! He's dead!

FATHER [*getting up and shouting at them*]. A fiction? Don't deceive yourselves! It's real! Reality, ladies and gentlemen! Reality! [*He too goes off behind the white backdrop, disconsolate.*]

DIRECTOR [*at the end of his rope*]. Fiction! Reality! Go to hell all of you! Lights! Lights! Lights!

> [*All at once the entire stage and the auditorium are flooded with brilliant light. The* DIRECTOR *heaves a sigh as if rid of an incubus, while all the others look at each other, stunned and lost.*]

Damn! Nothing like this has ever happened to me before! They've made me lose a whole day! [*He looks at his watch.*] You can all go now. There's nothing we can do now. It's too late to pick up the rehearsal again. I'll see you all this evening.

> [*The* ACTORS *take their leave. As soon as they're gone*]

Hey, electrician, turn off the lights!

> [*As soon as he has said this, the theater is plunged in complete darkness.*]

Hey, for God's sake, leave at least a little light so I can see where I'm walking.

> [*Suddenly, behind the backcloth, as if because of a bad connection, a green light comes on which projects, large and sharply outlined,*]

the shadows of the CHARACTERS, *except for the* BOY *and the* LITTLE
GIRL. *Seeing them, the* DIRECTOR *scurries from the stage, terrified.
At that instant this light goes off and on the stage the blue night
light mentioned earlier comes on. Slowly the* SON *comes from the
right side of the curtain, followed by the* MOTHER *with her arms
extended toward him. Then from the left side the* FATHER. *They stop
half way onto the stage and stand as if bemused. Lastly, the*
STEPDAUGHTER *comes from the left and runs toward one of the
stairways. On the first step she stops to look at the other three for
a moment and breaks into a coarse laugh. Then she hurries down
the stairs and runs up an aisle, stopping once more to laugh at the
other three still standing there. At last she rushes out of the auditorium. Even from the lobby her laughter can be heard.*

    Shortly after this the curtain falls.]

EUGENE O'NEILL

Long Day's Journey into Night†

For Carlotta, on our 12th Wedding Anniversary

*Dearest: I give you the original script of this play
of old sorrow, written in tears and blood. A sadly
inappropriate gift, it would seem, for a day
celebrating happiness. But you will understand. I
mean it as a tribute to your love and tenderness which
gave me the faith in love that enabled me to
face my dead at last and write this play—write it
with deep pity and understanding and forgiveness for
all the four haunted Tyrones.*

*These twelve years, Beloved One, have been a
Journey into Light—into love. You know my gratitude.
And my love!*

GENE

*Tao House
July 22, 1941.*

Characters

JAMES TYRONE
MARY CAVAN TYRONE, *his wife*
JAMES TYRONE, JR., *their elder son*
EDMUND TYRONE, *their younger son*
CATHLEEN, *second girl*

Scenes

ACT 1

Living room of the Tyrones' summer home 8:30 A.M. of a day in August,
   1912

ACT 2

SCENE 1: The same, around 12:45
SCENE 2: The same, about a half hour later

ACT 3

The same, around 6:30 that evening

ACT 4

The same, around midnight

Act One

SCENE—*Living room of* JAMES TYRONE'S *summer home on a morning in
August, 1912.*

   *At rear are two double doorways with portieres. The one at right leads
into a front parlor with the formally arranged, set appearance of a room
rarely occupied. The other opens on a dark, windowless back parlor, never
used except as a passage from living room to dining room. Against the
wall between the doorways is a small bookcase, with a picture of Shakespeare above it, containing novels by Balzac, Zola, Stendhal, philosophical and sociological works by Schopenhauer, Nietzsche, Marx,
Engels, Kropotkin, Max Stirner, plays by Ibsen, Shaw, Strindberg, poetry
by Swinburne, Rossetti, Wilde, Ernest Dowson, Kipling, etc.*

   *In the right wall, rear, is a screen door leading out on the porch which
extends halfway around the house. Farther forward, a series of three
windows looks over the front lawn to the harbor and the avenue that runs
along the water front. A small wicker table and an ordinary oak desk
are against the wall, flanking the windows.*

   *In the left wall, a similar series of windows looks out on the grounds
in back of the house. Beneath them is a wicker couch with cushions, its
head toward rear. Farther back is a large, glassed-in bookcase with sets
of Dumas, Victor Hugo, Charles Lever, three sets of Shakespeare, The
World's Best Literature in fifty large volumes, Hume's History of England, Thiers' History of the Consulate and Empire, Smollett's History
of England, Gibbon's Roman Empire and miscellaneous volumes of old
plays, poetry, and several histories of Ireland. The astonishing thing about*

these sets is that all the volumes have the look of having been read and reread.

The hardwood floor is nearly covered by a rug, inoffensive in design and color. At center is a round table with a green shaded reading lamp, the cord plugged in one of the four sockets in the chandelier above. Around the table within reading-light range are four chairs, three of them wicker armchairs, the fourth (at right front of table) a varnished oak rocker with leather bottom.

It is around 8:30. Sunshine comes through the windows at right.

As the curtain rises, the family have just finished breakfast.

MARY TYRONE *and her husband enter together from the back parlor, coming from the dining room.*

MARY *is fifty-four, about medium height. She still has a young, graceful figure, a trifle plump, but showing little evidence of middle-aged waist and hips, although she is not tightly corseted. Her face is distinctly Irish in type. It must once have been extremely pretty, and is still striking. It does not match her healthy figure but is thin and pale with the bone structure prominent. Her nose is long and straight, her mouth wide with full, sensitive lips. She uses no rouge or any sort of make-up. Her high forehead is framed by thick pure white hair. Accentuated by her pallor and white hair, her dark brown eyes appear black. They are unusually large and beautiful, with black brows and long curling lashes.*

What strikes one immediately is her extreme nervousness. Her hands are never still. They were once beautiful hands, with long, tapering fingers, but rheumatism has knotted the joints and warped the fingers, so that now they have an ugly crippled look. One avoids looking at them, the more so because one is conscious she is sensitive about their appearance and humiliated by her inability to control the nervousness which draws attention to them.

She is dressed simply but with a sure sense of what becomes her. Her hair is arranged with fastidious care. Her voice is soft and attractive. When she is merry, there is a touch of Irish lilt in it.

Her most appealing quality is the simple, unaffected charm of a shy convent-girl youthfulness she has never lost—an innate unworldly innocence.

JAMES TYRONE *is sixty-five but looks ten years younger. About five feet eight, broad-shouldered and deep-chested, he seems taller and slenderer because of his bearing, which has a soldierly quality of head up, chest out, stomach in, shoulders squared. His face has begun to break down but he is still remarkably good looking—a big, finely shaped head, a handsome profile, deep-set light-brown eyes. His grey hair is thin with a bald spot like a monk's tonsure.*

The stamp of his profession is unmistakably on him. Not that he indulges in any of the deliberate temperamental posturings of the stage star. He is by nature and preference a simple, unpretentious man, whose inclinations are still close to his humble beginnings and his Irish farmer forebears. But the actor shows in all his unconscious habits of speech, movement and gesture. These have the quality of belonging to a studied technique. His voice is remarkably fine, resonant and flexible, and he takes great pride in it.

His clothes, assuredly, do not costume any romantic part. He wears a threadbare, ready-made, grey sack suit and shineless black shoes, a collar-less shirt with a thick white handkerchief knotted loosely around his throat. There is nothing picturesquely careless about this get-up. It is commonplace shabby. He believes in wearing his clothes to the limit of usefulness, is dressed now for gardening, and doesn't give a damn how he looks.

He has never been really sick a day in his life. He has no nerves. There is a lot of stolid, earthy peasant in him, mixed with streaks of sentimental melancholy and rare flashes of intuitive sensibility.

TYRONE's *arm is around his wife's waist as they appear from the back parlor. Entering the living room he gives her a playful hug.*

TYRONE. You're a fine armful now, Mary, with those twenty pounds you've gained.

MARY [*smiles affectionately*]. I've gotten too fat, you mean, dear. I really ought to reduce.

TYRONE. None of that, my lady! You're just right. We'll have no talk of reducing. Is that why you ate so little breakfast?

MARY. So little? I thought I ate a lot.

TYRONE. You didn't. Not as much I'd like to see, anyway.

MARY [*teasingly*]. Oh you! You expect everyone to eat the enormous breakfast you do. No one else in the world could without dying of indigestion. [*She comes forward to stand by the right of table.*]

TYRONE [*following her*]. I hope I'm not as big a glutton as that sounds. [*With hearty satisfaction.*] But thank God, I've kept my appetite and I've the digestion of a young man of twenty, if I am sixty-five.

MARY. You surely have, James. No one could deny that.

[*She laughs and sits in the wicker armchair at right rear of table. He comes around in back of her and selects a cigar from a box on the table and cuts off the end with a little clipper. From the dining room* JAMIE's *and* EDMUND's *voices are heard.* MARY *turns her head that way.*]

Why did the boys stay in the dining room, I wonder? Cathleen must be waiting to clear the table.

TYRONE [*jokingly but with an undercurrent of resentment*]. It's a secret confab they don't want me to hear, I suppose. I'll bet they're cooking up some new scheme to touch the Old Man.

[*She is silent on this, keeping her head turned toward their voices. Her hands appear on the table top, moving restlessly. He lights his cigar and sits down in the rocker at right of table, which is his chair, and puffs contentedly.*]

There's nothing like the first after-breakfast cigar, if it's a good one, and this new lot have the right mellow flavor. They're a great bargain, too. I got them dead cheap. It was McGuire put me on to them.

MARY [*a trifle acidly*]. I hope he didn't put you on to any new piece of property at the same time. His real estate bargains don't work out so well.

TYRONE [*defensively*]. I wouldn't say that, Mary. After all, he was the one who advised me to buy that place on Chestnut Street and I made a quick turnover on it for a fine profit.

MARY [*smiles now with teasing affection*]. I know. The famous one stroke of good luck. I'm sure McGuire never dreamed— [*Then she pats his hand.*] Never mind, James. I know it's a waste of breath trying to convince you you're not a cunning real estate speculator.

TYRONE [*huffily*]. I've no such idea. But land is land, and it's safer than the stocks and bonds of Wall Street swindlers. [*Then placatingly*] But let's not argue about business this early in the morning.

[*A pause. The boys' voices are again heard and one of them has a fit of coughing.* MARY *listens worriedly. Her fingers play nervously on the table top.*]

MARY. James, it's Edmund you ought to scold for not eating enough. He hardly touched anything except coffee. He needs to eat to keep up his strength. I keep telling him that but he says he simply has no appetite. Of course, there's nothing takes away your appetite like a bad summer cold.

TYRONE. Yes, it's only natural. So don't let yourself get worried—

MARY [*quickly*]. Oh, I'm not. I know he'll be all right in a few days if he takes care of himself. [*As if she wanted to dismiss the subject but can't.*] But it does seem a shame he should have to be sick right now.

TYRONE. Yes, it is bad luck. [*He gives her a quick, worried look.*] But you mustn't let it upset you, Mary. Remember, you've got to take care of yourself, too.

MARY [*quickly*]. I'm not upset. There's nothing to be upset about. What makes you think I'm upset?

TYRONE. Why, nothing, except you've seemed a bit highstrung the past few days.

MARY [*forcing a smile*]. I have? Nonsense, dear. It's your imagination. [*With sudden tenseness.*] You really must not watch me all the time, James. I mean, it makes me self-conscious.

TYRONE [*putting a hand over one of her nervously playing ones*]. Now, now, Mary. That's your imagination. If I've watched you it was to admire how fat and beautiful you looked. [*His voice is suddenly moved by deep feeling.*] I can't tell you the deep happiness it gives me, darling, to see you as you've been since you came back to us, your dear old self again. [*He leans over and kisses her cheek impulsively—then turning back adds with a constrained air*] So keep up the good work, Mary.

MARY [*has turned her head away*]. I will, dear. [*She gets up restlessly and goes to the windows at right.*] Thank heavens, the fog is gone.

[*She turns back.*] I do feel out of sorts this morning. I wasn't able to get much sleep with that awful foghorn going all night long.

TYRONE. Yes, it's like having a sick whale in the back yard. It kept me awake, too.

MARY [*affectionately amused*]. Did it? You had a strange way of showing your restlessness. You were snoring so hard I couldn't tell which was the foghorn! [*She comes to him, laughing, and pats his cheek playfully.*] Ten foghorns couldn't disturb you. You haven't a nerve in you. You've never had.

TYRONE [*his vanity piqued—testily*]. Nonsense. You always exaggerate about my snoring.

MARY. I couldn't. If you could only hear yourself once—

[*A burst of laughter comes from the dining room. She turns her head, smiling.*]

What's the joke, I wonder?

TYRONE [*grumpily*]. It's on me. I'll bet that much. It's always on the Old Man.

MARY [*teasingly*]. Yes, it's terrible the way we all pick on you, isn't it? You're so abused! [*She laughs—then with a pleased, relieved air*] Well, no matter what the joke is about, it's a relief to hear Edmund laugh. He's been so down in the mouth lately.

TYRONE [*ignoring this—resentfully*]. Some joke of Jamie's, I'll wager. He's forever making sneering fun of somebody, that one.

MARY. Now don't start in on poor Jamie, dear. [*Without conviction*] He'll turn out all right in the end, you wait and see.

TYRONE. He'd better start soon, then. He's nearly thirty-four.

MARY [*ignoring this*]. Good heavens, are they going to stay in the dining room all day? [*She goes to the back parlor doorway and calls*] Jamie! Edmund! Come in the living room and give Cathleen a chance to clear the table.

[EDMUND *calls back,* "We're coming, Mama." *She goes back to the table.*]

TYRONE [*grumbling*]. You'd find excuses for him no matter what he did.

MARY [*sitting down beside him, pats his hand*]. Shush.

[*Their sons* JAMES, JR., *and* EDMUND *enter together from the back parlor. They are both grinning, still chuckling over what had caused their laughter, and as they come forward they glance at their father and their grins grow broader.*

JAMIE, *the elder, is thirty-three. He has his father's broad-shouldered, deep-chested physique, is an inch taller and weighs less, but appears shorter and stouter because he lacks* TYRONE'S *bearing and graceful carriage. He also lacks his father's vitality. The signs of premature disintegration are on him. His face is still good looking, despite marks of dissipation, but it has never been handsome like* TYRONE'S, *although* JAMIE *resembles him rather than his mother. He has fine brown eyes, their color midway between his father's lighter*

*and his mother's darker ones. His hair is thinning and already there
is indication of a bald spot like* TYRONE's. *His nose is unlike that
of any other member of the family, pronouncedly aquiline. Combined
with his habitual expression of cynicism it gives his countenance a
Mephistophelian cast. But on the rare occasions when he smiles
without sneering his personality possesses the remnant of a humorous, romantic, irresponsible Irish charm—that of the beguiling ne'er-
do-well, with a strain of the sentimentally poetic, attractive to
women and popular with men.*

He is dressed in an old sack suit, not as shabby as TYRONE's, *and
wears a collar and tie. His fair skin is sunburned a reddish, freckled
tan.*

EDMUND *is ten years younger than his brother, a couple of inches
taller, thin and wiry. Where* JAMIE *takes after his father, with little
resemblance to his mother,* EDMUND *looks like both his parents, but
is more like his mother. Her big, dark eyes are the dominant feature
in his long, narrow Irish face. His mouth has the same quality of
hypersensitiveness hers possesses. His high forehead is hers accentuated, with dark brown hair, sunbleached to red at the ends,
brushed straight back from it. But his nose is his father's and his
face in profile recalls* TYRONE's. EDMUND's *hands are noticeably like
his mother's, with the same exceptionally long fingers. They even
have to a minor degree the same nervousness. It is in the quality of
extreme nervous sensibility that the likeness of* EDMUND *to his mother
is most marked.*

*He is plainly in bad health. Much thinner than he should be,
his eyes appear feverish and his cheeks are sunken. His skin, in spite
of being sunburned a deep brown, has a parched sallowness. He
wears a shirt, collar and tie, no coat, old flannel trousers, brown
sneakers.*]

MARY [*turns smilingly to them, in a merry tone that is a bit forced*]. I've
been teasing your father about his snoring. [*To* TYRONE] I'll leave it
to the boys, James. They must have heard you. No, not you, Jamie.
I could hear you down the hall almost as bad as your father. You're
like him. As soon as your head touches the pillow you're off and ten
foghorns couldn't wake you.

[*She stops abruptly, catching* JAMIE's *eyes regarding her with an
uneasy, probing look. Her smile vanishes and her manner becomes
self-conscious.*]

Why are you staring, Jamie? [*Her hands flutter up to her hair.*] Is my
hair coming down? It's hard for me to do it up properly now. My
eyes are getting so bad and I never can find my glasses.

JAMIE [*looks away guiltily*]. Your hair's all right, Mama. I was only
thinking how well you look.

TYRONE [*heartily*]. Just what I've been telling her, Jamie. She's so fat
and sassy, there'll soon be no holding her.

EDMUND. Yes, you certainly look grand, Mama.

[*She is reassured and smiles at him lovingly. He winks with a kidding grin.*]

I'll back you up about Papa's snoring. Gosh, what a racket!

JAMIE. I heard him, too, [*He quotes, putting on a ham-actor manner.*] "The Moor, I know his trumpet."[1]

[*His mother and brother laugh.*]

TYRONE [*scathingly*]. If it takes my snoring to make you remember Shakespeare instead of the dope sheet on the ponies, I hope I'll keep on with it.

MARY. Now, James! You mustn't be so touchy.

[JAMIE *shrugs his shoulders and sits down in the chair on her right.*]

EDMUND [*irritably*]. Yes, for Pete's sake, Papa! The first thing after breakfast! Give it a rest, can't you?

[*He slumps down in the chair at left of table next to his brother. His father ignores him.*]

MARY [*reprovingly*]. Your father wasn't finding fault with you. You don't have to always take Jamie's part. You'd think you were the one ten years older.

JAMIE [*boredly*]. What's all the fuss about? Let's forget it.

TYRONE [*contemptuously*]. Yes, forget! Forget everything and face nothing! It's a convenient philosophy if you've no ambition in life except to—

MARY. James, do be quiet. [*She puts an arm around his shoulder— coaxingly.*] You must have gotten out of the wrong side of the bed this morning. [*To the boys, changing the subject.*] What were you two grinning about like Cheshire cats when you came in? What was the joke?

TYRONE [*with a painful effort to be a good sport*]. Yes, let us in on it, lads. I told your mother I knew damned well it would be one on me, but never mind that, I'm used to it.

JAMIE [*dryly*]. Don't look at me. This is the Kid's story.

EDMUND [*grins*]. I meant to tell you last night, Papa, and forgot it. Yesterday when I went for a walk I dropped in at the Inn—

MARY [*worriedly*]. You shouldn't drink now, Edmund.

EDMUND [*ignoring this*]. And who do you think I met there, with a beautiful bun on, but Shaughnessy, the tenant on that farm of yours.

MARY [*smiling*]. That dreadful man! But he is funny.

TYRONE [*Scowling*]. He's not so funny when you're his landlord. He's a wily Shanty Mick,[2] that one. He could hide behind a corkscrew. What's he complaining about now, Edmund—for I'm damned sure he's complaining. I suppose he wants his rent lowered. I let him have the place for almost nothing, just to keep someone on it, and he never pays that till I threaten to evict him.

---

1. From *Othello* 2.1.178.
2. "Mick" is slang for "Irishman." A "Shanty

Mick" is a poor Irishman as contrasted with a "Lace-curtain Mick" or middle-class Irishman.

EDMUND. No, he didn't beef about anything. He was so pleased with life he even bought a drink, and that's practically unheard of. He was delighted because he'd had a fight with your friend, Harker, the Standard Oil millionaire, and won a glorious victory.

MARY [with amused dismay]. Oh, Lord! James, you'll really have to do something—

TYRONE. Bad luck to Shaughnessy, anyway!

JAMIE [maliciously]. I'll bet the next time you see Harker at the Club and give him the old respectful bow, he won't see you.

EDMUND. Yes. Harker will think you're no gentleman for harboring a tenant who isn't humble in the presence of a king of America.

TYRONE. Never mind the Socialist gabble. I don't care to listen—

MARY [tactfully]. Go on with your story, Edmund.

EDMUND [grins at his father provocatively]. Well, you remember, Papa, the ice pond on Harker's estate is right next to the farm, and you remember Shaughnessy keeps pigs. Well, it seems there's a break in the fence and the pigs have been bathing in the millionaire's ice pond, and Harker's foreman told him he was sure Shaughnessy had broken the fence on purpose to give his pigs a free wallow.

MARY [shocked and amused]. Good heavens!

TYRONE [sourly, but with a trace of admiration]. I'm sure he did, too, the dirty scallywag. It's like him.

EDMUND. So Harker came in person to rebuke Shaughnessy. [He chuckles.] A very bonehead play! If I needed any further proof that our ruling plutocrats, especially the ones who inherited their boodle, are not mental giants, that would clinch it.

TYRONE [with appreciation, before he thinks]. Yes, he'd be no match for Shaughnessy. [Then he growls.] Keep your damned anarchist remarks to yourself. I won't have them in my house. [But he is full of eager anticipation.] What happened?

EDMUND. Harker had as much chance as I would with Jack Johnson.[3] Shaughnessy got a few drinks under his belt and was waiting at the gate to welcome him. He told me he never gave Harker a chance to open his mouth. He began by shouting that he was no slave Standard Oil could trample on. He was a King of Ireland, if he had his rights, and scum was scum to him, no matter how much money it had stolen from the poor.

MARY. Oh, Lord! [But she can't help laughing.]

EDMUND. Then he accused Harker of making his foreman break down the fence to entice the pigs into the ice pond in order to destroy them. The poor pigs, Shaughnessy yelled, had caught their death of cold. Many of them were dying of pneumonia, and several others had been taken down with cholera from drinking the poisoned water. He told Harker he was hiring a lawyer to sue him for damages. And he wound up by saying that he had to put up with poison ivy, ticks, potato bugs,

3. The then heavyweight champion.

snakes and skunks on his farm, but he was an honest man who drew the line somewhere, and he'd be damned if he'd stand for a Standard Oil thief trespassing. So would Harker kindly remove his dirty feet from the premises before he sicked the dog on him. And Harker did!

[*He and* JAMIE *laugh.*]

MARY [*shocked but giggling*]. Heavens, what a terrible tongue that man has!

TYRONE [*admiringly before he thinks*]. The damned old scoundrel! By God, you can't beat him! [*He laughs—then stops abruptly and scowls.*] The dirty blackguard! He'll get me in serious trouble yet. I hope you told him I'd be mad as hell—

EDMUND. I told him you'd be tickled to death over the great Irish victory, and so you are. Stop faking, Papa.

TYRONE. Well, I'm not tickled to death.

MARY [*teasingly*]. You are, too, James. You're simply delighted!

TYRONE. No, Mary, a joke is a joke, but—

EDMUND. I told Shaughnessy he should have reminded Harker that a Standard Oil millionaire ought to welcome the flavor of hog in his ice water as an appropriate touch.

TYRONE. The devil you did! [*Frowning.*] Keep your damned Socialist anarchist sentiments out of my affairs!

EDMUND. Shaughnessy almost wept because he hadn't thought of that one, but he said he'd include it in a letter he's writing to Harker, along with a few other insults he'd overlooked.

[*He and* JAMIE *laugh.*]

TYRONE. What are you laughing at? There's nothing funny— A fine son you are to help that blackguard get me into a lawsuit!

MARY. Now, James, don't lose your temper.

TYRONE [*turns on* JAMIE]. And you're worse than he is, encouraging him. I suppose you're regretting you weren't there to prompt Shaughnessy with a few nastier insults. You've a fine talent for that, if for nothing else.

MARY. James! There's no reason to scold Jamie.

[JAMIE *is about to make some sneering remark to his father, but he shrugs his shoulders.*]

EDMUND [*with sudden nervous exasperation*]. Oh, for God's sake, Papa! If you're starting that stuff again, I'll beat it. [*He jumps up.*] I left my book upstairs, anyway. [*He goes to the front parlor, saying disgustedly*] God, Papa, I should think you'd get sick of hearing yourself—

[*He disappears.* TYRONE *looks after him angrily.*]

MARY. You mustn't mind Edmund, James. Remember he isn't well.

[EDMUND *can be heard coughing as he goes upstairs.*]

[*She adds nervously*] A summer cold makes anyone irritable.

JAMIE [*genuinely concerned*]. It's not just a cold he's got. The Kid is damned sick.

[*His father gives him a sharp warning look but he doesn't see it.*]

MARY [*turns on him resentfully*]. Why do you say that? It *is* just a cold! Anyone can tell that! You always imagine things!

TYRONE [*with another warning glance at Jamie—easily*]. All Jamie meant was Edmund might have a touch of something else, too, which makes his cold worse.

JAMIE. Sure, Mama. That's all I meant.

TYRONE. Doctor Hardy thinks it might be a bit of malarial fever he caught when he was in the tropics. If it is, quinine will soon cure it.

MARY [*a look of contemptuous hostility flashes across her face*]. Doctor Hardy! I wouldn't believe a thing he said, if he swore on a stack of Bibles! I know what doctors are. They're all alike. Anything, they don't care what, to keep you coming to them. [*She stops short, overcome by a fit of acute self-consciousness as she catches their eyes fixed on her. Her hands jerk nervously to her hair. She forces a smile.*] What is it? What are you looking at? Is my hair—?

TYRONE [*puts his arm around her—with guilty heartiness, giving her a playful hug*]. There's nothing wrong with your hair. The healthier and fatter you get, the vainer you become. You'll soon spend half the day primping before the mirror.

MARY [*half reassured*]. I really should have new glasses. My eyes are so bad now.

TYRONE [*with Irish blarney*]. Your eyes are beautiful, and well you know it.

[*He gives her a kiss. Her face lights up with a charming, shy embarrassment. Suddenly and startlingly one sees in her face the girl she had once been, not a ghost of the dead, but still a living part of her.*]

MARY. You mustn't be so silly, James. Right in front of Jamie!

TYRONE. Oh, he's on to you, too. He knows this fuss about eyes and hair is only fishing for compliments. Eh, Jamie?

JAMIE [*his face has cleared, too, and there is an old boyish charm in his loving smile at his mother*]. Yes. You can't kid us, Mama.

MARY [*laughs and an Irish lilt comes into her voice*]. Go along with both of you! [*Then she speaks with a girlish gravity.*] But I did truly have beautiful hair once, didn't I, James?

TYRONE. The most beautiful in the world!

MARY. It was a rare shade of reddish brown and so long it came down below my knees. You ought to remember it, too, Jamie. It wasn't until after Edmund was born that I had a single gray hair. Then it began to turn white. [*The girlishness fades from her face.*]

TYRONE [*quickly*]. And that made it prettier than ever.

MARY [*again embarrassed and pleased*]. Will you listen to your father, Jamie—after thirty-five years of marriage! He isn't a great actor for nothing, is he? What's come over you, James? Are you pouring coals of fire on my head for teasing you about snoring? Well then, I take it all back. It must have been only the foghorn I heard.

[*She laughs, and they laugh with her. Then she changes to a brisk businesslike air.*]

But I can't stay with you any longer, even to hear compliments. I must see the cook about dinner and the day's marketing. [*She gets up and sighs with humorous exaggeration.*] Bridget is so lazy. And so sly. She begins telling me about her relatives so I can't get a word in edgeways and scold her. Well, I might as well get it over. [*She goes to the back-parlor doorway, then turns, her face worried again.*] You mustn't make Edmund work on the grounds with you, James, remember. [*Again with the strange obstinate set to her face.*] Not that he isn't strong enough, but he'd perspire and he might catch more cold.

[*She disappears through the back parlor.* TYRONE *turns on* JAMIE *condemningly.*]

TYRONE. You're a fine lunkhead! Haven't you any sense? The one thing to avoid is saying anything that would get her more upset over Edmund.

JAMIE [*shrugging his shoulders*]. All right. Have it your way. I think it's the wrong idea to let Mama go on kidding herself. It will only make the shock worse when she has to face it. Anyway, you can see she's deliberately fooling herself with that summer cold talk. She knows better.

TYRONE. Knows? Nobody knows yet.

JAMIE. Well, I do. I was with Edmund when he went to Doc Hardy on Monday. I heard him pull that touch of malaria stuff. He was stalling. That isn't what he thinks any more. You know it as well as I do. You talked to him when you went uptown yesterday, didn't you?

TYRONE. He couldn't say anything for sure yet. He's to phone me today before Edmund goes to him.

JAMIE [*slowly*]. He thinks it's consumption, doesn't he, Papa?

TYRONE [*reluctantly*]. He said it might be.

JAMIE [*moved, his love for his brother coming out*]. Poor kid! God damn it! [*He turns on his father accusingly.*] It might never have happened if you'd sent him to a real doctor when he first got sick.

TYRONE. What's the matter with Hardy? He's always been our doctor up here.

JAMIE. Everything's the matter with him! Even in this hick burg he's rated third class! He's a cheap old quack!

TYRONE. That's right! Run him down! Run down everybody! Everyone is a fake to you!

JAMIE [*contemptuously*]. Hardy only charges a dollar. That's what makes you think he's a fine doctor!

TYRONE [*stung*]. That's enough! You're not drunk now! There's no excuse— [*He controls himself—a bit defensively.*] If you mean I can't afford one of the fine society doctors who prey on the rich summer people—

JAMIE. Can't afford? You're one of the biggest property owners around here.

TYRONE. That doesn't mean I'm rich. It's all mortgaged—

JAMIE. Because you always buy more instead of paying off mortgages. If Edmund was a lousy acre of land you wanted, the sky would be the limit!

TYRONE. That's a lie! And your sneers against Doctor Hardy are lies! He doesn't put on frills, or have an office in a fashionable location, or drive around in an expensive automobile. That's what you pay for with those other five-dollars-to-look-at-your-tongue fellows, not their skill.

JAMIE [*with a scornful shrug of his shoulders*]. Oh, all right. I'm a fool to argue. You can't change the leopard's spots.

TYRONE [*with rising anger*]. No, you can't. You've taught me that lesson only too well. I've lost all hope you will ever change yours. You dare tell me what I can afford? You've never known the value of a dollar and never will. You've never saved a dollar in your life! At the end of each season you're penniless! You've thrown your salary away every week on whores and whiskey!

JAMIE. My salary! Christ!

TYRONE. It's more than you're worth, and you couldn't get that if it wasn't for me. If you weren't my son, there isn't a manager in the business who would give you a part, your reputation stinks so. As it is, I have to humble my pride and beg for you, saying you've turned over a new leaf, although I know it's a lie!

JAMIE. I never wanted to be an actor. You forced me on the stage.

TYRONE. That's a lie! You made no effort to find anything else to do. You left it to me to get you a job and I have no influence except in the theater. Forced you! You never wanted to do anything except loaf in barrooms! You'd have been content to sit back like a lazy lunk and sponge on me for the rest of your life! After all the money I'd wasted on your education, and all you did was get fired in disgrace from every college you went to!

JAMIE. Oh, for God's sake, don't drag up that ancient history!

TYRONE. It's not ancient history that you have to come home every summer to live on me.

JAMIE. I earn my board and lodging working on the grounds. It saves you hiring a man.

TYRONE. Bah! You have to be driven to do even that much! [*His anger ebbs into a weary complaint.*] I wouldn't give a damn if you ever displayed the slightest sign of gratitude. The only thanks is to have you sneer at me for a dirty miser, sneer at my profession, sneer at every damned thing in the world—except yourself.

JAMIE [*wryly*]. That's not true, Papa. You can't hear me talking to myself, that's all.

TYRONE [*stares at him puzzledly, then quotes mechanically*]. "Ingratitude, the vilest weed that grows"![4]

JAMIE. I could see that line coming! God, how many thousand times—! [*He stops, bored with their quarrel, and shrugs his shoulders.*] All right, Papa. I'm a bum. Anything you like, so long as it stops the argument.

TYRONE [*with indignant appeal now*]. If you'd get ambition in your head instead of folly! You're young yet. You could still make your mark. You had the talent to become a fine actor! You have it still. You're my son—!

JAMIE [*boredly*]. Let's forget me. I'm not interested in the subject. Neither are you.

[TYRONE *gives up.* JAMIE *goes on casually.*]

What started us on this? Oh, Doc Hardy. When is he going to call you up about Edmund?

TYRONE. Around lunch time. [*He pauses—then defensively.*] I couldn't have sent Edmund to a better doctor. Hardy's treated him whenever he was sick up here, since he was knee high. He knows his constitution as no other doctor could. It's not a question of my being miserly, as you'd like to make out. [*Bitterly.*] And what could the finest specialist in America do for Edmund, after he's deliberately ruined his health by the mad life he's led every since he was fired from college? Even before that when he was in prep school, he began dissipating and playing the Broadway sport to imitate you, when he's never had your constitution to stand it. You're a healthy hulk like me—or you were at his age—but he's always been a bundle of nerves like his mother. I've warned him for years his body couldn't stand it, but he wouldn't heed me, and now it's too late.

JAMIE [*sharply*]. What do you mean, too late? You talk as if you thought—

TYRONE [*guiltily explosive*]. Don't be a damned fool! I meant nothing but what's plain to anyone! His health has broken down and he may be an invalid for a long time.

JAMIE [*stares at his father, ignoring his explanation*]. I know it's an Irish peasant idea consumption is fatal. It probably is when you live in a hovel on a bog, but over here, with modern treatment—

TYRONE. Don't I know that! What are you gabbing about, anyway? And keep your dirty tongue off Ireland, with your sneers about peasants and bogs and hovels! [*Accusingly.*] The less you say about Edmund's sickness, the better for your conscience! You're more responsible than anyone!

JAMIE [*stung*]. That's a lie! I won't stand for that, Papa!

TYRONE. It's the truth! you've been the worst influence for him. He grew up admiring you as a hero! A fine example you set him! If you ever gave him advice except in the ways of rottenness, I've never heard of it! You made him old before his time, pumping him full of what you

---

4. Apparently a quotation from a well-known play, but I have not been able to trace which.

consider worldly wisdom, when he was too young to see that your mind was so poisoned by your own failure in life, you wanted to believe every man was a knave with his soul for sale, and every woman who wasn't a whore was a fool!

JAMIE [*with a defensive air of weary indifference again*]. All right. I did put Edmund wise to things, but not until I saw he'd started to raise hell, and knew he'd laugh at me if I tried the good advice, older brother stuff. All I did was make a pal of him and be absolutely frank so he'd learn from my mistakes that— [*He shrugs his shoulders—cynically.*] Well, that if you can't be good you can at least be careful. [*His father snorts contemptuously. Suddenly* JAMIE *becomes really moved.*]

That's a rotten accusation, Papa. You know how much the Kid means to me, and how close we've always been—not like the usual brothers! I'd do anything for him.

TYRONE [*impressed—mollifyingly*]. I know you may have thought it was for the best, Jamie. I didn't say you did it deliberately to harm him.

JAMIE. Besides it's damned rot! I'd like to see anyone influence Edmund more than he wants to be. His quietness fools people into thinking they can do what they like with him. But he's stubborn as hell inside and what he does is what he wants to do, and to hell with anyone else! What had I to do with all the crazy stunts he's pulled in the last few years—working his way all over the map as a sailor and all that stuff. I thought that was a damned fool idea, and I told him so. You can't imagine me getting fun out of being on the beach in South America, or living in filthy dives, drinking rotgut, can you? No, thanks! I'll stick to Broadway, and a room with a bath, and bars that serve bonded Bourbon.

TYRONE. You and Broadway! It's made you what you are! [*With a touch of pride.*] Whatever Edmund's done, he's had the guts to go off on his own, where he couldn't come whining to me the minute he was broke.

JAMIE [*stung into sneering jealousy*]. He's always come home broke finally, hasn't he? And what did his going away get him? Look at him now! [*He is suddenly shamefaced.*] Christ! That's a lousy thing to say. I don't mean that.

TYRONE [*decides to ignore this*]. He's been doing well on the paper. I was hoping he'd found the work he wants to do at last.

JAMIE [*sneering jealously again*]. A hick town rag! Whatever bull they hand you, they tell me he's a pretty bum reporter. If he weren't your son— [*Ashamed again.*] No, that's not true! They're glad to have him, but it's the special stuff that gets him by. Some of the poems and parodies he's written are damned good. [*Grudgingly again.*] Not that they'd ever get him anywhere on the big time. [*Hastily.*] But he's certainly made a damned good start.

TYRONE. Yes. He's made a start. You used to talk about wanting to become a newspaper man but you were never willing to start at the bottom. You expected—

JAMIE. Oh, for Christ's sake, Papa! Can't you lay off me!

TYRONE [*stares at him—then looks away—after a pause*]. It's damnable luck Edmund should be sick right now. It couldn't have come at a worse time for him. [*He adds, unable to conceal an almost furtive uneasiness*] Or for your mother. It's damnable she should have this to upset her, just when she needs peace and freedom from worry. She's been so well in the two months since she came home. [*His voice grows husky and trembles a little.*] It's been heaven to me. This home has been a home again. But I needn't tell you, Jamie.

[*His son looks at him for the first time with an understanding sympathy. It is as if suddenly a deep bond of common feeling existed between them in which their antagonisms could be forgotten.*]

JAMIE [*almost gently*]. I've felt the same way, Papa.

TYRONE. Yes, this time you can see how strong and sure of herself she is. She's a different woman entirely from the other times. She has control of her nerves—or she had until Edmund got sick. Now you can feel her growing tense and frightened underneath. I wish to God we could keep the truth from her, but we can't if he has to be sent to a sanatorium. What makes it worse is her father died of consumption. She worshiped him and she's never forgotten. Yes, it will be hard for her. But she can do it! She has the will power now! We must help her, Jamie, in every way we can!

JAMIE [*moved*]. Of course, Papa. [*Hesitantly.*] Outside of nerves, she seems perfectly all right this morning.

TYRONE [*with hearty confidence now*]. Never better. She's full of fun and mischief. [*Suddenly he frowns at JAMIE suspiciously.*] Why do you say, seems? Why shouldn't she be all right? What the hell do you mean?

JAMIE. Don't start jumping down my throat! God, Papa, this ought to be one thing we can talk over frankly without a battle.

TYRONE. I'm sorry, Jamie. [*Tensely.*] But go on and tell me—

JAMIE. There's nothing to tell. I was all wrong. It's just that last night— Well, you know how it is, I can't forget the past. I can't help being suspicious. Any more than you can. [*Bitterly.*] That's the hell of it. And it makes it hell for Mama! She watches us watching her—

TYRONE [*sadly*]. I know. [*Tensely.*] Well, what was it? Can't you speak out?

JAMIE. Nothing, I tell you. Just my damned foolishness. Around three o'clock this morning, I woke up and heard her moving around in the spare room. Then she went to the bathroom. I pretended to be asleep. She stopped in the hall to listen, as if she wanted to make sure I was.

TYRONE [*with forced scorn*]. For God's sake, is that all? She told me herself the foghorn kept her awake all night, and every night since

Edmund's been sick she's been up and down, going to his room to see how he was.

JAMIE [*eagerly*]. Yes, that's right, she did stop to listen outside his room. [*Hesitantly again.*] It was her being in the spare room that scared me. I couldn't help remembering that when she starts sleeping alone in there, it has always been a sign—

TYRONE. It isn't this time! It's easily explained. Where else could she go last night to get away from my snoring? [*He gives way to a burst of resentful anger.*] By God, how you can live with a mind that sees nothing but the worst motives behind everything is beyond me!

JAMIE [*stung*]. Don't pull that! I've just said I was all wrong. Don't you suppose I'm as glad of that as you are!

TYRONE [*mollifyingly*]. I'm sure you are, Jamie. [*A pause. His expression becomes somber. He speaks slowly with a superstitious dread.*] It would be like a curse she can't escape if worry over Edmund— It was in her long sickness after bringing him into the world that she first—

JAMIE. She didn't have anything to do with it!

TYRONE. I'm not blaming her.

JAMIE [*bitingly*]. Then who are you blaming? Edmund, for being born?

TYRONE. You damned fool! No one was to blame.

JAMIE. The bastard of a doctor was! From what Mama's said, he was another cheap quack like Hardy! You wouldn't pay for a first-rate—

TYRONE. That's a lie! [*Furiously.*] So I'm to blame! That's what you're driving at, is it? You evil-minded loafer!

JAMIE [*warningly as he hears his mother in the dining room*]. Ssh!
    [TYRONE *gets hastily to his feet and goes to look out the windows at right.* JAMIE *speaks with a complete change of tone.*]
Well, if we're going to cut the front hedge today, we'd better go to work.
    [MARY *comes in from the back parlor. She gives a quick, suspicious glance from one to the other, her manner nervously self-conscious.*]

TYRONE [*turns from the window—with an actor's heartiness*]. Yes, it's too fine a morning to waste indoors arguing. Take a look out the window, Mary. There's no fog in the harbor. I'm sure the spell of it we've had is over now.

MARY [*going to him*]. I hope so, dear. [*To* JAMIE, *forcing a smile.*] Did I actually hear you suggesting work on the front hedge, Jamie? Wonders will never cease! You must want pocket money badly.

JAMIE [*kiddingly*]. When don't I? [*He winks at her, with a derisive glance at his father.*] I expect a salary of at least one large iron man[5] at the end of the week—to carouse on!

MARY [*does not respond to his humor—her hands fluttering over the front of her dress*]. What were you two arguing about?

JAMIE [*shrugs his shoulders*]. The same old stuff.

5. A silver dollar.

MARY. I heard you say something about a doctor, and your father accusing you of being evil-minded.

JAMIE [*quickly*]. Oh, that. I was saying again Doc Hardy isn't my idea of the world's greatest physician.

MARY [*knows he is lying—vaguely*]. Oh. No, I wouldn't say he was, either. [*Changing the subject—forcing a smile.*] That Bridget! I thought I'd never get away. She told me all about her second cousin on the police force in St. Louis. [*Then with nervous irritation.*] Well, if you're going to work on the hedge why don't you go? [*Hastily.*] I mean, take advantage of the sunshine before the fog comes back. [*Strangely, as if talking aloud to herself.*] Because I know it will. [*Suddenly she is self-consciously aware that they are both staring fixedly at her—flurriedly, raising her hands.*] Or I should say, the rheumatism in my hands knows. It's a better weather prophet than you are, James. [*She stares at her hands with fascinated repulsion.*] Ugh! How ugly they are! Who'd ever believe they were once beautiful? [*They stare at her with a growing dread.*]

TYRONE [*takes her hands and gently pushes them down*]. Now, now, Mary. None of that foolishness. They're the sweetest hands in the world.

[*She smiles, her face lighting up, and kisses him gratefully. He turns to his son.*]

Come on Jamie. Your mother's right to scold us. The way to start work is to start work. The hot sun will sweat some of that booze fat off your middle.

[*He opens the screen door and goes out on the porch and disappears down a flight of steps leading to the ground. JAMIE rises from his chair and, taking off his coat, goes to the door. At the door he turns back but avoids looking at her, and she does not look at him.*]

JAMIE [*with an awkward, uneasy tenderness*]. We're all so proud of you, Mama, so darned happy.

[*She stiffens and stares at him with a frightened defiance. He flounders on.*]

But you've still got to be careful. You mustn't worry so much about Edmund. He'll be all right.

MARY [*with a stubborn, bitterly resentful look*]. Of course, he'll be all right. And I don't know what you mean, warning me to be careful.

JAMIE [*rebuffed and hurt, shrugs his shoulders*]. All right, Mama. I'm sorry I spoke.

[*He goes out on the porch. She waits rigidly until he disappears down the steps. Then she sinks down in the chair he had occupied, her face betraying a frightened, furtive desperation, her hands roving over the table top, aimlessly moving objects around. She hears EDMUND descending the stairs in the front hall. As he nears the bottom he has a fit of coughing. She springs to her feet, as if she wanted to run away from the sound, and goes quickly to the windows at right. She is looking out, apparently calm, as he enters from the*] *front parlor, a book in one hand. She turns to him, her lips set in a welcoming, motherly smile.*]

MARY. Here you are. I was just going upstairs to look for you.

EDMUND. I waited until they went out. I don't want to mix up in any arguments. I feel too rotten.

MARY [*almost resentfully*]. Oh, I'm sure you don't feel half as badly as you make out. You're such a baby. You like to get us worried so we'll make a fuss over you. [*Hastily.*] I'm only teasing, dear. I know how miserably uncomfortable you must be. But you feel better today, don't you? [*Worriedly, taking his arm.*] All the same, you've grown much too thin. You need to rest all you can. Sit down and I'll make you comfortable.

[*He sits down in the rocking chair and she puts a pillow behind his back.*]

There. How's that?

EDMUND. Grand. Thanks, Mama.

MARY [*kisses him—tenderly*]. All you need is your mother to nurse you. Big as you are, you're still the baby of the family to me, you know.

EDMUND [*takes her hand—with deep seriousness*]. Never mind me. You take care of yourself. That's all that counts.

MARY [*evading his eyes*]. But I am, dear. [*Forcing a laugh.*] Heavens, don't you see how fat I've grown! I'll have to have all my dresses let out. [*She turns away and goes to the windows at right. She attempts a light, amused tone.*] They've started clipping the hedge. Poor Jamie! How he hates working in front where everyone passing can see him. There go the Chatfields in their new Mercedes. It's a beautiful car, isn't it? Not like our secondhand Packard. Poor Jamie! He bent almost under the hedge so they wouldn't notice him. They bowed to your father and he bowed back as if he were taking a curtain call. In that filthy old suit I've tried to make him throw away. [*Her voice has grown bitter.*] Really, he ought to have more pride than to make such a show of himself.

EDMUND. He's right not to give a damn what anyone thinks. Jamie's a fool to care about the Chatfields. For Pete's sake, who ever heard of them outside this hick burg?

MARY [*with satisfaction*]. No one. You're quite right, Edmund. Big frogs in a small puddle. It is stupid of Jamie. [*She pauses, looking out the window—then with an undercurrent of lonely yearning.*] Still, the Chatfields and people like them stand for something. I mean they have decent, presentable homes they don't have to be ashamed of. They have friends who entertain them and whom they entertain. They're not cut off from everyone. [*She turns back from the window.*] Not that I want anything to do with them. I've always hated this town and everyone in it. You know that. I never wanted to live here in the first place, but your father liked it and insisted on building this house, and I've had to come here every summer.

EDMUND. Well, it's better than spending the summer in a New York hotel, isn't it? And this town's not so bad. I like it well enough. I suppose because it's the only home we've had.

MARY. I've never felt it was my home. It was wrong from the start. Everything was done in the cheapest way. Your father would never spend the money to make it right. It's just as well we haven't any friends here. I'd be ashamed to have them step in the door. But he's never wanted family friends. He hates calling on people, or receiving them. All he likes is to hobnob with men at the Club or in a barroom. Jamie and you are the same way, but you're not to blame. You've never had a chance to meet decent people here. I know you both would have been so different if you'd been able to associate with nice girls instead of— You'd never have disgraced yourselves as you have, so that now no respectable parents will let their daughters be seen with you.

EDMUND [*irritably*]. Oh, Mama, forget it! Who cares? Jamie and I would be bored stiff. And about the Old Man, what's the use of talking? You can't change him.

MARY [*mechanically rebuking*]. Don't call your father the Old Man. You should have more respect. [*Then dully.*] I know it's useless to talk. But sometimes I feel so lonely. [*Her lips quiver and she keeps her head turned away.*]

EDMUND. Anyway, you've got to be fair, Mama. It may have been all his fault in the beginning, but you know that later on, even if he'd wanted to, we couldn't have had people here— [*He flounders guiltily.*] I mean, you wouldn't have wanted them.

MARY [*wincing—her lips quivering pitifully*]. Don't. I can't bear having you remind me.

EDMUND. Don't take it that way! Please, Mama! I'm trying to help. Because it's bad for you to forget. The right way is to remember. So you'll always be on your guard. You know what's happened before. [*Miserably.*] God, Mama, you know I hate to remind you. I'm doing it because it's been so wonderful having you home the way you've been, and it would be terrible—

MARY [*strickenly*]. Please, dear. I know you mean it for the best, but— [*A defensive uneasiness comes into her voice again.*] I don't understand why you should suddenly say such things. What put it in your mind this morning?

EDMUND [*evasively*]. Nothing. Just because I feel rotten and blue, I suppose.

MARY. Tell me the truth. Why are you so suspicious all of a sudden?

EDMUND. I'm not!

MARY. Oh, yes you are. I can feel it. Your father and Jamie, too— particularly Jamie.

EDMUND. Now don't start imagining things, Mama.

MARY [*her hands fluttering*]. It makes it so much harder, living in this atmosphere of constant suspicion, knowing everyone is spying on me, and none of you believe in me, or trust me.

EDMUND. That's crazy, Mama. We do trust you.

MARY. If there was only some place I could go to get away for a day, or even an afternoon, some woman friend I could talk to—not about anything serious, simply laugh and gossip and forget for a while— someone besides the servants—that stupid Cathleen!

EDMUND [*gets up worriedly and puts his arm around her*]. Stop it, Mama. You're getting yourself worked up over nothing.

MARY. Your father goes out. He meets his friends in barrooms or at the Club. You and Jamie have the boys you know. You go out. But I am alone. I've always been alone.

EDMUND [*soothingly*]. Come now! You know that's a fib. One of us always stays around to keep you company, or goes with you in the automobile when you take a drive.

MARY [*bitterly*]. Because you're afraid to trust me alone! [*She turns on him—sharply.*] I insist you tell me why you act so differently this morning—why you felt you had to remind me—

EDMUND [*hesitates—then blurts out guiltily*]. It's stupid. It's just that I wasn't asleep when you came in my room last night. You didn't go back to your and Papa's room. You went in the spare room for the rest of the night.

MARY. Because your father's snoring was driving me crazy! For heaven's sake, haven't I often used the spare room as my bedroom? [*Bitterly.*] But I see what you thought. That was when—

EDMUND [*too vehemently*]. I didn't think anything!

MARY. So you pretended to be asleep in order to spy on me!

EDMUND. No! I did it because I knew if you found out I was feverish and couldn't sleep, it would upset you.

MARY. Jamie was pretending to be asleep, too, I'm sure, and I suppose your father—

EDMUND. Stop it, Mama!

MARY. Oh, I can't bear it, Edmund, when even you—! [*Her hands flutter up to pat her hair in their aimless, distracted way. Suddenly a strange undercurrent of revengefulness comes into her voice.*] It would serve all of you right if it was true!

EDMUND. Mama! Don't say that! That's the way you talk when—

MARY. Stop suspecting me! Please, dear! You hurt me! I couldn't sleep because I was thinking about you. That's the real reason! I've been so worried ever since you've been sick.

[*She puts her arms around him and hugs him with a frightened, protective tenderness.*]

EDMUND [*soothingly*]. That's foolishness. You know it's only a bad cold.

MARY. Yes, of course, I know that!

EDMUND. But listen, Mama. I want you to promise me that even if it should turn out to be something worse, you'll know I'll soon be all right again, anyway, and you won't worry yourself sick, and you'll keep on taking care of yourself—

MARY [*frightenedly*]. I won't listen when you're so silly! There's absolutely no reason to talk as if you expected something dreadful! Of course, I promise you. I give you my sacred word of honor! [*Then with a sad bitterness.*] But I suppose you're remembering I've promised before on my word of honor.

EDMUND. No!

MARY [*her bitterness receding into a resigned helplessness*]. I'm not blaming you, dear. How can you help it? How can any one of us forget? [*Strangely.*] That's what makes it so hard—for all of us. We can't forget.

EDMUND [*grabs her shoulder*]. Mama! Stop it!

MARY [*forcing a smile*]. All right, dear. I didn't mean to be so gloomy. Don't mind me. Here. Let me feel your head. Why, it's nice and cool. You certainly haven't any fever now.

EDMUND. Forget! It's you—

MARY. But I'm quite all right, dear. [*With a quick, strange, calculating, almost sly glance at him.*] Except I naturally feel tired and nervous this morning, after such a bad night. I really ought to go upstairs and lie down until lunch time and take a nap.

[*He gives her an instinctive look of suspicion—then, ashamed of himself, looks quickly away. She hurries on nervously.*]

What are you going to do? Read here? It would be much better for you to go out in the fresh air and sunshine. But don't get overheated, remember. Be sure and wear a hat.

[*She stops, looking straight at him now. He avoids her eyes. There is a tense pause. Then she speaks jeeringly*]

Or are you afraid to trust me alone?

EDMUND [tormentedly]. No! Can't you stop talking like that! I think you ought to take a nap. [*He goes to the screen door—forcing a joking tone.*] I'll go down and help Jamie bear up. I love to lie in the shade and watch him work.

[*He forces a laugh in which she makes herself join. Then he goes out on the porch and disappears down the steps. Her first reaction is one of relief. She appears to relax. She sinks down in one of the wicker armchairs at rear of table and leans her head back, closing her eyes. But suddenly she grows terribly tense again. Her eyes open and she strains forward, seized by a fit of nervous panic. She begins a desperate battle with herself. Her long fingers, warped and knotted by rheumatism, drum on the arms of the chair, driven by an insistent life of their own, without her consent.*]

[*Curtain*]

Act Two

Scene One

SCENE—*The same. It is around quarter to one. No sunlight comes into the room now through the windows at right. Outside the day is still fine but increasingly sultry, with a faint haziness in the air which softens the glare of the sun.*

EDMUND *sits in the armchair at left of table, reading a book. Or rather he is trying to concentrate on it but cannot. He seems to be listening for some sound from upstairs. His manner is nervously apprehensive and he looks more sickly than in the previous act.*

The second girl, CATHLEEN, *enters from the back parlor. She carries a tray on which is a bottle of bonded Bourbon, several whiskey glasses, and a pitcher of ice water. She is a buxom Irish peasant, in her early twenties, with a red-cheeked comely face, black hair and blue eyes—amiable, ignorant, clumsy, and possessed by a dense, well-meaning stupidity. She puts the tray on the table.* EDMUND *pretends to be so absorbed in his book he does not notice her, but she ignores this.*

CATHLEEN [*with garrulous familiarity*]. Here's the whiskey. It'll be lunch time soon. Will I call your father and Mister Jamie, or will you?

EDMUND [*without looking up from his book*]. You do it.

CATHLEEN. It's a wonder your father wouldn't look at his watch once in a while. He's a divil for making the meals late, and then Bridget curses me as if I was to blame. But he's a grand handsome man, if he is old. You'll never see the day you're as good looking—nor Mister Jamie, either. [*She chuckles.*] I'll wager Mister Jamie wouldn't miss the time to stop work and have his drop of whiskey if he had a watch to his name!

EDMUND [*gives up trying to ignore her and grins*]. You win that one.

CATHLEEN. And here's another I'd win, that you're making me call them so you can sneak a drink before they come.

EDMUND. Well, I hadn't thought of that—

CATHLEEN. Oh no, not you! Butter wouldn't melt in your mouth, I suppose.

EDMUND. But now you suggest it—

CATHLEEN [*suddenly primly virtuous*]. I'd never suggest a man or a woman touch drink, Mister Edmund. Sure, didn't it kill an uncle of mine in the old country. [*Relenting.*] Still, a drop now and then is no harm when you're in low spirits, or have a bad cold.

EDMUND. Thanks for handing me a good excuse. [*Then with forced casualness.*] You'd better call my mother, too.

CATHLEEN. What for? She's always on time without any calling. God bless her, she has some consideration for the help.

EDMUND. She's been taking a nap.

CATHLEEN. She wasn't asleep when I finished my work upstairs a while back. She was lying down in the spare room with her eyes wide open. She'd a terrible headache, she said.

EDMUND [*his casualness more forced*]. Oh well then, just call my father.

CATHLEEN [*goes to the screen door, grumbling good-naturedly*]. No wonder my feet kill me each night. I won't walk out in this heat and get sunstroke. I'll call from the porch. [*She goes out on the side porch, letting the screen door slam behind her, and disappears on her way to the front porch. A moment later she is heard shouting*] Mister Tyrone! Mister Jamie! It's time!

[EDMUND, *who has been staring frightenedly before him, forgetting his book, springs to his feet nervously.*]

EDMUND. God, what a wench!

[*He grabs the bottle and pours a drink, adds ice water and drinks. As he does so, he hears someone coming in the front door. He puts the glass hastily on the tray and sits down again, opening his book.* JAMIE *comes in from the front parlor, his coat over his arm. He has taken off collar and tie and carries them in his hand. He is wiping sweat from his forehead with a handkerchief.* EDMUND *looks up as if his reading was interrupted.* JAMIE *takes one look at the bottle and glasses and smiles cynically.*]

JAMIE. Sneaking one, eh? Cut out the bluff, Kid. You're a rottener actor than I am.

EDMUND [*grins*]. Yes, I grabbed one while the going was good.

JAMIE [*puts a hand affectionately on his shoulder*]. That's better. Why kid me? We're pals, aren't we?

EDMUND. I wasn't sure it was you coming.

JAMIE. I made the Old Man look at his watch. I was halfway up the walk when Cathleen burst into song. Our wild Irish lark! She ought to be a train announcer.

EDMUND. That's what drove me to drink. Why don't you sneak one while you've got a chance?

JAMIE. I was thinking of that little thing. [*He goes quickly to the window at right.*] The Old Man was talking to old Captain Turner. Yes, he's still at it. [*He comes back and takes a drink.*] And now to cover up from his eagle eye. He memorizes the level in the bottle after every drink. [*He measures two drinks of water and pours them in the whiskey bottle and shakes it up.*] There. That fixes it. [*He pours water in the glass and sets it on the table by* EDMUND.] And here's the water you've been drinking.

EDMUND. Fine! You don't think it will fool him, do you?

JAMIE. Maybe not, but he can't prove it. [*Putting on his collar and tie.*] I hope he doesn't forget lunch listening to himself talk. I'm hungry. [*He sits across the table from* EDMUND—*irritably.*] That's what I hate about working down in front. He puts on an act for every damned fool that comes along.

EDMUND [*gloomily*]. You're in luck to be hungry. The way I feel I don't care if I ever eat again.

JAMIE [*gives him a glance of concern*]. Listen, Kid. You know me. I've never lectured you, but Doctor Hardy was right when he told you to cut out the redeye.

EDMUND. Oh, I'm going to after he hands me the bad news this afternoon. A few before then won't make any difference.

JAMIE [*hesitates—then slowly*]. I'm glad you've got your mind prepared for bad news. It won't be such a jolt. [*He catches* EDMUND *staring at him.*] I mean, it's a cinch you're really sick, and it would be wrong dope to kid yourself.

EDMUND [*disturbed*]. I'm not. I know how rotten I feel, and the fever and chills I get at night are no joke. I think Doctor Hardy's last guess was right. It must be the damned malaria come back on me.

JAMIE. Maybe, but don't be too sure.

EDMUND. Why? What do you think it is?

JAMIE. Hell, how would I know? I'm no Doc. [*Abruptly.*] Where's Mama?

EDMUND. Upstairs.

JAMIE [*looks at him sharply*]. When did she go up?

EDMUND. Oh, about the time I came down to the hedge, I guess. She said she was going to take a nap.

JAMIE. You didn't tell me—

EDMUND [*defensively*]. Why should I? What about it? She was tired out. She didn't get much sleep last night.

JAMIE. I know she didn't.

[*A pause. The brothers avoid looking at each other.*]

EDMUND. That damned foghorn kept me awake, too. [*Another pause.*]

JAMIE. She's been upstairs alone all morning, eh? You haven't seen her?

EDMUND. No. I've been reading here. I wanted to give her a chance to sleep.

JAMIE. Is she coming down to lunch?

EDMUND. Of course.

JAMIE [*dryly*]. No of course about it. She might not want any lunch. Or she might start having most of her meals alone upstairs. That's happened, hasn't it?

EDMUND [*with frightened resentment*]. Cut it out, Jamie! Can't you think anything but—? [*Persuasively.*] You're all wrong to suspect anything. Cathleen saw her not long ago. Mama didn't tell her she wouldn't be down to lunch.

JAMIE. Then she wasn't taking a nap?

EDMUND. Not right then, but she was lying down, Cathleen said.

JAMIE. In the spare room?

EDMUND. Yes. For Pete's sake, what of it?

JAMIE [*bursts out*]. You damned fool! Why did you leave her alone so long? Why didn't you stick around?

EDMUND. Because she accused me—and you and Papa—of spying on her all the time and not trusting her. She made me feel ashamed. I know how rotten it must be for her. And she promised on her sacred word of honor—

JAMIE [*with a bitter weariness*]. You ought to know that doesn't mean anything.

EDMUND. It does this time!

JAMIE. That's what we thought the other times. [*He leans over the table to give his brother's arm an affectionate grasp.*] Listen, Kid, I know you think I'm a cynical bastard, but remember I've seen a lot more of this game than you have. You never knew what was really wrong until you were in prep school. Papa and I kept it from you. But I was wise ten years or more before we had to tell you. I know the game backwards and I've been thinking all morning of the way she acted last night when she thought we were asleep. I haven't been able to think of anything else. And now you tell me she got you to leave her alone upstairs all morning.

EDMUND. She didn't! You're crazy!

JAMIE [*placatingly*]. All right, Kid. Don't start a battle with me. I hope as much as you do I'm crazy. I've been as happy as hell because I'd really begun to believe that this time— [*He stops—looking through the front parlor toward the hall—lowering his voice, hurriedly.*] She's coming downstairs. You win on that. I guess I'm a damned suspicious louse. [*They grow tense with a hopeful, fearful expectancy.* JAMIE *mutters*] Damn! I wish I'd grabbed another drink.

EDMUND. Me, too.

[*He coughs nervously and this brings on a real fit of coughing.* JAMIE *glances at him with worried pity.* MARY *enters from the front parlor. At first one notices no change except that she appears to be less nervous, to be more as she was when we first saw her after breakfast, but then one becomes aware that her eyes are brighter, and there is a peculiar detachment in her voice and manner, as if she were a little withdrawn from her words and actions.*]

MARY [*goes worriedly to* EDMUND *and puts her arm around him*]. You mustn't cough like that. It's bad for your throat. You don't want to get a sore throat on top of your cold.

[*She kisses him. He stops coughing and gives her a quick apprehensive glance, but if his suspicions are aroused her tenderness makes him renounce them and he believes what he wants to believe for the moment. On the other hand,* JAMIE *knows after one probing look at her that his suspicions are justified. His eyes fall to stare at the floor, his face sets in an expression of embittered, defensive cynicism.* MARY *goes on, half sitting on the arm of* EDMUND's *chair, her arm around him, so her face is above and behind his and he cannot look into her eyes.*]

But I seem to be always picking on you, telling you don't do this and

don't do that. Forgive me, dear. It's just that I want to take care of
you.

EDMUND. I know, Mama. How about you? Do you feel rested?

MARY. Yes, ever so much better. I've been lying down ever since you
went out. It's what I needed after such a restless night. I don't feel
nervous now.

EDMUND. That's fine.

[*He pats her hand on his shoulder.* JAMIE *gives him a strange, almost
contemptuous glance, wondering if his brother can really mean this.*
EDMUND *does not notice but his mother does.*]

MARY [*in a forced teasing tone*]. Good heavens, how down in the mouth
you look, Jamie. What's the matter now?

JAMIE [*without looking at her*]. Nothing.

MARY. Oh, I'd forgotten you've been working on the front hedge. That
accounts for your sinking into the dumps, doesn't it?

JAMIE. If you want to think so, Mama.

MARY [*keeping her tone*]. Well, that's the effect it always has, isn't it?
What a big baby you are! Isn't he, Edmund?

EDMUND. He's certainly a fool to care what anyone thinks.

MARY [*strangely*]. Yes, the only way is to make yourself not care.

[*She catches* JAMIE *giving her a bitter glance and changes the subject.*]
Where is your father? I heard Cathleen call him.

EDMUND. Gabbing with old Captain Turner, Jamie says. He'll be late,
as usual.

[JAMIE *gets up and goes to the windows at right, glad of an excuse
to turn his back.*]

MARY. I've told Cathleen time and again she must go wherever he is
and tell him. The idea of screaming as if this were a cheap board-
inghouse!

JAMIE [*looking out the window*]. She's down there now. [*Sneeringly.*]
Interrupting the famous Beautiful Voice! She should have more
respect.

MARY [*sharply—letting her resentment toward him come out*]. It's you
who should have more respect! Stop sneering at your father! I won't
have it! You ought to be proud you're his son! He may have his faults.
Who hasn't? But he's worked hard all his life. He made his way up
from ignorance and poverty to the top of his profession! Everyone else
admires him and you should be the last one to sneer—you, who,
thanks to him, have never had to work hard in your life!

[*Stung,* JAMIE *has turned to stare at her with accusing antagonism.
Her eyes waver guiltily and she adds in a tone which begins to
placate*]

Remember your father is getting old, Jamie. You really ought to show
more consideration.

JAMIE. *I* ought to?

EDMUND [*uneasily*]. Oh, dry up, Jamie!

[JAMIE *looks out the window again.*]

And, for Pete's sake, Mama, why jump on Jamie all of a sudden?

MARY [*bitterly*]. Because he's always sneering at someone else, always looking for the worst weakness in everyone. [*Then with a strange, abrupt change to a detached, impersonal tone.*] But I suppose life has made him like that, and he can't help it. None of us can help the things life has done to us. They're done before you realize it, and once they're done they make you do other things until at last everything comes between you and what you'd like to be, and you've lost your true self forever.

[EDMUND *is made apprehensive by her strangeness. He tries to look up in her eyes but she keeps them averted.* JAMIE *turns to her—then looks quickly out of the window again.*]

JAMIE [*dully*]. I'm hungry. I wish the Old Man would get a move on. It's a rotten trick the way he keeps meals waiting, and then beefs because they're spoiled.

MARY [*with a resentment that has a quality of being automatic and on the surface while inwardly she is indifferent*]. Yes, it's very trying, Jamie. You don't know how trying. You don't have to keep house with summer servants who don't care because they know it isn't a permanent position. The really good servants are all with people who have homes and not merely summer places. And your father won't even pay the wages the best summer help ask. So every year I have stupid, lazy greenhorns to deal with. But you've heard me say this a thousand times. So has he, but it goes in one ear and out the other. He thinks money spent on a home is money wasted. He's lived too much in hotels. Never the best hotels, of course. Second-rate hotels. He doesn't understand a home. He doesn't feel at home in it. And yet, he wants a home. He's even proud of having this shabby place. He loves it here. [*She laughs—a hopeless and yet amused laugh.*] It's really funny, when you come to think of it. He's a peculiar man.

EDMUND [*again attempting uneasily to look up in her eyes*]. What makes you ramble on like that, Mama?

MARY [*quickly casual—patting his cheek*]. Why, nothing in particular, dear. It *is* foolish.

[*As she speaks,* CATHLEEN *enters from the back parlor.*]

CATHLEEN [*volubly*]. Lunch is ready, Ma'am, I went down to Mister Tyrone, like you ordered, and he said he'd come right away, but he kept on talking to that man, telling him of the time when—

MARY [*indifferently*]. All right, Cathleen. Tell Bridget I'm sorry but she'll have to wait a few minutes until Mister Tyrone is here.

[CATHLEEN *mutters,* "Yes, Ma'am," *and goes off through the back parlor, grumbling to herself.*]

JAMIE. Damn it! Why don't you go ahead without him? He's told us to.

MARY [*with a remote, amused smile*]. He doesn't mean it. Don't you know your father yet? He'd be so terribly hurt.

EDMUND [*jumps up—as if he was glad of an excuse to leave*]. I'll make
him get a move on. [*He goes out on the side porch. A moment later
he is heard calling from the porch exasperatedly.*] Hey! Papa! Come
on! We can't wait all day!

[MARY *has risen from the arm of the chair. Her hands play restlessly
over the table top. She does not look at* JAMIE *but she feels the
cynically appraising glance he gives her face and hands.*]

MARY [*tensely*]. Why do you stare like that?

JAMIE. You know. [*He turns back to the window.*]

MARY. I don't know.

JAMIE. Oh, for God's sake, do you think you can fool me, Mama? I'm
not blind.

MARY [*looks directly at him now, her face set again in an expression of
blank, stubborn denial*]. I don't know what you're talking about.

JAMIE. No? Take a look at your eyes in the mirror!

EDMUND [*coming in from the porch*]. I got Papa moving. He'll be
here in a minute. [*With a glance from one to the other, which his
mother avoids—uneasily.*] What's happened? What's the matter,
Mama?

MARY [*disturbed by his coming, gives way to a flurry of guilty, nervous
excitement*]. Your brother ought to be ashamed of himself. He's been
insinuating I don't know what.

EDMUND [*turns on* JAMIE]. God damn you!

[*He takes a threatening step toward him.* JAMIE *turns his back with
a shrug and looks out the window.*]

MARY [*more upset, grabs* EDMUND's *arm—excitedly*]. Stop this at once,
do you hear me? How dare you use such language before me! [*Abruptly her tone and manner change to the strange detachment she has
shown before.*] It's wrong to blame your brother. He can't help being
what the past has made him. Any more than your father can. Or you.
Or I.

EDMUND [*frightenedly—with a desperate hoping against hope*]. He's a
liar! It's a lie, isn't it, Mama?

MARY [*keeping her eyes averted*]. What is a lie? Now you're talking in
riddles like Jamie. [*Then her eyes meet his stricken, accusing look. She
stammers.*] Edmund! Don't! [*She looks away and her manner instantly
regains the quality of strange detachment—calmly.*] There's your father coming up the steps now. I must tell Bridget.

[*She goes through the back parlor.* EDMUND *moves slowly to his chair.
He looks sick and hopeless.*]

JAMIE [*from the window, without looking around*]. Well?

EDMUND [*refusing to admit anything to his brother yet—weakly defiant*].
Well, what? You're a liar.

[JAMIE *again shrugs his shoulders. The screen door on the front porch
is heard closing.* EDMUND *says dully*]

Here's Papa. I hope he loosens up with the old bottle.

[TYRONE *comes in through the front parlor. He is putting on his coat.*]

TYRONE. Sorry I'm late. Captain Turner stopped to talk and once he starts gabbing you can't get away from him.

JAMIE [*without turning—dryly*]. You mean once he starts listening.

[*His father regards him with dislike. He comes to the table with a quick measuring look at the bottle of whiskey. Without turning,* JAMIE *senses this.*]

It's all right. The level in the bottle hasn't changed.

TYRONE. I wasn't noticing that. [*He adds caustically*] As if it proved anything with you around. I'm on to your tricks.

EDMUND [*dully*]. Did I hear you say, let's all have a drink?

TYRONE [*frowns at him*]. Jamie is welcome after his hard morning's work, but I won't invite you. Doctor Hardy—

EDMUND. To hell with Doctor Hardy! One isn't going to kill me. I feel— all in, Papa.

TYRONE [*with a worried look at him—putting on a fake heartiness*]. Come along, then. It's before a meal and I've always found that good whiskey, taken in moderation as an appetizer, is the best of tonics.

[EDMUND *gets up as his father passes the bottle to him. He pours a big drink.* TYRONE *frowns admonishingly.*]

I said, in moderation.

[*He pours his own drink and passes the bottle to* JAMIE, *grumbling.*] It'd be a waste of breath mentioning moderation to you.

[*Ignoring the hint,* JAMIE *pours a big drink. His father scowls—then, giving it up, resumes his hearty air, raising his glass.*]

Well, here's health and happiness!

[EDMUND *gives a bitter laugh.*]

EDMUND. That's a joke!

TYRONE. What is?

EDMUND. Nothing. Here's how.

[*They drink.*]

TYRONE [*becoming aware of the atmosphere*]. What's the matter here? There's gloom in the air you could cut with a knife. [*Turns on* JAMIE *resentfully.*] You got the drink you were after, didn't you? Why are you wearing that gloomy look on your mug?

JAMIE [*shrugging his shoulders*]. You won't be singing a song yourself soon.

EDMUND. Shut up, Jamie.

TYRONE [*uneasy now—changing the subject*]. I thought lunch was ready. I'm hungry as a hunter. Where is your mother?

MARY [*returning through the back parlor, calls*]. Here I am. [*She comes in. She is excited and self-conscious. As she talks, she glances everywhere except at any of their faces.*] I've had to calm down Bridget. She's in a tantrum over your being late again, and I don't blame her. If your lunch is dried up from waiting in the oven, she said it served you right, you could like it or leave it for all she cared. [*With increasing excitement.*] Oh, I'm so sick and tired of pretending this is a home! You won't help me! You won't put yourself out the least bit! You don't know how to act in a home! You don't really want one! You never have wanted one—never since the day we were married! You should have remained a bachelor and lived in second-rate hotels and entertained your friends in barrooms! [*She adds strangely, as if she were now talking aloud to herself rather than to* TYRONE] Then nothing would ever have happened.

[*They stare at her.* TYRONE *knows now. He suddenly looks a tired, bitterly sad old man.* EDMUND *glances at his father and sees that he knows, but he still cannot help trying to warn his mother.*]

EDMUND. Mama! Stop talking. Why don't we go in to lunch.

MARY [*starts and at once the quality of unnatural detachment settles on her face again. She even smiles with an ironical amusement to herself*]. Yes, it is inconsiderate of me to dig up the past, when I know your father and Jamie must be hungry. [*Putting her arm around* EDMUND's *shoulder—with a fond solicitude which is at the same time remote.*] I do hope you have an appetite, dear. You really must eat more. [*Her eyes become fixed on the whiskey glass on the table beside him—sharply.*] Why is that glass there? Did you take a drink? Oh, how can you be such a fool? Don't you know it's the worst thing? [*She turns on* TYRONE.] You're to blame, James. How could you let him? Do you want to kill him? Don't you remember my father? He wouldn't stop after he was stricken. He said doctors were fools! He thought, like you, that whiskey is a good tonic! [*A look of terror comes into her eyes and she stammers*] But, of course, there's no comparison at all. I don't know why I—Forgive me for scolding you, James. One small drink won't hurt Edmund. It might be good for him, if it gives him an appetite.

[*She pats* EDMUND's *cheek playfully, the strange detachment again in her manner. He jerks his head away. She seems not to notice, but she moves instinctively away.*]

JAMIE [*roughly, to hide his tense nerves*]. For God's sake, let's eat. I've been working in the damned dirt under the hedge all morning. I've earned my grub. [*He comes around in back of his father, not looking at his mother, and grabs* EDMUND's *shoulder.*] Come on, Kid. Let's put on the feed bag.

[EDMUND *gets up, keeping his eyes averted from his mother. They pass her, heading for the back parlor.*]

TYRONE [*dully*]. Yes, you go in with your mother, lads. I'll join you in a second.

[*But they keep on without waiting for her. She looks at their backs with a helpless hurt and, as they enter the back parlor, starts to follow them.* TYRONE's *eyes are on her, sad and condemning. She feels them and turns sharply without meeting his stare.*]

MARY. Why do you look at me like that? [*Her hands flutter up to pat her hair.*] Is it my hair coming down? I was so worn out from last night. I thought I'd better lie down this morning. I drowsed off and had a nice refreshing nap. But I'm sure I fixed my hair again when I woke up. [*Forcing a laugh.*] Although, as usual, I couldn't find my glasses. [*Sharply.*] Please stop staring! One would think you were accusing me— [*Then pleadingly.*] James! You don't understand!

TYRONE [*with dull anger*]. I understand that I've been a God-damned fool to believe in you! [*He walks away from her to pour himself a big drink.*]

MARY [*her face again sets in stubborn defiance*]. I don't know what you mean by "believing in me." All I've felt was distrust and spying and suspicion. [*Then accusingly.*] Why are you having another drink? You never have more than one before lunch. [*Bitterly.*] I know what to expect. You will be drunk tonight. Well, it won't be the first time, will it—or the thousandth? [*Again she bursts out pleadingly.*] Oh, James, please! You don't understand! I'm so worried about Edmund! I'm so afraid he—

TYRONE. I don't want to listen to your excuses, Mary.

MARY [*strickenly*]. Excuses? You mean—? Oh, you can't believe that of me! You mustn't believe that, James! [*Then slipping away into her strange detachment—quite casually.*] Shall we not go into lunch, dear? I don't want anything but I know you're hungry.

[*He walks slowly to where she stands in the doorway. He walks like an old man. As he reaches her she bursts out piteously.*]

James! I tried so hard! I tried so hard! Please believe—!

TYRONE [*moved in spite of himself—helplessly*]. I suppose you did, Mary. [*Then grief-strickenly.*] For the love of God, why couldn't you have the strength to keep on?

MARY [*her face setting into that stubborn denial again*]. I don't know what you're talking about. Have the strength to keep on what?

TYRONE [*hopelessly*]. Never mind. It's no use now.

[*He moves on and she keeps beside him as they disappear in the back parlor.*]

[*Curtain*]

Scene Two

SCENE—*The same, about a half hour later. The tray with the bottle of whiskey has been removed from the table. The family are returning from lunch as the curtain rises.* MARY *is the first to enter from the back parlor. Her husband follows. He is not with her as he was in the similar entrance after breakfast at the opening of Act One. He avoids touching her or looking at her. There is condemnation in his face, mingled now with the beginning of an old weary, helpless resignation.* JAMIE *and* EDMUND *follow their father.* JAMIE'S *face is hard with defensive cynicism.* EDMUND *tries to copy this defense but without success. He plainly shows he is heartsick as well as physically ill.*

MARY is terribly nervous again, as if the strain of sitting through lunch with them had been too much for her. Yet at the same time, in contrast to this, her expression shows more of that strange aloofness which seems to stand apart from her nerves and the anxieties which harry them.

She is talking as she enters—a stream of words that issues casually, in a routine of family conversation, from her mouth. She appears indifferent to the fact that their thoughts are not on what she is saying any more than her own are. As she talks, she comes to the left of the table and stands, facing front, one hand fumbling with the bosom of her dress, the other playing over the table top. TYRONE lights a cigar and goes to the screen door, staring out. JAMIE fills a pipe from a jar on top of the bookcase at rear. He lights it as he goes to look out the window at right. EDMUND sits in a chair by the table, turned half away from his mother so he does not have to watch her.

MARY. It's no use finding fault with Bridget. She doesn't listen. I can't threaten her, or she'd threaten she'd leave. And she does do her best at times. It's too bad they seem to be just the times you're sure to be late, James. Well, there's this consolation: it's difficult to tell from her cooking whether she's doing her best or her worst. [*She gives a little laugh of detached amusement—indifferently.*] Never mind. The summer will soon be over, thank goodness. Your season will open again and we can go back to second-rate hotels and trains. I hate them, too, but at least I don't expect them to be like a home, and there's no housekeeping to worry about. It's unreasonable to expect Bridget or Cathleen to act is if this was a home. They know it isn't as well as we know it. It never has been and it never will be.

TYRONE [*bitterly without turning around*]. No, it never can be now. But it was once, before you—

MARY [*her face instantly set in blank denial*]. Before I what? [*There is a dead silence. She goes on with a return of her detached air.*] No, no. Whatever you mean, it isn't true, dear. It was never a home. You've always preferred the Club or a barroom. And for me it's always been as lonely as a dirty room in a one-night stand hotel. In a real home one is never lonely. You forget I know from experience what a home is like. I gave up one to marry you—my father's home. [*At once, through an association of ideas she turns to EDMUND. Her manner becomes tenderly solicitous, but there is the strange quality of detachment in it.*] I'm worried about you, Edmund. You hardly touched a thing at lunch. That's no way to take care of yourself. It's all right for me not to have an appetite. I've been growing too fat. But you must eat. [*Coaxingly maternal.*] Promise me you will, dear, for my sake.

EDMUND [*dully*]. Yes, Mama.

MARY [*pats his cheek as he tries not to shrink away*]. That's a good boy. [*There is another pause of dead silence. Then the telephone in the front hall rings and all of them stiffen startledly.*]

TYRONE [*hastily*]. I'll answer. McGuire said he'd call me. [*He goes out through the front parlor.*]

MARY [*indifferently*]. McGuire. He must have another piece of property on his list that no one would think of buying except your father. It doesn't matter any more, but it's always seemed to me your father could afford to keep on buying property but never to give me a home. [*She stops to listen as* TYRONE'*s voice is heard from the hall.*]

TYRONE. Hello. [*With forced heartiness.*] Oh, how are you, Doctor?

[JAMIE *turns from the window.* MARY'*s fingers play more rapidly on the table top.* TYRONE'*s voice, trying to conceal, reveals that he is hearing bad news.*]

I see— [*Hurriedly.*] Well, you'll explain all about it when you see him this afternoon. Yes, he'll be in without fail. Four o'clock. I'll drop in myself and have a talk with you before that. I have to go uptown on business, anyway. Goodbye, Doctor.

EDMUND [*dully*]. That didn't sound like glad tidings.

[JAMIE *gives him a pitying glance—then looks out the window again.* MARY'*s face is terrified and her hands flutter distractedly.* TYRONE *comes in. The strain is obvious in his casualness as he addresses* EDMUND.]

TYRONE. It was Doctor Hardy. He wants you to be sure and see him at four.

EDMUND [*dully*]. What did he say? Not that I give a damn now.

MARY [*bursts out excitedly*]. I wouldn't believe him if he swore on a stack of Bibles. You mustn't pay attention to a word he says, Edmund.

TYRONE [*sharply*]. Mary!

MARY [*more excitedly*]. Oh, we all realize why you like him, James! Because he's cheap! But please don't try to tell me! I know all about Doctor Hardy. Heaven knows I ought to after all these years. He's an ignorant fool! There should be a law to keep men like him from practicing. He hasn't the slightest idea— When you're in agony and half insane, he sits and holds your hand and delivers sermons on will power! [*Her face is drawn in an expression of intense suffering by the memory. For the moment, she loses all caution. With bitter hatred.*] He deliberately humiliates you! He makes you beg and plead! He treats you like a criminal! He understands nothing! And yet it was exactly the same type of cheap quack who first gave you the medicine—and you never knew what it was until too late! [*Passionately.*] I hate doctors! They'll do anything—anything to keep you coming to them. They'll sell their souls! What's worse, they'll sell yours, and you never know it till one day you find yourself in hell!

EDMUND. Mama! For God's sake, stop talking.

TYRONE [*shakenly*]. Yes, Mary, it's no time—

MARY [*suddenly is overcome by guilty confusion—stammers*]. I— Forgive me, dear. You're right. It's useless to be angry now. [*There is again a pause of dead silence. When she speaks again, her face has cleared and is calm, and the quality of uncanny detachment is in her voice and manner.*] I'm going upstairs for a moment, if you'll excuse me. I have to fix my hair. [*She adds smilingly*] That is if I can find my glasses. I'll be right down.

TYRONE [*as she starts through the doorway—pleading and rebuking*]. Mary!

MARY [*turns to stare at him calmly*]. Yes, dear? What is it?

TYRONE [*helplessly*]. Nothing.

MARY [*with a strange derisive smile*]. You're welcome to come up and watch me if you're so suspicious.

TYRONE. As if that could do any good! You'd only postpone it. And I'm not your jailor. This isn't a prison.

MARY. No. I know you can't help thinking it's a home. [*She adds quickly with a detached contrition*] I'm sorry, dear. I don't mean to be bitter. It's not your fault.

[*She turns and disappears through the back parlor. The three in the room remain silent. It is as if they were waiting until she got upstairs before speaking.*]

JAMIE [*cynically brutal*]. Another shot in the arm!

EDMUND [*angrily*]. Cut out that kind of talk!

TYRONE. Yes! Hold your foul tongue and your rotten Broadway loafer's lingo! Have you no pity or decency? [*Losing his temper.*] You ought to be kicked out in the gutter! But if I did it, you know damned well who'd weep and plead for you, and excuse you and complain till I let you come back.

JAMIE [*a spasm of pain crosses his face*]. Christ, don't I know that? No pity? I have all the pity in the world for her. I understand what a hard game to beat she's up against—which is more than you ever have! My lingo didn't mean I had no feeling. I was merely putting bluntly what we all know, and have to live with now, again. [*Bitterly.*] The cures are no damned good except for a while. The truth is there is no cure and we've been saps to hope— [*Cynically.*] They never come back!

EDMUND [*scornfully parodying his brother's cynicism*]. They never come back! Everything is in the bag! It's all a frame-up! We're all fall guys and suckers and we can't beat the game! [*Disdainfully.*] Christ, if I felt the way you do—!

JAMIE [*stung for a moment—then shrugging his shoulders, dryly*]. I thought you did. Your poetry isn't very cheery. Nor the stuff you read and claim you admire. [*He indicates the small bookcase at rear.*] Your pet with the unpronounceable name, for example.

EDMUND. Nietzsche.[6] You don't know what you're talking about. You haven't read him.

6. Friedrich Nietzsche (1844–1900), a German philosopher whose assault on traditional ideas and values was highly influential in the evolution of modernism.

JAMIE. Enough to know it's a lot of bunk!

TYRONE. Shut up, both of you! There's little choice between the philosophy you learned from Broadway loafers, and the one Edmund got from his books. They're both rotten to the core. You've both flouted the faith you were born and brought up in—the one true faith of the Catholic Church—and your denial has brought nothing but self-destruction!

[*His two sons stare at him contemptuously. They forget their quarrel and are as one against him on this issue.*]

EDMUND. That's the bunk, Papa!

JAMIE. We don't pretend, at any rate. [*Caustically.*] I don't notice you've worn any holes in the knees of your pants going to Mass.

TYRONE. It's true I'm a bad Catholic in the observance, God forgive me. But I believe! [*Angrily.*] And you're a liar! I may not go to church but every night and morning of my life I get on my knees and pray!

EDMUND [*bitingly*]. Did you pray for Mama?

TYRONE. I did. I've prayed to God these many years for her.

EDMUND. Then Nietzsche must be right. [*He quotes from Thus Spake Zarathustra.*] "God is dead: of His pity for man hath God died."

TYRONE [*ignores this*]. If your mother had prayed, too— She hasn't denied her faith, but she's forgotten it, until now there's no strength of the spirit left in her to fight against her curse. [*Then dully resigned.*] But what's the good of talk? We've lived with this before and now we must again. There's no help for it. [*Bitterly.*] Only I wish she hadn't led me to hope this time. By God, I never will again!

EDMUND. That's a rotten thing to say, Papa! [*Defiantly.*] Well, I'll hope! She's just started. It can't have got a hold on her yet. She can still stop. I'm going to talk to her.

JAMIE [*shrugs his shoulders*]. You can't talk to her now. She'll listen but she won't listen. She'll be here but she won't be here. You know the way she gets.

TYRONE. Yes, that's the way the poison acts on her always. Every day from now on, there'll be the same drifting away from us until by the end of each night—

EDMUND [*miserably*]. Cut it out, Papa! [*He jumps up from his chair.*] I'm going to get dressed. [*Bitterly, as he goes*]. I'll make so much noise she can't suspect I've come to spy on her. [*He disappears through the front parlor and can be heard stamping noisily upstairs.*]

JAMIE [*after a pause*]. What did Doc Hardy say about the Kid?

TYRONE [*dully*]. It's what you thought. He's got consumption.

JAMIE. God damn it!

TYRONE. There is no possible doubt, he said.

JAMIE. He'll have to go to a sanatorium.

TYRONE. Yes, and the sooner the better, Hardy said, for him and everyone around him. He claims that in six months to a year Edmund will be cured, if he obeys orders. [*He sighs—gloomily and resentfully.*] I never thought a child of mine— It doesn't come from my side of the family. There wasn't one of us that didn't have lungs as strong as an ox.

JAMIE. Who gives a damn about that part of it! Where does Hardy want to send him?

TYRONE. That's what I'm to see him about.

JAMIE. Well, for God's sake, pick out a good place and not some cheap dump!

TYRONE [*stung*]. I'll send him wherever Hardy thinks best!

JAMIE. Well, don't give Hardy your old over-the-hills-to-the-poorhouse song about taxes and mortgages.

TYRONE. I'm no millionaire who can throw money away! Why shouldn't I tell Hardy the truth?

JAMIE. Because he'll think you want him to pick a cheap dump, and because he'll know it isn't the truth—especially if he hears afterwards you've seen McGuire and let that flannel-mouth, gold-brick merchant sting you with another piece of bum property!

TYRONE [*furiously*]. Keep your nose out of my business!

JAMIE. This is Edmund's business. What I'm afraid of is, with your Irish bog-trotter idea that consumption is fatal, you'll figure it would be a waste of money to spend any more than you can help.

TYRONE. You liar!

JAMIE. All right. Prove I'm a liar. That's what I want. That's why I brought it up.

TYRONE [*his rage still smouldering*]. I have every hope Edmund will be cured. And keep your dirty tongue off Ireland! You're a fine one to sneer, with the map of it on your face!

JAMIE. Not after I wash my face. [*Then before his father can react to this insult to the Old Sod, he adds dryly, shrugging his shoulders*] Well, I've said all I have to say. It's up to you. [*Abruptly.*] What do you want me to do this afternoon, now you're going uptown? I've done all I can do on the hedge until you cut more of it. You don't want me to go ahead with your clipping, I know that.

TYRONE. No. You'd get it crooked, as you get everything else.

JAMIE. Then I'd better go uptown with Edmund. The bad news coming on top of what's happened to Mama may hit him hard.

TYRONE [*forgetting his quarrel*]. Yes, go with him, Jamie. Keep up his spirits, if you can. [*He adds caustically*] If you can without making it an excuse to get drunk!

JAMIE. What would I use for money? The last I heard they were still selling booze, not giving it away. [*He starts for the front-parlor door-way.*] I'll get dressed.

[*He stops in the doorway as he sees his mother approaching from the hall, and moves aside to let her come in. Her eyes look brighter, and her manner is more detached. This change becomes more marked as the scene goes on.*]

MARY [*vaguely*]. You haven't seen my glasses anywhere, have you, Jamie?

[*She doesn't look at him. He glances away, ignoring her question but she doesn't seem to expect an answer. She comes forward, addressing her husband without looking at him.*]

You haven't seem them, have you, James?

[*Behind her* JAMIE *disappears through the front parlor.*]

TYRONE [*turns to look out the screen door*]. No, Mary.

MARY. What's the matter with Jamie? Have you been nagging at him again? You shouldn't treat him with such contempt all the time. He's not to blame. If he'd been brought up in a real home, I'm sure he would have been different. [*She comes to the windows at right—lightly*]. You're not much of a weather prophet, dear. See how hazy it's getting. I can hardly see the other shore.

TYRONE [*trying to speak naturally*]. Yes, I spoke too soon. We're in for another night of fog, I'm afraid.

MARY. Oh, well, I won't mind it tonight.

TYRONE. No, I don't imagine you will, Mary.

MARY [*flashes a glance at him—after a pause*]. I don't see Jamie going down to the hedge. Where did he go?

TYRONE. He's going with Edmund to the Doctor's. He went up to change his clothes. [*Then, glad of an excuse to leave her.*] I'd better do the same or I'll be late for my appointment at the Club.

[*He makes a move toward the front-parlor doorway, but with a swift impulsive movement she reaches out and clasps his arm.*]

MARY [*a note of pleading in her voice*]. Don't go yet, dear. I don't want to be alone. [*Hastily.*] I mean, you have plenty of time. You know you boast you can dress in one-tenth the time it takes the boys. [*Vaguely.*] There is something I wanted to say. What is it? I've forgotten. I'm glad Jamie is going uptown. You didn't give him any money, I hope.

TYRONE. I did not.

MARY. He'd only spend it on drink and you know what a vile, poisonous tongue he has when he's drunk. Not that I would mind anything he said tonight, but he always manages to drive you into a rage, especially if you're drunk, too, as you will be.

TYRONE [*resentfully*]. I won't. I never get drunk.

MARY [*teasing indifferently*]. Oh, I'm sure you'll hold it well. You always have. It's hard for a stranger to tell, but after thirty-five years of marriage—

TYRONE. I've never missed a performance in my life. That's the proof! [*Then bitterly.*] If I did get drunk it is not you who should blame me. No man has ever had a better reason.

MARY. Reason? What reason? You always drink too much when you go to the Club, don't you? Particularly when you meet McGuire. He sees to that. Don't think I'm finding fault, dear. You must do as you please. I won't mind.

TYRONE. I know you won't. [*He turns toward the front parlor, anxious to escape.*] I've got to get dressed.

MARY [*again she reaches out and grasps his arm—pleading*]. No, please wait a little while, dear. At least, until one of the boys comes down. You will all be leaving me so soon.

TYRONE [*with bitter sadness*]. It's you who are leaving us, Mary.

MARY. I? That's a silly thing to say, James. How could I leave? There is nowhere I could go. Who would I go to see? I have no friends.

TYRONE. It's your own fault— [*He stops and sighs helplessly—persuasively.*] There's surely one thing you can do this afternoon that will be good for you, Mary. Take a drive in the automobile. Get away from the house. Get a little sun and fresh air. [*Injuredly.*] I bought the automobile for you. You know I don't like the damned things. I'd rather walk any day, or take a trolley. [*With growing resentment.*] I had it here waiting for you when you came back from the sanatorium. I hoped it would give you pleasure and distract your mind. You used to ride in it every day, but you've hardly used it at all lately. I paid a lot of money I couldn't afford, and there's the chauffeur I have to board and lodge and pay high wages whether he drives you or not. [*Bitterly.*] Waste! The same old waste that will land me in the poorhouse in my old age! What good did it do you? I might as well have thrown the money out the window.

MARY [*with detached calm*]. Yes, it was a waste of money, James. You shouldn't have bought a secondhand automobile. You were swindled again as you always are, because you insist on secondhand bargains in everything.

TYRONE. It's one of the best makes! Everyone says it's better than any of the new ones!

MARY [*ignoring this*]. It was another waste to hire Smythe, who was only a helper in a garage and had never been a chauffeur. Oh, I realize his wages are less than a real chauffeur's, but he more than makes up for that, I'm sure, by the graft he gets from the garage on repair bills. Something is always wrong. Smythe sees to that, I'm afraid.

TYRONE. I don't believe it! He may not be a fancy millionaire's flunky but he's honest! You're as bad as Jamie, suspecting everyone!

MARY. You mustn't be offended, dear. I wasn't offended when you gave me the automobile. I knew you didn't mean to humiliate me. I knew that was the way you had to do everything. I was grateful and touched. I knew buying the car was a hard thing for you to do, and it proved how much you loved me, in your way, especially when you couldn't really believe it would do me any good.

TYRONE. Mary! [*He suddenly hugs her to him—brokenly.*] Dear Mary! For the love of God, for my sake and the boys' sake and your own, won't you stop now?

MARY [*stammers in guilty confusion for a second*]. I—James! Please! [*Her strange, stubborn defense comes back instantly.*] Stop what? What are you talking about?

[*He lets his arm fall to his side brokenly. She impulsively puts her arm around him.*]

James! We've loved each other! We always will! Let's remember only that, and not try to understand what we cannot understand, or help things that cannot be helped—the things life has done to us we cannot excuse or explain.

TYRONE [as if he hadn't heard—bitterly]. You won't even try?

MARY [her arms drop hopelessly and she turns away—with detachment]. Try to go for a drive this afternoon, you mean? Why, yes, if you wish me to, although it makes me feel lonelier than if I stayed here. There is no one I can invite to drive with me, and I never know where to tell Smythe to go. If there was a friend's house where I could drop in and laugh and gossip awhile. But, of course, there isn't. There never has been. [Her manner becoming more and more remote.] At the Convent I had so many friends. Girls whose families lived in lovely homes. I used to visit them and they'd visit me in my father's home. But, naturally, after I married an actor—you know how actors were considered in those days—a lot of them gave me the cold shoulder. And then, right after we were married, there was the scandal of that woman who had been your mistress, suing you. From then on, all my old friends either pitied me or cut me dead. I hated the ones who cut me much less than the pitiers.

TYRONE [with guilty resentment]. For God's sake, don't dig up what's long forgotten. If you're that far gone in the past already, when it's only the beginning of the afternoon, what will you be tonight?

MARY [stares at him defiantly now]. Come to think of it, I do have to drive uptown. There's something I must get at the drugstore.

TYRONE [bitterly scornful]. Leave it to you to have some of the stuff hidden, and prescriptions for more! I hope you'll lay in a good stock ahead so we'll never have another night like the one when you screamed for it, and ran out of the house in your nightdress half crazy, to try and throw yourself off the dock!

MARY [tries to ignore this]. I have to get tooth powder and toilet soap and cold cream— [She breaks down pitiably.] James! You mustn't remember! You mustn't humiliate me so!

TYRONE [ashamed]. I'm sorry. Forgive me, Mary!

MARY [defensively detached again]. It doesn't matter. Nothing like that ever happened. You must have dreamed it.

[He stares at her hopelessly. Her voice seems to drift farther and farther away.]

I was so healthy before Edmund was born. You remember, James. There wasn't a nerve in my body. Even traveling with you season after season, with week after week of one-night stands, in trains without Pullmans, in dirty rooms of filthy hotels, eating bad food, bearing children in hotel rooms, I still kept healthy. But bearing Edmund was the last straw. I was so sick afterwards, and that ignorant quack of a cheap hotel doctor— All he knew was I was in pain. It was easy for him to stop the pain.

TYRONE. Mary! For God's sake, forget the past!

MARY [*with strange objective calm*]. Why? How can I? The past is the present, isn't it? It's the future, too. We all try to lie out of that but life won't let us. [*Going on.*] I blame only myself. I swore after Eugene died I would never have another baby. I was to blame for his death. If I hadn't left him with my mother to join you on the road, because you wrote telling me you missed me and were so lonely, Jamie would never have been allowed, when he still had measles, to go in the baby's room. [*Her face hardening.*] I've always believed Jamie did it on purpose. He was jealous of the baby. He hated him. [*As Tyrone starts to protest.*] Oh, I know Jamie was only seven, but he was never stupid. He'd been warned it might kill the baby. He knew. I've never been able to forgive him for that.

TYRONE [*with bitter sadness*]. Are you back with Eugene now? Can't you let our dead baby rest in peace?

MARY [*as if she hadn't heard him*]. It was my fault. I should have insisted on staying with Eugene and not have let you persuade me to join you, just becaue I loved you. Above all, I shouldn't have let you insist I have another baby to take Eugene's place, because you thought that would make me forget his death. I knew from experience by then that children should have homes to be born in, if they are to be good children, and women need homes, if they are to be good mothers. I was afraid all the time I carried Edmund. I knew something terrible would happen. I knew I'd proved by the way I'd left Eugene that I wasn't worthy to have another baby, and that God would punish me if I did. I never should have borne Edmund.

TYRONE [*with an uneasy glance through the front parlor*]. Mary! Be careful with your talk. If he heard you he might think you never wanted him. He's feeling bad enough already without—

MARY [*violently*]. It's a lie! I did want him! More than anything in the world! You don't understand! I meant, for his sake. He has never been happy. He never will be. Nor healthy. He was born nervous and too sensitive, and that's my fault. And now, ever since he's been so sick I've kept remembering Eugene and my father and I've been so frightened and guilty— [*Then, catching herself, with an instant change to stubborn denial*] Oh, I know it's foolish to imagine dreadful things when there's no reason for it. After all, everyone has colds and gets over them.

[TYRONE *stares at her and sighs helplessly. He turns away toward the front parlor and sees* EDMUND *coming down the stairs in the hall.*]

TYRONE [*sharply, in a low voice*]. Here's Edmund. For God's sake try and be yourself—at least until he goes! You can do that much for him!

[*He waits, forcing his face into a pleasantly paternal expression. She waits frightenedly, seized again by a nervous panic, her hands flut-*

*tering over the bosom of her dress, up to her throat and hair, with
a distracted aimlessness. Then, as* EDMUND *approaches the doorway,
she cannot face him. She goes swiftly away to the windows at left
and stares out with her back to the front parlor.* EDMUND *enters. He
has changed to a ready-made blue serge suit, high stiff collar and
tie, black shoes. With an actor's heartiness.*]

Well! You look spic and span. I'm on my way up to change, too.
[*He starts to pass him.*]

EDMUND [*dryly*]. Wait a minute, Papa. I hate to bring up disagreeable
topics, but there's the matter of carfare. I'm broke.

TYRONE [*starts automatically on a customary lecture*]. You'll always be
broke until you learn the value— [*Checks himself guiltily, looking at
his son's sick face with worried pity.*] But you've been learning, lad.
You worked hard before you took ill. You've done splendidly. I'm
proud of you.

[*He pulls out a small roll of bills from his pants pocket and carefully
selects one.* EDMUND *takes it. He glances at it and his face expresses
astonishment. His father again reacts customarily—sarcastically.*]

Thank you. [*He quotes*] "How sharper than a serpent's tooth it
is—"[7]

EDMUND. "To have a thankless child." I know. Give me a chance, Papa.
I'm knocked speechless. This isn't a dollar. It's a ten spot.

TYRONE [*embarrassed by his generosity*]. Put it in your pocket. You'll
probably meet some of your friends uptown and you can't hold your
end up and be sociable with nothing in your jeans.

EDMUND. You meant it? Gosh, thank you, Papa. [*He is genuinely pleased
and grateful for a moment—then he stares at his father's face with
uneasy suspicion.*] But why all of a sudden—? [*Cynically.*] Did Doc
Hardy tell you I was going to die? [*Then he sees his father is bitterly
hurt.*] No! That's a rotten crack. I was only kidding, Papa. [*He puts
an arm around his father impulsively and gives him an affectionate
hug.*] I'm very grateful. Honest, Papa.

TYRONE [*touched, returns his hug*]. You're welcome, lad.

MARY [*suddenly turns to them in a confused panic of frightened anger*].
I won't have it! [*She stamps her foot.*] Do you hear, Edmund! Such
morbid nonsense! Saying you're going to die! It's the books you read!
Nothing but sadness and death! Your father shouldn't allow you to
have them. And some of the poems you've written yourself are even
worse! You'd think you didn't want to live! A boy of your age with
everything before him! It's just a pose you get out of books! You're
not really sick at all!

TYRONE. Mary! Hold your tongue!

MARY [*instantly changing to a detached tone*]. But, James, it's absurd of
Edmund to be so gloomy and make such a great to-do about nothing.
[*Turning to* EDMUND *but avoiding his eyes—teasingly affectionate.*]

7. *King Lear* 1.4.288–89.

Never mind, dear. I'm on to you. [*She comes to him.*] You want to be petted and spoiled and made a fuss over, isn't that it? You're still such a baby.

[*She puts her arm around him and hugs him. He remains rigid and unyielding. Her voice begins to tremble.*]

But please don't carry it too far, dear. Don't say horrible things. I know it's foolish to take them seriously but I can't help it. You've got me—so frightened.

[*She breaks and hides her face on his shoulder, sobbing. Edmund is moved in spite of himself. He pats her shoulder with an awkward tenderness.*]

EDMUND. Don't Mother. [*His eyes meet his father's.*]

TYRONE [*huskily—clutching at hopeless hope*]. Maybe if you asked your mother now what you said you were going to— [*He fumbles with his watch.*] By God, look at the time! I'll have to shake a leg.

[*He hurries away through the front parlor.* MARY *lifts her head. Her manner is again one of detached motherly solicitude. She seems to have forgotten the tears which are still in her eyes.*]

MARY. How do you feel, dear? [*She feels his forehead.*] Your head is a little hot, but that's just from going out in the sun. You look ever so much better than you did this morning. [*Taking his hand.*] Come and sit down. You mustn't stand on your feet so much. You must learn to husband your strength.

[*She gets him to sit and she sits sideways on the arm of his chair, an arm around his shoulder, so he cannot meet her eyes.*]

EDMUND [*starts to blurt out the appeal he now feels is quite hopeless*]. Listen, Mama—

MARY [*interrupting quickly*]. Now, now! Don't talk. Lean back and rest. [*Persuasively.*] You know, I think it would be much better for you if you stayed home this afternoon and let me take care of you. It's such a tiring trip uptown in the dirty old trolley on a hot day like this. I'm sure you'd be much better off here with me.

EDMUND [*dully*]. You forget I have an appointment with Hardy. [*Trying again to get his appeal started.*] Listen, Mama—

MARY [*quickly*]. You can telephone and say you don't feel well enough. [*Excitedly*] It's simply a waste of time and money seeing him. He'll only tell you some lie. He'll pretend he's found something serious the matter because that's his bread and butter. [*She gives a hard sneering little laugh.*] The old idiot! All he knows about medicine is to look solemn and preach will power!

EDMUND [*trying to catch her eyes*]. Mama! Please listen! I want to ask you something! You— You're only just started. You can still stop. You've got the will power! We'll all help you. I'll do anything! Won't you, Mama?

MARY [*stammers pleadingly*]. Please don't—talk about things you don't understand!

EDMUND [*dully*]. All right, I give up. I knew it was no use.

MARY [*in blank denial now*]. Anyway, I don't know what you're referring
to. But I do know you should be the last one— Right after I returned
from the sanatorium, you began to be ill. The doctor there had warned
me I must have peace at home with nothing to upset me, and all I've
done is worry about you. [*Then distractedly.*] But that's no excuse!
I'm only trying to explain. It's not an excuse! [*She hugs him to her—
pleadingly.*] Promise me, dear, you won't believe I made you an
excuse.

EDMUND [*bitterly*]. What else can I believe?

MARY [*slowly takes her arm away—her manner remote and objective
again*]. Yes, I suppose you can't help suspecting that.

EDMUND [*ashamed but still bitter*]. What do you expect?

MARY. Nothing, I don't blame you. How could you believe me—when
I can't believe myself? I've become such a liar. I never lied about
anything once upon a time. Now I have to lie, especially to myself.
But how can you understand, when I don't myself. I've never understood anything about it, except that one day long ago I found I could
no longer call my soul my own. [*She pauses—then lowering her voice
to a strange tone of whispered confidence.*] But some day, dear, I will
find it again—some day when you're all well, and I see you healthy
and happy and successful, and I don't have to feel guilty any more—
some day when the Blessed Virgin Mary forgives me and gives me
back the faith in Her love and pity I used to have in my convent
days, and I can pray to Her again—when She sees no one in the
world can believe in me even for a moment any more, then She
will believe in me, and with Her help it will be so easy. I will
hear myself scream with agony, and at the same time I will laugh
because I will be so sure of myself. [*Then as* EDMUND *remains hopelessly silent, she adds sadly*] Of course, you can't believe that, either.
[*She rises from the arm of his chair and goes to stare out the windows
at right with her back to him—casually.*] Now I think of it, you might
as well go uptown. I forgot I'm taking a drive. I have to go the
drugstore. You would hardly want to go there with me. You'd be so
ashamed.

EDMUND [*brokenly*]. Mama! Don't!

MARY. I suppose you'll divide that ten dollars your father gave you with
Jamie. You always divide with each other, don't you? Like good sports.
Well, I know what he'll do with his share. Get drunk someplace
where he can be with the only kind of woman he understands or likes.
[*She turns to him, pleading frightenedly.*] Edmund! Promise me you
won't drink! It's so dangerous! You know Doctor Hardy told you—

EDMUND [*bitterly*]. I thought he was an old idiot.

MARY [*pitifully*]. Edmund!

    [JAMIE's *voice is heard from the front hall,* "Come on, Kid, let's beat
it."]

    [MARY's *manner at once becomes detached again.*] Go on, Edmund.

Jamie's waiting. [*She goes to the front-parlor doorway.*] There comes
your father downstairs, too.

[TYRONE's *voice calls,* "Come on, Edmund."]

MARY [*kisses him with detached affection*]. Goodbye, dear. If you're
coming home for dinner, try not to be late. And tell your father. You
know what Bridget is.

[*He turns and hurries away.* TYRONE *calls from the hall,* "Goodbye,
Mary," *and then* JAMIE, *"Goodbye, Mama."*]

[*She calls back*] Goodbye. [*The front screen door is heard closing after
them. She comes and stands by the table, one hand drumming on it,
the other fluttering up to pat her hair. She stares about the room with
frightened, forsaken eyes and whispers to herself*] It's so lonely here.
[*Then her face hardens into bitter self-contempt.*] You're lying to yourself again. You wanted to get rid of them. Their contempt and disgust
aren't pleasant company. You're glad they're gone. [*She gives a little
despairing laugh.*] Then Mother of God, why do I feel so lonely?

[*Curtain*]

Act Three

SCENE—*The same. It is around half past six in the evening. Dusk is
gathering in the living room, an early dusk due to the fog which has
rolled in from the Sound and is like a white curtain drawn down outside
the windows. From a lighthouse beyond the harbor's mouth, a foghorn
is heard at regular intervals, moaning like a mournful whale in labor,
and from the harbor itself, intermittently, comes the warning ringing of
bells on yachts at anchor.*

*The tray with the bottle of whiskey, glasses, and pitcher of ice water
is on the table, as it was in the pre-luncheon scene of the previous act.*

MARY *and the second girl,* CATHLEEN, *are discovered. The latter is
standing at left of table. She holds an empty whiskey glass in her hand
as if she'd forgotten she had it. She shows the effects of drink. Her stupid,
good-humored face wears a pleased and flattered simper.*

MARY *is paler than before and her eyes shine with unnatural brilliance.
The strange detachment in her manner has intensified. She has hidden
deeper within herself and found refuge and release in a dream where
present reality is but an appearance to be accepted and dismissed un-
feelingly—even with a hard cynicism—or entirely ignored. There is at
times an uncanny gay, free youthfulness in her manner, as if in spirit
she were released to become again, simply and without self-consciousness,
the naive, happy, chattering schoolgirl of her convent days. She wears
the dress into which she had changed for her drive to town, a simple,
fairly expensive affair, which would be extremely becoming if it were not
for the careless, almost slovenly way she wears it. Her hair is no longer
fastidiously in place. It has a slightly disheveled, lopsided look. She talks*

to CATHLEEN *with a confiding familiarity, as if the second girl were an old, intimate friend. As the curtain rises, she is standing by the screen door looking out. A moan of the foghorn is heard.*

MARY [*amused—girlishly*]. That foghorn! Isn't it awful, Cathleen?

CATHLEEN [*talks more familiarly than usual but never with intentional impertinence because she sincerely likes her mistress*]. It is indeed, Ma'am. It's like a banshee.

MARY [*goes on as if she hadn't heard. In nearly all the following dialogue there is the feeling that she has* CATHLEEN *with her merely as an excuse to keep talking*]. I don't mind it tonight. Last night it drove me crazy. I lay awake worrying until I couldn't stand it any more.

CATHLEEN. Bad cess[8] to it. I was scared out of my wits riding back from town. I thought that ugly monkey, Smythe, would drive us in a ditch or against a tree. You couldn't see your hand in front of you. I'm glad you had me sit in back with you, Ma'am. If I'd been in front with that monkey— He can't keep his dirty hands to himself. Give him half a chance and he's pinching me on the leg or you-know-where—asking your pardon, Ma'am, but it's true.

MARY [*dreamily*]. It wasn't the fog I minded, Cathleen. I really love fog.

CATHLEEN. They say it's good for the complexion.

MARY. It hides you from the world and the world from you. You feel that everything has changed, and nothing is what it seemed to be. No one can find or touch you any more.

CATHLEEN. I wouldn't care so much if Smythe was a fine, handsome man like some chauffeurs I've seen—I mean, if it was all in fun, for I'm a decent girl. But for a shriveled runt like Smythe—! I've told him, you must think I'm hard up that I'd notice a monkey like you. I've warned him, one day I'll give a clout that'll knock him into next week. And so I will!

MARY. It's the foghorn I hate. It won't let you alone. It keeps reminding you and warning you, and calling you back. [*She smiles strangely.*] But it can't tonight. It's just an ugly sound. It doesn't remind me of anything. [*She gives a teasing, girlish laugh.*] Except, perhaps, Mr. Tyrone's snores. I've always had such fun teasing him about it. He has snored ever since I can remember, especially when he's had too much to drink, and yet he's like a child, he hates to admit it. [*She laughs, coming to the table.*] Well, I suppose I snore at times, too, and I don't like to admit it. So I have no right to make fun of him, have I? [*She sits in the rocker at right of table.*]

CATHLEEN. Ah, sure, everybody healthy snores. It's a sign of sanity, they say. [*Then, worriedly.*] What time is it, Ma'am? I ought to go back in the kitchen. The damp is in Bridget's rheumatism and she's like a raging divil. She'll bite my head off. [*She puts her glass on the table and makes a movement toward the back parlor.*]

8. Irish for "luck."

MARY [*with a flash of apprehension*]. No, don't go, Cathleen. I don't want to be alone, yet.

CATHLEEN. You won't be for long. The Master and the boys will be home soon.

MARY. I doubt if they'll come back for dinner. They have too good an excuse to remain in the barrooms where they feel at home.

[*Cathleen stares at her, stupidly puzzled. Mary goes on smilingly.*] Don't worry about Bridget. I'll tell her I kept you with me, and you can take a big drink of whiskey to her when you go. She won't mind then.

CATHLEEN [*grins—at her ease again*]. No, Ma'am. That's the one thing can make her cheerful. She loves her drop.

MARY. Have another drink yourself, if you wish, Cathleen.

CATHLEEN. I don't know if I'd better, Ma'am. I can feel what I've had already. [*Reaching for the bottle.*] Well, maybe one more won't harm. [*She pours a drink.*] Here's your good health, Ma'am. [*She drinks without bothering about a chaser.*]

MARY [*dreamily*]. I really did have good health once, Cathleen. But that was long ago.

CATHLEEN [*worried again*]. The Master's sure to notice what's gone from the bottle. He has the eye of a hawk for that.

MARY [*amusedly*]. Oh, we'll play Jamie's trick on him. Just measure a few drinks of water and pour them in.

CATHLEEN [*does this—with a silly giggle*]. God save me, it'll be half water. He'll know by the taste.

MARY [*indifferently*]. No, by the time he comes home he'll be too drunk to tell the difference. He has such a good excuse, he believes, to drown his sorrows.

CATHLEEN [*philosophically*]. Well, it's a good man's failing. I wouldn't give a trauneen[9] for a teetotaler. They've no high spirits. [*Then, stupidly puzzled.*] Good excuse? You mean Master Edmund, Ma'am? I can tell the Master is worried about him.

MARY [*stiffens defensively—but in a strange way the reaction has a mechanical quality, as if it did not penetrate to real emotion*]. Don't be silly, Cathleen. Why should he be? A touch of grippe is nothing. And Mr. Tyrone never is worried about anything, except money and property and the fear he'll end his days in poverty. I mean, deeply worried. Because he cannot really understand anything else. [*She gives a little laugh of detached, affectionate amusement.*] My husband is a very peculiar man, Cathleen.

CATHLEEN [*vaguely resentful*]. Well, he's a fine, handsome, kind gentleman just the same, Ma'am. Never mind his weakness.

MARY. Oh, I don't mind. I've loved him dearly for thirty-six years. That proves I know he's lovable at heart and can't help being what he is, doesn't it?

9. Irish for a thing of little value; perhaps a small coin.

CATHLEEN [*hazily reassured*]. That's right, Ma'am. Love him dearly, for any fool can see he worships the ground you walk on. [*Fighting the effect of her last drink and trying to be soberly conversational.*] Speaking of acting, Ma'am, how is it you never went on the stage?

MARY [*resentfully*]. I? What put that absurd notion in your head? I was brought up in a respectable home and educated in the best convent in the Middle West. Before I met Mr. Tyrone I hardly knew there was such a thing as a theater. I was a very pious girl. I even dreamed of becoming a nun. I've never had the slightest desire to be an actress.

CATHLEEN [*bluntly*]. Well, I can't imagine you a holy nun, Ma'am. Sure, you never darken the door of a church, God forgive you.

MARY [*ignores this*]. I've never felt at home in the theater. Even though Mr. Tyrone has made me go with him on all his tours, I've had little to do with the people in his company, or with anyone on the stage. Not that I have anything against them. They have always been kind to me, and I to them. But I've never felt at home with them. Their life is not my life. It has always stood between me and— [*She gets up—abruptly.*] But let's not talk of old things that couldn't be helped. [*She goes to the porch door and stares out.*] How thick the fog is. I can't see the road. All the people in the world could pass by and I would never know. I wish it was always that way. It's getting dark already. It will soon be night, thank goodness. [*She turns back— vaguely.*] It was kind of you to keep me company this afternoon, Cathleen. I would have been lonely driving uptown alone.

CATHLEEN. Sure, wouldn't I rather ride in a fine automobile than stay here and listen to Bridget's lies about her relations? It was like a vacation, Ma'am. [*She pauses—then stupidly.*] There was only one thing I didn't like.

MARY [*vaguely*]. What was that, Cathleen?

CATHLEEN. The way the man in the drugstore acted when I took in the prescription for you. [*Indignantly.*] The impidence of him!

MARY [*with stubborn blankness*]. What are you talking about? What drugstore? What prescription? [*Then hastily, as Cathleen stares in stupid amazement.*] Oh, of course, I'd forgotten. The medicine for the rheumatism in my hands. What did the man say? [*Then with indifference.*] Not that it matters, as long as he filled the prescription.

CATHLEEN. It mattered to me, then! I'm not used to being treated like a thief. He gave me a long look and says insultingly, "Where did you get hold of this?" and I says, "It's none of your damned business, but if you must know, it's for the lady I work for, Mrs. Tyrone, who's sitting out in the automobile." That shut him up quick. He gave a look out at you and said, "Oh," and went to get the medicine.

MARY [*vaguely*]. Yes, he knows me. [*She sits in the armchair at right rear of table. She adds in a calm, detached voice*] I have to take it because there is no other that can stop the pain—*all* the pain—I mean, in my hands. [*She raises her hands and regards them with*

melancholy sympathy. There is no tremor in them now.] Poor hands!
You'd never believe it, but they were once one of my good points,
along with my hair and eyes, and I had a fine figure, too. [*Her tone
has become more and more far-off and dreamy.*] They were a musician's
hands. I used to love the piano. I worked so hard at my music in the
Convent—if you can call it work when you do something you love.
Mother Elizabeth and my music teacher both said I had more talent
than any student they remembered. My father paid for special lessons.
He spoiled me. He would do anything I asked. He would have sent
me to Europe to study anything I asked. He would have sent me to
Europe to study after I graduated from the Convent. I might have
gone—if I hadn't fallen in love with Mr. Tyrone. Or I might have
become a nun. I had two dreams. To be a nun, that was the more
beautiful one. To become a concert pianist, that was the other.

    [*She pauses, regarding her hands fixedly.* CATHLEEN *blinks her eyes
    to fight off drowsiness and a tipsy feeling.*]

I haven't touched a piano in so many years. I couldn't play with such
crippled fingers, even if I wanted to. For a time after my marriage I
tried to keep up my music. But it was hopeless. One-night stands,
cheap hotels, dirty trains, leaving children, never having a home—
[*She stares at her hands with fascinated disgust.*] See, Cathleen, how
ugly they are! So maimed and crippled! You would think they'd been
through some horrible accident! [*She gives a strange little laugh.*] So
they have, come to think of it. [*She suddenly thrusts her hands behind
her back.*] I won't look at them. They're worse than the foghorn for
reminding me— [*Then with defiant self-assurance.*] But even they
can't touch me now. [*She brings her hands from behind her back and
deliberately stares at them—calmly.*] They're far away. I see them,
but the pain has gone.

CATHLEEN [*stupidly puzzled*]. You've taken some of the medicine? It
made you act funny, Ma'am. If I didn't know better, I'd think you'd
a drop taken.

MARY [*dreamily*]. It kills the pain. You go back until at last you are
beyond its reach. Only the past when you were happy is real. [*She
pauses—then as if her words had been an evocation which called back
happiness she changes in her whole manner and facial expression. She
looks younger. There is a quality of an innocent convent girl about
her, and she smiles shyly.*] If you think Mr. Tyrone is handsome now,
Cathleen, you should have seen him when I first met him. He had
the reputation of being one of the best looking men in the country.
The girls in the Convent who had seen him act, or seen his photographs used to rave about him. He was a great matinee idol then,
you know. Women used to wait at the stage door just to see him come
out. You can imagine how excited I was when my father wrote me
he and James Tyrone had become friends, and that I was to meet
him when I came home for Easter vacation. I showed the letter to

all the girls, and how envious they were! My father took me to see
him act first. It was a play about the French Revolution and the
leading part was a nobleman. I couldn't take my eyes off him. I wept
when he was thrown in prison—and then was so mad at myself because
I was afraid my eyes and nose would be red. My father had said we'd
go backstage to his dressing room right after the play, and so we did.
[*She gives a little excited, shy laugh.*] I was so bashful and all I could
do was stammer and blush like a little fool. But he didn't seem to
think I was a fool. I know he liked me the first moment we were
introduced. [*Coquettishly.*] I guess my eyes and nose couldn't have
been red, after all. I was really very pretty then, Cathleen. And he
was handsomer than my wildest dream, in his makeup-up and his
nobleman's costume that was so becoming to him. He was different
from all ordinary men, like someone from another world. at the same
time he was simple, and kind, and unassuming, not a bit stuck-up
or vain. I fell in love right then. So did he, he told me afterwards. I
forgot all about becoming a nun or a concert pianist. All I wanted
was to be his wife. [*She pauses, staring before her with unnaturally
bright, dreamy eyes, and a rapt, tender, girlish smile.*] Thirty-six years
ago, but I can see it as clearly as if it were tonight! We've loved each
other ever since. And in all those thirty-six years, there has never
been a breath of scandal about him. I mean, with any other woman.
Never since he met me. That has made me very happy, Cathleen.
It has made me forgive so many other things.

CATHLEEN [*fighting tipsy drowsiness—sentimentally*]. He's a fine gentleman and you're a lucky woman. [*Then, fidgeting.*] Can I take the
drink to Bridget, Ma'am? It must be near dinnertime and I ought to
be in the kitchen helping her. If she don't get something to quiet her
temper, she'll be after me with the cleaver.

MARY [*with a vague exasperation at being brought back from her dream*].
Yes, yes, go. I don't need you now.

CATHLEEN [*with relief*]. Thank you, Ma'am. [*She pours out a big drink
and starts for the back parlor with it.*] You won't be alone long. The
Master and the boys—

MARY [*impatiently*]. No, no, they won't come. Tell Bridget I won't wait.
You can serve dinner promptly at half past six. I'm not hungry but
I'll sit at the table and we'll get it over with.

CATHLEEN. You ought to eat something, Ma'am. It's a queer medicine
if it takes away your appetite.

MARY [*has begun to drift into dreams again—reacts mechanically*]. What
medicine? I don't know what you mean. [*In dismissal*] You better
take the drink to Bridget.

CATHLEEN. Yes, Ma'am.

[*She disappears through the back parlor. MARY waits until she hears
the pantry door close behind her. Then she settles back in relaxed
dreaminess, staring fixedly at nothing. her arms rest limply along
the arms of the chair, her hands with long, warped, swollen-*

knuckled, sensitive fingers drooping in complete calm. It is growing dark in the room. There is a pause of dead quiet. Then from the world outside comes the melancholy moan of the foghorn, followed by a chorus of bells, muffled by the fog, from the anchored craft in the harbor. Mary's face gives no sign she has heard, but her hands jerk and the fingers automatically play for a moment on the air. She frowns and shakes her head mechanically as if a fly had walked across her mind. She suddenly loses all the girlish quality and is an aging, cynically sad, embittered woman.]

MARY [*bitterly*]. You're a sentimental fool. What is so wonderful about that first meeting between a silly romantic schoolgirl and a matinee idol? You were much happier before you knew he existed, in the Convent when you used to pray to the Blessed Virgin. [*Longingly.*] If I could only find the faith I lost, so I could pray again! [*She pauses— then begins to recite the Hail Mary in a flat, empty tone.*] "Hail, Mary, full of grace! The Lord is with Thee; blessed art Thou among women." [*Sneeringly*] You expect the Blessed Virgin to be fooled by a lying dope fiend reciting words! You can't hide from her! [*She springs to her feet. Her hands fly up to pat her hair distractedly*] I must go upstairs. I haven't taken enough. When you start again you never know exactly how much you need. [*She goes toward the front parlor— then stops in the doorway as she hears the sound of voices from the front path. She starts guiltily.*] That must be them— [*She hurries back to sit down. Her face sets in stubborn defensiveness—resentfully.*] Why are they coming back? They don't want to. And I'd much rather be alone. [*Suddenly her whole manner changes. She becomes pathetically relieved and eager.*] Oh, I'm so glad they've come! I've been so horribly lonely!

[*The front door is heard closing and* TYRONE *calls uneasily from the hall.*]

TYRONE. Are you there, Mary?

[*The light in the hall is turned on and shines through the front parlor to fall on* MARY.]

MARY [*rises from her chair, her face lighting up lovingly—with excited eagerness*]. I'm here, dear. In the living room. I've been waiting for you.

[TYRONE *comes in through the front parlor.* EDMUND *is behind him.* TYRONE *has had a lot to drink but beyond a slightly glazed look in his eyes and a trace of blur in his speech, he does not show it.* EDMUND *has also had more than a few drinks without much apparent effect, except that his sunken cheeks are flushed and his eyes look bright and feverish. They stop in the doorway to stare appraisingly at her. What they see fulfills their worst expectations. But for the moment* MARY *is unconscious of their condemning eyes. She kisses her husband and then* EDMUND. *Her manner is unnaturally effusive. They submit shrinkingly. She talks excitedly.*]

I'm so happy you've come. I had given up hope. I was afraid you wouldn't come home. It's such a dismal, foggy evening. It must be much more cheerful in the barrooms uptown, where they are people you can talk and joke with. No, don't deny it. I know how you feel. I don't blame you a bit. I'm all the more grateful to you for coming home. I was sitting here so lonely and blue. Come and sit down.

[*She sits at left rear of table,* EDMUND *at left of table, and* TYRONE *in the rocker at right of it.*]

Dinner won't be ready for a minute. You're actually a little early. Will wonders never cease. Here's the whiskey, dear. Shall I pour a drink for you? [*Without waiting for a reply she does so.*] And you, Edmund? I don't want to encourage you, but one before dinner, as an appetizer, can't do any harm. [*She pours a drink for him. They make no move to take the drinks. She talks on as if unaware of their silence.*] Where's Jamie? But, of course, he'll never come home so long as he has the price of a drink left. [*She reaches out and clasps her husband's hand—sadly.*] I'm afraid Jamie has been lost to us for a long time, dear. [*Her face hardens.*] But we mustn't allow him to drag Edmund down with him, as he's like to do. He's jealous because Edmund has always been the baby—just as he used to be of Eugene. He'll never be content until he makes Edmund as hopeless a failure as he is.

EDMUND [*miserably*]. Stop talking, Mama.

TYRONE [*dully*]. Yes, Mary, the less you say now— [*Then to* EDMUND, *a bit tipsily.*] All the same there's truth in your mother's warning. Beware of that brother of yours, or he'll poison life for you with his damned sneering serpent's tongue!

EDMUND [*as before*]. Oh, cut it out, Papa.

MARY [*goes on as if nothing had been said*]. It's hard to believe, seeing Jamie as he is now, that he was ever my baby. Do you remember what a healthy, happy baby he was, James? The one-night stands and filthy trains and cheap hotels and bad food never made him cross or sick. He was always smiling or laughing. He hardly ever cried. Eugene was the same, too, happy and healthy, during the two years he lived before I let him die through my neglect.

TYRONE. Oh, for the love of God! I'm a fool for coming home!

EDMUND. Papa! Shut up!

MARY [*smiles with detached tenderness at* EDMUND]. It was Edmund who was the crosspatch[1] when he was little, always getting upset and frightened about nothing at all. [*She pats his hand—teasingly.*] Everyone used to say, dear, you'd cry at the drop of a hat.

EDMUND [*cannot control his bitterness*]. Maybe I guessed there was a good reason not to laugh.

TYRONE [*reproving and pitying*]. Now, now, lad. You know better than to pay attention—

---

1. A cranky, ill-tempered person.

MARY [*as if she hadn't heard—sadly again*]. Who would have thought Jamie would grow up to disgrace us. You remember, James, for years after he went to boarding school, we received such glowing reports. Everyone liked him. All his teachers told us what a fine brain he had, and how easily he learned his lessons. Even after he began to drink and they had to expel him, they wrote us how sorry they were, because he was so likable and such a brilliant student. They predicted a wonderful future for him if he would only learn to take life seriously. [*She pauses—then adds with a strange, sad detachment*] It's such a pity. Poor Jamie! It's hard to understand— [*Abruptly a change comes over her. Her face hardens and she stares at her husband with accusing hostility.*] No, it isn't at all. You brought him up to be a boozer. Since he first opened his eyes, he's seen you drinking. Always a bottle on the bureau in the cheap hotel rooms! And if he had a nightmare when he was little, or a stomach-ache, your remedy was to give him a teaspoonful of whiskey to quiet him.

TYRONE [*stung*]. So I'm to blame because that lazy hulk has made a drunken loafer of himself? Is that what I came home to listen to? I might have known! When you have the poison in you, you want to blame everyone but yourself!

EDMUND. Papa! You told me not to pay attention. [*Then, resentfully.*] Anyway it's true. You did the same thing with me. I can remember that teaspoonful of booze every time I woke up with a nightmare.

MARY [*in a detached reminiscent tone*]. Yes, you were continually having nightmares as a child. You were born afraid. Because I was so afraid to bring you into the world. [*She pauses—then goes on with the same detachment.*] Please don't think I blame your father, Edmund. He didn't know any better. He never went to school after he was ten. His people were the most ignorant kind of poverty-stricken Irish. I'm sure they honestly believed whiskey is the healthiest medicine for a child who is sick or frightened.

[TYRONE *is about to burst out in angry defense of his family but* EDMUND *intervenes.*]

EDMUND [*sharply*]. Papa! [*Changing the subject.*] Are we going to have this drink or aren't we?

TYRONE [*controlling himself—dully*]. You're right. I'm a fool to take notice. [*He picks up his glass listlessly.*] Drink hearty, lad.

[EDMUND *drinks but* TYRONE *remains staring at the glass in his hand.* EDMUND *at once realizes how much the whiskey has been watered. He frowns, glancing from the bottle to his mother—starts to say something but stops.*]

MARY [*in a changed tone—repentantly*]. I'm sorry if I sounded bitter, James. I'm not. It's all so far away. But I did feel a little hurt when you wished you hadn't come home. I was so relieved and happy when you came, and grateful to you. It's very dreary and sad to be here alone in the fog with night falling.

TYRONE [*moved*]. I'm glad I came, Mary, when you act like your real
self.

MARY. I was so lonesome I kept Cathleen with me just to have someone
to talk to. [*Her manner and quality drift back to the shy convent girl
again.*] Do you know what I was telling her, dear? About the night
my father took me to your dressing room and I first fell in love with
you. Do you remember?

TYRONE [*deeply moved—his voice husky*]. Can you think I'd ever forget,
Mary?

[EDMUND *looks away from them, sad and embarrassed.*]

MARY [*tenderly*]. No. I know you still love me, James, in spite of
everything.

TYRONE [*his face works and he blinks back tears—with quiet intensity*].
Yes! As God is my judge! Always and forever, Mary!

MARY. And I love you, dear, in spite of everything.

[*There is a pause in which* EDMUND *moves embarrassedly. The strange
detachment comes over her manner again as if she were speaking
impersonally of people seen from a distance.*]

But I must confess, James, although I couldn't help loving you, I
would never have married you if I'd known you drank so much. I
remember the first night your barroom friends had to help you up to
the door of our hotel room, and knocked and then ran away before
I came to the door. We were still on our honeymoon, do you
remember?

TYRONE [*with guilty vehemence*]. I don't remember! It wasn't on our
honeymoon! And I never in my life had to be helped to bed, or missed
a performance!

MARY [*as though he hadn't spoken*]. I had waited in that ugly hotel room
hour after hour. I kept making excuses for you. I told myself it must
be some business connected with the theater. I knew so little about
the theater. Then I became terrified. I imagined all sorts of horrible
accidents. I got on my knees and prayed that nothing had happened
to you—and then they brought you up and left you outside the door.
[*She gives a little, sad sigh.*] I didn't know how often that was to
happen in the years to come, how many times I was to wait in ugly
hotel rooms. I became quite used to it.

EDMUND [*bursts out with a look of accusing hate at his father*]. Christ!
No wonder—! [*He controls himself—gruffly*] When is dinner, Mama?
It must be time.

TYRONE [*overwhelmed by shame which he tries to hide, fumbles with his
watch*]. Yes. It must be. Let's see. [*He stares at his watch without
seeing it. Pleadingly.*] Mary! Can't you forget—?

MARY [*with detached pity*]. No, dear. But I forgive. I always forgive you.
So don't look so guilty. I'm sorry I remembered out loud. I don't
want to be sad, or to make you sad. I want to remember only the
happy part of the past. [*Her manner drifts back to the shy, gay convent*

girl.] Do you remember our wedding, dear? I'm sure you've completely forgotten what my wedding gown looked like. Men don't notice such things. They don't think they're important. But it was important to me, I can tell you! How I fussed and worried! I was so excited and happy! My father told me to buy anything I wanted and never mind what it cost. The best is none too good, he said. I'm afraid he spoiled me dreadfully. My mother didn't. She was very pious and strict. I think she was a little jealous. She didn't approve of my marrying— especially an actor. I think she hoped I would become a nun. She used to scold my father. She'd grumble, "You never tell me, never mind what it costs, when I buy anything! You've spoiled that girl so, I pity her husband if she ever marries. She'll expect him to give her the moon. She'll never make a good wife." [*She laughs affectionately.*] Poor mother! [*She smiles at* TYRONE *with a strange, incongruous coquetry.*] But she was mistaken, wasn't she, James? I haven't been such a bad wife, have I?

TYRONE [*huskily, trying to force a smile*]. I'm not complaining, Mary.

MARY [*A shadow of vague guilt crosses her face*]. At least, I've loved you dearly, and done the best I could—under the circumstances. [*The shadow vanishes and her shy, girlish expression returns.*] That wedding gown was nearly the death of me and the dressmaker, too! [*She laughs.*] I was so particular. It was never quite good enough. At last she said she refused to touch it any more or she might spoil it, and I made her leave so I could be alone to examine myself in the mirror. I was so pleased and vain. I thought to myself, "Even if your nose and mouth and ears are a trifle too large, your eyes and hair and figure, and your hands, make up for it. You're just as pretty as any actress he's ever met, and you don't have to use paint." [*She pauses, wrinkling her brow in an effort of memory.*] Where is my wedding gown now, I wonder? I kept it wrapped up in tissue paper in my trunk. I used to hope I would have a daughter and when it came time for her to marry— She couldn't have bought a lovelier gown, and I knew, James, you'd never tell her, never mind the cost. You'd want her to pick up something at a bargain. It was made of soft, shimmering satin, trimmed with wonderful old duchesse lace, in tiny ruffles around the neck and sleeves, and worked in with the folds that were draped round in a bustle effect at the back. The basque was boned and very tight. I remember I held my breath when it was fitted, so my waist would be as small as possible. My father even let me have duchesse lace on my white satin slippers, and lace with the orange blossoms in my veil. Oh, how I loved that gown! It was so beautiful! Where is it now, I wonder? I used to take it out from time to time when I was lonely, but it always made me cry, so finally a long while ago— [*She wrinkles her forehead again.*] I wonder where I hid it? Probably in one of the old trunks in the attic. Some day I'll have to look.

[*She stops, staring before her.* TYRONE *sighs, shaking his head hope-*

lessly, and attempts to catch his son's eye, looking for sympathy, but EDMUND *is staring at the floor.*]

TYRONE [*forces a casual tone*]. Isn't it dinner time, dear? [*With a feeble attempt at teasing.*] You're forever scolding me for being late, but now I'm on time for once, it's dinner that's late. [*She doesn't appear to hear him. He adds, still pleasantly*] Well, if I can't eat yet, I can drink. I'd forgotten I had this.

[*He drinks his drink.* EDMUND *watches him.* TYRONE *scowls and looks at his wife with sharp suspicion—roughly.*]

Who's been tampering with my whiskey? The damned stuff is half water! Jamie's been away and he wouldn't overdo his trick like this, anyway. Any fool could tell— Mary, answer me! [*With angry disgust.*] I hope to God you haven't taken to drink on top of—

EDMUND. Shut up, Papa! [*To his mother, without looking at her.*] You treated Cathleen and Bridget, isn't that it, Mama?

MARY [*with indifferent casualness*]. Yes, of course. They work hard for poor wages. And I'm the housekeeper, I have to keep them from leaving. Besides, I wanted to treat Cathleen because I had her drive uptown with me and sent her to get my prescription filled.

EDMUND. For God's sake, Mama! You can't trust her! Do you want everyone on earth to know?

MARY [*her face hardening stubbornly*]. Know what? That I suffer from rheumatism in my hands and have to take medicine to kill the pain? Why should I be ashamed of that? [*Turns on* EDMUND *with a hard, accusing antagonism—almost a revengeful enmity.*] I never knew what rheumatism was before you were born! Ask your father!

[EDMUND *looks away, shrinking into himself.*]

TYRONE. Don't mind her, lad. It doesn't mean anything. When she gets to the stage where she gives the old crazy excuse about her hands she's gone far away from us.

MARY [*turns on him—with a strangely triumphant, taunting smile*]. I'm glad you realize that, James! Now perhaps you'll give up trying to remind me, you and Edmund! [*Abruptly, in a detached, matter-of-fact tone.*] Why don't you light the light, James? It's getting dark. I know you hate to, but Edmund has proved to you that one bulb burning doesn't cost much. There's no sense letting your fear of the poorhouse make you too stingy.

TYRONE [*reacts mechanically*]. I never claimed one bulb cost much! It's having them on, one here and one there, that makes the Electric Light Company rich. [*He gets up and turns on the reading lamp—roughly.*] But I'm a fool to talk reason to you. [*To* EDMUND.] I'll get a fresh bottle of whiskey, lad, and we'll have a real drink. [*He goes through the back parlor.*]

MARY [*with detached amusement*]. He'll sneak around to the outside cellar door so the servants won't see him. He's really ashamed of keeping his whiskey padlocked in the cellar. Your father is a strange man, Edmund. It took many years before I understood him. You must try to understand and forgive him, too, and not feel contempt because he's closefisted. His father deserted his mother and their six children a year or so after they came to America. He told them he had a premonition he would die soon, and he was homesick for Ireland, and wanted to go back there to die. So he went and he did die. He must have been a peculiar man, too. Your father had to go to work in a machine shop when he was only ten years old.

EDMUND [*protests dully*]. Oh, for Pete's sake, Mama. I've heard Papa tell that machine shop story ten thousand times.

MARY. Yes, dear you've had to listen, but I don't think you've ever tried to understand.

EDMUND [*ignoring this—miserably*]. Listen, Mama! You're not so far gone yet you've forgotten everything. You haven't asked me what I found out this afternoon. Don't you care a damn?

MARY [*shakenly*]. Don't say that! You hurt me, dear!

EDMUND. What I've got is serious, Mama. Doc Hardy knows for sure now.

MARY [*stiffens into scornful, defensive stubbornness*]. That lying old quack! I warned you he'd invent—!

EDMUND [*miserably dogged*]. He called in a specialist to examine me, so he'd be absolutely sure.

MARY [*ignoring this*]. Don't tell me about Hardy! If you heard what the doctor at the sanatorium, who really knows something, said about how he'd treated me! He said he ought to be locked up! He said it was a wonder I hadn't gone mad! I told him I had once, that time I ran down in my nightdress to throw myself off the dock. You remember that, don't you? And yet you want me to pay attention to what Doctor Hardy says. Oh, no!

EDMUND [*bitterly*]. I remember, all right. It was right after that Papa and Jamie decided they couldn't hide it from me any more. Jamie told me. I called him a liar! I tried to punch him in the nose. But I knew he wasn't lying. [*His voice trembles, his eyes begin to fill with tears.*] God, it made everything in life seem rotten!

MARY [*pitiably*]. Oh, don't. My baby! You hurt me so dreadfully!

EDMUND [*dully*]. I'm sorry, Mama. It was you who brought it up. [*Then with a bitter, stubborn persistence.*] Listen, Mama. I'm going to tell you whether you want to hear or not. I've got to go to a sanatorium.

MARY [*dazedly, as if this was something that had never occurred to her*]. Go away? [*Violently.*] No! I won't have it! How dare Doctor Hardy advise such a thing without consulting me! How dare your father allow him! What right has he? You are my baby! Let him attend to Jamie! [*More and more excited and bitter.*] I know why he wants you sent to a sanatorium. To take you from me! He's always tried to do that. He's been jealous of every one of my babies! He kept finding ways to make me leave them. That's what caused Eugene's death.

He's been jealous of you most of all. He knew I loved you most because—

EDMUND [*miserably*]. Oh, stop talking crazy, can't you, Mama! Stop trying to blame him. And why are you so against my going away now? I've been away a lot, and I've never noticed it broke your heart!

MARY [*bitterly*]. I'm afraid you're not very sensitive, after all. [*Sadly.*] You might have guessed, dear, that after I knew you knew—about me—I had to be glad whenever you were where you couldn't see me.

EDMUND [*brokenly*]. Mama! Don't! [*He reaches out blindly and takes her hand—but he drops it immediately, overcome by bitterness again.*] All this talk about loving me—and you won't even listen when I try to tell you how sick—

MARY [*with an abrupt transformation into a detached bullying motherliness.*]. Now, now. That's enough! I don't care to hear because I know it's nothing but Hardy's ignorant lies.

[*He shrinks back into himself. She keeps on in a forced, teasing tone but with an increasing undercurrent of resentment.*]

You're so like your father, dear. You love to make a scene out of nothing so you can be dramatic and tragic. [*With a belittling laugh.*] If I gave you the slightest encouragement, you'd tell me next you were going to die—

EDMUND. People do die of it. Your own father—

MARY [*sharply*]. Why do you mention him? There's no comparison at all with you. He had consumption. [*Angrily.*] I hate you when you become gloomy and morbid! I forbid you to remind me of my father's death, do you hear me?

EDMUND [*his face hard—grimly*]. Yes, I hear you, Mama. I wish to God I didn't! [*He gets up from his chair and stands staring condemningly at her—bitterly.*] It's pretty hard to take at times, having a dope fiend for a mother!

[*She winces—all life seeming to drain from her face, leaving it with the appearance of a plaster cast. Instantly EDMUND wishes he could take back what he has said. He stammers miserably.*]

Forgive me, Mama. I was angry. You hurt me.

[*There is a pause in which the foghorn and the ships' bells are heard.*]

MARY [*goes slowly to the windows at right like an automaton—looking out, a blank, far-off quality in her voice*]. Just listen to that awful foghorn. And the bells. Why is it fog makes everything sound so sad and lost, I wonder?

EDMUND [*brokenly*]. I—I can't stay here. I don't want any dinner.

[*He hurries away through the front parlor. She keeps staring out the window until she hears the front door close behind him. Then she comes back and sits in her chair, the same blank look on her face.*]

MARY [*vaguely*]. I must go upstairs. I haven't taken enough. [*She pauses—then longingly.*] I hope, sometime, without meaning it, I will take an overdose. I never could do it deliberately. The Blessed Virgin would never forgive me, then.

[*She hears* TYRONE *returning and turns as he comes in, through the back parlor, with a bottle of whiskey he has just uncorked. He is fuming.*]

TYRONE [*wrathfully*]. The padlock is all scratched. That drunken loafer has tried to pick the lock with a piece of wire, the way he's done before. [*With satisfaction, as if this was a perpetual battle of wits with his elder son.*] But I've fooled him this time. It's a special padlock a professional burglar couldn't pick. [*He puts the bottle on the tray and suddenly is aware of* EDMUND's *absence.*] Where's Edmund?

MARY [*with a vague far-away air*]. He went out. Perhaps he's going uptown again to find Jamie. He still has some money left, I suppose, and it's burning a hole in his pocket. He said he didn't want any dinner. He doesn't seem to have any appetite these days. [*Then stubbornly.*] But it's just a summer cold.

[TYRONE *stares at her and shakes his head helplessly and pours himself a big drink and drinks it. Suddenly it is too much for her and she breaks out and sobs.*]

Oh, James, I'm so frightened! [*She gets up and throws her arms around him and hides her face on his shoulder—sobbingly.*] I know he's going to die!

TYRONE. Don't say that! It's not true! They promised me in six months he'd be cured.

MARY. You don't believe that! I can tell when you're acting! And it will be my fault. I should never have borne him. It would have been better for his sake. I could never hurt him then. He wouldn't have had to know his mother was a dope fiend—and hate her!

TYRONE [*his voice quivering*]. Hush, Mary, for the love of God! He loves you. He knows it was a curse put on you without your knowing or willing it. He's proud you're his mother! [*Abruptly as he hears the pantry door opening.*] Hush, now! Here comes Cathleen. You don't want her to see you crying.

[*She turns quickly away from him to the windows at right, hastily wiping her eyes. A moment later* CATHLEEN *appears in the back-parlor doorway. She is uncertain in her walk and grinning woozily.*]

CATHLEEN [*starts guiltily when she sees* TYRONE—*with dignity*]. Dinner is served, Sir. [*Raising her voice unnecessarily.*] Dinner is served, Ma'am. [*She forgets her dignity and addresses* TYRONE *with good-natured familiarity.*] So you're here, are you? Well, well. Won't Bridget be in a rage! I told her the Madame said you wouldn't be home. [*Then reading accusation in his eye.*] Don't be looking at me that way. If I've a drop taken, I didn't steal it. I was invited. [*She turns with huffy dignity and disappears through the back parlor.*]

TYRONE [*sighs—then summoning his actor's heartiness*]. Come along, dear. Let's have our dinner. I'm hungry as a hunter.

MARY [*comes to him—her face is composed in plaster again and her tone is remote*]. I'm afraid you'll have to excuse me, James. I couldn't possibly eat anything. My hands pain me dreadfully. I think the best thing for me is to go to bed and rest. Good night, dear. [*She kisses him mechanically and turns toward the front parlor.*]

TYRONE [*harshly*]. Up to take more of that God-damned poison, is that it? You'll be like a mad ghost before the night's over!

MARY [*starts to walk away—blankly*]. I don't know what you're talking about, James. You say such mean, bitter things when you've drunk too much. You're as bad as Jamie or Edmund.

[*She moves off through the front parlor. He stands a second as if not knowing what to do. He is a sad, bewildered, broken old man. He walks wearily off through the back parlor toward the dining room.*]

[*Curtain*]

Act Four

SCENE—*The same. It is around midnight. The lamp in the front hall has been turned out, so that now no light shines through the front parlor. In the living room only the reading lamp on the table is lighted. Outside the windows the wall of fog appears denser than ever. As the curtain rises, the foghorn is heard, followed by the ships' bells from the harbor.*

TYRONE *is seated at the table. He wears his pince-nez, and is playing solitaire. He has taken off his coat and has on an old brown dressing gown. The whiskey bottle on the tray is three-quarters empty. There is a fresh full bottle on the table, which he has brought from the cellar so there will be an ample reserve at hand. He is drunk and shows it by the owlish, deliberate manner in which he peers at each card to make certain of its identity, and then plays it as if he wasn't certain of his aim. His eyes have a misted, oily look and his mouth is slack. But despite all the whiskey in him, he has not escaped, and he looks as he appeared at the close of the preceding act, a sad, defeated old man, possessed by hopeless resignation.*

As the curtain rises, he finishes a game and sweeps the cards together. He shuffles them clumsily, dropping a couple on the floor. He retrieves them with difficulty, and starts to shuffle again, when he hears someone entering the front door. He peers over his pince-nez through the front parlor.

TYRONE [*his voice thick*]. Who's that? Is it you, Edmund?

[EDMUND's *voice answers curtly, "Yes." Then he evidently collides with something in the dark hall and can be heard cursing. A moment later the hall lamp is turned on.* TYRONE *frowns and calls*]

Turn that light out before you come in.

[*But* EDMUND *doesn't. He comes in through the front parlor. He is drunk now, too, but like his father he carries it well, and gives little physical sign of it except in his eyes and a chip-on-the-shoulder aggressiveness in his manner.* TYRONE *speaks, at first with a warm, relieved welcome.*]

You're a fine one to run away and leave me to sit alone here all night when you know— [*With sharp irritation.*] I told you to turn out that light! We're not giving a ball. There's no reason to have the house ablaze with electricity at this time of night, burning up money!

EDMUND [*angrily*]. Ablaze with electricity! One bulb! Hell, everyone keeps a light on in the front hall until they go to bed. [*He rubs his knee.*] I damned near busted my knee on the hat stand.

TYRONE. The light from here shows in the hall. You could see your way well enough if you were sober.

EDMUND. If *I* was sober? I like that!

TYRONE. I don't give a damn what other people do. If they want to be wasteful fools, for the sake of show, let them be!

EDMUND. One bulb! Christ, don't be such a cheap skate! I've proved by figures if you left the light bulb on all night it wouldn't be as much as one drink!

TYRONE. To hell with your figures! The proof is in the bills I have to pay!

EDMUND [*sits down opposite his father—contemptuously*]. Yes, facts don't mean a thing, do they? What you want to believe, that's the only truth! [*Derisively.*] Shakespeare was an Irish Catholic, for example.

TYRONE [*stubbornly*]. So he was. The proof is in his plays.

EDMUND. Well he wasn't, and there's no proof of it in his plays, except to you! [*Jeeringly.*] The Duke of Wellington, there was another good Irish Catholic!

TYRONE. I never said he was a good one. He was a renegade but a Catholic just the same.

EDMUND. Well, he wasn't. You just want to believe no one but an Irish Catholic general could beat Napoleon.

TYRONE. I'm not going to argue with you. I asked you to turn out that light in the hall.

EDMUND. I heard you, and as far as I'm concerned it stays on.

TYRONE. None of your damned insolence! Are you going to obey me or not?

EDMUND. Not! If you want to be a crazy miser put it out yourself!

TYRONE [*with threatening anger*]. Listen to me! I've put up with a lot from you because from the mad things you've done at times I've thought you weren't quite right in your head. I've excused you and never lifted my hand to you. But there's a straw that breaks the camel's back. You'll obey me and put out that light or, big as you are, I'll give you a thrashing that'll teach you—! [*Suddenly he remembers Edmund's illness and instantly becomes guilty and shamefaced.*] Forgive me, lad. I forgot— You shouldn't goad me into losing my temper.

EDMUND [*ashamed himself now*]. Forget it, Papa. I apologize, too. I had

no right being nasty about nothing. I am a bit soused, I guess. I'll
put out the damned light. [*He starts to get up.*]

TYRONE. No, stay where you are. Let it burn. [*He stands up abruptly—
and a bit drunkenly—and begins turning on the three bulbs in the
chandelier, with a childish, bitterly dramatic self-pity.*] We'll have
them all on! Let them burn! To hell with them! The poorhouse is
the end of the road, and it might as well be sooner as later! [*He finishes
turning on the lights.*]

EDMUND [*has watched this proceeding with an awakened sense of humor—
now he grins, teasing affectionately*]. That's a grand curtain. [*He
laughs.*] You're a wonder, Papa.

TYRONE [*sits down sheepishly—grumbles pathetically*]. That's right, laugh
at the old fool! The poor old ham! But the final curtain will be in
the poorhouse just the same, and that's not comedy! [*Then as* EDMUND
is still grinning, he changes the subject.] Well, well, let's not argue.
You've got brains in that head of yours, though you do your best to
deny them. You'll live to learn the value of a dollar. You're not like
your damned tramp of a brother. I've given up hope he'll ever get
sense. Where is he, by the way?

EDMUND. How would I know?

TYRONE. I thought you'd gone back uptown to meet him.

EDMUND. No. I walked out to the beach. I haven't seen him since this
afternoon.

TYRONE. Well, if you split the money I gave you with him, like a fool—

EDMUND. Sure I did. He's always staked me when he had anything.

TYRONE. Then it doesn't take a soothsayer to tell he's probably in the
whorehouse.

EDMUND. What of it if he is? Why not?

TYRONE [*contemptuously*]. Why not, indeed. It's the fit place for him.
If he's ever had a loftier dream than whores and whiskey, he's never
shown it.

EDMUND. Oh, for Pete's sake, Papa! If you're going to start that stuff,
I'll beat it. [*He starts to get up.*]

TYRONE [*placatingly*]. All right, all right, I'll stop. God knows, I don't
like the subject either. Will you join me in a drink?

EDMUND. Ah! Now you're talking!

TYRONE [*passes the bottle to him—mechanically*]. I'm wrong to treat you.
You've had enough already.

EDMUND [*pouring a big drink—a bit drunkenly*]. Enough is *not* as good
as a feast. [*He hands back the bottle.*]

TYRONE. It's too much in your condition.

EDMUND. Forget my condition! [*He raises his glass.*] Here's how.

TYRONE. Drink hearty. [*They drink.*] If you walked all the way to the
beach you must be damp and chilled.

EDMUND. Oh, I dropped in at the Inn on the way out and back.

TYRONE. It's not a night I'd pick for a long walk.

EDMUND. I loved the fog. It was what I needed. [*He sounds more tipsy and looks it.*]

TYRONE. You should have more sense than to risk—

EDMUND. To hell with sense! We're all crazy. What do we want with sense? [*He quotes from Dowson[2] sardonically.*]

> "They are not long, the weeping and the laughter,
> Love and desire and hate:
> I think they have no portion in us after
> We pass the gate.
>
> They are not long, the days of wine and roses:
> Out of a misty dream
> Our path emerges for a while, then closes
> Within a dream."

[*Staring before him.*] The fog was where I wanted to be. Halfway down the path you can't see this house. You'd never know it was here. Or any of the other places down the avenue. I couldn't see but a few feet ahead. I didn't meet a soul. Everything looked and sounded unreal. Nothing was what it is. That's what I wanted—to be alone with myself in another world where truth is untrue and life can hide from itself. Out beyond the harbor, where the road runs along the beach, I even lost the feeling of being on land. The fog and the sea seemed part of each other. It was like walking on the bottom of the sea. As if I had drowned long ago. As if I was a ghost belonging to the fog, and the fog was the ghost of the sea. It felt damned peaceful to be nothing more than a ghost within a ghost. [*He sees his father staring at him with mingled worry and irritated disapproval. He grins mockingly.*] Don't look at me as if I'd gone nutty. I'm talking sense. Who wants to see life as it is, if they can help it? It's the three Gorgons[3] in one. You look in their faces and turn to stone. Or it's Pan.[4] You see him and you die—that is, inside you—and have to go on living as a ghost.

TYRONE [*impressed and at the same time revolted*]. You have a poet in you but it's a damned morbid one! [*Forcing a smile.*] Devil take your pessimism. I feel low-spirited enough. [*He sighs.*] Why can't you remember your Shakespeare and forget the third-raters. You'll find what you're trying to say in him—as you'll find everything else worth saying. [*He quotes, using his fine voice.*] "We are such stuff as dreams are made on, and our little life is rounded with a sleep."[5]

---

2. Ernest Dowson (1867–1900), perhaps the best of the English "decadent" poets. The poem is entitled "Envoy (*Vitae summa brevis spem nos vetat incohare longam* ["The brief span of life prevents us from having long-range hope"—from Horace, *Odes* 1.4.15])."

3. Stheno, Euryale, and Medusa. In Greek myth-

ology these sisters with serpents for hair were so terrifying that the sight of them was enough to turn the beholder to stone.

4. In Greek mythology a god of forests, flocks of animals, and shepherds.

5. From *The Tempest* 4.1.57–58.

EDMUND [*ironically*]. Fine! That's beautiful. But I wasn't trying to say that. We are such stuff as manure is made on, so let's drink up and forget it. That's more my idea.

TYRONE [*disgustedly*]. Ach! Keep such sentiments to yourself. I shouldn't have given you that drink.

EDMUND. It did pack a wallop, all right. On you, too. [*He grins with affectionate teasing.*] Even if you've never missed a performance! [*Aggressively.*] Well, what's wrong with being drunk? It's what we're after, isn't it? Let's not kid each other, Papa. Not tonight. We know what we're trying to forget. [*Hurriedly.*] But let's not talk about it. It's no use now.

TYRONE [*dully*]. No. All we can do is try to be resigned—again.

EDMUND. Or be so drunk you can forget. [*He recites, and recites well, with bitter, ironical passion, the Symons' translation of Baudelaire's prose poem.*[6]] "Be always drunken. Nothing else matters: that is the only question. If you would not feel the horrible burden of Time weighing on your shoulders and crushing you to the earth, be drunken continually.

Drunken with what? With wine, with poetry, or with virtue, as you will. But be drunken.

And if sometimes, on the stairs of a palace, or on the green side of a ditch, or in the dreary solitude of your own room, you should awaken and the drunkenness be half or wholly slipped away from you, ask of the wind, or of the wave, or of the star, or of the bird, or of the clock, of whatever flies, or sighs, or rocks, or sings, or speaks, ask what hour it is; and the wind, wave, star, bird, clock, will answer you: 'It is the hour to be drunken! Be drunken, if you would not be martyred slaves of Time; be drunken continually! With wine, with poetry, or with virtue, as you will.' "

[*He grins at his father provocatively.*]

TYRONE [*thickly humorous*]. I wouldn't worry about the virtue part of it, if I were you. [*Then disgustedly.*] Pah! It's morbid nonsense! What little truth is in it you'll find nobly said in Shakespeare. [*Then appreciatively.*] But you recited it well, lad. Who wrote it?

EDMUND. Baudelaire.

TYRONE. Never heard of him.

EDMUND [*grins provocatively*]. He also wrote a poem about Jamie and the Great White Way.

TYRONE. That loafer! I hope to God he misses the last car and has to stay uptown!

EDMUND [*goes on, ignoring this*]. Although he was French and never saw Broadway and died before Jamie was born. He knew him and Little Old New York just the same. [*He recites the Symons' translation of Baudelaire's "Epilogue."*]

6. Arthur Symons (1865–1945), another English "decadent." Charles Baudelaire (1821–67) was a French "decadent" poet.

"With heart at rest I climbed the citadel's
Steep height, and saw the city as from a tower,
Hospital, brothel, prison, and such hells,

Where evil comes up softly like a flower.
Thou knowest, O Satan, patron of my pain,
Not for vain tears I went up at that hour;

But like an old sad faithful lecher, fain
To drink delight of that enormous trull
Whose hellish beauty makes me young again.

Whether thou sleep, with heavy vapours full,
Sodden with day, or, new apparelled, stand
In gold-laced veils of evening beautiful,

I love thee, infamous city! Harlots and
Hunted have pleasures of their own to give,
The vulgar herd can never understand."

TYRONE [*with irritable disgust*]. Morbid filth! Where the hell do you get your taste in literature? Filth and despair and pessimism! Another atheist, I suppose. When you deny God, you deny hope. That's the trouble with you. If you'd get down on your knees—

EDMUND [*as if he hadn't heard—sardonically*]. It's a good likeness of Jamie, don't you think, hunted by himself and whiskey, hiding in a Broadway hotel room with some fat tart—he likes them fat—reciting Dowson's Cynara to her. [*He recites derisively, but with deep feeling.*]

"All night upon mine heart I felt her warm heart beat,
Night-long within mine arms in love and sleep she lay;
Surely the kisses of her bought red mouth were sweet;
But I was desolate and sick of an old passion,
When I awoke and found the dawn was gray:
I have been faithful to thee, Cynara! in my fashion."[7]

[*Jeeringly*] And the poor fat burlesque queen doesn't get a word of it, but suspects she's being insulted! And Jamie never loved any Cynara, and was never faithful to a woman in his life, even in his fashion! But he lies there, kidding himself he is superior and enjoys pleasures "the vulgar herd can never understand"! [*He laughs.*] It's nuts—completely nuts!

TYRONE [*vaguely—his voice thick*]. It's madness, yes. If you'd get on your knees and pray. When you deny God, you deny sanity.

EDMUND [*ignoring this*]. But who am I to feel superior? I've done the same damned thing. And it's no more crazy than Dowson himself, inspired by an absinthe hangover, writing it to a dumb barmaid, who thought he was a poor crazy souse, and gave him the gate to marry

7. Dowson's title for the poem is "*Non Sum Qualis Eram Bonae Sub Regno Cynarae*" ["I'm not such as I was under the reign of the good Cynara"—from Horace, *Odes* 4.1.3–4].

a waiter! [*He laughs—then soberly, with genuine sympathy.*] Poor Dowson. Booze and consumption got him. [*He starts and for a second looks miserable and frightened. Then with defensive irony.*] Perhaps it would be tactful of me to change the subject.

TYRONE [*thickly*]. Where you get your taste in authors—That damned library of yours! [*He indicates the small bookcase at rear.*] Voltaire, Rousseau, Schopenhauer, Nietzsche, Ibsen! Atheists, fools, and madmen! And your poets! This Dowson, and this Baudelaire, and Swinburne and Oscar Wilde, and Whitman and Poe! Whoremongers and degenerates! Pah! When I've three good sets of Shakespeare there [*he nods at the large bookcase*] you could read.

EDMUND [*provocatively*]. They say he was a souse, too.

TYRONE. They lie! I don't doubt he liked his glass—it's a good man's failing—but he knew how to drink so it didn't poison his brain with morbidness and filth. Don't compare him with the pack you've got in there. [*He indicates the small bookcase again.*] Your dirty Zola! And your Dante Gabriel Rossetti who was a dope fiend! [*He starts and looks guilty.*]

EDMUND [*with defensive dryness*]. Perhaps it would be wise to change the subject. [*A pause.*] You can't accuse me of not knowing Shakespeare. Didn't I win five dollars from you once when you bet me I couldn't learn a leading part of his in a week, as you used to do in stock in the old days. I learned Macbeth and recited it letter perfect, with you giving me the cues.

TYRONE [*approvingly*]. That's true. So you did. [*He smiles teasingly and sighs.*] It was a terrible ordeal, I remember, hearing you murder the lines. I kept wishing I'd paid over the bet without making you prove it.

[*He chuckles and* EDMUND *grins. Then he starts as he hears a sound from upstairs—with dread.*]

Did you hear? She's moving around. I was hoping she'd gone to sleep.

EDMUND. Forget it! How about another drink?

[*He reaches out and gets the bottle, pours a drink and hands it back. Then with a strained casualness, as his father pours a drink.*]

When did Mama go to bed?

TYRONE. Right after you left. She wouldn't eat any dinner. What made you run away?

EDMUND. Nothing. [*Abruptly raising his glass.*] Well, here's how.

TYRONE [*mechanically*]. Drink hearty, lad.

[*They drink.* TYRONE *again listens to sounds upstairs—with dread.*]

She's moving around a lot. I hope to God she doesn't come down.

EDMUND [*dully*]. Yes. She'll be nothing but a ghost haunting the past by this time. [*He pauses—then miserably.*] Back before I was born—

TYRONE. Doesn't she do the same with me? Back before she ever knew me. You'd think the only happy days she's ever known were in her father's home, or at the Convent, praying and playing the piano.

[*Jealous resentment in his bitterness.*] As I've told you before, you must take her memories with a grain of salt. Her wonderful home was ordinary enough. Her father wasn't the great, generous, noble Irish gentleman she makes out. He was a nice enough man, good company and a good talker. I liked him and he liked me. He was prosperous enough, too, in his wholesale grocery business, an able man. But he had his weakness. She condemns my drinking but she forgets his. It's true he never touched a drop till he was forty, but after that he made up for lost time. He became a steady champagne drinker, the worst kind. That was his grand pose, to drink only champagne. Well, it finished him quick—that and the consumption— [*He stops with a guilty glance at his son.*]

EDMUND [*sardonically*]. We don't seem able to avoid unpleasant topics, do we?

TYRONE [*sighs sadly*]. No. [*Then with a pathetic attempt at heartiness.*] What do you say to a game or two of Casino, lad?

EDMUND. All right.

TYRONE [*shuffling the cards clumsily*]. We can't lock up and go to bed till Jamie comes on the last trolley—which I hope he won't—and I don't want to go upstairs, anyway, till she's asleep.

EDMUND. Neither do I.

TYRONE [*keeps shuffling the cards fumblingly, forgetting to deal them*]. As I was saying, you must take her tales of the past with a grain of salt. The piano playing and her dream of becoming a concert pianist. That was put in her head by the nuns flattering her. She was their pet. They loved her for being so devout. They're innocent women, anyway, when it comes to the world. They don't know that not one in a million who shows promise ever rises to concert playing. Not that your mother didn't play well for a schoolgirl, but that's no reason to take it for granted she could have—

EDMUND [*sharply*]. Why don't you deal, if we're going to play.

TYRONE. Eh? I am. [*Dealing with very uncertain judgment of distance.*] And the idea she might have become a nun. That's the worst. Your mother was one of the most beautiful girls you could ever see. She knew it, too. She was a bit of a rogue and a coquette, God bless her, behind all her shyness and blushes. She was never made to renounce the world. She was bursting with health and high spirits and the love of loving.

EDMUND. For God's sake, Papa! Why don't you pick up your hand?

TYRONE [*picks it up—dully*]. Yes, let's see what I have here.

[*They both stare at their cards unseeingly. Then they both start.* TYRONE *whispers.*]

Listen!

EDMUND. She's coming downstairs.

TYRONE [*hurriedly*]. We'll play our game. Pretend not to notice and she'll soon go up again.

EDMUND [*staring through the front parlor—with relief*]. I don't see her.
She must have started down and then turned back.

TYRONE. Thank God.

EDMUND. Yes. It's pretty horrible to see her the way she must be now.
[*With bitter misery*] The hardest thing to take is the blank wall she
builds around her. Or it's more like a bank of fog in which she hides
and loses herself. Deliberately, that's the hell of it! You know something in her does it deliberately—to get beyond our reach, to be rid
of us, to forget we're alive! It's as if, in spite of loving us, she hated
us!

TYRONE [*remonstrates gently*]. Now, now, lad. It's not her. It's the
damned poison.

EDMUND [*bitterly*]. She takes it to get that effect. At least, I know she
did this time! [*Abruptly.*] My play, isn't it? Here. [*He plays a card.*]

TYRONE [*plays mechanically—gently reproachful*]. She's been terribly
frightened about your illness, for all her pretending. Don't be too
hard on her, lad. Remember she's not responsible. Once that cursed
poison gets a hold on anyone—

EDMUND [*his face grows hard and he stares at his father with bitter
accusation*]. It never should have gotten a hold on her! I know damned
well she's not to blame! And I know who is! You are! Your damned
stinginess! If you'd spent money for a decent doctor when she was so
sick after I was born, she'd never have known morphine existed!
Instead you put her in the hands of a hotel quack who wouldn't admit
his ignorance and took the easiest way out, not giving a damn what
happened to her afterwards! All because his fee was cheap! Another
one of your bargains!

TYRONE [*stung—angrily*]. Be quiet! How dare you talk of something you
know nothing about! [*Trying to control his temper.*] You must try to
see my side of it, too, lad. How was I to know he was that kind of a
doctor? He had a good reputation—

EDMUND. Among the souses in the hotel bar, I suppose!

TYRONE. That's a lie! I asked the hotel proprietor to recommend the
best—

EDMUND. Yes! At the same time crying poorhouse and making it plain
you wanted a cheap one! I know your system! By God, I ought to
after this afternoon!

TYRONE [*guiltily defensive*]. What about this afternoon?

EDMUND. Never mind now. We're talking about Mama! I'm saying no
matter how you excuse yourself you know damned well your stinginess
is to blame—

TYRONE. And I say you're a liar! Shut your mouth right now, or—

EDMUND [*ignoring this*]. After you found out she'd been made a morphine
addict, why didn't you send her to a cure then, at the start, while she
still had a chance? No, that would have meant spending some money!
I'll bet you told her all she had to do was use a little will power! That's

what you still believe in your heart, in spite of what doctors, who really know something about it, have told you!

TYRONE. You lie again! I know better than that now! But how was I to know then? What did I know of morphine? It was years before I discovered what was wrong. I thought she'd never got over her sickness, that's all. Why didn't I send her to a cure, you say? [Bitterly.] Haven't I? I've spent thousands upon thousands in cures! A waste. What good have they done her? She always started again.

EDMUND. Because you've never given her anything that would help her want to stay off it! No home except this summer dump in a place she hates and you've refused even to spend money to make this look decent, while you keep buying more property, and playing sucker for every con man with a gold mine, or a silver mine, or any kind of get-rich-quick swindle! You've dragged her around on the road, season after season, on one-night stands, with no one she could talk to, waiting night after night in dirty hotel rooms for you to come back with a bun on after the bars closed! Christ, is it any wonder she didn't want to be cured. Jesus, when I think of it I hate your guts!

TYRONE [strickenly]. Edmund! [Then in a rage.] How dare you talk to your father like that, you insolent young cub! After all I've done for you.

EDMUND. We'll come to that, what you're doing for me!

TYRONE [looking guilty again—ignores this]. Will you stop repeating your mother's crazy accusations, which she never makes unless it's the poison talking? I never dragged her on the road against her will. Naturally, I wanted her with me. I loved her. And she came because she loved me and wanted to be with me. That's the truth, no matter what she says when she's not herself. And she needn't have been lonely. There was always the members of my company to talk to, if she'd wanted. She had her children, too, and I insisted, in spite of the expense, on having a nurse to travel with her.

EDMUND [bitterly]. Yes, your one generosity, and that because you were jealous of her paying too much attention to us, and wanted us out of your way! It was another mistake, too! If she'd had to take care of me all by herself, and had that to occupy her mind, maybe she'd have been able—

TYRONE [goaded into vindictiveness]. Or for that matter, if you insist on judging things by what she says when she's not in her right mind, if you hadn't been born she'd never— [He stops ashamed.]

EDMUND [suddenly spent and miserable]. Sure. I know that's what she feels, Papa.

TYRONE [protests penitently]. She doesn't! She loves you as dearly as ever mother loved a son! I only said that because you put me in such a God-damned rage, raking up the past, and saying you hate me—

EDMUND [dully]. I didn't mean it, Papa. [He suddenly smiles—kidding *a bit drunkenly.*] I'm like Mama, I can't help liking you, in spite of everything.

TYRONE [*grins a bit drunkenly in return*]. I might say the same of you. You're no great shakes as a son. It's a case of "A poor thing but mine own."[8]

[*They both chuckle with real, if alcoholic, affection.* TYRONE *changes the subject.*]

What's happened to our game? Whose play is it?

EDMUND. Yours, I guess.

[TYRONE *plays a card which* EDMUND *takes and the game gets forgotten again.*]

TYRONE. You musn't let yourself be too downhearted, lad, by the bad news you had today. Both the doctors promised me, if you obey orders at this place you're going, you'll be cured in six months, or a year at most.

EDMUND [*his face hard again*]. Don't kid me. You don't believe that.

TYRONE [*too vehemently*]. Of course I believe it! Why shouldn't I believe it when both Hardy and the specialist—?

EDMUND. You think I'm going to die.

TYRONE. That's a lie! You're crazy!

EDMUND [*more bitterly*]. So why waste money? That's why you're sending me to a state farm—

TYRONE [*in guilty confusion*]. What state farm? It's the Hilltown Sanatorium, that's all I know, and both doctors said it was the best place for you.

EDMUND [*scathingly*]. For the money! That is, for nothing, or practically nothing. Don't lie, Papa! You know damned well Hilltown Sanatorium is a state institution! Jamie suspected you'd cry poorhouse to Hardy and he wormed the truth out of him.

TYRONE [*furiously*]. That drunken loafer! I'll kick him out in the gutter! He's poisoned your mind against me ever since you were old enough to listen!

EDMUND. You can't deny it's the truth about the state farm, can you?

TYRONE. It's not true the way you look at it! What if it is run by the state? That's nothing against it. The state has the money to make a better place than any private sanatorium. And why shouldn't I take advantage of it? It's my right—and yours. We're residents. I'm a property owner. I help to support it. I'm taxed to death—

EDMUND [*with bitter irony*]. Yes, on property valued at a quarter of a million.

TYRONE. Lies! It's all mortgaged!

EDMUND. Hardy and the specialist know what you're worth. I wonder what they thought of you when they heard you moaning poorhouse and showing you wanted to wish me on charity!

8. From *As You Like It* 5.4.57–58.

TYRONE. It's a lie! All I told them was I couldn't afford any millionaire's sanatorium because I was land poor. That's the truth!

EDMUND. And then you went to the Club to meet McGuire and let him stick you with another bum piece of property! [As TYRONE starts to deny.] Don't lie about it! We met McGuire in the hotel bar after he left you. Jamie kidded him about hooking you, and he winked and laughed!

TYRONE [lying feebly]. He's a liar if he said—

EDMUND. Don't lie about it! [With gathering intensity.] God, Papa, ever since I went to sea and was on my own, and found out what hard work for little pay was, and what it felt like to be broke, and starve, and camp on park benches because I had no place to sleep, I've tried to be fair to you because I knew what you'd been up against as a kid. I've tried to make allowances. Christ, you have to make allowances in this damned family or go nuts! I have tried to make allowances for myself when I remember all the rotten stuff I've pulled! I've tried to feel like Mama that you can't help being what you are where money is concerned. But God Almighty, this last stunt of yours is too much! It makes me want to puke! Not because of the rotten way you're treating me. To hell with that! I've treated you rottenly, in my way, more than once. But to think when it's a question of your son having consumption, you can show yourself up before the whole town as such a stinking old tightwad! Don't you know Hardy will talk and the whole damned town will know! Jesus, Papa, haven't you any pride or shame? [Bursting with rage.] And don't think I'll let you get away with it! I won't go to any damned state farm just to save you a few lousy dollars to buy more bum property with! You stinking old miser—! [He chokes huskily, his voice trembling with rage, and then is shaken by a fit of coughing.]

TYRONE [has shrunk back in his chair under this attack, his guilty contrition greater than his anger. He stammers]. Be quiet! Don't say that to me! You're drunk! I won't mind you. Stop coughing, lad. You've got yourself worked up over nothing. Who said you had to go to this Hilltown place? You can go anywhere you like. I don't give a damn what it costs. All I care about is to have you get well. Don't call me a stinking miser, just because I don't want doctors to think I'm a millionaire they can swindle.

[EDMUND has stopped coughing. He looks sick and weak. His father stares at him frightenedly.]

You look weak, lad. You'd better take a bracer.

EDMUND [grabs the bottle and pours his glass brimfull—weakly]. Thanks. [He gulps down the whiskey.]

TYRONE [pours himself a big drink, which empties the bottle, and drinks it. His head bows and he stares dully at the cards on the table— vaguely]. Whose play is it? [He goes on dully, without resentment.] A stinking old miser. Well, maybe you're right. Maybe I can't help being, although all my life since I had anything I've thrown money over the bar to buy drinks for everyone in the house, or loaned money to sponges I knew would never pay it back— [*With a loose-mouthed sneer of self-contempt*] But, of course, that was in barrooms, when I was full of whiskey. I can't feel that way about it when I'm sober in my home. It was at home I first learned the value of a dollar and the fear of the poorhouse. I've never been able to believe in my luck since. I've always feared it would change and everything I had would be taken away. But still, the more property you own, the safer you think you are. That may not be logical, but it's the way I have to feel. Banks fail, and your money's gone, but you think you can keep land beneath your feet. [*Abruptly his tone becomes scornfully superior.*] You said you realized what I'd been up against as a boy. The hell you do! How could you? You've had everything—nurses, schools, college, though you didn't stay there. You've had food, clothing. Oh, I know you had a fling of hard work with your back and hands, a bit of being homeless and penniless in a foreign land, and I respect you for it. But it was a game of romance and adventure to you. It was play.

EDMUND [*dully sarcastic*]. Yes, particularly the time I tried to commit suicide at Jimmie the Priest's, and almost did.

TYRONE. You weren't in your right mind. No son of mine would ever— You were drunk.

EDMUND. I was stone cold sober. That was the trouble. I'd stopped to think too long.

TYRONE [*with drunken peevishness*]. Don't start your damned atheist morbidity again! I don't care to listen. I was trying to make plain to you— [*Scornfully.*] What do you know of the value of a dollar? When I was ten my father deserted my mother and went back to Ireland to die. Which he did soon enough, and deserved to, and I hope he's roasting in hell. He mistook rat poison for flour, or sugar, or something. There was gossip it wasn't by mistake but that's a lie. No one in my family ever—

EDMUND. My bet is, it wasn't by mistake.

TYRONE. More morbidness! Your brother put that in your head. The worst he can suspect is the only truth for him. But never mind. My mother was left, a stranger in a strange land, with four small children, me and a sister a little older and two younger than me. My two older brothers had moved to other parts. They couldn't help. They were hard put to it to keep themselves alive. There was no damned romance in our poverty. Twice we were evicted from the miserable hovel we called home, with my mother's few sticks of furniture thrown out in the street, and my mother and sisters crying. I cried, too, though I tried hard not to, because I was the man of the family. At ten years old! There was no more school for me. I worked twelve hours a day in a machine shop, learning to make files. A dirty barn of a place where rain dripped through the roof, where you roasted in summer, and there was no stove in winter, and your hands got numb with cold, where the only light came through two small filthy windows, so on grey days I'd have to sit bent over with my eyes almost touching the files in order to see! You talk of work! And what do you think I got for it? Fifty cents a week! It's the truth! Fifty cents a week! And my poor mother washed and scrubbed for the Yanks by the day, and my older sister sewed, and my two younger stayed at home to keep the house. We never had clothes enough to wear, nor enough food to eat. Well I remember one Thanksgiving, or maybe it was Christmas, when some Yank in whose house mother had been scrubbing gave her a dollar extra for a present, and on the way home she spent it all on food. I can remember her hugging and kissing us and saying with tears of joy running down her tired face: "Glory be to God, for once in our lives we'll have enough for each of us!" [*He wipes tears from his eyes.*] A fine, brave, sweet woman. There never was a braver or finer.

EDMUND [*moved*]. Yes, she must have been.

TYRONE. Her one fear was she'd get old and sick and have to die in the poorhouse. [*He pauses—then adds with grim humor*] It was in those days I learned to be a miser. A dollar was worth so much then. And once you've learned a lesson, it's hard to unlearn it. You have to look for bargains. If I took this state farm sanatorium for a good bargain, you'll have to forgive me. The doctors did tell me it's a good place. You must believe that, Edmund. And I swear I never meant you to go there if you didn't want to. [*Vehemently.*] You can choose any place you like! Never mind what it costs! Any place I can afford. Any place you like—within reason.

[*At this qualification, a grin twitches* EDMUND'S *lips. His resentment has gone. His father goes on with an elaborately offhand, casual air.*]

There was another sanatorium the specialist recommended. He said it had a record as good as any place in the country. It's endowed by a group of millionaire factory owners, for the benefit of their workers principally, but you're eligible to go there because you're a resident. There's such a pile of money behind it, they don't have to charge much. It's only seven dollars a week but you get ten times that value. [*Hastily.*] I don't want to persuade you to anything, understand. I'm simply repeating what I was told.

EDMUND [*concealing his smile—casually*]. Oh, I know that. It sounds like a good bargain to me. I'd like to go there. So that settles that. [*Abruptly he is miserably desperate again—dully.*] It doesn't matter a damn now, anyway. Let's forget it! [*Changing the subject.*] How about our game? Whose play is it?

TYRONE [*mechanically*]. I don't know. Mine, I guess. No, it's yours.

[EDMUND *plays a card. His father takes it. Then about to play from his hand, he again forgets the game.*]

Yes, maybe life overdid the lesson for me, and made a dollar worth too much, and the time came when that mistake ruined my career as a fine actor. [*Sadly.*] I've never admitted this to anyone before, lad, but tonight I'm so heartsick I feel at the end of everything, and what's the use of fake pride and pretense. That God-damned play I bought for a song and made such a great success in—a great money success—it ruined me with its promise of an easy fortune. I didn't want to do anything else, and by the time I woke up to the fact I'd become a slave to the damned thing and did try other plays, it was too late. They had identified me with that one part, and didn't want me in anything else. They were right, too. I'd lost the great talent I once had through years of easy repetition, never learning a new part, never really working hard. Thirty-five to forty thousand dollars net profit a season like snapping your fingers! It was too great a temptation. Yet before I bought the damned thing I was considered one of the three or four young actors with the greatest artistic promise in America. I'd worked like hell. I'd left a good job as a machinist to take supers' parts because I loved the theater. I was wild with ambition. I read all the plays ever written. I studied Shakespeare as you'd study the Bible. I educated myself. I got rid of an Irish brogue you could cut with a knife. I loved Shakespeare. I would have acted in any of his plays for nothing, for the joy of being alive in his great poetry. And I acted well in him. I felt inspired by him. I could have been a great Shakespearean actor, if I'd kept on. I know that! In 1874 when Edwin Booth came to the theater in Chicago where I was leading man, I played Cassius to his Brutus one night, Brutus to his Cassius the next, Othello to his Iago, and so on. The first night I played Othello, he said to our manager, "That young man is playing Othello better than I ever did!" [*Proudly.*] That from Booth, the greatest actor of his day or any other! And it was true! And I was only twenty-seven years old! As I look back on it now, that night was the high spot in my career. I had life where I wanted it! And for a time after that I kept on upward with ambition high. Married your mother. Ask her what I was like in those days. Her love was an added incentive to ambition. But a few years later my good bad luck made me find the big money-maker. It wasn't that in my eyes at first. It was a great romantic part I knew I could play better than anyone. But it was a great box office success from the start—and then life had me where it wanted me—at from thirty-five to forty thousand net profit a season! A fortune in those days— or even in these. [*Bitterly.*] What the hell was it I wanted to buy, I wonder, that was worth— Well, no matter. It's a late day for regrets. [*He glances vaguely at his cards.*] My play, isn't it?

EDMUND [*moved, stares at his father with understanding—slowly*]. I'm glad you've told me this, Papa. I know you a lot better now.

TYRONE [*with a loose, twisted smile*]. Maybe I shouldn't have told you. Maybe you'll only feel more contempt for me. And it's a poor way to convince you of the value of a dollar. [*Then as if this phrase automatically aroused an habitual association in his mind, he glances up at the chandelier disapprovingly.*] The glare from those extra lights hurts my eyes. You don't mind if I turn them out, do you? We don't need them, and there's no use making the Electric Company rich.

EDMUND [*controlling a wild impulse to laugh—agreeably*]. No, sure not. Turn them out.

TYRONE [*gets heavily and a bit waveringly to his feet and gropes uncertainly for the lights—his mind going back to its line of thought*]. No, I don't know what the hell it was I wanted to buy. [*He clicks out one bulb.*] On my solemn oath, Edmund, I'd gladly face not having an acre of land to call my own, nor a penny in the bank— [*He clicks out another bulb.*] I'd be willing to have no home but the poorhouse in my old age if I could look back now on having been the fine artist I might have been.

[*He turns out the third bulb, so only the reading lamp is on, and sits down again heavily.* EDMUND *suddenly cannot hold back a burst of strained, ironical laugher.* TYRONE *is hurt.*]

What the devil are you laughing at?

EDMUND. Not at you, Papa. At life. It's so damned crazy.

TYRONE [*growls*]. More of your morbidness! There's nothing wrong with life. It's we who— [*He quotes.*] "The fault, dear Brutus, is not in our stars, but in ourselves that we are underlings."[9] [*He pauses—then sadly.*] The praise Edwin Booth gave my Othello. I made the manager put down his exact words in writing. I kept it in my wallet for years. I used to read it every once in a while until finally it made me feel so bad I didn't want to face it any more. Where is it now, I wonder? Somewhere in this house. I remember I put it away carefully—

EDMUND [*with a wry ironical sadness*]. It might be in an old trunk in the attic, along with Mama's wedding dress. [*Then as his father stares at him, he adds quickly*] For Pete's sake, if we're going to play cards, let's play.

[*He takes the card his father had played and leads. For a moment, they play the game, like mechanical chess players. Then* TYRONE *stops, listening to a sound upstairs.*]

TYRONE. She's still moving around. God knows when she'll go to sleep.

EDMUND [*pleads tensely*]. For Christ's sake, Papa, forget it!

[*He reaches out and pours a drink.* TYRONE *starts to protest, then gives it up.* EDMUND *drinks. He puts down the glass. His expression changes. When he speaks it is as if he were deliberately giving way to drunkenness and seeking to hide behind a maudlin manner.*]

Yes, she moves above and beyond us, a ghost haunting the past, and here we sit pretending to forget, but straining our ears listening for the slightest sound, hearing the fog drip from the eaves like the uneven tick of a rundown, crazy clock—or like the dreary tears of a trollop

9. From *Julius Caesar* 1.2.140–41.

spattering in a puddle of stale beer on a honky-tonk table top! [*He laughs with maudlin appreciation.*] Not so bad, that last, eh? Original, not Baudelaire. Give me credit! [*Then with alcoholic talkativeness.*] You've just told me some high spots in your memories. Want to hear mine? They're all connected with the sea. Here's one. When I was on the Squarehead square rigger, bound for Buenos Aires. Full moon in the Trades. The old hooker driving fourteen knots. I lay on the bowsprit, facing astern, with the water foaming into spume under me, the masts with every sail white in the moonlight, towering high above me. I became drunk with the beauty and singing rhythm of it, and for a moment I lost myself—actually lost my life. I was set free! I dissolved in the sea, became white sails and flying spray, became beauty and rhythm, became moonlight and the ship and the high dim-starred sky! I belonged, without past or future, within peace and unity and a wild joy, within something greater than my own life, or the life of Man, to Life itself! To God, if you want to put it that way. Then another time, on the American Line, when I was lookout on the crow's nest in the dawn watch. A calm sea, that time. Only a lazy ground swell and a slow drowsy roll of the ship. The passengers asleep and none of the crew in sight. No sound of man. Black smoke pouring from the funnels behind and beneath me. Dreaming, not keeping lookout, feeling alone, and above, and apart, watching the dawn creep like a painted dream over the sky and sea which slept together. Then the moment of ecstatic freedom came. The peace, the end of the quest, the last harbor, the joy of belonging to a fulfillment beyond men's lousy, pitiful, greedy fears and hopes and dreams! And several other times in my life, when I was swimming far out, or lying alone on a beach, I have had the same experience. Became the sun, the hot sand, green seaweed anchored to a rock, swaying in the tide. Like a saint's vision of beatitude. Like the veil of things as they seem drawn back by an unseen hand. For a second you see—and seeing the secret, are the secret. For a second there is meaning! Then the hand lets the veil fall and you are alone, lost in the fog again, and you stumble on toward nowhere, for no good reason! [*He grins wryly.*] It was a great mistake, my being born a man, I would have been much more successful as a seal gull or a fish. As it is, I will always be a stranger who never feels at home, who does not really want and is not really wanted, who can never belong, who must always be a little in love with death!

TYRONE [*stares at him—impressed*]. Yes, there's the makings of a poet in you all right. [*Then protesting uneasily*] But that's morbid craziness about not being wanted and loving death.

EDMUND [*sardonically*]. The *makings* of a poet. No, I'm afraid I'm like the guy who is always panhandling for a smoke. He hasn't even got the makings. He's got only the habit. I couldn't touch what I tried to tell you just now. I just stammered. That's the best I'll ever do. I mean, if I live. Well, it will be faithful realism, at least. Stammering is the native eloquence of us fog people.

[*A* pause. *Then they both jump startledly as there is a noise from outside the house, as if someone had stumbled and fallen on the front steps.* EDMUND *grins.*]

Well, that sounds like the absent brother. He must have a peach of a bun on.

TYRONE [*scowling*]. That loafer! He caught the last car, bad luck to it. [*He gets to his feet.*] Get him to bed, Edmund. I'll go out on the porch. He has a tongue like an adder when he's drunk. I'd only lose my temper.

[*He goes out the door to the side porch as the front door in the hall bangs shut behind* JAMIE. EDMUND *watches with amusement* JAMIE's *wavering progress through the front parlor.* JAMIE *comes in. He is very drunk and woozy on his legs. His eyes are glassy, his face bloated, his speech blurred, his mouth slack like his father's, a leer on his lips.*]

JAMIE [*swaying and blinking in the doorway—in a loud voice*]. What ho! What ho!

EDMUND [*sharply*]. Nix on the loud noise!

JAMIE [*blinks at him*]. Oh, hello, Kid. [*With great seriousness*] I'm as drunk as a fiddler's bitch.

EDMUND [*dryly*]. Thanks for telling me your great secret.

JAMIE [*grins foolishly*]. Yes. Unneshesary information Number one, eh? [*He bends and slaps at the knees of his trousers.*] Had serious accident. The front steps tried to trample on me. Took advantage of fog to waylay me. Ought to be a lighthouse out there. Dark in here, too. [*Scowling.*] What the hell is this, the morgue? Lesh have some light on sibject. [*He sways forward to the table, reciting Kipling.*[1]]

"Ford, ford, ford o' Kabul river,
Ford o' Kabul river in the dark!
Keep the crossing-stakes beside you, an' they will surely guide you
'Cross the ford o' Kabul river in the dark."

[*He fumbles at the chandelier and manages to turn on the three bulbs.*] Thash more like it. To hell with old Gaspard.[2] Where is the old tightwad?

EDMUND. Out on the porch.

JAMIE. Can't expect us to live in the Black Hole of Calcutta. [*His eyes fix on the full bottle of whiskey.*] Say! Have I got the d.t.'s? [*He reaches out fumblingly and grabs it.*] By God, it's real. What's matter with the Old Man tonight? Must be ossified to forget he left this out. Grab

---

1. Rudyard Kipling (1865–1936), an extremely successful writer of fiction and poetry, much of which deals with Britain's adventures in empire in Indian and Africa.

2. A character in the operetta *The Bells of Corneville* (1877), by Robert Planquette, not *The Bells* by Leopold Lewis, as the later reference suggests.

opportunity by the forelock. Key to my success. [*He slops a big drink into a glass.*]

EDMUND. You're stinking now. That will knock you stiff.

JAMIE. Wisdom from the mouth of babes. Can the wise stuff, Kid. You're still wet behind the ears. [*He lowers himself into a chair, holding the drink carefully aloft.*]

EDMUND. All right. Pass out if you want to.

JAMIE. Can't, that's the trouble. Had enough to sink a ship, but can't sink. Well, here's hoping. [*He drinks.*]

EDMUND. Shove over the bottle. I'll have one, too.

JAMIE [*with sudden, big-brotherly solicitude, grabbing the bottle*]. No, you don't. Not while I'm around. Remember doctor's orders. Maybe no one else gives a damn if you die, but I do. My kid brother. I love your guts, Kid. Everything else is gone. You're all I've got left. [*Pulling bottle closer to him.*] So no booze for you, if I can help it. [*Beneath his drunken sentimentality there is a genuine sincerity.*]

EDMUND [*irritably*]. Oh, lay off it.

JAMIE [*is hurt and his face hardens*]. You don't believe I care, eh? Just drunken bull. [*He shoves the bottle over.*] All right. Go ahead and kill yourself.

EDMUND [*seeing he is hurt—affectionately*]. Sure I know you care, Jamie, and I'm going on the wagon. But tonight doesn't count. Too many damned things have happened today. [*He pours a drink.*] Here's how. [*He drinks.*]

JAMIE [*sobers up momentarily and with a pitying look*]. I know, Kid. It's been a lousy day for you. [*Then with sneering cynicism.*] I'll bet old Gaspard hasn't tried to keep you off booze. Probably give you a case to take with you to the state farm for pauper patients. The sooner you kick the bucket, the less expense. [*With contemptuous hatred.*] What a bastard to have for a father! Christ, if you put him in a book, no one would believe it!

EDMUND [*defensively*]. Oh, Papa's all right, if you try to understand him— and keep your sense of humor.

JAMIE [*cynically*]. He's been putting on the old sob act for you, eh? He can always kid you. But not me. Never again. [*Then slowly*] Although, in a way, I do feel sorry for him about one thing. But he has even that coming to him. He's to blame. [*Hurriedly.*] But to hell with that. [*He grabs the bottle and pours another drink, appearing very drunk again.*] That lash drink's getting me. This one ought to put the lights out. Did you tell Gaspard I got it out of Doc Hardy this sanatorium is a charity dump?

EDMUND [*reluctantly*]. Yes. I told him I wouldn't go there. It's all settled now. He said I can go anywhere I want. [*He adds, smiling without resentment*] Within reason, of course.

JAMIE [*drunkenly imitating his father*]. Of course, lad. Anything within reason. [*Sneering.*] That means another cheap dump. Old Gaspard, the miser in "The Bells," that's a part he can play without make-up.

EDMUND [*irritably*]. Oh, shut up, will you. I've heard that Gaspard stuff a million times.

JAMIE [*shrugs his shoulders—thickly*]. Aw right, if you're shatisfied—let him get away with it. It's your funeral—I mean, I hope it won't be.

EDMUND [*changing the subject*]. What did you do uptown tonight? Go to Mamie Burns?

JAMIE [*very drunk, his head nodding*]. Sure thing. Where else could I find suitable feminine companionship? And love. Don't forget love. What is a man without a good woman's love? A God-damned hollow shell.

EDMUND [*chuckles tipsily, letting himself go now and be drunk*]. You're a nut.

JAMIE [*quotes with gusto from Oscar Wilde's "The Harlot's House"*].[3]

> "Then, turning to my love, I said,
> 'The dead are dancing with the dead,
> The dust is whirling with the dust.'
>
> But she—she heard the violin,
> And left my side and entered in:
> Love passed into the house of lust.
>
> Then suddenly the tune went false,
> The dancers wearied of the waltz . . ."

[*He breaks off, thickly.*] Not strictly accurate. If my love was with me, I didn't notice it. She must have been a ghost. [*He pauses.*] Guess which one of Mamie's charmers I picked to bless me with her woman's love. It'll hand you a laugh, Kid. I picked Fat Violet.

EDMUND [*laughs drunkenly*]. No, honest? Some pick! God, she weighs a ton. What the hell for, a joke?

JAMIE. No joke. Very serious. By the time I hit Mamie's dump I felt very sad about myself and all the other poor bums in the world. Ready for a weep on any old womanly bosom. You know how you get when John Barleycorn turns on the soft music inside you. Then, soon as I got in the door, Mamie began telling me all her troubles. Beefed how rotten business was, and she was going to give Fat Violet the gate. Customers didn't fall for Vi. Only reason she'd kept her was she could play the piano. Lately Vi's gone on drunks and been too boiled to play, and was eating her out of house and home, and although Vi was a goodhearted dumbbell, and she felt sorry for her because she didn't know how the hell she'd make a living, still business was business, and she couldn't afford to run a home for fat tarts. Well, that made me feel sorry for Fat Violet, so I squandered two bucks of your dough to escort her upstairs. With no dishonorable intentions what-

3. Oscar Wilde (1856–1900), a poet, playwright, novelist, and celebrated wit, was also associated with the English "decadents."

ever. I like them fat, but not that fat. All I wanted was a little heart-to-heart talk concerning the infinite sorrow of life.

EDMUND [*chuckles drunkenly*]. Poor Vi! I'll bet you recited Kipling and Swinburne and Dowson and gave her "I have been faithful to thee, Cynara, in my fashion."

JAMIE [*grins loosely*]. Sure—with the Old Master, John Barleycorn, playing soft music. She stood it for a while. Then she got good and sore. Got the idea I took her upstairs for a joke. Gave me a grand bawling out. Said she was better than a drunken bum who recited poetry. Then she began to cry. So I had to say I loved her because she was fat, and she wanted to believe that, and I stayed with her to prove it, and that cheered her up, and she kissed me when I left, and said she'd fallen hard for me, and we both cried a little more in the hallway, and everything was fine, except Mamie Burns thought I'd gone bughouse.

EDMUND [*quotes derisively*].

> "Harlots and
> Hunted have pleasures of their own to give,
> The vulgar herd can never understand."[4]

JAMIE [*nods his head drunkenly*]. Egzackly! Hell of a good time, at that. You should have stuck around with me, Kid. Mamie Burns inquired after you. Sorry to hear you were sick. She meant it, too. [*He pauses—then with maudlin humor, in a ham-actor tone.*] This night has opened my eyes to a great career in store for me, my boy! I shall give the art of acting back to the performing seals, which are its most perfect expression. By applying my natural God-given talents in their proper sphere, I shall attain the pinnacle of success! I'll be the lover of the fat woman in Barnum and Bailey's circus!

[EDMUND *laughs.* JAMIE's *mood changes to arrogant disdain.*]

Pah! Imagine me sunk to the fat girl in a hick town hooker shop! Me! Who have made some of the best-lookers on Broadway sit up and beg! [*He quotes from Kipling's "Sestina of the Tramp-Royal."*]

> "Speakin' in general, I 'ave tried 'em all,
> The 'appy roads that take you o'er the world."

[*With sodden melancholy.*] No so apt. Happy roads is bunk. Weary roads is right. Get you nowhere fast. That's where I've got—nowhere. Where everyone lands in the end, even if most of the suckers won't admit it.

EDMUND [*derisively*]. Can it! You'll be crying in a minute.

JAMIE [*starts and stares at his brother for a second with bitter hostility—thickly*]. Don't get—too damned fresh. [*Then abruptly.*] But you're right. To hell with repining! Fat Violet's a good kid. Glad I stayed

---

4. From Baudelaire's "Epilogue," *Petits Poèmes en Prose* (1869).

with her. Christian act. Cured her blues. Hell of a good time. You should have stuck with me, Kid. Taken your mind off your troubles. What's the use coming home to get the blues over what can't be helped. All over—finished now—not a hope! [*He stops, his head nodding drunkenly, his eyes closing—then suddenly he looks up, his face hard, and quotes jeeringly.*]

> "If I were hanged on the highest hill,
> Mother o'mine, O mother o' mine!
> I know whose love would follow me still . . ."[5]

EDMUND [*violently*]. Shut up!

JAMIE [*in a cruel, sneering tone with hatred in it*]. Where's the hophead? Gone to sleep?

[EDMUND *jerks as if he'd been struck. There is a tense silence.* EDMUND's *face looks stricken and sick. Then in a burst of rage he springs from his chair.*]

EDMUND. You dirty bastard!

[*He punches his brother in the face, a blow that glances off the cheekbone. For a second* JAMIE *reacts pugnaciously and half rises from his chair to do battle, but suddenly he seems to sober up to a shocked realization of what he has said and he sinks back limply.*]

JAMIE [*miserably*]. Thanks, Kid. I certainly had that coming. Don't know what made me—booze talking— You know me, Kid.

EDMUND [*his anger ebbing*]. I know you'd never say that unless— But God, Jamie, no matter how drunk you are, it's no excuse! [*He pauses—miserably.*] I'm sorry I hit you. You and I never scrap—that bad. [*He sinks back on his chair.*]

JAMIE [*huskily*]. It's all right. Glad you did. My dirty tongue. Like to cut it out. [*He hides his face in his hands—dully.*] I suppose it's because I feel so damned sunk. Because this time Mama had me fooled. I really believed she had it licked. She thinks I always believe the worst, but this time I believed the best. [*His voice flutters.*] I suppose I can't forgive her—yet. It meant so much. I'd begun to hope, if she'd beaten the game, I could, too. [*He begins to sob, and the horrible part of his weeping is that it appears sober, not the maudlin tears of drunkenness.*]

EDMUND [*blinking back tears himself*]. God, don't I know how you feel! Stop it, Jamie!

JAMIE [*trying to control his sobs*]. I've known about Mama so much longer than you. Never forget the first time I got wise. Caught her in the act with a hypo. Christ, I'd never dreamed before that any women but whores took dope! [*He pauses.*] And then this stuff of you getting consumption. It's got me licked. We've been more than brothers. You're the only pal I've ever had. I love your guts. I'd do anything for you.

5. From Kipling's "Mother o' Mine," his dedication to *The Light That Failed* (1891).

EDMUND [*reaches out and pats his arm*]. I know that, Jamie.

JAMIE [*his crying over—drops his hands from his face—with a strange bitterness*]. Yet I'll bet you've heard Mama and old Gaspard spill so much bunk about my hoping for the worst, you suspect right now I'm thinking to myself that Papa is old and can't last much longer, and if you were to die, Mama and I would get all he's got, and so I'm probably hoping—

EDMUND [*indignantly*]. Shut up, you damned fool! What the hell put that in your nut? [*He stares at his brother accusingly.*] Yes, that's what I'd like to know. What put that in your mind?

JAMIE [*confusedly—appearing drunk again*]. Don't be a dumbbell! What I said! Always suspected of hoping for the worst. I've got so I can't help— [*Then drunkenly resentful.*] What are you trying to do, accuse me? Don't play the wise guy with me! I've learned more of life than you'll ever know! Just because you've read a lot of highbrow junk, don't think you can fool me! You're only an overgrown kid! Mama's baby and Papa's pet! The family White Hope! You've been getting a swelled head lately. About nothing! About a few poems in a hick town newspaper! Hell, I used to write better stuff for the Lit magazine in college! You better wake up! You're setting no rivers on fire! You let hick town boobs flatter you with bunk about your future—

[*Abruptly his tone changes to disgusted contrition.* EDMUND *has looked away from him, trying to ignore this tirade.*]

Hell, Kid, forget it. That goes for Sweeny.[6] You know I don't mean it. No one is prouder you've started to make good. [*Drunkenly assertive.*] Why shouldn't I be proud? Hell, it's purely selfish. You reflect credit on me. I've had more to do with bringing you up than anyone. I wised you up about women, so you'd never be a fall guy, or make any mistakes you didn't want to make! And who steered you on to reading poetry first? Swinburne, for example? I did! And because I once wanted to write, I planted it in your mind that someday you'd write! Hell, you're more than my brother. I made you! You're my Frankenstein![7]

[*He has risen to a note of drunken arrogance.* EDMUND *is grinning with amusement now.*]

EDMUND. All right, I'm your Frankenstein. So let's have a drink. [*He laughs.*] You crazy nut!

JAMIE [*thickly*]. I'll have a drink. Not you. Got to take care of you. [*He reaches out with a foolish grin of doting affection and grabs his brother's hand.*] Don't be scared of this sanatorium business. Hell, you can beat that standing on your head. Six months and you'll be in the pink. Probably haven't got consumption at all. Doctors lot of fakers. Told me years ago to cut out booze or I'd soon be dead—and here I

6. A simple, gullible person.
7. A reference to Mary Shelley's novel of terror *Frankenstein* (1817), in which Dr. Frankenstein creates a "man," rather than is created, as Jamie says.

am. They're all con men. Anything to grab your dough. I'll bet this state farm stuff is political graft game. Doctors get a cut for every patient they send.

EDMUND [*disgustedly amused*]. You're the limit! At the Last Judgment, you'll be around telling everyone it's in the bag.

JAMIE. And I'll be right. Slip a piece of change to the Judge and be saved, but if you're broke you can go to hell!

[*He grins at this blasphemy and* EDMUND *has to laugh.* JAMIE *goes on.*]

"Therefore put money in thy purse."[8] That's the only dope. [*Mockingly.*] The secret of my success! Look what it's got me!

[*He lets* EDMUND's *hand go to pour a big drink, and gulps it down. He stares at his brother with bleary affection—takes his hand again and begins to talk thickly but with a strange, convincing sincerity.*]

Listen, Kid, you'll be going away. May not get another chance to talk. Or might not be drunk enough to tell you truth. So got to tell you now. Something I ought to have told you long ago—for your own good.

[*He pauses—struggling with himself.* EDMUND *stares, impressed and uneasy.* JAMIE *blurts out*]

Not drunken bull, but "in vino veritas"[9] stuff. You better take it seriously. Want to warn you—against me. Mama and Papa are right. I've been rotten bad influence. And worst of it is, I did it on purpose.

EDMUND [*uneasily*]. Shut up! I don't want to hear—

JAMIE. Nix, Kid! You listen! Did it on purpose to make a bum of you. Or part of me did. A big part. That part that's been dead so long. That hates life. My putting you wise so you'd learn from my mistakes. Believed that myself at times, but it's a fake. Made my mistakes look good. Made getting drunk romantic. Made whores fascinating vampires instead of poor, stupid, diseased slobs they really are. Made fun of work as sucker's game. Never wanted you succeed and make me look even worse by comparison. Wanted you to fail. Always jealous of you. Mama's baby, Papa's pet! [*He stares at* EDMUND *with increasing enmity.*] And it was your being born that started Mama on dope. I know that's not your fault, but all the same, God damn you, I can't help hating your guts—!

EDMUND [*almost frightenedly*]. Jamie! Cut it out! You're crazy!

JAMIE. But don't get wrong idea, Kid. I love you more than I hate you. My saying what I'm telling you now proves it. I run the risk you'll hate me—and you're all I've got left. But I didn't mean to tell you that last stuff—go that far back. Don't know what made me. What I wanted to say is, I'd like to see you become the greatest success in the world. But you'd better be on your guard. Because I'll do my damnedest to make you fail. Can't help it. I hate myself. Got to take

---

8. From *Othello* 1.3.352.   9. "In wine there is truth."

revenge. On everyone else. Especially you. Oscar Wilde's "Reading Gaol" has the dope twisted. The man was dead and so he had to kill the thing he loved.[1] That's what it ought to be. The dead part of me hopes you won't get well. Maybe he's even glad the game has got Mama again! He wants company, he doesn't want to be the only corpse around the house! [*He gives a hard, tortured laugh.*]

EDMUND. Jesus, Jamie! You really have gone crazy!

JAMIE. Think it over and you'll see I'm right. Think it over when you're away from me in the sanatorium. Make up your mind you've got to tie a can to me—get me out of your life—think of me as dead—tell people, "I had a brother, but he's dead." And when you come back, look out for me. I'll be waiting to welcome you with that "my old pal" stuff, and give you the glad hand, and at the first good chance I get stab you in the back.

EDMUND. Shut up! I'll be God-damned if I'll listen to you any more—

JAMIE [*as if he hadn't heard*]. Only don't forget me. Remember I warned you—for your sake. Give me credit. Greater love hath no man than this, that he saveth his brother from himself. [*Very drunkenly, his head bobbing.*] That's all. Feel better now. Gone to confession. Know you absolve me, don't you, Kid? You understand. You're a damned fine kid. Ought to be. I made you. So go and get well. Don't die on me. You're all I've got left. God bless you, Kid. [*His eyes close. He mumbles*] That last drink—the old K.O.

[*He falls into a drunken doze, not completely asleep.* EDMUND *buries his face in his hands miserably.* TYRONE *comes in quietly through the screen door from the porch, his dressing gown wet with fog, the collar turned up around his throat. His face is stern and disgusted but at the same time pitying.* EDMUND *does not notice his entrance.*]

TYRONE [*in a low voice*]. Thank God he's asleep.

[EDMUND *looks up with a start.*]

I thought he'd never stop talking. [*He turns down the collar of his dressing gown.*] We'd better let him stay where he is and sleep it off.

[EDMUND *remains silent.* TYRONE *regards him—then goes on.*]

I heard the last part of his talk. it's what I've warned you. I hope you'll heed the warning, now it comes from his own mouth.

[EDMUND *gives no sign of having heard.* TYRONE *adds pityingly*]

But don't take it too much to heart, lad. He loves to exaggerate the worst of himself when he's drunk. He's devoted to you. It's the one good thing left in him. [*He looks down on* JAMIE *with a bitter sadness.*] A sweet spectacle for me! My first-born, who I hoped would bear my name in honor and dignity, who showed such brilliant promise!

EDMUND [*miserably*]. Keep quiet, can't you, Papa?

TYRONE [*pours a drink*]. A waste! A wreck, a drunken hulk, done with and finished!

---

1. Oscar Wilde's line in "The Ballad of Reading Gaol" is "Yet each man kills the thing he loves."

[*He drinks.* JAMIE *has become restless, sensing his father's presence, struggling up from his stupor. Now he gets his eyes open to blink up at* TYRONE. *The latter moves back a step defensively, his face growing hard.*]

JAMIE [*suddenly points a finger at him and recites with dramatic emphasis*].

> "Clarence is come, false, fleeting, perjured Clarence,
> That stabbed me in the field by Tewksbury.
> Seize on him, Furies, take him into torment."[2]

[*Then resentfully.*] What the hell are you staring at? [*He recites sardonically from Rossetti.*]

> "Look in my face. My name is Might-Have-Been;
> I am also called No More, Too Late, Farewell."[3]

TYRONE. I'm well aware of that, and God knows I don't want to look at it.

EDMUND. Papa! Quit it!

JAMIE [*derisively*]. Got a great idea for you, Papa. Put on revival of "The Bells" this season. Great part in it you can play without make-up. Old Gaspard, the miser!

[TYRONE *turns away, trying to control his temper.*]

EDMUND. Shut up, Jamie!

JAMIE [*jeeringly*]. I claim Edwin Booth never saw the day when he could give as good a performance as a trained seal. Seals are intelligent and honest. They don't put up any bluffs about the Art of Acting. They admit they're just hams earning their daily fish.

TYRONE [*stung, turns on him in a rage*]. You loafer!

EDMUND. Papa! Do you want to start a row that will bring Mama down? Jamie, go back to sleep! You've shot off your mouth too much already.

[TYRONE *turns away.*]

JAMIE [*thickly*]. All right, Kid. Not looking for argument. Too damned sleepy.

[*He closes his eyes, his head nodding.* TYRONE *comes to the table and sits down, turning his chair so he won't look at* JAMIE. *At once he becomes sleepy, too.*]

TYRONE [*heavily*]. I wish to God she'd go to bed so that I could, too.

[*Drowsily.*] I'm dog tired. I can't stay up all night like I used to. Getting old—old and finished. [*With a bone-cracking yawn.*] Can't keep my eyes open. I think I'll catch a few winks. Why don't you do the same, Edmund? It'll pass the time until she—

[*His voice trails off. His eyes close, his chin sags, and he begins to breathe heavily through his mouth.* EDMUND *sits tensely. He hears something and jerks nervously forward in his chair, staring through the front parlor into the hall. He jumps up with a hunted, distracted*

2. From *Richard III* 1.4.55–57.
3. From Dante Gabriel Rossetti's sonnet "A Su-

perscription," sonnet 97 in *The House of Life* (1870).

expression. It seems for a second he is going to hide in the back parlor. Then he sits down again and waits, his eyes averted, his hands gripping the arms of his chair. Suddenly all five bulbs of the chandelier in the front parlor are turned on from a wall switch, and a moment later someone starts playing the piano in there—the opening of one of Chopin's simpler waltzes, done with a forgetful, stiff-fingered groping, as if an awkward schoolgirl were practicing it for the first time. TYRONE *starts to wide-awakeness and sober dread, and* JAMIE's *head jerks back and his eyes open. For a moment they listen frozenly. The playing stops as abruptly as it began, and* MARY *appears in the doorway. She wears a sky-blue dressing gown over her nightdress, dainty slippers with pompons on her bare feet. Her face is paler than ever. Her eyes look enormous. They glisten like polished black jewels. The uncanny thing is that her face now appears so youthful. Experience seems ironed out of it. It is a marble mask of girlish innocence, the mouth caught in a shy smile. Her white hair is braided in two pigtails which hang over her breast. Over one arm, carried neglectfully, trailing on the floor, as if she had forgotten she held it, is an old-fashioned white satin wedding gown, trimmed with duchesse lace. She hesitates in the doorway, glancing round the room, her forehead puckered puzzledly, like someone who has come to a room to get something but has become absent-minded on the way and forgotten what it was. They stare at her. She seems aware of them merely as she is aware of other objects in the room, the furniture, the windows, familiar things she accepts automatically as naturally belong there but which she is too preoccupied to notice.*]

JAMIE [*breaks the cracking silence—bitterly, self-defensively sardonic*]. The Mad Scene. Enter Ophelia![4]

   [*His father and brother both turn on him fiercely.* EDMUND *is quicker. He slaps* JAMIE *across the mouth with the back of his hand.*]

TYRONE [*his voice trembling with suppressed fury*]. Good boy, Edmund. The dirty blackguard! His own mother!

JAMIE [*mumbles guiltily, without resentment*]. All right, Kid. Had it coming. But I told you how much I'd hoped— [*He puts his hands over his face and begins to sob.*]

TYRONE. I'll kick you out in the gutter tomorrow, so help me God. [*But* JAMIE's *sobbing breaks his anger, and he turns and shakes his shoulder, pleading.*] Jamie, for the love of God, stop it!

   [*Then* MARY *speaks, and they freeze into silence again, staring at her. She has paid no attention whatever to the incident. It is simply a part of the familiar atmosphere of the room, a background which does not touch her preoccupation; and she speaks aloud to herself, not to them.*]

MARY. I play so badly now. I'm all out of practice. Sister Theresa will

4. *Hamlet* 4.1.

give me a dreadful scolding. She'll tell me it isn't fair to my father when he spends so much mooney for extra lessons. She's quite right, it isn't fair, when he's so good and generous, and so proud of me. I'll practice every day from now on. But something horrible has happened to my hands. The fingers have gotten so stiff— [*She lifts her hands to examine them with a frightened puzzlement.*] The knuckles are all swollen. They're so ugly. I'll have to go to the Infirmary and show Sister Martha. [*With a sweet smile of affectionate trust.*] She's old and a little cranky, but I love her just the same, and she has things in her medicine chest that'll cure anything. She'll give me something to rub on my hands, and tell me to pray to the Blessed Virgin, and they'll be well again in no time. [*She forgets her hands and comes into the room, the wedding gown trailing on the floor. She glances around vaguely, her forehead puckered again.*] Let me see. What did I come here to find? It's terrible, how absentminded I've become. I'm always dreaming and forgetting.

TYRONE [*in a stifled voice*]. What's that she's carrying, Edmund?

EDMUND [*dully*]. Her wedding gown, I suppose.

TYRONE. Christ! [*He gets to his feet and stands directly in her path—in anguish.*] Mary! Isn't it bad enough—? [*Controlling himself—gently persuasive.*] Here, let me take it, dear. You'll only step on it and tear it and get it dirty dragging it on the floor. Then you'd be sorry afterwards.

  [*She lets him take it, regarding him from somewhere far away within herself, without recognition, without either affection or animosity.*]

MARY [*with the shy politeness of a well-bred young girl toward an elderly gentleman who relieves her of a bundle*]. Thank you. You are very kind. [*She regards the wedding gown with a puzzled interest.*] It's a wedding gown. It's very lovely, isn't it? [*A shadow crosses her face and she looks vaguely uneasy.*] I remember now. I found it in the attic hidden in a trunk. But I don't know what I wanted it for. I'm going to be a nun—that is, if I can only find— [*She looks around the room, her forehead puckered again.*] What is it I'm looking for? I know it's something I lost. [*She moves back from* TYRONE, *aware of him now only as some obstacle in her path.*]

TYRONE [*in hopeless appeal*]. Mary!

  [*But it cannot penetrate her preoccupation. She doesn't seem to hear him. He gives up helplessly, shrinking into himself, even his defensive drunkenness taken from him, leaving him sick and sober. He sinks back on his chair, holding the wedding gown in his arms with an unconscious clumsy, protective gentleness.*]

JAMIE [*drops his hand from his face, his eyes on the table top. He has suddenly sobered up, too—dully*]. It's no good, Papa. [*He recites from Swinburne's "A Leave-taking"[5] and does it well, simply but with a bitter sadness.*]

5. From the *Poems and Ballads* (1866) of Algernon Swinburne (1837–1909).

"Let us rise up and part; she will not know.
Let us go seaward as the great winds go,
Full of blown sand and foam; what help is here?
There is no help, for all these things are so,
And all the world is bitter as a tear.
And how these things are, though ye strove to show,
She would not know."

MARY [*looking around her*]. Something I miss terribly. It can't be altogether lost. [*She starts to move around in back of* JAMIE's *chair.*]
JAMIE [*turns to look up into her face—and cannot help appealing pleadingly in his turn*]. Mama! [*She does not seem to hear. He looks away
hopelessly.*] Hell! What's the use? It's no good. [*He recites from "A
Leave-taking" again with increased bitterness.*]

"Let us go hence, my songs; she will not hear.
Let us go hence together without fear;
Keep silence now, for singing-time is over,
And over all old things and all things dear.
She loves not you nor me as all we love her.
Yea, though we sang as angels in her ear,
She would not hear."

MARY [*looking around her*]. Something I need terribly. I remember when
I had it I was never lonely nor afraid. I can't have lost it forever, I
would die if I thought that. Because then there would be no hope.
[*She moves like a sleepwalker, around the back of* JAMIE's *chair, then
forward toward left front, passing behind* EDMUND.]
EDMUND [*turns impulsively and grabs her arm. As he pleads he has the
quality of a bewilderedly hurt little boy*]. Mama! It isn't a summer
cold! I've got consumption!
MARY [*for a second he seems to have broken through to her. She trembles
and her expression becomes terrified. She calls distractedly, as if giving
a command to herself*]. No! [*And instantly she is far away again. She
murmurs gently but impersonally*] You must not try to touch me. You
must not try to hold me. It isn't right, when I am hoping to be a
nun.
    [*He lets his hand drop from her arm. She moves left to the front end
    of the sofa beneath the windows and sits down, facing front, her
    hands folded in her lap, in a demure schoolgirlish pose.*]
JAMIE [*gives* EDMUND *a strange look of mingled pity and jealous gloating*].
You damned fool. It's no good. [*He recites again from the Swinburne
poem.*]

"Let us go hence, go hence; she will not see.
Sing all once more together; surely she,
She too, remembering days and words that were,

Will turn a little toward us, sighing; but we,
We are hence, we are gone, as though we had not been there.
Nay, and though all men seeing had pity on me,
She would not see."

TYRONE [*trying to shake off his hopeless stupor*]. Oh, we're fools to pay
any attention. It's the damned poison. But I've never known her to
drown herself in it as deep as this. [*Gruffly.*] Pass me that bottle,
Jamie. And stop reciting that damned morbid poetry. I won't have it
in my house!

[JAMIE *pushes the bottle toward him. He pours a drink without
disarranging the wedding gown he holds carefully over his other arm
and on his lap, and shoves the bottle back.* JAMIE *pours his and
passes the bottle to* EDMUND, *who, in turn, pours one.* TYRONE *lifts
his glass and his sons follow suit mechanically, but before they can
drink* MARY *speaks and they slowly lower their drinks to the table,
forgetting them.*]

MARY [*staring dreamily before her. Her face looks extraordinarily youthful
and innocent. The shyly eager, trusting smile is on her lips as she talks
aloud to herself*]. I had a talk with Mother Elizabeth. She is so sweet
and good. A saint on earth. I love her dearly. It may be sinful of me
but I love her better than my own mother. Because she always understands, even before you say a word. Her kind blue eyes look right
into your heart. You can't keep any secrets from her. You couldn't
deceive her, even if you were mean enough to want to. [*She gives a
little rebellious toss of her head—with girlish pique.*] All the same, I
don't think she was so understanding this time. I told her I wanted
to be a nun. I explained how sure I was of my vocation, that I had
prayed to the Blessed Virgin to make me sure, and to find me worthy.
I told Mother I had had a true vision when I was praying in the shrine
of Our Lady of Lourdes, on the little island in the lake. I said I knew,
as surely as I knew I was kneeling there, that the Blessed Virgin had
smiled and blessed me with her consent. But Mother Elizabeth told
me I must be more sure than that, even, that I must prove it wasn't
simply my imagination. She said, If I was so sure, then I wouldn't
mind putting myself to a test by going home after I graduated, and
living as other girls lived, going out to parties and dances and enjoying
myself; and then if after a year or two I still felt sure, I could come
back to see her and we would talk it over again. [*She tosses her head—
indignantly.*] I never dreamed Holy Mother would give me such
advice! I was really shocked. I said, of course, I would do anything
she suggested, but I knew it was simply a waste of time. After I left
her, I felt all mixed up, so I went to the shrine and prayed to the
Blessed Virgin and found peace again because I knew she heard my
prayer and would always love me and see no harm ever came to me
so long as I never lost my faith in her. [*She pauses and a look of*

growing uneasiness comes over her face. She passes a hand over her forehead as if brushing cobwebs from her brain—vaguely.] That was in the winter of senior year. Then in the spring something happened to me. Yes, I remember. I fell in love with James Tyrone and was so happy for a time.

[*She stares before her in a sad dream.* TYRONE *stirs in his chair.* EDMUND *and* JAMIE *remain motionless.*]

[*Curtain*]

BERTOLT BRECHT

Mother Courage and Her Children†

A Chronicle of the Thirty Years War

Characters (in order of appearance)

Prologue

MOTHER COURAGE   SWISS CHEESE
EILIF   CATHERINE

Scene One

RECRUITING OFFICER   SERGEANT

Scene Two

COOK   COMMANDER   CHAPLAIN

Scene Three

ORDNANCE OFFICER   SERGEANT
YVETTE POTTIER   ONE EYE
SOLDIER   COLONEL
(TWO SUPERS)

Scene Four

CLERK   OLDER SOLDIER   YOUNGER SOLDIER

Scene Five

FIRST SOLDIER   PEASANT
SECOND SOLDIER   PEASANT WOMAN

Scene Six

SOLDIER *(singing)*

Scene Seven: no new characters

† From COLLECTED PLAYS, Volume 5, by Bertolt Brecht. Copyright © 1972 by Stefan S. Brecht. Reprinted by permission of Pantheon Books, a Division of Random House, Inc. English version by Eric Bentley. Copyright 1955, 1959, 1961, by Eric Bentley.

Scene Eight

OLD WOMAN	VOICES (*two*)
YOUNG MAN	SOLDIER
(ONE SUPER)	

Scene Nine
VOICE

Scene Ten
VOICE (*girl singing*)

Scene Eleven

LIEUTENANT	OLD PEASANT
FIRST SOLDIER	PEASANT WOMAN
SECOND SOLDIER	YOUNG PEASANT

Scene Twelve: no new characters

THE TIME   1624–1636
THE PLACE   *Sweden, Poland, Germany*

Prologue

The wagon of a vivandière.[1] MOTHER COURAGE *sitting on it, singing. Her dumb daughter* CATHERINE *beside her playing the mouth organ. The wagon is drawn by her two sons,* EILIF *and* SWISS CHEESE, *who join in the refrain.*

Here's Mother Courage and her wagon!
    Hey, Captain, let them come and buy!
Beer by the keg! Wine by the flagon!
    Let your men drink before they die!
Sabres and swords are hard to swallow:
    First you must give them beer to drink.
Then they can face what is to follow—
    But let 'em swim before they sink!
        Christians, awake! The winter's gone!
        The snows depart. The dead sleep on.
        And though you may not long survive
        Get out of bed and look alive!

Your men will march till they are dead, sir,
    But cannot fight unless they eat.
The blood they spill for you is red, sir,
    What fires that blood is my red meat.
For meat and soup and jam and jelly
    In this old cart of mine are found:
So fill the hole up in your belly

---

1. Formerly a woman who supplied provisions and liquors to troops in the field.

Before you fill one underground.
Christians awake! The winter's gone!
The snows depart. The dead sleep on.
And though you may not long survive
Get out of bed and look alive!

Scene One

SPRING, 1624, IN DALARNA, SWEDEN, KING GUSTAVUS
ADOLPHUS IS RECRUITING FOR THE CAMPAIGN IN PO-
LAND. THE PROVISIONER ANNA FIERLING, KNOWN AS
CANTEEN ANNA OR MOTHER COURAGE, LOSES A SON.[2]

A highway in the neighborhood of a town. A top SERGEANT *and a* RECRUIT-
ING OFFICER *stand shivering.*

OFFICER. How the hell can you line up a squadron in *this* place? You
know what I keep thinking about, Sergeant? Suicide. I'm supposed
to slap four platoons together by the twelfth—four platoons the
Chief's asking for! And they're so friendly around here I'm scared to
sleep nights. Suppose I do get my hands on some character and squint
at him so I don't notice he's chicken breasted and has varicose veins.
I get him drunk and relaxed, he signs on the dotted line. I pay for
the drinks, he steps outside for a minute. I get a hunch I should
follow him to the door, and am I right! Off he's shot like a louse
from a scratch. You can't take a man's word any more, Sergeant.
There's no loyalty left in the world, no trust, no faith, no sense of
honor. I'm losing my confidence in mankind, Sergeant.
SERGEANT. What they could use round here is a good war. What else
can you expect with peace running wild all over the place? You know
what the trouble with peace is? No organization. When do you get
organization? In a war. Peace is one big waste of equipment. Anything
goes, no one gives a god damn. See the way they eat? Cheese on rye,
bacon on the cheese? Disgusting! How many horses they got in this
town? How many young men? Nobody knows! They haven't bothered
to count 'em!! That's peace for you!!! I been in places where they
haven't had a war in seventy years and you know what? The people
can't remember their own names! They don't know who they are! It
takes a war to fix all that. In a war everyone registers, everybody's
name's on a list, their shoes are stacked, their corn's in the bag, you
count it all up—cattle, men, et cetera—and take it away! Yeah, that's
the story—no organization, no war!
OFFICER. It's the God's truth.

2. The scene headings in block capitals are projected on a front curtain. In the scene itself the
location is indicated by large black letters hanging
from the flies (*e.g.*, Sweden in this first scene)
[*Translator's note*].

SERGEANT. Course, a war's like every real good deal, hard to get going. But when it's on the road, it's a pisser—everybody's scared off peace—like a crapshooter that keeps fading to cover his loss. Course, *until* it gets going, they're just as scared off war—afraid to try anything new.

OFFICER. Look, a wagon! Two women and a couple of young punks. Stop the old lady, Sergeant. And if there's nothing doing this time, you won't catch *me* freezing my ass in the April wind!

MOTHER COURAGE [*entering with her three children as in the prologue*]. Good day to you, Sergeant!

SERGEANT [*barring the way*]. Good day! Who do you think you are?

MOTHER COURAGE. Tradespeople! [*She prepares to go.*]

SERGEANT. Halt! Where are you riffraff from?

EILIF. The Second Protestant Regiment.

SERGEANT. Where are your papers?

MOTHER COURAGE. Papers?

SWISS CHEESE. But this is Mother Courage!

SERGEANT. Never heard of her. Where'd she get a name like that?

MOTHER COURAGE. They call me Mother Courage because I was afraid I'd be ruined, so I drove through the bombardment of Riga like a madwoman, with fifty loaves of bread in my cart. They were getting moldy, I couldn't please myself.

SERGEANT. No funny business! Where are your papers?

MOTHER COURAGE [*rummaging among a mass of papers in a tin box, and clambering down from her cart*]. Here, Sergeant! Here's a whole Bible I got in Altötting to wrap cucumbers in, and a map of Moravia, God knows if I'll ever get there, it's good enough for the cat if I don't. And here's a document to say my horse hasn't got hoof and mouth disease; too bad he died on us, he cost fifteen gilders, thank God I didn't pay it. Is that enough paper?

SERGEANT. Are you making a pass at me? Well, you got another guess coming. You got to have a license and you know it.

MOTHER COURAGE. Show a little respect for a lady and don't go telling these grown children of mine I'm making a pass at you, it's not proper, what would I want with *you*? My license in the Second Protestant Regiment is an honest face, even if *you* wouldn't know how to read it. I'll have no rubber stamp on it neither.

OFFICER. There's insubordination for you, my dear Sergeant! [*To* MOTHER COURAGE.] Do you know what we need in the army?

    [MOTHER COURAGE *starts to reply but he doesn't let her.*]
Discipline!

MOTHER COURAGE. I'd have said frankfurters.

SERGEANT. Name?

MOTHER COURAGE. Anna Fierling.

SERGEANT. So you're all Fierlings?

MOTHER COURAGE. What do you mean? I was talking about me.

SERGEANT. And I was talking about your children!

MOTHER COURAGE. Must they all have the same name! [*Indicating the elder son.*] This boy, for instance, his name is Eilif Noyocki—for the good reason that his father always said his name was Koyocki or Moyocki. The boy remembers him to this day, only it's another one he remembers to this day, a Frenchman with a pointed beard. Anyhow he certainly has his father's brains—that man would have the pants off a farmer's behind before he knew what had happened. So we all have our own names.

SERGEANT. You're all called something different?

MOTHER COURAGE. Are you pretending you don't get it?

SERGEANT [*indicating* SWISS CHEESE]. He's Chinese, I suppose?

MOTHER COURAGE. Wrong again. A Swiss.

SERGEANT. After the Frenchman?

MOTHER COURAGE. Frenchman? I don't know any Frenchman. Don't confuse the issue or we'll be here all day. He's a Swiss but he happens to be called Feyos, a name that has nothing to do with his father, who was called something else; he was a military engineer, if you please, and a drunkard.

[SWISS CHEESE *nods, beaming, and even* CATHERINE *is amused.*]

SERGEANT. Then how come his name's Feyos?

MOTHER COURAGE. No harm meant, Sergeant, but you have no imagination. Of course he's called Feyos—when he came I was with a Hungarian, he didn't mind a bit, he had a floating kidney, though he never touched a drop, he was a very honest man. The boy takes after him.

SERGEANT. But he wasn't his father!

MOTHER COURAGE. I said he took after him. I call him Swiss Cheese because he's good at pulling the wagon. [*Indicating her daughter.*] She's called Catherine Haupt. Half German.

SERGEANT. A nice family I must say.

MOTHER COURAGE. We've seen the whole world together, my wagon and me.

SERGEANT [*writing*]. We'll need all that in writing. You are from Bamberg in Bavaria. How do you come to be in this place?

MOTHER COURAGE. I can't wait till the war decides to come to Bavaria.

OFFICER [*to* EILIF]. And you two oxen pull the cart. Jacob Ox and Esau Ox! Do you ever get out of harness?

EILIF. Can I smack him in the puss, Mother? I'd like to.

MOTHER COURAGE. No, you can't, you stay where you are. And now, gentlemen, what about a fine pair of pistols? Or a belt—yours is practically worn through, Sergeant.

SERGEANT. I'm after something else. I see these boys are straight as birch trees, broad in the chest, strong of limb—what are specimens like that doing out of the army I'd like to know?

MOTHER COURAGE [*rapidly*]. It's no use, Sergeant: the soldier's life is not for sons of mine!

OFFICER. Why not? It means money. It means fame. Peddling boots is woman's work. [*To* EILIF.] Just step up here and let me see if that's muscle or chicken fat.

MOTHER COURAGE. Chicken fat. Give him a good hard look and he'll fall over.

OFFICER. And kill a calf while he's falling if there's one in the way. [*He tries to hustle* EILIF *off.*]

MOTHER COURAGE. Will you let him alone? He's not for you!

OFFICER. He called my face a puss, that's an insult. The two of us will now go out in the field and settle this affair like men of honor.

EILIF. Don't worry, I can handle him, Mother.

MOTHER COURAGE. Stay here, you trouble maker! Never happy unless you're in a fight. [*To the* OFFICER.] He has a knife in his boot and he knows how to use it.

OFFICER. I'll draw it out of him like a milk tooth. Come on, young fellow!

MOTHER COURAGE. Officer, I'll report you to the colonel, he'll throw you in jail. The lieutenant is courting my daughter!

SERGEANT. Take it easy, brother. [*To* MOTHER COURAGE.] What have you got against the service? Wasn't his father a soldier? Didn't he die a soldier's death? You said so yourself.

MOTHER COURAGE. Yes, he's dead, but this one's just a baby, and you'll lead him to the slaughter for me, I know you. You'll get five gilders for him.

OFFICER. First thing you know, you'll have a new cap and knee boots, how about it?

EILIF. Not from you, thanks.

MOTHER COURAGE. "Come on, let's go fishing," said the angler to the worm. [*To* SWISS CHEESE.] Run, and tell everybody they're trying to steal your brother! [*She draws a knife.*] Now try and steal him! And I'll let you have it. I'll cut you down like dogs! Using *him* in your war! We sell linen, we sell ham, we're peaceful people!

SERGEANT. You're peaceful all right, your knife proves it. Why, you should be ashamed of yourself. Give me that knife, you hag! You admit you live off the war, what else *would* you live off? Tell me: how can we have a war without soldiers?

MOTHER COURAGE. Do they have to be mine?

SERGEANT. So that's it. The war should swallow the pits and spit out the peach, huh? Your brood should get fat off the war, and the poor war shouldn't ask a thing in return; it can look after itself, huh? Call yourself Mother Courage and then get scared of the war—your bread-winner? Your sons aren't scared, I know that much.

EILIF. No war can scare me.

SERGEANT. Why should it? Look at me: the soldier's life hasn't done me any harm, has it? I enlisted at seventeen.

MOTHER COURAGE. You haven't reached seventy.

SERGEANT. I will, though.

MOTHER COURAGE. Above ground?

SERGEANT. Are you trying to rile me, telling me I'll die?

MOTHER COURAGE. Suppose it's the truth? Suppose I can see it's your fate? Suppose I know you're just a corpse on furlough?

SWISS CHEESE. She has second sight. Everyone says so. She can look into the future.

OFFICER. Then go look into the sergeant's future, it might amuse him.

SERGEANT. I don't believe in that stuff.

MOTHER COURAGE. Your helmet!

[*He gives her his helmet.*]

SERGEANT. It means about as much as a crap in the grass. But anything for a laugh.

MOTHER COURAGE [*takes a sheet or parchment and tears it in two pieces*]. Eilif, Swiss Cheese, and Catherine, so should we all be torn asunder if we let ourselves be drawn too deep into the war! [*To the* SERGEANT.] For you, I'll make an exception, and do it free. Death is black. I draw a black cross on this piece of paper.

SWISS CHEESE. And the other she leaves blank, see?

MOTHER COURAGE. Then I fold them, put them in the helmet, and shuffle them up—mixed up like we all are from our mother's womb on. And now you draw and find out the answer.

[*The* SERGEANT *hesitates.*]

OFFICER [*to* EILIF]. I don't take just anybody, I'm particular, they all say so. And you're full of punch, I like that.

SERGEANT [*fishing into the helmet*]. It's a lot of bunk. Hogwash!

SWISS CHEESE. He's drawn the black cross. His number's up!

OFFICER. Don't let them frighten you, there aren't enough bullets to go round.

SERGEANT [*hoarsely*]. You swindled me.

MOTHER COURAGE. You swindled yourself, the day you enlisted. And now we must drive on, there isn't a war every day in the week, we got to get to work.

SERGEANT. Hell and damnation, you're not getting away with this. We're taking that bastard of yours with us, we'll make a soldier of him.

EILIF. I'd like that, Mother.

MOTHER COURAGE. Shut up, you Finnish devil!

EILIF. And Swiss Cheese would like to be a soldier too.

MOTHER COURAGE. That's news to me. I see I'll have to draw lots for all three of you. [*She goes to the back to draw crosses on the slips.*]

OFFICER [*to* EILIF]. People've been saying the Swedish soldier is religious. That's malicious gossip. I can't tell you how much damage it's done us. We only sing on Sunday. One verse of a hymn. And then only if you have a voice.

MOTHER COURAGE [*returns with the slips and throws them into the* SERGEANT'*s helmet*]. Run away from their mother would they, the devils, and off to war like a cat to cream? Just let me consult these slips and they'll see the world's no promised land with its "Join up, son, you're officer material!" [*She thrusts the helmet at* EILIF.] There, take yours, Eilif.

[*He does so. As he unfolds the paper she snatches it from him.*]

There you are, a cross! If he's a soldier, his number's up, that's for sure.

OFFICER [*still talking to* EILIF]. If you're wetting your pants, I'll try your brother.

MOTHER COURAGE. Now take yours, Swiss Cheese. You're a safer bet because you're my *good* boy.

[*He draws his lot.*]

Why do you look so strangely at it? It *must* be blank. [*She takes it from him.*]

A cross? Oh, Swiss Cheese, there's no saving you either—unless you're a good boy through and through every minute of every day! Just look, Sergeant, a black cross, isn't it?

SERGEANT. Another cross. But I don't see why *I* got one, I always stay well in the rear. [*To the* OFFICER.] It can't be a trick, it gets her own children.

MOTHER COURAGE [*to* CATHERINE]. And now all I have left is you, you're a cross in yourself, but you have a kind heart. [*She holds the helmet up but takes the paper herself.*] Oh! I could give up in despair! I can't be right, I must have made a mistake. Don't be *too* kind, Catherine, don't be too kind, there's a cross in your path! [*Breaking the mood.*] So now you all know: always be very careful! And now, we'll get in and drive on. [*She climbs on to the wagon.*]

OFFICER [*to* SERGEANT]. Do something.

SERGEANT. I don't feel so well.

OFFICER. Maybe you caught a cold when you took your helmet off. Try doing business with her. [*Aloud.*] That belt, Sergeant, you could at least take a look at it, after all they live by trade, don't they, these good people? Hey, you! The sergeant will buy the belt!

MOTHER COURAGE. Half a gilder. Worth four times the price.

SERGEANT. It's not even a new one. But there's too much wind here, I'll go look at it behind your wagon.

MOTHER COURAGE. It doesn't seem windy to me.

SERGEANT. Hey, maybe it is worth half a gilder at that, there's silver on it.

MOTHER COURAGE [*following him back of the wagon*]. A solid six ounces worth.

OFFICER [*to* EILIF]. I can let you have some cash in advance, come on!

[EILIF *is undecided.*]

MOTHER COURAGE [*behind the wagon with the* SERGEANT]. Half a gilder then, quick.

SERGEANT. I still don't see why I had to draw a cross. I told you I always stay in the rear, it's the only place that's safe. You send the others on ahead to win the laurels of victory or the glory of heroic defeat as the case may be. You've ruined my afternoon.

MOTHER COURAGE. You mustn't take on so. Here, have a shot of brandy. [*She gives him some.*] And go right on staying in the rear. Half a gilder.

OFFICER [*has taken* EILIF *by the arm and is drawing him upstage*]. Ten gilders in advance and you're a soldier of the king, my lad, a stout fellow! The women'll be mad about you. And you can smack me in the puss because I insulted you.

[*Both leave.*]

[CATHERINE *makes harsh noises.*]

MOTHER COURAGE. Coming, Catherine, coming! The sergeant's just paying his bill. [*She bites the half gilder.*] To me, Sergeant, all money is suspect, but your half gilder's okay. Now we'll be off. Where's Eilif?

SWISS CHEESE. Gone with the recruiting officer.

MOTHER COURAGE [*stops in her tracks, a pause, then*]. Oh, you simpleton! [*To* CATHERINE.] And you could do nothing about it, you're dumb.

SERGEANT. Take a shot yourself, Mother. That's how it goes. Your son's a soldier, he might do worse.

MOTHER COURAGE [*motions* CATHERINE *down from the wagon*]. You must help your brother now, Catherine.

[*Brother and sister get into harness together and pull the wagon,* MOTHER COURAGE *beside them.*]

SERGEANT [*Looking after them*].

If from the war you'd like to borrow
Remember: the debt must be paid tomorrow!

Scene Two

IN THE YEARS 1625 AND 1626 MOTHER COURAGE JOURNEYS THROUGH POLAND IN THE BAGGAGE TRAIN OF THE SWEDISH ARMY. SHE MEETS HER SON AGAIN BEFORE WALLHOF CASTLE. OF THE SUCCESSFUL SALE OF A CAPON AND GREAT DAYS FOR THE BRAVE SON.

Tent of the Swedish Commander. Kitchen next to it. Sound of cannon. The COOK *is quarreling with* MOTHER COURAGE *who is trying to sell him a capon.*

COOK [*who has a Dutch accent*]. Sixty hellers for that paltry poultry?

MOTHER COURAGE. Paltry poultry? Why, he's the fattest fowl you ever saw! I see no reason why I shouldn't get sixty hellers for him—this Commander can eat till the cows come home.

COOK. They're ten hellers a dozen on every street corner.

MOTHER COURAGE. A capon like this on every street corner! With a siege going on and people all skin and bones? Maybe you can get a field rat! I said maybe. Because we're all out of *them* too. Didn't you see the soldiers running five deep after one hungry little field rat? All right then, in a siege, my price for a giant capon is fifty hellers.

COOK. But we're not "in a siege," we're doing the besieging, it's the other side that's "in a siege" . . .

MOTHER COURAGE. A fat lot of difference that makes, *we* don't have a thing to eat either. They took everything in the town with them before all this started, and now they've nothing to do but eat and drink. It's us I'm worried about. Look at the farmers round here, they haven't a thing.

COOK. Sure they have. They hide it.

MOTHER COURAGE. They have not! They're ruined. They're so hungry I've seen 'em digging up roots to eat. I could boil your leather belt and make their mouths water with it. That's how things are round here. And I'm supposed to let a capon go for forty hellers!

COOK. Thirty. Not forty, I said thirty hellers.

MOTHER COURAGE. I say this is no ordinary chicken. It was a talented animal, so I hear. It would only feed when they played it some music. In fact, it had its own way of marching. It was so intelligent it could count. Forty hellers is too much for all this? I know *your* problem: if you don't find something to eat and quick, the Chief will—cut—your—fat—head—off!

COOK. All right, just watch. [*He takes a piece of beef and lays his knife on it.*] Here's a piece of beef, I'm going to roast it. I give you one more chance.

MOTHER COURAGE. Roast it, go ahead, it's only one year old.

COOK. One *day* old! Yesterday it was a cow. I saw it running around.

MOTHER COURAGE. In that case it must have started stinking before it died.

COOK. I don't care if I have to cook it five hours. [*He cuts into it.*]

MOTHER COURAGE. Put plenty of pepper in.

[*The* SWEDISH COMMANDER, *a* CHAPLAIN *and* EILIF *enter the tent.*]

COMMANDER [*clapping* EILIF *on the shoulder*]. In the Commander's tent with you, Eilif my son! Sit at my right hand, you happy warrior! You've played a hero's part, you've served the Lord in his own Holy War,[3] *that's* the thing! And you'll get a gold bracelet out of it when we take the town if *I* have any say in the matter! We come to save their souls and what do they do, the filthy, irreligious sons of bitches? Drive their cattle away from *us*, while they stuff their priests with beef

<hr>

3. The Thirty Years War was in large part a religious war in which German Protestant princes with the help of France, Sweden, England, and Denmark fought against the Hapsburgs and Catholic princes of the Holy Roman Empire.

at both ends! But you showed 'em. So here's a can of red wine for you, we'll drink together!

[*They do so.*]

The chaplain gets the dregs, he's religious. Now what would you like for dinner, my hearty?

EILIF. How about a slice of meat?

COOK. Nothing to eat, so he brings company to eat it!

[MOTHER COURAGE *makes him stop talking, she wants to listen.*]

COMMANDER. Cook, meat!

EILIF. Tires you out, skinning peasants. Gives you an appetite.

MOTHER COURAGE. Dear God, it's my Eilif!

COOK. Who?

MOTHER COURAGE. My eldest. It's two years since I saw him, he was stolen from me right off the street. He must be in high favor if the Commander's invited him to dinner. And what do you have to eat? Nothing. You hear what the Commander's guest wants? Meat! Better take my advice, buy the capon. The price is one gilder.

COMMANDER [*who has sat down with* EILIF *and the* CHAPLAIN, *roaring*]. Cook! Dinner, you pig, or I'll have your head!

COOK. This is blackmail. Give me the damn thing!

MOTHER COURAGE. Paltry poultry like this?

COOK. You were right. Give it here. It's highway robbery, fifty hellers.

MOTHER COURAGE. I said one gilder. Nothing's too high for my eldest, the Commander's guest of honor.

COOK. Well, you might at least pluck the damn thing till I have a fire going.

MOTHER COURAGE [*sitting down to pluck the capon*]. I can't wait to see his face when he sees me. This is my brave son. I also have a stupid one but he's honest. The daughter is nothing. At least, she doesn't talk; we must be thankful for small mercies.

COMMANDER. Have another glass, my son, it's my favorite Falernian. There's only one cask left—two at the most—but it's worth it to meet a soldier that still believes in God! Our chaplain here just looks on, he only preaches, he hasn't a clue how anything gets done. So now, Eilif my son, give us the details: tell us how you fixed the peasants and grabbed the twenty bullocks.

EILIF. Well, it was like this. I found out that the peasants had hidden their oxen and—on the sly and chiefly at night—had driven them into a certain wood. The people from the town were to pick them up there. I let them get their oxen in peace—they ought to know better than me where they are, I said to myself. Meanwhile I made my men crazy for meat. Their rations were short and I made sure they got shorter. Their mouths'd water at the sound of any word beginning with M, like mother.

COMMANDER. Smart kid.

EILIF. Not bad. The rest was a snap. Only the peasants had clubs and outnumbered us three to one and made a murderous attack on us. Four of them drove me into a clump of trees, knocked my good sword from my hand, and yelled, "Surrender!" What now, I said to myself, they'll make mincemeat of me.

COMMANDER. What did you do?

EILIF. I laughed.

COMMANDER. You what?

EILIF. I laughed. And so we got to talking. I came right down to business and said: "Twenty gilders an ox is too much, I bid fifteen." Like I wanted to buy. That foxed 'em. So while they were scratching their heads, I reached for my good sword and cut 'em to pieces. Necessity knows no law, huh?

COMMANDER. What do *you* say, keeper of souls?

CHAPLAIN. Strictly speaking, that saying is not in the Bible. Our Lord made five hundred loaves out of five so that no such necessity would arise. When he told men to love their neighbors, their bellies were full. Nowadays things are different.

COMMANDER [*laughing*]. Quite different. A swallow of wine for those wise words, you pharisee![4] [*To* EILIF.] You cut 'em to pieces in a good cause, our fellows were hungry and you gave 'em to eat. Doesn't it say in the Bible "Whatsoever thou doest to the least of these my children, thou doest unto me?" And what *did* you do to 'em? You got 'em the best steak dinner they ever tasted.

EILIF. I reached for my good sword and cut 'em to pieces.

COMMANDER. You have the makings of a Julius Caesar, why, you should be presented to the King!

EILIF. I've seen him—from a distance of course. He seemed to shed a light all around. I must try to be like him!

COMMANDER. I think you're succeeding, my boy! Oh, Eilif, you don't know how I value a brave soldier like you!

[*He takes him to the map.*]

Take a look at our position, Eilif, it isn't all it might be, is it?

MOTHER COURAGE [*who has been listening and is now plucking angrily at her capon*]. He must be a very bad commander.

COOK. Just a greedy one. Why bad?

MOTHER COURAGE. Because he needs *brave* soldiers, that's why. If his plan of campaign was any good, why would he need *brave* soldiers, wouldn't plain, ordinary soldiers do? Whenever there are great virtues, it's a sure sign something's wrong.

COOK. You mean, it's a sure sign something's right.

MOTHER COURAGE. I mean what I say. Listen. When a king is a stupid king and leads his soldiers into a trap, they need this virtue of courage. When he's tightfisted and hasn't enough soldiers, the few he does have need the heroism of Hercules—another virtue. And if he's a

---

4. A sanctimonious, hypocritical person.

sloven and doesn't give a damn about anything, they have to fend for themselves and be wise as serpents or they're through. Loyalty's another virtue and you need plenty of it if the king's always asking too much of you. But in a good country the virtues wouldn't be necessary. Everybody could be quite ordinary, middling, and, for all of me, cowards.

COMMANDER. I bet your father was a soldier.

EILIF. I've heard he was a great soldier. My mother warned me. I know a song about that.

COMMANDER. Sing it to us. [*Roaring.*] Bring that meat!

EILIF. It's called *The Song of the Fishwife and the Soldier.* [*He sings and at the same time does a war dance with his sabre.*]

> To a soldier lad comes an old fishwife
>   And this old fishwife, says she:
> A gun will shoot, a knife will knife,
>   You will drown if you fall in the sea.
> Keep away from the ice if you want my advice,
>   Says the old fishwife, says she.
> The soldier laughs and loads his gun
> Then grabs his knife and starts to run:
>   It's the life of a hero for me!
> From the north to the south I shall march through the land
> With a knife at my side and a gun in my hand!
>   Says the soldier lad, says he.
>
> When the lad defies the fishwife's cries
>   The old fishwife, says she:
> The young are young, the old are wise,
>   You will drown if you fall in the sea.
> Don't ignore what I say or you'll rue it one day!
>   Says the old fishwife, says she.
> But gun in hand and knife at side
> The soldier steps into the tide:
>   It's the life of a hero for me!
> When the new moon is shining on shingle roofs white
> We are all coming back, go and pray for that night!
>   Says the soldier lad, says he.
>
> And the fishwife old does what she'd told:
>   Down upon her knees drops she.
> When the smoke is gone, the air is cold,
>   Your heroic deeds won't warm me!
> See the smoke, how it goes! May God scatter his foes!
>   Down upon her knees drops she.
> But gun in hand and knife at side
> The lad is swept out by the tide:
>   He floats with the ice to the sea.
> And the new moon is shining on shingle roofs white

But the lad and his laughter are lost in the night:
    He floats with the ice to the sea.

COMMANDER. What a kitchen I've got! There's no end to the liberties they take!

EILIF [*has entered the kitchen and embraced his mother*]. To see you again! Where are the others?

MOTHER COURAGE [*in his arms*]. Happy as ducks in a pond. Swiss Cheese is paymaster with the Second Protestant Regiment, so at least he isn't in the fighting. I couldn't keep him out altogether.

EILIF. Are your feet holding up?

MOTHER COURAGE. I've a bit of trouble getting my shoes on in the morning.

COMMANDER [*who has come over*]. So, you're his mother! I hope you have more sons for me like this fellow.

EILIF. If I'm not the lucky one: you sit there in the kitchen and hear your son being feasted!

MOTHER COURAGE. Yes, I heard all right. [*Gives him a box on the ear.*]

EILIF. Because I took the oxen?

MOTHER COURAGE. No. Because you didn't surrender when the four peasants let fly at you and tried to make mincemeat of you! Didn't I teach you to take care of yourself? Finnish devil!

[*The* COMMANDER *and the* CHAPLAIN *stand laughing in the doorway.*]

Scene Three

THREE YEARS PASS AND MOTHER COURAGE, WITH PARTS OF A FINNISH REGIMENT, IS TAKEN PRISONER. HER DAUGHTER IS SAVED, HER WAGON LIKEWISE, BUT HER HONEST SON DIES.

A camp. The regimental flag is flying from a pole. Afternoon. All sorts of wares hanging on the wagon. MOTHER COURAGE's *clothes line is tied to the wagon at one end, to a cannon at the other. She and* CATHERINE *are folding the wash on the cannon. At the same time she is bargaining with an* ORDNANCE OFFICER *over a bag of bullets.* SWISS CHEESE, *in paymaster's uniform now, looks on.* YVETTE POTTIER, *a very good-looking young person, is sewing at a colored hat, a glass of brandy before her. She is in stocking feet. Her red boots are near by.*

OFFICER. I'm letting you have the bullets for two gilders. Dirt cheap. 'Cause I need the money. The Colonel's been drinking with the officers for three days and we're out of liquor.

MOTHER COURAGE. They're army property. If they find 'em on me, I'll be courtmartialed. You sell your bullets, you bastards, and send your men out to fight with nothing to shoot with.

OFFICER. Aw, come on, one good turn deserves another.

MOTHER COURAGE. I won't take army stuff. Not at *that* price.

OFFICER. You can resell 'em for five gilders, maybe eight, to the Ordnance Officer of the Fourth Regiment. All you have to do is give him a receipt for twelve. He hasn't a bullet left.

MOTHER COURAGE. Why don't you do it yourself?

OFFICER. I don't trust him. We're friends.

MOTHER COURAGE [*takes the bag*]. Give it here. [*To* CATHERINE.] Take it round the back and pay him a gilder and a half. [*As the* OFFICER *protests.*] I said a gilder and a half!

> [CATHERINE *drags the bag away. The* OFFICER *follows.* MOTHER COURAGE *speaks to* SWISS CHEESE]

Here's your underwear back, take care of it; it's October now, autumn may come at any time; I purposely don't say it must come, I've learnt from experience there's nothing that must come, not even the seasons. But your books *must* balance now you're the regimental paymaster. *Do* they balance?

SWISS CHEESE. Yes, Mother.

MOTHER COURAGE. Don't forget they made you paymaster because you're honest and so simple you'd never think of running off with the cash. Don't lose that underwear.

SWISS CHEESE. No, Mother. I'll put it under the mattress. [*He starts to go.*]

OFFICER. I'll go with you, paymaster.

MOTHER COURAGE. Don't teach him how to finagle!

> [*Without a good-by the* OFFICER *leaves with* SWISS CHEESE.]

YVETTE [*waving to him*]. You might at least say good-by!

MOTHER COURAGE [to YVETTE]. I don't like that. *He's* no sort of company for my Swiss Cheese. But the war's not making a bad start. Before all the different countries get into it, four or five years'll have gone by like nothing. If I look ahead and make no mistakes, business will be good. Don't you know you shouldn't drink in the morning with your illness?

YVETTE. Who says I'm ill? That's libel!

MOTHER COURAGE. They all say so.

YVETTE. They're all liars. I'm desperate, Mother Courage. They all avoid me like a stinking fish. Because of those lies. So what am I fixing my hat for? [*She throws it down.*] That's why I drink in the morning; I never used to, it gives you crow's feet, but now it's all one, every man in the regiment knows me. I should have stayed home when my first was unfaithful. But pride isn't for the likes of us, you eat dirt or down you go.

MOTHER COURAGE. Now don't you start in again with your friend Peter and how it all happened—in front of my innocent daughter.

YVETTE. She's the one that should hear it. So she'll get hardened against love.

MOTHER COURAGE. That's something no one ever gets hardened against.

YVETTE. He was an army cook, blond, a Dutchman, but thin. Catherine, beware of thin men! I didn't. I didn't even know he'd had another girl before me and she called him Peter Piper because he never took his pipe out of his mouth the whole time, it meant so little to him. [*She sings* THE CAMP FOLLOWER'S SONG.]

> Scarce seventeen was I when
> > The foe came to our land
> And laid aside his saber
> > And took me by the hand.
> > > And we performed by day
> > > The sacred rite of May
> > > And we performed by night
> > > Another sacred rite.
> > > The regiment, well exercised,
> > > Presented arms, then stood at ease,
> > > Then took us off behind the trees
> > > Where we fraternized.
>
> Each of us had her foe and
> > A cook fell to my lot.
> I hated him by daylight
> > But in the dark did not.
> > > So we perform by day
> > > The sacred rite of May
> > > And we perform by night
> > > That other sacred rite.
> > > The regiment, well exercised,
> > > Presents its arms, then stands at ease,
> > > Then takes us off behind the trees
> > > Where we fraternize.
>
> Ecstasy filled my heart, O
> > My love seemed heaven-born!
> But why were people saying
> > It was not love but scorn?
> > > The springtime's soft amour
> > > Through summer may endure
> > > But swiftly comes the fall
> > > And winter ends it all.
> > > December came. All of the men
> > > Filed past the trees where once we hid
> > > Then quickly marched away and did
> > > Not come back again.

I made the mistake of running after him, I never found him. It's ten years ago now. [*With swaying gait she goes behind the wagon.*]

MOTHER COURAGE. You're leaving your hat.

YVETTE. For the birds.

MOTHER COURAGE. Let this be a lesson to you, Catherine, never start anything with a soldier. Love *is* like a heavenly dove, so watch out! He tells you he'd like to kiss the ground under your feet—did you wash 'em yesterday, while we're on the subject? And then if you don't look out, your number's up, you're his slave for life. Be glad you're dumb, Catherine: you'll never contradict yourself, you'll never want to bite your tongue off because you spoke out of turn. Dumbness is a gift from God. Here comes the Commander's Cook, what's biting him?

[*Enter the* COOK *and the* CHAPLAIN.]

CHAPLAIN. I bring a message from your son Eilif. The Cook came with me. You've made, ahem, an impression on him.

COOK. I thought I'd get a little whiff of the balmy breeze.

MOTHER COURAGE. Get it then, and welcome. But what does Eilif want? I've no money to spare.

CHAPLAIN. Actually, I have something to tell his brother, the paymaster.

MOTHER COURAGE. He isn't here. And he isn't anywhere else either. He's not his brother's paymaster, and I won't have him led into temptation. [*She takes money from the purse at her belt.*] Give him this. It's a sin. He's speculating in mother love, he ought to be ashamed of himself.

COOK. Not for long. He has to go with his regiment now—to his death maybe. Send some more money, or you'll be sorry. You women are hard—and sorry afterward. A glass of brandy wouldn't cost very much, but you don't give it, and six feet under goes your man and you can't dig him up again.

CHAPLAIN. All very touching, my dear Cook, but to fall in this war is not a misfortune, it's a blessing. This is a holy war. Not just any old war but a religious one, and therefore pleasing unto God.

COOK. Sure. In one sense it's a war because there's fleecing, bribing, plundering, not to mention a little raping, but it's different from all other wars because it's a holy war. That's clear. All the same, it makes you thirsty.

CHAPLAIN [*to* MOTHER COURAGE, *pointing at the* COOK]. I tried to hold him off but he said you'd bewitched him. He dreams about you.

COOK [*lighting a clay pipe*]. Brandy from the fair hand of a lady, that's for me. And don't embarrass me any more: the stories the chaplain was telling on the way over still have me blushing.

MOTHER COURAGE. A man of his cloth! I must get you both something to drink or you'll be making improper advances out of sheer boredom.

CHAPLAIN. That is indeed a temptation, said the Court Chaplain, and gave way to it. [*Turning toward* CATHERINE *as he strolls around.*] And who is this captivating young person?

MOTHER COURAGE. She's not a captivating young person, she's a respectable young person.

[*The* CHAPLAIN *and the* COOK *go with* MOTHER COURAGE *behind the cart.*]

MOTHER COURAGE. The trouble here in Poland is that the Poles *would* keep meddling. It's true our Swedish King moved in on them with man, beast, and wagon, but instead of maintaining the peace the Poles were always meddling in their own affairs. They attacked the Swedish King when he was in the act of peacefully withdrawing. So they were guilty of a breach of the peace and their blood is on their own heads.

CHAPLAIN. Anyway, our Gustavus Adolphus was thinking of nothing but their freedom. The German Kaiser enslaved them all, Poles and Germans alike, so our King *had* to liberate them.

COOK. Just what *I* think. Your health! Your brandy is first rate, I'm never mistaken in a face.

[CATHERINE *looks after them, leaves the washing, and goes to the hat, picks it up, sits down, and takes up the red boots.*]

And the war is a holy war.

[*Singing while* CATHERINE *puts the boots on.*]

"A mighty fortress is our God . . ." [*He sings a verse or so of Luther's hymn.*] And talking of King Gustavus, this freedom he tried to bring to Germany cost him a pretty penny. Back in Sweden he had to levy a salt tax, the poorer folks didn't like it a bit. Then, too, he had to lock up the Germans and even cut their heads off, they clung so to slavery and their Kaiser. Of course, if no one had *wanted* to be free, the King wouldn't have had any fun. First it was just Poland he tried to protect from bad men, specially the Kaiser, then his appetite grew with eating, and he ended protecting Germany too.

CHAPLAIN. He had one thing in his favor anyway: the Word of God. Or they could have said he did it all for himself and for profits. He has a clear conscience, that man.

COOK [*with heavy irony*]. Yes. He always put conscience first.

CHAPLAIN. It's plain you're no Swede, or you'd speak differently of the Hero King!

MOTHER COURAGE. What's more, you eat his bread.

COOK. I don't eat his bread. I bake his bread.

MOTHER COURAGE. He can never be conquered, and I'll tell you why: his men believe in him. [*Earnestly.*]

To hear the big fellows talk, they wage the war from fear of God and for all things bright and beautiful, but just look into it, and you'll see they're not so silly: they want a good profit out of it, or else the little fellows like you and me wouldn't back 'em up.

COOK. Surely.

CHAPLAIN [*indicating the Protestant flag*]. And as a Dutchman you'd do well to see which flag's flying here before you express an opinion!

MOTHER COURAGE. All good Protestants for ever!

COOK. A health!

[CATHERINE *has begun to strut around with* YVETTE's *hat on, copying* YVETTE's *sexy walk. Suddenly cannon and shots. Drums.* MOTHER COURAGE, *the* COOK, *and the* CHAPLAIN *rush round to the front of*

the cart, the two last with glasses in their hands. The ORDNANCE
OFFICER *and a* SOLDIER *come running to the cannon and try to push
it along.*]

MOTHER COURAGE. What's the matter? Let me get my wash off that gun,
you slobs! [*She tries to do so.*]

OFFICER. The Catholics! Surprise attack! We don't know if we can get
away! [*To the* SOLDIER.] Get that gun! [*Runs off.*]

COOK. For heaven's sake! I must go to the Commander. Mother Courage,
I'll be back in a day or two—for a short conversation. [*Rushes off.*]

MOTHER COURAGE. Hey, you're leaving your pipe!

COOK [*off*]. Keep it for me, I'll need it!

MOTHER COURAGE. This *would* happen when we were just making
money.

CHAPLAIN. Well, I must be going too. Yes, if the enemy's so close, it
can be dangerous. "Blessed are the peacemakers," a good slogan in
wartime! If only I had a cloak.

MOTHER COURAGE. I'm lending no cloaks. Not even to save a life I'm
not. I've had experience in that line.

CHAPLAIN. But I'm in special danger. Because of my religion!

MOTHER COURAGE [*brings him a cloak*]. It's against my better judgment.
Now run!

CHAPLAIN. I thank you, you're very generous, but maybe I'd better stay
and sit here. If I run, I might attract the enemy's attention. I might
arouse suspicion.

MOTHER COURAGE [to the SOLDIER]. Let it alone, you dope, who's going
to pay you for this? It'll cost you your life, let me hold it for you.

SOLDIER [*running away*]. You're my witness: I tried!

MOTHER COURAGE. I'll swear to it! [*Seeing* CATHERINE *with the hat.*]
What on earth are you up to—with a whore's hat! Take it off this
minute! Are you crazy? With the enemy coming? [*She tears the hat
off her head.*] Do you want them to find you and make a whore of
you? And she has the boots on too, straight from Babylon, I'll soon
fix that. [*She tries to get them off.*] Oh God, Chaplain, help me with
these boots, I'll be right back! [*She runs to the wagon.*]

YVETTE [*entering and powdering her face*]. What's that you say; the
Catholics are coming? Where's my hat? Who's been trampling on
it!? I can't run around in that, what will they think of me? And I've
no mirror either. [*To the* CHAPLAIN, *coming very close.*] How do I
look—too much powder?

CHAPLAIN. Just, er, right.

YVETTE. And where are my red boots?

[*She can't find them because* CATHERINE *is hiding her feet under her
skirt.*]

I left them here! Now I've got to go barefoot to my tent, it's a scandal!
[*Exit.*]

[SWISS CHEESE *comes running in carrying a cash box.*]

MOTHER COURAGE [*enters with her hands covered with ashes*]. [*To* CATH-ERINE.] Ashes! [*To* SWISS CHEESE.] What you got there?

SWISS CHEESE. The regimental cash box.

MOTHER COURAGE. Throw it away! Your paymastering days are over!

SWISS CHEESE. It's a trust! [*He goes to the back.*]

MOTHER COURAGE [*to the* CHAPLAIN]. Off with your pastor's coat, Chaplain, or they'll recognize you, cloak or no cloak.

[*She is rubbing ashes into* CATHERINE's *face.*]

Keep still. A little dirt, and you're safe. When a soldier sees a clean face, there's one more whore in the world. Specially a Catholic soldier. That should do, it looks like you've been rolling in muck. Don't tremble. Nothing can happen to you now. [*To* SWISS CHEESE.] Where have you left that cash?

SWISS CHEESE. I thought I'd just put it in the wagon.

MOTHER COURAGE [*horrified*]. What!? In my wagon? God punish you for a prize idiot! If I just look away for a moment! They'll hang all three of us!

SWISS CHEESE. Then I'll put it somewhere else. Or escape with it.

MOTHER COURAGE. You'll stay right here. It's too late.

CHAPLAIN [*still changing his clothes*]. For Heaven's sake: the Protestant flag!

MOTHER COURAGE [*taking down the flag*]. I don't notice it any more, I've had it twenty-five years.

[*The sound of cannon grows.*]

[*Three days later. Morning. The cannon is gone.* MOTHER COURAGE, CATHERINE, *the* CHAPLAIN *and* SWISS CHEESE *sit anxiously eating.*]

SWISS CHEESE. This is the third day I've been sitting here doing nothing, and the Sergeant, who's always been patient with me, may be slowly beginning to ask, "Where on earth is Swiss Cheese with that cash box?"

MOTHER COURAGE. Be glad they're not on the scent.

CHAPLAIN. What about me? I can't hold service here or I'll be in hot water. It is written, "Out of the abundance of the heart, the tongue speaketh." But woe is me if *my* tongue speaketh!

MOTHER COURAGE. That's how it is. Here you sit—one with his religion, the other with his cash box, I don't know which is more dangerous.

CHAPLAIN. We're in God's hands now!

MOTHER COURAGE. I hope we're not as desperate as *that*, but it *is* hard to sleep at night. 'Course it'd be easier if *you* weren't here, Swiss Cheese, all the same I've not done badly. When they questioned me, I always asked where I could buy holy candles a bit cheaper. I know these things because Swiss Cheese's father was a Catholic and made jokes about it. They didn't quite believe me but they needed a canteen, so they winked an eye. Maybe it's all for the best. We're prisoners. But so are lice in fur.

CHAPLAIN. The milk is good. As far as quantity goes, we may have to reduce our Swedish appetites somewhat. We are defeated.

MOTHER COURAGE. Who's defeated? The defeats and victories of the fellows at the top aren't always defeats and victories for the fellows at the bottom. Not at all. There've been cases where a defeat is a victory for the fellows at the bottom, it's only their honor that's lost, nothing serious. In Livonia once, our Chief took such a knock from the enemy, in the confusion I got a fine gray mare out of the baggage train, it pulled my wagon seven months—till we won and there was inventory. But in general both defeat and victory are a costly business for us that haven't got much. The best thing is for politics to kind of get stuck in the mud. [*To* SWISS CHEESE.] Eat!

SWISS CHEESE I don't like it. How will the Sergeant pay his men?

MOTHER COURAGE. Soldiers in flight don't get paid.

SWISS CHEESE. Well, they could claim to be. No pay, no flight. They can refuse to budge.

MOTHER COURAGE. Swiss Cheese, your sense of duty worries me. I've brought you up to be honest because you're not very bright. But don't go too far! And now I'm going with the Chaplain to buy a Catholic flag and some meat. A good thing they let me continue in business. In business you ask what price, not what religion. Protestant pants keep you just as warm. [*She disappears into the wagon.*]

CHAPLAIN. She's worried about the cash box. Up to now they've ignored us—as if we were part of the wagon—but can it last?

SWISS CHEESE. I can get rid of it.

CHAPLAIN. That's almost *more* dangerous. Suppose you're seen. They have spies. Yesterday morning one jumped out of the very hole I was relieving myself in. I was so off guard I almost broke out in prayer—*that* would have given me away all right! I believe their favorite way of finding a Protestant is smelling his, um, excrement. The spy was a little brute with a bandage over one eye.

MOTHER COURAGE [*clambering out of the wagon with a basket*]. I've found you out, you shameless hussy! [*She holds up* YVETTE's *red boots in triumph.*] Yvette's red boots! She just snitched them—because you went and told her she was a captivating person. [*She lays them in the basket.*] Stealing Yvette's boots! But *she* disgraces herself for money, *you* do it for nothing—for pleasure! Save your proud peacock ways for peacetime!

CHAPLAIN. I don't find her proud.

MOTHER COURAGE. I like her when people say "I never noticed the poor thing." I like her when she's a stone in Dalarna where there's nothing but stones. [*To* SWISS CHEESE.] Leave the cash box where it is, do you hear? And pay attention to your sister, she needs it. Between the two of you, you'll be the death of me yet; I'd rather take care of a bag of fleas.

[*She leaves with the* CHAPLAIN. CATHERINE *clears the dishes away.*]

SWISS CHEESE. Not many days more when you can sit in the sun in your shirtsleeves.

[CATHERINE *points to a tree.*]

Yes, the leaves are yellow already.

[*With gestures,* CATHERINE *asks if he wants a drink.*]

I'm not drinking, I'm thinking. [*Pause.*] She says she can't sleep. So I *should* take the cash box away. I've found a place for it. I'll keep it in the mole hole by the river till the time comes. I might get it tonight before sunrise and take it to the regiment. How far can they have fled in three days? The Sergeant's eyes'll pop out of his head. "You've disappointed me most pleasantly, Swiss Cheese," he'll say, "I trust you with the cash box and *you* bring it back!" Yes, Catherine, I *will* have a glass now!

[*When* CATHERINE *reappears behind the wagon two men confront her. One of them is a sergeant. The other doffs his hat and flourishes it in a showy greeting. He has a bandage over one eye.*]

THE MAN WITH THE BANDAGE. Good morning, young lady. Have you seen a staff officer from the Second Protestant Regiment?

[*Terrified,* CATHERINE *runs away, spilling her brandy. The two men look at each other and then withdraw after seeing* SWISS CHEESE.]

SWISS CHEESE [*starting up from his reflections*]. You're spilling it! What's the matter with you, can't you see where you're going? I don't understand you. Anyway, I must be off, I've decided it's the thing to do.

[*He stands up. She does all she can to make him aware of the danger he is in. He only pushes her away.*]

I'd like to know what you mean. I know you mean well, poor thing, you just can't get it out. And don't trouble yourself about the brandy; I'll live to drink so much of it, what's one glass? [*He takes the cash box out of the wagon and puts it under his coat.*] I'll be right back. But don't hold me up or I'll have to scold you. Yes, I know you mean well. If you only could speak!

[*When she tries to hold him back he kisses her and pulls himself free. Exit. She is desperate and runs up and down, emitting little sounds.* MOTHER COURAGE *and the* CHAPLAIN *return.* CATHERINE *rushes at her mother.*]

MOTHER COURAGE. What *is* it, what *is* it, Catherine? Control yourself! Has someone done something to you? Where is Swiss Cheese? [*To the* CHAPLAIN.] Don't stand around, get that Catholic flag up!

[*She takes a Catholic flag out of her basket and the* CHAPLAIN *runs it up the pole.*]

CHAPLAIN [*bitterly*]. All good Catholics forever!

MOTHER COURAGE. Now, Catherine, calm down and tell all about it, your mother understands. What, that little bastard of mine's taken the cash box away? I'll box his ears for him, the rascal! Now take your time and don't try to talk, use your hands. I don't like it when you howl like a dog, what'll the Chaplain think of you? See how shocked he looks. A man with one eye was here?

CHAPLAIN. That fellow with one eye is an informer! Have they caught Swiss Cheese?

[CATHERINE *shakes her head, shrugs her shoulders.*]

This is the end.

[*Voices off. The two men bring in* SWISS CHEESE.]

SWISS CHEESE. Let me go. I've nothing on me. You're breaking my shoulder! I am innocent.

SERGEANT. This is where he comes from. These are his friends.

MOTHER COURAGE. Us? Since when? [*Putting things in her basket.*]

SWISS CHEESE. I don't even know 'em. I was just getting my lunch here. Ten hellers it cost me. Maybe you saw me sitting on that bench. It was too salty.

SERGEANT. Who *are* you people, anyway?

MOTHER COURAGE. Law abiding citizens! It's true what he says. He bought his lunch here. And it was too salty.

SERGEANT. Are you pretending you don't know him?

MOTHER COURAGE. I can't know all of them, can I? *I* don't ask, "What's your name and are you a heathen?" If they pay up, they're not heathens to me. Are you a heathen?

SWISS CHEESE. Oh, no!

CHAPLAIN. He sat there like a law-abiding chap and never once opened his mouth. Except to eat. Which is necessary.

SERGEANT. Who do you think *you* are?

MOTHER COURAGE. Oh, he's my barman. And you're thirsty, I'll bring you a glass of brandy; you must be footsore and weary!

SERGEANT. No brandy on duty. [*To* SWISS CHEESE.] You were carrying something. You must have hidden it by the river. We saw the bulge in your shirt.

MOTHER COURAGE. Sure it was him?

SWISS CHEESE. I think you mean another fellow. There *was* a fellow with something under his shirt, I saw him. I'm the wrong man.

MOTHER COURAGE. I think so too. It's a misunderstanding. Could happen to anyone. Oh, I know what people are like, I'm Mother Courage, you've heard of me, everyone knows about me, and I can tell you this: he looks honest.

SERGEANT. We're after the regimental cash box. And we know what the man looks like who's been keeping it. We've been looking for him two days. It's you.

SWISS CHEESE. No, it's not!

SERGEANT. And if you don't shell out, you're dead, see? Where is it?

MOTHER COURAGE [*urgently*]. 'Course he'd give it to you to save his life. He'd up and say, I do have it, here it is, you're stronger than me. He's not *that* stupid. Speak, little stupid, the Sergeant's giving you a chance!

SWISS CHEESE. What if I don't have it?

SERGEANT. Come with us. We'll get it out of you.

[*They take him off.*]

MOTHER COURAGE [*shouting after them*]. He'd tell you! He's not *that* stupid! And leave his shoulder alone!! [*She runs after them.*]

[*The same evening. The* CHAPLAIN *and* CATHERINE *are rinsing glasses and polishing knives.*]

CHAPLAIN. Cases of people getting caught like this are by no means unknown in the history of religion. I am reminded of the Passion of Our Lord and Savior. There's an old song about it. [*He sings The Song of the Hours.*]

> In the first hour of the day
> Simple Jesus Christ was
> Halèd as a murderer
> Before the heathen Pilate.
>
> Pilate found no fault in him
> No cause to condemn him
> So he sent the Lord away.
> Let King Herod see him!
>
> Hour the third: the Son of God
> Was with scourges beaten
> And they set a crown of thorns
> On the head of Jesus.
>
> And they dressed him as a king
> Joked and jested at him
> And the cross to die upon
> He himself must carry.
>
> Six: they stripped Lord Jesus bare.
> To the cross they nailed him.
> When the blood came gushing, he
> Prayed and loud lamented.
>
> From their neighbor crosses, thieves
> Mocked him like the others.
> And the bright sun crept away
> Not to see such doings.
>
> Nine: Lord Jesus cried aloud
> That he was forsaken!
> In a sponge upon a pole
> Vinegar was fed him.
>
> Then the Lord gave up the ghost
> And the earth did tremble.
> Temple curtain split in twain.
> Cliffs fell in the ocean.

Evening: they broke the bones
Of the malefactors.
Then they took a spear and pierced
The side of gentle Jesus.

And the blood and water ran
And they laughed at Jesus.
Of this simple son of man
Such and more they tell us.

MOTHER COURAGE [*entering, excited*]. It's life and death. But the Sergeant will still listen to us. The only thing is, he mustn't know it's our Swiss Cheese, or they'll say we helped him. It's only a matter of money, but where can *we* get money? Wasn't Yvette here? I met her on the way over. She's picked up a Colonel! Maybe he'll buy her a canteen business!

CHAPLAIN. You'd sell the wagon, everything?

MOTHER COURAGE. Where else would I get the money for the Sergeant?

CHAPLAIN. What are you to live off?

MOTHER COURAGE. That's just it.

[*Enter* YVETTE POTTIER *with a hoary old* COLONEL.]

YVETTE [*embracing* MOTHER COURAGE]. *Dear* Mistress Courage, we meet again! [*Whispering.*] He didn't say no. [*Aloud.*] This is my friend, my, um, business adviser. I happened to hear you might like to sell your wagon. Due to special circumstances. I'd like to think about it.

MOTHER COURAGE. I want to pawn it, not sell it. And nothing hasty. In war time you don't find another wagon like that so easy.

YVETTE [*disappointed*]. Only pawn it? I thought you wanted to sell, I don't know if I'm interested. [*To the* COLONEL.] What do *you* think, my dear?

COLONEL. I quite agree with you, honey bun.

MOTHER COURAGE. It's only for pawn.

YVETTE. I thought you *had* to have the money.

MOTHER COURAGE [*firmly*]. I do have to have it. But I'd rather wear my feet off looking for an offer than just sell. We live off the wagon.

COLONEL. Take it, take it!

YVETTE. My friend thinks I should go ahead, but I'm not sure—if it's only for pawn. You think we should buy it outright, don't you?

COLONEL. I do, bunny, I do!

MOTHER COURAGE. Then you must find something that's for sale.

YVETTE. Yes, we can go around looking for something. I *love* going around looking, I *love* going around with you, Poldy . . .

COLONEL. Really? You do?

YVETTE. Oh, it's *lovely!* I could take *weeks* of it!

COLONEL. Really? You could?

YVETTE. If you get the money, when are you thinking of paying it back?

MOTHER COURAGE. In two weeks. Maybe in one.

YVETTE. I can't make up my mind. Poldy, advise me, *chéri!*
> [*She takes the* COLONEL *to one side.*]
> She'll *have* to sell, don't worry. That lieutenant—the blond one—
> you know the one I mean—he'll lend me the money. He's *mad* about
> me, he says I remind him of someone. What do you advise?

COLONEL. Oh, I have to warn you against *him*. He's no good. He'll
exploit the situation. I told you, bunny, I told you *I'd* buy you something, didn't I tell you that?

YVETTE. I simply can't let you!

COLONEL. Oh, please, please!

YVETTE. Well, if you think the lieutenant might exploit the situation I
will let you!

COLONEL. I do think so.

YVETTE. So you advise me to?

COLONEL. I do, bunny, I do!

YVETTE [*returning to* MOTHER COURAGE]. My friend says all right. Write
me out a receipt saying the wagon's mine when the two weeks are
up—with everything in it. I'll just run through it all now, the two
hundred gilders can wait. [*To the* COLONEL.] You go on ahead to the
camp, I'll follow, I must go over all this so nothing'll be missing later
from *my* wagon!

COLONEL. Wait, I'll help you up! [*He does so.*] Come soon, honey-
bunny! [*Exit.*]

MOTHER COURAGE. Yvette, Yvette!

YVETTE. There aren't many boots left!

MOTHER COURAGE. Yvette, this is no time to go through the wagon,
yours or not yours. You promised you'd talk to the Sergeant about
Swiss Cheese. There isn't a minute to lose. He's up before the court
martial one hour from now.

YVETTE. I just want to check through these shirts.

MOTHER COURAGE [*dragging her down the steps by the skirt*]. You hyena,
Swiss Cheese's life's at stake! And don't say who the money comes
from. Pretend he's your sweetheart, for heaven's sake, or we'll all get
it for helping him.

YVETTE. I've arranged to meet One Eye in the bushes. He must be there
by now.

CHAPLAIN. And don't hand over all two hundred, a hundred and fifty's
sure to be enough.

MOTHER COURAGE. I'll thank you to keep your nose out of this, I'm not
doing *you* out of your porridge. Now run, and no haggling, remember
his life's at stake.
> [*She pushes* YVETTE *off.*]

CHAPLAIN. I didn't want to talk you into anything, but what are we going
to live on? You have an unmarriageable daughter round your neck.

MOTHER COURAGE. I'm counting on that cash box, smart alec. They'll
pay his expenses out of it.

CHAPLAIN. You think she can work it?

MOTHER COURAGE. It's to her interest: I pay out the two hundred and she gets the wagon. She knows what she's doing, she won't have her colonel on the string forever. Catherine, go and clean the knives, use pumice stone. [*To the* CHAPLAIN.] And don't *you* stand around like Jesus in Gethsemane. Get a move on, wash those glasses. There'll be over fifty cavalrymen here tonight, can't you just hear them grumbling, "Isn't walking terrible, oh my poor feet!" I think they'll let us have him. Thanks be to God they're corruptible. They're not wolves, they're human and after money. God is merciful, and men are bribable, that's how His will is done on earth as it is in Heaven. Corruption is our only hope. As long as there's corruption, there'll be merciful judges and even the innocent may get off!

YVETTE [*comes panting in*]. They'll do it for two hundred if you make it snappy, these things change from one minute to the next. I'd better take One Eye to my colonel right now. He confessed he had the cash box, they put the thumb screws on him. But he threw it in the river when he noticed them coming up behind him. So it's gone. Shall I run and get the money from my colonel?

MOTHER COURAGE. The cash box gone? How'll I ever get my two hundred back?

YVETTE. So you thought you could get it from the cash box? I *would* have been sunk. Not a hope, Mother Courage. If you want your Swiss Cheese, you'll have to pay. Or should I let the whole thing drop, so you can keep your wagon?

MOTHER COURAGE. What can I do? I *can't* pay two hundred. You *should* have haggled with them. I must hold on to something, or any passer-by can kick me in the ditch. Go and say I'll pay a hundred and twenty or the deal's off. Even at that I lose the wagon.

YVETTE. They won't do it. And anyway, One Eye's in a hurry. He looks over his shoulder the whole time, he's so worked up. Hadn't I better give them the whole two hundred?

MOTHER COURAGE [*desperate*]. I can't pay it! I've been working thirty years. She's twenty-five and still no husband, I have her to think of. So leave me alone, I know what I'm doing. A hundred and twenty or no deal.

YVETTE. You know best. [*Runs off.*]

> [MOTHER COURAGE *turns away and slowly walks a few paces to the rear. Then she turns round, looks neither at the* CHAPLAIN *nor at her daughter, and sits down to help* CATHERINE *polish the knives.*]

MOTHER COURAGE. You'll have your brother back. I *will* pay two hundred—if I have to. With eighty gilders we could pack a hamper with goods and begin over. It wouldn't be the end of the world.

CHAPLAIN. The Bible says, the Lord will provide.

MOTHER COURAGE [*to* CATHERINE]. You must rub them dry.

YVETTE [*comes running on*]. They won't do it. I warned you. He said the drums would roll any second now and that's the sign a verdict has been pronounced. I offered a hundred and fifty, he didn't even shrug his shoulders. I could hardly get him to stay there while I came to you.

MOTHER COURAGE. Tell him, I'll pay two hundred. Run!

[YVETTE *runs.* MOTHER COURAGE *sits, silent. The* CHAPLAIN *has stopped doing the glasses.*]

I believe—I haggled too long.

[*In the distance, a roll of drums. The* CHAPLAIN *stands up and walks toward the rear.* MOTHER COURAGE *remains seated. It grows dark. It gets light again.* MOTHER COURAGE *has not moved.*]

YVETTE [*appears, pale*]. Now you've done it—with your haggling. You can keep the wagon now. He got eleven bullets, that's all. I don't know why I still bother about you, you don't deserve it, but I just happened to learn they don't think the cash box is really in the river. They suspect it's here, they think you're connected with him. I think they mean to bring him here to see if you give yourself away when you see him. I warn you not to know him or we're in for it. And I better tell you straight, they're right behind me. Shall I keep Catherine away?

[MOTHER COURAGE *shakes her head.*]

Does she know? Maybe she never heard the drums or didn't understand.

MOTHER COURAGE. She knows. Bring her.

[YVETTE *brings* CATHERINE, *who walks over to her mother and stands by her.* MOTHER COURAGE *takes her hand. Two men come on with a stretcher; there is a sheet on it and something underneath. Beside them, the* SERGEANT. *They put the stretcher down.*]

SERGEANT. Here's a man we don't know the name of. But he has to be registered to keep the records straight. He bought a meal from you. Look at him, see if you know him. [*He pulls back the sheet.*] Do you know him?

[MOTHER COURAGE *shakes her head.*]

What? You never saw him before he took that meal?

[MOTHER COURAGE *shakes her head.*]

Lift him up. Throw him on the junk heap. He has no one that knows him.

[*They carry him off.*]

Scene Four

MOTHER COURAGE SINGS *THE SONG OF THE GREAT CAPITULATION.*

Outside an officer's tent, MOTHER COURAGE *waits.* A CLERK *looks out of the tent.*

CLERK. You want to speak to the captain? I know you. You had a Protestant paymaster with you, he was hiding out. Better make no complaint here.

MOTHER COURAGE. I will too! I'm innocent and if I give up it'll look like I have a bad conscience. They cut everything in my wagon to ribbons with their sabers and then claimed a fine of five thalers for nothing and less than nothing.

CLERK. For your own good, keep your trap shut. We haven't many canteens, so we let you stay in business, especially if you've had a bad conscience and have to pay a fine now and then.

MOTHER COURAGE. I'm going to lodge a complaint.

CLERK. As you wish. Wait here till the captain has time. [*Withdraws into the tent.*]

YOUNG SOLDIER [*comes storming in*]. Screw the captain! Where *is* the son-of-a-bitch? Snitching my reward, spending it on brandy for his whores, I'll rip his belly open!

OLDER SOLDIER [*coming after him*]. Shut your hole, you'll wind up in the stocks.

YOUNG SOLDIER. Come out, you thief, I'll make lamb chops out of you! I was the only one in the squad who swam the river and *he* grabs my money, I can't even buy a beer. Come on out! And let me slice you up!

OLDER SOLDIER. Holy Christ, he'll destroy himself!

YOUNG SOLDIER. Let me go or I'll run *you* down too. This thing has got to be settled!

OLDER SOLDIER. Saved the colonel's horse and didn't get the reward. He's young, he hasn't been at it long.

MOTHER COURAGE. Let him go. He doesn't have to be chained, he's not a dog. Very reasonable to want a reward. Why else should he want to shine?

YOUNG SOLDIER. He's in there pouring it down! You're all chickens. I done something special, I want the reward!

MOTHER COURAGE. You man, don't scream at *me*, I have my own troubles.

YOUNG SOLDIER. He's whoring on my money and I'm hungry! I'll murder him!

MOTHER COURAGE. I understand: you're hungry. You're angry: I understand that too.

YOUNG SOLDIER. It's no use you talking, I won't stand for injustice!

MOTHER COURAGE. You're quite right. But how long for? How long won't you stand injustice for? One hour? Or two? You haven't asked yourself that, have you? And yet it's the main thing. It's a misery to sit in the stocks. Especially if you leave it till then to decide you do stand for injustice.

YOUNG SOLDIER. I don't know why I listen to you. Screw that captain! Where is he?

MOTHER COURAGE. You listen because you know I'm right. Your rage has calmed down already. It was a short one and you'd need a long one. But where would you find it?

YOUNG SOLDIER. Are you trying to say it's not right to ask for the money?

MOTHER COURAGE. Just the opposite. I only say, your rage won't last. You'll get nowhere with it, it's a pity. If your rage was a long one, I'd urge you on. Slice him up, I'd advise you. But what's the use if you *don't* slice him up because you feel your tail between your legs? You stand there and the captain lets you have it.

OLDER SOLDIER. You're quite right, he's nuts.

YOUNG SOLDIER. All right, we'll see whether I slice him up or not.
[*Draws his sword.*] When he comes out, I slice him up!

CLERK [*looking out*]. The captain will be right out. [*In the tone of military command.*] Be seated!

[*The* YOUNG SOLDIER *sits.*]

MOTHER COURAGE. What did I tell you? They know us inside out, they know their business. Be seated! And we sit. Oh, you needn't be embarrassed in front of me, I'm no better. We don't stick our necks out, do we? We're too well paid to keep 'em in. Let me tell you about the Great Capitulation.

[*She sings* The Song of the Great Capitulation.]

Long, long ago, a green beginner
   I thought myself a special case.
(None of your ordinary, run of the mill girls, with my looks and my
       talent and my love of the higher things!)
I picked a hair out of my dinner
   And put the waiter in his place.
(All or nothing. Anyway, never the second best. I am the master of
      my fate. I'll take no orders from no one.)
Then a little bird whispers!
     The bird says: "Wait a year or so
     And marching with the band you'll go
     Keeping in step, now fast, now slow,
     And piping out your little spiel.
     Then one day the battalions wheel
     And you go down upon your knees
     To God Almighty if you please!"

My friend, before that year was over
   I'd learned to drink their cup of tea.
(Two children round your neck and the price of bread and what all!)
When they were through with me, moreover,
   They had me where they wanted me.
(You must get in with people. If you scratch my back, I'll scratch
        yours. Never stick your neck out!)
Then a little bird whispered!
     The bird says: "Scarce a year or so
     And marching with the band she'd go
     Keeping in step, now fast, now slow,
     And piping out her little spiel.
     Then one day the battalions wheel
     And she goes down upon her knees
     to God Almighty if you please!"

Our plans are big, our hopes colossal.
   We hitch our wagon to a star.
(Where there's a will, there's a way. You can't hold a good man down.)
"We can lift mountains," says the apostle.
   And yet: how heavy one cigar!
(You must cut your coat according to your cloth.)
That little bird whispers!
     The bird says: "Wait a year or so
     And marching with the band we go
     Keeping in step, now fast, now slow,
     And piping out our little spiel.
     Then one day the battalions wheel
     And we go down upon our knees
     To God Almighty if you please!"

MOTHER COURAGE. And so I think you should stay here with your sword
   drawn if you're set on it and your anger is big enough. You have good
   cause, I admit. But if your anger is a short one, you'd better go.

YOUNG SOLDIER. Aw, shove it!

   [He stumbles off, the other soldier following him.]

CLERK [sticks his head out]. The captain is here. You can lodge your
   complaint.

MOTHER COURAGE. I've thought better of it. I'm not complaining.

   [Exit. The CLERK looks after her, shaking his head.]

Scene Five

TWO YEARS HAVE PASSED. THE WAR COVERS WIDER AND
WIDER TERRITORY. FOREVER ON THE MOVE THE LITTLE
WAGON CROSSES POLAND, MORAVIA, BAVARIA, ITALY,
AND AGAIN BAVARIA. 1631. TILLY'S[5] VICTORY AT LEIPZIG
COSTS MOTHER COURAGE FOUR SHIRTS.

5. Jean T'Serlaes Tilly (1559–1632), a Flemish general in the service of the Catholics.

The wagon stands in a war-ruined village. Faint military music from the distance. Two soldiers are being served at a counter by CATHERINE *and* MOTHER COURAGE. *One of them has a woman's fur coat about his shoulders.*

MOTHER COURAGE. What, you can't pay? No money, no schnapps! They can play a victory march, they should pay their men.

FIRST SOLDIER. I want my schnapps! I arrived too late for plunder. The Chief allowed one hour to plunder the town, it's a swindle. He's not inhuman, he says. So I guess they bought him off.

CHAPLAIN [*staggering in*]. There are more in the farmhouse. A whole family of peasants. Help me someone, I need linen!

[*The* SECOND SOLDIER *goes with him.* CATHERINE *is getting very excited. She tries to get her mother to bring linen out.*]

MOTHER COURAGE. I have none. I sold all my bandages to the regiment. I'm not tearing up my officer's shirts for these people.

CHAPLAIN [*calling over his shoulder*]. I said I need linen!

MOTHER COURAGE [*stopping* CATHERINE *from entering the wagon*]. Not a thing! They have nothing and they pay nothing!

CHAPLAIN [*to a woman he is carrying in*]. Why did you stay out there in the line of fire?

WOMAN. Our farm——

MOTHER COURAGE. Think they'd ever let go of *any*thing? And now I'm supposed to pay. Well, I won't!

FIRST SOLDIER. They're Protestants, why should they be Protestants?

MOTHER COURAGE. Protestant, Catholic, what do *they* care? Their farm's gone, that's what.

SECOND SOLDIER. They're not Protestants anyway, they're Catholics.

FIRST SOLDIER. In a bombardment we can't pick and choose.

PEASANT [*brought on by* CHAPLAIN]. My arm's gone.

CHAPLAIN. Where's that linen?

MOTHER COURAGE. I can't give you any. With all I have to pay out— taxes, duties, bribes . . .

[CATHERINE *takes up a board and threatens her mother with it, emitting gurgling sounds.*]

Are you out of your mind? Put that board down or I'll fetch you one, you lunatic! I'm giving nothing, I don't dare, I have myself to think of.

[*The* CHAPLAIN *lifts her bodily off the steps of the wagon and sets her down on the ground. He takes out shirts from the wagon and tears them in strips.*]

My shirts, my officer's shirts!

[*From the house comes the cry of a child in pain.*]

PEASANT. The child's still in there!

[CATHERINE *runs in.*]

MOTHER COURAGE. Hold her back, the roof may fall in!

CHAPLAIN. I'm not going back in there!

MOTHER COURAGE. My officer's shirts, half a gilder apiece! I'm ruined.

[CATHERINE *brings a baby out of the ruins.*]

MOTHER COURAGE. Another baby to drag around, you must be pleased with yourself. Give it to its mother this minute!

[CATHERINE *is rocking the child and half humming a lullaby.*]

CHAPLAIN [*bandaging*]. The blood's coming through.

MOTHER COURAGE. There she sits, happy as a lark in all this! [*Shouting toward the music.*] Stop that music, I can see your victory all right!

[*Seeing* FIRST SOLDIER *trying to make off with the bottle he's been drinking from.*]

Stop, you pig, if you want *another* victory you must pay for it!

FIRST SOLDIER. I'm broke.

MOTHER COURAGE [*tearing the fur coat off him*]. Then leave this, it's stolen goods anyhow.

[CATHERINE *rocks the child and raises it high above her head.*]

Scene Six

BEFORE THE CITY OF INGOLSTADT IN BAVARIA MOTHER COURAGE ATTENDS THE FUNERAL OF THE FALLEN COMMANDER, TILLY. CONVERSATIONS TAKE PLACE ABOUT WAR HEROES AND THE DURATION OF THE WAR. THE CHAPLAIN COMPLAINS THAT HIS TALENTS ARE LYING FALLOW AND CATHERINE GETS THE RED BOOTS. THE YEAR IS 1632.

The inside of a canteen tent. The inner side of a counter at the rear. Rain. In the distance, drums and funeral music. The CHAPLAIN *and the* REGIMENTAL CLERK *are playing checkers.* MOTHER COURAGE *and her* DAUGHTER *are taking inventory.*

CHAPLAIN. The funeral procession is just starting out.

MOTHER COURAGE. Pity about the Chief—twenty-two pairs, socks—getting killed that way. They say it was an accident. There was a fog over the fields that morning, and the fog was to blame. The Chief called up another regiment, told 'em to fight to the death, rode back again, missed his way in the fog, went forward instead of back, and ran straight into a bullet in the thick of the battle! [A *whistle from the rear. She goes to the counter. To a soldier.*] It's a disgrace the way you're all skipping your Commander's funeral! [*She pours a drink.*]

CLERK. They shouldn't have handed the money out before the funeral. Now the men are all getting drunk instead of going to it.

CHAPLAIN [to the CLERK]. Don't you have to be there?

CLERK. I stayed away because of the rain.

MOTHER COURAGE. It's different for you, the rain might spoil your uniform.

VOICE FROM THE COUNTER. Service! One brandy!

MOTHER COURAGE. Your money first. No, you *can't* come inside the tent, not with those boots; you can drink outside, rain or no rain. I only let officers in here. [To the CLERK.] The Chief had his troubles lately, I hear. There was unrest in the second regiment because he didn't pay 'em but said it was a holy war and they must fight it for free.

CHAPLAIN [as music continues]. Now they're filing past the body.

MOTHER COURAGE. I feel sorry for a commander or an emperor like that—when maybe he had something special in mind, something they'd talk about in times to come, something they'd raise a statue to him for. The conquest of the world now, *that's* a goal for a commander, he couldn't do better than *that*, could he? . . . Lord, worms have got into the biscuit. . . . In short he works his hands to the bone and then it's all spoiled by the common riffraff that only wants a jug of beer or a bit of company, not the higher things in life. The finest plans have always been spoiled by the littleness of them that should carry them out. Even emperors can't do it all by themselves. They count on support from their soldiers and the people round about. Am I right?

CHAPLAIN [laughing]. You're right, Mother Courage, till you come to the soldiers. They do what they can. Those fellows outside, for example, drinking their brandy in the rain, I'd trust 'em to fight a hundred years, one war after another, two at once if necessary. And I wasn't trained as a Commander.

MOTHER COURAGE. . . . Seventeen leather belts . . . Then you don't think the war might end?

CHAPLAIN. Because a Commander's dead? Don't be childish, they're a dime a dozen. There are always heroes.

MOTHER COURAGE. Well, I wasn't asking just for the sake of argument. I was wondering if I should buy up a lot of supplies. They happen to be cheap right now. But if the war ended, I might just as well throw them away.

CHAPLAIN. I realize you are serious, Mother Courage. Well, there have always been people going around saying someday the war will end. I say, you can't be sure the war will *ever* end. Of course it may have to pause occasionally—for breath, as it were—it can even meet with an accident—nothing on this earth is perfect—a war of which we could say it left nothing to be desired will probably never exist. A war can come to a sudden halt—from unforeseen causes—you can't think of everything—a little oversight, and the war's in the hole, and someone's got to pull it out again! The someone is the Emperor or the King or the Pope. They're such friends in need, the war has really nothing to worry about, it can look forward to a prosperous future.

A SOLDIER [*sings at the counter*].

> A schnapps, host, quick, make haste!
> A soldier's no time to waste,
> Must be for his Kaiser fighting!

Make it a double, this is a holiday.

MOTHER COURAGE. If I was sure you're right . . .

CHAPLAIN. Think it out for yourself, how *could* the war end?

SOLDIER.

> Your breast, girl, quick, make haste!
> A soldier's no time to waste,
> Must be to Moravia riding!

CLERK [*of a sudden*]. What about peace? Yes, peace. I'm from Bohemia, I'd like to get home once in a while.

CHAPLAIN. You would, would you? Dear old peace! What happens to the hole when the cheese is gone?

CLERK. In the long run you can't live without peace!

CHAPLAIN. Well, I'd say there's peace even in war, war has its . . . islands of peace. For war satisfies *all* needs, even those of peace, yes, they're provided for, or the war couldn't keep going. In war—as in the very thick of peace—you can take a crap, and between one battle and the next there's always a beer, and even on the march you can catch a nap—on your elbow maybe, in a gutter—something can always be managed. Of course you can't play cards during an attack, but neither can you while plowing the fields in peace-time; it's when the victory's won that there are possibilities. And can't you be fruitful and multiply in the very midst of slaughter—behind a barn or some place? Nothing can keep you from it very long in any event. And so the war has your offspring and can carry on. War is like love, it always finds a way. Why *should* it end?

> [CATHERINE *has stopped working. She stares at the* CHAPLAIN.]

MOTHER COURAGE. Then I *will* buy those supplies, I'll rely on you.

> [CATHERINE *suddenly bangs a basket of glasses down on the ground and runs out.* MOTHER COURAGE *laughs.*]

Lord, Catherine's still going to wait for peace. I promised her she'll get a husband—when it's peace. [*Runs after her.*]

CLERK [*standing up*]. I win. You were talking. You pay.

MOTHER COURAGE [*returning with* CATHERINE]. Be sensible, the war'll go on a bit longer, and we'll make a bit more money, then peace'll be all the nicer. Now you go into the town, it's not ten minutes walk, and bring the things from the Golden Lion, just the more expensive ones, we can get the rest later in the wagon. It's all arranged, the clerk will go with you, most of the soldiers are at the funeral, nothing can happen to you. Do a good job, don't lose anything, Catherine, think of your trousseau!

[CATHERINE *ties a cloth round her head and leaves with the* CLERK.]

CHAPLAIN. You don't mind her going with the clerk?

MOTHER COURAGE. She's not so pretty anyone would want to ruin her.

CHAPLAIN. The way you run your business and always come through is nothing short of commendable, Mother Courage—I see how you got your name.

MOTHER COURAGE. Poorer people need courage. They're lost, that's why. That they even get up in the morning is something—in *their* plight. Or that they plow a field—in war time. Or that they have an Emperor and a Pope, what courage *that* takes, when you can lose your life by it! The poor! They hang each other one by one, they slaughter each other in the lump, so if they want to look each other in the face once in a while—well, it takes courage, that's all. [*She sits, takes a small pipe from her pocket and smokes it.*] You might chop me a bit of firewood.

CHAPLAIN [*reluctantly taking his coat off and preparing to chop wood*]. Properly speaking, I'm a pastor of souls, not a woodcutter.

MOTHER COURAGE. But I don't have a soul. And I do need wood.

CHAPLAIN. What's that little pipe you've got there?

MOTHER COURAGE. Just a pipe.

CHAPLAIN. I think it's a very particular pipe.

MOTHER COURAGE. Oh?

CHAPLAIN. The cook's pipe in fact. Our Swedish Commander's cook.

MOTHER COURAGE. If you know, why beat about the bush?

CHAPLAIN. Because I don't know if you've been *aware* that's what you've been smoking. It was possible you just rummaged among your belongings and your fingers just lit on a pipe and you just took it. In pure absent-mindedness.

MOTHER COURAGE. How do you know that's not it?

CHAPLAIN. It isn't. You *are* aware of it. [*He brings the ax down on the block with a crash.*]

MOTHER COURAGE. What if I was?

CHAPLAIN. I must give you a warning, Mother Courage, it's my duty. You are unlikely ever again to see the gentleman but that's no pity, you're in luck. Mother Courage, he did not impress me as trustworthy. On the contrary.

MOTHER COURAGE. Really? He was such a nice man.

CHAPLAIN. Well! So that's what you call a nice man. I do not. [*The ax falls again.*] Far be it from me to wish him ill, but I cannot—cannot—describe him as nice. No, no, he's a Don Juan, a cunning Don Juan. Just look at that pipe if you don't believe me. You must admit it tells everything about him.

MOTHER COURAGE. I see nothing special in it. It's been, um, used.

CHAPLAIN. It's bitten half-way through! He's a man of great violence! It is the pipe of a man of great violence, you can see *that* if you've any judgment left! [*He deals the block a tremendous blow.*]

MOTHER COURAGE. Don't bite my chopping block halfway through!

CHAPLAIN. I told you I had no training as a woodcutter. The care of souls was my field. Around here my gifts and capabilities are grossly misused. In physical labor my god-given talents find no—um—adequate expression—which is a sin. You haven't heard me preach. Why, I can put such spirit into a regiment with a single sermon that the enemy's a mere flock of sheep to them and their own lives no more than smelly old shoes to be thrown away at the thought of final victory! God has given me the gift of tongues. I can preach you out of your senses!

MOTHER COURAGE. I need my senses, what would I do without them?

CHAPLAIN. Mother Courage, I have often thought that—under a veil of plain speech—you conceal a heart. You are human, you need . . . warmth.

MOTHER COURAGE. The best way of warming this tent is to chop plenty of firewood.

CHAPLAIN. You're changing the subject. Seriously, my dear Courage, I sometimes ask myself how it would be if our relationship should be somewhat more firmly . . . cemented. I mean, now the wind of war has whirled us so strangely together.

MOTHER COURAGE. The cement's pretty firm already. I cook your meals. And you lend a hand—at chopping firewood, for instance.

CHAPLAIN [*going over to her, gesturing with the ax*]. You know what I mean by a close relationship. It has nothing to do with heating and woodcutting and such base necessities. Let your heart speak!

MOTHER COURAGE. Don't come at me like that with your ax, that'd be *too* close a relationship!

CHAPLAIN. This is no laughing matter, I am in earnest. I've thought it all over.

MOTHER COURAGE. Dear Chaplain, be a sensible fellow. I like you, and I don't want to heap coals of fire on your head. All I'm after is to bring me and my children through in that wagon. Now chop the firewood and we'll be warm of an evening, which is quite a lot these days. What's that?

[*She stands up.* CATHERINE *enters breathless with a nasty wound above her eye and brow. She is letting everything fall, parcels, leather goods, a drum, etc.*]

Catherine, what is it? Were you attacked? On the way back? It's not serious, only a flesh wound, I'll bandage it up for you, and you'll be better within the week. Didn't the clerk walk you back? That's because you're a good girl, he thought they'd leave you alone. The wound really isn't deep, it won't show, though I wouldn't mind if it did. The pretty girls have a bad time, they get dragged around till they're finished off, and the other ones get left alone. I've seen so many with pretty faces and they looked like something that would scare a wolf in no time. They can't go behind a tree without getting scared. They lead a horrible life. It's like with the trees: the straight and tall ones are cut down for roof timber while the crooked ones are left to enjoy life. That's it, now it's all bandaged. Now I've got something for you, I've been keeping it, just watch. [*She digs* YVETTE POTTIER's *red boots out of a bag.*] You see? You always wanted 'em and now you have 'em. Put them on before I think twice about it. [*She helps her.*] It won't show at all! The boots have kept well, I cleaned them good before I put them away.

[CATHERINE *leaves the shoes and creeps into the wagon.*]

CHAPLAIN [*when she's gone*]. I hope she won't be disfigured?

MOTHER COURAGE. There'll be a scar. She needn't wait for peace now.

CHAPLAIN. She didn't let them get any of the stuff from her.

MOTHER COURAGE. Maybe I shouldn't have been so strict with her. If only I ever knew what went on inside her head. One time she stayed out all night, once in all the years. I could never get out of her what happened, I racked my brains for quite a while. [*She picks up the things* CATHERINE *spilled and sorts them angrily.*] This is war. A nice source of income to have!

[*Cannon shots.*]

CHAPLAIN. Now they're lowering the Commander in his grave! A historic moment.

MOTHER COURAGE. It's a historic moment to me when they hit my daughter over the eye. She's all but finished now, she'll get no husband, and she's so crazy for children! Even her dumbness comes from the war. A soldier stuck something in her mouth when she was little. I'll not see Swiss Cheese again, and where my Eilif is the Good Lord knows. Curse the war!

Scene Seven

A *highway. The* CHAPLAIN *and* CATHERINE *are pulling the wagon. It is dirty and neglected, though there are new goods hung round it.*

MOTHER COURAGE [*walking beside the wagon and drinking heavily from a flask at her waist*]. I won't have my war all spoiled for me! It destroys the weak, does it? Well, what does peace do for 'em? Huh? [*She sings her song.*]

> So cheer up, boys, the rose is fading
> When victory comes you may be dead
> A war is just the same as trading
> But not with cheese—with steel and lead!

> Christians, awake! The winter's gone!
> The snows depart, the dead sleep on.
> And though you may not long survive
> Get out of bed and look alive!

[*And the wagon moves on.*]

Scene Eight

1632. IN THIS SAME YEAR GUSTAVUS ADOLPHUS[6] FELL IN THE BATTLE OF LÜTZEN. THE PEACE THREATENS MOTHER COURAGE WITH RUIN. HER BRAVE SON PERFORMS ONE HEROIC DEED TOO MANY AND COMES TO A SHAMEFUL END.

A camp. A summer morning. In front of the wagon, an old woman and her son. The son is dragging a large bag of bedding.

MOTHER COURAGE [*from inside the wagon*]. Must you come at the crack of dawn?

YOUNG MAN. We've been walking all night, twenty miles it was, we have to be back today.

MOTHER COURAGE [*still inside*]. What do I want with bed feathers? Take 'em to the town!

YOUNG MAN. At least wait till you see 'em.

OLD WOMAN. Nothing doing here either, let's go.

YOUNG MAN. And let 'em sign away the roof over our heads for taxes? Maybe she'll pay three gilders if you throw in that bracelet.

    [*Bells start ringing.*]

    You hear, Mother?

VOICES [*from the rear*]. It's peace! The King of Sweden's killed!

MOTHER COURAGE [*sticking her head out of the wagon. She hasn't done her hair yet*]. Bells! What are the bells for, middle of the week?

CHAPLAIN [*crawling out from under the wagon*]. What's that they're shouting?

YOUNG MAN. It's peace.

CHAPLAIN. Peace!?

MOTHER COURAGE. Don't tell me peace has broken out—when I've just gone and bought all these supplies!

CHAPLAIN [*calling, toward the rear*]. Is it peace?

VOICE [*from a distance*]. Yes, the war stopped three weeks ago!

CHAPLAIN [*to MOTHER COURAGE*]. Or why would they ring the bells?

VOICE. A great crowd of Lutherans have just arrived with wagons—they brought the news.

6. The hero-king leader of the Swedes (1594–1632).

YOUNG MAN. It's peace, Mother.

　　[*The* OLD WOMAN *collapses.*]

What's the matter?

MOTHER COURAGE [*back in the wagon*]. Catherine, it's peace! Put on your black dress, we're going to church, we owe it to Swiss Cheese!

YOUNG MAN. The people here say so too, the war's over.

　　[*The* OLD WOMAN *stands up, dazed.*]

I'll get the harness shop going again now, I promise you. Everything'll be all right, father will get his bed back. . . . Can you walk? [*To the* CHAPLAIN.] She felt sick, it was the news. She didn't believe there'd ever be peace again. Father always said there would. We're going home.

　　[*They leave.*]

MOTHER COURAGE [*off*]. Give her a schnapps!

CHAPLAIN. They've left already.

MOTHER COURAGE [*still off*]. What's going on in the camp over there?

CHAPLAIN. They're all getting together, I think I'll go over. Shall I put my pastor's clothes on again?

MOTHER COURAGE. Better get the exact news first, and not risk being taken for the antichrist. I'm glad about the peace even though I'm ruined. At least I've got two of my children through the war. Now I'll see my Eilif again.

CHAPLAIN. And who may this be coming down from the camp? Well, if it isn't our Swedish Commander's cook!

COOK [*somewhat bedraggled, carrying a bundle*]. Who's here? The Chaplain!

CHAPLAIN. Mother Courage, a visitor!

　　[MOTHER COURAGE *clambers out.*]

COOK. Well, I promised I'd come over for a brief conversation as soon as I had time. I didn't forget your brandy, Mrs. Fierling.

MOTHER COURAGE. Mr. Lamp, the Commander's cook! After all these years! Where is Eilif?

COOK. Isn't he here yet? He went on ahead yesterday, he was on his way over.

CHAPLAIN. I *will* put my pastor's clothes on. [*He goes behind the wagon.*]

MOTHER COURAGE. He may be here any minute then. [*Calls toward the wagon*] Catherine, Eilif's coming! Bring a glass of brandy for the Cook, Catherine!

　　[CATHERINE *doesn't come.*]

Pull your hair over it and have done, the Cook's no stranger. She won't come out. Peace is nothing to her, it was too long coming. Well, one more schnapps!

COOK. Dear old peace!

　　[*He and* MOTHER COURAGE *sit.*]

MOTHER COURAGE. Cook, you come at a bad time: I'm ruined.

COOK. What? That's terrible!

MOTHER COURAGE. The peace has broken my neck. On the Chaplain's advice I've gone and bought a lot of supplies. Now everybody's leaving and I'm holding the bag.

COOK. How ever could you listen to the Chaplain? If I'd had time—but the Catholics were too quick—I'd have warned you against him. He's a windbag. Well, so now he's the big wheel round here!

MOTHER COURAGE. He's been doing the dishes for me and helping with the wagon.

COOK. I'll bet he has. And I'll bet he's told you a few of his jokes. He has a most unhealthy attitude to women. I tried to influence him but it was no good. He isn't sound.

MOTHER COURAGE. Are you sound?

COOK. If I'm nothing else, I'm sound. Your health!

MOTHER COURAGE. Sound! Only one person around here was ever sound, and I never had to slave as I did then. He sold the blankets off the children's beds in autumn. You aren't recommending yourself if you *admit* you're sound.

COOK. You fight tooth and nail, don't you? I like that.

MOTHER COURAGE. Don't tell me you dream of my teeth and nails.

COOK. Well, here we sit, while the bells of peace do ring, and you pour your famous brandy as only you know how.

MOTHER COURAGE. I don't think much of the bells of peace at the moment. I don't see how they can hand out all this pay that's in arrears. And then where shall I be with my famous brandy? Have you all been paid?

COOK [*hesitating*]. Not exactly. That's why we disbanded. In the circumstances, I thought, why stay? For the time being, I'll look up a couple of friends. So here I am.

MOTHER COURAGE. In other words, you're broke.

COOK [*annoyed by the bells*]. It's about time they stopped that racket! I'd like to set myself up in some business. I'm fed up with being their cook. I'm supposed to make do with tree roots and shoe leather, and then they throw the soup in my face. Being a cook nowadays is a dog's life. I'd sooner do war service, but of course it's peace now. We'll discuss it later.

MOTHER COURAGE. Oh, Cook, it's a dog's life.

COOK [*as the* CHAPLAIN *turns up, wearing his old costume*]. We'll discuss it.

CHAPLAIN. The coat's pretty good. Just a few moth holes.

COOK. I don't know why you take the trouble. You won't find another job. Who could you incite now to earn an honorable wage or risk his life for a cause? Besides I have a bone to pick with you.

CHAPLAIN. Have you?

COOK. I have. You advised a lady to buy superfluous goods on the pretext that the war would never end.

CHAPLAIN [*hotly*]. I'd like to know what business it is of yours?

COOK. It's unprincipled behavior! How can you give unwanted advice? And interfere with the conduct of other people's businesses?

CHAPLAIN. Who's interfering now, I'd like to know? [*Haughtily to* MOTHER COURAGE.] I had no idea you were such a close friend of this gentleman and had to account to *him* for everything.

MOTHER COURAGE. Now don't get excited. The Cook's giving his personal opinion. You can't deny your war was a lemon.

CHAPLAIN. You mustn't take the name of peace in vain. Remember, you're a hyena of the battlefield!

MOTHER COURAGE. A what!?

COOK. If you insult my girl friend, you'll have to reckon with me!

CHAPLAIN. I am *not* speaking to you, your intentions are only too transparent! [*To* MOTHER COURAGE.] But when I see *you* take peace between finger and thumb like a snotty old hanky, my humanity rebels! It shows that you want war, not peace, for what you get out of it. But don't forget the proverb: he who sups with the devil must use a long spoon!

MOTHER COURAGE. Remember what one fox said to another that was caught in a trap? "If you stay there, you're just asking for trouble!" There isn't much love lost between me and the war. And when it comes to calling me a hyena, you and I part company.

CHAPLAIN. Then why all this grumbling about the peace just as everyone's heaving a sigh of relief? Is it just for the junk in your wagon?

MOTHER COURAGE. My goods are not junk. I live off them.

CHAPLAIN. You live off war. Exactly.

COOK [*to the* CHAPLAIN]. As a grown man, you should know better than to go around advising people. [*To* MOTHER COURAGE.] Now, in your situation you'd be smart to get rid of certain goods at once—before the prices sink to zero. Get ready and get going, there isn't a moment to lose!

MOTHER COURAGE. That's sensible advice, I think I'll take it.

CHAPLAIN. Because the Cook says so.

MOTHER COURAGE. Why didn't *you* say so? He's right, I must get to the market. [*She climbs into the wagon.*]

COOK. One up for me, Chaplain. You have no presence of mind. You should have said, "*I* gave you advice? Why, I was just talking politics!" And you shouldn't take me on as a rival. Cockfights are not becoming to your cloth.

CHAPLAIN. If you don't shut your trap, I'll murder you, whether it's becoming or not!

COOK [*taking his boots off and unwinding the wrappings on his feet*]. If you hadn't degenerated into a godless tramp, you could easily be quite a success these days. Cooks won't be needed, there's nothing to cook, but there's plenty to believe, and people'll go right on believing it.

CHAPLAIN [*changing his tone*]. Cook, please don't drive me out! Since I became a tramp, I'm a somewhat better man. I couldn't preach to 'em any more. So where should I go?

[YVETTE POTTIER *enters, decked out in black, with a stick. She is much older, fatter, and heavily powdered. Behind her, a servant.*]

YVETTE. Hullo, everybody! Is this Mother Courage's establishment?

CHAPLAIN. Quite right. And with whom have we the pleasure?

YVETTE. I am Madame Colonel Starhemberg, good people. Where's Mother Courage?

CHAPLAIN [*calling to the wagon*]. Madame Colonel Starhemberg wants to speak with you!

MOTHER COURAGE [*from inside*]. Coming!

YVETTE [*calling*]. It's Yvette!

MOTHER COURAGE [*inside*]. Yvette!

YVETTE. Just to see how you're getting on!

[*As the* COOK *turns round in horror.*]

Peter!

COOK. Yvette!

YVETTE. Of all things! How did *you* get here?

COOK. On a cart.

CHAPLAIN. Well! You know each other? Intimately?

YVETTE. I'll say! [*Scrutinizing the* COOK.] You're fat.

COOK. For that matter, *you're* no beanpole.

YVETTE. Anyway, nice meeting you, tramp. Now I can tell you what I think of you.

CHAPLAIN. Do that, tell him all, but wait till Mother Courage comes out.

COOK. Now don't make a scene . . .

MOTHER COURAGE [*comes out, laden with goods*]. Yvette!

[*They embrace.*]

But why are you in mourning?

YVETTE. Doesn't it suit me? My husband, the colonel, died several years ago.

MOTHER COURAGE. The old fellow that nearly bought my wagon?

YVETTE. Naw, not him—his older brother!

MOTHER COURAGE. Good to see one person who got somewhere in the war.

YVETTE. I've had my ups and downs.

MOTHER COURAGE. Don't let's talk badly of Colonels. They make money like hay.

CHAPLAIN. If I were you, I'd put my shoes on again. You promised to give us your opinion of this gentleman.

COOK. Now, Yvette, don't make a stink!

MOTHER COURAGE. He's a friend of mine, Yvette.

YVETTE. He's—Peter Piper, that's what!

MOTHER COURAGE. What!?

COOK. Cut the nicknames. My name's Lamp.

MOTHER COURAGE [*laughing*]. Peter Piper? Who turned the women's heads? I'll have to sit down. And I've been keeping your pipe for you.

CHAPLAIN. And smoking it.

YVETTE. Lucky I can warn you against him. He's a bad lot. You won't find a worse on the whole coast of Flanders. He got more girls in trouble than . . .

COOK. That's a long time ago, it isn't true any more.

YVETTE. Stand up when you talk to a lady! Oh, how I loved that man! And all the time he was having a little bowlegged brunette. He got *her* in trouble too, of course.

COOK. I seem to have brought *you* luck!

YVETTE. Shut your trap, you hoary ruin! And you take care, Mother Courage, this type is still dangerous even in decay!

MOTHER COURAGE [*to* YVETTE]. Come with me, I must get rid of this stuff before the prices fall.

YVETTE [*concentrating on* COOK]. Miserable cur!

MOTHER COURAGE. Maybe you can help me at army headquarters, you have contacts.

YVETTE. Damnable whore hunter!

MOTHER COURAGE [*shouting into the wagon*]. Catherine, church is all off, I'm going to market!

YVETTE. Inveterate seducer!

MOTHER COURAGE [*still to* CATHERINE]. When Eilif comes, give him something to drink!

YVETTE. I've put an end to your tricks, Peter Piper, and one day—in a better life than this—the Lord God will reward me! [*She sniffs.*] Come, Mother Courage!

[*Leaves with* MOTHER COURAGE. *Pause.*]

CHAPLAIN. As our text this morning let us take the saying, the mills of God grind slowly. And you complain of my jokes!

COOK. I have no luck. I'll be frank, I was hoping for a good hot dinner, I'm starving. And now they'll be talking about me, and she'll get a completely wrong picture. I think I should go before she comes back.

CHAPLAIN. I think so too.

COOK. Chaplain, the peace makes me sick. Mankind must perish by fire and sword, we're born and bred in sin! Oh, how I wish I was roasting a great fat capon for the Commander—God knows where *he's* got to—with mustard sauce and those little yellow carrots. . . .

CHAPLAIN. Red cabbage—with capon, red cabbage.

COOK. You're right. But he always wanted yellow carrots.

CHAPLAIN. He never understood a thing.

COOK. You always put plenty away.

CHAPLAIN. Under protest.

COOK. Anyway, you must admit, those were the days.

CHAPLAIN. Yes, that I might admit.

COOK. Now you've called her a hyena, there's not much future for you here either. What are you staring at?

CHAPLAIN. It's Eilif!

[*Followed by two soldiers with halberds,* EILIF *enters. His hands are fettered. He is white as chalk.*]

What's happened to you?

EILIF. Where's Mother?

CHAPLAIN. Gone to town.

EILIF. They said she was here. I was allowed a last visit.

COOK [*to the soldiers*]. Where are you taking him?

SOLDIER. For a ride.

[*The other soldier makes the gesture of throat cutting.*]

CHAPLAIN. What has he done?

SOLDIER. He broke in on a peasant. The wife is dead.

CHAPLAIN. Eilif, how could you?

EILIF. It's no different. It's what I did before.

COOK. That was in wartime.

EILIF. Shut your hole. Can I sit down till she comes?

SOLDIER. No.

CHAPLAIN. It's true. In wartime they honored him for it. He sat at the Commander's right hand. It was bravery. Couldn't we speak with the provost?

SOLDIER. What's the use? Stealing cattle from a peasant, what's brave about that?

COOK. It was just dumb.

EILIF. If I'd been dumb, I'd have starved, smarty.

COOK. So you were bright and paid for it.

CHAPLAIN. At least we must bring Catherine out.

EILIF. Let her alone. Just give me some brandy.

SOLDIER. No.

CHAPLAIN. What shall we tell your mother?

EILIF. Tell her it was no different. Tell her it was the same. Aw, tell her nothing.

[*The soldiers take him away.*]

CHAPLAIN. I'll come with you, I'll . . .

EILIF. I don't need a priest!

CHAPLAIN. You don't know—yet. [*Follows him.*]

COOK [*calling after him*]. I'll have to tell her, she'll want to see him!

CHAPLAIN. Better tell her nothing. Or maybe just that he was here, and he'll return, maybe tomorrow. Meantime I'll be back and can break the news.

[*Leaves quickly. The* COOK *looks after him, shakes his head, then walks uneasily around. Finally, he approaches the wagon.*]

COOK. Hi! Won't you come out? You want to run away from the peace, don't you? Well, so do I! I'm the Swedish Commander's cook, remember me? I was wondering if you got anything to eat in there— while we're waiting for your mother. I wouldn't mind a bit of bacon— or even bread—just to pass the time. [*He looks in.*] She's got a blanket over her head.

[*The thunder of cannon.*]

MOTHER COURAGE [*running, out of breath, still carrying the goods*]. Cook, the peace is over, the war's on again, has been for three days! I didn't get rid of this stuff after all, thank God! There's a shooting match in the town already—with the Lutherans. We must get away with the wagon. Pack, Catherine! What's on *your* mind? Something the matter?

COOK. Nothing.

MOTHER COURAGE. But there is, I see it in your face.

COOK. Eilif was here. Only he had to go away again.

MOTHER COURAGE. He was here? Then we'll see him on the march. I'll be with our side this time. How'd he look?

COOK. The same.

MOTHER COURAGE. He'll *never* change. And the war couldn't get *him*, he's bright. Help me with the packing. [*She starts it.*] Did he tell you anything? Is he in good with the captain? Did he tell you about his heroic deeds?

COOK [*darkly*]. He's done one of them over again.

MOTHER COURAGE. Tell me about it later.

[CATHERINE *appears.*]

Catherine, the peace is all through, we're on the move again. [*To the* COOK.] What *is* biting you?

COOK. I'll enlist.

MOTHER COURAGE. A good idea. Where's the Chaplain?

COOK. In the town. With Eilif.

MOTHER COURAGE. Stay with us a while, Mr. Lamp, I need a bit of help.

COOK. This Yvette thing . . .

MOTHER COURAGE. Hasn't done you any harm at all in my eyes. Just the opposite. Where there's smoke, there's fire, they say. You'll come?

COOK. I won't say no.

MOTHER COURAGE. The twelfth regiment's under way. Into harness with you! Maybe I'll see Eilif before the day is out, just think! Well, it wasn't such a long peace, we can't grumble. Let's go!

[*They move off.* MOTHER COURAGE *sings.*]

> Up hill, down dale, past dome and steeple,
> My wagon always moves ahead.
> The war can care for all its people
> So long as there is steel and lead.
> Though steel and lead are stout supporters
> A war needs human beings too.
> Report today to your headquarters!
> If it's to last, this war needs you!
> Christians, awake! The winter's gone!
> The snows depart, the dead sleep on.
> And though you may not long survive
> Get out of bed and look alive!

Scene Nine

THE HOLY WAR HAS LASTED SIXTEEN YEARS AND GER-
MANY HAS LOST HALF ITS INHABITANTS. THOSE WHO ARE
SPARED IN BATTLE DIE BY PLAGUE. OVER ONCE BLOOM-
ING COUNTRYSIDE HUNGER RAGES. TOWNS ARE BURNED
DOWN. WOLVES PROWL THE EMPTY STREETS. IN THE AU-
TUMN OF 1634 WE FIND MOTHER COURAGE IN THE
FICHTELGEBIRGE NOT FAR FROM THE ROAD THE SWED-
ISH ARMY IS TAKING. WINTER HAS COME EARLY AND IS
HARD. BUSINESS IS BAD. ONLY BEGGING REMAINS. THE
COOK RECEIVES A LETTER FROM UTRECHT AND IS SENT
PACKING.

*In front of a half-ruined parsonage. Early winter. A gray morning. Gusts
of wind.* MOTHER COURAGE *and the* COOK *at the wagon in shabby clothes.*

COOK. There are no lights on, no one's up.

MOTHER COURAGE. But it's a parsonage. The parson'll have to leave his
feather bed and go ring the bells. Then he'll have himself a hot soup.

COOK. Where'll he get it from? The whole village is starving.

MOTHER COURAGE. The house is lived in. There was a dog barking.

COOK. If the parson has anything, he'll stick to it.

MOTHER COURAGE. Maybe if we sang him something . . .

COOK. I've had enough. Anna, I didn't tell you, a letter came from
Utrecht. My mother died of cholera, the inn is mine. There's the
letter, if you don't believe me.

MOTHER COURAGE [*reading*]. Mr. Lamp, I'm tired of wandering, too. I
feel like a butcher's dog taking meat to my customers and getting
none myself. I've nothing more to sell and people have nothing to
pay for it. In Saxony someone tried to saddle me with a chestful of
books in return for two eggs. And in Württemberg they would have
let me have their plough for a bag of salt. Nothing grows any more,
only thorn bushes. I hear they've even caught nuns committing
robbery.

COOK. The world's dying out.

MOTHER COURAGE. Sometimes I see myself driving through hell with
this wagon and selling brimstone. And sometimes I'm driving through
heaven handing out provisions to wandering souls! If only we could
find a place where there's no shooting, me and my children—what's
left of 'em—we might rest up a while.

COOK. We could open this inn together. Think about it, Courage. My
mind's made up. With or without you, I'm leaving for Utrecht. And
today at that.

MOTHER COURAGE. I must talk to Catherine, it's sudden.

[CATHERINE *emerges from the wagon.*]

Catherine, I've something to tell you. The cook and I want to go to Utrecht, he's been left an inn. We'd be sure of our dinner: nice, hm? And you'd have a bed, what do you think of *that?* This is a dog's life, on the road, you might be killed any time, even now you're covered with lice. . . . I think we'll decide to go, Catherine.

COOK. Anna, I must have a word with you alone.

MOTHER COURAGE. Go back inside, Catherine.

[CATHERINE *does so.*]

COOK. I'm interrupting because there's a misunderstanding, Anna. I thought I wouldn't have to say it right out, but I see I must. If you're bringing *her,* it's all off.

[CATHERINE *has her head out of the back of the wagon and is listening.*]

MOTHER COURAGE. You mean I leave Catherine behind?

COOK. What do you think? There's no room in the inn, it isn't one of those places with three counters. If the two of us stand on our hindlegs we can earn a living, but three's too many. Let Catherine keep your wagon.

MOTHER COURAGE. I was thinking she might find a husband in Utrecht.

COOK. Don't make me laugh. With that scar? And old as she is? And dumb?

MOTHER COURAGE. Not so loud!

COOK. Loud or soft, what is, is. That's another reason I can't have her in the inn, the customers wouldn't like it.

MOTHER COURAGE. Not so loud, I said!

COOK. There's a light in the parsonage, we can sing now!

[*They go over toward the wall.*]

MOTHER COURAGE. How could she pull the wagon by herself? The war frightens her. She has terrible dreams. I hear her groan at night, especially after battles. What she sees in her dreams I don't know. The other day I found a hedgehog with her that we'd run over.

COOK. The inn's too small. [*Calling.*] Worthy Sir, menials, and all within! We now present the song of Solomon, Julius Caesar, and other great souls who came to no good, so you can see we're law-abiding folk too, and have a hard time getting by, especially in winter.

[*He sings:* The Song of the Great Souls of this Earth]

> You've heard of wise old Solomon
>   You know his history.
> He thought so little of this earth
> He cursed the hour of his birth
>   Declaring: all is vanity.
> How very wise was Solomon!
>   But ere night came and day did go
> This fact was clear to everyone:
>   It was his wisdom that had brought him low.
> *Better for you if you have none.*

For the virtues are dangerous in this world, as our fine song tells.
You're better off without, you have a nice life, breakfast included—
a good hot soup maybe. . . . I'm an example of a man who's not had
any, and I'd like some, I'm a soldier, but what good did my bravery
do me in all those battles? None at all. I might just as well have wet
my pants like a coward and stayed home. For why?

> And Julius Caesar, who was brave,
>> You saw what came of him.
> He sat like God on an altar-piece
>> And yet they tore him limb from limb
> While his prestige did still increase!
> "Et tu, Brute, I am undone!"
>> And ere night came and day did go
> This fact was clear to everyone:
>> It was his bravery that brought him low
> *Better for you if have none.*

[*Under his breath.*]
They don't even look out.
[*Aloud.*]
Worthy Sir, menials, and all within! You should say, no, courage
isn't the thing to fill a man's belly, try honesty, that should be worth
a dinner, at any rate it must have *some* effect. Let's see.

> You all know honest Socrates
>> Who always spoke the truth.
> They owed him thanks for that, you'd think,
> Yet they put hemlock in his drink
>> And swore that he was bad for youth.
> How honest was the people's son!
>> But ere night came and day did go
> This fact was clear to everyone:
>> It was his honesty that brought him low.
> *Better for you if you have none.*

Yes, we're told to be unselfish and share what we have but what if
we have nothing? And those who do share it don't have an easy time
either, for what's left when you're through sharing? Unselfishness is
a very rare virtue—it doesn't pay.

> Unselfish Martin[7] could not bear
>> His fellow creature's woes.
>> He met a beggar in the snows
> And gave him half his cloak to wear:
>> So both of them fell down and froze.
> What an unselfish paragon!
>> But ere night came and day did go

7. Saint Martin of Tours (c.316–97). One of the tales told about him is that he gave his cloak to a
beggar on a snowy day.

> This fact was clear to everyone:
> > It was unselfishness that brought him low.
> > *Better for you if you have none.*

That's how it is with us. We're law-abiding folk, we keep to ourselves, don't steal, don't kill, don't burn the place down. And in this way we sink lower and lower and the song proves true and there's no soup going. And if we were different, if we were thieves and killers, maybe we could eat our fill! For virtues bring no reward, only vices. Such is the world, need it be so?

> > God's Ten Commandments we have kept
> > > And acted as we should.
> > > It has not done us any good.
> > O you who sit beside a fire
> > Please help us now: our need is dire!
> > Strict godliness we've always shown
> > > But ere night came and day did go
> > This fact was clear to every one:
> > > It was our godliness that brought us low.
> > *Better for you if you have none.*

VOICE [*from above*]. You there! Come up! There's some soup here for you!

MOTHER COURAGE. Lamp, I couldn't swallow a thing. Was that your last word?

COOK. Yes, Anna. Think it over.

MOTHER COURAGE. There's nothing to think over.

COOK. You're going to be silly, but what can I do? I'm not inhuman, it's just that the inn's a small one. And now we must go up, or it'll be no soup here too, and we've been singing in the cold for nothing.

MOTHER COURAGE. I'll get Catherine.

COOK. Better stick something in your pocket for her. If there are three of us, they won't like it.

[*Exeunt.*]

[CATHERINE *clambers out of the wagon with a bundle. She makes sure they're both gone. Then, on a wagon wheel, she lays out a skirt of her mother's and a pair of the* COOK's *pants side by side and easy to see. She has just finished, and has picked her bundle up, when* MOTHER COURAGE *returns.*]

MOTHER COURAGE [*with a plate of soup*]. Catherine! Stay where you are, Catherine! Where do you think you're going with that bundle? [*She examines the bundle.*] She's packed her things. Were you listening? I told him there was nothing doing, he can *have* Utrecht and his lousy inn, what would *we* want with a lousy inn? [*She sees the skirt and pants.*] Oh, you're a stupid girl, Catherine, what if I'd seen that and you gone?

[*She takes hold of* CATHERINE, *who's trying to leave.*]

And don't think I've sent him packing on your account. It was the wagon. You can't part us, I'm too used to it, *you* didn't come into it, it was the wagon. Now we're leaving, and we'll put the cook's things here where he'll find 'em, the stupid man. [*She clambers up and throws a couple of things down to go with the pants.*] There! He's fired! The last man I'll take into *this* business! Now let's you and me be going. Get into harness. This winter'll pass—like all the others.

[*They harness themselves to the wagon, turn it around, and start out. A gust of wind. Enter the* cook, *still chewing. He sees his things.*]

Scene Ten

On the highway. mother courage *and* catherine *are pulling the wagon. They come to a prosperous farmhouse. Someone inside is singing* The Song of Shelter.

> In March a tree we planted
> To make the garden gay.
> In June we were enchanted:
> A lovely rose was blooming
> The balmy air perfuming!
> Blest of the gods are they
> Who have a garden gay!
> In June we were enchanted.
>
> When snow falls helter-skelter
> And loudly blows the storm
> Our farmhouse gives us shelter.
> The winter's in a hurry
> But we've no cause to worry.
> Cosy are we and warm
> Though loudly blows the storm
> Our farmhouse gives us shelter.

[mother courage *and* catherine *have stopped to listen. Then they start out again.*]

Scene Eleven

JANUARY, 1636. CATHOLIC TROOPS THREATEN THE PROTESTANT TOWN OF HALLE. THE STONES BEGIN TO TALK. MOTHER COURAGE LOSES HER DAUGHTER AND JOURNEYS ONWARD ALONE. THE WAR IS NOT YET NEAR ITS END.

The wagon, very far gone now, stands near a farmhouse with a straw roof. It is night. Out of the wood come a LIEUTENANT *and* THREE SOLDIERS *in full armor.*

LIEUTENANT. And there mustn't be a sound. If anyone yells, cut him down.

FIRST SOLDIER. But we'll have to knock—if we want a guide.

LIEUTENANT. Knocking's a natural noise, it's all right, could be a cow hitting the wall of the cowshed.

[*The* SOLDIERS *knock at the farmhouse door. An old* PEASANT WOMAN *opens. A hand is clapped over her mouth. Two* SOLDIERS *enter.*]

MAN'S VOICE. What is it?

[*The* SOLDIERS *bring out an* OLD PEASANT *and his son.*]

LIEUTENANT [*pointing to the wagon on which* CATHERINE *has appeared*]. There's one.

[*A* SOLDIER *pulls her out.*]

Is this everybody that lives here?

PEASANTS [*alternating*]. That's our son. And that's a girl that can't talk. Her mother's in town buying up stocks because the shopkeepers are running away and selling cheap. They're canteen people.

LIEUTENANT. I'm warning you. Keep quiet. One sound and you'll have a sword in your ribs. And I need someone to show us the path to the town. [*Points to the* YOUNG PEASANT.] You! Come here!

YOUNG PEASANT. I don't know any path!

SECOND SOLDIER [*grinning*]. He don't know any path!

YOUNG PEASANT. I don't help Catholics.

LIEUTENANT [*to* SECOND SOLDIER]. Show him your sword.

YOUNG PEASANT [*forced to his knees, a sword at his throat*]. I'd rather die!

SECOND SOLDIER [*again mimicking*]. He'd rather die!

FIRST SOLDIER. I know how to change his mind. [*Walks over to the cowshed.*] Two cows and a bull. Listen, you. If you aren't going to be reasonable, I'll saber your cattle.

YOUNG PEASANT. Not the cattle!

PEASANT WOMAN [*weeping*]. Spare the cattle, Captain, or we'll starve!

LIEUTENANT. If he must be pigheaded!

FIRST SOLDIER. I think I'll start with the bull.

YOUNG PEASANT [*to the old one*]. Do I have to?

[*The* OLDER ONE *nods.*]

I'll do it.

PEASANT WOMAN. Thank you, thank you, Captain, for sparing us, for ever and ever, Amen.

[*The old man stops her going on thanking him.*]

FIRST SOLDIER. I knew the bull came first all right!

[*Led by the* YOUNG PEASANT, *the* LIEUTENANT *and the* SOLDIERS *go on their way.*]

OLD PEASANT. I wish we knew what it was. Nothing good, I guess.

PEASANT WOMAN. Maybe they're just scouts. What are you doing?

OLD PEASANT [*setting a ladder against the roof and climbing up*]. I'm seeing if they're alone. [*On the roof.*] Things are moving—all over. I can see armor. And a cannon. There must be more than a regiment. God have mercy on the town and all within!

PEASANT WOMAN. Are there lights in the town?

OLD PEASANT. No, they're all asleep. [*He climbs down.*] There'll be an attack, and they'll all be slaughtered in their beds.

PEASANT WOMAN. The watchman'll give warning.

OLD PEASANT. They must have killed the watchman in the tower on the hill or he'd have sounded his horn before this.

PEASANT WOMAN. If there were more of us . . .

OLD PEASANT. But being that we're alone with that cripple . . .

PEASANT WOMAN. There's nothing we can do, is there?

OLD PEASANT. Nothing.

PEASANT WOMAN. We can't get down there. In the dark.

OLD PEASANT. The whole hillside's swarming with 'em.

PEASANT WOMAN. We could give a sign?

OLD PEASANT. And be cut down for it?

PEASANT WOMAN. No, there's nothing we can do. [*To* CATHERINE.] Pray, poor thing, pray! There's nothing we can do to stop this bloodshed, so even if you can't talk, at least pray! He hears, if no one else does. I'll help you. [ALL *kneel,* CATHERINE *behind.*] Our Father, which art in Heaven, hear our prayer, let not the town perish with all that lie therein asleep and fearing nothing. Wake them, that they rise and go to the walls and see the foe that comes with fire and sword in the night down the hill and across the fields. God protect our mother and make the watchman not sleep but wake ere it's too late. And save our son-in-law too, O god, he's there with his four children, let them not perish, they're innocent, they know nothing, one of them's not two years old, the eldest is seven.

   [CATHERINE *rises, troubled.*]

Heavenly Father, hear us, only Thou canst help us or we die, for we are weak and have no sword nor nothing; we cannot trust our own strength but only Thine, O Lord; we are in Thy hands, our cattle, our farm, and the town too, we're all in Thy hands, and the foe is nigh unto the walls with all his power.

   [CATHERINE *unperceived, has crept off to the wagon, has taken something out of it, put it under her skirt, and has climbed up the ladder to the roof.*]

Be mindful of the children in danger, especially the little ones, be mindful of the old folk who cannot move, and of all Christian souls, O Lord.

OLD PEASANT. And forgive us our trespasses as we forgive them that trespass against us. Amen.

   [*Sitting on the roof,* CATHERINE *takes a drum from under her skirt, and starts to beat it.*]

PEASANT WOMAN. Heavens, what's she doing?

OLD PEASANT. She's out of her mind!

PEASANT WOMAN. Bring her down, quick!

[*The* OLD PEASANT *runs to the ladder but* CATHERINE *pulls it up on the roof.*]

She'll get us in trouble.

OLD PEASANT. Stop it this minute, you silly cripple!

PEASANT WOMAN. The soldiers'll come!

OLD PEASANT [*looking for stones*]. I'll stone you!

PEASANT WOMAN. Have you no pity, don't you have a heart? We have relations there too, four grandchildren, but there's nothing we can do. If they find us now, it's the end, they'll stab us to death!

[CATHERINE *is staring into the far distance, toward the town. She goes on drumming.*]

PEASANT WOMAN [*to the* PEASANT]. I told you not to let that riffraff in your farm. What do *they* care if we lose our cattle?

LIEUTENANT [*running back with* SOLDIERS *and* YOUNG PEASANT]. I'll cut you all to bits!

PEASANT WOMAN. We're innocent, sir, there's nothing we can do. She did it, a stranger!

LIEUTENANT. Where's the ladder?

OLD PEASANT. On the roof.

LIEUTENANT [*calling*]. Throw down the drum. I order you! [*To* PEASANTS.] You're all in this, but you won't live to tell the tale.

OLD PEASANT. They've been cutting down fir trees around here. If we bring a tall enough trunk we can knock her off the roof. . . .

FIRST SOLDIER [*to the* LIEUTENANT]. I beg leave to make a suggestion. [*He whispers something to the* LIEUTENANT, *who nods. To* CATHERINE.] Listen, you! We have an idea—for your own good. Come down and go with us to the town. Show us your mother and we'll spare her.

[CATHERINE *replies with more drumming.*]

LIEUTENANT [*pushing him away*]. She doesn't trust you, no wonder with your face. [*He calls up to* CATHERINE.] Hey, you! Suppose I give you my word? I'm an officer, my word's my bond!

[CATHERINE *again replies with drumming—harder this time.*]

Nothing is sacred to her.

FIRST SOLDIER. This can't go on, they'll sure as hell hear it in the town.

LIEUTENANT. We must make another noise with something. Louder than that drum. What can we make a nose with?

FIRST SOLDIER. But we mustn't make a noise!

LIEUTENANT. A harmless noise, fool, a peacetime noise!

OLD PEASANT. I could start chopping wood.

LIEUTENANT. That's it!

[*The* PEASANT *brings his ax and chops away.*]

Chop! Chop harder! Chop for your life! It's not enough. [*To* FIRST SOLDIER.] You chop too!

OLD PEASANT. I've only one ax.

LIEUTENANT. We must set fire to the farm. Smoke her out.

OLD PEASANT. That's no good, Captain, when they see fire from the town, they'll know everything.

[CATHERINE *is laughing now and drumming harder than ever.*]

LIEUTENANT. She's laughing at us, that's too much, I'll have her guts if it's the last thing I do. Bring a musket!

[*Two* SOLDIERS *off.*]

PEASANT WOMAN. I have it, Captain. That's their wagon over there, Captain. If we smash that, she'll stop. It's all they have, Captain.

LIEUTENANT [*to the* YOUNG PEASANT]. Smash it! [*Calling*] If you don't stop that noise, we'll smash up your wagon!

[*The* YOUNG PEASANT *deals the wagon a couple of feeble blows with a board.*]

PEASANT WOMAN [*to* CATHERINE]. Stop, you little beast!

[CATHERINE *stares at the wagon and pauses. Noises of distress come out of her. She goes on drumming.*]

LIEUTENANT. Where are those sonsofbitches with that gun?

FIRST SOLDIER. They can't have heard anything in the town or we'd hear their cannon.

LIEUTENANT [*calling*]. They don't hear you. And now we're going to shoot you. I'll give you one more chance: throw down that drum!

YOUNG PEASANT [*dropping the board, screaming to* CATHERINE]. Don't stop now! Go on, go on, go on . . .

[*The* SOLDIER *knocks him down and stabs him.* CATHERINE *starts crying but goes on drumming.*]

PEASANT WOMAN. Not in the back, you're killing him!

[*The* SOLDIERS *arrive with the musket.*]

LIEUTENANT. Set it up! [*Calling while the musket is set up on forks.*] Once for all: stop that drumming!

[*Still crying,* CATHERINE *is drumming as hard as she can.*]

Fire!

[*The soldiers fire.* CATHERINE *is hit. She gives the drum another feeble beat or two, then collapses.*]

LIEUTENANT. That's an end to the noise.

[*But the last beats of the drum are lost in the din of cannon from the town. Mingled with the thunder of cannon, alarm-bells are heard in the distance.*]

FIRST SOLDIER. She made it.

Scene Twelve

Toward morning. The drums and pipes of troops on the march, receding. In front of the wagon MOTHER COURAGE *sits by* CATHERINE's *body. The peasants of the last scene are standing near.*

PEASANTS [*one sentence apiece*]. You must leave. There's only one regiment to go. You can never get away by yourself.
MOTHER COURAGE. Maybe she's asleep. [*She sings.*]

> Lullay, lullay, what's that in the hay?
> The neighbor's kids cry but mine are gay.
> The neighbor's kids are dressed in dirt:
> Your silks were cut from an angel's skirt.
> They are all starving: you have a cake;
> If it's too stale, you need but speak.
> Lullay, lullay, what's rustling there?
> One lad fell in Poland. The other is where?

You shouldn't have told her about the children.
PEASANTS. If you hadn't gone off to the town to get your cut, maybe it
   wouldn't have happened.
MOTHER COURAGE. I'm glad she can sleep.
PEASANTS [*one sentence apiece*]. She's not asleep, it's time you realized.
   She's through. You must get away. There are wolves in these parts.
   And the bandits are worse.
MOTHER COURAGE [*standing up*]. That's right.
PEASANTS. Have you no one now?
MOTHER COURAGE. Yes. My son Eilif.
PEASANTS. Find him then. Leave *her* to us. We'll give her a proper
   burial. You needn't worry.
MOTHER COURAGE. Here's a little money for the expenses. [*Harnessing
   herself to the wagon.*] I hope I can pull the wagon by myself. Yes, I'll
   manage, there's not much in it now.
   [*Another regiment passes with pipe and drum.*]
MOTHER COURAGE. Hey! Take me with you!!
   [*She starts pulling the wagon. Soldiers are heard singing.*]

> Dangers, surprises, devastations—
>   The war takes hold and will not quit.
> But though it last three generations
>   We shall get nothing out of it.
> Starvation, filth, and cold enslave us.
>   The army robs us of our pay.
> Only a miracle can save us
>   And miracles have had their day.
>   Christians, awake! The winter's gone!
>   The snows depart. The dead sleep on.
>   And though you may not long survive
>   Get out of bed and look alive!

SAMUEL BECKETT

Happy Days†

Act One

*Expanse of scorched grass rising centre to low mound. Gentle slopes down
to front and either side of stage. Back an abrupter fall to stage level.
Maximum of simplicity and symmetry.*

Blazing light.

*Very pompier trompe-l'oeil[1] backcloth to represent unbroken plain and
sky receding to meet in far distance.*

Imbedded up to above her waist in exact centre of mound, WINNIE.
*About fifty, well preserved, blond for preference, plump, arms and shoul-
ders bare, low bodice, big bosom, pearl necklet. She is discovered sleeping,
her arms on the ground before her, her head on her arms. Beside her on
ground to her left a capacious black bag, shopping variety, and to her
right a collapsible collapsed parasol, beak of handle emerging from
sheath.*

To her right and rear, lying asleep on ground, hidden by mound,
WILLIE.

*Long pause. A bell rings piercingly, say ten seconds, stops. She does
not move. Pause. Bell more piercingly, say five seconds. She wakes. Bell
stops. She raises her head, gazes front. Long pause. She straightens up,
lays her hands flat on ground, throws back her head and gazes at zenith.
Long pause.*

WINNIE [*gazing at zenith*]. Another heavenly day. [*Pause. Head back
level, eyes front, pause. She clasps hands to breast, closes eyes. Lips
move in inaudible prayer, say ten seconds. Lips still. Hands remain
clasped. Low.*] For Jesus Christ sake Amen. [*Eyes open, hands unclasp,
return to mound. Pause. She clasps hands to breast again, closes eyes,
lips move again in inaudible addendum, say five seconds. Low.*] World
without end Amen. [*Eyes open, hands unclasp, return to mound.*

† Reprinted by permission of Grove Weidenfeld,
a division of Wheatland Corporation. Copyright
© 1961 by Grove Press, Inc.; renewed © 1989 by
Samuel Beckett.
1. A routine, unexceptional treatment of the "unbroken plain and sky," to give the illusion of depth.

Pause.] Begin, Winnie. [*Pause.*] Begin your day, Winnie. [*Pause. She turns to bag, rummages in it without moving it from its place, brings out toothbrush, rummages again, brings out flat tube of tooth-paste, turns back front, unscrews cap of tube, lays cap on ground, squeezes with difficulty small blob of paste on brush, holds tube in one hand and brushes teeth with other. She turns modestly aside and back to her right to spit out behind mound. In this position her eyes rest on* WILLIE. *She spits out. She cranes a little further back and down. Loud.*] Hoo-oo! [*Pause. Louder.*] Hoo-oo! [*Pause. Tender smile as she turns back front, lays down brush.*] Poor Willie—[*examines tube, smile off*]—running out—[*looks for cap*]—ah well—[*finds cap*]—can't be helped—[*screws on cap*]—just one of those old things—[*lays down tube*]—another of those old things—[*turns towards bag*]—just can't be cured—[*rummages in bag*]—cannot be cured—[*brings out small mirror, turns back front*]—ah yes—[*inspects teeth in mirror*]—poor dear Willie—[*testing upper front teeth with thumb, indistinctly*]—good Lord!—[*pulling back upper lip to inspect gums, do.*]—good God!—[*pulling back corner of mouth, mouth open, do.*]—ah well—[*other corner, do.*]—no worse—[*abandons inspection, normal speech*]—no better, no worse—[*lays down mirror*]—no change—[*wipes fingers on grass*]—no pain—[*looks for toothbrush*]—hardly any—[*takes up toothbrush*]—great thing that—[*examines handle of brush*]—noth-ing like it—[*examines handle, reads*]—pure . . . what?—[*pause*]—what?—[*lays down brush*]—ah yes—[*turns toward bag*]—poor Wil-lie—[*rummages in bag*]—no zest—[*rummages*]—for anything—[*brings out spectacles in case*]—no interest—[*turns back front*]—in life—[*takes spectacles from case*]—poor dear Willie—[*lays down case*]—sleep for ever—[*opens spectacles*]—marvellous gift—[*puts on spectacles*]—nothing to touch it—[*looks for toothbrush*]—in my opin-ion—[*takes up toothbrush*]—always said so—[*examines handle of brush*]—wish I had it—[*examines handle, reads*]—genuine . . . pure . . . what?—[*lays down brush*]—blind next—[*takes off spectacles*]—ah well—[*lays down spectacles*]—seen enough—[*feels in bodice for handkerchief*]—I suppose—[*takes out folded handkerchief*]—by now—[*shakes out handkerchief*]—what are those wonderful lines—[*wipes one eye*]—woe woe is me—[*wipes the other*]—to see what I see—[2][*looks for spectacles*]—ah yes—[*takes up spectacles*]—wouldn't miss it—[*starts polishing spectacles, breathing on lenses*]—or would

---

2. The lines are Ophelia's as she witnesses what she understands to be Hamlet's madness (3.1.158ff.):

O, what a noble mind is here o'erthrown!
The courtier's, scholar's, soldier's eye, tongue, sword,

Th'expectancy and rose of the fair state,
The glass of fashion and the mould of form,
Th'observed of all observers—quite, quite down!
* * * O woe is me
T'have seen what I have seen, see what I see!

I?—[*polishes*]—holy light[3]—[*polishes*]—bob up out of dark—[*polishes*]—blaze of hellish light. [*Stops polishing, raises face to sky, pause, head back level, resumes polishing, stops polishing, cranes back to her right and down.*] Hoo-oo! [*Pause. Tender smile as she turns back front and resumes polishing. Smile off.*] Marvellous gift—[*stops polishing, lays down spectacles*]—wish I had it—[*folds handkerchief*]—ah well—[*puts handkerchief back in bodice*]—can't complain—[*looks for spectacles*]—no no—[*takes up spectacles*]—mustn't complain—[*holds up spectacles, looks through lens*]—so much to be thankful for—[*looks through other lens*]—no pain—[*puts on spectacles*]—hardly any—[*looks for toothbrush*]—wonderful thing that—[*takes up toothbrush*]—nothing like it]—[*examines handle of brush*]—slight headache sometimes—[*examines handle, reads*]—guaranteed . . . genuine . . . pure . . . what?—[*looks closer*]—genuine pure . . . —[*takes handkerchief from bodice*]—ah yes—[*shakes out handkerchief*]—occasional mild migraine—[*starts wiping handle of brush*]—it comes—[*wipes*]—then goes—[*wiping mechanically*]—ah yes—[*wiping*]—many mercies—[*wiping*]—great mercies—[*stops wiping, fixed lost gaze, brokenly*]—prayers perhaps not for naught—[*pause, do.*]—first thing—[*pause, do.*]—last thing—[*head down, resumes wiping, stops wiping, head up, calmed, wipes eyes, folds handkerchief, puts it back in bodice, examines handle of brush, reads*]—fully guaranteed . . . genuine pure . . . — [*looks closer*]—genuine pure . . . [*Takes off spectacles, lays them and brush down, gazes before her.*] Old things. [*Pause.*] Old eyes. [*Long pause.*] On, Winnie. [*She casts about her, sees parasol, considers it at length, takes it up and develops from sheath a handle of surprising length. Holding butt of parasol in right hand she cranes back and down to her right to hang over* WILLIE.] Hoo-oo! [*Pause.*] Willie! [*Pause.*] Wonderful gift. [*She strikes down at him with beak of parasol.*] Wish I had it. [*She strikes again. The parasol slips from her grasp and falls behind mound. It is immediately restored to her by* WILLIE'S *invisible hand.*] Thank you, dear. [*She transfers parasol to left hand, turns back front and examines right palm.*] Damp. [*Returns parasol to right hand, examines left palm.*] Ah well, no worse. [*Head up, cheerfully.*] No better, no worse, no change. [*Pause. Do.*] No pain. [*Cranes back to look down at* WILLIE, *holding parasol by butt as before.*] Don't go off on me again now dear will you please, I may need you.[*Pause.*] No hurry, no hurry, just don't curl up on me again. [*Turns back front, lays down parasol, examines palms together, wipes*

---

3. The first of several allusions to Milton's *Paradise Lost* with its opposition of the "holy light" of paradise and the darkness and "hellish light" of hell. Book 3 begins with the invocation

Hail holy light, offspring of heaven first-born,
Or the eternal coeternal beam

May I express thee unblamed? since God is light,
And never but in unapproached light
Dwelt from eternity.

See the first line of act 2.

them on grass.] Perhaps a shade off colour just the same. [*Turns to bag, rummages in it, brings out revolver, holds it up, kisses it rapidly, puts it back, rummages, brings out almost empty bottle of red medicine, turns back front, looks for spectacles, puts them on, reads label.*] Loss of spirits . . . lack of keenness . . . want of appetite . . . infants . . . children . . . adults . . . six level . . . tablespoonfuls daily—[*head up, smile*]—the old style!—[*smile off, head down, reads*]—daily . . . before and after . . . meals . . . instantaneous . . . [*looks closer*] . . . improvement. [*Takes off spectacles, lays them down, holds up bottle at arm's length to see level, unscrews cap, swigs it off head well back, tosses cap and bottle away in* WILLIE'*s direction. Sound of breaking glass.*] Ah that's better! [*Turns to bag, rummages in it, brings out lipstick, turns back front, examines lipstick.*] Running out. [*Looks for spectacles.*] Ah well. [*Puts on spectacles, looks for mirror.*] Musn't complain. [*Takes up mirror, starts doing lips.*] What is that wonderful line? [*Lips.*] Oh fleeting joys—[*lips*]—oh something lasting woe.[4] [*Lips. She is interrupted by disturbance from* WILLIE. *He is sitting up. She lowers lipstick and mirror and cranes back and down to look at him. Pause. Top back of* WILLIE'*s bald head, trickling blood, rises to view above slope, comes to rest.* WINNIE *pushes up her spectacles. Pause. His hand appears with handkerchief, spreads it on skull, disappears. Pause. The hand appears with boater, club ribbon, settles it on head, rakish angle, disappears. Pause.* WINNIE *cranes a little further back and down.*] Slip on your drawers, dear, before you get singed. [*Pause.*] No? [*Pause.*] Oh I see, you still have some of that stuff left. [*Pause.*] Work it well in, dear. [*Pause.*] Now the other. [*Pause. She turns back front, gazes before her. Happy expression.*] Oh this is going to be another happy day! [*Pause. Happy expression off. She pulls down spectacles and resumes lips.* WILLIE *opens newspaper, hands invisible. Tops of yellow sheets appear on either side of his head.* WINNIE *finishes lips, inspects them in mirror held a little further away.*] Ensign crimson. [WILLIE *turns page.* WINNIE *lays down lipstick and mirror, turns towards bag.*] Pale flag.[5]

    [WILLIE *turns page.* WINNIE *rummages in bag, brings out small ornate brimless hat with crumpled feather, turns back front, straightens hat, smooths feather, raises it towards head, arrests gesture as* WILLIE *reads.*]

WILLIE. His Grace and Most Reverend Father in God Dr Carolus Hunter dead in tub.

    [*Pause.*]

WINNIE [*gazing front, hat in hand, tone of fervent reminiscence*]. Charlie Hunter! [*Pause.*] I close my eyes—[*she takes off spectacles and does*

---

4. From *Paradise Lost* 10.741–42: " * * * O fleeting joys / Of Paradise, dear bought with lasting woes."
5. "Ensign crimson" and "pale flag" are phrases from the lines with which Romeo discovers Juliet in the tomb. Although he thinks her dead, he says, "Thou art not conquered; beauty's ensign yet / Is crimson in they lips and in thy cheeks / And death's pale flag is not advanced there" (5.3.94–96).

so, hat in one hand, spectacles in other, WILLIE *turns page*]—and am sitting on his knees again, in the back garden at Borough Green, under the horse-beech. [*Pause. She opens eyes, puts on spectacles, fiddles with hat.*] Oh the happy memories!

[*Pause. She raises hat towards head, arrests gesture as* WILLIE *reads.*]

WILLIE. Opening for smart youth.

[*Pause. She raises hat towards head, arrests gesture, takes off spectacles, gazes front, hat in one hand, spectacles in other.*]

WINNIE. My first ball! [*Long pause.*] My second ball! [*Long pause. Closes eyes.*] My first kiss! [*Pause.* WILLIE *turns page.* WINNIE *opens eyes.*] A Mr Johnson, or Johnston, or perhaps I should say John*stone.* Very bushy moustache, very tawny. [*Reverently.*] Almost ginger! [*Pause.*] Within a toolshed, though whose I cannot conceive. We had no toolshed and he most certainly had no toolshed. [*Closes eyes.*] I see the piles of pots. [*Pause.*] The tangles of bast. [*Pause.*] The shadows deepening among the rafters.

[*Pause. She opens eyes, puts on spectacles, raises hat towards head, arrests gesture as* WILLIE *reads.*]

WILLIE. Wanted bright boy.

[*Pause.* WINNIE *puts on hat hurriedly, looks for mirror.* WILLIE *turns page.* WINNIE *takes up mirror, inspects hat, lays down mirror, turns towards bag. Paper disappears.* WINNIE *rummages in bag, brings out magnifying-glass, turns back front, looks for toothbrush. Paper reappears, folded, and begins to fan* WILLIE's *face, hand invisible.* WINNIE *takes up toothbrush and examines handle through glass.*]

WINNIE. Fully guaranteed . . . [WILLIE *stops fanning*] . . . genuine pure . . . [*Pause.* WILLIE *resumes fanning.* WINNIE *looks closer, reads.*] Fully guaranteed . . . [WILLIE *stops fanning*] . . . genuine pure . . . [*Pause.* WILLIE *resumes fanning.* WINNIE *lays down glass and brush, takes handkerchief from bodice, takes off and polishes spectacles, puts on spectacles, looks for glass, takes up and polishes glass, lays down glass, looks for brush, takes up brush and wipes handle, lays down brush, puts handkerchief back in bodice, looks for glass, takes up glass, looks for brush, takes up brush and examines handle through glass.*] Fully guaranteed . . . [WILLIE *stops fanning*] . . . genuine pure . . . [*pause,* WILLIE *resumes fanning*] . . . hog's [WILLIE *stops fanning, pause*] . . . setae. [*Pause.* WINNIE *lays down glass and brush, paper disappears,* WINNIE *takes off spectacles, lays them down, gazes front.*] Hog's setae. [*Pause.*] That is what I find so wonderful, that not a day goes by— [*smile*]—to speak in the old style—[*smile off*]—hardly a day, without some addition to one's knowledge however trifling, the addition I mean, provided one takes the pains. [WILLIE's *hand reappears with a postcard which he examines close to eyes.*] And if for some strange reason no further pains are possible, why then just close the eyes— [*she does so*]—and wait for the day to come—[*opens eyes*]—the happy day to come when flesh melts at so many degrees and the night of

the moon has so many hundred hours. [*Pause.*] That is what I find
so comforting when I lose heart and envy the brute beast. [*Turning
towards* WILLIE.] I hope you are taking in—[*She sees postcard, bends
lower.*] What is that you have there, Willie, may I see? [*She reaches
down with hand and* WILLIE *hands her card. The hairy forearm appears
above slope, raised in gesture of giving, the hand open to take back,
and remains in this position till card is returned.* WINNIE *turns back
front and examines card.*] Heavens what are they up to! [*She looks for
spectacles, puts them on and examines card.*] No but this is just genuine
pure filth! [*Examines card.*] Make any nice-minded person want to
vomit! [*Impatience of* WILLIE's *fingers. She looks for glass, takes it up
and examines card through glass. Long pause.*] What does that creature
in the background think he's doing? [*Looks closer.*] Oh no really!
[*Impatience of fingers. Last long look. She lays down glass, takes edge
of card between right forefinger and thumb, averts head, takes nose
between left forefinger and thumb.*] Pah! [*Drops card.*] Take it away!
[WILLIE's *arm disappears. His hand reappears immediately, holding
card.* WINNIE *takes off spectacles, lays them down, gazes before her.
During what follows* WILLIE *continues to relish card, varying angles
and distance from his eyes.*] Hog's setae. [*Puzzled expression.*] What
exactly is a hog? [*Pause. Do.*] A sow of course I know, but a hog
. . . [*Puzzled expression off.*] Oh well what does it matter, that is what
I always say, it will come back, that is what I find so wonderful, all
comes back. [*Pause.*] All? [*Pause.*] No, not all. [*Smile.*] No no. [*Smile
off.*] Not quite. [*Pause.*] A part. [*Pause.*] Floats up, one fine day, out
of the blue. [*Pause.*] That is what I find so wonderful. [*Pause. She
turns towards bag. Hand and card disappear. She makes to rummage
in bag, arrests gesture.*] No. [*She turns back front. Smile.*] No no.
[*Smile off.*] Gently Winnie. [*She gazes front.* WILLIE's *hand reappears,
takes off hat, disappears with hat.*] What then? [*Hand reappears, takes
handkerchief from skull, disappears with handkerchief. Sharply, as to
one not paying attention.*] Winnie! [WILLIE *bows head out of sight.*]
What *is* the alternative? [*Pause.*] What *is* the al— [WILLIE *blows nose
loud and long, head and hands invisible. She turns to look at him.
Pause. Head reappears. Pause. Hand reappears with handkerchief,
spreads it on skull, disappers. Pause. Hand reappears with boater,
settles it on head, rakish angle, disappears. Pause.*] Would I had let
you sleep on. [*She turns back front. Intermittent plucking at grass,
head up and down, to animate following.*] Ah yes, if only I could
bear to be alone, I mean prattle away with not a soul to hear. [*Pause.*]
Not that I flatter myself you hear much, no Willie, God forbid.
[*Pause.*] Days perhaps when you hear nothing. [*Pause.*] But days too
when you answer. [*Pause.*] So that I may say at all times, even when
you do not answer and perhaps hear nothing, Something of this is
being heard, I am not merely talking to myself, that is in the wil-

derness, a thing I could never bear to do—for any length of time. [*Pause.*] That is what enables me to go on, go on talking that is. [*Pause.*] Whereas if you were to die—[*smile*]—to speak in the old style—[*smile off*]—or go away and leave me, then what would I do, what *could* I do, all day long, I mean between the bell for waking and the bell for sleep? [*Pause.*] Simply gaze before me with compressed lips. [*Long pause while she does so. No more plucking.*] Not another word as long as I drew breath, nothing to break the silence of this place. [*Pause.*] Save possibly, now and then, every now and then, a sigh into my looking-glass. [*Pause.*] Or a brief . . . gale of laughter, should I happen to see the old joke again. [*Pause. Smile appears, broadens and seems about to culminate in laugh when suddenly replaced by expression of anxiety.*] My hair! [*Pause.*] Did I brush and comb my hair? [*Pause.*] I may have done. [*Pause.*] Normally I do. [*Pause.*] There is so little one *can* do. [*Pause.*] One does it all. [*Pause.*] All one can. [*Pause.*] Tis only human. [*Pause.*] Human nature. [*She begins to inspect mound, looks up.*] Human weakness. [*She resumes inspection of mound, looks up.*] Natural weakness. [*She resumes inspection of mound.*] I see no comb. [*Inspects.*] Nor any hairbrush. [*Looks up. Puzzled expression. She turns to bag, rummages in it.*] The comb is here. [*Back front. Puzzled expression. Back to bag. Rummages.*] The brush is here. [*Back front. Puzzled expression.*] Perhaps I put them back, after use. [*Pause. Do.*] But normally I do not put things back, after use, no, I leave them lying about and put them back all together, at the end of the day. [*Smile.*] To speak in the old style. [*Pause.*] The sweet old style.[6] [*Smile off.*] And yet . . . I seem . . . to remember . . . [*Suddenly careless.*] Oh well, what does it matter, that is what I always say, I shall simply brush and comb them later on, purely and simply, I have the whole—[*Pause. Puzzled.*] Them? [*Pause.*] Or it? [*Pause.*] Brush and comb it? [*Pause.*] Sounds improper somehow. [*Pause. Turning a little towards* WILLIE.] What would you say, Willie? [*Pause. Turning a little further.*] What would you say, Willie, speaking of your hair, them or it? [*Pause.*] The hair on your head, I mean. [*Pause. Turning a little further.*] The hair on your head, Willie, what would you say speaking of the hair on your head, them or it?

[*Long pause.*]

WILLIE. It.

WINNIE [*turning back front, joyful*]. Oh you are going to talk to me today, this is going to be a happy day! [*Pause. Joy off.*] Another happy day. [*Pause.*] Ah well, where was I, my hair, yes, later on, I shall be thankful for it later on. [*Pause.*] I have my—[*raises hands to hat*]—

6. Here Winnie seems to merge the "old style" as a way of reckoning time by days, weeks, etc., with a memory of Dante's *"dolce stil nuovo,"* the sweet new style of writing of the Renaissance, now become the "sweet old style."

yes, on, my hat on—[*lowers hands*]—I cannot take it off now. [*Pause.*] To think there are times one cannot take off one's hat, not if one's life were at stake. Times one cannot put it on, times one cannot take it off. [*Pause.*] How often I have said, Put on your hat now, Winnie, there is nothing else for it, take off your hat now, Winnie, like a good girl, it will do you good, and did not. [*Pause.*] Could not. [*Pause. She raises hand, frees a strand of hair from under hat, draws it towards eye, squints at it, lets it go, hand down.*] Golden you called it, that day, when the last guest was gone—[*hand up in gesture of raising a glass*]—to your golden . . . may it never . . . [*voice breaks*] . . . may it never . . . [*Hand down. Head down. Pause. Low.*] That day. [*Pause. Do.*] What day? [*Pause. Head up. Normal voice.*] What now? [*Pause.*] Words fail, there are times when even they fail. [*Turning a little towards* WILLIE.] Is that not so, Willie? [*Pause. Turning a little further.*] Is not that so, Willie, that even words fail, at times? [*Pause. Back front.*] What is one to do then, until they come again? Brush and comb the hair, if it has not been done, or if there is some doubt, trim the nails if they are in need of trimming, these things tide one over. [*Pause.*] That is what I mean. [*Pause.*] That is all I mean. [*Pause.*] That is what I find so wonderful, that not a day goes by—[*smile*]—to speak in the old style—[*smile off*]—without some blessing—[WILLIE *collapses behind slope, his head disappears,* WINNIE *turns towards event*]—in disguise. [*She cranes back and down.*] Go back into your hole now, Willie, you've exposed yourself enough. [*Pause.*] Do as I say, Willie, don't lie sprawling there in this hellish sun, go back into your hole. [*Pause.*] Go on now, Willie. [WILLIE *invisible starts crawling left towards hole.*] That's the man. [*She follows his progress with her eyes.*] Not head first, stupid, how are you going to turn? [*Pause.*] That's it . . . right round . . . now . . . back in. [*Pause.*] Oh I know it is not easy, dear, crawling backwards, but it is rewarding in the end. [*Pause.*] You have left your vaseline behind. *She watches as he crawls back for vaseline.*] The lid! [*She watches as he crawls back towards hole. Irritated.*] Not head first, I tell you! [*Pause.*] More to the right. [*Pause.*] The *right*, I said. [*Pause. Irritated.*] Keep your tail down, can't you! [*Pause.*] Now. [*Pause.*] There! [*All these directions loud. Now in her normal voice, still turned towards him.*] Can you hear me? [*Pause.*] I beseech you, Willie, just yes or no, can you hear me, just yes or nothing.

[*Pause.*]

WILLIE. Yes.

WINNIE [*turning front, same voice*]. And now?

WILLIE [*irritated*]. Yes.

WINNIE [*less loud*]. And now?

WILLIE [*more irritated*]. Yes.

WINNIE [*still less loud*]. And now? [*A little louder.*] And now?

WILLIE [*violently*]. Yes!

WINNIE [*same voice*]. Fear no more the heat o' the sun.[7] [*Pause.*] Did
you hear that?

WILLIE [*irritated*]. Yes.

WINNIE [*same voice*]. What? [*Pause.*] What?

WILLIE [*more irritated*]. Fear no more.

   [*Pause.*]

WINNIE [*same voice*]. No more what? [*Pause.*] Fear no more what?

WILLIE [*violently*]. Fear no more!

WINNIE [*normal voice, gabbled*]. Bless you Willie I do appreciate your
goodness I know what an effort it costs you, now you may relax I
shall not trouble you again unless I am obliged to, by that I mean
unless I come to the end of my own resources which is most unlikely,
just to know that in theory you can hear me even though in fact you
don't is all I need, just to feel you there within earshot and conceivably
on the qui vive[8] is all I ask, not to say anything I would not wish you
to hear or liable to cause you pain, not to be just babbling away on
trust as it is were not knowing and something gnawing at me. [*Pause
for breath.*] Doubt. [*Places index and second finger on heart area,
moves them about, brings them to rest.*] Here. [*Moves them slightly.*]
Abouts. [*Hand away.*] Oh no doubt the time will come when before
I can utter a word I must make sure you heard the one that went
before and then no doubt another come another time when I must
learn to talk to myself a thing I could never bear to do such wilderness.
[*Pause.*] Or gaze before me with compressed lips. [*She does so.*] All
day long. [*Gaze and lips again.*] No. [*Smile.*] No no. [*Smile off.*]
There is of course the bag. [*Turns towards it.*] There will always be
the bag. [*Back front.*] Yes, I suppose so. [*Pause.*] Even when you are
gone, Willie. [*She turns a little towards him.*] You *are* going, Willie,
aren't you? [*Pause. Louder.*] You *will* be going soon, Willie, won't
you? [*Pause. Louder.*] Willie! [*Pause. She cranes back and down to
look at him.*] So you have taken off your straw, that is wise. [*Pause.*]
You do look snug, I must say, with your chin on your hands and the
old blue eyes like saucers in the shadows. [*Pause.*] Can you see me
from there I wonder, I still wonder. [*Pause.*] No? [*Back front.*] Oh I
know it does not follow when two are gathered together—[*faltering*]—
in this way—[*normal*]—that because one sees the other the other sees
the one, life has taught me that . . . too. [*Pause.*] Yes, life I suppose,
there is no other word. [*She turns a little towards him.*] Could you
see me, Willie, do you think, from where you are, if you were to

---

7. The first line of the dirge sung by Imogen's
brothers in *Cymbeline* when they think she's
dead:

Fear no more the heat of the sun,
   Nor the furious winter's rages;
Thou thy worldly task hast done,

Home art gone, and ta'en thy wages:
Golden lads and girls all must,
As chimney-sweepers, come to dust.
   (4.2.258–64)

8. "On the alert."

raise your eyes in my direction? [*Turns a little further.*] Lift up your eyes to me, Willie, and tell me can you see me, do that for me, I'll lean back as far as I can. [*Does so. Pause.*] No? [*Pause.*] Well never mind. [*Turns back painfully front.*] The earth is very tight today, can it be I have put on flesh, I trust not. [*Pause. Absently, eyes lowered.*] The great heat possibly. [*Starts to pat and stroke ground.*] All things expanding, some more than others. [*Pause. Patting and stroking.*] Some less. [*Pause. Do.*] Oh I can well imagine what is passing through your mind, it is not enough to have to listen to the woman, now I must look at her as well. [*Pause. Do.*] Well it is very understandable. [*Pause. Do.*] Most understandable. [*Pause. Do.*] One does not appear to be asking a great deal, indeed at times it would seem hardly possible—[*voice breaks, falls to a murmur*]—to ask less—of a fellow-creature—to put it mildly—whereas actually—when you think about it—look into your heart—see the other—what he needs—peace—to be left in peace—then perhaps the moon—all this time—asking for the moon. [*Pause. Stroking hand suddenly still. Lively.*] Oh I say, what have we here? [*Bending head to ground, incredulous.*] Looks like life of some kind! [*Looks for spectacles, puts them on, bends closer. Pause.*] An emmet! [*Recoils. Shrill.*] Willie, an emmet, a live emmet! [*Seizes magnifying-glass, bends to ground again, inspects through glass.*] Where's it gone? [*Inspects.*] Ah! [*Follows its progress through grass.*] Has like a little white ball in its arms. [*Follows progress. Hand still. Pause.*] It's gone in. [*Continues a moment to gaze at spot through glass, then slowly straightens up, lays down glass, takes off spectacles and gazes before her, spectacles in hand. Finally.*] Like a little white ball. [*Long pause. Gesture to lay down spectacles.*]

WILLIE. Eggs.

WINNIE [*arresting gesture*]. What?

    [*Pause.*]

WILLIE. Eggs. [*Pause. Gesture to lay down glasses.*] Formication.

WINNIE [*arresting gesture*]. What?

    [*Pause.*]

WILLIE. Formication.

    [*Pause. She lays down spectacles, gazes before her. Finally.*]

WINNIE [*murmur*]. God. [*Pause.* WILLIE *laughs quietly. After a moment she joins in. They laugh quietly together.* WILLIE *stops. She laughs on a moment alone.* WILLIE *joins in. They laugh together. She stops.* WILLIE *laughs on a moment alone. He stops. Pause. Normal voice.*] Ah well what a joy in any case to hear you laugh again, Willie, I was convinced I never would, you never would. [*Pause.*] I suppose some people might think us a trifle irreverent, but I doubt it.[*Pause.*] How can one better magnify the Almightly than by sniggering with him at his little jokes, particularly the poorer ones? [*Pause.*] I think you would back me up there, Willie. [*Pause.*] Or were we perhaps diverted by two quite different things? [*Pause.*] Oh well, what does it matter, that is what I always say, so long as one . . . you know . . . what is that wonderful line . . . laughing wild . . . something something laughing wild amid severest woe.⁹ [*Pause.*] And now? [*Long pause.*] Was I lovable once, Willie? [*Pause.*] Was I ever lovable? [*Pause.*] Do not misunderstand my question, I am not asking you if you loved me, we know all about that, I am asking you if you found me lovable— at one stage. [*Pause.*] No? [*Pause.*] You can't? [*Pause.*] Well I admit it is a teaser. And you have done more than your bit already, for the time being, just lie back now and relax, I shall not trouble you again unless I am compelled to, just to know you are there within hearing and conceivably on the semi-alert is . . . er . . . paradise enow.¹ [*Pause.*] The day is now well advanced. [*Smile.*] To speak in the old style. [*Smile off.*] And yet it is perhaps a little soon for my song. [*Pause.*] To sing too soon is a great mistake, I find. [*Turning towards bag.*] There is of course the bag. [*Looking at bag.*] The bag. [*Back front.*] Could I enumerate its contents? [*Pause.*] No. [*Pause.*] Could I, if some kind person were to come along and ask, What all have you got in that big black bag, Winnie? give an exhaustive answer? [*Pause.*] No. [*Pause.*] The depths in particular, who knows what treasures. [*Pause.*] What comforts. [*Turns to look at bag.*] Yes, there is the bag. [*Back front.*] But something tells me, Do not overdo the bag, Winnie, make use of it of course, let it help you . . . along, when stuck, by all means, but cast your mind forward, something tells me, cast your mind forward, Winnie, to the time when words must fail—[*she closes eyes, pause, opens eyes*]—and do not overdo the bag. [*Pause. She turns to look at bag.*] Perhaps just one quick dip. [*She turns back front, closes eyes, throws out left arm, plunges hand in bag and brings out revolver. Disgusted.*] You again! [*She opens eyes, brings revolver front and contemplates it. She weighs it in her palm.*] You'd think the weight of this thing would bring it down among the . . . last rounds. But no. It doesn't. Ever uppermost, like Browning.² [*Pause.*]

---

9. From Thomas Gray's *Ode on a Distant Prospect of Eton* (1742, 1747). The crucial stanza is:

Ambition this shall tempt to rise,
    Then whirl the wretch from high,
To bitter Scorn a sacrifice,
    And grinning Infamy.
And hard unkindness' alter'd eye,
    That mocks the tear it forc'd to flow:
And keen Remorse with blood defil'd,
And moody Madness laughing wild
    Amid severest woe.

The poem ends with the lines, " * * * where

ignorance is bliss, / 'Tis folly to be wise."
1. This phrase recalls Edward Fitzgerald's translation of *The Rubáiyát of Omar Khayyám,* a very popular poem among the Victorians. The phrase occurs in the lines

A Book of Verses underneath the Bough,
A Jug of Wine, a Loaf of Bread—and Thou
Beside me singing in the Wilderness—
    Ah, Wilderness were Paradise enow.
        (Rubáiyát 12)

2. The allusion to is Browning's *Paracelsus:* "I say confusedly what comes uppermost" (3.372).

Brownie . . . [*Turning a little towards* WILLIE.] Remember Brownie,
Willie? [*Pause.*] Remember how you used to keep on at me to take
it away from you? Take it away, Winnie, take it away, before I put
myself out of my misery. [*Back front. Derisive.*] Your misery! [*To
revolver.*] Oh I suppose it's a comfort to know you're there, but I'm
tired of you. [*Pause.*] I'll leave you out, that's what I'll do. [*She lays
revolver on ground to her right.*] There, that's your home from this
day out. [*Smile.*] The old style! [*Smile off.*] And now? [*Long pause.*]
Is gravity what it was, Willie, I fancy not. [*Pause.*] Yes, the feeling
more and more that if I were not held—[*gesture*]—in this way, I
would simply float up into the blue. [*Pause.*] And that perhaps some
day the earth will yield and let me go, the pull is so great, yes, crack
all round me and let me out. [*Pause.*] Don't you ever have that feeling,
Willie, of being sucked up? [*Pause.*] Don't you have to cling on
sometimes, Willie? [*Pause. She turns a little towards him.*] Willie.
   [*Pause.*]
WILLIE. *Sucked* up?
WINNIE. Yes love, up into the blue, like gossamer. [*Pause.*] No? [*Pause.*]
You don't? [*Pause.*] Ah well, natural laws, natural laws, I suppose it's
like everything else, it all depends on the creature you happen to be.
All I can say is for my part is that for me they are not what they were
when I was young and . . . foolish and . . . [*faltering, head down*]
. . . beautiful . . . possibly . . . lovely . . . in a way . . . to look at.
[*Pause. Head up.*] Forgive me, Willie, sorrow keeps breaking in.
[*Normal voice.*] Ah well what a joy in any case to know you are there,
as usual, and perhaps awake, and perhaps taking all this in, some of
all this, what a happy day for me . . . it will have been. [*Pause.*] So
far. [*Pause.*] What a blessing nothing grows, imagine if all this stuff
were to start growing. [*Pause.*] Imagine. [*Pause.*] Ah yes, great mercies.
[*Long pause.*] I can say no more. [*Pause.*] For the moment. [*Pause.
Turns to look at bag. Back front. Smile.*] No no. [*Smile off. Looks at
parasol.*] I suppose I might—[*takes up parasol*]—yes, I suppose I might
. . . hoist this thing now. [*Begins to unfurl it. Following punctuated
by mechanical difficulties overcome.*] One keeps putting off—putting
up—for fear of putting up—too soon—and the day goes by—quite
by—without one's having put up—at all. [*Parasol now fully open.
Turned to her right she twirls it idly this way and that.*] Ah yes, so
little to say, so little to do, and the fear so great, certain days, of
finding oneself . . . left, with hours still to run, before the bell for
sleep, and nothing more to say, nothing more to do, that the days go
by, certain days go by, quite by, the bell goes, and little or nothing
said, little or nothing done. [*Raising parasol.*] That is the danger.
[*Turning front.*] To be guarded against. [*She gazes front, holding up
parasol with right hand. Maximum pause.*] I used to perspire freely.
[*Pause.*] Now hardly at all. [*Pause.*] The heat is much greater. [*Pause.*]
The perspiration much less. [*Pause.*] That is what I find so wonderful.

[*Pause.*] The way man adapts himself. [*Pause.*] To changing conditions. [*She transfers parasol to left hand. Long pause.*] Holding up wearies the arm. [*Pause.*] Not if one is going along. [*Pause.*] Only if one is at rest. [*Pause.*] That is a curious observation. [*Pause.*] I hope you heard that, Willie, I should be grieved to think you had not heard that. [*She takes parasol in both hands. Long pause.*] I am weary, holding it up, and I cannot put it down. [*Pause.*] I am worse off with it up than with it down, and I cannot put it down. [*Pause.*] Reason says, Put it down, Winnie, it is not helping you, put the thing down and get on with something else. [*Pause.*] I cannot. [*Pause.*] I cannot move. [*Pause.*] No, something must happen, in the world, take place, some change, I cannot, if I am to move again. [*Pause.*] Willie. [*Mildly.*] Help. [*Pause.*] No? [*Pause.*] Bid me put this thing down, Willie, I would obey you instantly, as I have always done, honoured and obeyed. [*Pause.*] Please, Willie. [*Mildly.*] For pity's sake. [*Pause.*] No? [*Pause.*] You can't? [*Pause.*] Well I don't blame you, no, it would ill become me, who cannot move, to blame my Willie because he cannot speak. [*Pause.*] Fortunately I am in tongue again. [*Pause.*] That is what I find so wonderful, my two lamps, when one goes out the other burns brighter. [*Pause.*] Oh yes, great mercies. [*Maximum pause. The parasol goes on fire. Smoke, flames if feasible. She sniffs, looks up, throws parasol to her right behind mound, cranes back to watch it burning. Pause.*] Ah earth you old extinguisher. [*Back front.*] I presume this has occurred before, though I cannot recall it. [*Pause.*] Can you, Willie? [*Turns a little towards him.*] Can you recall this having occurred before? [*Pause. Cranes back to look at him.*] Do you know what has occurred, Willie? [*Pause.*] Have you gone off on me again? [*Pause.*] I do not ask if you are alive to all that is going on, I merely ask if you have not gone off on me again. [*Pause.*] Your eyes appear to be closed, but that has no particular significance we know. [*Pause.*] Raise a finger, dear, will you please, if you are not quite senseless. [*Pause.*] Do that for me, Willie please, just the little finger, if you are still conscious. [*Pause. Joyful.*] Oh all five, you are a darling today, now I may continue with an easy mind. [*Back front.*] Yes, what ever occurred that did not occur before and yet . . . I wonder, yes, I confess I wonder. [*Pause.*] With the sun blazing so much fiercer down, and hourly fiercer, is it not natural things should go on fire never known to do so, in this way I mean, spontaneous like. [*Pause.*] Shall I myself not melt perhaps in the end, or burn, oh I do not mean necessarily burst in to flames, no, just little by little be charred to a black cinder, all this—[*ample gesture of arms*]—visible flesh. [*Pause.*] On the other hand, did I ever know a temperate time? [*Pause.*] No. [*Pause.*] I speak of temperate times and torrid times, they are empty words. [*Pause.*] I speak of when I was not yet caught—in this way—and had my legs and had the use of my legs, and could seek out a shady place, like you, when I was tired of the sun, or a sunny place when I was tired of the shade, like you, and they are all empty words. [*Pause.*] It is no hotter today than yesterday, it will be no hotter tomorrow than today, how could it, and so on back into the far past, forward into the far future. [*Pause.*] And should one day the earth cover my breasts, then I shall never have seen my breasts, no one ever seen my breasts. [*Pause.*] I hope you caught something of that, Willie, I should be sorry to think you had caught nothing of all that, it is not every day I rise to such heights. [*Pause.*] Yes, something seems to have occurred, something has seemed to occur, and nothing has occurred, nothing at all, you are quite right, Willie. [*Pause.*] The sunshade will be there again tomorrow, beside me on this mound, to help me through the day. [*Pause. She takes up mirror.*] I take up this little glass, I shiver it on a stone—[*does so*]—I throw it away—[*does so far behind her*]—it will be in the bag again tomorrow, without a scratch, to help me through the day. [*Pause.*] No, one can do nothing. [*Pause.*] That is what I find so wonderful, the way things . . . [*voice breaks, head down*] . . . things . . . so wonderful. [*Long pause, head down. Finally turns, still bowed, to bag, brings out unidentifiable odds and ends, stuffs them back, fumbles deeper, brings out finally musical-box, winds it up, turns it on, listens for a moment holding it in both hands, huddled over it, turns back front, straightens up and listens to tune, holding box to breast with both hands. It plays the Waltz Duet "I love you so" from* The Merry Widow. *Gradually happy expression. She sways to the rhythm. Music stops. Pause. Brief burst of hoarse song without words—musical-box tune—from* WILLIE. *Increase of happy expression. She lays down box.*] Oh this will have been a happy day! [*She claps hands.*] Again, Willie, again! [*Claps.*] Encore, Willie, please! [*Pause. Happy expression off.*] No? You won't do that for me? [*Pause.*] Well it is very understandable, very understandable. One cannot sing just to please someone, however much one loves them, no, song must come from the heart, that is what I always say, pour out from the inmost, like a thrush. [*Pause.*] How often I have said, in evil hours, Sing now, Winnie, sing your song, there is nothing else for it, and did not. [*Pause.*] Could not. [*Pause.*] No, like the thrush, or the bird of dawning, with no thought of benefit, to oneself or anyone else. [*Pause.*] And now? [*Long pause. Low.*] Strange feeling. [*Pause. Do.*] Strange feeling that someone is looking at me. I am clear, then dim, then gone, then dim again, then clear again, and so on, back and forth, in and out of someone's eye. [*Pause. Do.*] Strange? [*Pause. Do.*] No, here all is strange. [*Pause. Normal voice.*] Something says, Stop talking now, Winnie, for a minute, don't squander all your words for the day, stop talking and do something for a change, will you? [*She raises hands and holds them open before her eyes. Apostrophic.*] Do something! [*She closes hands.*] What claws! [*She turns to bag, rummages in it, brings out finally a nailfile, turns back front and begins to file nails. Files for a time in silence, then the*

following punctuated by filing.] There floats up—into my thoughts—
a Mr Shower—a Mr and perhaps a Mrs Shower—no—they are holding hands—his fiancée then more likely—or just some—loved one.
[*Looks closer at nails.*] Very brittle today. [*Resumes filing.*] Shower—
Shower—does the name mean anything—to you, Willie—evoke any
reality, I mean—for you, Willie—don't answer if you don't—feel up
to it—you have done more—than your bit—already—Shower—
Shower. [*Inspects filed nails.*] Bit more like it. [*Raises head, gazes
front.*] Keep yourself nice, Winnie, that's what I always say, come
what may, keep yourself nice. [*Pause. Resumes filing.*] Yes—
Shower—Shower—[*stops filing, raises head, gazes front, pause*]—or
Cooker, perhaps I should say Cooker. [*Turning a little towards
WILLIE.*] Cooker, Willie, does Cooker strike a chord? [*Pause. Turns
a little further. Louder.*] Cooker, Willie, does Cooker ring a bell, the
name Cooker? [*Pause. She cranes back to look at him. Pause.*] Oh
really! [*Pause.*] Have you no handkerchief, darling? [*Pause.*] Have
you no delicacy? [*Pause.*] Oh, Willie, you're not eating it! Spit it out,
dear, spit it out! [*Pause. Back front.*] Ah well, I suppose it's only
natural. [*Break in voice.*] Human. [*Pause. Do.*] What *is* one to do?
[*Head down. Do.*] All day long. [*Pause. Do.*] Day after day. [*Pause.
Head up. Smile. Calm.*] The old style! [*Smile off. Resumes nails.*]
No, done him. [*Passes on to next.*] Should have put on my glasses.
[*Pause.*] Too late now. [*Finishes left hand, inspects it.*] Bit more
human. [*Starts right hand. Following punctuated as before.*] Well
anyway—this man Shower—or Cooker—no matter—and the
woman—hand in hand—in the other hands bags—kind of big brown
grips—standing there gaping at me—and at last this man Shower—
or Cooker—ends in er anyway—stake my life on that—What's she
doing? he says—What's the idea? he says—stuck up to her diddies in
the bleeding ground—coarse fellow—What does it mean? he says—
What's it meant to mean?—and so on—lot more stuff like that—
usual drivel—Do you hear me? he says—I do, she says, God help
me—What do you mean, he says, God help you? [*Stops filing, raises
head, gazes front.*] And you, she says, what's the idea of you, she
says, what are you meant to mean? It is because you're still on your
two flat feet, with your old ditty full of tinned muck and changes of
underwear, dragging me up and down this fornicating wilderness,
coarse creature, fit mate—[*with sudden violence*]—let go of my hand
and drop for God's sake, she says, drop! [*Pause. Resumes filing.*] Why
doesn't he dig her out? he says—referring to you, my dear—What
good is she to him like that?—What good is he to her like that?—
and so on—usual tosh—Good! she says, have a heart for God's sake—
Dig her out, he says, dig her out, no sense in her like that—Dig her
out with what? she says—I'd dig her out with my bare hands, he
says—must have been man and—wife. [*Files in silence.*] Next thing
they're away—hand in hand—and the bags—dim—then gone—last

human kind—to stray this way. [*Finishes right hand, inspects it, lays down file, gazes front.*] Strange thing, time like this, drift up into the mind. [*Pause.*] Strange? [*Pause.*] No, here all is strange. [*Pause.*] Thankful for it in any case. [*Voice breaks.*] Most thankful. [*Head down. Pause. Head up. Calm.*] Bow and raise the head, bow and raise, always that. [*Pause.*] And now? [*Long pause. Starts putting things back in bag, toothbrush last. This operation, interrupted by pauses as indicated, punctuates following.*] It is perhaps a little soon— to make ready—for the night—[*stops tidying, head up, smile*]—the old style!—[*smile off, resumes tidying*]—and yet I do—make ready for the night—feeling it at hand—the bell for sleep—saying to myself— Winnie—it will not be long now, Winnie—until the bell for sleep. [*Stops tidying, head up.*] Sometimes I am wrong. [*Smile.*] But not often. [*Smile off.*] Sometimes all is over, for the day, all done, all said, all ready for the night, and the day not over, far from over, the night not ready, far, far from ready. [*Smile.*] But not often. [*Smile off.*] Yes, the bell for sleep, when I feel it at hand, and so make ready for the night—[*gesture*]—in this way, sometimes I am wrong— [*smile*]—but not often. [*Smile off. Resumes tidying.*] I used to think— I say I used to think—that all these things—put back into the bag— if too soon—put back too soon—could be taken out again—if nec- essary—if needed—and so on—indefinitely—back into the bag—back out of the bag—until the bell—went. [*Stops tidying, head up, smile.*] But no. [*Smile broader.*] No no. [*Smile off. Resumes tidying.*] I suppose this—might seem strange—this—what shall I say—this what I have said—yes—[*she takes up revolver*]—strange—[*she turns to put revolver in bag*]—were it not—[*about to put revolver in bag she arrests gesture and turns back front*]—were it not—[*she lays down revolver to her right, stops tidying, head up*]—that all seems strange. [*Pause.*] Most strange. [*Pause.*] Never any change. [*Pause.*] And more and more strange. [*Pause. She bends to mound again, takes up last object, i.e. toothbrush, and turns to put it in bag when her attention is drawn to disturbance from* WILLIE. *She cranes back and to her right to see. Pause.*] Weary of your hole, dear? [*Pause.*] Well I can understand that. [*Pause.*] Don't forget your straw. [*Pause.*] Not the crawler you were, poor darling. [*Pause.*] No, not the crawler I gave my heart to. [*Pause.*] The hands and knees, love, try the hands and knees. [*Pause.*] The knees! The knees! [*Pause.*] What a curse, mobility! [*She follows with eyes his progress towards her behind mound, i.e. towards place he occupied at beginning of act.*] Another foot, Willie, and you're home. [*Pause as she observes last foot.*] Ah! [*Turns back front labo- riously, rubs neck.*] Crick in my neck admiring you. [*Rubs neck.*] But it's worth it, well worth it. [*Turning slightly towards him.*] Do you know what I dream sometimes? [*Pause.*] What I dream sometimes, Willie. [*Pause.*] That you'll come round and live this side where I could see you. [*Pause. Back front.*] I'd be a different woman. [*Pause.*]

Unrecognizable. [*Turning slightly towards him.*] Or just now and then, come round this side just every now and then and let me feast on you. [*Back front.*] But you can't, I know. [*Head down.*] I know. [*Pause. Head up.*] Well anyway—[*looks at toothbrush in her hand*]—can't be long now—[*looks at brush*]—until the bell. [*Top back of* WILLIE'*s head appears above slope.* WINNIE *looks closer at brush.*] Fully guaranteed . . . [*head up*] . . . what's this it was? [WILLIE'*s hand appears with handkerchief, spreads it on skull, disappears.*] Genuine pure . . . fully guaranteed . . . [WILLIE'*s hand appears with boater, settles it on head, rakish angle, disappears*] . . . genuine pure . . . ah! hog's setae. [*Pause.*] What is a hog exactly? [*Pause. Turns slightly towards* WILLIE.] What exactly is a hog, Willie, do you know, I can't remember. [*Pause. Turning a little further, pleading.*] What *is* a hog, Willie, please!

[*Pause.*]

WILLIE. Castrated male swine. [*Happy expression appears on* WINNIE'*s face.*] Reared for slaughter.

[*Happy expression increases.* WILLIE *opens newspaper, hands invisible. Tops of yellow sheets appear on either side of his head.* WINNIE *gazes before her with happy expression.*]

WINNIE. Oh this *is* a happy day! This will have been another happy day! [*Pause.*] After all. [*Pause.*] So far.

[*Pause. Happy expression off.* WILLIE *turns page. Pause. He turns another page. Pause.*]

WILLIE. Opening for smart youth.

[*Pause.* WINNIE *takes off hat, turns to put it in bag, arrests gesture, turns back front. Smile.*]

WINNIE. No. [*Smile broader.*] No no. [*Smile off. Puts on hat again, gazes front, pause.*] And now? [*Pause.*] Sing. [*Pause.*] Sing your song, Winnie. [*Pause.*] No? [*Pause.*] Then pray. [*Pause.*] Pray your prayer, Winnie.

[*Pause.* WILLIE *turns page. Pause.*]

WILLIE. Wanted bright boy.

[*Pause.* WINNIE *gazes before her.* WILLIE *turns page. Pause. Newspaper disappears. Long pause.*]

WINNIE. Pray your old prayer, Winnie.

[*Long pause.*]

[CURTAIN]

Act Two

Scene as before.

WINNIE *imbedded up to neck, hat on head, eyes closed. Her head, which she can no longer turn, nor bow, nor raise, faces front motionless throughout act. Movements of eyes as indicated.*

Bag and parasol as before. Revolver conspicuous to her right on mound. Long pause.
Bell rings loudly. She opens eyes at once. Bell stops. She gazes front. Long pause.

WINNIE. Hail, holy light. [*Long pause. She closes her eyes. Bell rings loudly. She opens eyes at once. Bell stops. She gazes front. Long smile. Smile off. Long pause.*] Someone is looking at me still. [*Pause.*] Caring for me still. [*Pause.*] That is what I find so wonderful. [*Pause.*] Eyes on my eyes. [*Pause.*] What is that unforgettable line? [*Pause. Eyes right.*] Willie. [*Pause. Louder.*] Willie. [*Pause. Eyes front.*] May one still speak of time? [*Pause.*] Say it is a long time now, Willie, since I saw you. [*Pause.*] Since I heard you. [*Pause.*] May one? [*Pause.*] One does. [*Smile.*] The old style! [*Smile off.*] There is so little one can speak of. [*Pause.*] One speaks of it all. [*Pause.*] All one can. [*Pause.*] I used to think . . . [*pause*] . . . I say I used to think that I would learn to talk alone. [*Pause.*] By that I mean to myself, the wilderness. [*Smile.*] But no. [*Smile broader.*] No no. [*Smile off.*] Ergo you are there. [*Pause.*] Oh no doubt you are dead, like the others, no doubt you have died, or gone away and left me, like the others, it doesn't matter, you are there. [*Pause. Eyes left.*] The bag too is there, the same as ever, I can see it. [*Pause. Eyes right. Louder.*] The bag is there, Willie, as good as ever, the one you gave me that day . . . to go to market. [*Pause. Eyes front.*] That day. [*Pause.*] What day? [*Pause.*] I used to pray. [*Pause.*] I say I used to pray. [*Pause.*] Yes, I must confess I did. [*Smile.*] Not now. [*Smile broader.*] No no. [*Smile off. Pause.*] Then . . . now . . . what difficulties here, for the mind. [*Pause.*] To have been always what I am—and so changed from what I was. [*Pause.*] I am the one, I say the one, then the other. [*Pause.*] Now the one, then the other. [*Pause.*] There is so little one can say, one says it all. [*Pause.*] All one can. [*Pause.*] And no truth in it anywhere. [*Pause.*] My arms. [*Pause.*] My breasts. [*Pause.*] What arms? [*Pause.*] What breasts? [*Pause.*] Willie. [*Pause.*] What Willie? [*Sudden vehement affirmation.*] My Willie! [*Eyes right, calling.*] Willie! [*Pause. Louder.*] Willie! [*Pause. Eyes front.*] Ah well, not to know, not to know for sure, great mercy, all I ask. [*Pause.*] Ah yes . . . then . . . now . . . beechen green[3] . . . this . . . Charlie . . . kisses . . . this . . . all that . . . deep trouble for the mind. [*Pause.*] But it does not trouble mine. [*Smile.*] Not now. [*Smile broader.*] No no. [*Smile off. Long pause. She closes eyes. Bell rings loudly. She opens eyes. Pause.*] Eyes float up that seem to close in peace . . . to see . . . in peace. [*Pause.*] Not mine. [*Smile.*] Not now. [*Smile broader.*] No no. [*Smile off. Long pause.*] Willie. [*Pause.*] Do you think the earth has

---

3. This phrase recalls the first stanza of Keats's "Ode to a Nightingale," in which the speaker, numbed by unhappiness, is summoned from a "melodious plot / of beechen green" by the bird singing of its happiness (1.8–9).

lost its atmosphere, Willie? [*Pause.*] Do you, Willie? [*Pause.*] You
have no opinion? [*Pause.*] Well that is like you, you never had any
opinion about anything. [*Pause.*] It's understandable. [*Pause.*] Most.
[*Pause.*] The earthball. [*Pause.*] I sometimes wonder. [*Pause.*] Perhaps
not quite all. [*Pause.*] There always remains something. [*Pause.*] Of
everything. [*Pause.*] Some remains. [*Pause.*] If the mind were to go.
[*Pause.*] It won't of course. [*Pause.*] Not quite. [*Pause.*] Not mine.
[*Smile.*] Not now. [*Smile broader.*] No no. [*Smile off. Long pause.*]
It might be the eternal cold. [*Pause.*] Everlasting perishing cold.
[*Pause.*] Just chance, I take it, happy chance. [*Pause.*] Oh yes, great
mercies, great mercies. [*Pause.*] And now? [*Long pause.*] The face.
[*Pause.*] The nose. [*She squints down.*] I can see it . . . [*squinting
down*] . . . the tip . . . the nostrils . . . breath of life . . . that curve
you so admired . . . [*pouts*] . . . a hint of lip . . . [*pouts again*] . . .
if I pout them out . . . [*sticks out tongue*] . . . the tongue of course
. . . you so admired . . . if I stick it out . . . [*sticks it out again*]
. . . the tip . . . [*eyes up*] . . . suspicion of brow . . . eyebrow . . .
imagination possibly . . . [*eyes left*] . . . cheek . . . no . . . [*eyes right*]
. . . no . . . [*distends cheeks*] . . . even if I puff them out . . . [*eyes
left, distends cheeks again*] . . . no . . . no damask.[4] [*Eyes front.*]
That is all. [*Pause.*] The bag of course . . . [*eyes left*] . . . a little
blurred perhaps . . . but the bag. [*Eyes front. Offhand.*] The earth
of course and sky. [*Eyes right.*] The sunshade you gave me . . . that
day . . . [*pause.*] . . . that day . . . the lake . . . the reeds. [*Eyes
front. Pause.*] What day? [*Pause.*] What reeds? [*Long pause. Eyes
close. Bell rings loudly. Eyes open. Pause. Eyes right.*] Brownie of
course. [*Pause.*] You remember Brownie, Willie, I can see him.
[*Pause.*] Brownie is there, Willie, beside me. [*Pause. Loud.*] Brownie
is there, Willie. [*Pause. Eyes front.*] That is all. [*Pause.*] What would
I do without them? [*Pause.*] What would I do without them, when
words fail? [*Pause.*] Gaze before me, with compressed lips. [*Long
pause while she does so.*] I cannot. [*Pause.*] Ah yes, great mercies,
great mercies. [*Long pause. Low.*] Sometimes I hear sounds. [*Listening expression. Normal voice.*] But not often. [*Pause.*] They are a
boon, sounds are a boon, they help me . . . through the day. [*Smile.*]
The old style! [*Smile off.*] Yes, those are happy days, when there are
sounds. [*Pause.*] When I hear sounds. [*Pause.*] I used to think . . .
[*pause.*] . . . I say I used to think they were in my head. [*Smile.*] But
no. [*Smile broader.*] No no. [*Smile off.*] That was just logic. [*Pause.*]
Reason. [*Pause.*] I have not lost my reason. [*Pause.*] Not yet. [*Pause.*]
Not all. [*Pause.*] Some remains. [*Pause.*] Sounds. [*Pause.*] Like little
. . . sunderings, little falls . . . apart. [*Pause. Low.*] It's things, Willie.
[*Pause. Normal voice.*] In the bag, outside the bag. [*Pause.*] Ah yes,

---

4. Winnie's correction to "damask [cheek]" could
allude to *Twelfth Night* and Viola, who, in disguise
" * * * never told her love, / But let concealment
like a worm i' th' bud / Feed on her damask cheek"
(2.4.110–12).

things have their life, that is what I always say, *things* have a life. [*Pause.*] Take my looking-glass, it doesn't need me. [*Pause.*] The bell. [*Pause.*] It hurts like a knife. [*Pause.*] A gouge. [*Pause.*] One cannot ignore it. [*Pause.*] How often . . . [*pause.*] . . . I say how often I have said, Ignore it, Winnie, ignore the bell, pay no heed, just sleep and wake, sleep and wake, as you please, open and close the eyes, as you please, or in the way you find most helpful. [*Pause.*] Open and close the eyes, Winnie, open and close, always that. [*Pause.*] But no. [*Smile.*] Not now. [*Smile broader.*] No no. [*Smile off. Pause.*] What now? [*Pause.*] What now, Willie? [*Long pause.*] There is my story of course, when all else fails. [*Pause.*] A life. [*Smile.*] A long life. [*Smile off.*] Beginning in the womb, where life used to begin, Mildred has memories, she will have memories, of the womb, before she dies, the mother's womb. [*Pause.*] She is now four or five already and has recently been given a big waxen dolly. [*Pause.*] Fully clothed, complete outfit. [*Pause.*] Shoes, socks, undies, complete set, frilly frock, gloves. [*Pause.*] White mesh. [*Pause.*] A little white straw hat with a chin elastic. [*Pause.*] Pearly necklet. [*Pause.*] A little picture-book with legends in real print to go under her arm when she takes her walk. [*Pause.*] China blue eyes that open and shut. [*Pause. Narrative.*] The sun was not well up when Milly rose, descended the steep . . . [*pause.*] . . . slipped on her nightgown, descended all alone the steep wooden stairs, backwards on all fours, though she had been forbidden to do so, entered the . . . [*pause.*] . . . tiptoed down the silent passage, entered the nursery and began to undress Dolly. [*Pause.*] Crept under the table and began to undress Dolly. [*Pause.*] Scolding her . . . the while. [*Pause.*] Suddenly a mouse—[*Long pause.*] Gently, Winnie. [*Long pause. Calling.*] Willie! [*Pause. Louder.*] Willie! [*Pause. Mild reproach.*] I sometimes find your attitude a little strange, Willie, all this time, it is not like you to be wantonly cruel. [*Pause.*] Strange? [*Pause.*] No. [*Smile.*] Not here. [*Smile broader.*] Not now. [*Smile off.*] And yet . . . [*Suddenly anxious.*] I do hope nothing is amiss. [*Eyes right, loud.*] Is all well, dear? [*Pause. Eyes front. To herself.*] God grant he did not go in head foremost! [*Eyes right, loud.*] You're not stuck, Willie? [*Pause. Do.*] You're not jammed, Willie? [*Eyes front, distressed.*] Perhaps he is crying out for help all this time and I do not hear him! [*Pause.*] I do of course hear cries. [*Pause.*] But they are in my head surely. [*Pause.*] Is it possible that . . . [*Pause. With finality.*] No no, my head was always full of cries. [*Pause.*] Faint confused cries. [*Pause.*] They come. [*Pause.*] Then go. [*Pause.*] As on a wind. [*Pause.*] That is what I find so wonderful. [*Pause.*] They cease. [*Pause.*] Ah yes, great mercies, great mercies. [*Pause.*] The day is now well advanced. [*Smile. Smile off.*] And yet it is perhaps a little soon for my song. [*Pause.*] To sing too soon is fatal, I always find. [*Pause.*] On the other hand it is possible to leave it too late. [*Pause.*] The bell goes for sleep and one has not sung. [*Pause.*] The whole day has flown—[*smile, smile off*]—flown by, quite by, and no song of any class, kind of description. [*Pause.*] There is a problem here. [*Pause.*] One cannot sing . . . just like that, no. [*Pause.*] It bubbles up, for some unknown reason, the time is ill chosen, one chokes it back. [*Pause.*] One says, Now is the time, it is now or never, and one cannot. [*Pause.*] Simply cannot sing. [*Pause.*] Not a note. [*Pause.*] Another thing, Willie, while we are on this subject. [*Pause.*] The sadness after song. [*Pause.*] Have you run across that, Willie? [*Pause.*] In the course of your experience. [*Pause.*] No? [*Pause.*] Sadness after intimate sexual intercourse one is familiar with of course. [*Pause.*] You would concur with Aristotle there, Willie, I fancy. [*Pause.*] Yes, that one knows and is prepared to face. [*Pause.*] But after song . . . [*Pause.*] It does not last of course. [*Pause.*] That is what I find so wonderful. [*Pause.*] It wears away. [*Pause.*] What are those exquisite lines? [*Pause.*] Go forget me why should something o'er that something shadow fling . . . go forget me . . . why should sorrow . . . brightly smile . . . go forget me . . . never hear me . . . sweetly smile . . . brightly sing[5] . . . [*Pause. With a sigh.*] One loses one's classics. [*Pause.*] Oh not all. [*Pause.*] A part. [*Pause.*] A part remains. [*Pause.*] That is what I find so wonderful, a part remains, of one's classics, to help one through the day. [*Pause.*] Oh yes, many mercies, many mercies. [*Pause.*] And now? [*Pause.*] And now, Willie? [*Long pause.*] I call to the eye of the mind[6] . . . Mr. Shower—or Cooker. [*She closes her eyes. Bell rings loudly. She opens her eyes. Pause.*] Hand in hand, in the other hands bags. [*Pause.*] Getting on . . . in life. [*Pause.*] No longer young, not yet old. [*Pause.*] Standing there gaping at me. [*Pause.*] Can't have been a bad bosom, he says, in its day. [*Pause.*] Seen worse shoulders, he says, in my time. [*Pause.*] Does she feel her legs? he says. [*Pause.*] Is there any life in her legs? he says. [*Pause.*] Has she anything on underneath? he says. [*Pause.*] Ask her, he says, I'm shy. [*Pause.*] Ask her what? she says. [*Pause.*] Is there any life in her legs. [*Pause.*] Has she anything on underneath. [*Pause.*] Ask her yourself, she says. [*Pause. With sudden violence.*] Let go of me for Christ sake and drop! [*Pause. Do.*] Drop dead! [*Smile.*] But no. [*Smile broader.*] No no. [*Smile off.*] I watch them recede. [*Pause.*] Hand in hand—and the bags. [*Pause.*] Dim. [*Pause.*] Then gone. [*Pause.*] Last

---

5. Winnie quotes, or misquotes, the first stanza of a poem by Charles Wolfe (1791–1823), a minor Irish poet:

> Go! forget me, why should sorrow
>   O'er that brow a shadow fling?
> Go! forget me—and tomorrow
>   Brightly smile, and sweetly sing.
> Smile—though I shall not be near thee;
> Sing—though I shall never hear thee.
> May thy soul with pleasure shine,
> Lasting as the gloom of mine.

6. Winnie here quotes the opening of Yeats's "At the Hawk's Well," where the poet calls on the audience to supply the props and scenery for the play.

human kind—to stray this way. [*Pause.*] Up to date. [*Pause.*] And
now? [*Pause. Low.*] Help. [*Pause. Do.*] Help, Willie. [*Pause. Do.*]
No? [*Long pause. Narrative.*] Suddenly a mouse . . . [*Pause.*] Suddenly a mouse ran up her little thigh and Mildred, dropping Dolly
in her fright, began to scream—[WINNIE *gives a sudden piercing
scream*]—and screamed and screamed—[WINNIE *screams twice*]—
screamed and screamed and screamed and screamed till all came
running, in their night attire, papa, mamma, Bibby and . . . old
Annie, to see what was the matter . . . [*pause*] . . . what on earth
could possibly be the matter. [*Pause.*] Too late. [*Pause.*] Too late.
[*Long pause. Just audible.*] Willie. [*Pause. Normal voice.*] Ah well,
not long now, Winnie, can't be long now, until the bell for sleep.
[*Pause.*] Then you may close your eyes, then you *must* close your
eyes—and keep them closed. [*Pause.*] Why say that again? [*pause*] I
used to think . . . [*Pause.*] . . . I say I used to think there was no
difference between one fraction of a second and the next. [*pause*] I
used to say . . . [*Pause.*] . . . I say I used to say, Winnie, you are
changeless, there is never any difference between one fraction of a
second and the next. [*Pause.*] Why bring that up again? [*Pause.*] There
is so little one can bring up, one brings up all. [*Pause.*] All one can.
[*Pause.*] My neck is hurting me. [*Pause. With sudden violence.*] My
neck is hurting me! [*Pause.*] Ah that's better. [*With mild irritation.*]
Everything within reason. [*Long pause.*] I can do no more. [*Pause.*]
Say no more. [*Pause.*] But I must say more. [*Pause.*] Problem here.
[*Pause.*] No, something must move, in the world, I can't any more.
[*Pause.*] A zephyr. [*Pause.*] A breath. [*Pause.*] What are those im-
mortal lines? [*Pause.*] It might be the eternal dark. [*Pause.*] Black
night without end. [*Pause.*] Just chance, I take it, happy chance.
[*Pause.*] Oh yes, abounding mercies. [*Long pause.*] And now? [*Pause.*]
And now, Willie? [*Long pause.*] That day. [*Pause.*] The pink fizz.
[*Pause.*] The flute glasses. [*Pause.*] The last guest gone. [*Pause.*] The
last bumper with the bodies nearly touching. [*Pause.*] The look. [*Long
pause.*] What day? [*Long pause.*] What look? [*Long pause.*] I hear
cries. [*Pause.*] Sing. [*Pause.*] Sing your old song, Winnie.
    [*Long pause. Suddenly alert expression. Eyes switch right.* WILLIE's
    *head appears to her right round corner of mound. He is on all fours,
    dressed to kill—top hat, morning coat, striped trousers, etc., white
    gloves in hand. Very long bushy white Battle of Britain moustache.
    He halts, gazes front, smooths moustache. He emerges completely
    from behind mound, turns to his left, halts, looks up at* WINNIE. *He
    advances on all fours towards centre, halts, turns head front, gazes
    front, strokes moustache, straightens tie, adjusts hat, advances a
    little further, halts, takes off hat and looks up at* WINNIE. *He is now
    not far from centre and within her field of vision. Unable to sustain
    effort of looking up he sinks head to ground.*]
WINNIE [*mondaine*]. Well this is an unexpected pleasure! [*Pause.*] Re-

minds me of the day you came whining for my hand. [*Pause.*] I worship you, Winnie, be mine. [*He looks up.*] Life a mockery without Win. [*She goes off into a giggle.*] What a get up, you do look a sight! [*Giggles.*] Where are the flowers?[7] [*Pause.*] That smile today. [WILLIE *sinks head.*] What's that on your neck, an anthrax?[8] [*Pause.*] Want to watch that, Willie, before it gets a hold on you. [*Pause.*] Where were you all this time? [*Pause.*] What were you doing all this time? [*Pause.*] Changing? [*Pause.*] Did you not hear me screaming for you? [*Pause.*] Did you get stuck in your hole? [*Pause. He looks up.*] That's right, Willie, look at me. [*Pause.*] Feast your old eyes, Willie. [*Pause.*] Does anything remain? [*Pause.*] Any remains? [*Pause.*] No? [*Pause.*] I haven't been able to look after it, you know. [*He sinks his head.*] You are still recognizable, in a way. [*Pause.*] Are you thinking of coming to live this side now . . . for a bit maybe? [*Pause.*] No? [*Pause.*] Just a brief call? [*Pause.*] Have you gone deaf, Willie? [*Pause.*] Dumb? [*Pause.*] Oh I know you were never one to talk, I worship you Winnie be mine and then nothing from that day forth only titbits from Reynolds' News. [*Eyes front. Pause.*] Ah well, what matter, that's what I always say, it will have been a happy day, after all, another happy day. [*Pause.*] Not long now, Winnie. [*Pause.*] I hear cries. [*Pause.*] Do you ever hear cries, Willie? [*Pause.*] No? [*Eyes back on* WILLIE.] Willie. [*Pause.*] Look at me again, Willie. [*Pause.*] Once more, Willie. [*He looks up. Happily.*] Ah! [*Pause. Shocked.*] What ails you, Willie, I never saw such an expression! [*Pause.*] Put on your hat, dear, it's the sun, don't stand on ceremony, I won't mind. [*He drops hat and gloves and starts to crawl up mound towards her. Gleeful.*] Oh I say, this is terrific! [*He halts, clinging to mound with one hand, reaching up with the other.*] Come on, dear, put a bit of jizz into it, I'll cheer you on. [*Pause.*] Is it me you're after, Willie . . . or is it something else? [*Pause.*] Do you want to touch my face . . . again? [*Pause.*] Is it a kiss you're after, Willie . . . or is it something else? [*Pause.*] There was a time when I could have given you a hand. [*Pause.*] And then a time before that again when I did give you a hand. [*Pause.*] You were always in dire need of a hand, Willie. [*He slithers back to foot of mound and lies with face to ground.*] Brrum! [*Pause. He rises to hands and knees, raises his face towards her.*] Have another go, Willie, I'll cheer you on. [*Pause.*] Don't look at me like that! [*Pause. Vehement.*] Don't look at me like that! [*Pause. Low.*] Have you gone off your head, Willie? [*Pause. Do.*] Out of your poor old wits, Willie?

[*Pause.*]

WILLIE [*just audible*]. Win.

---

7. In his manuscript notes Beckett makes clear that he was thinking here of Robert Herrick's "To the Virgins, to Make Much of Time" and the senti- ment crystallized in the line "Gather ye rosebuds while ye may."

8. A carbuncle or boil.

[*Pause.* WINNIE'*s eyes front. Happy expression appears, grows.*]

WINNIE. Win! [*Pause.*] Oh this *is* a happy day, this will have been another happy day! [*Pause.*] After all. [*Pause.*] So far. [*Pause. She hums tentatively beginning of song, then sings softly, musical-box tune.*]

> Though I say not
> What I may not
> Let you hear,
> Yet the swaying
> Dance is saying,
> Love me dear!
> Every touch of fingers
> Tells me what I know,
> Says for you,
> It's true, it's true,
> You love me so![9]

[*Pause. Happy expression off. She closes her eyes. Bell rings loudly. She opens her eyes. She smiles, gazing front. She turns her eyes, smiling, to* WILLIE, *still on his hands and knees looking up at her. Smile off. They look at each other. Long pause.*]

[CURTAIN]

---

9. The waltz-duet from *The Merry Widow* by Ferenc Lehar (1870–1948).

BACKGROUNDS AND CRITICISM

EMILE ZOLA

Preface to *Thérèse Raquin*†

It is by no means my intention to make my play a rallying standard. It
has striking shortcomings, toward which no one is more severe than
myself; if I were to criticize it, there would be only one thing I should
not attack: the author's very obvious desire to bring the theatre into closer
relation with the great movement toward truth and experimental science
which has since the last century been on the increase in every manifestation of the human intellect. The movement was started by the new
methods of science; thence, Naturalism revolutionized criticism and
history, in submitting man and his works to a system of precise analysis,
taking into account all circumstances, environment, and "organic
cases." Then, in turn, art and letters were carried along with the current:
painting became realistic—our landscape school killed the historical
school—; the novel, that social and individual study with its extremely
loose frame-work, after growing and growing, took up all the activities
of man, absorbing little by little the various classifications made in the
rhetorics of the past. These are all undeniable facts. We have now come
to the birth of the true, that is the great, the only force of the century.
Everything advances in a literary epoch. Whoever wishes to retreat or
turn to one side, will be lost in the general dust. This is why I am
absolutely convinced that in the near future the Naturalist movement
will take its place in the realm of the drama, and bring with it the power
of reality, the new life of modern art.

In the theater, every innovation is a delicate matter. Literary revolutions are slow in making themselves felt. And it is only logical that
this should be the last citadel of falsehood: where the true belongs. The
public as a whole resents having its habits changed, and the judgments
which it passes have all the brutality of a death-sentence. But there
comes a time when the public itself becomes an accomplice of the
innovators; this is when, imbued with the new spirit, weary of the same
stories repeated to it countless times, it feels an imperious desire for
youth and originality.

I may be mistaken, but I believe that this is the situation of our public
today. The historical drama is in its death-throes, unless something new
comes to its assistance: that corpse needs new blood. It is said that the
operetta and the dramatic fantasy have killed the historical drama. This
is not so: the historical drama is dying a natural death, of its own
extravagances, lies, and platitudes. If comedy still maintains its place
amid the general disintegration of the stage, it is because comedy clings
closer to actual life, and is often true. I defy the last of the Romanticists

† 1873. From *European Theories of the Drama* by Barrett Clark. Copyright 1943 by Barrett H. Clark.
Reprinted by permission of Crown Publishers, Inc. Pp. 377–79.

to put upon the stage a heroic drama; at the sight of all the paraphernalia of armor, secret doors, poisoned wines and the rest, the audience would only shrug its shoulders. And melodrama, that bourgeois offspring of the romantic drama, is in the hearts of the people more dead than its predecessor; its false sentiment, its complications of stolen children and discovered documents, its impudent gasconnades, have finally rendered it despicable, so that any attempt to revive it proves abortive. The great works of 1830[1] will always remain advance-guard works, landmarks in a literary epoch, superb efforts which laid low the scaffoldings of the classics. But, now that everything is torn down, and swords and capes rendered useless, it is time to base our works on truth. To substitute the Romantic for the Classic tradition would be a refusal to take advantage of the liberty acquired by our forbears. There should no longer be any school, no more formulas, no standards of any sort; there is only life itself, an immense field where each may study and create as he likes.

I am attempting no justification of my own cause, I am merely expressing my profound conviction—upon which I particularly insist—that the experimental and scientific spirit of the century will enter the domain of the drama, and that in it lies its only possible salvation. Let the critics look about them and tell me from what direction help is to be expected, or a breath of life, to rehabilitate the drama? Of course, the past is dead. We must look to the future, and the future will have to do with the human problem studied in the frame-work of reality. We must cast aside fables of every sort, and delve into the living drama of the two-fold life of the character and its environment, bereft of every nursery tale, historical trapping, and the usual conventional stupidities. The decayed scaffoldings of the drama of yesterday will fall of their own accord. We must clear the ground. The well-known receipts for the tying and untying of an intrigue have served their time; now we must seek a simple and broad picture of men and things, such as Molière might write. Outside of a few scenic conventions, all that is now known as the "science of the theater" is merely a heap of clever tricks, a narrow tradition that serves to cramp the drama, a ready-made code of language and hackneyed situations, all known and planned out beforehand, which every original worker will scorn to use.

Naturalism is already stammering its first accents on the stage. I shall not cite any particular work, but among the plays produced during these past two years, there are many that contain the germ of the movement whose approach I have prophesied. I am not taking into account plays by new authors, I refer especially to certain plays of dramatists who have grown old in the *métier*, who are clever enough to realize the new transformation that is taking place in our literature. The drama will either die, or become modern and realistic.

1. In the French theater the Romantic revolt led by Victor Hugo and Alexandre Dumas [*Editor*].

It is under the influence of these ideas that I have dramatized *Thérèse Raquin*. As I have said, there are in that novel a subject, characters and *milieu* constituting, to my mind, excellent elements for the tentative of which I have dreamed. I tried to make of it a purely human study, apart from every other interest, and go straight to the point; the action did not consist in any story invented for the occasion, but in the inner struggles of the characters; there was no logic of facts, but a logic of sensation and sentiment; and the dénouement was the mathematical result of the problem as proposed. I followed the novel step by step; I laid the play in the same room, dark and damp, in order not to lose relief or the sense of impending doom; I chose supernumerary fools, who were unnecessary from the point of view of strict technique, in order to place side by side with the fearful agony of my protagonists the drab life of every day; I tried continually to bring my setting into perfect accord with the occupations of my characters, in order that they might not *play*, but rather *live*, before the audience. I counted, I confess, and with good reason, on the intrinsic power of the drama to make up, in the minds of the audience, for the absence of intrigue and the usual details. The attempt was successful, and for that reason I am more hopeful for the plays I *shall* write than for *Thérèse Raquin*. I publish this play with vague regret, and with a mad desire to change whole scenes.

The critics were wild: they discussed the play with extreme violence. I have nothing to complain of, but rather thank them. I gained by hearing them praise the novel from which the play was taken, the novel which was so badly received by the press when it was first published. To-day the novel is good, and the drama is worthless. Let us hope that the play would be good were I able to extract something from it that the critics should declare bad. In criticism, you must be able to read between the lines. For instance, how could the old champions of 1830 be indulgent toward *Thérèse Raquin*? Supposing even that my merchant's wife were a queen and my murderer wore an apricot-colored cloak? And if at the last Thérèse and Laurent should take poison from a golden goblet filled to the brim with Syracusan wine? But that nasty little shop! And those lower middle-class shop-keepers that presume to participate in a drama of their own in their own house, with their oilcloth table-cover! It is certain that the last of the Romanticists, even if they found some talent in my play, would have denied it absolutely, with the beautiful injustice of literary passion. Then there were the critics whose beliefs were in direct opposition to my own; these very sincerely tried to persuade me that I was wrong to burrow in a place which was not their own. I read these critics carefully; they said some excellent things, and I shall do my best to profit by some of their utterances which particularly appealed to me. Finally, I have to thank those sympathetic critics, of my own age, those who share my hopes, because, sad to say, one rarely finds support among one's elders: one must grow along with one's own generation, be pushed ahead by the one that follows, and attain the idea and the manner of the time. * * *

ANTONIN ARTAUD

No More Masterpieces†

One of the reasons for the asphyxiating atmosphere in which we live without possible escape or remedy—and in which we all share, even the most revolutionary among us—is our respect for what has been written, formulated, or painted, what has been given form, as if all expression were not at last exhausted, were not at a point where things must break apart if they are to start anew and begin fresh.

We must have done with this idea of masterpieces reserved for a self-styled elite and not understood by the general public; the mind has no such restricted districts as those so often used for clandestine sexual encounters.

Masterpieces of the past are good for the past: they are not good for us. We have the right to say what has been said and even what has not been said in a way that belongs to us, a way that is immediate and direct, corresponding to present modes of feeling, and understandable to everyone.

It is idiotic to reproach the masses for having no sense of the sublime, when the sublime is confused with one or another of its formal manifestations, which are moreover always defunct manifestations. And if for example a contemporary public does not understand *Oedipus Rex*, I shall make bold to say that it is the fault of *Oedipus Rex* and not of the public.

In *Oedipus Rex* there is the theme of incest and the idea that nature mocks at morality and that there are certain unspecified powers at large which we would do well to beware of, call them *destiny* or anything you choose.

There is in addition the presence of a plague epidemic which is a physical incarnation of these powers. But the whole in a manner and language that have lost all touch with the rude and epileptic rhythm of our time. Sophocles speaks grandly perhaps, but in a style that is no longer timely. His language is too refined for this age, it is as if he were speaking beside the point.

However, a public that shudders at train wrecks, that is familiar with earthquakes, plagues, revolutions, wars; that is sensitive to the disordered anguish of love, can be affected by all these grand notions and asks only to become aware of them, but on condition that it is addressed in its

† From *The Theater and Its Double* by Antonin Artaud, pp. 74–83. Reprinted by permission of Grove Weidenfeld, a division of Wheatland Corporation. Copyright © 1958 by Grove Press, Inc,

own language, and that its knowledge of these things does not come to it through adulterated trappings and speech that belong to extinct eras which will never live again.

Today as yesterday, the public is greedy for mystery: it asks only to become aware of the laws according to which destiny manifests itself, and to divine perhaps the secret of its apparitions.

Let us leave textual criticism to graduate students, formal criticism to esthetes, and recognize that what has been said is not still to be said; that an expression does not have the same value twice, does not live two lives; that all words, once spoken, are dead and function only at the moment when they are uttered, that a form, once it has served, cannot be used again and asks only to be replaced by another, and that the theater is the only place in the world where a gesture, once made, can never be made the same way twice. ·

If the public does not frequent our literary masterpieces, it is because those masterpieces are literary, that is to say, fixed; and fixed in forms that no longer respond to the needs of the time.

Far from blaming the public, we ought to blame the formal screen we interpose between ourselves and the public, and this new form of idolatry, the idolatry of fixed masterpieces which is one of the aspects of bourgeois conformism.

This conformism makes us confuse sublimity, ideas, and things with the forms they have taken in time and in our minds—in our snobbish, precious, aesthetic mentalities which the public does not understand.

How pointless in such matters to accuse the public of bad taste because it relishes insanities, so long as the public is not shown a valid spectacle; and I defy anyone to show me *here* a spectacle valid—valid in the supreme sense of the theater—since the last great romantic melodramas, i.e., since a hundred years ago.

The public, which takes the false for the true, has the sense of the true and always responds to it when it is manifested. However it is not upon the stage that the true is to be sought nowadays, but in the street; and if the crowd in the street is offered an occasion to show its human dignity, it will always do so.

If people are out of the habit of going to the theater, if we have all finally come to think of theater as an inferior art, a means of popular distraction, and to use it as an outlet for our worst instincts, it is because we have learned too well what the theater has been, namely, falsehood and illusion. It is because we have been accustomed for four hundred years, that is since the Renaissance, to a purely descriptive and narrative theater—storytelling psychology; it is because every possible ingenuity has been exerted in bringing to life on the stage plausible but detached beings, with the spectacle on one side, the public on the other—and because the public is no longer shown anything but the mirror of itself.

Shakespeare himself is responsible for this aberration and decline, this disinterested idea of the theater which wishes a theatrical performance to leave the public intact, without setting off one image that will shake the organism to its foundations and leave an ineffaceable scar.

If, in Shakespeare, a man is sometimes preoccupied with what transcends him, it is always in order to determine the ultimate consequences of this preoccupation within him, i.e., psychology.

Psychology, which works relentlessly to reduce the unknown to the known, to the quotidian and the ordinary, is the cause of the theater's abasement and its fearful loss of energy, which seems to me to have reached its lowest point. And I think both the theater and we ourselves have had enough of psychology.

I believe furthermore that we can all agree on this matter sufficiently so that there is no need to descend to the repugnant level of the modern and French theater to condemn the theater of psychology.

Stories about money, worry over money, social careerism, the pangs of love unspoiled by altruism, sexuality sugar-coated with an eroticism that has lost its mystery have nothing to do with the theater, even if they do belong to psychology. These torments, seductions, and lusts before which we are nothing but Peeping Toms gratifying our cravings, tend to go bad, and their rot turns to revolution: we must take this into account.

But this is not our most serious concern.

If Shakespeare and his imitators have gradually insinuated the idea of art for art's sake, with art on one side and life on the other, we can rest on this feeble and lazy idea only as long as the life outside endures. But there are too many signs that everything that used to sustain our lives no longer does so, that we are all mad, desperate, and sick. And I call for *us* to react.

This idea of a detached art, of poetry as a charm which exists only to distract our leisure, is a decadent idea and an unmistakable symptom of our power to castrate.

Our literary admiration for Rimbaud, Jarry, Lautréamont,[1] and a few others, which has driven two men to suicide, but turned into café gossip for the rest, belongs to this idea of literary poetry, of detached art, of neutral spiritual activity which creates nothing and produces nothing; and I can bear witness that at the very moment when that kind of personal poetry which involves only the man who creates it and only at the moment he creates it broke out in its most abusive fashion, the theater was scorned more than ever before by poets who have never had the sense of direct and concerted action, nor of efficacity, nor of danger.

We must get rid of our superstitious valuation of texts and *written* poetry. Written poetry is worth reading once, and then should be destroyed. Let the dead poets make way for others. Then we might even come to see that it is our veneration for what has already been created,

1. Arthur Rimbaud (1854–91), Alfred Jarry (1873–1907), and Isidore Ducasse, count of Lautréamont (1846–70) were poets of the symbolist movement in France. All three lived unconventional, sensational lives [*Editor*].

however beautiful and valid it may be, that petrifies us, deadens our responses, and prevents us from making contact with that underlying power, call it thought-energy, the life force, the determinism of change, lunar menses, or anything you like. Beneath the poetry of the texts, there is the actual poetry, without form and without text. And just as the efficacity of masks in the magic practices of certain tribes is exhausted—and these masks are no longer good for anything except museums—so the poetic efficacity of a text is exhausted; yet the poetry and the efficacity of the theater are exhausted least quickly of all, since they permit the *action* of what is gesticulated and pronounced, and which is never made the same way twice.

It is a question of knowing what we want. If we are prepared for war, plague, famine, and slaughter we do not even need to say so, we have only to continue as we are; continue behaving like snobs, rushing en masse to hear such and such a singer, to see such and such an admirable performance which never transcends the realm of art (and even the Russian ballet at the height of its splendor never transcended the realm of art), to marvel at such and such an exhibition of painting in which exciting shapes explode here and there but at random and without any genuine consciousness of the forces they could rouse.

The empiricism, randomness, individualism, and anarchy must cease.

Enough of personal poems, benefitting those who create them much more than those who read them.

Once and for all, enough of this closed, egoistic, and personal art.

Our spiritual anarchy and intellectual disorder is a function of the anarchy of everything else—or rather, everything else is a function of this anarchy.

I am not one of those who believe that civilization has to change in order for the theater to change; but I do believe that the theater, utilized in the highest and most difficult sense possible, has the power to influence the aspect and formation of things: and the encounter upon the stage of two passionate manifestations, two living centers, two nervous magnetisms is something as entire, true, even decisive, as, in life, the encounter of one epidermis with another in a timeless debauchery.

That is why I propose a theater of cruelty.—With this mania we all have for depreciating everything, as soon as I have said, "cruelty," everybody will at once take it to mean "blood." But "*theater of cruelty*" means a theater difficult and cruel for myself first of all. And, on the level of performance, it is not the cruelty we can exercise upon each other by hacking at each other's bodies, carving up our personal anatomies, or, like Assyrian emperors, sending parcels of human ears, noses, or neatly detached nostrils through the mail, but the much more terrible and necessary cruelty which things can exercise against us. We are not free. And the sky can still fall on our heads. And the theater has been created to teach us that first of all.

Either we will be capable of returning by present-day means to this superior idea of poetry and poetry-through-theater which underlies the Myths told by the great ancient tragedians, capable once more of entertaining a religious idea of the theater (without meditation, useless contemplation, and vague dreams), capable of attaining awareness and a possession of certain dominant forces, of certain notions that control all others, and (since ideas, when they are effective, carry their energy with them) capable of recovering within ourselves those energies which ultimately create order and increase the value of life, or else we might as well abandon ourselves now, without protest, and recognize that we are no longer good for anything but disorder, famine, blood, war, and epidemics.

Either we restore all the arts to a central attitude and necessity, finding an analogy between a gesture made in painting or the theater, and a gesture made by lava in a volcanic explosion, or we must stop painting, babbling, writing, or doing whatever it is we do.

I propose to bring back into the theater this elementary magical idea, taken up by modern psychoanalysis, which consists in effecting a patient's cure by making him assume the apparent and exterior attitudes of the desired condition.

I propose to renounce our empiricism of imagery, in which the unconscious furnishes images at random, and which the poet arranges at random too, calling them poetic and hence hermetic images, as if the kind of trance that poetry provides did not have its reverberations throughout the whole sensibility, in every nerve, and as if poetry were some vague force whose movements were invariable.

I propose to return through the theater to an idea of the physical knowledge of images and the means of inducing trances, as in Chinese medicine which knows, over the entire extent of the human anatomy, at what points to puncture in order to regulate the subtlest functions.

Those who have forgotten the communicative power and magical mimesis of a gesture, the theater can reinstruct, because a gesture carries its energy with it, and there are still human beings in the theater to manifest the force of the gesture made.

To create art is to deprive a gesture of its reverberation in the organism, whereas this reverberation, if the gesture is made in the conditions and with the force required, incites the organism and, through it, the entire individuality, to take attitudes in harmony with the gesture.

The theater is the only place in the world, the last general means we still possess of directly affecting the organism and, in periods of neurosis and petty sensuality like the one in which we are immersed, of attacking this sensuality by physical means it cannot withstand.

If music affects snakes, it is not on account of the spiritual notions it offers them, but because snakes are long and coil their length upon the earth, because their bodies touch the earth at almost every point; and because the musical vibrations which are communicated to the earth affect them like a very subtle, very long massage; and I propose to treat the spectators like the snakecharmer's subjects and conduct them *by means of their organisms* to an apprehension of the subtlest notions.

At first crude means, which will gradually be refined. These immediate crude means will hold their attention at the start.

That is why in the "theater of cruelty" the spectator is in the center and the spectacle surrounds him.

In this spectacle the sonorisation is constant: sounds, noises, cries are chosen first for their vibratory quality, then for what they represent.

Among these gradually refined means light is interposed in its turn. Light which is not created merely to add color or to brighten, and which brings its power, influence, suggestions with it. And the light of a green cavern does not sensually dispose the organism like the light of a windy day.

After sound and light there is action, and the dynamism of action: here the theater, far from copying life, puts itself whenever possible in communication with pure forces. And whether you accept or deny them, there is nevertheless a way of speaking which gives the name of "forces" to whatever brings to birth images of energy in the unconscious, and gratuitous crime on the surface.

A violent and concentrated action is a kind of lyricism: it summons up supernatural images, a bloodstream of images, a bleeding spurt of images in the poet's head and in the spectator's as well.

Whatever the conflicts that haunt the mind of a given period, I defy and spectator to whom such violent scenes will have transferred their blood, who will have felt in himself the transit of a superior action, who will have seen the extraordinary and essential movements of his thought illuminated in extraordinary deeds—the violence and blood having been placed at the service of the violence of the thought—I defy that spectator to give himself up, once outside the theater, to ideas of war, riot, and blantant murder.

So expressed, this idea seems dangerous and sophomoric. It will be claimed that example breeds example, that if the attitude of cure induces cure, the attitude of murder will induce murder. Everything depends upon the manner and the purity with which the thing is done. There is a risk. But let it not be forgotten that though a theatrical gesture is violent, it is disinterested; and that the theater teaches precisely the uselessness of the action which, once done, is not to be done, and the superior use of the state unused by the action and which, *restored*, produces a purification.

I propose then a theater in which violent physical images crush and hypnotize the sensibility of the spectator seized by the theater as by a whirlwind of higher forces.

A theater which, abandoning psychology, recounts the extraordinary, stages natural conflicts, natural and subtle forces, and presents itself first of all as an exceptional power of redirection. A theater that induces trance, as the dances of Dervishes induce trance, and that addresses itself to the organism by precise instruments, by the same means as those of certain tribal music cures which we admire on records but are incapable or originating among ourselves.

There is a risk involved, but in the present circumstances I believe it is a risk worth running. I do not believe we have managed to revitalize the world we live in, and I do not believe it is worth the trouble of clinging to; but I do propose something to get us out of our marasmus, instead of continuing to complain about it, and about the boredom, inertia, and stupidity of everything.

BERT O. STATES

Expressionism and After†

* * *

When drama arrives at the point where it is about people who dream, rather than act, it is on the verge of giving birth to the dream play, or to the drama of the interior of the human mind. (I am putting aside the obvious example of Strindberg here because his is such a clear case of a dramatist who broke one form [naturalism] and moved, more or less wholesale, to another [surrealism]. The best treatment of this journey to the interior has been written by Raymond Williams, who argues that the "break" between naturalism and the various nonrealisms that succeeded it must be seen not in "the look of the stage" but as the steady evolution of a "structure of feeling" based on "a passion for truth, in strictly human and contemporary terms." Thus broadly conceived, the naturalist drama is "one of the great revolutions in human consciousness: to confront the human drama in its immediate setting, without reference to 'outside' forces and powers.[1] There is always, he says, "a precise internal relation" between a structure of feeling and its set of stylistic conventions, and the naturalist drive toward its constantly evolving truth often found it necessary to slough off conventions because they were no longer true enough—all of which gave the product the look of a new "ism." Being a sort of scientist, the naturalist found himself in the position of the physicist searching for the elementary particle: every time he thought he had found it, a still more elementary particle signaled its existence. Or, today's truth is tomorrow's received idea; today's realism is tomorrow's melodrama. Thus naturalism moved increasingly inward to subtler and more subjective kinds of experience, creating its own conventions or borrowing them from earlier forms as it advanced. To abbreviate a complex metamorphosis: once realism had perfected the fusion of psychology and scenery—finding, as it were, the mind's con-

---

† From *Great Reckonings in Little Rooms: On the Phenomenology of Theatre.* Pp. 82–89. Copyright © 1985 The Regents of the University of California. Reprinted with permission of the University of California Press.

1. Raymond Williams, *The Drama from Ibsen to Brecht* (New York, 1969), p. 334.

struction in the environment—the next step was immanent. The clearest moment of conventional transformation, or at least the most important for the theater, is expressionism, which, Williams says, is realism turned inside out. Once you have trapped your protagonist in one of these *real* rooms, leaving him (or her) in the posture of Munch's creature in *The Cry*,[2] you take away the room—which is no longer *real* enough—and reconstruct it as the visible extension of his ravaged state of mind. For example, as the story of a woman who dreams of living dangerously, imagine an expressionistic *Hedda Gabler*[3] that takes place in the barrel of a dueling pistol; or a *Cherry Orchard*[4] set among trees that gradually turn into telegraph poles and industrial smokestacks.

The refreshing thing about Williams's approach is that it enables us to see an evolution as a continual process rather than as something that began and ended as a manifestation of style. However distinctive the look of the expressionistic stage, it was doing the work of the naturalist premise either in its pessimistic aspect (with respect to society's victimization of the individual) or in its essentialist aspect (with respect to its intense concern for the state of the soul). Above all, it was still representational in the sense that is sought to depict faithfully its experience "in human and contemporary terms." The distinctive thing about the naturalists and the expressionists was that theirs was an art of fierce signification—meaning that if the play was interesting, if the audience drew its breath in outrage or astonishment, it was because the stage was directly plugged into life. What the spectator was seeing was his own rooms or the inside of his own head. It is important to remember how different this conception of art was from that of the neoclassicists, or even the romantics, who presumably viewed plays as achieving, or not achieving, a perfection of traditional form, a just representation of eternal nature, or as a freedom to mix forms on the theory that what was good enough for eternal nature was good enough for art. From the standpoint of the new militancy, whether expressionist or naturalist, classicism was summed up by Ernst Toller as "the expression of self-contained superior calm,"[5] and romanticism by Zola as "the restless regret of the old world."[6]

---

2. A painting by the Norwegian Edvard Munch (1863–1944) with a figure in the foreground with his mouth open in a cry of pain and the shape of his mouth repeated in the setting behind him [*Editor*].

3. A play by Ibsen (1890) that deals with a woman morbidly preoccupied with the arid limitations of her bourgeois life but lacking the courage to break with it [*Editor*].

4. A play be Chekhov (1904) set on a country estate that its owners refuse to sell in part because they cannot bear the idea that it will be adapted to modern needs and its famous cherry orchard be destroyed [*Editor*].

5. Ernst Toller, "Hoppla, Such is Life," in *Playwrights on Playwriting*, p. 226. [Toller (1893–1939) was a leading dramatist in the German Expressionist movement just after World War I—*Editor*.]

6. Zola, "Naturalism and the Stage," p. 117. Of course, we must bear in mind that this "organistic" idea could also be extended in the reverse direction. That is, what we are here calling naturalism cannot be cleanly separated from the "structure of feeling" of romanticism. For example, romanticism's strong theme of the imprisonment of the noble hero (e.g. Kleist's Prince of Homburg) gets carried over into naturalism in the imprisonment of the bourgeois protagonist (Hedda Gabler, the Rosmers, Ivanov) in the sociological trap of his or her living room. The romantic hero's discovery, usually while in prison, of his true self and his freedom of soul more or less disappears in naturalism and is replaced by the escape from society through the side door of suicide. (See my review of Victor Brombert's *The Romantic Prison*: "The Piranesi Effect: Alone and Well in Prison," *Hudson Review* 32 [Winter 1979–80]: 615–20). * * *

It would be absurd to conflate naturalism and expressionism as styles, or to maintain that expressionism, as a style, did not have an influence on later naturalism, as a "passion for truth." The other side of this argument is that expressionism (including its sister "isms"), whatever its origins in naturalistic truth seeking, represented an almost atomic release of stylistic energy. One is always impressed by the sanity of E. H. Gombrich in these duck/rabbit matters of style and content. Particularly, I think of his image of the artist as a man with a paint box and a method who goes out into nature not to paint what he sees but to see what he knows how to paint. Beyond this image of the individual talent wearing the spectacles of his own tradition, however, there is the matter of the tradition's own evolution which, though composed of a sucession of individual talents, resembles a biological lifecycle. If a tradition, like an organism, is to remain vital, it follows that it must feed on something. But styles, Gombrich says, are like languages: they are inevitably limited in the number and kinds of questions they allow the artist to ask.[7] * * * And it is quite possible to see naturalism, as a rigidly mimetic style, entering a stage of crisis at about the turn of the century. There are two aspects to this crisis. The first we have discussed sufficiently: the idea that naturalism, as a style, could no longer answer the questions raised by its own discoveries (how, for example, to display what is inside the human head). The second has to do with the artistic, as opposed to the scientific problem, and it might simply be called a crisis of self-perfection. Ostensibly, the naturalist's art is marked by the disappearance of style; and though we can speak, on other levels, of the style of an Ibsen or a Chekhov, naturalism was a style in which the artist disappeared, or pretended he had never been there at all. As a result, we tend to think of naturalism not as a kind of beauty but as a form of journalism which, like the newspaper, has an endless fund of new subjects and, being a thing invisible itself, is precisely as interesting as its subject's social relevance. But if we regard the theater as an institution of pleasure—that is, as something for the eye and the ear to enjoy as a species of beauty—we can see wherein naturalism was exposed to the same vicissitudes of fashion as lesser and more ostentatious movements. I say there was a crisis of self-perfection not because the world was tiring of Ibsen and Chekhov, or because there was no social work left for naturalism to do, but because there was nothing *new* it could do, as a mature style, without repeating itself to death. And it seems to be a characteristic of art movements that they must have something new to do, and as they become essentially perfect in form they sense the end of inventiveness and begin generating their own opponents or, if you wish, their own heirs.

It is usually, and in another sense quite validly, said that their opponents generate themselves on their own from the outside, like the

7. E.H. Gombrich, *Art and Illusion: A Study in the Psychology of Pictorial Representation* (New York, 1965), p. 90.

poor rising against an aristocracy, thus giving rise to new movements. But we should not allow the noisy wars between the naturalists and the expressionists to obscure the fact that above, or beneath, all "isms" is the internal continuity of the art itself. This is implicit in Picasso's remark: "We are all Modern-Style artists. . . . Because even if you are against a movement, you're still part of it. The pro and the con are, after all, two aspects of the same movement."[8] Perhaps we may describe the historical movement of an art form as a stream that flows and changes direction at the speed of its stylistic momentum. By this I refer to the art's ability to explore the possibilities of its own image system—and art abhors an unused possibility as nature abhors a vacuum—to sense the approach of the system's collapse, to reconstitute itself of new materials, to transmigrate, like Antony's crocodile, when the elements are out of it, in order to protect itself against the great deadener of its own habit. Lurking in the word *convention*, which is art's only language, is always the danger of the conventional, or the degeneration of the convention into unintentional self-parody. Perhaps this is very fanciful morphology, but I am not concerned here with giving art movements a transcendent consciousness; rather, I am interested in the sense in which revolutions originate from within the stylistic paradigm, a little as the bank clerk learns banking from the inside and then runs off with the funds. Expressionism was an inside job in the sense that it was prepared from naturalism's principle that drama arises from the conflict of individuals and institutions. Expressionism did not in the least kill off naturallism, either as a style or as a structure of feeling; nor did it affect the popularity or durability of major naturalist writers (Chekhov had barely reached Europe); it made it possible for naturalism to remain alive, temporarily in the back seat while it reconstructed itself from "new fundamentals," as Kuhn might say.[9]

The difference between art paradigms and scientific paradigms is that art rarely discards any previous achievement. We do not discard naturalism as we discard the concept of a Ptolemaic universe[1] and replace it with the "correct" Copernican view.[2] Naturalism doesn't become invalid; it simply leads to something else and then it quietly absorbs that something else into its own practice, as we see, in different ways, in the plays of expressionists like Kaiser, Wedekind, and Strindberg,[3] and today in the theatrical naturalism of playwrights like David Rabe, Sam She-

8. Françoise Gilot and Carlton Lake, *Life with Picasso* (New York, 1964), pp. 75–76.

9. Thomas S. Kuhn, a theorist about scientific revolutions discussed earlier by States in this book. Kuhn's book is *The Copernican Revolution: Planetary Astronomy in the Development of Western Thought* (Cambridge, Mass., 1957) [*Editor*].

1. The system formulated by Ptolemy about 140 A.D. that postulated that the earth was the fixed center of the universe while the stars were fixed in a sphere around it with yet another sphere, the

Prime Mover, which caused the sphere of stars to move around the earth, outside that [*Editor*].

2. The Copernican system, the work of Nicolaus Copernicus (1473–1547), postulated a sun-centered universe and the earth's daily rotation. It challenged earlier science and religious dogma and laid the foundation for modern astronomy [*Editor*].

3. Georg Kaiser (1878–1945) and Frank Wedekind (1864–1918) were German playwrights; August Strindberg (1849–1916) a Swedish playwright [*Editor*].

pard, and John Guare.[4] To sum up: with expressionism the drama abruptly reeentered the world of style; moreover, a style precisely equipped to dissolve naturalism's dense centripetal mass and return the stage to the kind of epic time/space options it had enjoyed in Shakespeare's day. If expressionism, as a content, was naturalism turned inside out, as a style it was naturalism cut into pieces somewhat along the lines of Tristan Tzara's newspaper-poems:[5] an art of sudden juxtapositions as opposed to an art of gradual transition; and most important, a style that could juxtapose various degrees of realism and nonrealism, from the filthiest cellar of hard-core naturalism to the most flagrant symbolism.

4. David Rabe (1940–), Sam Shepard (1943–), and John Guare (1938–) are American playwrights [Editor].

5. Tzara (1896–1963), a Rumanian poet, was the chief spokesman for Dadaism, an extreme form of nonrealistic art. One of Tzara's specialties was "sound poems" consisting of snippets of newspaper articles selected at random and then read aloud [Editor].

Henrik Ibsen and *The Wild Duck*

HENRIK IBSEN

Letters and Speeches†

To Georg Brandes[1]

Dresden, December 20, 1870

Dear Georg Brandes, You have been in my thoughts every day lately. I heard of your illness both from Councilor Hegel and from the Norwegian papers, but I did not write to you since I was afraid you might still be too weak to receive letters. Your kind note received yesterday has, however, quite reassured me. Many thanks for thinking of me!

You ask what you ought to undertake in the future. I can tell you: in the immediate future you must undertake nothing at all. You must give your mind a holiday for an indefinite period. You must lie still and grow strong. You see, these illnesses bring a blessing with them—the condition in which one comes out of them! A glorious time awaits you when you begin to regain your strength. I know this from personal experience. All evil thoughts had left me; I felt like eating only the lightest and most delicate foods—anything coarse, I thought, would taint me. It is an indescribable state of thankfulness and well-being.

And when you have grown strong and fit again, then what will you do? Why, then you will do what you must do. A nature such as yours has no choice.

I am not going to write you a long letter; that would not be good for you. And you had better not write to me for some time yet.

I was in Copenhagen last summer. You have many, many friends and adherents there; perhaps more than you realize. If you are away for

† Excerpts from *Ibsen, Letters and Speeches*, edited by Evert Sprinchorn. Pp. 105–7, 108, 109, 114–16, 226, 227, 337–38. Copyright © 1964 by Evert Sprinchorn. Reprinted by permission of Hill & Wang, a division of Farrar, Straus and Giroux, Inc.

1. A Danish literary critic (1842–1927) who was at this time ill with typhoid in Rome [*Editor*].

a while, so much the better; one always gains something by being missed.

They have finally taken Rome away from us human beings and given it to the politicians.[2] Where shall we take refuge now? Rome was the one sanctuary in Europe, the only place that enjoyed true freedom—freedom from the tyranny of political freedom. I do not think I shall visit it again after what has happened. All that was delightful—the unsophisticatedness, the dirt—all that will disappear. For every statesman who crops up there, an artist will be ruined. And the glorious longing for liberty—that is at an end now. Yes—I for one must confess that the only thing I love about liberty is the struggle for it; I care nothing for the possession of it.

One morning some time ago my new work [on Julian the Apostate] became strikingly clear to me; and in my exuberance I dashed off a letter to you. But I never sent it. The mood did not last long, and when it was over, the letter was useless.

Moreover, the historic events of today are claiming a large share of my thoughts. The old illusory France has been smashed to bits, and as soon as the new, *de facto* Prussia is also smashed too, we shall enter the age of the future in one leap. How the old ideas will come tumbling about our ears! And it is high time they did. Up till now we have been living on nothing but crumbs from the revolutionary table of last century, and I think we have been chewing on that stuff long enough. The old terms must be invested with new meaning, and given new explanations. Liberty, equality, and fraternity are no longer what they were in the days of the late-lamented guillotine. This is what the politicians will not understand; and that is why I hate them. They want only their own special revolutions—external revolutions, political revolutions, etc. But that is only dabbling. What is really needed is a revolution of the human spirit. And in this *you* shall be one of those who take the lead. But the first thing to do is to get that fever out of your system.

Your devoted friend,
Henrik Ibsen

To Georg Brandes

Dresden, February 17, 1871

Dear Brandes, I suspected that my long silence would make you angry. But I confidently trust that our relations are such that they will stand the strain. In fact, I have a decided feeling that a brisk correspondence would be much more dangerous to our friendship. Once we have actually met, many things will assume another aspect; much will be cleared up on both sides. Until then I really run the danger of exhibiting myself to you through my casual remarks in quite a wrong light. You philosophers can prove black is white—and I have to desire to allow myself

---

2. Rome had recently been annexed by the new Italian republic after a plebiscite [*Editor*].

to be reduced, per correspondence, to a stone or a cock—even if it is possible to restore me after an oral explanation to the rank of a human being [a reference to Holberg's *Erasmus Montanus*]. In your previous letter you ironically admire my undisturbed mental equilibrium under the present conditions. There we have the stone! And now in your last friendly (?) note, you make me out a hater of liberty. The cock! The fact is that my mind is relatively calm because I regard France's present misfortune as the greatest good fortune that could befall her. As to liberty, I take it that our disagreement is a disagreement about words. I shall never agree to making liberty synonymous with political liberty. What you call liberty, I call liberties; and what I call the struggle for liberty is nothing but the steady, vital growth and pursuit of the very conception of liberty. He who possesses liberty as something already achieved possesses it dead and soulless; for the essence of the idea of liberty is that it continue to develop steadily as men pursue it and make it part of their being. Anyone who stops in the middle of the struggle and says, "Now I have it," shows that he has lost it. It is exactly this tendency to stop dead when a certain given amount of liberty has been acquired that is characteristic of the political state—and it is this that I said was not good.

Of course it is a benefit to possess the right to vote, the right of self-taxation, etc. But who benefits? The citizen, not the individual. Now, there is absolutely no logical necessity for the individual to be a citizen. On the contrary—the state is the curse of the individual. How did Prussia purchase its strength as a state? By absorbing the spirit of the individual into a political and geographical conception. The waiter makes the best soldier. Now, turn to the Jewish nation, the nobility of the human race. How has it managed to preserve itself—in its isolation, in its poetry—despite all the barbarity of the outside world? Because it had no state to burden it. Had the Jewish people remained in Palestine, it would long since have been ruined in the process of construction, like all the other nations. The state must be abolished! In that revolution I will take part. Undermine the idea of the state; make willingness and spriritual kinship the only essentials for union—and you have the beginning of a liberty that is of some value. Changing one form of government for another is merely a matter of toying with various degrees of the same thing—a little more or a little less. Folly, all of it.

Yes, dear friend, the great thing is not to allow oneself to be frightened by the venerableness of institutions. The state has its roots in time: it will reach its height in time. Greater things than it will fall; all religion will fall. Neither standards of morality nor of art are eternal. What is there that we are really obliged to hold on to? Who will vouch for it that two and two do not make five up on Jupiter?

I cannot and will not enlarge upon these points in a letter. My best thanks for your poem! It is not the last one you will write. The poet's calling proclaims itself in every line. You overestimate me, but I set that down to our friendship. But thank you, thank you! Keep me ever so in your thoughts. I shall not fail you! * * *

Yours sincerely,
Henrik Ibsen

To Georg Brandes

Dresden, September 24, 1871

Dear Brandes, I always read your letters with strangely mixed feelings. They are more like poems than letters. What you write strikes me like a cry of distress from one who has been left the sole survivor in some great lifeless desert. And I cannot but rejoice, and thank you, that you direct this cry to me. But on the other hand, I begin to worry. I ask myself: "What will such a mood lead to?" And I have nothing to comfort myself with but the hope that it is only temporary. You seem to me to be passing through the same crisis that I passed through when I began to write *Brand*. I am convinced that you, too, will find the medicine that will drive the disease out of your system.

Energetic productivity is an excellent remedy. What I recommend for you is a thoroughgoing, full-blooded egoism, which will force you for a time to regard yourself and your work as the only things of consequence in this world, and everything else as simply nonexistent. Now, don't take this as evidence of something brutal in my nature! There is no way in which you can benefit society more than by coining the metal you have in yourself. I have never really had a very great feeling for solidarity. In fact, I have allowed it in my mental cargo only because it is a traditional article of belief. If one had the courage to throw it overboard altogether, one would be getting rid of the ballast that weighs most heavily on the personality. There are actually moments when the whole history of the world reminds one of a sinking ship; the only thing to do is save oneself.

Nothing will come from special reforms. The whole human race is on the wrong track. That is the trouble. Is there really anything tenable in the present situation—with its unattainable ideals, etc.? All of human history reminds me of a cobbler who doesn't stick to his last but goes on the stage to act. And we have made a fiasco in both the roles of hero and lover. The only part in which we have shown a little talent is that of the naive comic; and with our more highly developed self-consciousness we shall no longer be fitted even for that. I do not believe that things are better in other countries. The masses, both at home and abroad, have absolutely no understanding of higher things.

And so I should raise a banner, should I? My dear friend, I would be putting on the same kind of performance Louis Napoleon did when he landed at Boulogne with an eagle on his head.[3] Later, when the

---

3. In 1840 Louis Napoleon, seeking to end his exile and to assume the throne of France, made a foolish and theatrical descent on Boulogne. He was captured, tried, and imprisoned [*Translator's note*].

hour of his destiny struck, he didn't need any eagle. In the course of my work on Julian,[4] I have become a fatalist in a way; yet this play will be a kind of banner. But do not worry—this will not be a tendentious work. I explore the characters, their conflicting plans, the plot, and do not concern myself with the moral of the whole—always assuming, however, that by the moral of the story you do not mean its philosophy. You can take it for granted that the philosophy will burst forth as the final verdict on the struggle and on the victory. But this is too abstract to make much sense. You must look at the work itself.

Your last letter on this subject did not cause me any uneasiness. In the first place, I was prepared for such misgivings on your part; and in the second, I am not handling the subject in the way you assume.

I have received you book [probably *Criticisms and Portraits*], and all I can say is that I return to it again and again. It is incomprehensible to me, my dear, good Brandes, that you of all people can be despondent. Very few have received the call of the spirit as clearly and unmistakably as you have. What is the use of despairing? Have you any right to do so? But don't think I don't understand you perfectly.

. . . And now in conclusion accept my heartfelt thanks for your visit to Dresden. Those were festive hours for me. Best wishes for health, courage, happiness—everything good!

Yours sincerely,
Henrik Ibsen

Speech at the Banquet in Stockholm

Stockholm, September 24, 1887

Ladies and Gentlemen: I thank you most deeply for all the friendliness, for the welcoming spirit and the understanding that I have once again received proofs of here. It is a great joy to feel that one belongs to a greater country. But to reply fully to all the words of praise that I have just heard lies outside and beyond my power. There is, however, one point in particular that I should like to consider for a moment. It has been said that I, too, have contributed, and in a prominent way, to bringing about a new era in our countries. I believe, on the contrary, that the time in which we now live might with quite as good reason be described as a conclusion, and that something new is about to be born from it. For I believe that the teaching of natural science about evolution is also valid as regards the spiritual aspects of life. I believe that the time is not far off when political and social conceptions will cease to exist in their present forms, and that from both of them there will arise a unity, which for a while will contain within itself the conditions for the happiness of mankind. I believe that poetry, philosophy, and religion will

4. Flavius Claudius Julianus, or Julian the Apostate (331–63). As emperor of Rome he opposed Christianity in an attempt to revive classical paganism. Ibsen treated his rebellion in *Emperor and Galilean* (1864–73) [*Editor*].

be merged in a new category and become a new vital force, of which we who are living now can have no clear conception.

It has been said of me on different occasions that I am a pessimist. And so I am insofar as I do not believe in the everlastingness of human ideals. But I am also an optimist insofar as I firmly believe in the capacity for the propagation and development of ideals. Especially, to be more definite, I believe that the ideals of our time, while disintegrating, are tending toward what in my play *Emperor and Galilean* I designated "the third kingdom." Therefore, permit me to drink a toast to the future— to that which is to come. We are assembled here on a Saturday night. Following it, comes the day of rest, the holiday, the holy day—whichever you wish to call it. For my part I shall be content with my week's work, a lifelong week, if it can serve to prepare the spirit for tomorrow. But above all I shall be most content if it will serve to strengthen the spirit for that week of work that inevitably follows.

Thank you.

Speech at the Banquet of the Norwegian League for Women's Rights

Christiania, May 26, 1898

I am not a member of the Women's Rights League. Whatever I have written has been without any conscious thought of making propaganda. I have been more the poet and less the social philosopher than people generally seem inclined to believe. I thank you for the toast, but must disclaim the honor of having consciously worked for the women's rights movement. I am not even quite clear as to just what this women's rights movement really is. To me it has seemed a problem of mankind in general. And if you read my books carefully you will understand this. True enough, it is desirable to solve the woman problem, along with all the others; but that has not been the whole purpose. My task has been the *description of humanity*. To be sure, whenever such a description is felt to be reasonably true, the reader will read his own feelings and sentiments into the work of the poet. These are then attributed to the poet; but incorrectly so. Every reader remolds the work beautifully and neatly, each according to his own personality. Not only those who write but also those who read are poets. They are collaborators. They are often more poetical than the poet himself.

With these reservations, let me thank you for the toast you have given me. I do indeed recognize that women have an important task to perform in the particular directions this club is working along. I will express my thanks by proposing a toast to the League for Women's Rights, wishing it progress and success.

The task always before my mind has been to advance our country and to give our people a higher standard. To achieve this, two factors are important. It is for the *mothers*, by strenuous and sustained labor, to awaken a conscious feeling of *culture* and *discipline*. This feeling must be awakened before it will be possible to lift the people to a higher plane. It is the women who shall solve the human problem. As mothers they shall solve it. And only in that capacity can they solve it. Here lies a great task for woman. My thanks! And success to the League for Women's Rights!

M. C. BRADBROOK

[The Wild Duck]†

The old view of *The Wild Duck* was that it presented the obverse case of *A Doll's House* and *Ghosts*, and gave a timely warning against fanatic innovators. In this view the centre of the play lies in the mistakes of Gregers and the diagnosis of Relling, the only two characters capable of judgment or of moral decision. This is its "problem". As Shaw puts it:

> Now an interesting play cannot in the nature of things mean anything but a play in which problems of conduct and character of personal importance to the audience are raised and suggestively discussed.[1]

Three times Gregers the idealist crosses swords with Relling the psychologist and the play ends with their mutual defiance. The structure depends on Gregers' interventions; he is responsible not only for the breach between Gina and Hjalmer but also for the suggestion which drives Hedvig to her death. It may be that Gregers was a more interesting figure to contemporaries than he is today; but the fact is that although Gregers sets the play in motion, he is not the centre of interest. Ibsen himself seems to have shifted his ground as he wrote. We have indeed his ówn word that he did not think in terms of "problems," "Everything which I have written as a poet has had its origin in a frame of mind and situation in life. I never wrote because I had, as they say, 'found a good subject' ", and in explanation of the artists's attitude to science: "What we, the uninitiated, do not possess as knowledge, we possess, I believe, to a certain degree, as intuition or instinct." He goes on to say that there is a kind of family likeness between scientists and artists of the same period, just as in portraits—he observes—there is a type characteristic of a given period, independent of any school of painters. Ibsen's own anticipation of psychological discoveries is itself a testimony to his theory; the most striking instance is *The Sea Woman*.

Ibsen would therefore in any case have repudiated the idea that in

† From M. C. Bradbrook, *Ibsen The Norwegian*, London, 1948. Pp. 102–7. Copyright 1946. Reprinted by permission of the publishers, Chatto and Windus, Ltd.
1. *The Quintessence of Ibsenism.*

The Wild Duck he was being merely instructive. But it does appear that he began with the notion of a satiric comedy, rather in the mood of *An Enemy of the People*. The first act is out of key with what follows, although it is an excellent sketch of provincial good society in all its smug solidarity—a society which has made catspaws of the weak, as Ibsen had already depicted. Wehrle the elder is another Consul Bernick. In this society Gregers is playing the part of social reformer, and, as in all literature of the time, from *Aurora Leigh* to *Beauchamp's Career*, the way of the social reformer is thorny indeed. On the other hand, the social reformer is conscious of the nobility of his vocation, and is thus enabled to withstand all the fiery darts of the wicked and to hurl a pretty dart in turn. Miss Aurora Leigh—a notable social reformer—bids Lady Waldemar remember how

> You sold that poisonous porridge called your soul,

and, beside her invective, Greger's words to old Wehrle sound almost filial.[2] But the force of these scenes is almost lost upon the reader of today.

In a sense, of course, Gregers is a permanent figure; he is the man who has found the entire solution to life in a creed, whether that of Marx or Freud, the Oxford Group or Yoga. He is Brand turned inside out.[3] He saw his mother as right and his father as wrong. He feels wronged by his father, and at the same time morbidly conscious of a duty towards Hjalmer, so he is driven to interference. In none of his highminded attempts does he pay any attention to the delicate human material he is handling—being what Hedda Gabler called "a specialist."[4] Nevertheless, Relling's brutalities are beside the mark. Gregers himself is mentally abnormal and, as he hints, physically a doomed man.

The play begins with his story; but the Ekdals run away with it. Ibsen said in a letter to his publisher, "The characters of *The Wild Duck* have endeared themselves to me," and by the characters, he clearly meant the Ekdals. Relling does his best to keep the play on a straight line with his sermon on the life-fantasy—in which he was anticipated by Francis Bacon,[5] but in the later acts Gregers is chiefly a "feed" to the Ekdals; he knits up an episode, or evokes a confidence from Hjalmer or Hedvig, but has little independent life.

The Ekdals gleam with vitality, even the sodden old Lieutenant. They are complex people who have simple minds. In the scene where old Ekdal decides to show Gregers the wild duck, they infect one another

2. *Aurora Leigh* was written by Mrs. Browning in 1857.
3. The reforming hero of an earlier play by Ibsen [*Editor*].
4. In *Hedda Gabler* Hedda applies the term to her husband to suggest his narrowness within cultivated limits and to explain the tedium of his company [*Editor*].

5. "Doth any man doubt that if there were taken out of men's minds vain opinions, flattering hopes, false valuations, imaginations as one would, and the like, but it would leave the minds of a number of men poor shrunken things, full of melancholy and indisposition, unpleasing to themselves" (*Essay: "Of Truth"*).

with excitement, until at last Hjalmer, who had begun by being rather ashamed of his hobby, joins in the chorus.

> *Lieut. Ekdal*: That's where the rabbits go at night, old man!
> *Gregers*: No, really? you've got rabbits too?
> *Lieut. Ekdal*: Yes, you can well believe we've got rabbits. He's asking if we've got rabbits, Hjalmer! Aha! But now comes the great thing, look you! Now for it! Look out, Hedvig! Stand here: like that: now look in. Do you see a basket full of straw?
> *Gregers*: Yes. And I see there's a bird in the basket.
> *Lieut. Ekdal*: Aha—"a bird!"!
> *Gregers*: Isn't it a duck?
> *Lieut. Ekdal*: Yes, you can bet it's a duck!
> *Hjalmer*: But WHAT SORT of a duck, do you think?
> *Hedvig*: It's not an ordinary duck——
> *Lieut. Ekdal*: Sh! Sh!

In this second act, the charm and absurdity of the Ekdals are enhanced by their innocent self-deceptions. The old man pretending he wants his hot water only for his ink, Hjalmer crying "No beer at a moment like this! Give me my flute!" are safe in the hands of their womenfolk, practising the ancient conspiratorial art of "managing father." What is humiliation for Nora becomes a game for Gina and Hedvig. It is a housecraft handed down from mother to daughter with the family recipes and ranging from maxims like "Feed the brute"—"Beer, father! lovely cool beer!" cries Hedvig—to that genuine faith in the Great Inventor which only the simple and childish could entertain, but which is the basis of Hjalmer's well-being. For he is a timid soul, easily snubbed, and needs the constant worship of his family to keep him in good heart. Hence his fretfulness at any suggestion of criticism; he feels betrayed from within the citadel.

Unsparingly as he is exposed, Hjalmer is not condemned. He, too, has endeared himself to Ibsen. He is not a Pecksniff or even a Skimpole[6]—rather he is a Micawber. When his preparation for heroic flight is punctured by Gina's "But what about all the rabbits?" he first cries desparingly. "What! have I got to take all the rabbits with me?" but almost at once wrests the alarming situation to his own advantage— "Father must get used to it. There are higher things than rabbits, which I have had to give up." His meanest act is when he gets Hedvig to finish his work so that he can potter in the attic, but salves his conscience by saying: "Don't hurt your eyes, do you hear? I'm not going to answer for it: you must decide for yourself, and so I warn you."

But his relish of the "patent contrivance" and his passionate concern about "a new path to the water-trough" are at least evidence of

6. Characters in Dickens' *Martin Chuzzlewit* and *Bleak House*, respectively; both contemptible hypocrites [*Editor*].

livsglaeden[7] if not of *arbeitsglaeden*.[8] He is so childish that he asks only for a part to play and an audience to applaud. Old Wehrle's cast-off mistress and her child are the perfect audience—docile, responsive, uncritical. His anger when he first suspects Hedvig not to be his is blind, savage and genuine.

> *Hjalmer:* My home's in ruins! (*Bursts into tears*) Gregers, I
> have no child now!
> *Hedvig:* What's that? Father! Father!
> *Gina:* Look at that now!
> *Hjalmer:* Don't come near me, Hedvig! Go away . . . I can't
> bear to see her. Ah . . . her eyes . . . Goodbye.
> *Hedvig (screams):* No! No! Don't leave me!
> *Gina:* Look at the child, Hjalmer! Look at the child!
> *Hjalmer:* I won't! I can't! I'm going—away from all this.

But his later cruelty is false play-acting. "In these last minutes in my old home I wish to be free from—intruders!" "Does he mean me, mother?" asks Hedvig, trembling. In his last explanation to Gregers, Hjalmer admits his dependence on her love and hero-worship, a little too clearly to be completely in character. "There is that terrible doubt—perhaps Hedvig never really loved me . . ." and he makes up a fantasy of how Hedvig had all the time been really laughing at him and deceiving him. The appetite for proof of affection is begotten of anxiety, and in this confession, Hjalmer becomes pitiable, because he, too, is seen to be bankrupt, and broken. Selfish and parasitic as his love was, it sprang from and satisfied his deepest need.

Hjalmer is both a tragic and a comic figure: Hedvig, like Antigone and Cordelia, is the victim who redeems. She is a mere child, saying prayers for the wild duck "that it may be preserved from all harm," and making her deep-laid plans to keep father in good humour. But she is mysterious too: like the wild duck, no one knows "where she came from, or who her friends are"—it is essentially an open question whether she is Hjalmer's child or old Wehrle's; and she is subject to strange adolescent tides of feeling that rise "from the ocean depths." Hedvig's piteous limitations leave her exposed to catastrophe. She does believe in Hjalmer, as no one but a child could do. He is her God and when he betrays her, she is terror-stricken with all the final black despair of childhood. Gregers, in prompting her to kill the wild duck, uses the language of religion. It is to be a witness-bearing, a ritual sacrifice, to propitiate Hjalmer, the offended God. And so when Hjalmer presents his final "demand of the ideal"—"If I were to say, 'Hedvig, art willing to give up this *life* for me?'—thanks, you'd soon see the answer!" Hedvig puts the pistol to her own breast and fires. Yet it is unresolved whether she died in grief or as a sacrifice; from an adolescent impulse to self-destruc-

---

7. "Joy of life" [*Editor*].   8. "Joy of work" [*Editor*].

tion, or a childish desire for revenge—"I'll die and *then* you'll be sorry."

Her death is catastrophic, the only unambiguous event in the play; yet its causes are veiled. It is not related to the previous action by the kind of iron chain that draws on Osvald's death.[9] It is a shock yet inevitable. Gina, gathering the remnants of her poor tenderness, speaks the last word: "The child mustn't lie out here to be looked at. She shall go in her own little room, my pet."

The most mysterious and potent symbol of all is not a human character but the wild duck itself. Each of the characters has something in common with the wild duck's story, but that story reflects all the scattered lights of the play and focuses them in one. The potency and power of the wild duck is that of the ghost in *Hamlet*, or the witches in *Macbeth*: it unites and concentrates the implications which lie behind the action of individuals.

Relling's final gibe at Gregers belongs to another world—the world of judgments, views and reason; the greatness of this play is that it moves upon so many levels simultaneously. Ibsen was no longer limited by his own chosen technique. The freedom and scope of *The Wild Duck* are a symptom of that increasing depth of humanity and generosity which was taking Ibsen further and further from the doctrinal and the propagandist. "Dramatic categories," he observed, "are elastic and must accommodate themselves to literary fact." The characters had endeared themselves to him and the dramatic category was modified accordingly, so that even the weakest is allowed to hint that he too has known "the ocean's depths."

DOROTHEA KROOK

[The Wild Duck]†

* * *

In *The Wild Duck*, the equivalent of the act of shame [to Hedda Gabler's] is not single and simple; rather it is positively double or twofold. The disastrous idealism of Gregers Werle in seeking to make Hjalmar face the truth about his child Hedvig's illegitimate birth is one side of it; the other side is the illusion in which Hjalmar Ekdal himself lives. This fool's paradise, however, is not what Gregers supposed it to be, and from this misunderstanding springs the whole tragic irony of the central action of the play. The irony has nothing to do with Hjalmar's not knowing the truth about his wife and Hedvig; it has to do with his not knowing

---

9. A character in Ibsen's *Ghosts* [Editor].
† From *Elements of Tragedy*, "Border Cases: Ibsen's A *Doll's House, Hedda Gabler, The Wild* *Duck*, and *The Master Builder*," New Haven and London, 1969. Pp. 98–106. Reprinted by permission of the publishers, Yale University Press.

the truth about himself. The shamefulness of his situation is not that he has been deceived about a child that is not his (which is shameful in a purely conventional, unreal sense), but that he is self-deceived, believing himself to be the breadwinner of the family when he is no such thing, and playing the part of the strong man toward his wife and child when he is in fact weak, vain and egotistical, and insufferably complacent.

The matter of this self-deception is a point that needs emphasis, because there has been a tendency in recent discussions of the play to minimize almost out of existence all that is repellent about Hjalmar and his domestic situation, and as a consequence to see no virtue at all in the misguided efforts of the abstract idealist, Gregers Werle.[1] But the text does not to my mind admit of this partisan interpretation. Hjalmar's egotism, vanity, and complacency are exhibited in sufficient detail to leave no doubt about the way we are meant to view him; nor are we left in any doubt that his state of self-deception is a fatal moral disability. On the other side, the virtue in Gregers Werle's misguided idealism is simply that it is the truth he is concerned about. Since we are expected to believe, suspending disbelief for the moment if necessary, that the pursuit of truth is in itself a virtue, there is that amount of virtue in what Gregers tries to do for Hjalmar, even though, being thoroughly mistaken in the circumstances, his efforts end in disaster.

This, I suggest, is a more accurate view of the central situation which in this play is the equivalent of the traditional act of shame. It is confirmed—negatively at least—by the comments of that cynical choric commentator, Relling, who cannot find words bitter and disparaging enough to express his loathing for the abstract idealism of Gregers Werle, but is at the same time at pains to expose Hjalmar's self-deception as savagely as he exposes Gregers' fanatical love of truth. Rellings's view is not to be wholly identified with Ibsen's (I will return to this point), but he does expose one aspect of the total situation as Ibsen meant us to see it.

Concerning Gregers Werle's idealism, it is perhaps enough to say that Ibsen's exposure of it is brilliantly incisive, and indeed one of the best things in the play. To the question, Why is Gregers' love of truth false and therefore destructive? The play gives a clear and powerfully convincing answer. It is false because it ignores the vital matter of human resources, of the capacity of human beings to receive the truth. Gregers is proffering a truth which is beyond the powers of the recipient (Hjalmar) to use for his salvation, and it can therefore only destroy him. His idealism is abstract—viciously abstract—because it takes no account of the actual moral and spiritual capacity of the individual recipient; and this proves that the abstract idealist himself is, with all his moralism, insensitive and obtuse. The pessimistic side of Ibsen's exposure—the

1. See, for instance, M. C. Bradbrook, *Ibsen the Norwegian* (London, 1948), pp. 104–7.

theme that "men cannot endure too much reality"—must not be minimized, for it contributes its share to the final doubt about the play as a tragedy. But insofar as the play is successful, it is so at least partly because the anti-idealism theme bears the stamp of the authentically tragic.

The basic "shameful" situation in this play, then, is a composite of the fool's paradise in which Hjalmar lives and the world of abstract truth (also a fool's paradise) in which Gregers lives. It is the impact of one upon the other that precipitates the spectacle of tragic suffering, of which the principal vessel is the child Hedvig. The suffering begins with Hedvig's anguish when Hjalmar rejects her on discovering that she is not his child; it is taken a stage further when Gregers Werle suggests to her that she kill the wild duck—as an act of propitiation, presumably, to her incensed father; and it ends with her taking her own life—a sacrificial death intended to affirm the power of her love for the father who has rejected her.

This is the main action of the play reduced to its barest outlines. It leaves out of account, among other things, the complicated symbolism of the wild duck (which I do not find completely successful), and the subsidiary theme of the sins of the fathers visited upon the children (a favorite theme of Ibsen's, here symbolized in Hedvig's weak sight which she has inherited from Old Werle, her real father). Up to this point, the play is as fully tragic as may be desired. The equivalent of the act of shame—the condition of self-deception in which Hjalmar and Gregers each helplessly flounder—is thoroughly representative of the human condition. Self-deception is one of the fundamental human infirmities, and being also one of the most subtle and insidious, it is peculiarly dangerous and destructive, indeed, almost illimitable in its tragic possibilities. As to the suffering, the child Hedvig's anguish when she is rejected by the man she has always thought of and loved as her father is intense, real, and very moving; The mother Gina's, though pitched in a lower key, is also real and moving; and Hjalmar's is neither real nor moving—but this is consistent with the design of the whole action, in which not he but Hedvig is the principal vessel of the tragic suffering.

At what point, then, does the doubt arise that *The Wild Duck* may fall short of being fully tragic? It comes, I suggest, in the very last passages of the play, into which are compressed the third and fourth elements of tragedy: the knowledge generated by the suffering, and the affirmation of the dignity of man and the worthwhileness of human life issuing from or implicit in the suffering so illuminated by knowledge. The relevant action begins at the point at which Hedvig's body is carried in, and Hjalmar cries out in an anguish and shame which (we feel) is at last completely genuine:

> RELLING. The bullet has entered the breast . . .
> GINA   (*bursting into tears*). My child, my child!

GREGERS *(huskily)*. In the ocean's depths.

HJALMAR *(springing up)*. No, no, she must live! Oh, for
    heaven's sake, Relling—only a moment—just long
    enough to let me tell her how inexpressibly I loved
    her all the time!

RELLING. It has reached the heart. Internal haemorrhage. She
    died on the spot.

HJALMAR. And I drove her from me like a hunted animal!
    And she crept into the loft in terror and died, for
    love of me *(sobbing)*. Never able to put it right
    now! Never able to tell her! *(Clenching his hands
    and shrieking to heaven.)* Ah, Thou above! If Thou
    art there! Why hast Thou done this thing to me!

GINA.   Hush, hush; you mustn't say things like that. We
    didn't deserve to keep her, I expect. (p. 258) [76][2]

And so on. Then, presently, comes the crucial last dialogue between
Hjalmar and Gina before they make their final exit:

GINA.   Help me with her, Hjalmar.
    (Hjalmar and Gina lift Hedvig between them.)

HJALMAR *(as they carry her away)*. Oh, Gina, Gina, can you
    bear it?

GINA.   We must help one another, Hjalmar. Now we have
    equal shares in her, haven't we? (p. 259) [76]

From this alone, it is indeed not easy to know whether the profound
shock administered to his complacency by Hedvig's death has brought,
or will bring, genuine self-knowledge to Hjalmar. Yet the internal evi-
dences, it seems to me, point to the more hopeful possibility. Hjalmar's
grief (one could argue) is so uncharacteristically genuine here, and his
remarks to Gina so uncharacteristically simple and sincere (especially
in the last little colloquy), that one feels this may be the beginning of
salvation for him. He really does seem to have taken that first step towards
the self-knowledge which for him would mean the end of his vanity,
egotism and complacency, and so the end of the real fool's paradise in
which he has been living. If this has in fact happened, it is his recognition
of the redemptive power of love (figured in Hedvig's sacrificial death)
which has effected his release from self-deception. Up to this point in
the play, therefore, Hedvig's death would seem not to have been in vain;
and if Ibsen had ended his play here, it would I think be possible to
argue that the implicit affirmation of tragedy had in fact been made,
and made with complete psychological and dramatic veracity—that is,
in the only way in which it could be made through a dramatic vehicle
like Hjalmar Ekdal. But the play goes on, and what follows, the last

2. Quotations from *The Wild Duck* are from Henrik Ibsen, *Three Plays*, trans. Una Ellis-Fermor (London,
1950). [Page references to this Norton Critical Edition are given in brackets.]

dialogue between Relling and Gregers Werle, puts all in doubt again. Relling and Gregers are alone on the stage:

GREGERS. Hedvig has not died in vain. Did you see how sorrow called out what was noblest in him?

RELLING. Most people are noble in the presence of death. But how long do you suppose his nobility will last in him?

GREGERS. Surely it will last and increase all his life!

RELLING. Before the year is out little Hedvig will be nothing more to him than a fine subject to declaim on.

GREGERS. You dare to say that of Hjalmar Ekdal!

RELLING. We will talk about it again when the first grass is showing on her grave. Then you'll hear him delivering himself of fine phrases about "the child torn untimely from her father's heart," and see him wallowing in emotion and self-pity.

GREGERS. If you are right and I am wrong, then life is not worth living.

RELLING. Oh, life would be tolerable enough, even so, if we could only be rid of these infernal duns who come to us poor people's doors with their claim of the ideal.

GREGERS *(looking in front of him)*. In that case, I am glad my destiny is what it is.

RELLING. May I ask—what *is* your destiny?

GREGERS *(on the point of going)*. To be thirteenth at table.

RELLING. I wonder . . . (pp. 259–60) [76–77]

The ambiguity of this passage rests on the fact, already touched on, that Relling as choric commentator is not to be fully identified with Ibsen himself. This may be decisively argued from the mere passage of Hedvig in the action of the drama. If Ibsen's own view were identical with Relling's, he would be incapable of giving us Hedvig and Hedvig's sacrificial death as the potentially redemptive element in his fable. Such phenomena have no place in the view of life adopted by the Rellings of this world, and since Ibsen does present Hedvig and Hedvig's death, we must infer that his own view is more inclusive than Relling's, and so not to be identified with it.

If this claim is correct, it follows that Relling's word cannot be taken as necessarily the last word on the situation, but only as one possible view of it. Therefore, his bitter gloomy prophecy about Hjalmar's back-sliding ("Before the year is out little Hedvig will be nothing more to him than a fine subject to declaim on") need not be taken as the truth about Hjalmar that Ibsen wishes us to believe. And it goes without saying that Gregers Werle's view of the situation—his faith in the beauty and nobility of Hjalmar's self-knowledge, repentance, and expiation—is not to be taken at its face value either. Gregers' simple-mindedness has already been sufficiently exposed to make it obviously impossible to accept his as the true interpretation.

Thus, faced with the perfect ambiguity of this last scene, we may well ask, Where in *The Wild Duck* is there an affirmation of the kind required in tragedy, and, if it is made, what exactly is it that is affirmed? We are given only Relling's characteristically pessimistic view of the situation and Gregers' characteristically optimistic view of it. There Ibsen leaves it. Hedvig's sacrificial death, which could have yielded the saving self-knowledge that those steeped in self-deception (Hjalmar and Gregers Werle) needed to be redeemed, has no such effect after all, or cannot with certainty be said to have this effect. And where there is such uncertainty about a fact so crucial to this play that it affects intimately the very possibility of a final affirmation of life, there the tragic effect has not been achieved, and *The Wild Duck*, viewed as a potential tragedy, remains (like *Hedda Gabler*) another of Ibsen's interesting failures.

* * *

Anton Chekhov
and
Three Sisters

ANTON CHEKHOV

Letters†

To Maria Kiseleva[1]

January 14, 1887, Moscow

* * * It is true that the world teems with "scoundrels—male and female." Human nature is imperfect and it would therefore be strange to observe only the righteous in this world. Certainly, to believe that literature bears the responsiblity for digging up the "pearls" from the heap of muck would mean rejecting literature itself. Literature is called artistic when it depicts life as it actually is. Its aim is absolute and honest truth. To constrict its function to such a specialty as digging for "pearls" is as fatal for it as if you were to require Levitan[2] to draw a tree and omit the dirty bark and yellowing foilage. I agree that the "pearl" theory is a good thing, but surely a man of letters is not a pastry cook, nor an expert on cosmetics, nor an entertainer; he is a responsible person, under contract to his conscience and the consciousness of his duty; being in for a penny he has to be in for a pound, and no matter how distressing he finds it, he is in duty bound to battle with his fastidiousness and soil his imagination with the grime of life. He is like any ordinary reporter. What would you say if a reporter, out of a feeling of squeamishness or from the desire to give pleasure to his readers, would describe only honest city administrators, high-minded matrons and virtuous railroad magnates?

† Excerpts from *The Selected Letters of Anton Chekhov*, edited by Lillian Hellman. Pp. 19, 20, 54, 55, 133, 137–39. Copyright © 1955 and renewal copyright © 1983 by Lillian Hellman. Reprinted by permission of Farrar, Straus & Giroux, Inc. From *Letters of Anton Tchekhov to his Family and Friends*, translated by Constance Garnett, New York, 1920, Pp. 99, 100, 300, 318–20.

1. Wife of a rich, cultured country gentleman from whom in the 1880s the Chekhovs rented a cottage [*Editor*].
2. Isaak Levitan (1861–1900), a landscape painter [*Editor*].

To chemists there is nothing unclean in this world. A man of letters should be as objective as a chemist; he has to renounce ordinary
subjectivity and realize that manure piles play a very respectable role in
a landscape and that evil passions are as inherent in life as good ones.
* * *

Devotedly and respectfully,
A. *Chekhov*

To Alexei Suvorin[3]

May 30, 1888, Sumy

* * * You write that the talk about pessimism and Kisochka's[4] story
in no way develop or solve the problem of pessimism. It seems to me
that it is not up to writers to solve such questions as God, pessimism
and so on. The job of the writer is to depict only who, how and under
what circumstances people have spoken or thought about God or pessimism. The artist should not be a judge of his characters or of what
they say, but only an objective observer. I heard a confused, indecisive
talk by two Russians on pessimism and so must convey this conversation
in the same form in which I heard it, but it is up to the jury, i.e., the
readers, to give it an evaluation. My job is only to be talented, i.e., to
be able to throw light upon some figures and speak their language.
Shcheglov-Leontiev[5] finds fault with me for having ended my story with
the sentence: "You can't appraise anything in this world!" In his opinion
the artist-psychologist *must* analyze—that's why he's a psychologist. But
I don't agree with him. It is high time for writing folk, especially artists,
to admit you can't appraise anything in this world, as Socrates did in
his day, and Voltaire. The crowd thinks it knows and understands everything: and the more stupid it is, the broader seems to be its scope. If
the artist, in whom the crowd believes, dares to declare that he does not
understand what he sees, that alone comprises deep knowledge in the
domain of thought and a good step ahead . . .

What a letter I've concocted! I must end. Give my regards to Anna
Ivanovna, Nastya and Borya. . . . Goodbye, keep well, and may God
be good to you.

Your sincerely devoted
A. Chekhov

To Alexei Suvorin

October 27, 1888, Moscow

* * * In conversation with my literary colleagues I always insist that
it is not the artist's business to solve problems that require a specialist's
knowledge. It is a bad thing if a writer tackles a subject he does not

---

3. Editor of the *New Times*, a conservative newspaper in St. Petersburg [*Editor*].
4. A character in Chekhov's story *The Lights*

[*Editor*].
5. Ivan Leontiev (1856–1911), a playwright and
novelist [*Editor*].

understand. We have specialists for dealing with special questions: it is their business to judge of the commune, of the future of capitalism, of the evils of drunkenness, of boots, of the diseases of women. An artist must only judge of what he understands, his field is just as limited as that of any other specialist—I repeat this and insist on it always. That in his sphere there are no questions, but only answers, can only be maintained by those who have never written and have had no experience of thinking in images. An artist observes, selects, guesses, combines—and this in itself presupposes a problem: unless he had set himself a problem from the very first there would be nothing to conjecture and nothing to select. To put it briefly, I will end by using the language of psychiatry: if one denies that creative work involves problems and purposes, one must admit that an artist creates without premeditation or intention, in a state of aberration; therefore, if an author boasted to me of having written a novel, without a preconceived design, under a sudden inspiration, I should call him mad.

You are right in demanding that an artist should take an intelligent attitude to his work, but you confuse two things: *solving a problem* and *stating a problem correctly*. It is only the second that is obligatory for the artist. In "Anna Karenin"[6] and "Evgeny Onyegin"[7] not a single problem is solved, but they satisfy you completely because all the problems are correctly stated in them. It is the business of the judge to put the right questions, but the answers must be given by the jury according to their own lights. * * *

A. Chekhov

To Alexei Suvorin

December 9, 1890, Moscow

* * * God's earth is good. It is only we on it who are bad. How little justice and humility we have, how poor our understanding of patriotism! A drunken, worn-out, good-for-nothing husband loves his wife and children, but what good is this love? The newspapers tell us we love our mighty land, but how does this love express itself? Instead of knowledge, there is insolence and boundless conceit, instead of labor, idleness and caddishness; there is no justice, the understanding of honor does not go beyond "the honor of the uniform," a uniform usually adorning our prisoners' dock. We must work, the hell with everything else. The important thing is that we must be just, and all the rest will be added unto us.

I want terribly to speak with you. My soul is in upheaval. I don't want to see anyone but you, because you are the only one I can talk to. The hell with Pleshcheyev.[8] And the hell with the actors, too.

6. Novel by Leo Tolstoy (1828–1910) [*Editor*].
7. Long poem by Alexander Pushkin (1799–1837) [*Editor*].

8. Alexei Pleshcheyev (1825–93), a prominent poet and essayist with whom Chekhov frequently differed [*Editor*].

I got your telegrams in deplorable condition, all of them torn . . . God keep you.

Yours,
A. Chekhov

To Anatol Koni[9]

January 26, 1891, St. Petersburg

Dear Sir,

I have not answered your letter in a hurry, as I am not leaving St. Petersburg before Saturday.

I shall attempt to describe in detail the situation of Sakhalin[1] children and adolescents. It is extraordinary. I saw hungry children, thirteen-year-old mistresses, girls of fifteen pregnant. Little girls enter upon prostitution at the age of twelve, sometimes before the coming of menstruation. The church and the school exist only on paper, the children are educated instead by their environment and convict atmosphere. By the way, I wrote down a conversation I had with a ten-year old boy. I was taking the census of the village of Upper Armundan; its inhabitants are to a man beggars, and notorious as reckless stoss players. I entered a hut: the parents were not at home, and on a bench sat a towheaded little fellow, round-shouldered, barefooted, in a brown study. We started talking:

I. What is your father's name?
He. I don't know.
I. How's that? You live with your father and don't know his name? You ought to be ashamed of yourself.
He. He isn't my real father.
I. What do you mean—not real?
He. He's living with Mom.
I. Does your mother have a husband or is she a widow?
He. A widow. She came here on account of her husband.
I. What do you mean by that?
He. She killed him.
I. Do you remember your father?
He. No. I'm illegitimate. She gave birth to me on Kara.

A prisoner, in foot shackles, who had murdered his wife, was with us on the Amur boat to Sakhalin. His poor half-orphaned daughter, a little girl of about six, was with him. I noticed that when the father went down from the upper to the lower deck, where the toilet was, his guard and daughter followed; while the former sat in the toilet the armed soldier and the little girl stood at the door. When the prisoner climbed

9. A liberal lawyer and public official (1844–1927) [*Editor*].   1. An island off the Pacific coast of Siberia used for criminals and political prisoners [*Editor*].

the staircase on his way back, the little girl clambered up and held on to his fetters. At night the little girl slept in a heap with the convicts and soldiers. Then I remember attending a funeral in Sakhalin. The wife of a transported criminal, who had left for Nikolayevsk, was being buried. Around the open grave stood four convicts as pallbearers—ex officio; the island treasurer and I in the capacity of Hamlet and Horatio, roamed about the cemetery; the dead woman's lodger, a Circassian, who had nothing else to do; and a peasant woman prisoner, who was here out of pity; she had brought along two children of the deceased—one an infant and the other little Alyosha, a boy of four dressed in a woman's jacket and blue pants with brightly colored patches on the knees. It was cold, raw, there was water in the grave, and the convicts stood around laughing. The sea was visible. Alyosha looked at the grave with curiosity; he wanted to wipe his chilly nose, but the long sleeves of the jacket got in the way. While the grave was being filled I asked him, "Where is your mother, Alyosha?"

He waved his arm like a gentleman who had lost at cards, laughed and said, "Buried!"

The prisoners laughed; the Circassian turned to us and asked what he was to do with the children, as he was not obliged to take care of them.

I did not come upon infectious diseases in Sakhalin, there was very little congenital syphilis, but I did see children blind, filthy, covered with rashes—all maladies symptomatic of neglect.

Of course I shall not solve the children's problem, and I don't know what should be done. But it seems to me you will not get anywhere with charity and leftovers from prison appropriations and other sums. To my way of thinking, it is harmful to approach this important problem by depending upon charity, which in Russia is a casual affair, or upon nonexistent funds. I should prefer to have the government be financially responsible.

My Moscow address is c/o Firgang, M. Dmitrovka Street.

Permit me to thank you for your cordiality and for your promise to visit me and to remain,

Your sincerely respectful and devoted,
A. Chekhov

To Alexei Suvorin

March 17, 1892, Melihovo.

* * * Ah, my dear fellow, if only you could take a holiday! Living in the country is inconvenient. The insufferable time of thaw and mud is beginning, but something marvellous and moving is taking place in nature, the poetry and novelty of which makes up for all the discomforts of life. Every day there are surprises, one better than another. The starlings have returned, everywhere there is the gurgling of water, in

places where the snow has thawed the grass is already green. The day drags on like eternity. One lives as though in Australia, somewhere at the ends of the earth; one's mood is calm, contemplative, and animal, in the sense that one does not regret yesterday or look forward to to-morrow. From here, far away, people seem very good, and that is natural, for in going away into the country we are not hiding from people but from our vanity, which in town among people is unjust and active beyond measure. Looking at the spring, I have a dreadful longing that there should be paradise in the other world. In fact, at moments I am so happy that I superstitiously pull myself up and remind myself of my creditors, who will one day drive me out of the Australia I have so happily won * * *

A. Chekhov

To Alexei Suvorin

November 25, 1892, Melihovo

It is easy to understand you, and there is no need for you to abuse yourself for obscurity of expression. You are a hard drinker, and I have regaled you with sweet lemonade, and you, after giving the lemonade its due, justly observe that there is no spirit in it. That is just what is lacking in our productions—the alcohol which could intoxicate and subjugate, and you state that very well. Why not? Putting aside "Ward No. 6"[2] and myself, let us discuss the matter in general, for that is more interesting. Let us discuss the general causes, if that won't bore you, and let us include the whole age. Tell me honestly, who of my con-temporaries—that is, men between thirty and forty-five—have given the world one single drop of alcohol? Are not Korolenko, Nadson, and all the playwrights of to-day, lemonade? Have Ryepin's or Shishkin's pic-tures turned your head? Charming, talented, you are enthusiastic; but at the same time you can't forget that you want to smoke. Science and technical knowledge are passing through a great period now, but for our sort it is a flabby, stale, and dull time. We are stale and dull ourselves . . . The causes of this are not to be found in our stupidity, our lack of talent, or our insolence, as Burenin imagines, but in a disease which for the artist is worse than syphilis or sexual exhaustion. We lack "some-thing," that is true, and that means that, lift the robe of our muse, and you will find within an empty void. Let me remind you that the writers, who we say are for all time or are simply good, and who intoxicate us, have one common and very important characteristic; they are going towards something and are summoning you towards it, too, and you feel not with your mind, but with your whole being, that they have some object, just like the ghost of Hamlet's father, who did not come and disturb the imagination for nothing. Some have more immediate objects—the abolition of serfdom, the liberation of their country, pol-

2. A short story by Chekhov [Editor].

itics, beauty, or simply vodka, like Denis Davydov; others have remote objects—God, life beyond the grave, the happiness of humanity, and so on. The best of them are realists and paint life as it is, but, through every line's being soaked in the consciousness of an object, you feel, besides life as it is, the life which ought to be, and that captivates you. And we? We! We paint life as it is, but beyond that—nothing at all. . . . Flog us and we can do no more! We have neither immediate nor remote aims, and in our soul there is a great empty space. We have no politics, we do not believe in revolution, we have no God, we are not afraid of ghosts, and I personally am not afraid even of death and blindness. One who wants nothing, hopes for nothing, and fears nothing, cannot be an artist. Whether it is a disease or not—what it is does not matter; but we ought to recognize that our position is worse than a governor's. I don't know how it will be with us in ten or twenty years—then circumstances may be different, but meanwhile it would be rash to expect of us anything of real value, apart from the question whether we have talent or not. We write mechanically, merely obeying the long-established arrangement in accordance with which some men go into the government service, others into trade, others write. . . . Grigorovitch and you think I am clever. Yes, I am at least so far clever as not to conceal from myself my disease, and not to deceive myself, and not to cover up my own emptiness with other people's rags, such as the ideas of the sixties, and so on. I am not going to throw myself like Garshin over the bannisters, but I am not going to flatter myself with hopes of a better future either. I am not to blame for my disease, and it's not for me to cure myself, for this disease, it must be supposed, has some good purpose hidden from us, and is not sent in vain. * * *

A. Chekhov

ROBERT BRUSTEIN

[Chekhov's Dramaturgy in *The Three Sisters*]†

Anton Chekhov is the gentlest and the most impersonal of all the great modern dramatists, but there is one sense in which he does align himself on the side of his characters—insofar as they are cultured individuals, constituting the last stronghold of enlightenment against the enroaching mediocrity, vulgarity, and illiteracy of Russian life. For against these forces of darkness—the environment of his plays—he directs a vigorous personal revolt. Chekhov himself was passionately addicted to "culture"—by which he meant not intellectuality (he finds the intelligentsia

† From "Forward" by Robert Brustein of *Chekhov: The Major Plays*, translated by Ann Dunnigan. Copyright © 1964 by Robert Brustein. Pp. vii– xxii. Reprinted by arrangement with New American Library, a Division of Penguin Books USA Inc., New York, New York.

"hypocritical, false, hysterical, poorly educated,and indolent"), but rather a mystical compound of humanity, decency, kindness, intelligence, education, accomplishment,and will. It is by these standards that he usually measures the worth of human beings. In a long letter to his brother Nikolay, Chekhov begins by accusing him of an "utter lack of culture," and then proceeds to define the characteristics of truly cultured people in a revelatory manner. Such people, he notes, "respect the human personality, and are therefore always forbearing, gentle, courteous, and compliant. They will overlook noise, and cold, and overdone meat, and the presence of strangers in their house. . . . They are sincere and fear untruth like the very devil. . . . They do not make fools of themselves in order to arouse sympathy. . . . They are not vain. . . . They develop an esthetic sense." Cautioning Nikolay "not to fall below the level of your environment," Chekhov counsels him, "What you need is constant work, day and night, eternal reading, study, willpower."

Chekhov, who had peasant blood himself, foresaw that cultured individuals might arise from any class of society, however humble, but he did not (like Tolstoy) idealize the peasantry, and the crude utilitarianism of the middle class filled him with disgust. If he is aggrieved by any general fact of Russian life, it is the cancerous growth of slovenliness, filth, stupidity, and cruelty among the mass of men; and if he despises the sluggishness and indolence of his upper-class characters, then this is because they, too, are gradually being overwhelmed by the tide, lacking the will to stem it. For if the Russian gentry represents beauty without use, the Russian environment is characterized by use without beauty; and those with the necessary willpower are often utterly without the necessary culture or education. It is this conflict between the cultured upper classes and their stupefying environment—between the forces of light and the forces of darkness—that provides the basic substance of most of Chekhov's plays.

Thus, while David Magarshack, the author of *Chekhov, The Dramatist*,[1] somewhat overstates the case by saying that Chekhov's mature plays are dramas of "courage and hope," he is perfectly right to emphasize the moral purpose behind Chekhov's imitation of reality. Chekhov never developed any program for "life as it should be." His revolt, like that of most great artists, is mainly negative. And it is a mistake to interpret the occasional expressions of visionary optimism that conclude his plays as evidence of "courage and hope" (they are more like desperate defenses against nihilism and despair). Yet it is also wrong to assume that Chekhov shares the pessimism that pervades his plays or the despondency of his defeated characters. Everyone who knew him testified to his gaiety, humor, and buoyancy, and if he always expected the worst, he always hoped for the best. Chekhov the realist was required to transcribe accurately the appalling conditions of provincial life without false affirmations or baseless optimism; but Chekhov the moralist has a sneaking

1. Gloucester, Mass: Peter Smith, 1960.

belief in change. In short, Chekhov expresses his revolt not by depicting the ideal, which would have violated his sense of reality, and not by merely imitating the real, which would have violated his sense of moral purpose, but by criticizing the real at the same time that he is representing it. He will not comment on reality; he will permit reality to comment on itself. And so it is that while the surfaces of his plays seem drenched with *tedium vitae*[2] and spiritual vapors, the depths are charged with energy and dissent.

These depths are also charged with melodrama. For although this is a mode that Chekhov deplores as unnatural, he smuggles his personal commentary into his plays by means of a hidden melodramatic configuration. Actually, Chekhov uses melodramatic devices all through his career—suicides, duels, attempted murders, love triangles, interrupted love scenes—and, trying to combat his weakness for exciting act curtains, he is constantly working to excise the unnatural from his art. (After *The Cherry Orchard*, he crows triumphantly that there is "not a single pistol shot in it.") On the other hand, all of his mature dramatic works, and especially *The Cherry Orchard*, are constructed on the same melodramatic pattern—the conflict between a despoiler and his victims—while the action of the plays follows the same melodramatic development—the gradual dispossession of the victims from their rightful inheritance.

This external conflict can be more easily observed if we strip away everything extraneous to the (hidden) plot, ignoring for a moment, Chekhov's explorations of motive and character. In *The Sea Gull*, Trigorin seduces and ruins Nina; Mme. Arkadina spiritually dispossesses Treplyov, her Hamlet-like son. In *Uncle Vanya*, Yelena steals Sonya's secret love, Astrov, while Serebryakov robs Sonya of her inheritance and produces in Vanya a soul-killing disillusionment. In *The Three Sisters*, Natasha gradually evicts the Prozorov family from their provincial house. And in *The Cherry Orchard*, Lopakhin dispossesses Mme. Ranevskaya and Gaev, taking over their orchard as acreage for summer cottages. In each case, the central act of dispossession is symbolized through some central image, representing what is being ravished, stolen, or destroyed. In *The Sea Gull*, it is the bird that Treplyov kills, identified with Nina, who is also destroyed by a man with "nothing better to do." In *Uncle Vanya*, it is the forest, "a picture of gradual and unmistakable degeneration," associated with the lives of the family, degenerating through sheer inertia. In *The Three Sisters*, it is the Prozorov house, eventually hollowed out by Natasha as though by a nest of termites. And in *The Cherry Orchard*, of course, it is the famous orchard, hacked to pieces by the commercial ax. With the possible exception of *The Sea Gull*, each play dramatizes the triumph of the forces of darkness over the forces of enlightenment, the degeneration of culture in the crude modern world.

What prevents us from seeing these melodramatic configurations is

---

2. "The wearisomeness of life" [*Editor*].

the extraordinary way in which they have been concealed. Technically, Chekhov's most effective masking device is to bury the plot (Magarshack's concept of the "indirect action") so that violent acts and emotional climaxes occur offstage or between the acts. In this way, he manages to avoid the melodramatic crisis and to obscure the external conflict, ducking the event and concentrating on the denouement. Secondly, Chekhov concludes the action before the conventional melodramatic reversal— the triumphant victory of virtue over vice; in its place, he substitutes a reversal of his own invention, in which the defeated characters, shuffling off the old life, begin to look forward to the new. Most important, however, he refuses to cast his characters in conventional hero-villain roles. In the buried plot, Chekhov's despoilers act while his victims suffer; but by subordinating plot to character, Chekhov diverts our attention from process to motive and makes us suspend our judgment of the action.

Chekhov also dilutes the melodramatic pathos by qualifying our sympathy for the victims. In most cases, they seem largely responsible for whatever happens to them. This is not to say, as some have said, that we do not sympathize with their unhappy lot; we do, but since Chekhov highlights their inertia, irresponsibility, and waste, we also deplore their helpless inability to resist their fate. Carefully balancing pathos with irony, Chekhov avoids the stock responses of conventional theatre, deflecting the emphasis from the melodramatic to the natural and the atomspheric, wrapping layers of commonplace detail around extremely climactic events.

And this is precisely the effect that Chekhov aims to achieve. "Let the things that happen onstage," he writes, "be just as complex and yet just as simple as they are in life. For instance, people are having a meal at table, just having a meal, but at the same time their happiness is being created, or their lives are being smashed up." The placid surface of existence, then, is to be a masking device for his controlled manipulation of human fatality; the trivial course of the daily routine is to disguise his sense of process, development, and crisis. Chekhov is so successful in achieving these goals that English and American critics often condemn his plays as vague, actionless, and formless. They have been blinded by Chekhov's extraordinary atmospheric power and his capacity to evoke, through rhythmic sound effects (scratching pens, guitar music, sneezes, songs, etc.), a poetic illusion of fluid reality.

Beneath this surface, Chekhov's work has the tensile strength of a steel girder, the construction being so subtle that it is almost invisible. And while his characters seem to exist in isolated pockets of vacancy, they are all integral parts of a close network of interlocking motives and effects. Thus, while the dialogue seems to wander aimlessly into discussions of cold samovars, the situation in Moscow, and the temperature of the earth, it is economically performing a great number of essential dramatic functions: revealing character, furthering the action, uncovering the theme, evoking in the spectators a mood identical with that of the characters, and diverting attention from the melodramatic events that are erupting under the smooth surface of life. Through this original and inimitable technique, Chekhov manages to exercise his function both as a realist and as a moralist, and to express his resistance to certain aspects of modern life in enduring esthetic form.

All of Chekhov's mature works are masterpieces, but *The Three Sisters* perhaps provides the most stunning example of his dramatic approach. Completed late in 1900, almost four years after *Uncle Vanya*, it was written mostly in the Crimea, where Chekhov had retired to recuperate from the tuberculosis that was soon to prove fatal to him. One year before, he had published "In the Ravine," a short story with enough similarities to the play to suggest that it was a preparatory sketch. The location of the story is a provincial village called Ukleyevo, so ordinary and banal that it is identified to visitors as the place "where the deacon ate all the caviare at the funeral"—nothing more stimulating has ever happened there. Yet, as usual with Chekhov, extraordinary events take place in this commonplace setting. The most important development, for our purposes, is the progress of the woman, Aksinya—married to one of the two sons of Tsybukin, an elderly, generous shopkeeper. Aksinya, contemptuous of the family, parades wantonly about the town in low-necked dresses and is openly conducting an affair with a rich factory owner. When Tsybukin's unmarried son weds a girl named Lipa—a quiet, frightened, gentle peasant woman—Aksinya becomes intensely jealous; when Lipa gives birth to a baby boy, Aksinya scalds it with a ladle of boiling water, killing both the infant and the hopes of the family. Instead of being punished, however, Aksinya continues to flourish in the town, finally turning her father-in-law and his family out of their own house.

From this story, Chekhov apparently derived his idea for Natalya Ivanovna, the lustful, ambitious, and predatory woman who eventually disinherits the gentle Prozorovs—an action played out against the background of a provincial town so petty, vulgar, and boring that it has the power to degrade its most cultured inhabitants. *The Three Sisters* is richer, more complex, and more ambiguous than "In the Ravine"; Chekhov smooths the melodramatic wrinkles of the story by toning down the adulterous villainy of Natasha-Aksinya; he enriches the story by adding a military background and transforming the petit-bourgeois Tsybukins into the leisured, upper-class Prozorovs. But the basic outline is the same; and so is Chekhov's careful balancing of the internal and external influences on character, an element of all his mature work. In *Ivanov*, the decline of the hero was mostly determined from within, and Borkin's theory that "it's your environment that's killing you" was rejected as a thoughtless cliché. But in *The Three Sisters*, environment plays a crucial role in the gradual defeat of the central characters, while their own psychological failings are kept relatively muted.

The forces of evil, in fact, are quite inexorable in this work, making the Chekhovian pathos more dominant than usual. Chekhov, according to Stanislavsky, was amazed at the first reading of the play by the Art Theatre, because, in the producer's words, "he had written a happy comedy and all of us considered the play a tragedy and even wept over it." Stanislavsky is probably exaggerating Chekhov's response. Rather than considering it a "happy comedy," he was very careful to call *The Three Sisters* a "drama," the only such classification, as Magarshack notes, among his works. The play is certainly no tragedy, but it is the gloomiest Chekhov ever wrote. Certainly, the author introduces very little of his customary buffoonery. Though the play has its pantaloons, they are too implicated in the events of the house to evoke from us more than occasional smiles: Kulygin, for example, with his genial pedantry and maddening insensitivity to sorrow, is nevertheless a rather pathetic cuckold; and the alcoholic Chebutykin, for all his absurdity, eventually develops into a withdrawn and nihilistic figure. Furthermore, an atmosphere of doom seems to permeate the household, lifted only during brief festive moments; even these are quickly brought to an end by the ominous Natasha. Despite Magarshack's desire to read the play as "a *gay* affirmation of life," there is little that is gay or affirmative about it. Chekhov displays his usual impatience with the delusions of his central characters, but they are more clearly victims than most such figures. And while they undoubtedly are partially responsible for their fates (which explains why Chekhov did not want Stanislavsky's actors to grow maudlin over them), much of the responsibility belongs to Natasha, who represents the dark forces eating away at their lives.

For Natasha is the most malevolent figure Chekhov ever created—a pretentious bourgeois *arriviste* without a single redeeming trait. Eveyone emphasizes her vulgarity, vengefulness, and lack of culture, and even Andrey, who leans over backward to be fair, sees in her "a small, blind, sort of thick-skinned animal. In any case, she's not a human being." Natasha is a malignant growth in a benevolent organism, and her final triumph, no matter how Chekhov tries to disguise it, is the triumph of pure evil. Despite the thick texture of the play, then, neatly woven into the tapestry is an almost invisible thread of action: the destruction of the Prozorovs by Natasha. From the moment she enters the house, at the end of Act I, to accept Andrey's proposal of marriage, until she has secured her control at the end of the play, the process of dispossession continued with relentless motion.

It takes place, however, by steady degrees. Andrey has mortgaged the house to the bank in order to pay his gambling debts, but Natasha, a much more dangerous adversary than a bank, takes over from there. Not only has she "grabbed all the money" (presumably the mortgage money), but she is engaged, throughout the play, in shifting the family from room to room, until she has finally shifted them out of the house entirely. Natasha's ambitions proceed under the guise of maternal solicitude and love of order; and never have such qualities seemed so thoroughly repellent. In the second act, she is planning to move Irina into Olga's room so that little Bobik will have a warmer nursery; in the third act, she offers to evict Anfisa, the old family servant, because she has outlived her usefulness (Natasha's unfeeling utilitarianism is among her most inhuman traits); and in the last act—with Olga and Anfisa installed in a government flat and Irina having moved to a furnished room—she is preparing to move Andrey out of his room to make way for baby Sophie. Since Sophie is probably the child of Protopopov, Natasha's lover, the dispossession has been symbolically completed. It will not be long before it is literally completed, and Andrey, the last of the Prozorovs, is ejected from the house altogether.

Chekhov illustrates this process through a careful manipulation of the setting. The first three acts take place in interiors that grow progressively more confined, the third act being laid in the room of Olga and Irina, cramped with people, screens, and furniture. But the last act is laid outdoors. The exterior setting tells the story visually: the family is now out of their own home; Andrey pushes the baby carriage around the house in widening circles; and Protopopov (never seen) is comfortably installed *inside*, in the drawing room with Natasha. Natasha, however, has not yet finished, for she is determined to violate the outdoors as well. Popping out of the house for a moment, she expresses her determination to cut down the fir and maple trees that Tuzenbakh admires so much, an act of despoliation that foreshadows a similar act in *The Cherry Orchard*.

The contrast between Natasha and the Prozorovs is demonstrated by the difference in their manners—Natasha's vulgarity is amply documented by her French affectations and her abuse of the servants. An even better contrast is provided during the fire that is raging in town at the beginning of the third act. In this scene, Chekhov sets off Natasha's *arriviste* pretensions against the instinctual humanity of the Prozorovs by comparing their attitudes toward the victims of the conflagration. In accordance with Chekhov's description of the cultured in his letter to Nikolay ("They will overlook . . . the presence of strangers in their house"), the sisters generously offer their hospitality to those without homes, but Natasha is more occupied with fears that her children will catch some disease. When she considers the homeless, she thinks of them as objects to be patronized—"Indeed, we should always be ready to help the poor, that's the duty of the rich"—and talks about joining a committee for the assistance of the victims, that impersonal, dehumanized approach to charity invented by the middle class less out of generosity than out of status-seeking and guilt.

Since the fire is an external crisis introduced to heighten (and at the same time draw attention from) the crisis occurring within, it also illustrates Natasha's destructive tendencies. The fire is closely identified with that conflagration that is destroying the Prozorov household; the fate of the victims anticipates that of the family (they are out on the street); and Natasha symbolically links the two events. As Natasha marches through her room with a candle, Masha suggests this link by saying: "She goes about looking as if it were she who had started the fire." But at the same time that Natasha is a symbolic arsonist, she is also a symbolic fire extinguisher. Always on the lookout for fear something goes wrong, she stalks through the house, snuffing out candles—snuffing, too, all laughter and pleasure in the family. Pleading baby Bobik's health, she puts an end to the Carnival party; for like Serebryakov (who similarly throws cold water on the musical interlude planned by Yelena and Sonya in *Uncle Vanya*), she functions to extinguish joy, and to spread gloom and despair.

The conflict between Natasha and the Prozorovs, needless to say, is always kept indistinct. Andrey and the sisters are either too polite or too deeply involved in their own problems to comment much on Natasha's activities, and while she and the family brush each other frequently throughout the play, they never break into open argument. Instead of dramatizing the Prozorovs' relations with Natasha, Chekhov defines them against the background of their surroundings, concentrating on the wasting away of this potentially superior family in a coarse and sordid environment. On the other hand, Natasha is really the personification of this environment—a native of the town who lives in the house—and so both she and the environment are actually related forces converging on the same objects. Thus, the surface and the depths of *The Three Sisters* follow parallel lines of development. The gradual dispossession of the Prozorovs by Natasha is the buried action, while their gradual deterioration in their surroundings proceeds above. In each case, the conflict between culture and vulgarity provides the basic theme.

This conflict is clear from the opening lines of the play, when the three sisters—a doleful portrait in blue, black, and white—first reveal their dissatisfaction with the present by reflecting, nostalgically, on the life of the past. A highly educated Moscow family, the Prozorovs were geographically transplanted eleven years before when their father, a brigadier general, took command of an artillery unit in the provinces. As the action proceeds, Chekhov shows how the family following the father's death, has tried to adapt to their new surroundings: Olga by teaching school, Masha by marrying the local schoolmaster, Irina by working in a variety of civil jobs, Andrey by marrying Natasha and joining the District Board. All these attempts at assimilation are, however, unsuccessful. And regarding their present life as a kind of involuntary banishment, they are now uncomfortably suspended between their idealization of the past and resentment over their depressing provincial existence.

The past, of course, is closely identified with Moscow, seen through a haze of memory as a city of sun, flowers, refinement, and sensibility—in short, of *culture*—as opposed to the cold, stupidity, and dreariness of their town. Their vision of Moscow, like their hopes of returning, is, of course, delusionary—an idle dream with which we are meant to have little patience—and their endless complaining is neither courageous nor attractive. Still, their shared apprehension of the pettiness, drabness, and conformity of their provincial district is terrifyingly accurate. As Andrey describes it:

> Our town has been in existence now for two hundred years, there are a hundred thousand people in it, and not one who isn't exactly like all the others, not one saint, either in the past or in the present, not one scholar, not one artist, no one in the least remarkable who could inspire envy or a passionate desire to imitate him. . . . and an overwhelmingly vulgar influence weighs on the children, the divine spark is extinguished in them, and they become the same pitiful, identical corpses as their fathers and mothers. . . .

In this speech—which may have been intended as an attack on the audience (Chekhov stipulated that Andrey, while speaking it, "must almost threaten the audience with his fists")—Andrey is clearly expressing Chekhov's revolt against the appalling conditions of the provincial town. It is a place in which any man of sensibility is bound to feel "a stranger, and lonely," for it is without culture, without art, without humanity, without excellence; its "overwhelmingly vulgar influence" has the power to brutalize all who live within its circumference. The influence of the town, in it most extreme state, is shown on Chebutykin, who takes refuge from his disillusionment in alcohol and newspapers and from his professional incompetence in a profound nihilism: "Maybe it only appears that we exist, but, in fact, we are not here." For just as the Prozorovs respond to their surroundings by weaving the illusion of Moscow, so Chebutykin responds by declaring that nothing in the world is real, and that "it doesn't matter."

The Prozorovs are aware that the town is brutalizing them, too, which accounts for their growing despair. Masha—dressed in black to illustrate her depression—is perpetually bored; Irina is perpetually tired; Olga suffers from perpetual headaches. As for Andrey, their gifted brother, he trails his life along with no apparent aim, followed by the senile Ferapont, as by an ignominious Nemesis. In this lifeless atmosphere, they are drying up, their culture falling from them like shreds of dead skin—each, in turn, will ask, "Where has it all gone?" For whatever might have made them seem unusual in Moscow is here merely a superfluous layer—useless, unnecessary, and gradually being forgotten. Andrey, carefully trained for a distinguished university career, holds a position in which his education is meaningless. Masha, once an accomplished pianist, now "has forgotten" how to play—just as Chebutykin has "forgotten" his medical training—just as the entire family is forgetting the accomplishments of their hopeful youth. Thus, the Prozorovs alternate between hysteria and despair, their hopes disintegrating in an environment where everything is reduced to zero:

> IRINA. [*sobbing*] Where? Where has it all gone? Where is it? Oh, my God, my God! I have forgotten everything, I've forgotten . . . it's all muddled in my head. . . . I can't remember how to say window or floor in Italian. I'm forgetting everything, every day I forget, and life is slipping by, never to return, never, we shall never go to Moscow. . . . I see that we shall never go. . . .

Life is slipping by, and time, like a cormorant, is devouring hopes, illusions, expectations, consuming their minds, souls, and bodies in its tedious-rapid progress toward death.

While their culture is being forgotten, however, the Prozorovs do try to preserve a pocket of civilization in this dreary wasteland; their house is open to limited forms of intellectual discussion and artistic activity. Generally, the discussions at the Prozorovs' reflect the banality of the surrounding area (Solyony's and Chebutykin's heated argument over *chehartma* and *cheremsha* is typical), but occasionally, genuine ideas seem to come out of these soirées. Attending the discussions are the Prozorovs' cultural allies, the military officers stationed in town. Chekhov, according to Stanislavsky, looked on the military as the bearers of a cultural mission, since, coming into the farthest corners of the provinces, they brought with them new demands on life, knowledge, art, happiness, and joy." Masha suggests Chekhov's attitudes when she observes the difference between the crude townspeople and the more refined soldiers: "Among civilians generally, there are so many coarse, impolite, ill-bred people," but "in our town the most decent, the most honorable and well-bred people are all in the army." Her attraction to Colonel Vershinin is partially explained by his superior refinement, for he is associated in her mind with the old Muscovite charm and glamour. In part, he probably reminds her of her father (also identified with culture), for he lived on the same street, was an officer in her father's brigade, and has now taken command of her father's old battery. Attracted to educated men (she married Kulygin because she mistakenly thought him "the cleverest of men"), Masha unquestionably finds a suitable intellectual companion in Vershinin; even their courtship reveals their cultural affinities—he hums a tune to which she hums a reply. Magarshack calls this "the most original love declaration in the whole history of the stage"—actually, Congreve's Mirabel and Millamant[3] employ much the same device, when he completes a Lovelace verse that she has begun—but in both cases, the couples signify their instinctual rapport and their superior sophistication to other suitors.

While Masha tries to find expression through an extramarital affair

3. William Congreve (1670–1729), an English playwright, perhaps the most polished writer of the type of play called the "comedy of manners." The leading characters in his *The Way of the World* (1700) are Mirabel and Millamant [*Editor*].

that is doomed to failure, Irina tries to discover a substitute commitment in her work. In this, her spiritual partner, though she doesn't love him, is Tuzenbakh, because he too seeks salvation in work, finally, in a Tolstoyan gesture, resigning his commission for a job in a brickyard. Irina's faith in the dignity of labor, however, is gradually destroyed by depressing jobs in a telegraph office and on the Town Council—in this district, work can have no essential meaning or purpose. In the last act, Irina looks forward to "a new life" as a schoolteacher; but we have Olga's enervating academic career as evidence that this "new life" will be just as unfulfilling as the old. And when Tuzenbakh is killed in a duel with Solyony (*his* despoiler), even the minor consolations of a loveless marriage are denied her.

Everything, in fact, fails the family in *The Three Sisters*. And as their culture fades and their lives grow grayer, the forces of darkness and illiteracy move in like carrion crows, ready to pick the last bones. There is some doubt, however, whether this condition is permanent. The question the play finally asks is whether the defeat of the Prozorovs has any ultimate meaning: will their suffering eventually influence their surroundings in any positive way? The question is never resolved in the play, but it is endlessly debated by Vershinin and Tuzenbakh, whose opinions contrast as sharply as their characters. Vershinin—an extremely unhappy soul—holds to optimistic theories, while Tuzenbakh—inexplicably merry—is more profoundly pessimistic.[4] This conflict, though usually couched in general terms, is secretly connected with the fate of the Prozorovs. When Masha, for example, declares, "We know a great deal that is useless," Vershinin takes the opportunity to expound his view:

> It seems to me that there is not and cannot be a town so dull and depressing that a clever, educated person would be useless. Let us suppose that among the hundred thousand inhabitants of this town, which, of course, is backward and uncouth, there are only three people such as you. It goes without saying that you cannot vanquish the ignorant masses around you; in the course of your life, little by little, you will have to give way and be lost in that crowd of a hundred thousand; life will stifle you, but all the same, you will not disappear, you will not be without influence. After you there may appear perhaps six like you, then twelve, and so on, untill finally, your kind will become the majority. In two to three hundred years life on this earth will be unimaginably beautiful, wonderful.

Vershinin, in short—anticipating the eventual transformation of the surrounding area by people like the Prozorovs—believes in the progres-

4. Chekhov may be dramatizing a paradox here that he once expounded to Lydia Avilova in the course of explaining the alleged gloominess of his themes and characters: "It has always been pointed out to me that somber, melancholy people always write gaily, while the works of cheerful souls are always depressing." Chekhov, like Tuzenbakh, is a cheerful soul with a gloomy point of view.

sive march of civilization toward perfection. And this perfection will be based on the future interrelationship of the benighted mass and the cultured elite ("If, don't you know, we could add culture to the love of work, and love of work to culture.")—a synthesis of beauty and utility.

Tuzenbakh, on the other hand, is more skeptical. Seeing no special providence in the fall of a sparrow or the flight of migratory cranes, he doubts the ability of anyone to influence anything:

> Not only in two or three hundred years, but in a million years, life will be just the same . . . it doesn't change, it remains constant, following its own laws, which do not concern us, or which, in any case, you will never get to know.

Vershinin's view awakens hope that there is some ultimate meaning to life. Tuzenbakh's leads to stoicism and tragic resignation. It is the recurrent conflict between the progressive and the static interpretation of history, and its outcome remains insoluble.

In the last act, in fact, both views are recapitulated without being reconciled. The military is leaving the town—a sad departure, because it signifies not only the end of Masha's affair with Vershinin but also the disintegration of the last cultural rampart. Tuzenbakh anticipates that "dreadful boredom" will descend upon the town, and Andrey notes (reminding us of Natasha's symbolic role) that "it's as though someone put a hood over it." The end of the Prozorov way of life has almost come. Masha has turned obsessive and hysterical; Olga is installed in a position she loathes; Andrey, likened to an expensive bell that has fallen and smashed, has become hag-ridden and mediocre. Only Irina preserves some hope, but even these hopes are soon to be dashed. The entire family is finally facing the truth: "Nothing turns out as we would have it"—the dream of Moscow will never be realized, the mass of darkness has overwhelmed them. In the requiem that concludes the play, the three sisters meditate on the future, just as, in the beginning of the play, they reflected on the past, while Andrey pushes the carriage, Kulygin bustles, and Chebutykin hums softly to himself.

Their affirmations, showing the strong influence of Vershinin's view of life, are inexplicably hopeful and expectant. Masha expresses her determination to endure; Irina has faith that a "time will come when everyone will know what all this is for"; and Olga affirms that "our sufferings will turn into joy for those who live after us, happiness and peace will come to this earth, and then they will remember kindly and bless those who are living now." The gay band music played by the military evokes in the three sisters the will to live. But the music slowly fades away. Will hope fade away as well? Olga's anxious questioning of life ("If only we knew—if only we knew!") is—as if to suggest this—antiphonally answered by Chebutykin's muttered denials ("It doesn't matter, it doesn't matter!"), the skepticism of Tuzenbakh reduced to its most nihilistic form. And on this double note—the dialectic of hope and despair in a situation of defeat—Chekhov's darkest play draws to its close.

In *The Three Sisters*, Chekhov depicts the prostration of the cultured elite before the forces of darkness; in *The Cherry Orchard*, he examines the same problem from a comic-ironic point of view. Written while he was dying with great difficulty, *The Cherry Orchard* is the most farcical of Chekhov's full-length works, and so it was intended. In 1901, when the play was just beginning to take shape in his mind, he wrote to Olga Knipper: "The next play I write for the Art Theatre will definitely be funny, very funny—at least in intention." The last phrase was probably a sally aimed at Stanislavsky (Chekhov deplored his tendency to turn "my characters into crybabies"), and through Stanislavsky did, in fact, eventually misinterpret *The Cherry Orchard* as a somber study of Russian life, Chekhov always insisted on calling it "not a drama but a comedy; in places almost a farce."

The importance of the comic element in the play suggests that Chekhov is emphasizing the other side of his revolt. Instead of merely evoking sympathy for the victims of the social conflict, he is now satirizing them as well; instead of blackening the character of the despoiler, he is drawing him with a great deal more depth and balance. The change is one of degree—Chekhov has not reversed his earlier position, he has merely modified it—and the dispossession of the victims still evokes strains of pathos that we should not ignore. But in *The Cherry Orchard* Chekhov is more impatient with his cultured idlers; and their eventual fate seems more fitting and more just.

In all of his plays, on the other hand, Chekhov's revolt remains two-edged, for it is directed both against his leisured characters, too will-less to resist their own liquidation, and also against the dark environment that drags them under. Thus Chekhov's revolt may change in emphasis and attack, but it is always fixed on the fate of the cultured classes in the modern world. This is the great "problem" of his plays—and it is a problem that, in keeping with his artistic creed, he undertakes not to solve but simply to present correctly. Confronting the same world as the other modern dramatists—a world without God and, therefore, without meaning—Chekhov has no remedy for the disease of contemporary life. Ibsen speaks of the importance of one's calling, and Strindberg of resignation. But even Chekhov's panacea of work is ultimately ineffectual before the insupportable fact of death.

Still, despite the bleakness of his vision, Chekhov possesses a deeper humanity than any other modern dramatist. For while he never fails to examine the desperate absurdity of his characters, he never loses sight of the qualities that make them fully alive: "My holy of holies," he writes, "are the human body, health, intelligence, talent, inspiration, love, and the most absolute freedom—freedom from despotism and lies." Chekhov himself embodies these qualities so perfectly that no one has even been able to write of him without the most profound affection and love; and he, the author, remains the most profound character in his fiction. Because of his hatred of untruth, Chekhov will not arouse false hopes about the future of mankind—but because he is humane to the marrow of his bones, he manages to increase our expectations of the human race. Coupling sweetness of temper with toughness of mind, Chekhov makes his work an extraordinary compound of morality and reality, rebellion and acceptance, irony and sympathy—evoking a singular affirmation even in the darkest despair. There are more powerful playwrights in the modern theatre—artists with greater range, wider variety, more intellectual power—but there are none more warm and generous, and none who bring the drama to a higher realization of its human role.

THOMAS R. WHITAKER

[The Three Sisters] †

Immediately the three of them: dark-blue, white, and black. Olga speaking. Olga in her teacher's uniform, moving about the drawing room with nervous lassitude, school-exercises in hand, wide awake but as if in a dream: "Father died just a year ago today. . . ." Speaking to whom? Expecting no answer from Irina, that shimmer of white lost in thought by the sunny window. Not even glancing toward Masha—your foreground figure, blackly ensconced in a downstage chair, hat on her lap, absorbed in a book. ". . . very cold and it was snowing. It seemed to me I would never live through it; and you were lying there quite still. . . ." Behind the upstage columns, just beyond your focus of attention, a maid beginning to lay the table in the ball-room. "And now—a year's gone by, and we talk about it so easily. . . ." We? Irina still not answering, Masha not looking up. Then the clock striking. You listen: How many of you listen? "The clock struck twelve then, too." Silence—in which you can almost hear . . . And now Olga recalling (for whom?) how the band played as they carried father to the cemetery.

"Why must we bring up all those memories?" Irina now speaking: part of a *we* that had been silently shared, after all, but resisted? Masha still rather firmly not looking up. Refusing to? Behind the columns, nearly inaudible to you, three men now chatting. Olga turning to the window, exclaiming over the spring warmth but at once going back to the past—to the spring now eleven years ago when they left Moscow. This morning her heart leapt with joy: she wanted so much to go home again. "Go home to Moscow!" And a smile now playing over Irina's face. From upstage, fragments of talk: "Small chance of that!" "Of

† From "Dreaming the Music," *Fields of Play in Modern Drama*. Copyright © 1977 Princeton University Press. Excerpt, pp. 82–89 reprinted with permission of Princeton University Press.

course, it's nonsense." Masha suddenly whistling a snatch of yearning melody. A sharp reproof from Olga. Masha silent, rigid. And now Olga recalling defensively her headaches, her gloom, her weakness, day by day for the past four years.

As you follow this increasingly intricate counterpoint of echoes and reversals, abortive talk and shared silence, you recall Gorky's[1] verdict after a performance by the Moscow Art Theater: "This is music—not acting." But it's a music, you now begin to realize, that is itself a mode of action—and one that is already unfolding its own meaning. Seldom confronting each other directly, these people are always exchanging oblique responses, unacknowledged echoes, tacit resistances. Solitude is certainly not—as some have called it—their essential condition. Don't they allow a chronic inadvertence to distort or disrupt the silent reciprocity of which they are all fitfully aware? (They? But aren't they almost *we*—for you who sit silently with them?) Even in turning away, they don't listen only to themselves. They want to be aware of their distance from others, to hear themselves being absent from just this continuous music of existence in which you find them immersed. Stanislavsky[2] must have been wrong: they don't want gaiety. They want to *want* gaiety. They want to remain within some poignant dream of the past or of the merely possible. But you were wrong, too: they aren't weakwilled. Lost in thought, or addressing the air, or suddenly whistling, they fix themselves in subtle opposition to the present. And yet, even the absence they seek has a consoling mutuality: "It seemed to me I would never live through it," Olga has said; "and you had fainted and were lying there quite still, just as if you were dead." Don't they want somehow to hear themselves being absent together?

But in this resistance to a living present, what various life! There is Masha—remaining aloof even after the men come downstage, but radiating a blocked vitality that now speaks in those haunting lines from Pushkin: "A green oak grows by a curving shore, / And round that oak hangs a golden chain." And Chebutykin—now coyly giving Irina that most inappropriate samovar because he is still carrying on a fantasied romance with her dead mother. And Solyony—ostentatiously playing Lermontov or the sinister boor because of his painful shyness. (Just as the shy Natasha who is soon to enter will learn to play the domestic tyrant? What irrelevant moralism tempted you to think that pathetic pair more willful or malign than anyone else? Don't they simply escape into a different dream?) And there is the competent but glib Vershinin—now meeting the sisters, joking about the distant past or future, spinning out charming words so that he won't think of that histrionically suicidal wife who is a painful image of their shared condition, and increasingly

1. Maxim Gorky (1868–1936), a friend of Chekhov's and the only Russian playwright to flourish under both the tsarist and the Soviet regimes [*Editor*].
2. Konstantin Stanislavsky (1863–1938), a Russian actor, producer, and teacher; he founded, among other things, the Moscow Art Theatre in 1898 with Nemirovich-Danchenko. Among his greatest achievements were his productions of Chekhov's plays [*Editor*].

glancing toward Masha (And, yes, Masha has reversed her decision to leave the party. Won't the affair toward which they are already drifting—as she tries not to think of her histrionically pedantic husband—be their own dream of shared absence, a dream as hypnotic as those lines from Pushkin?) And now Andrey, the capable brother who has "such a bad habit"—as Olga has just told Vershinin—"always walking away." (For just that reason, Natasha's embarrassed running away from the luncheon table will soon easily trap him into proposing a domestic flight into shared absence.) And finally Kulygin—the leaden chain about Masha's green oak, maintaining himself precariously in the pompous academic dream toward which he had once tempted her schoolgirl romanticiscm. (And yet when he almost relaxes don't you glimpse through the mask an ironically compassionate eye?)

As the group moves into the ball-room for luncheon, leaving Irina behind with Tusenbach, you realize that you have neglected to play that ugly little lieutenant within this unfolding panorama of compulsive inadvertence. Is that because he seems the most genuinely attentive person in this drawing-room—ready enough to join in with Vershinin's philosophizing, but ready also, as his remark to Irina now makes explicit, to understand even the Solyony who taunts him and will one day kill him? Surely Tusenbach doesn't want merely to *want* gaiety? But listen more closely as he now plays the perennially rejected lover: "Oh, I long so passionately for life, to work and aspire, and all this longing is part of my love for you, Irina." No, he hasn't even heard her say a moment ago that she doesn't want to hear such talk. Though aware of his own absurdity, he too wants to hear himself being absent—with her.

Now they have all gone behind the upstage columns, leaving the drawing-room appropriately empty. Fragments of talk reach you. Two lieutenants enter and take pictures of the various company. And is this, then, Chekhov's picture of our necessary condition? Can he do nothing but smilingly lament, with that Dr. Dorn in *The Sea Gull*: "But what can I do . . . ? Tell me, what can I do?" Many have said so—and you have agreed. Tolstoy, you recall, couldn't read many pages of *Three Sisters*. "Where does it all lead us?" he asked. But the script isn't the play, and the play is more than a picture. Hasn't it been inviting and requiring of you, through its increasingly panoramic focus and its developing counterpoint of disjunctive speeches and gestures, exactly what these people resist: that you open yourself to the full music of our existence in mutuality? In *Rosmersholm*,[3] where you spy upon spying characters, the dramatic structure tempts you to join them in trying to possess the field of play as an intellectual object. But *Three Sisters* frustrates any such analytic observation—and even seems to empty you of that possessive "me." Detective work here would only distract from the revelatory pattern of present trivia. What happens instead? A wid-

3. A play by Ibsen [*Editor*].

ening of your peripheral attention, a listening in quiet alertness to the jagged texture of this music—and to the harmonies produced by the gestures through which these people construct for themselves a dream of shared need.

The play's style has been leading you into an alternative mode of witnessing—a norm rendered more subtly and immediately than if it were consigned to a *raisonneur* like Krouschov in *The Wood Demon*.[4] And witnessing, as you have seen, is itself a fundamental action. Josiah Royce[5] said somewhere, "Finite beings are always such as they are in virtue of an *inattention* which at present blinds them to their actual relations to God and to one another." Leaving "God" aside, as it seems, *Three Sisters* explores something like that intuition. In their willed in-attention, its people experience one another as distant or nonexistent. They experience space as constriction or separation, time as not-yet or a slipping-away, the world itself as the constant threat of nothingness. But through you the play has been disclosing time and space as an expanding *now*, a moving yet simultaneous apprehension of these var-iously self-closed subjective worlds which are really one.

And yet, have you really been an empty alertness to the "now?" Haven't you limited your attention to a poignantly realistic fiction, to what you call the "people" in that drawing-room? But those "people" are living masks for the actors, whose attention to your present field has alerted you to the more abortive reciprocity that they are playing—and so enabling you indirectly to play. At this moment Andrey and Natasha seem lost in their awkward embrace, unaware of the newly arrived officers who stare in amusement. But the actors are sharing with you that quietly farcical closing tableau, in which years of pain are ironically implicit. Stanislavsky knew very well the great importance of "public solitude" as a technique for the Chekhovian actor. And he also knew that the actor must sustain, while "penetrating into the most secret places" of his character's heart, an "unbroken flow" of communion with his stage partners, with objects, and with the audience. Only a style founded upon such communion can enable the cast of *Three Sisters* to present, within and beyond these masks of distraction and self-obsession, our mutual immanence.

Of course, for the actors and for you, the play's apparent realism combines its intimate penetration with a clarifying distance. Could you hear this music if immersed in it as Tusenbach must be? But then isn't your own point of view itself an absurd fiction, the contemplative equiv-alent of what the characters more damagingly seek? If so, you must now be experiencing your own version of the play's "spine" or objective: to hear ourselves being absent from the silent music of presence. You stop short. Does *Three Sisters* ask you to abandon the theater—in order to become genuinely present to your own life? "I saw a wonderful play last

4. An early play by Chekhov [*Editor*].   5. An American philosopher and psychologist (1855–1916) [*Editor*].

night," says Lopakhin in *The Cherry Orchard*. "It was so funny." To which Lyubov retorts: "It probably wasn't funny at all. Instead of going to plays, you should take a good look at yourself. . . ." Advice, certainly, which that histrionic lady might better take than give!

But despite such ambivalences in Chekhov's homeopathic art, which seeks to cure illusion through illusion, your own life is nowhere but *here* for the moment. And this performance is now inviting you to open yourself more fully. In the second act, Andrey will tell Natasha that there's nothing to talk about and will then confess his disappointment to the deaf Ferapont. Masha and Vershinin will exchange flattering complaints about tedious men and complaining wives. Tusenbach, who dreams of work, will chatter of his patience to an Irina who thinks only of the exhaustion to which her own dream of work has led. Vershinin will pretend to debate Tusenbach about the existence of happiness, and Chebutykin will squabble with Solyony about whether a roast is a roast or an onion is an onion. And, after Tusenbach has got drunk to prepare for a night of trashy piano-playing that Natasha has already vetoed, after Solyony has forced words of love and Natasha words of maternal anxiety upon the perturbed Irina, Olga will bring to the tired and frustrated company a splitting headache and the report that the whole town is talking of Andrey. But you? You will have to listen closely to the counterpoint between all this inattentive loquacity and the action of performance itself.

Through an evasive complaining or yearning that nourishes the very predicaments on which it feeds, the characters will increasingly justify their sense of being helpless victims of circumstance. But the actors, by rendering the nuances of this subtext with such affectionate realism, will utterly transform each instance of self-closure—from Natasha's and Andrey's non-conversation to the final moments in which Irina ignores Kulygin, who ignores Vershinin, who ignores Olga, who ignores everyone. As the characters confirm their prisons, sometimes thinking of an illusory key called "tomorrow," the actors will be leading you to understand from the inside—in all their tempting ease or seeming necessity—those momentary maneuvers of turning off or away that enable us gradually to construct some trap of habit, addiction, or catastrophic role-playing from which no ordinary act of attention can then free us. And won't your own painful exhilaration, as the second act sputters to its close, indicate that you will have doubly shared the spectrum of self-isolating moods generated here by such maneuvers: the self-pity of Andrey and Chebutykin, the fatuous if self-ironc verbosity of Vershinin, Tusenbach, and Kulygin, the cruel petulance of Natasha and Solyony, the hysterical indecisiveness of Masha, the sick anxiety of Olga, and the numb exhaustion of Irina?

You will then be prepared to act and witness, in the context appropriately provided by a disastrous fire of unknown origin, some yet more painful consequences of that willed and often quite lucid inattention.

Most obviously, of course, in the generous but weary Olga—who will withdraw from Natasha's rude attack into a near faint, leave the room to avoid the spectacle of the drunken Chebutykin, block out Masha's literary confession of love by insisting from behind a night-screen that she can't hear, and finally utter no word at all from behind that screen as Andrey makes his defiant confession of guilt. But the despairing Irina, too, will now be merely curt with Chebutykin, won't notice for some time that Tusenbach has fallen asleep, and will say nothing in response to either Masha's confession or Andrey's. And even Masha, who so eagerly answers Vershinin's snatch of song, will then dismiss Tusenbach and Kulygin in bored irritation, sit in silence as Olga consoles Irina, confess her love in phrases intended mainly for her own ears, and walk out (again answering Vershinin's music) just as Andrey proposes a family conference. Won't Irina's pleading curtain-line sum up for you then, not just her desire to escape from their shared predicament, but also the interior action that has repeatedly constituted that predicament? "Let's go!"

The last act, of course, will bring that performed action full circle— to an unresolved dissonance. The military band will play, Chebutykin will hum, and the sisters will utter their various cries, as ex-lieutenant Tusenbach is now carried to the cemetery. But the action of performance, far from being circular, will have moved through an expanding present to disclose all that was implicit in the plays' opening scene. And suddenly you foresee, just before the end, a moment of harmony between the music so imperfectly known by the *dramatis personae* and that being disclosed through the play's total form of acting and witnessing. Thanks to Solyony's catastrophic role-playing, thanks also to the repeatedly endorsed decorum of evasion that lets affairs of "honor" as well as "love" proceed as if unnoticed, death is now imminent. And amid a conversation designed mainly to hide from each other and from themselves their full awareness of such a possibility, Tusenbach will turn to Irina— and he who plays Tusenbach will turn to her who plays Irina—and say: "Really, I feel fine. I feel as if I were seeing those pine trees and maples and birches for the first time in my life. They all seem to be looking at me, waiting for something." And they are. They are waiting for Tusenbach to wake up from your daily sleepwalking. They are inviting you to listen. . . .

And you turn to her: "The music of silence?"

George Bernard Shaw
and
Candida

GEORGE BERNARD SHAW

Ideals and Idealists†

We have seen that as Man grows through the ages, he finds himself bolder by the growth of his courage: that is, of his spirit (for so the common people name it), and dares more and more to love and trust instead of to fear and fight. But his courage has other effects: he also raises himself from mere consciousness to knowledge by daring more and more to face facts and tell himself the truth. For in his infancy of helplessness and terror he could not face the inexorable; and facts being of all things the most inexorable, he masked all the threatening ones as fast as he discovered them; so that now every mask requires a hero to tear it off. The king of terrors, Death, was the Arch-Inexorable: Man could not bear the dread of that. He must persuade himself that Death can be propitiated, circumvented, abolished. How he fixed the mask of personal immortality on the face of Death for this purpose we all know. And he did the like with all disagreeables as long as they remained inevitable. Otherwise he must have gone mad with terror of the grim shapes around him, headed by the skeleton with the scythe and hour-glass. The masks were his ideals, as he called them; and what, he would ask, would life be without ideals? Thus he became an idealist, and remained so until he dared to begin pulling the masks off and looking the spectres in the face—dared, that is, to be more and more a realist. But all men are not equally brave; and the greatest terror prevailed whenever some realist bolder than the rest laid hands on a mask which they did not yet dare to do without.

We have plenty of these masks around us still: some of them more fantastic than any of the Sandwich Islanders' masks in the British Museum. In our novels and romances especially we see the most beautiful

† From George Bernard Shaw, *The Quintessence of Ibsenism*, London, 1891. Pp. 19–30.

of all the masks: those devised to disguise the brutalities of the sexual instinct in the earlier stages of its development and to soften the rigorous aspect of the iron laws by which Society regulates its gratification. When the social organism becomes bent on civilization, it has to force marriage and family life on the individual, because it can perpetuate itself in no other way whilst love is still known only by fitful glimpses, the basis of sexual relationship being in the main mere physical appetite. Under these circumstances men try to graft pleasure on necessity by desperately pretending that the institution forced upon them is a congenial one, making it a point of public decency to assume always that men spontaneously love their kindred better than their chance acquaintances, and that the woman once desired is always desired: also that the family is woman's proper sphere, and that no really womanly woman ever forms an attachment, or even knows what it means, until she is requested to do so by a man. Now if anyone's childhood has been embittered by the dislike of his mother and the ill-temper of his father; if his wife has ceased to care for him and he is heartily tired of his wife; if his brother is going to law with him over the division of the family property, and his son acting in studied defiance of his plans and wishes, it is hard for him to persuade himself that passion is eternal and that blood is thicker than water. Yet if he tells himself the truth, all his life seems a waste and a failure by the light of it. It comes then to this, that his neighbors must either agree with him that the whole system is a mistake, and discard it for a new one, which cannot possibly happen until social organization so far outgrows the institution that Society can perpetuate itself without it; or else they must keep him in countenance by resolutely making believe that all the illusions with which it has been masked are realities.

For the sake of precision, let us imagine a community of a thousand persons, organized for the perpetuation of the species on the basis of the British family as we know it at present. Seven hundred of them, we will suppose, find the British family arrangement quite good enough for them. Two hundred and ninety-nine find it a failure, but must put up with it since they are in a minority. The remaining person occupies a position to be explained presently. The 299 failures will not have the courage to face the fact that they are irremediable failures, since they cannot prevent the 700 satisfied ones from coercing them into conformity with the marriage law. They will accordingly try to persuade themselves that, whatever their own particular domestic arrangements may be, the family is a beautiful and holy natural institution. For the fox not only declares that the grapes he cannot get are sour: he also insists that the sloes he *can* get are sweet. Now observe what has happened. The family as it really is is a conventional arrangement, legally enforced, which the majority, because it happens to suit them, think good enough for the minority, whom it happens not to suit at all. The family as a beautiful and holy natural institution is only a fancy picture of what every family would be if everybody was to be suited, invented by the minority as a mask for the reality, which in its nakedness is intolerable to them. We call this sort of fancy picture an Ideal; and the policy of forcing individuals to act on the assumption that all ideals are real, and to recognize and accept such action as standard moral conduct, absolutely valid under all circumstances, contrary conduct or any advocacy of it being discountenanced and punished as immoral, may therefore be described as the policy of Idealism. Our 299 domestic failures are therefore become idealists as to marriage; and in proclaiming the ideal in fiction, poetry, pulpit and platform oratory, and serious private conversation, they will far outdo the 700 who comfortably accept marriage as a matter of course, never dreaming of calling it an "institution," much less a holy and beautiful one, and being pretty plainly of opinion that Idealism is a crackbrained fuss about nothing. The idealists, hurt by this, will retort by calling them Philistines. We then have our society classified as 700 Philistines and 299 idealists, leaving one man unclassified: the man strong enough to face the truth the idealists are shirking.

Such a man says of marriage, "This thing is a failure for many of us. It is insufferable that two human beings, having entered into relations which only warm affection can render tolerable, should be forced to maintain them after such affections have ceased to exist, or in spite of the fact that they have never arisen. The alleged natural attractions and repulsions upon which the family ideal is based do not exist; and it is historically false that the family was founded for the purpose of satisfying them. Let us provide otherwise for the social ends which the family subserves, and then abolish its compulsory character altogether." What will be the attitude of the rest to this outspoken man? The Philistines will simply think him mad. But the idealists will be terrified beyond measure at the proclamation of their hidden thought—at the presence of the traitor among the conspirators of silence—at the rending of the beautiful veil they and their poets have woven to hide the unbearable face of the truth. They will crucify him, burn him, violate their own ideals of family affection by taking his children away from him, ostracize him, brand him as immoral, profligate, filthy, and appeal against him to the despised Philistines, specially idealized for the occasion as Society. How far they will proceed against him depends on how far his courage exceeds theirs. At his worst, they call him cynic and paradoxer: at his best they do their utmost to ruin him, if not to take his life. Thus, purblindly courageous moralists like Mandeville and Larochefoucauld,[1] who merely state unpleasant facts without denying the validity of current ideals, and who indeed depend on those ideals to make their statements piquant, get off with nothing worse than this name of cynic, the free use of which is a familiar mark of the zealous idealist. But take the case

---

1. Bernard Mandeville (c. 1670–1733) was a satirist and philosopher, the author of *The Fable of the Bees* (1714). François de la Rochefoucauld (1613–80) was a French moralist and writer of maxims [*Editor*].

of the man who has already served us as an example: Shelley. The idealists did not call Shelley a cynic: they called him a fiend until they invented a new illusion to enable them to enjoy the beauty of his lyrics, this illusion being nothing less than the pretence that since he was at bottom an idealist himself, his ideals must be identical with those of Tennyson and Longfellow, neither of whom ever wrote a line in which some highly respectable ideal was not implicit.[2]

Here the admission that Shelley, the realist, was an idealist too, seems to spoil the whole argument. And it certainly spoils its verbal consistency. For we unfortunately use this word ideal indifferently to denote both the institution which the ideal masks and the mask itself thereby producing desperate confusion of thought, since the institution may be an effete and poisonous one, whilst the mask may be, and indeed generally is, an image of what we would fain have in its place. If the existing facts, with their masks on, are to be called ideals, and the future possibilities which the masks depict are also to be called ideals—if, again, the man who is defending existing institutions by maintaining their identity with their masks is to be confounded under one name with the man who is striving to realize the future possibilities by tearing the mask and the thing masked asunder, then the position cannot be intelligibly described by mortal pen: you, and I, reader, will be at cross purposes at every sentence unless you allow me to distinguish pioneers like Shelley and Ibsen as realists from the idealists of my imaginary community of one thousand. If you ask why I have not allotted the terms the other way, and called Shelley and Ibsen idealists and the conventionalists realists, I reply that Ibsen himself, though he has not formally made the distinction, has so repeatedly harped on conventions and conventionalists as ideals and idealists that if I were now perversely to call them realities and realists, I should confuse readers of The Wild Duck and Rosmersholm more than I should help them. Doubtless I shall be reproached for puzzling people by thus limiting the meaning of the term ideal. But what, I ask, is that inevitable passing perplexity compared to the inextricable tangle I must produce if I follow the custom, and use the word indiscriminately in its two violently incompatible senses? If the term realist is objected to on account of some of its modern associations, I can only recommend you, if you must associate it with something else than my own description of its meaning (I do not deal in definitions), to associate it, not with Zola and Maupassant, but with Plato.

2. The following are examples of the two stages of Shelley criticism: "We feel as if one of the darkest of the fiends had been clothed with a human body to enable him to gratify his enmity against the human race, and as if the supernatural atrocity of his hate were only heightened by his power to do injury. So strongly has this impression dwelt upon our minds that we absolutely asked a friend, who had seen this individual, to describe him to us—as if a cloven hoof, or horn, or flames from the mouth, must have marked the external appearance of so bitter an enemy of mankind" (*Literary Gazette*, 19 May 1821). "A beautiful and ineffectual angel, beating his luminous wings in vain" (Matthew Arnold, in the Preface of his selection of poems by Byron, dated 1881).

The 1881 opinion is much sillier than the 1821 opinion. Further samples will be found in the articles of Henry Salt, one of the few writers on Shelley who understand his true position as a social pioneer.

Now let us return to our community of 700 Philistines, 299 idealists, and 1 realist. The mere verbal ambiguity against which I have just provided is as nothing beside that which comes of any attempt to express the relations of these three sections, simple as they are, in terms of the ordinary systems of reason and duty. The idealist, higher in the ascent of evolution than the Philistine, yet hates the highest and strikes at him with a dread and rancor of which the easygoing Philistine is guiltless. The man who has risen above the danger and the fear that his acquisitiveness will lead him to theft, his temper to murder, and his affections to debauchery: this is he who is denounced as an arch-scoundrel and libertine, and thus confounded with the lowest because he is the highest. And it is not the ignorant and stupid who maintain this error, but the literate and the cultured. When the true prophet speaks, he is proved to be both rascal and idiot, not by those who have never read of how foolishly such learned demonstrations have come off in the past, but by those who have themselves written volumes on the crucifixions, the burnings, the stonings, the beheadings and hangings, the Siberia transportations, the calumny and ostracism which have been the lot of the pioneer as well as of the camp follower. It is from men of established literary reputation that we learn that William Blake[3] was mad, that Shelley was spoiled by living in a low set, that Robert Owen[4] was a man who did not know the world, that Ruskin[5] was incapable of comprehending political economy, that Zola was a mere blackguard, and that Ibsen was "a Zola with a wooden leg." The great musician, accepted by the unskilled listener, is vilified by his fellow-musicians: it was the musical culture of Europe that pronounced Wagner the inferior of Mendelssohn and Meyerbeer. The great artist finds his foes among the painters, and not among the men in the street: it was the Royal Academy which placed forgotten nobodies above Burne Jones.[6] It is not rational that it should be so; but it is so, for all that.

The realist at last loses patience with ideals altogether, and sees in them only something to blind us, something to numb us, something to murder self in us, something whereby, instead of resisting death, we can disarm it by committing suicide. The idealist, who has taken refuge with the ideals because he hates himself and is ashamed of himself, thinks that all this is so much the better. The realist, who has come to have a deep respect for himself and faith in the validity of his own will, thinks it so much the worse. To the one, human nature, naturally corrupt, is held back from ruinous excesses only by self-denying conformity to the ideals. To the other these ideals are only swaddling clothes which man has outgrown, and which insufferably impede his movements. No wonder the two cannot agree. The idealist says, "Realism means egotism;

3. An English poet and mystic (1757–1827) [Editor].
4. A Welsh social reformer (1771–1858) who improved the quality of his workers' lives by paying high wages and generally upgrading working conditions in the mills and who nonetheless made profits [Editor].
5. John Ruskin (1819–1900), an English art and social critic who attacked laissez-faire economics [Editor].
6. An English painter (1833–98) [Editor].

and egotism means depravity." The realist declares that when a man abnegates the will to live and be free in a world of the living and free, seeking only to conform to ideals for the sake of being, not himself, but "a good man," then he is morally dead and rotten, and must be left unheeded to abide his resurrection, if that by good luck arrive before his bodily death. Unfortunately, this is the sort of speech that nobody but a realist understands. It will be more amusing as well as more convincing to take an actual example of an idealist criticising a realist.

Letters

To William Archer†

[29 Fitzroy Square W]
[Undated: assigned to 21st April 1898]

[Dear Archer][1]

When Eugene, with his apprehensive faculty raised to the highest sensitiveness by his emotional state, hears that long speech of Candida's about the household, he takes the whole thing in, grasps for the first time what it really means, what the conditions of such love are, and how it is essentially the creature of limitations which are far transcended in his own nature. He sees at once that no such life and no such love are possible for him, and instantly leaves them all far behind him. To put it another way, he jumps to the position from which the Master-builder saw that it was all over with the building of happy homes for human beings. He looks at the comfort and sweetness and happiness that has just been placed before him at its best, and turns away from it, exclaiming with absolute conviction, "Life is nobler than that." Thus Candida's sympathy with his supposed sorrow is entirely thrown away. If she were to alter her decision and offer herself to him he would be unspeakably embarrassed and terrified. When he says "Out into the night with me," he does not mean the night of despair and darkness, but the free air and holy starlight which is so much more natural an atmosphere to him than this stuffy fireside warmth of mothers and sisters and wives and so on. It may be that this exposition may seem to you to destroy all the pathos and sanity of the scene; but from no other point of view could it have been written. A perfect dramatic command, either of character or situation, can only be obtained from some point of view that transcends both. The absolute fitness which is the secret of the effectiveness of the ending of "Candida," would be a mere sham if it meant nothing more than a success for Morell at the cost of a privation for Eugene. Further, any such privation would take all the point from

† From *Bernard Shaw: Collected Letters, 1898–1910*, ed. Dan H. Laurence, London, 1972. P. 33. Reprinted with the permission of the publishers, Max Reinhardt Ltd.

1. William Archer (1856–1924), an English drama critic and a staunch proponent of the new drama of writers like Ibsen and Shaw [*Editor*].

Candida's sub-consciousness of the real state of affairs; for you will observe that Candida knows all along perfectly well that she is no mate for Eugene, and instinctively relies on that solid fact to pull him through when he is going off, as she thinks, broken-hearted. The final touch of comedy is the femininely practical reason that she gives for their incompatibility.

* * *

To James Huneker†

10 Adelphi Terrace WC
6th April 1904

Dear Huneker[1]

Dont ask me conundrums about that very immoral female Candida. Observe the entry of Mr Burgess. "Youre not the lady as hused to typewrite for him." "No." "Naaaoww: *she* was younger." And therefore Candida sacked her. Prossy is a very highly selected young person indeed, devoted to Morell to the extent of helping in kitchen, but to him the merest pet rabbit, unable to get the smallest hold on him. Candida is as unscrupulous as Siegfried:[2] Morell himself at last sees that "no law will bind her." She seduces Eugene just exactly as far as it is worth her while to seduce him. She is a woman without "character" in the conventional sense. Without brains and strength of mind she would be a wretched slattern & voluptuary. She is straight for natural reasons, not for conventional ethical ones. Nothing can be more coldbloodedly reasonable than her farewell to Eugene. "All very well, my lad; but I dont quite see myself at 50 with a husband of 35." It is just this freedom from emotional slop, this unerring wisdom on the domestic plane, that makes her so completely mistress of the situation.

Then consider the poet. She makes a man of him finally by shewing him his own strength—that David must do without poor Uriah's wife.[3] And then she pitches in her picture of the home, the onions & the tradesmen & the cossetting of big baby Morell. The New York Hausfrau thinks it a little paradise; but the poet rises up and says "Out, then, into the night with me"—Tristan's holy night.[4] If this greasy fool's paradise is happiness, then I give it to you with both hands: "life is nobler than that." That is "the poet's secret." The young things in front weep to see the poor boy going out lonely & brokenhearted in the cold night to save the properties of New England Puritanism; but he is really a god going back to his heaven, proud, unspeakably contemptuous of the "happiness"

† From *Bernard Shaw: Collected Letters (1898–1910)*, ed. Dan H. Laurence, London, 1972. Pp. 415–16. Reprinted with the permission of the publishers, Max Reinhardt, Ltd.
1. James Huneker (1860–1921) was an American critic of music, drama, and art [Editor].
2. The hero of the German epic *The Nibelungen Lied* [Editor].

3. In the Bible David does not do without Bathsheba, Uriah's wife [Editor].
4. One of the famous pair of lovers Tristan and Isolde. Tristan's "holy night" is the night of oblivion he longed to share with Isolde in their love-death in Richard Wagner's opera *Tristan und Isolde* (1859) [Editor].

he envied in the days of his blindness, clearly seeing that he has higher business on hand than Candida. She has a little quaint intuition of the completeness of his cure: she says "he has learnt to do without happiness."

As I should certainly be lynched by the infuriated Candidamaniacs if this view of the case were made known, I confide it to your discretion. I tell it to you because it is an interesting example of the way in which a scene which could be conceived & written only by transcending the ordinary notion of the relations between the persons, nevertheless stirs the ordinary emotions to a very high degree, all the more because the language of the poet, to those who have not the clue to it, is mysterious & bewildering & therefore worshipful. I divined it myself before I found out the whole truth about it.

[Benjamin] Tucker[5] is a very decent fellow; but he persists, like most intellectuals, in dictating conditions to a world which has to organize itself in obedience to laws of life which he doesnt understand any more than you or I. Individualism is all very well as a study product; *but that is not what is happening.* Society is integrating, not individualizing; and it is better to lay hold of what it is doing & make the best of it than sit complaining that it wont do something else. Trusts are most excellent things—as superior to competitive shopkeeperism as symphonies are to cornet solos; but they need more careful scoring & longer rehearsal & better conducting. The only individualism worth looking at now is breeding the race & getting rid of the promiscuity & profligacy called marriage.

Is there such a thing in America as a decent publisher—one whom I could trust, in reason, to sell my books on commission if I manufactured them myself. I am tired of wasting time negotiating with fools who are afraid to publish the Superman,[6] & rogues who want to get too soft a bargain over it. It is copyrighted all safely; but it lies there dead whilst McClures & Harpers & the like funk it, and others want to grab it for ever & ever.

yrs
G. Bernard Shaw

CHARLES A. CARPENTER

The Quintessence of Shaw's Ethical Position†

The controlling currents of idea and intention that run through all of a writer's works, whatever his subject, form, or strategy, are extremely hard to discern when the writer is as prolific and wide-ranging as Bernard

5. Benjamin Tucker (1854–1939) was an anarchist writer and publisher and a friend of Shaw's [*Editor*].

6. His play *Man and Superman* (1901–3) [*Editor*].
† Revised from the first edition of this anthology and printed here by permission of the author.

Shaw. What is his fundamental bent? What are the basic ingredients of his thought? What are the constant elements among the innumerable variables in his essays and plays? These questions have never been answered adequately, perhaps for the simple reason that few critics have elected to deal with the vast, word-encumbered realm of Shaw's motives, purposes, and doctrines. Those who have, moreover, too often describe its more curious and remote extremities, then acknowledge that its center must lie somewhere between—if indeed there is one at all. I believe there is. At one of the critics' favorite extremities, Shaw was an odd type of semi-mystic: an impassioned but distinctly unpoetic artist who claimed to be possessed by a "world-betterment craze."[1] At another, he was a coldly cerebral (though unsystematic) philosopher: a leading advocate of the theory that a cosmic force is gradually turning life into a "vortex of pure thought." At dead center, however, Shaw was much less an artist or a philosopher than an intense rhetorician, a journalistic "battering ram."[2] No matter what guise he presented himself in, he was always trying to provoke human beings to behave in certain ways. This is why critics complain that his compulsions as an artist are not typically poetic and his edicts as a philosopher not sufficiently abstract. Both are conditioned by his predominant desire to influence human conduct. His orientation is pervasively and profoundly ethical.

Shaw's first book-length essay, *The Quintessence of Ibsenism*, contains the core of his ideas in relatively uncomplicated form. Despite its subject—and its value as an analysis of that subject—the book is still an uncamouflaged piece of Shavian propaganda. In a preface, Shaw speaks of it as "the living word of a man delivering a message to his own time."[3] In the text, he even scolds Ibsen for deviating from the straight Shaw line. Not that he ignored the actual import of Ibsen's plays; rather, he looked for—and found—the "ism" that tallied with his own.

Shaw once defended this practice, and his rationale offers an illuminating glimpse of his basic ethical convictions. In 1905, his newly authorized biographer, Archibald Henderson, earnestly told him that he was determined to write a "just" as well as accurate book. Shaw replied:

> Be as accurate as you can; but as to being just, who are you that you should be just? . . . Write boldly according to your bent: say what you WANT to say and not what you think you ought to say or what is right or just or any such arid nonsense. You are not God Almighty; and nobody will expect justice from you or any other superhuman attribute. This affected,

---

1. Shaw says in his postscript to Frank Harris's *Bernard Shaw* (New York, 1931), p. 428, that "a passion of pure political *Weltverbesserungswahn* [worldbettermentcraze] . . . is my own devouring malady."
2. He once declared: "The theatre is my battering ram as much as the platform or the press" (*Col-*

lected Letters, 1874–1897, ed. Dan H. Laurence [New York, 1965], p. 722).
3. Shaw, *Major Critical Essays* (London, 1932), p. 5. Further references to the edition of *The Quintessence of Ibsenism* in this essay will be given in the text.

> manufactured, artificial conscience of morality and justice and
> so on is of no use for the making of works of art: for that you
> must have the real conscience that gives a man courage to
> fulfil his will by saying what he likes.[4]

Shaw follows his own advice so conspicuously in his study of Ibsen that it has earned the label The Quintessence of Shaw.

The thesis of *The Quintessence of Ibsenism*, and the main root of Shaw's ethical convictions, is that man must follow "not the abstract law but the living will" (p. 122). He must cast off the "artificial conscience" imposed upon him by his misguided belief in the validity of moral codes and social institutions, and must replace it with a "real conscience" that springs from his own aspirations and convictions. Both the negative and positive sides of this dictum are fundamental elements in Shaw's thought from *My Dear Dorothea* (1878) to *Everybody's Political What's What?* (1944). Let us first consider the negative, or destructive, side.

Shaw's overriding purpose in life was to promote "world-betterment": the gradual movement of society and man to higher and higher forms of organization. In the *Quintessence*, he argues that the forces striving for evolution are continually obstructed by "abstract law," variously referred to as "institutions," "ideals of goodness," or simply "duty." He explains how the conflict inevitably occurs within society: "social progress takes effect through the replacement of old institutions by new ones; and since every institution involves the recognition of the duty of conforming to it, progress must involve the repudiation of an established duty at every step" (p. 17). But in the *Quintessence* as a whole Shaw calls for much more than the destruction of outmoded institutions and codes. He finally wants to eliminate the very basis of man's tendency to cherish ideals: the assumption, normally unquestioned, that people ought to direct their lives by some set of ethical absolutes. In his opinion, "abstract law" in the broadest sense is the major deterrent to evolution. Moreover, Shaw rejects the possibility that ideal institutions may be developed. He is a world-*betterer*, a meliorist, not an idealist in any sense. As such, he recognizes that the further improvement of society and mankind is feasible at any level of advancement, and he actively strives for that improvement.

The positive, constructive side of his ethical convictions is grounded in "the living will." He defines the will not mainly as a restraining faculty (our "will power"), but rather as man's passionate desire to accomplish what he wants to. As such, it becomes the immediate stimulant of all forms of evolution. To Shaw, as to Schopenhauer, the human will reflects a cosmic *Wille zu leben*, a force as real as gravity, even though it can be discerned only through its effects. Shaw does not stop where Schopenhauer does, however; his will to live is also a will to live

4. Henderson, *George Bernard Shaw: Man of the Century* (New York, 1956), p. xxv.

better—ultimately a drive to improve the conditions of life for everyone. Manifesting what M. H. Abrams terms "the genetic habit of mind," he regards Being as Becoming, and instinctively reads an upward movement into the process. According to this meliorist view, human volition is the specific agent of a cosmic drive for world-betterment. When neither inhibited nor misled by "ideals," Shaw says, the will acts as "our old friend the soul or spirit of man," hopefully doing the work of a power analogous to the Holy Spirit (p. 20n.). But it also operates collectively, within an ever-growing "social organism" (p. 25). There it serves as the final measure of the validity of institutions, since none will be workable in the long run which are not constructed to fulfil man's will (p. 20). In sum, the gradual fulfilment of individual wills actually constitutes the growth of the social organism, and thus makes possible the physical, mental, and spiritual evolution of mankind.

But man cannot fulfil his will simply by following its promptings blindly. As Shaw's spokesman Don Juan points out in the dream scene of *Man and Superman*, it needs a brain to steer it to its goal. Shaw believes that the human mind has the potential capacity to direct the will at once successfully and economically. In the *Quintessence* he remarks: "Only the other day our highest boast was that we were reasonable human beings. Today we laugh at that conceit, and see ourselves as wilful creatures. [But] ability to reason accurately is as desirable as ever; for by accurate reasoning only can we calculate our actions so as to do what we intend to do: that is, to fulfil our will" (p. 22). Even in Shaw's basically irrationalist conception, the intellect has an indispensable evolutionary function and must therefore be developed as fully as possible. The will to live better demands a change in life as it is, or gives birth to the image of a better life; the intellect ponders the why and the wherefore. As Shaw once explained it, reason does not determine the destination, but it searches for the shortest way.[5] The highly intellectual "philosophic man," as Don Juan puts it, is a person who "seeks in contemplation to discover the inner will of the world, in invention to discover the means of fulfilling that will, and in action to do that will by the so-discovered means."

To carry on its work effectively, the mind must first of all free itself from illusory ideals. Many times in the *Quintessence*, Shaw declares that men and women (especially the latter) must repudiate duty, which restricts the mind and thereby obstructs the fulfilment of the will; they must regard ideals as "only swaddling clothes which man has outgrown, and which insufferably impede his movements" (p. 31). At best, he should try to attain a state of "vigilant openmindedness" (p. 123). But the intellect requires more than mere freedom from the inhibiting pressures of abstract law. It also requires materials with which to formulate the higher modes of life that the will hints at and campaigns for. These

5. *The Intelligent Woman's Guide to Socialism and Capitalism* (New York, 1928), p. 365.

materials are ideas. To Shaw, ideas are the stepping-stones of progress, since by means of them the individual visualizes the paths that his will may follow. Not only are they the materials that the mind creates (via the imagination), then deliberately works with as the hand works with tools; they also have lives of their own, independent of man, and thus "wills" of their own. As a result, ideas have peculiar powers of intruding themselves into the mind and implanting themselves there, with or without man's conscious consent.[6] Shaw defends his whole approach to Ibsen's plays by insisting that "the existence of a discoverable and perfectly definite thesis in a poet's work by no means depends on the completeness of his own intellectual consciousness of it" (p. 12). He even explains away the heretic atmosphere of Darwinian fatalism in some of the plays by maintaining that Ibsen's "prophetic belief in the spontaneous growth of the will" made him a Shavian meliorist despite his nod to the theory of natural selection (p. 53). Shaw's view of ideas as both usable materials and wilful entities is remarkably appropriate to his evolutionary doctrine.

At the risk of oversimplifying, then, we can say that this doctrine consists of three basic elements. The human will, mankind's link with a cosmic force, channels the evolutionary impulse; the intellect, a distinctively human faculty in its advanced form, looks for the most efficient way to fulfil the will; and ideas, man-made articles which yet exist apart from their inventors, are the alternative paths that the intellect considers in its search. These elements are the fundamental ingredients of Shaw's ethical aims, the directives for human conduct which he believes will enable himself and others to contribute markedly to world-betterment, and which permeate his works as artist and rhetorician. Each element has its corresponding aim. First, Shaw attempts to eliminate the main obstruction that the will encounters, a sense of duty to established moral and social codes. Second, he tries to strengthen and refine the human brain so that it will become as efficient an instrument of the will as possible. And third, he seeks to supply those brains with ideas that might prove useful in the process of evolution. In short, he consistently aims to destroy ideals, to cultivate the intellect, and to implant ideas.

These three ethical convictions pervade Shaw's work from beginning to end. My purpose has been to single them out and put them in some sort of order, not to defend this assertion at length. Still, let us observe them in action through one highly significant piece of prose, Shaw's concluding statement about what he preferred to call the quintessence of Ibsenism. Ibsen's attack on ideals, he announces, is clear evidence that true religion is reviving after its suppression at the hands of Darwinists. He continues:

6. Particularly ideas in the form of jokes, Shaw says in a chapter he added to *The Quintessence of Ibsenism* in 1913: a "general law of the evolution of ideas" is that "every jest is an earnest in the womb of time" (p. 126).

[Ibsen] is on the side of the prophets in having devoted himself to shewing [*sic*] that the spirit or will of Man is constantly outgrowing the ideals, and that therefore thoughtless conformity to them is constantly producing results no less tragic than those which follow thoughtless violation of them. Thus the main effect of his plays is to keep before the public the importance of being always prepared to act immorally [that is, in opposition to currently accredited ideals]. . . . He protests against the ordinary assumption that there are certain moral institutions which justify all means used to maintain them, and insists that the supreme end shall be the inspired, eternal, ever growing one, not the external unchanging, artificial one; not the letter but the spirit; not the contract but the object of the contract; not the abstract law but the living will. And because the will to change our habits and thus defy morality arises before the intellect can reason out any racially beneficent purpose in the change, there is always an interval during which the individual can say no more than that he wants to behave immorally because he likes, and because he will feel constrained and unhappy if he acts otherwise. For this reason it is enormously important that we should "mind our own business" and let other people do as they like unless we can prove some damage beyond the shock to our feelings and prejudices. . . . The plain working truth is that it is not only good for people to be shocked occasionally, but absolutely necessary to the progress of society that they should be shocked pretty often. . . . The need for freedom of evolution is the sole basis of toleration, . . . the sole reason for not burning heretics and sending every eccentric person to the madhouse. . . . (pp. 121–23)

What Ibsen insists on is that there is no golden rule; that conduct must justify itself by its effect upon life and not by its conformity to any rule or ideal. And since life consists in the fulfilment of the will, which is constantly growing, and cannot be fulfilled today under the conditions which secured its fulfilment yesterday, he claims afresh the old Protestant right of private judgment in questions of conduct as against all institutions, the so-called Protestant Churches themselves included.

Here I must leave the matter, merely reminding those who may think that I have forgotten to reduce Ibsenism to a formula for them, that its quintessence is that there is no formula. (p. 125)

Strictly speaking, there is no formula for Shavianism either. But from the ethical perspective that his work invites, the entire Shavian canon is permeated by his emphasis on destroying ideals, cultivating the intellect, and implanting ideas as the principal means to the "supreme end" of evolution.

WILLIAM IRVINE

[*Candida*]†

* * *

Essentially, [*Candida*] is Ibsen's "Doll's House" turned upside down. Ibsen had shown that unhappiness results when a husband treats his wife as a doll. Shaw points out that happiness may result when a wife treats her husband as a doll. His Nora sees her husband as he really is—and retains him. In fact, there is a great scene in which Nora, like the Lady from the Sea, chooses between her husband and another man. But even more than it resembles "A Doll's House" and "The Lady from the Sea," "Candida" resembles Shaw's own *Love among the Artists*.[1] Yet more desperately unmarried and more desperately unsuccessful at thirty-eight, Shaw returns to the same double problem of marriage and genius and essentially the same triangle situation—and turns a crude juvenility into a masterpiece.

Fortunately, "Candida" has so many excellences that it does not need to be understood to be enjoyed. Acted by Janet Achurch at the Independent Theatre, it soon became a success, but it is still, next perhaps to "Major Barbara," the most widely misunderstood of all Shaw's dramas. As late as 1944, Mr. E. R. Bentley regards Candida as a kind of black-widow spider. The best that can be said is that the play is being progressively more ingeniously and acutely misunderstood. The commonest mistake is to regard Candida's choice as genuine and real. As a matter of fact, Shaw has taken pains not to present her with a choice. Eugene could have been twenty-eight; he is eighteen. He could have been Jovian and red-bearded, like Jack Tanner; he is "slight, effeminate, with a delicate childish voice."[2] His grotesque shyness and absurd cowardice are cruelly if comically insisted on to make the audience see that he could not possibly win a hardheaded woman like Candida. So far as the Morell marriage is concerned, Eugene merely precipitates the conflict between husband and wife; he is no more than a catalytic agent in the domestic rearrangement of atoms. For the real action of "Candida" is based on a very old dramatic device: a misunderstanding. In the course

† William Irvine, "Adventures in Success," from *The Universe of* G.B.S. Pp. 174–178. Copyright 1949 William Irvine; copyright renewed 1977 Mrs. William Irvine. (Russell & Russell, N.Y., 1968) Reprinted with permission of Macmillan Publishing Company.
1. An early novel of Shaw's (1887–88) [*Editor*].
2. Shaw, "Candida," *Plays: Pleasant and Unpleasant: II, Pleasant*, p. 102 [145]. Norton Critical Edition page numbers are in brackets.

of the play, husband and wife come for the first time genuinely to
understand each other and their actual relationship.

In the opening scenes we learn a good deal about the Reverend Morell.
Toward Prossy and Lexy, he is wise and indulgent; toward Burgess,
vigorous and frank. "He is a first rate clergyman, able to say what he
likes to whom he likes, to lecture people without setting himself up
against them, to impose his authority on them without humiliating
them."[3] We learn also that he considers his wife the rock and foundation
of his happiness. Meanwhile, she has been down in the country with
her children for three weeks. Eugene Marchbanks, a young poet and a
friend of the family, has been visiting them there. He comes back
thoroughly in love with her, and she, with her mind and ideas thoroughly
aired out by him. Conceiving love as a romantic ecstasy which has
nothing to do with the domesticities of peeling onions and trimming
lamps and little to do with the sublunary detail of physical possession,
he cannot understand how a woman like Candida can have any feeling
for a windbag like James Morell. He tells James so without delay, having
first declared his own love. Morell meets this youthful outburst with
magnificent condescension and indulgence. And yet he has apparently
himself noticed in Candida's attitude toward him something disturbing,
which he has always been reluctant to understand. He concludes an
oratorical appeal with: "There are so many things to make us doubt, if
once we let our understanding be troubled. Even at home, we sit as if
in camp, encompassed by a hostile army of doubts. Will you play the
traitor and let them in on me?"[4] Eugene certainly does not come to the
rescue: "Is it like this for her always? . . . Do you think a woman's soul
can live on your talent for preaching?" Slashing about with truths that
are quite irrelevant to Candida's marriage, he cuts deep into the clergyman's self-confidence and therefore into the latter's faith in his wife's
love. For James's idea of love is as romantically conventional as Eugene's
is romantically poetic. It is an honest, money-down, value-received
conception. He possesses Candida's love partly because as a pure woman
and a good wife she owes it; and much more, because as a husband,
father, and provider, he has earned it.

And what kind of woman is Candida? She is, as Shaw says, "unerring
wisdom [one might almost say, Benthamite rationalism and detachment]
on the domestic-plane,"[5] a realist placed between two romantics, whom
she regards with maternal indulgence. Hard facts are her specialty, and
the great facts in her life are sex and the home. Therefore she trades a
little on her good looks and her good figure, and she regards the great

3. *Ibid*, p. 86 [135].
4. *Ibid*, p. 110 [151].
5. Huneker, James, "The Truth about Candida,"
Metropolitan Magazine, vol. XX (1904), p. 635.
[This letter was republished by Dan H. Laurence
in *Bernard Shaw: Collected Letters (1898–1910)*,

pp. 415–16. "Benthamite rationalism" alludes to
the Utilitarianism of Jeremy Bentham (1748–
1832), which argued that all actions, political and
personal, should be governed by the goal of "the
greatest good for the greatest number"—*Editor.*]

world beyond her fireside as somewhat shadowy and unreal. Moreover, she is herself a woman of strong instincts. Shaw writes that "without brains and strength of mind she would be a wretched slattern or voluptuary."[6] It is significant that she has married a physically powerful and handsome man. The maternal instinct is particularly strong. And here both Shaw and his critics have gone too far. The stage directions and the symbolism of the play indicate that she is to be regarded primarily as the mother-woman. Her maternal indulgence toward the adult male infant is stressed to the point of objectionable omniscience. Granted that she is predominantly maternal in outward manner and psychological attitude; that the maternal manner, in a beautiful and intelligent woman, is charming to most men—and indeed it is often simply a reassuringly innocent disguise for sex—nevertheless, Candida is much more than a schematization of the mother instinct. If, for example, she were attracted to men simply for their weakness, she would be most fascinated by Lexy, who has nothing but weaknesses. Obviously, she loves Morell because he has been, in some respects at least, stronger and wiser than she. It is clearly indicated that he has formed her mind and therefore encouraged her in that freedom from convention which, he recognizes, will cause her to leave him at once if she is not held by love. Here Chesterton's comment is more accurate than the author's own. He finds in the play

> the reality of the normal wife's attitude to the normal husband, an attitude which is . . . insanely unselfish and yet quite cynically clear-sighted. . . . She regards him in some strange fashion at once as a warrior who must make his way and as an infant who is sure to lose his way. The man has emotions which exactly correspond; sometimes looking down at his wife and sometimes up at her; for marriage is like a splendid game of see-saw.[7]

But if Candida sincerely admires her husband, why, when she observes his melancholy after the skirmish with Eugene, does she attack him with such sharp and unfeeling gaiety? She assures him that his work does no good, that his parishioners do not mind him the least bit, that he positively abets them in evil by his sermons, which make them feel good without being good. And all the women are in love with him. "And you," she adds, "are in love with preaching because you do it so beautifully. And you think it's all enthusiasm for the kingdom of Heaven on earth; and so do they. You dear silly!"[8]

This is all new to James, because it is all new to Candida. She has just got it from Eugene. But why isn't she disturbed by it, both for herself and for her husband? Partly, perhaps, because she feels that a little truth

6. *Loc. cit.*
7. Chesterton, G. K., *George Bernard Shaw*, John Lane, The Bodley Head, Ltd. London, 1909, pp. 121–23.
8. Shaw, "Candida." *Plays: Pleasant and Unpleasant: II, Pleasant*, p. 164 [163].

will be good for James's complacency. But much more, because her rational detachment limits her sympathetic insight; she cannot understand why everybody should not relish truth as keenly as she. And finally, because the masculine world outside is not very real: whether James is winning actual or imaginary victories is not extremely important.

She is equally detached in discussing with Morell Eugene's love for her. Will Eugene forgive her for allowing him to learn what love is from a bad woman? "Forgive you for what?" exclaims her husband. For not having taught him herself, of course. Her decision has been the result of a very Benthamite calculation in moral mathematics. She explains to her husband that she is restrained not by her purity or his preaching but by the preponderant claim of her love for him.

In her too confident superiority and her present subservience to Eugene's thought, she has missed all the storm signals. She does not dream that James cannot grasp her combination of steadfast affection with clear-sighted detachment, that he has understood every word in a personal, emotional context. Morell, on the other hand, is convinced that she cannot love him, since she does not love him for his reasons. The misunderstanding is complete. When she approaches him, he waves her off, telling her with anguish in his voice that she must not touch him. From this point on, Shaw manipulates events to forestall any clarification between husband and wife, until Morell, tortured and degraded by uncertainty and suspicion, demands a "choice" between himself and Marchbanks.

This, the great scene of the play is, as M. Hamon observes, no more than an appearance for Candida but an agonizing reality for the two men. The spectator is also on the very knife-edge of suspense, for he perceives that Candida, having in her turn been disillusioned about James's conception of their marriage, is beside herself with indignation. "And pray, my lords and masters," she cries, "what have you to offer for my choice? I am up for auction, it seems. What do you bid, James?"[9] His complacency, though badly shaken, is still monumental, and he is still wedded to his illusions. He replies with "proud humility" and magnificently restrained oratory:

> I have nothing to offer you but my strength for your defence,
> my honesty of purpose for your surety, my ability and industry
> for your livelihood, and my authority and position for your
> dignity. That is all it becomes a man to offer to a woman.

At length she decides superbly, "I give myself to the weaker of the two,"[1] which is of course Morell. The spectacle of his bewildered suffering, now showing clearly through the polished speaker and the glossy Christian, has changed her anger to sympathy, but the sense of outrage remains. She must set him right, not with Eugene's truths but with those which are fundamental to her self-respect:

9. *Ibid*, p. 155 [180].　　　　　　1. *Ibid*, p. 156 [180].

Ask James's mother and his three sisters what it cost to save
James the trouble of doing anything but be strong and clever
and happy. Ask me what it costs to be James's mother and
three sisters and wife and mother to his children all in one.
. . . I build a castle of comfort and indulgence and love for
him, and stand sentinel always to keep little vulgar cares out.
I make him master here, though he does not know it.[2]

Candida has been called a prig and Shaw a preacher for this speech.
Yet she must have made it, even though the curtain had fallen and the
audience, preceding Eugene, had gone out into the night. It is this grave
explanation which makes the play a comedy: now we know how it will
be with the Morells in the future; we know also that Candida correctly
evaluates her husband, for she can afford to tell him his weakness and
her strength. Crushing as the outcome has been to his self-confidence,
he is at least temporarily humble and grateful. Clearly, his wife believes
that he will rise above his humiliating victory—and indeed men like
Morell, however noble, have an automatic apparatus for manufacturing
self-esteem.

"Candida" is also a study of genius in relation to worldly success and
happiness. Burgess is bitter satire. He represents the very worst and
shabbiest to whom the world permits the prestige of success. Morell, on
the other hand, is the very best that the world admires. He has all the
obvious weaknesses and will eventually succeed because he cannot help
it. Finally, Eugene is a genius. He has all the obvious weaknesses and
will eventually succeed because the world cannot prevent him. In the
extremity of defeat and suffering, he rises suddenly to a realization of
his destiny, and rejecting the mere happiness of Candida and her husband, goes out into the night, so that at the very close of the play the
theme of the loneliness and self-sufficiency of genius surges up to dom-
inance. Admirably effective as a dramatic instrument, Eugene is psychologically the least satisfactory character in "Candida." As a lover he
is, as Chesterton observes, too turgid in his speeches and too finicky
about onions. As a genius, he is perhaps too much Shelley made over
to fit the definition of a Shavian realist. He "dares to love and trust"
and at the same time sees facts without illusion. In so far he tends to
inconsistency.

* * *

2. *Ibid*, pp. 157–58 [181].

August Strindberg
and
The Ghost Sonata

AUGUST STRINDBERG

Paradise Regained†

I reckon the summer and autumn of 1895—in spite of everything—among the happy resting places of my turbulent life. All my undertakings prospered, unknown friends brought food to me as the ravens did to Elijah.[1] Money came to me of itself. I was able to buy books, natural-history specimens, and, among other things, a microscope that unveiled for me the secrets of life.

Lost to the world by renouncing the empty pleasure of Paris, I lived entirely within my own quarter of the city. Each morning I visited the departed in the Cemetery of Montparnasse, and afterwards walked down to the Luxembourg Gardens to say good morning to my flowers. Now and then some countryman of mine, on a visit to Paris, would call and invite me out to luncheon or to the theatre on the other side of the river. I always refused, as the right bank was forbidden territory. To me it represented the 'world' in the true sense of the word, the world of the living and of earthly vanity.

The fact was that a kind of religion had developed in me, though I was quite unable to formulate it. It was a spiritual state rather than an opinion founded upon theories, a hotch-potch of impressions that were far from being condensed into thoughts.

I had bought a Roman missal, and this I read and meditated over. The Old Testament comforted but also chastised me in a somewhat confused way, while the New Testament left me cold. This did not prevent a Buddhist work from making a far greater impression on me than all other sacred books, as it put the value of actual suffering far

---

† This and "Tribulations" are from August Strindberg, *Inferno*, translated by Mary Sandback, London, 1962. Pp. 42–44, 164–68.

1. Hiding from the wrath of Ahab, Elijah was fed by ravens each morning and each evening (1 Kings 17.6) [*Editor*].

higher than that of mere abstention. Buddha had had the courage to give up his wife and children when he was in the prime of life and enjoying the happiness of married bliss, whereas Christ had avoided all contact with the legitimate pleasures of this world.

In other respects I did not brood upon the emotions that possessed me. I remained detached, let things take their course, and granted to myself the same freedom that I was bound to accord to others.

The great event in Paris that season was the call to arms raised by the critic Brunetière[2] about the bankruptcy of science. I had been well acquainted with the natural sciences since my childhood and had tended towards Darwinism. But I had discovered how unsatisfying can be the scientific approach that recognizes the exquisite mechanism of the world but denies the existence of a mechanic. The weakness of the theory was revealed by the universal degeneration of science, which had marked out for itself a boundary line beyond which no one was allowed to go.

'We have solved all problems, the Universe has no secrets left.'

This presumptuous lie had annoyed me even in 1880, and for the past fifteen years I had been engaged upon revising the natural sciences. Thus, in 1884, I had cast doubts upon the accepted theory of the composition of the atmosphere, and upon the identification of the nitrogen found in the air with that obtained by breaking down a compound of nitrogen. In 1891 I had gone to the Laboratory of Physical Science in Lund to compare the spectra of these two kinds of nitrogen, which I knew differed. Need I describe the sort of reception I got from the mechanistic men of science there? But with the year 1895 came the discovery of argon, which proved the rightness of the suppositions I had already advanced and infused new life into the investigations that had been interrupted by my rash marriage.

No, science had not gone bankrupt, only science that was out of date and distorted. Brunetière was right, though he was wrong.

Meanwhile, whereas all were agreed in recognizing the unity of matter and called themselves monists without really being so, I went further, drew the ultimate conclusions of this doctrine, and eliminated the boundaries between matter and what was called the spirit. In my book *Antibarbarus* I had discussed the psychology of sulphur and interpreted it in the light of its ontogeny—that is to say, the embryonic development of sulphur.

For further information I refer those interested to my book *Sylva Sylvarum*, published in 1896, in which, proudly aware of my clairvoyant faculty, I penetrated to the very heart of the secrets of creation, especially those of the animal and vegetable kingdoms. I would also refer them to my essay. *In the Cemetery* (included in *Printed and Unprinted*) which

2. Ferdinand Brunetière (1849–1906) [*Editor*].

shows how in solitude and in suffering I was brought back to a faltering apprehension of God and immortality.

Tribulations

Shut up in that little city of the Muses, without any hope of getting away, I fought out a terrible battle with the enemy, my own self.

Each morning when I took my walk along the ramparts shaded by plane trees, the sight of the huge, red lunatic asylum reminded me of the danger I had escaped and of the future, should I suffer a relapse. By revealing to me the true nature of the terrors that had beset me during the past year, Swedenborg[1] had set me free from the electrical experts, the practitioners of the black arts, the wizards, the envious gold makers, and the fear of insanity. He had shown me the only way to salvation: to seek out the demons in their lair, within myself, and to destroy them by—repentance. Balzac,[2] as the prophet's adjutant, had taught me in his Séraphita that 'remorse is the impotent emotion felt by the man who will sin again; repentance alone is effective, and brings everything to an end'.

To repent, then! But was not that to repudiate Providence, that had chosen me to be its scourge? Was it not to say to the Powers: 'You have misdirected my fate, you have allowed me to be born with a mission to punish, to overthrow idols, to raise the standard of revolt, and then you have withdrawn your protection and left me alone to recant and thus to earn ridicule. Do you now ask me to submit, to apologize, to make amends?'

Fantastic, but exactly the vicious circle that I foresaw in my twentieth year when I wrote my play *Master Olof*, which I now see as the tragedy of my own life. What is the good of having dragged out a laborious existence for thirty years only to learn by experience what I had already anticipated? In my youth I was a true believer and you made of me a free-thinker. Of the free-thinker you made an atheist, of the atheist a monk. Inspired by the humanitarians, I extolled socialism. Five years later you showed me the absurdity of socialism. You have cut the ground from under all my enthusiasms, and suppose that I now dedicate myself to religion, I know for a certainty that before ten years have passed you will prove to me that religion is false.

Are not the Gods jesting with us mortals, and is that why we too, sharing the jest, are able to laugh in the most tormented moments of our lives?

How can you require that we take seriously something that appears to be no more than a colossal jest?

1. Emanuel Swedenborg (1688–1772), a Swedish philosopher, scientist, theologian, and mystic [Editor].

2. Honoré de Balzac (1799–1850), French nov- elist. His novella *Séraphita* is an eccentric work among his novels and stories, heavily philosophical with a mystical bias [Editor].

Jesus Christ our Saviour, what is it that he saved? Look at our Swedish pietists, the most Christian of all Christians, those pale, wicked, terror-stricken creatures, who cannot smile and who look like maniacs. They seem to carry a demon in their hearts and, mark you, most of their leaders end up in prison as malefactors. Why should their Lord have delivered them over to the enemy? Is religion a punishment, and is Christ the spirit of vengeance?

All the ancient Gods reappeared as demons at a later date, The dwellers in Olympus became evil spirits. Odin and Thor, the Devil himself, Prometheus—Lucifer, the Bringer of Light, degenerated into Satan. Is it possible—God forgive me—that even Christ has been transformed into a demon? He has brought death to reason, to the flesh, to beauty, to joy, to the purest feelings of affection of which mankind is capable. He has brought death to the virtues of fearlessness, valour, glory, love, and mercy.

The sun shines, daily life goes on in its accustomed way, the sound of men at their everyday tasks raises our spirits. It is at such moments that the courage to revolt rears up and we fling our challenge and our doubts at Heaven.

But at night, when silence and solitude fall about us, our arrogance is dissipated, we hear our heart-beats and feel a weight on our chests. Then go down on your knees in the bush of thorns outside your window, go; find a doctor or seek out some comrade who will sleep with you in the same room.

Enter your room alone at night-time and you will find that someone has got there before you. You will not see him, but you will feel his presence. Go to the lunatic asylum and consult the psychiatrist. He will talk to you of neurasthenia, paranoia, angina pectoris, and the like, but he will never cure you.

Where will you go, then, all you who suffer from sleeplessness, and you who walk the streets waiting for the sun to rise?

The Mills of the Universe, the Mills of God, these are two expressions that are often used.

Have you had in your ears the humming that resembles the noise of a water-mill? Have you noticed, in the stillness of the night, or even in broad daylight, how memories of your past life stir and are resurrected, one by one or two by two? All the mistakes you have made, all your crimes, all your follies, that make you blush to your very ear-tips, bring a cold sweat to your brow and send shivers down your spine. You relive the life you have lived, from your birth to the very day that is. You suffer again all the sufferings you have endured, you drink again all the cups of bitterness you have so often drained. You crucify your skeleton, as there is no longer any flesh to mortify. You send your spirit to the stake, as your heart is already burned to ashes.

Do you recognize the truth of all this?

There are the Mills of God, that grind slow but grind exceeding small—and black. You are ground to powder and you think it is all over. But no, it will begin again and you will be put through the mill once more.

Be happy. That is the Hell here on earth, recognized by Luther,[3] who esteemed it a high honour that he should be ground to powder on this side of the empyrean.

Be happy and grateful.

What is to be done? Must you humble yourself?

But if you humble yourself before mankind you will arouse their arrogance, since they will then believe themselves to be better than you are, however great their villainy.

Must you then humble yourself before God? But it is an insult to the All-Highest to drag Him down to the level of a planter who rules over slaves.

Pray! What? Will you arrogate to yourself the right to bend the will of the Eternal and His decrees, by flattery and by servility?

Seek God and find the Devil. That is what has happened to me.

I have done penance, I have mended my ways, but no sooner do I begin the work of resoling my soul than I have to add yet another patch. If I put on new heels the uppers split. There is no end to it.

If I give up drinking and come home sober at nine o'clock of an evening to a glass of milk, my room is full to overflowing with all manner of demons, who pluck me from my bed and smother me under the bedclothes. If, on the other hand, I come home drunk, towards midnight, I fall asleep like a little angel and wake up in the morning as fresh as a young god, ready to work like a galley-slave.

If I shun women unwholesome dreams come upon me at night. If I train myself to think well of my friends, if I confide my secrets to them or give them money, I am betrayed, and if I lose my temper over a breach of faith it is always I who am punished.

I try to love mankind in the mass, I close my eyes to their faults, and, with limitless forbearance, forgive them their meanness and their back-biting, and then, one fine day, I find that I am an accomplice. If I withdraw from the company of people I consider bad I am immediately attacked by the demon of solitude. If I then seek for better friends I fall in with worse.

Furthermore, when I vanquish my evil passions, and reach at least some measure of tranquility by my abstinence, I experience a feeling of self-satisfaction that makes me think I am superior to my fellow men, and this is the mortal sin of egotism, which brings down instant punishment.

How are we to explain the fact that each apprenticeship in virtue is followed by a new vice?

3. Martin Luther (1483–1546), a German monk and theologian; a leader of the Protestant reformation [*Editor*].

Swedenborg solves this riddle when he says that vices are the punish-
ments man incurs for more serious sins. For instance, those who are
greedy of power are doomed to the Hell of Sodomy. If we admit that
the theory holds good we must endure our vices and profit by the remorse
that accompanies them as things that will help us to settle our final
account.

Consequently, to seek to be virtuous is like attempting to escape from
our prison and our torments. This is what Luther was trying to say in
article XXXIX of his reply to the Papal Bull of excommunication, where
he proclaims that 'The Souls in Purgatory sin incessantly, since they
are trying to gain peace and to avoid their torments.'

Similarly in article XXXIV: 'To struggle against the Turks is nothing
more that rising in rebellion against God, who is chastising us for our
sins throughout the medium of the Turks.'

Thus it is clear that 'all our good deeds are mortal sins', and that 'the
world must be sinful in the eyes of God, and must understand that no
one can become good except by the grace of God'.

Therefore, O my brethren, you must suffer without hope of a single
lasting happiness in this life, since we are already in Hell. We must not
reproach the Lord if we see innocent little children suffer. None of us
can know why, but divine justice makes us suppose that it is because of
sins committed before ever they arrived in this world. Let us rejoice in
our torments which are so many debts repaid, and let us believe that it
is out of pure compassion that we are kept in ignorance of the primordial
reasons for our punishment.

Author's Note [to A *Dream Play*]†

In this dream play, as in his former dream play *To Damascus*, the Author
has sought to reproduce the disconnected but apparently logical form
of a dream. Anything can happen; everything is possible and probable.
Time and space do not exist; on a slight groundwork of reality, imagination spins and weaves new patterns made up of memories, experiences,
unfettered fancies, absurdities and improvisations.

The characters are split, double and multiply; they evaporate, crys-
tallise, scatter and converge. But a single consciousness hold sway over
them all—that of the dreamer. For him there are no secrets, no incon-
gruities, no scruples and no law. He neither condemns nor acquits, but
only relates, and since on the whole, there is more pain than pleasure
in the dream, a tone of melancholy, and of compassion for all living
things, runs through the swaying narrative. Sleep, the liberator, often
appears as a torturer—and is thus reconciled with reality. For however
agonising real life may be, at this moment, compared with the tor-
menting dream, it is a joy.

† From August Strindberg, *Six Plays of Strindberg*, translated by Elizabeth Sprigge. Copyright © 1955
by Elizabeth Sprigge. Reprinted by permission of Curtis Brown, Ltd.

MILTON A. MAYS

Strindberg's *Ghost Sonata:* Parodied Fairy Tale on Original Sin†

Despite a good deal of interest in Strindberg's *The Ghost Sonata*, critics, as Evert Sprinchorn puts it, "seem reluctant to declare that the play possesses any great coherence."[1] There has been, in fact, a marked willingness to take the dodge that "dreams needn't make sense": doubly specious, since plays are not dreams, however "dreamlike," and even dreams have, if not logic, a psychologic. The many readers who find *The Ghost Sonata* one of the most exciting pieces in modern drama—however much avoided by pusillanimous directors—are surely correct. The play, that is to say, for all its admitted redundancies and even symbolic nonsequiturs, must have a thematic and symbolic coherence. The thesis here advanced—which by no means explains everything—is that *The Ghost Sonata* takes as its main structural mode the fairy tale, that it is in fact a parodied fairy tale of sorts, and that this form is the means of saying something about Original Sin.

Strindberg's was a basically religious consciousness, and a fascination with the concept of Original Sin would seem a natural corollary of his known obsessive fascination with guilt, especially marked in the chamber plays. *The Burned House*, which immediately precedes our play in the group, and is closely associated with it in the writing, turns on a question of the guilty past, and is full of allusions to the Garden, the Tree of Knowledge, and the loss of an (equivocal) childhood innocence. *The Ghost Sonata*, with that hallucinatory clarity peculiar to the surrealistic work, focuses on the universality and inescapability of guilt, bearing down on "innocent" and "sinful" alike in a debacle which seems fully as terrible as the pagan retribution rejected by the play—and this despite the concluding unction of the Student's words on patience and hope, accompanied by "a white light," Böcklin, and "soft, sweet, melancholy" music.[2]

Early in Scene I when the Old Man begins to open out the insanely complicated relationships binding the inmates of the Colonel's house, the Student says, "It's like a fairy story." Hummel, in replying, "My whole life's like a book of fairy stories . . . held together by one thread, and the main theme constantly recurs," seems to corroborate their genre and hints that his story—and our play—is about something specific. Seen in broad relief, *The Ghost Sonata* contains all the elements of the fairy story, and it is this which gives it a kind of structural cohesiveness

† From *Modern Drama* 10 (September 1967) 2: 189–94. Reprinted with permission of the publisher.
1. August Strindberg, *The Chamber Plays* (Minneapolis, 1962), p. xix.

2. Most of the quotations from *The Ghost Sonata* are in the Otto Reinert translation in *Modern Drama* (Boston, 1961); occasional use has been made of the Sprinchorn edition cited above.

not found in the other chamber plays, which seem to spill their symbols into a void. We have a poor but heroic youth, and one, moreover, especially blessed or singled out by destiny (a "Sunday child" with the gift of second sight). Our Student is enraptured of a beautiful and high-born maiden, who lives in a "castle" imagined by the Student to enclose all his life's desires. He thinks his suit is hopeless, but a "fairy godfather" with an aura of immense and mysterious powers appears and promises him an entrée to "doors and hearts." In Scene II we discover, as we might have expected, that there are "ogres" in the castle who have the maid in thrall; but the fairy godfather is prepared to do them battle. In the third scene we would further expect the fairy princess and hero to be united and "live happily ever after." Just how true—and false—to the facts of the play this outline is should be apparent; yet in the play's relation to this submerged paradigm, I am suggesting, lies much of its meaning.

For the fairy tale, after all, is a projection of the return-to-Paradise wish. Whatever his ill fortune (symbolic of the fallen world), the hero's desert is always good (he is naturally good, an erect Adam), and the powers that be, somehow always recognizing this, return him and his Eve, the princess (who has sufferd her trials as well), to Paradise, shutting the golden doors of "they lived happily ever after" firmly before our inquisitive eyes. In *The Ghost Sonata* Strindberg uses parody and dis-tortion of the fairy tale to make it say the opposite thing: that guilt is contagious, innocence non-existent, or, if in some sense real (the girl), it is "sick" and "doomed," "suffering for no fault" of its own. In Adam's fall, sinned we all. Nor is there any Paradise to be regained in the last act. The Student says of the girl's house: "I thought it was paradise itself that first time I saw you coming in here." But the flowers in the "paradise" are poisonous; it is in fact a place of ordeals, where no dreams come true. In sum, despite the vague appeal of the Student (who seems in these last moments of the play to have stepped out of the character of hero and into the function of *raisonneur*) to a "Liberator" who will waken the innocent girl to "a sun that does not burn, in a home without dust by friends without stain, by a love without a flaw"—despite this perhaps rather sentimental gesture, the force of the play is compacted into a metaphor for Original Sin: it is expressive of the agony of "this world of illusion, guilt, suffering, and death . . . endless change, dis-appointment, and pain."

Strindberg's meaning in the play is put both abstractly and concretely: both in discursive "talk," such as we have rather too much of in the Stu-dent's last speeches, and in the most vivid symbols, such as the vampire cook—a disturbing contribution of paranoia to art. The Student *says* that "The curse lies over the whole of creation, over life itself"; but this allu-sion to the fallen world is only effective because we have seen the "haunted" old house, in which the very air is tainted, "charged with crime," so that its inmates, guilty and innocent alike, are withering away.

It has been said that "the fairy tale's miracles occur on the material plane; on the spiritual plane (affections; characters; justice; love) law abides."[3] *The Ghost Sonata* is a fairy tale parodied and distorted. We have not witnessed this play for long before getting a disturbing sense that nothing is quite right, that even a "spiritual logic" is being tampered with. Is the Old Man, Hummel, a benefactor, or a self-serving user of other people, after power—or what? That is, is he good fairy or wicked witch? There are abundant hints to shake our confidence in Hummel, the most startling of which is the first sounding of the vampire-motif when Hummel takes the Student's hand in his icy hand, and the Student struggles to free himself, saying, "You are taking all my strength. You are freezing me." Variations on this theme occur throughout the play, of course: "vampirism" is a multiplex symbol for vicarious gratification ("enjoy life so that I can watch, at least from a distance"), for enslaving others by a knowledge of their guilty secrets (Johansson, the Colonel), or by a sense of obligation (the Student) or by usury. Hummel is a "blood-sucker" both metaphorically, on the surreal level of "sucking the marrow out of the house," and economically (the debts of the Consul and the Colonel).

There is, if anything, a redundancy of suggestion of evil identity for the Student's ostensible benefactor: he is a pagan god in a chariot, a wizard, an "old devil." Hummel's Mephistophelean character is underlined by his saying to the Student, "Serve me and you shall have power."

STUDENT. Is it a bargain? Am I to sell my soul?

And when the Student, after hearing something disturbing about Hummel from Johansson, his servant, decides to escape from him, the girl drops her bracelet out of the window, the Student returns it, and there is no more talk of escape. The girl serves Hummel's purpose in a sense as Gretchen does Mephisto's. (And both women are destroyed, though I am not suggesting the parallel be taken any further.)

The question of the essential nature of Hummel remains a difficult one. He is clearly the most dynamic character in the play, the one who seems to make everything happen. With the Student as the "arm to do [his] will" Hummel will enter the Colonel's house and "expose the crimes" there so that the girl (his daughter by the Colonel's wife), withering away in the evil atmosphere, can live again in health with the Student. All is for the young couple; Hummel's cleansing revenge is to involve the "ghosts" only. But by Scene II we are as suspicious of Hummel's intention as is the Mummy. In any case, realistic criteria of character consistency and continuity of action are mostly irrelevant in this play. If we are unsure what Hummel's "real" purpose with regard to the "innocents" is, we are no more sure how his defeat by the Mummy has influenced the outcome of the play in Scene III. Are the Mummy,

3. *Dictionary of World Literary Terms*, Joseph T. Shipley, ed. (London, 1955) , p. 155.

the Colonel, and the others versus the Old Man two groups of equally evil figures who mutually destroy each other? This would seem to leave the field clear for the blossoming of young love, the ghost house purged. But before we can understand more fully why this is not the case, the Student must be considered.

The role of the Student in *The Ghost Sonata* also has its curious features. Does the play's conclusion leave him saved or damned? A survivor—the only one—or a victim? Or is he, by the conclusion of the play, not a protagonist at all, but dramatist's *raisonneur*, as suggested above? It seems to me that in his final speeches he does assume the function of authorial surrogate, but that there is a certain fitness to this: like Strindberg, the Student is an innocent trying to believe in an unfallen world in the face of the horrors of real existence. He is an Adam-figure, a "Sunday child," who, when he first saw the house of his beloved on Sunday morning—the "first day of creation"—thought it was paradise. But he is a fairy tale hero ejected from his fairy tale world—and a cruelly parodied hero at that. His dream of bliss is all bourgeois: " 'Think of living up there in the top flat, with a beautiful young wife, two pretty little children and an income of twenty thousand crowns a year.' " The conclusion of Scene I is also parodistic, and splendid theater: Hummel, standing in his wheel chair which is drawn in by the beggars, cries: "Hail the noble youth who, at the risk of his own life, saved so many in yesterday's accident. Three cheers for Arkenholtz!" This scene is followed by a nice tableau of the beggars baring their heads, the girl waving her hankerchief, the old woman rising at her window, and the maid hoisting the flag. Strains of a bizarre slapstick are found throughout the play; the audience should laugh, but not over-confidently.

The girl and the Student—fairy tale hero and princess—do not figure in Scene II, where the ogres or witches fight. At least one consequence of Hummel's defeat follows the fairy tale pattern: Johansson, his servant, is "freed from slavery" by his death, as the victims of the enchanter or wicked witch always are. Alone with his beloved in the Hyacinth Room in Scene III, the Student's expectations are clearly for speedy achievement of his heart's desire. "We are wedded," he says; but his Eve must disillusion him. This place is not what it seems; it is no paradise, and no fairy-tale "ever-after," but is "bewitched"—"bedeviled" we might more literally call the post-lapsarian world. Hummel—"old Adam" as well as "old Nick"?—may be dead (literally by his own hand, as Adam was in effect), but his influence lives on after him. "This room is called the room of ordeals," says the girl; "It looks beautiful, but it is full of defects." We are placed on earth to work out our salvation; and earth's beauties are no end in themselves, but illusory, mutable ("defective"). The metaphor for this in *The Ghost Sonata* is domestic—if insane. The Student's "paradise" was domestic; his fate is the domestic demented; instead of "they lived happily ever after," we see the fairy princess at the kitchen sink, in effect. It is not the real world, but the domestic-surreal, this house with servants who un-clean, cooks who un-feed; but the surreal can be taken as measure of the recoil of the tender soul (Strindberg, the Student) from real life. As the Student says in closing only in the imagination is there anything which fulfills its promise. The Student, rather like his creator, is Adam who refuses to accept his ejection, symbolically as well as psychologically the child who refuses to grow up. ("Where are honor and faith? In fairy-tales and children's fancies.") "I asked you to become my wife in a home full of poetry and song and music. Then the Cook came . . ." says the Student. "What have we to do with the kitchen?" he asks the girl, who replies, "realistically," "We must eat." The Student reflects Stindberg's neurotic fastidiousness, well known, toward the "lower functions"; and eating, by the mechanism known to psychologists as "displacement," can represent the sexual function, also profoundly disturbing to Strindberg: "It is always in the kitchen quarters that the seed-leaves of the children are nipped, if it has not already happened in the bedroom." The Student wants to live in a garden with his bride, but this garden is "poison": "You have poisoned me and I have given the poison back to you," says the Student. But perhaps the "sickness" is in fact the "Student's": It is the recoil of a pathological romanticism upon itself which sees the earth as "this madhouse, this prison, this charnel house." Strindberg, like his surrogate, the Student, desires the fairy-tale princess in a "home full of poetry and song and music"—a home with no "kitchen quarters," only conservatory. That this whole fairy-tale gone crazy is a projection of the Student's we may take as admitted in his saying that he is a man born with one of those "poisons that open the eyes"—or does it "destroy the sight"?—"for I cannot see what is ugly as beautiful, nor call evil good."

As the girl enumerates all the tasks which weigh her down, the Student cries out again and again for "Music!"—music to drown out the sounds of real life. But it is no more possible to do so than it is for Strindberg to ring in "soft, sweet, and melancholy" music at the end of his play in order to effect a resolution. The emotion we depart with is fear trembling on the brink of hysteria, the image that of the grinning vampire cook. No vague promises of a "Liberator," a waking to a "sun that does not burn, in a home without dust, by friends without stain, by a love without a flaw" can salve over the fact, of which *The Ghost Sonata* is the gripping symbol, that "a curse lies over the whole of creation, over life itself." Out of his own conflict between paradise and the fallen world, fairy-tale and reality, Strindberg has made stunning drama.

GERALD PARKER

[The Ghost Sonata]†

*   *   *

The Ghost Sonata is a much simpler, less theatrically ambitious work than *To Damascus*; however, the controlling rhythm and form of this work owes much to the sense of a revitalized *mise en scène* that we find in many parts of the earlier play. Both the visual aspects and the language of *Ghost Sonata* are orchestrated in such a fashion as to make theatrically lucid the underlying motifs and to establish on the sensory level alone an experience of extraordinary range and effectiveness. That is to say, the *mise en scène* operates meaningfully with "the force of an assistant and accompaniment," helping to embody the rhythm of thought and feeling which the main action manifests; and the *mise en scène*, as a totality, possesses a certain sensual quality, which, as sub-textual,[1] automatically elicits a response not unlike that demanded by music and painting.

For this reason, although Strindberg has carefully fused in this play "vision" and form, the structure of *Ghost Sonata* possesses a certain duality. On the one hand, there is the straightforward pattern of spiritual action: the Student's entrance into a house wherein he discovers first of all an observer (in Scenes One and Two) and secondly as an active participant (in Scene Three through his relationship with the Girl) the "curse" which "lies over the whole of creation, over life itself." This action is cadential, tending, as Susanne Langer puts it in her analysis of the tragic rhythm, "to an absolute close."[2] This "close" is the death of the Girl, and the Student's acquiescence to what is unmistakably a Schopenhauerian awareness[3] of the hellishness of life. Again, in Thomas Mann's words, "every expression of the will to live has always something of the infernal about it, being itself a metaphysical stupidity, a frightful error, *the* sin."[4] The action of the play is, then, on this primary level of "idea" entirely spiritual, and, as in the case of *To Damascus*, the controlling pattern is that of a quest. In Schopenhauer's terms, the first two scenes embody the *principium individuationis*[5] with all its turmoil and divisions: here we are made to share the observing Student's apprehension of hell on earth. In the last scene, the Student fails to "save" the Girl, fails to effect through *action* in the phenomenal world any sort of redemption. However, in the last moments of the play, a kind of "elevation" is manifested, not through action, but in "being." Scho-

---

† From "The Spectator Seized by the Theatre: Strindberg's *The Ghost Sonata*," *Modern Drama* 14 (1972): 379–86. Reprinted with permission of the publisher.

1. That is, serving to organize and focus by means beneath the surface level of the play [*Editor*].

2. Susanne Langer, *Feeling and Form* (New York, 1953), p. 351.

3. An awareness that we create it ourselves [*Editor*].

4. *Essays by Thomas Mann*, pp. 268–69.

5. "Principle of individuation" [*Editor*].

penhauer describes the "Nirvana" of his vision thus: "What lends to everything tragic, in whatever form it may appear, its peculiar impetus to elevation, is the dawning realization that the world, that life cannot grant any true satisfaction, and hence they do not deserve our attachment: in this consists the tragic spirit: hence it leads to resignation.[6]

Such fearful resignation is the emotion informing the Student's concluding prayer to the Liberator death (considered as a sleep) and to the "wise and gentle Buddha," as well as his total awareness of "this world of illusion, guilt, suffering and death, this world of endless change, disappointment, and pain." If Schopenhauer's philosophy is of some assistance to the illumination of such spiritual action, likewise is the Oriental concept of the tension between the qualities of *Samsāra* and *Nirvana*, a concept with which Strindberg was likely familiar, indeed, which is hinted at through the presence of the seated Buddha. Nirvana is a state reached "when a man becomes annihilated from his attributes" and thus "attains to perfect subsistence."[7] Samsāra, on the other hand, is the wheel of birth and death, the realm of "eternal succession and coincidence of evolution and involution."[8] The Student acquires through observation in Scene Two a growing awareness of the overpowering force of this realm, and, as expressed in the *Vimala-kīrti Sūtra*, rather than initially shrinking from experience, he "plunges himself into the ever rushing current of Samsāra and sacrifices himself to save his fellow creatures from being eternally drowned in it."[9] His efforts, however, are futile, and his defeat is registered in a despair from which the concluding resignation springs.

Although this primary pattern of action is distinctly spiritual, the play, particularly in the first two scenes, and mainly through the appearance of the Cook in the third, is as fully expressive of the tensions of the material-social world as are the earlier realist plays by Strindberg. The spiritual action is lucidly portrayed through the gradual disappearance of the social context so evident in the opening scenes, especially in the complicated exposition by Hummel. As in Ibsen's late plays, the spiritual quest is firmly located in the familiar context of class and family strife, economics, and sex. And, as in such plays as *The Master Builder* and *When We Dead Awaken*,[1] this context is gradually transcended—largely because it represents the scene of personal choice and action which prove ineffectual as redemptive sources in the light of the appealing "metaphysical stupidity" of any expression of the will to live, that is, the will to choose and act. To a considerable extent, the three scenes depict this transcendence of the phenomenal world of action and choice by way of the gradual elimination of characters until only the Student

6. Schopenhauer, *The World as Will and Idea*, II, Chapter 27. Quoted by Walter Kaufmann, *Tragedy and Philosophy* (New York, 1968), p. 292.
7. Ananda K. Coomaraswamy, *Buddha and the*

Gospel of Buddhism (New York, 1964), p. 244.
8. *Ibid.*, p. 195.
9. *Ibid.*, pp. 244–45.
1. Late plays by Ibsen [*Editor*].

and the Girl remain in a sofly lit room visited occasionally by the vampire-like Cook.

Valency remarks that the "underlying narrative is fantastically complex. The relation of its three parts is neither close nor entirely apparent."[2] There is certainly no denying the truth of this first assertion if we centre upon the bizarre complications of Hummel, the Colonel, the Colonel's wife ("White and shrivelled into a Mummy") and the Girl in the Hyacinth Room. These complications are related by Hummel to the Student in Scene One, and are revealed further in the ghostly gathering of Scene Two. Hummel admits the "fairy-tale" quality of his narration to the Student, admits the near impossibility of disentangling the threads of earlier action and the current relationships among the characters. "My whole life's like a book of fairy stories," he says; "And although the stories are different, they are held together by one thread, and the main theme constantly occurs."[3] This main theme is the stultifying stagnation of lives buttressed by lies, deceit, crime, sin and sorrow—lives fettered in every direction by subjugation to the soul-destroying forces resulting from the *principium individuationis* and the world it has brought forth, "born of greed and compulsion . . . a thing to shudder at." The "underlying narrative" *is* complex in the telling, but perfectly lucid as the embodiment of this main theme. Like the Student, we are under no obligation to deliberately sort through the complications and arrive at a clear pattern of *temporal* action: we are meant, surely, to share his confusion, his admission to Hummel "I don't understand any of this." In the theatre, the exposition by Hummel in the first scene and the more public admissions of crime and guilt in the second have a cumulative *sensory* effect; the complications become too involved for immediate rational comprehension and become, theatrically at one level, "mere sound." We are reminded of this use of language in the banquet scene of *To Damascus*, and, perhaps, of a similar use of language and complicated exposition in the plays of Ionesco.[4]

Despite this grotesquely abstruse temporal level of action, the more important spiritual pattern of action is never lost sight of. This spiritual pattern is made evident through the gradual transcendence of the social context, and through the arrangement of the visual elements in the total *mise en scène*. Evidence of the movement from the familiar to the strange, from the temporal to the spiritual, is provided by the visual pattern which tends from the opening out-door, sun-lit scene with the façade of a house, a street complete with drinking fountain, bench and advertisement column, to the Round Room of Scene Two with familiar (though oddly juxtaposed—as in surrealist art) interior objects (a stove, pendulum clock, candelabra, cupboard) and the almost claustrophobic

2. Maurice Valency, *The Flower and the Castle: An Introduction to Modern Drama* (New York and London, 1963) 348 [*Editor*].

3. *The Ghost Sonata*, in *Six Plays by Strindberg*, trans. Elizabeth Sprigge (New York, 1955), p. 274.

4. See also the use of complicated exposition in the first scenes of Betti's *Corruption in the Palace of Justice*.

impression of enclosure, to, finally, the Hyacinth Room with its general "exotic and oriental" effect, its clusters of vari-coloured hyacinths, and the dominating presence of a large seated Buddha.

In the course of this visual movement, the highly detailed and more overtly social context of the opening gives place to interior settings: first of all to the almost surreal Round Room, which, in a sense, functions like the single room setting of such plays as *Miss Julie*[5] or Ibsen's *Ghosts* (that is, as a room which seems symbolically to portray the environmental dimensions and entrapment of modern man), and secondly, to another, but stranger interior which is far more "cosmic" in its symbolic implications. The sun-lit effects of Scene One, with shadows giving emphasis to the angular shapes produced by the house façade and the various street details (not to mention the array of objects seen within the house) give place to, first of all the darkly grim second scene, and then to the more subtly orchestrated harmony of coloured flowers and the striking effect of the Buddha from whose lap "rises the stem of a shallot (*Allium ascalonicum*), bearing its globular cluster of white, starlike flowers."

If the first scene is reminiscent of the visual effects of such a realist painting as Degas' *Cotton Market in New Orleans*, the final scene is reminiscent of Gaugin's *Where do we come from? Where are we? Where are we going?* (1897—a picture, incidentally, which seems to reflect something of the spiritual quest dimension of *Ghost Sonata*. In each of these scenes we never completely lose sight of the others. Scene One portrays vague interior details which become visually clearer in each of the following. In Scene Two, hints of the Hyacinth Room appear off to one side, where we see the Girl reading. In Scene Three, the door to the Round Room is left open, and we see the seated Colonel and Mummy, "inactive and silent," and have a slight glimpse of the death-screen used for Hummel. Thus the transitions are not, visually, totally abrupt. Finally, all these visual presentations, which correspond so well to the general pattern of action described earlier, are made to dissolve into a single effect, which in a carefully devised production might pick up certain forms and colours already impressed upon our eyes. As the Student's last prayer is concluded, Böcklin's *Isle of the Dead* appears, the small solitary figures, gloomy shadows, isolated gold-lit temples of this painting displacing the varied impressions of both familiar and strange which the three scenes visually manifested.

In addition to such an overall visual pattern is the pattern of sound which likewise reinforces, "with the force of an assistant and accompaniment" the main action of the play. Apart from the wide range of voices (as sounds or intonations) throughout the play, this pattern is composed of the sound of bells, an organ, a clock, street noises, a harp, the loud pounding on a table. Like the visual details, these sounds are orchestrated to reflect the movement from the "familiar" to the strange

5. An earlier, realistic play by Strindberg [*Editor*].

and spiritual. In the course of the play, the bells, organ and general street noises of Scene One give place to the more discordant sounds of Scene Two (produced mainly by the voices) and, finally, to the more lyrical sounds of Scene Three, which is framed by the harp-accompanied song, "I saw the sun." The final sound is that of "music, soft, sweet, and melancholy" as the Böcklin picture slowly pervades the entire visual plane. Undoubtedly, Artaud is right in his production plans for this play in suggesting a considerable magnification of sound effects.[6] For instance, to reinforce the steamship bells which are heard at the beginning (an image which, incidentally, is echoed in the small boat carrying passengers in Böcklin's painting) Artaud suggest that "A constant noise of water will be heard, loud at times, to the point of obsession." Artaud also suggests that the return of Hummel with the Beggars, in Scene One, should take place "in a great din. The old man will begin his invocations from very far off, and the beggars will answer him in several stages. At each call the crutches will be heard knocking rhythmically, sometimes on the ground, sometimes against the walls, in a very distinct cadence. Their vocal calls, and the beat of their crutches will be punctuated towards the end by a bizarre sound, as of a monstrous tongue violently knocking against a hole in the teeth."

The play affords many such instances when exaggerated sounds could be employed effectively. The close of Scene One is, perhaps, the most striking instance of an unnerving violence in the play. The relative calm of the opening dialogue in this scene rises rapidly into a crescendo of voices and excitement. The ghostly figures in the house rise and gesture, announcing their real presence, as Hummel stands in his wheel chair, drawn and followed by the beggars, screaming "Hail to noble youth!" Such a crescendo is repeated twice more in the play. In Scene Two, the silence of the group is suddenly broken by Hummel as he begins to function more formidably as the exposer of lies and crimes. His speech is punctuated with silences of varying length, until he rises again—as in Scene One—to a crescendo augmented by the magnified sound of the clock ("ticking like a death-watch beetle in the wall"), and by the horrendous striking of the table with one of his crutches. This crescendo is broken by the Mummy who stops the clock and in a normal voice proceeds to expose Hummel himself. The scene then subsides in intensity as Hummel gradually loses his forceful manner, and becomes, himself, a grotesque parrot. In Scene Three, after a most lyrical beginning, the disturbing sounds of Scene Two are echoed first of all by the Cook's presence and the Student's violent reaction to her, and secondly, the crescendo is apparent in the course of the Student's relation of the events of the earlier scene to the Girl.

Generally speaking, these deliberately spaced crescendo rhythms together with the various auditory juxtapositions (particularly of the lyrical

6. Antonin Artaud, "Production Plan for Strindberg's Ghost Sonata," Tulane Drama Review, VIII, no. 2 (1963–64), pp. 50ff.

and the dissonant) contribute to a total sound pattern of wide range and expressiveness; in addition, the overall pattern of sound functions as does the visual in the manner of an assistant and accompaniment to the main spiritual action. The auditory and the visual together constitute "beneath language," as Artaud advocated, "a subterranean current of impressions, correspondences, and analogies." As components of the *mise en scène*, they assist the main action, and they possess a certain sub-textual quality which elicits a response not unlike that demanded by music and painting. In no other single play by Strindberg is there such clear evidence of an advanced aesthetic to a considerable degree expressive of Ionesco's assertion that "The theatre is visual as much as it is auditory. It is not a series of images, like the cinema, but a construction, a moving architecture of scenic images."[7]

Ionesco once wrote that

> For me, a play does not consist in the description of the development of a story—that would be writing a novel or a film. A play is a structure that consists of a series of states of consciousness or situations, which become intensified, grow more and more dense, then get entangled, either to be disentangled again or to end in unbearable inextricability. . . . All my plays have their origin in two fundamental states of consciousness: now the one, now the other is predominant, and sometimes they are combined. These basic states of consciousness are an awareness of evanescence and of solidity, of emptiness and of too much presence, of the unreal transparency of the world and its opacity, of light and of thick darkness.[8]

An account of a play's structure in such terms will first of all indicate the theatrical functioning of such auditory and visual components of the *mise en scène* as have been discussed; and secondly, will give clearer definition to that movement and rhythm of a play which operates in the theatre somewhat independently of the principle narrative thread or action. Frequently in Strindberg's plays, certainly in such a work as *The Inferno*,[9] we can appreciate a sense of form based upon such a rhythm of "states of consciousness" as Ionesco describes. In *The Ghost Sonata*, the close of Scene One, the exposing of Hummel in Scene Two, and the Student's narration to the Girl in Scene Three are three significant instances of "states of consciousness" which "become intensified, grow more and more dense, then get entangled either to be disentangled again

7. Eugène Ionesco, "Discovering the Theatre," in *Theatre in the Twentieth Century*, ed. R. W. Corrigan (New York, 1963), p. 126.
8. *Notes and Counternotes*, (New York, 1964), p. 86.
9. *The Inferno*, of course, has something of a chronological form, rooted, as it is, in autobiography. Nonetheless, throughout *The Inferno*, Strindberg exhibits a highly visual and auditory sensitivity which is evidenced both in the many detailed descriptive passages of the work and in the effect of what is *observed* or *heard* upon Strindberg's psyche. This work, then, has a kind of "form" related to, yet also independent of the sequential and chronological.

or to end in unbearable inextricability." The exposition by Hummel in Scene One surely induces in the Student–and in the audience—a sense of "unbearable inextricability" not unlike the "expository" passages in Ionesco's *The Bald Soprano* or the accumulation of questions in *The Lesson* (where the Student responds physically to words which have become like solid objects enclosing her). The close of Scene One also possesses something of the gradual rhythm of intensification and relaxation of tension that we find in *The Chairs*.[1] On this level, the form of *The Ghost Sonata* is a continuous modulation of sound and silence, of intensification and relaxation, of a sense of evanescence and "too much presence." Such a modulation is theatrically orchestrated through tension and release which is related to, yet also independent of the more lucid and "straightforward" spiritual action of the play.

1. Another play by Ionesco, which, like *The Bald Soprano* and *The Lesson*, is propelled by a kind of nonlogic that becomes a special logic [*Editor*].

Luigi Pirandello
and
Six Characters in Search
of an Author

LUIGI PIRANDELLO

From Umorismo†

The humorist is best defined by his special capacity for reflection, a kind of reflection that typically generates a sense of contradiction, perplexity, uncertainty, a certain wavering state of consciousness. It is precisely this that distinguishes him from the comic writer, the ironist, and the satirist. A sense of contradiction does not breed in them; if it were to, it would lead the comic writer to seize on some abnormality or other and would defeat the comic be making his laugher bitter; it would defeat the ironic because the ironist's wholly verbal contradiction between what he says and what he wishes to be understood would no longer be merely verbal, but real and substantial; it would defeat the satiric because it would put an end to the disdain and aversion for reality which are satire's reason for being. Not that the humorist is pleased by reality! It is sufficient for him that he be pleased by it only for a little while, so that, reflecting on his own pleasure, he might destroy it.

By nature fine and sharp, this reflection insinuates itself everywhere and unmakes everything: every semblance of feeling, every visionary fancy, every appearance of reality, every illusion. Guy de Maupassant[1] used to say that human thought "goes around like a fly in a bottle." All phenomena are either illusory or inexplicable—their reason for being escapes us. That objective value which we commonly presume to attribute to our knowledge of the world and of ourselves does not exist; it's a continuous illusory construction.

But let's consider the struggle between illusion and the humorist's

† From Luigi Pirandello, *Umorismo* (The Mondadori Edition), Rome, 1960. Pp. 145–57. Reprinted by permission of the Pirandello Estate and Toby Cole, Agent. Translated by Anthony Caputi. 1. French novelist and short-story writer (1850–93) [*Editor*].

reflection, illusion which also insinuates itself everywhere, constructing in its own way, and this reflection which one by one unmakes these constructions.

Let's begin with what illusion does for each one of us, with the construction, that is, which each of us by means of illusion makes of himself for himself. Do we see ourselves as we are, in our true, undiluted reality, and not as we wish to be? By means of a trick worked inside us, spontaneously, the product of hidden tendencies or of unconscious imitation, do we not in good faith believe ourselves different from what substantially we are? And yet we think, we work, and we live according to this fictional and even sincere interpretation of ourselves.

Now reflection can discover in this illusory construction as much for the comic writer and the satirist as for the humorist. But the comic writer will merely laugh at it, contenting himself with deflating the metaphor of ourselves that illusion spontaneously creates, while the satirist will be offended by it. Not the humorist: through the ridiculousness of the discovery he will see its serious and painful side. He will dismantle the construction, but not merely to laugh at it; and even though he laughs, he will sympathize instead of being offended.

Reflection has taught the comic writer and the satirist how much thread the spider of experience takes from social life in composing the web of mentality in this or that individual, and how this web supports, often envelops, what is called the moral sense. What is, fundamentally, the internal social structure of what is called convention? A system of elements derived from convenience, they reply, in which morality is almost always sacrificed. The humorist goes deeper and, without getting angry, laughs at discovering how with the greatest good faith, indeed ingenuously, we are induced by the impulsive working of fancy to believe that this responsibility and that moral sentiment are true, in themselves, when, in reality, they are only the responsibilites and sentiments of convention, that is, based on convenience. And he goes still further and discovers that even the need for a thing to appear worse than it actually is can become conventional, if being a member of some social group requires that one display ideals and feelings appropriate to the group yet contrary and inferior to the private feelings of the one who particpates in it.

The communal lie provides a more practicable basis on which to reconcile jarring tendencies, conflicting feelings, and opposing opinions than one which openly and explicitly tolerates dissent and opposition; indeed, falsehood seems altogether more effective than truthfulness in that it can unite, whereas veracity separates. Moreover, none of this prevents falsehood, even as it is tacitly unmasked and recognized, from enlisting this same veracity as a guarantee of its efficacy and in this way making hypocrisy seem like honesty. Reserve, discretion, the practice of letting others believe more than one says or does, silence itself when accompanied by a knowledge of the conditions which justify it—oh unforgettable Conte Zio of the Secret Council![2]—all these arts are met frequently in practical life; so too are the practice of not revealing what one is thinking, of letting others believe that one thinks less of oneself than one actually does, of pretending that one is thought to be different from what, at bottom, one is. . . .

The more one's own weakness is felt in the struggle for life the more important becomes the need for reciprocal deceit. The simulation of strength, of honesty, of sympathy, of prudence, in fact, of each of the major virtues relating to truthfulness, is a form of adaptation, a service-able tool for use in the struggle. The humorist readily collects the various impersonations used in the life-struggle; he amuses himself by unmasking them. But he does not become angry: life is like that! While the soci-ologist describes social life as it appears in external observations, the humorist, armed with his instinctive shrewdness, shows how profoundly different the appearances are from the intimate private life of its mem-bers. Yet one lies in psychological matters just as one does in social ones, and the lie to ourselves, as we knowingly live only on the surface of our psychic being, is a result of the social lie. The spirit that ponders itself is a solitary spirit; but inward solitude is never so great that the influence of everyday life, with the dissimulations and transfiguring arts that characterize it, does not penetrate the consciousness of even the solitary spirit. There lives in our spirit the spirit of the race or of the collectivity of which we are a part; we respond, unconsciously, to the pressure of others, to their ways of judging, their ways of feeling and functioning.

Further, just as simulation and dissimulation dominate in the social world, the less evidently as they become more habitual, so we simulate and dissimulate with ourselves, now halving and now multiplying our-selves. We are driven by vanity to appear different from the person we give form to in society, and we take refuge from the analysis which, revealing this vanity, would prompt the bite of conscience and humiliate us before ourselves. But the humorist performs this analysis for us; it is his function to unmask all vanities and to represent society, as Thackeray did in *Vanity Fair*.

Moreover, the humorist knows perfectly well that in the long run the pretence of logic frequently overcomes actual logical coherence in us. Even as we pretend, in theory, to be logical men, the logic of action is capable of belying the logic of thought, capable of demonstrating that a belief held with absolute sincerity is a sham. Habit, imitation, irre-sponsibility, and mental laziness compete to create misunderstanding. And even when logic rigorously informs our reasoning processes, with respect and love, let's assume, for certain fixed ideals, the reason is not always honest in its treatment of them. Is the true and exclusive source of our ideals and of our perseverance in cultivating them only to be

---

2. A character in Alessandro Manzoni's *The Betrothed*; a master in the arts of dissimulation [*Editor*].

found in pure, disinterested reason? Or is it more consistent with reality to suspect that sometimes they are evaluated, not by an objective and rational criterion, but by special emotional impulses and obscure tendencies?

The barriers and limits that we set on our consciousness are also illusory: they are the conditions for our relative individuality, but actually they have no existence. And this applies not only to us such as we are now and live in ourselves now, but also to us such as we were previously and lived then and felt and reasoned with thoughts and emotions long since forgotten, cancelled, spent in our present consciousness, but which with a jolt, a sudden turmoil of spirit, can still spring to life to reveal in us an unsuspected being within our present being. The limits of our private memory and consciousness are not rigidly fixed; beyond lie further memories and perceptions and reasonings. What we are aware of in ourselves is only a part, and perhaps a small part, of what we are. At certain unusual moments we come upon so many surprising things within ourselves—perceptions, reasonings, states of consciousness, things actually beyond the relative limits of our normal conscious existence. Certain ideals which we think we have put aside and believe no longer capable of exerting influence on our thoughts, emotions, and actions perhaps continue to survive, if not in a pure, intellectual form, on a stratum of their own, re-enforced by emotional tendencies and habit. Certain tendencies which we believe ourselves free of can be real motives for action, while new beliefs which we think we hold truly and deeply have no practical influence on us.

It is precisely the variety of tendencies that goes to make up the personality which ultimately forces the conclusion that the individual spirit is not one. How can we affirm that it is one, in fact, if passion and reason, instinct and will, indistinct tendencies, and ideals constitute numerous separate and mobile systems functioning so that the individual, now living by this one, now by that, now by some compromise between two or more psychic orientations, seems as if he contained several different and even opposed spirits, several conflicting personalities? There is no man, Pascal[3] observed, who differs from another more than, in time, he differs from himself. The spirit in its natural state contradicts the historical concept of the human spirit. Its life is a moving equilibrium, a continuous rising and falling away of emotions, tendencies, ideas, an incessant fluctuation between conflicting ends, an oscillation between such opposing poles as hope and fear, true and false, beautiful and ugly, just and unjust. If in the obscure image of the future a bright design for action suddenly appears, or the flower of delight vaguely glimmers, it is not long before our memory of the past, that avenger in the name of experience, appears, usually dim and sad, or our riotous sense of the present intervenes and restrains our too lively

---

3. Blaise Pascal (1623–62), French mathematician and philosopher [*Editor*].

imagination. This struggle between memories, hopes, forebodings, perceptions, and ideals can be seen as a struggle among spirits who oppose the domination of a firm and definitive personality.

Here is an important functionary who believes himself and who is in fact, poor soul, a man of honor. In him the moral spirit dominates. Yet one fine day instinct, like a primal beast crouched in the depths of each of us, lets fly with a kick at the moral spirit, and this man of honor steals. Oh, he himself, poor soul, is the first, shortly afterwards, to be stupefied by what has happened, to weep, to ask himself in despair: "How, how were you ever able to do such a thing?" But yes, my dear sir, you have stolen. And that one there? An upright man, indeed, an exceedingly good man: yes, my dear sir, he has killed. Moral idealism furnished his personality with a spirit which conflicted with his instinct and even to some extent with his emotions; it bodied forth an acquired spirit which fought the inherited one, which, in turn, left briefly to itself, seized suddenly on theft and crime.

Life is a continuous flux and we seek to arrest it, to fix it in stable and determined forms, inside and outside us, because we are already fixed forms, forms which move in the midst of immobile ones and which can therefore follow the flux of life until, as it gradually becomes rigid, the movement, which has already slowed down little by little, ceases. The forms in ourselves by which we seek to arrest and fix this continuous flux are the concepts and ideals which we would like to keep consistent, all the pretenses we create, the conditions, the state in which we endeavor to stabilize ourselves. But inside ourselves, in what we call the soul, which is the center of our lives, the flux continues, indistinct, sliding under the barriers we have set up, beyond the limits we have imposed, fashioning a consciousness and constructing a personality for us. At certain violent moments, assailed by the flux, all our make-believe forms crumble miserably; and even what does not slither under the barriers and beyond the limits, even what is clearly a part of us, what we have channelled into the affections and duties we have assumed and the habits we have marked out for ourselves, overflows in certain moments of fullness and throws everything into confusion.

There are reckless spirits who, almost continuously in a state of melting and blending, resist congealing or hardening into this or that form of personality. But even for the more placid ones who have settled into one form or other the melting and blending is always possible.

Even our own bodies, fixed perpetually in their immutable features, can sometimes represent a torture for the moving, melting spirit. Why must we be just like this, we sometimes ask ourselves at the mirror, with this face and this body? We raise a hand, unconsciously, and the gesture remains suspended. It seems strange that *we* have done it. *We are seeing ourselves live*. With this suspended gesture we can liken ourselves to a statue, to that statue of the ancient orator, for example, which one sees in a niche as one ascends the staircase of the Quirinale.[4] With a scroll in one hand and the other extended in a sober gesture, how distressed and amazed he seems to have remained there, in stone, for all those centuries, suspended in that attitude, before all those people who have ascended, who ascend, and who will ascend that staircase!

In certain moments of interior silence, in which our spirit divests itself of its habitual pretences and our eyes become sharper and more penetrating, we see ourselves in life, and life itself, as if in a sterile nudity, and we are troubled; we feel ourselves assaulted by a strange impression, as if, in a flash, a different reality from that which we normally perceive were clarifying itself, a living reality beyond human sight, outside the forms of human reason. At such times the fabric of daily existence, almost suspended in the void of our interior silence, appears with blinding clarity to be without sense and purpose; and as all our habitual sham connections for sentiments and images are disjointed and broken up, the new reality seems horrible in its impassive and mysterious severity. The inward void gets larger, goes beyond the limits of our body, becomes a void around us, a strange emptiness, like a pause in time and in life, as if our interior silence were sinking into the abysses of mystery. With a supreme effort we try to re-acquire our normal consciousness of things, to re-establish the usual ties between them, to re-connect ideas, to feel ourselves alive again in the usual way, as before. But in this normal consciousness, in these re-connected ideas, in this habitual sense of life, we can no longer have faith because by now we know that they compromise a deception for the purpose of living, that beneath them is something else which man cannot confront except at the cost of dying or going mad. The whole experience has taken only an instant, but its impression endures in us for a long time, like a dizziness to which is contrasted the stability, however unreal in actuality, of things—ambitious, paltry appearances. The life that wanders about, small and habitual, among these appearances seems almost to be no longer real, to be a mechanical fantasmagoria. How can we give it importance? How can we respect it?

Today we are, tomorrow we are not. What sort of face have they given us with which to play the role of someone alive? An ugly nose? What misery to have to carry around an ugly nose all one's life . . . It's fortunate that in the long run we cease to notice it. Others notice it, it's true, when we have succeeded in believing that we have a beautiful nose; and then we can no longer understand why they laugh when they look at us. They are such fools! We console ourselves by noticing what ears that one has and what lips that other, yet they are not aware of them and they have the nerve to laugh at us. Masks, masks . . . A puff of wind and they pass and make way for others. That poor cripple there . . . Who is he? To run towards death on crutches . . . Here life crushes

4. A palace on one of Rome's seven hills, currently the residence of the president of the Republic [Editor].

someone's foot; there it pulls out someone's eye . . . A wooden leg, a glass eye, and forward! Everyone tidies up his mask as best he can— that is, the exterior mask. But inside there is still that other, which often does not agree with the exterior one.

Nothing is true! The sea is true, yes, and the mountain, and the stone, and the blade of grass; but man? Eternally masked, without wishing to be or knowing it, by those very things that he in good faith believes himself to be: handsome, good, gracious, generous, unhappy. To think of all this is to laugh; yes, laugh. What does a dog do when he has overcome the first fever of living? He eats and sleeps; he lives as he can live, as he must live. He closes his eyes patiently and lets time pass; he's cold if it's cold, hot if it's hot; and if they kick him, he takes it because this too is a sign of his lot. But man? Even as an old man he always has fever: he is delirious and he is not aware of it; he cannot do less than assume a pose, even, somehow, to beguile himself with; and with his imagination he creates things, a great many things, which he needs to believe and needs to take seriously.

He is helped in this by a certain infernal little machine that nature gave him and adjusted to him inwardly as a conspicuous proof of its benevolence. In the interests of their health men ought to have let it rust, ought never to have started it, or touched it. But no. Certain individuals felt so proud and deemed themselves so happy to have it that they quickly dedicated themselves with relentless zeal to perfecting it. Aristotle wrote a book about it, a graceful little treatise that is still adopted in the schools because children learn how to play with toys so quickly and well. It's a kind of pump and filter which puts the brain in communication with the heart. The esteemed philosophers call it logic.

By means of logic the brain pumps feelings from the heart and extracts ideas. The feeling passes through the filter and leaves whatever it contains that is hot and cloudy; then it is refrigerated, purified, and i-de-a-lized. By this process a poor feeling, initially evoked by a particular circumstance, by some occurrence or other, often a sorrowful one, now pumped and filtered by this little machine used by the brain, becomes an abstract, general idea. And what follows? It follows that we not only must worry about this particular circumstance and that passing occurrence, but we also must poison our lives with the concentrated extract, the corrosive sublimate of logical deduction. Many unfortunates believe that in this way we shall cure the world of all its ills: they pump and filter, pump and filter, until their hearts are as dry as cork and their brains are like cabinets in a pharmacy, full of those little bottles with the black label bearing the skull and crossbones and the legend "Poison."

Man does not have an idea or an absolute conception of life, but a sense of it that is mutable and variable, depending on the times, circumstances, and chance. Now logic, abstracting ideas from feelings tends to fix what is mobile, mutable, and fluid, tends to give an absolute value to what is relative. It makes worse an evil that is already grave to begin with. For the root of our trouble is precisely that we have a sense of life. The tree lives but does not feel: for it the earth, sun, air, light, wind, and rain are not things beyond it. Man, on the other hand, is at birth endowed with the sad privilege of feeling himself alive, and this leads to that happy illusion by which he accepts his inward sense of life, mutable and variable as it is, as if it were a reality outside him.

The ancients told the story that Prometheus stole a spark from the sun to make a gift of it to men. Now the sense we have of life is precisely this Promethean spark of the fable. It causes us to see ourselves lost on the earth; it projects all around us a more or less full circle of light beyond which is dark shadow, the fearful shadow that would not exist if it were not for the lighted spark within us, a shadow, however, that we must unfortunately believe real as long as the spark lives in our breast. When it is extinguished at the last by the breath of death, what has apparently been a shadow will gather us up for good; after the smoky day of illusion perpetual night will receive us. Or, even then, perhaps, we shall continue to be at the mercy of Being, which will have broken only the futile forms of reason. All that shadow, that enormous mystery on which so many philosophers have speculated in vain and which now science, though it denies its interest in it, does not exclude, will it not be, perhaps, finally a deception like any other, a trick played by our minds, a fantasy that comes to nothing? What if ultimately all this mystery does not exist outside us, but only within us, and necessarily within us by virtue of the famous privilege of our sense of life? What if death were only the breath that extinguishes this sense in us, this sense so painful and terrifying because it is limited, defined by the circle of fictional shadow beyond the slight orbit of faint light which we project around us and within which our life remains as if imprisoned, as if excluded for a time from the universal, eternal life which it seems to us we must one day re-enter? What if actually we are already there and there we shall remain, though no longer with this sense of exile that aggrieves us? Is not this limit also illusory and relative to the scant light of our individuality? Perhaps we have always lived, always shall live with all of life; perhaps even now, in our present form, we participate in all the manifestations of the universe. We do not know it and we do not see it because unfortunately the Promethean spark enables us to see only that little which it illuminates.

Tomorrow a humorist could picture Prometheus on his rock in the Caucasus in the act of pondering sadly his lighted torch and perceiving in it, at last, the fatal cause of his infinite suffering. He has finally understood that Zeus is no other than a vain fantasm of his own creating, a pitiable deception, the shadow of his own body projected in gigantic dimensions in the sky precisely because he holds the torch burning in his hand. Zeus would disappear on one condition only, on condition that Prometheus extinguish his torch. But he does not know how, he does not wish it, he cannot; and the shadow remains, terrifying and tyrannical, for all men who do not succeed in understanding the fatal deception.

Thus the conflict proves itself irremovable and unresolvable, like shadow and substance. In this brief humorist vision we have seen it enlarge itself gradually, go beyond the limits of our individual being whence it takes root, and extend itself around us. Reflection, which sees in everything a construction that is either illusory, or pretended, or fictional, discovers it and by shrewd, subtle, minute analysis disassembles and unmakes it.

One of the greatest humorists, without knowing it, was Copernicus,[5] who disassembled, not really the machine of the universe, but the proud image which we had made of it. * * * It was the discovery of the telescope, yet another infernal little machine which could make a pair with the one that nature made us a present of, which administered the coup de grace to us. But we invented this one so as not to be inferior. While the eye looks at one end, through the smaller lense, and sees enlarged what nature had providentially intended us to see small, what does our soul do? It leaps to look through the other end, through the larger lense. In this way the telescope becomes a terrible instrument which overwhelms the earth and man and all our glories and grandeur.

It is fortunate that humorist reflection does provoke a sense of contradiction: in this case it says, "But is man really as little as the reversesd telescope causes us to see him? If he can understand and conceive of his infinite littleness, that means he understands and conceives of the infinite grandeur of the universe. How, then, can we say that man is a small creature?" Yet it is also true that if man believes himself great and a humorist comes to know it, he can go the way of Gulliver and be both a giant in Lilliput and a toy among the giants of Brobdingnag.[6]

ANTHONY CAPUTI

[Six Characters in Search of an Author]†

* * *

Six Characters has proved difficult for readers and critics largely because it resists what To Find Oneself[1] lends itself to readily, a relatively easy translation into ideas. Despite its look of allegory or parable, it is in fact

5. Nicolaus Copernicus (1473–1543), the Polish cleric and astronomer who developed the theory of a sun-centered universe, thus subverting the claims of religion and earlier astronomy and providing the basis for modern astronomy [Editor].
6. Jonathan Swift's hero in Gulliver's Travels (1726), first entitled Travels into Several Remote Nations of the World; Gulliver is a giant among the diminutive Lilliputians and a mite among the giant Brobdingnagians [Editor].

† From "The Theatrical Matrix of Experience," Pirandello and the Crisis of Modern Consciousness, Urbana and Chicago, 1988. Pp. 114–19. Reprinted with permission of the publishers, the University of Illinois Press.

1. A later play by Pirandello (1932).

neither. On the contrary, it can best be described, perhaps, as a sur-realistic expression of a tension, but of a tension experienced so that the details of its articulation are far more prominent than any of the ideas implicit in it. This is the tension we meet in Pirandello's first reference to the subject when in a letter to Stefano he speaks of six characters who pursue him, show him their wounds, and insist that he write a novel about them, while he chases them away.[2] Tilgher[3] also appears to have identified it in his account of the play's debt to futurism: "*Six Characters* . . . is the strongest attempt made . . . to realize scenically an entirely inward state of spirit, to discompose and project on the stage the planes and various phases of a continuously flowing process of consciousness, according to a method similar to that by which the futurist painters discompose light and planes."[4] Unfortunately, Tilgher then found that purpose wanting because it did not provide a resolution by moving to what he called "universal values."[5] Actually, Pirandello is perfectly ex-plicit about the nature of this dramatic action and is himself the most helpful commentator on its density.

It is strange that so few critics have taken notice of his remarks in the essay written in 1925, "How and Why I Wrote *Six Characters in Search of an Author*" ("Come e Perché Ho Scritto *Sei Personaggi in Cerca d'Autore*"). His explanation is not simple, but it goes straight to the heart of the matter by establishing that the play is about characters in search of but not finding an author and accordingly not finding the life-as-form an author could give them; it is about, in other words, impulses to life refused. "I wanted to show six characters in search of an author. The drama does not succeed in being represented precisely because the author they are searching for is lacking; instead, what is represented is the play of their vain attempt, with all that it has about it of the tragic because these six characters have been refused." A little further along he describes the action of the play as "the drama of being in search of an author, [of being] refused."[6]

Now a great deal of the confusion about the play traces to a failure to understand this as a purpose to create a dramatic tension and not to mount an argument. Pirandello's explanation, for example, that he had originally rejected the characters because he could not find their "par-ticular sense of life" or "universal value" has misled some critics into concluding that he was mainly interested in the process of artistic cre-ation. But to settle for that is to ignore that ultimately he did find a "particular sense of life" and "universal value" in the circumstance of

2. "Lettere al Figlio Stefano durante la Guerra," *Sipario*, VII, no. 80 (July 1952), 37 (the letter was written on 23 July 1917). (All translations are the editor's.)

3. Adriano Tilgher (1887–1941), an Italian critic and philosopher, the first major writer to take up Pirandello's cause.

4. The article "Ratti e Pirandello" first appeared in the newspaper *La Stampa* (21, 22 May 1921).

5. He makes the point in *Il Problema Centrale*, ed. Alessandro D'Amico (Genoa, 1973), pp. 129–31.

6. The article first appeared in *Comoedia* 7 (1 Jan. 1925): 5–10, then as the Preface of *Six Characters* in *Maschere Nude*, ed. Silvio D'Amico, *Opere di Luigi Pirandello*, I Classici Italiani Contemporanei (Milan, 1958), 4.34–46. Pp. 38–40.

characters searching and being refused. He even goes so far as to describe the activity of searching while being refused as tragic, and as we shall see, he used this term to characterize the painful necessity of struggling between the extremes of movement and form. In the essay he reverts to his usual account of how the "life germs" or "vital germs" become characters who then need the "form" of a dramatic action to live, who need, in other words, to be theatricalized. As he put it as early as 1921 in a letter to Tilgher, the life of the six characters is "infused but not yet expressed, not yet 'constructed.' "[7] He accepts them for this play only when he sees their universal value here consists in the act of their searching for an author who will put them in a play and thus enable them to live and in their not finding this "coordinating spirit." To put this another way, Pirandello has here described an action that while containing a great many of the issues that have long interested him, positions its characters between being, with its impulses to live in a form, and form itself; he has created an image of life as a play that never quite gets put on. It does not matter that it is a painful play: it *is* the play of these characters.

To begin with, it is very important that the characters have come not to narrate—they, and especially the Father, are contemptuous of mere words—but to play out their story, to reify their lives in the only way available to them or to any of us, as action. They are different from the members of the theater company because they are narrowly held to the limited series of events that the playwright had devised for them before abandoning them. Unlike the actors, who, as the Father explains in act 3, can change and for whom even the events of their lives can change as these events are forgotten or seen with different eyes,[8] the characters cannot change. The Father is particularly sensitve on this point because he wishes desperately to free himself from the definition that the Step-Daughter and the given events of their story impose on him, an unjust definition, he insists, which leaves him "suspended," "in pillory." But all the characters are similarly fixed, and Pirandello underscores this fixedness in the stage direction amplified in the version of 1925 to include the suggestion that the characters wear light masks.

> *All this should sharpen the underlying meaning of the play. The characters should not in fact seem like phantasms, but like created realities, unchanging constructions of the imagination, and therefore more substantial and real than the unstable nat- uralness of the actors. The masks should help give the impression of faces fashioned by art, each fixed in the expression of its fundamental emotion, whether it be remorse for the FATHER, vengeance for the STEPDAUGHTER, disdain for the SON, or acute grief for the MOTHER. She could have fixed wax tears in the*

7. Leonardo Sciascia, *Pirandello e il Pirandellismo* (Palermo, 1953), p. 90.   8. P. [248] in this text.

*swellings around her eyes and down her cheeks such as we see
in sculptured and painted images of the Mater Dolorosa in
church.*[9]

The characters are to be understood, therefore, as different from human beings because fixed, but cognate creations in that like humans they hover between the impulse to have form and theatrical form itself.

Six Characters is about living in this state of suspended animation. Its power and excitement trace primarily to the image of the characters searching, struggling, held in a kind of dynamic incompleteness. That is not to say, of course, that their encounter with the actors does not occasion a good deal of commentary: it does. But the comments on words and the multiplicity of selves and the eternal struggle between movement and form and the elusiveness of truth and reality serve rather to focus and deepen the central image than to define it. That image is essentially defined by the characters' encounter with the actors and their attempts and failure to find in the Manager the "coordinating spirit" who will give them life in a theatricalization of their story.

The series of disclosures in act 1, after the Father's first line, "We are here in search of an author," traces a dizzying descent first into a sphere of incomplete realization and then into a volcanic domestic situation. As the Father and the Step-Daughter rapidly piece together the past that has led to their present anguish, they show themselves to be under tremendous pressure to live their drama. The Father, while recognizing the multiple selves that huddle within him, wishes to actualize through living it a more adequate version of his moral nature than his Step-Daughter's idea of him and the events of their story allow. The Step-Daughter, meanwhile, bursts with eagerness to play the meeting with the Father at Madame Pace's so as to live the full dimensions of her nausea: "I'm dying, I tell you, of the mania to live it, to see it, this scene."[1] These imperatives invest these two characters with a conspicuous intensity. But even the Mother and Son, though far more passive, are capable of great intensity when aroused.

Throughout the play this intensity contrasts sharply with the hazy flaccidity of the actors. In a letter to Ruggeri[2] in 1936 concerning a projected production of the play, Pirandello reiterated the emphasis of his additions to the version of 1925: "It will be necessary to avoid the error that has always been committed of making the characters appear like shadows or phantasms instead of as superior and more potent beings because 'created realities,' forms of art fixed forever, immutable, almost statues in contrast with the mobile naturalness, changeable and almost fluid, of the actors."[3] And within the play the characters themselves recoil from the disparity between their sense of themselves and the

9. Pp. [214–15].
1. P. [237].
2. Ruggero Ruggeri (1871–1953), the leading Ital-

ian actor of Pirandello's day.
3. "Lettere di Pirandello a Ruggero Ruggeri," *Il Dramma*, XXXI (Aug.–Sept. 1955), 70.

theatricalized versions of them proposed by the actors. Even as the Manager assigns the roles, the Father perceives the falsity: "I no longer know what to say to you. . . . I already begin . . . I don't know, to hear as false, as if they were other sounds, my own words."[4] The Step-Daughter laughs outright at the actors' impersonations. Throughout the play the characters keep screaming for truth—"The truth! The truth, *signore!*"—while the Manager keeps reminding them that the theater can produce only a limited truth. A great deal of the represented action of the play consists of this struggle: the characters on the one hand demanding to live completely, the actors on the other almost foppishly acquiescent in compromise. Moreover, the energy generated by that opposition is experienced directly by us, mediated, as Gino Rizzo has shrewdly argued, by no interpreting voice.[5] The tension produced by the characters' failure to achieve some kind of rapprochement with the actors is at the heart of the play's power.

That Pirandello's conception stressed the concreteness of this action, of the characters "in search of an author" and "refused," is supported by his revisions of the play. Despite such passages of Tilgherian analysis as that in "How and Why I Wrote *Six Characters in Search of an Author*," in which he expounds on the "immanent conflict with vital movement and form" and numerous passages of commentary within the play itself, the changes to be found in the definitive version of 1925 all serve to solidify the surface of the action. Long speeches are broken up or eliminated; stage directions are amplified; awkward choral speeches like the Step-Daughter's speech on the theater at the beginning of act 2 in the first version are set into the action less conspicuously; important moments like the concluding image of the Manager leaving the theater are opened up. In the first version of the conclusion the Manager, left on stage as the others carry off the dead child, simply screams in exasperation that he has lost a whole day. In the final version once he is alone he instructs the electrician to turn out the lights and then complains when they go out that he might at least leave him enough to see by.

> *Suddenly, behind the backcloth . . . a green light comes on, which projects, large and sharply outlined, the shadows of the characters, except for the* BOY *and the* LITTLE GIRL. *Seeing them, the* DIRECTOR *scurries from the stage, terrified. At that instant this light goes off and on the stage the blue night light mentioned earlier comes on. Slowly the* SON *comes from the right side of the curtain, followed by the* MOTHER *with her arms extended toward him. Then from the left side the* FATHER. *They stop half way onto the stage and stand as if bemused. Lastly, the* STEPDAUGHER *comes from the left and runs toward one of the stairways. On the first step she stops to look at the other three*

4. P. [232].

5. "Luigi Pirandello in Search of a Total Theatre," *Italian Quarterly*, XXII, no. 5 (1968), 3–26.

*for a moment and breaks into a coarse laugh. Then she hurries
down the stairs and runs up an aisle, stopping once more to
laugh at the other three still standing there. At last she rushes
out of the auditorium. Even from the lobby her laughter can
be heard.*
      Shortly after this the curtain falls.[6]

These additions to the closing image intensify the sense of chasm that
lies just beyond the represented action of the search and the failure to
find an author. The action is not only unresolved, as so many Piran-
dellian actions are; it is played against a future that is felt acutely as a
blank. Life as a play that never gets put on, life as a state of suspended
animation between a mania to live and a theatricalization that even
before it is achieved is known to be inadequate, is vexed further by the
sense that it is played in anticipation of a future like an abyss. This facet
of the action, however abstract in the telling, is also in the image and
part of the play's extraordinary immediacy and directness.

Altogether, the dramatic action that Pirandello has devised here is his
most masterful embodiment of his vision of life as theater. The device
of bringing a group of dramatic characters face to face with a theatrical
company and then having them experiment with playing the drama that
for the characters is their life provides, among other things, numerous
opportunities to show figures standing apart from their lives and commenting on them. In the course of these commentaries, as the characters
review and mull over details, we see them contemplate their lives as
theatricalizations. When they are asked to stand aside so that the actors
can take their parts, they object, as we have seen, to inaccuracies and
distortions. At other times they ponder with fascination and horror the
details that fix their experience, details like the Mother's scream at finding
the Step-Daughter in an embrace with her husband. As they review the
theatrical progress toward the scream, they underscore how theatrical
detail gives substance to the event.

> FATHER. . . . all our passion must culminate in her final
>   scream. [*Again indicating the* MOTHER.]
> STEPDAUGHTER. It's still ringing in my ears. It drove me mad,
>   that scream!—You can have me acted as you wish, sir—it
>   doesn't matter. Even dressed. As long as . . . my arms—
>   only my arms—are bare. So that, look, standing like this
>   [*she goes to the* FATHER *and puts her head on his chest*], with
>   my head resting like this, and my arms like this around his
>   neck, I see here, in my arms, a vein throbbing. And then
>   as if only that living vein disgusts me, I shut my eyes, like
>   this, and bury my head in his chest. [*Turning to the*
>   MOTHER.] Scream! Scream, Mama! [*She buries her head in*

6. Pp. [255–56].

the FATHER's *chest and with her shoulders hunched as if to*
fend off the scream, she goes on in a voice of stifled pain.]
Scream the way you screamed then!

MOTHER [*hurling herself on them to separate them*]. No, my
darling! My darling daughter! [*And after having separated*
her from him] You brute! She's my daughter! Don't you see
she's my daughter?[7]

Now in much the way this passage positions inner promptings and
external event so the whole dynamic by which impulse struggles to
expression is kept before us, the play as a whole generates an acute
consciousness of experience struggling, without success, to complete
itself in theatrical form.

* * *

WYLIE SYPHER

Cubist Drama†

When Luigi Pirandello wrote *Six Characters in Search of an Author* in
1921, he called it a "comedy in the making." It is a very highbrow study
of oscillation of appearances in the theatre. Just as the cubist broke up
the object into various planes, or as photomontage gave its own sort of
polyphonic vision by means of combined shots, so Pirandello offers a
compound image in drama. He surrenders the literary subject while the
cubist is surrendering the ancedote, and treats his theatre as a plane
intersecting art and life, explaining in his prefatory note that "the whole
complex of theatrical elements, characters and actors, author and actor-
manager or director, dramatic critics and spectators (external or involved)
present every possible conflict." He is concerned with the collision between art and actuality, the theatrical crisis where the imitation of life
and life itself appear as a passage between events on the stage and events
in our existence. His play is a research into the plural aspects of identity,
and he concludes that there are many possible levels of reality at which
things can happen. He has penetrated the old theatrical plot by thought,
much as the cubist penetrated objects, and having conceived his problem
as an encounter of art with life, he has discovered a "way to resolve it
by means of a new perspective"—a perspective like a flat-pattern cubist
illusion.

In *Six Characters* the action (which is not a "play" at all) improvises
upon certain events in life as being art. While a company of actors is
rehearsing a play—by Pirandello himself, for the planes of reality begin
to shift at once—six members of a family (father, mother, legitimate

7. P. [245].
† From *Rococo to Cubism in Art and Literature*,
by Wylie Sypher. Pp. 289–94. Copyright © 1960
by Wylie Sypher. Reprinted by permission of Random House, Inc.

and illegitimate children) enter the bare stage and ask to be allowed to act out (or "realize") the drama of their lives; for an author has conceived them but not written them into any script. Theirs is a history of a broken home caused by the mother's infidelity. Against the manager's inclination, against the inclination of the actors, the six characters try to represent their sad lives in acted form, which at once brings the difficulty that they cannot interpret for the professionals the meaning of the plot they have lived and are attempting to realize. "The drama," explains the Father, "is in us, and we are the drama." In other words, theatre breaks down. The effort of the characters to represent themselves on the stage is finally blocked when one of the six, the unhappy Boy, in a fit of despair, shoots himself. Some of the professional actors take this to be an artistic climax; but it is a genuine suicide. The Father shouts "Pretence? Reality, sir, reality!" By this time the director does not care: "Pretence? Reality? To hell with it all. . . . I've lost a whole day over these people, a whole day!" The ambiguity of the illusion is emphasized when at the close of the second "act" a stage hand drops the curtain by mistake, leaving the Father and the director in front of it, before the footlights, isolated from both audience and the "characters" and other actors. The end of the first act comes when the director, to gather his wits, calls off rehearsal—which is not rehearsal at all, but an equivocal passage from life that is being translated into art by characters who wish to express their life in dramatic form.

By refusing the momentum of plot Pirandello is left with the formal art-problem of writing a drama about the writing of a drama, a final purification of the nineteenth-century problem of treating life as art, or taking the art-view of life. Like the cubist painting about the painting of a painting, Pirandello's play is a sort of *tableau-tableau* showing the relation between actuality and its representation. The cubists used the textures of actuality in the form of collage to bring their art-structure into proper focus; and they used it impromptu. Sometimes they quoted a few legible details of objects in a frankly photographic way so that the clichés of painting could be better contrasted with the functions of flat-pattern perspective. In thus avoiding the tyranny of the literary subject they discovered what Piet Mondrian[1] a little later emphasized, that "the expression of reality cannot be the same as reality." Into his formal study of the writing of a drama Pirandello has deliberately inserted a good many theatrical clichés as a sort of collage: the professional actors, whose vocation is like that of the traditional model or lay figure used by painters, rely on all the customary mechanisms of the stage; and the director takes the attitude of the commercial theatre toward doing a play. He fails entirely to mediate between the professional troupe who are rehearsing a Pirandello script and the six displaced characters who have blundered into the commercial theatre from reality.

These six belong to life yet at the same time they do not belong to

1. A Dutch painter (1872–1944). His fame rests on his geometric style consisting of black lines in a gridlike pattern to outline colored or white rectangular shapes [*Editor*].

it; they are like the things Picasso[2] "assassinated" in the interest of total representation. Their impromptu appearance on the "legitimate" stage is a double exposure of reality and illusion. There is also the bona-fide audience (which may or may not represent actual life). All these levels of representation are held together in a simultaneous perspective of transparent dramatic planes to be read in many directions at the same time. The final test, of course, is whether the events of life are susceptible of being interpreted by drama anyhow, or whether the experience of the six characters can be realized until they appear in some artistic composition. The Boy's suicide is a shocking collage. We cannot say that these persons exist off the stage; and we cannot say they live on the stage. Above all, what is the stage? Hamlet had already raised Pirandello's questions about drama's being a mere dream of passion. The six characters, the director, the actors rehearsing Pirandello come into every sort of encounter. If the six exist at all, they do so in some state of emergence. When they enter, "a tenuous light surrounds them, almost as if irradiated by them—the faint breath of their fantastic reality." This is their cubist iridescence of form.

The instant the six appear, the planes of representation are displaced. The Father tries to state their situation: "The drama consists finally in this: when that mother re-enters my house, her family born outside of it, and shall we say *superimposed* on the original, ends with the death of the little girl, the tragedy of the boy, and the flight of the elder daughter. It cannot go on, because it is foreign to its surroundings. So after much torment, we three remain: I, the mother, that son." But the Son stands in the background refusing to be identified with the rest of the six, commenting upon the whole enterprise as being merely "Literature." In vain the Father protests, "Literature indeed! This is life, this is passion." Yet the Son will not take his part in any theatrical representation; nor does he belong to life either. "Mr. Manager," he insists, "I am an 'unrealized' character, dramatically speaking; and I find myself not at all at ease in their company. Leave me out of it, I beg you." There he is, a figure to be fitted into the composition against his will, adding a further difficult dimension as if he had broken loose from the terms of the problem as Pirandello posed it. We cannot even place him as collage.

For the Father the drama lies in taking a point of view on events—a prehension, Whitehead[3] would call it. He argues, "For the drama lies all in this—in the conscience that I have, that each one of us has. We believe this conscience to be a single thing, but it is many-sided. There is one for this person, and another for that. Diverse consciences. So we have this illusion of being one person for all, of having a personality that is unique in all our acts. But it isn't true. We see this when, tragically perhaps, in something we do we are, as it were, suspended, caught up

2. Pablo Picasso (1881–1973), a Spanish painter, a pioneer in and the master of the various modes of avant-garde expression [*Editor*].

3. Alfred North Whitehead (1861–1947), an English philosopher [*Editor*].

in the air on a kind of hook." This is the cubist suspension of the object. When the Father sees the professional actors trying to play his "role," speaking his "part" in the clichés of their art, he exclaims, getting more and more confused, "I don't know what to say to you. Already I begin to hear my own words ring false, as if they had another sound."

Pirandello invites us to examine texture of his drama exactly as the cubist invites us to examine the contrasting textures in his painting, the very invitation raising doubt about holding the mirror up to nature. The most "natural" scene in the rehearsal comes when two of the characters, Madam Pace and the Step-Daughter, begin to speak so quietly and casually that the actors—who are trying to learn the "parts"—object it's impossible to play the scene that way. The director agrees: "Acting is our business here. Truth up to a certain point, but no farther." Pirandello thus parodies Cézanne's[4] approach to art: "I have not tried to reproduce nature," Cézanne said: "I have represented it." The manager wishes a single, simple illusion of reality. The Father points out that any such illusion makes drama only "a kind of game." Naturally the actors think it no game: "We are serious actors," they protest; they are artists. In desperation the Father then asks, "I should like to request you to abandon this game of art which you are accustomed to play here with your actors, and to ask you seriously once again: who are you?" The director, badly upset by this remark, resents having his identity questioned by a mere dramatic character: "A man who calls himself a character comes and asks me who I am." By the Father's reply, Pirandello hints that represented forms may be more real than actualities: "A character, sir, may always ask a man who he is. Because a character has really a life of his own. . . ." The reality may be an appearance; as the Father says, "You must not count overmuch on your reality as you feel it today, since, like that of yesterday, it may prove an illusion for you tomorrow." Gide[5] would agree, and T. S. Eliot,[6] who writes

> You are not the same people who left that station
> Or who will arrive at any terminus. . . .
>
> ("Dry Salvages")

Pirandello is only characteristic of the many others in modern theatre who have tried to break through the boundaries between the stage and life; and besides, the problem became a traditional one anyhow after Hamlet's advice to the players. This does not, however, make it less contemporary.[7]

With Pirandello it was almost obsessive, and coincided with the cubist

4. Paul Cézanne (1839–1906), French painter and one of the most important influences on modern art [Editor].
5. André Gide (1869–1951), French novelist [Editor].
6. Anglo-American poet (1888–1965) [Editor].
7. Perhaps the most notable recent attempt to break the barriers between theatre and life is the "epic" theatre of Bertolt Brecht, a discussion of which might obscure (or a least greatly retard) matters here because of Brecht's involvements with Marxist ideology. However, Brecht's epic theatre is technically an extension of the cubist methods in Pirandello, as the excellent account in John Willett's *Theatre of Bertolt Brecht*, London, 1959, explains. Willett describes how Brecht uses montage, and fractures the continuity of his drama by counterpointing effects, deliber-

analysis of illusion and reality. *Each In His Own Way* (1923) returns to the dramatic illusion "based upon an episode in real life." In this play the audience takes part, for among them are "real" persons whose lives have been dramatized in the "play" going on behind the footlights. These persons, objecting that "the author has taken it from real life," gather in the "lobby" after the first act to attack Pirandello and to break up the performance on the stage, which deals with a love affair between "a certain Moreno Woman" and "Baron Nuti," whose names have been in the newspapers. The directions Pirandello wrote for this interlude show how he was experimenting with multidimensional theatre:

> This scene in the lobby—Spectators coming out of a theatre— will show what was first presented on the stage as life itself to be a fiction of art; and the substance of the comedy will accordingly be pushed back, as it were, into a secondary plane of actuality or reality. . . . The Moreno Woman and Baron Nuti are present in the theatre among the spectators. Their appearance, therefore, suddenly and violently establishes a plane of reality still closer to real life, leaving the spectators who are discussing the fictitious reality of the staged play on a plane midway between. In the interlude at the end of the second act these three planes of reality will come into conflict with one another, as the participants in the drama of real life attack the participants in the comedy, the Spectators, meantime, trying to interfere.

Pirandello "destroys" drama much as the cubists destroyed conventional things. He will not accept as authentic "real" people or the cliché of the theatre any more than the cubist accepts as authentic the "real" object, the cliché of deep perspective, the contour of volumes seen in the light of the studio—or under sunlight either. The object, say Gleizes and Metzinger,[8] has no absolute form; it is only a passage in possible relationships, with many relevances that are never fixed. Except by a blunder we cannot drop the curtain on Pirandello's drama because there is no clear boundary between life and art. Nor can the cubist painter isolate or define his object. He can, however, represent its emergence into reality.

---

ately interrupting the action by songs and using the film for background and subtitles. Brecht subjects his audience to a sort of shock treatment by his so-called *Verfremdungseffekt* ("V-effect")— "jerking" the actor out of relationship, breaking the illusion of the conventional theatre, making the spectators continually reorient themselves by unfamiliar changing angles. Above all Brecht is analytical, and has said of his plays, "The process of showing must itself be shown." He writes a "non-Aristotelian" drama and has said of his presentations, "I am the Einstein of the new stage form." Willett has treated all these questions in relation to Brecht's social realism and his use of the new music of Kurt Weill, Milhaud, and others. Eisenstein has had his influence on Brecht, also, as well as the Japanese Nō play. But it is difficult to talk of Brecht's theatre apart from his social point of view.

8. Authors of an influential book on cubism: *Du Cubisme* (Paris, 1912, 1947) [*Editor*].

Eugene O'Neill
and
Long Day's Journey into Night

EUGENE O'NEILL

From the *New York Tribune*, February 13, 1921 †

Diff'rent, as I see it, is merely a tale of the eternal, romantic idealist who is in all of us—the eternally defeated one. In our innermost hearts we all wish ourselves and others to be "Diff'rent." We are all more or less "Emmas"[1]—the more or less depending on our talent for compromise. Either we try in desperation to clutch our dream at the last by deluding ourselves with some tawdry substitute; or, having waited the best part of our lives, we find the substitute time mocks us with too shabby to accept. In either case we are tragic figures, and also fit subjects for the highest comedy, were one sufficiently detached to write it.

I have been accused of unmitigated gloom. Is this a pessimistic view of life? I do not think so. There is a skin deep optimism and another higher optimism, not skin deep, which is usually confounded with pessimism. To me, the tragic alone has that significant beauty which is truth. It is the meaning of life—and the hope. The noblest is eternally the most tragic. The people who succeed and do not push on to a greater failure are the spiritual middle classers. Their stopping at success is the proof of their compromising insignificance. How pretty their dreams must have been! The man who pursues the mere attainable should be sentenced to get it—and keep it. Let him rest on his laurels and enthrone him in a Morris chair, in which laurels and hero may wither away together. Only through the unattainable does man achieve a hope worth living and dying for—and so attain himself. He with the spiritual guerdon of a hope in hopelessness, is nearest to the stars and the rainbow's foot.

This may seem to be soaring grandiloquently—and somewhat platitudinously—far above "a poor thing but mine own"[2] like *Diff'rent*;

---

† Reprinted by permission

1. Emma Crosby, a character in *Diff'rent* [Editor].

2. The line is Touchstone's reference to his country girl friend, Audrey, in *As You Like It*, 5.4.57–58 [Editor].

but one must state one's religion first in order not to be misunderstood, even if one makes no rash boast of always having the strength to live up to it.

Diff'rent whatever its faults may be, has the virtue of sincerity. It is the truth, the inevitable truth, of the lives of the people in it as I see and know them. Whether it is psychoanalytically exact or not I will leave more dogmatic students of Freud and Jung than myself (or than Freud and Jung) to decide. It is life, nevertheless. I stick out for that— life that swallows all formulas. Some critics have said that Emma would not do this thing, would undoubtedly do that other. By Emma they must mean "a woman." But Emma is Emma. She is a whaling captain's daughter in a small New England seacoast town—surely no feminist. She is universal only in the sense that she reacts definitely to a definite sex-suppression, as every woman might. The form her reaction takes is absolutely governed by her environment and her own character. Let the captious be sure they know their Emmas as well as I do before they tell me how she would act.

There are objections to my end; but given Caleb and Emma the end to me is clearly inevitable. The youthful Emma refuses to accept the compromise of a human being for her dream Caleb. As the years go by she lives alone with her dream lover, the real Caleb fading into a friend. But suddenly she realizes youth is gone and the possibility of her dream lover forevermore. She snatches after him in a panic— and gets a Benny. She must re-create her god in this lump of mud. When it finally is brought home to her that mud is mud, she cries after the real Caleb, seeing him now for the first time. But he is gone. There is nothing for her to do but follow him. As for Caleb, he dies because it is not in him to compromise. He belongs to the old iron school of Nantucket-New Bedford whalemen whose slogan was "A dead whale or a stove boat." The whale in this case is transformed suddenly into a malignant Moby Dick who has sounded to depths forever out of reach. Caleb's boat is stove, his quest is ended. He goes with his ship.

There are objections to the play as pathological, but I protest that is putting the accent where none was intended, where only contributing circumstance was meant. And someone has said to me that all the people in the play were either degenerates or roughs—at which I was properly stunned, because I consider all of the characters, with the exception of Benny, to be perfectly regular human beings even as you and I. Dividing folks into moral castes has never been one of my favorite moral occupations.

And then there was someone, I have heard, who attributed to the author Caleb's remark that "folks be all crazy and rotten to the core." Upon which I grab the shoelace (but did they have them, though?) of the author of Hamlet, and going aloft to the dizzy height of his instep, inquire pipingly whether it was he or Macbeth who said, "It is a tale told by an idiot, full of sound and fury, signifying nothing."

Damn the optimists anyway! They make life so darned hopeless!

Letters to George Jean Nathan†

[*On* Welded]

Brook Farm / Ridgefield, Connecticut / May 7, 1923

Dear Nathan:

Nevertheless, I am convinced "Welded" is the best yet. I'm glad to get Mencken's[1] letter but I must confess the greater part of his comment seems irrelevant as criticism of my play. To point out its weakness as realism (in the usual sense of that word) is to confuse what is obviously part of my deliberate intention.

Damn that word, "realism"! When I first spoke to you of the play as a "last word in realism," I meant something "really real," in the sense of being spiritually true, not meticulously life-like—an interpretation of actuality by a distillation, an elimination of most realistic trappings, an intensification of human lives into clear symbols of truth.

Here's an example: Mencken says: "The man haranguing the street-walker is surely not a man who ever actually lived." Well, he surely is to me and, what is more to my point, he is also much more than that. He is Man dimly aware of recurring experience, groping for the truth behind the realistic appearances of himself, and of love and life. For the moment his agony gives him vision of the truth behind the real.

I can't agree that the speeches in this scene are "banal" or the ideas "rubber stamp." In fact, I'm positive it's the deepest and truest, as well as the best written scene I've ever done. Perhaps it isn't "plausible"—but the play is about love as a life-force, not as an intellectual conception, and the plausibilities of realism don't apply. Reason has no business in the theatre anyway, any more than it has in a church. They are both either below—or above it.

But I won't rave on. I'll grant this much for your criticisms—that parts of the dialogue are still, I find, "speechy" and artificial but that will all be gone over and fixed. It's the slopping-over of too much eagerness to say it all.

Thank Mencken for me for reading it. I'm sorry it didn't "knock him dead" to repay him for his trouble.

---

† The first two letters to Nathan are in the collection at the Cornell University Library and are reprinted by permission of the Cornell University Library and O'Neill Library Estate (Yale Committee on Library Property). The third letter was published in George Jean Nathan, *Intimate Note-*

books (New York: Alfred A. Knopf, Inc., 1932) and is reprinted by permission of The O'Neill Library Estate. Nathan (1882–1958) was for many years the dean of New York drama critics.

1. H. L. Mencken (1880–1956), an American journalist, editor, essayist, and critic [*Editor*].

Well, just wait until you see it played! (if it's done right). I'm hoping that may make you recant.

My best to you both.
Sincerely,
Eugene O'Neill

[On Desire Under the Elms]

"Camprea" / South Shore, Paget W. / Bermuda / March 26, 1925
Dear Nathan:
   * * * What I think everyone missed in "Desire" is the quality in it I set most store by—the attempt to give an epic tinge to New England's inhibited life-lust, to make its inexpressiveness poetically expressive, to release it. It's just that—the poetical (in the broadest and deepest sense) vision illuminating even the most sordid and mean blind alleys of life—which I'm convinced is, and is to be, *my* concern and justification as a dramatist. * * *

Sincerely,
Eugene O'Neill

[On the Playwright Today]

The playwright today must dig at the roots of the sickness of today as he feels it—the death of the Old God and the failure of science and materialism to give any satisfying new One for the surviving primitive religious instinct to find a meaning for life in, and to comfort its fears of death with. It seems to me that anyone trying to do big work nowadays must have this big subject behind all the little subjects of his plays or novels, or he is simply scribbling around on the surface of things and has no more real status than a parlor entertainer.

[A Conversational Remark]†

Most modern plays are concerned with the relation between man and man, but that does not interest me at all. I am interested only in the relation between man and God.

A Letter to Arthur Hobson Quinn‡

It's not in me to pose much as a "misunderstood one," but it does seem discouragingly (that is, if one lacked a sense of ironic humor!)

† From *Nine Plays by Eugene O'Neill*, with an introduction by Joseph Wood Krutch. Copyright 1932 and renewed 1960 by Random House, Inc. P. xvii. Reprinted by permission of Random House, Inc.
‡ From a letter to Arthur Hobson Quinn pub-lished in Quinn's *A History of American Drama*, Volume II (New York: F. S. Crofts and Company, 1945). P. 199. Reprinted by permission of The O'Neill Library Estate. Quinn (1875–1960) was a professor of English and historian of the American drama.

evident to me that most of my critics don't want to see what I'm trying to do or how I'm trying to do it, although I flatter myself that end and means are characteristic, individual and positive enough not to be mistaken for anyone's else, or for those of any "modern" or "pre-modern" school. To be called a "sordid realist" one day, a "grim, pessimistic Naturalist" the next, a "lying Moral Romanticist" the next, etc. is quite perplexing—not to add the *Times* editorial that settled *Desire* once and for all by calling it a "Neo-Primitive," a Mastisse of the drama, as it were! So I'm really longing to explain and try and convince some sympathetic ear that I've tried to make myself a melting pot for all these methods, seeing some virtues for my ends in each of them, and thereby, if there is enough real fire in me, boil down to my own technique. But where I feel myself most neglected is just where I set most store by myself—as a bit of a poet, who has labored with the spoken word to evolve original rhythms of beauty, where beauty apparently isn't—*Jones, Ape, God's Chillun, Desire*, etc.—and to see the transfiguring nobility of tragedy, in as near the Greek sense as one can grasp it, in seemingly the most ignoble, debased lives. And just here is where I am a most confirmed mystic, too, for I'm always, always trying to interpret Life in terms of lives, never just lives in terms of character. I'm always acutely conscious of the Force behind—Fate, God, our biological past creating our present, whatever one calls it—Mystery certainly—and of the one eternal tragedy of Man in his glorious, self-destructive struggle to make the Force express him instead of being, as an animal is, an infinitesimal incident in its expression. And my profound conviction is that this is the only subject worth writing about and that it is possible—or can be— to develop a tragic expression in terms of transfigured modern values and symbols in the theatre which may to some degree bring home to members of a modern audience their ennobling identity with the tragic figures on the stage. Of course, this is very much of a dream, but where the theatre is concerned, one must have a dream, and the Greek dream in tragedy is the noblest ever!

From an Interview with Oliver M. Sayler

The theatre to me *is* life—the substance and interpretation of life. . . . [And] life is struggle, often, if not usually, unsuccessful struggle; for most of us have something within us which prevents us from accomplishing what we dream and desire. And then, as we progress, we are always seeing further than we can reach. I suppose that is one reason why I have come to feel so indifferent toward political and social movements of all kinds. Time was when I was an active socialist, and, after that, a philosophical anarchist. But today I can't feel that anything like that really matters. It is rather amusing to me to see how seriously some people take politics and social questions and how much they expect of them. Life as a whole is changed very little, if at all, as a result of their course. It seems to me that, as far as we can judge, man is much the same creature, with the same primal emotions and ambitions and motives, the same powers and the same weaknesses, as in the time when the Aryan race started toward Europe from the slopes of the Himalayas. He has become better acquainted with those powers and those weaknesses, and he is learning ever so slowly how to control them. The birth-cry of the higher men is almost audible, but they will not come by tinkering with externals or by legislative or social fiat. They will come at the command of the imagination and the will.

HAROLD CLURMAN

[Long Day's Journey into Night]†

1956

Eugene O'Neill wrote *Long Day's Journey into Night* in 1940. Since it is a painfully autobiographical work, he did not wish to have it published or performed until twenty-five years after his death. His wife, Carlotta Monterey O'Neill, to whom the play is touchingly dedicated, has consented to have it published and performed three years after his death. I believe she was right. Who knows what such a play—or any play—will mean twenty-five years after an author's death? At the present moment, the play is a precious gift to us—regardless of its ultimate value.

I say this, though on a first reading I cannot determine what I actually think of it as a work of art or simply as a play. I am moved and fascinated by it in a personal way. The fact that the Swedes were held by it and that they did not complain of its four and one-half hours of playing length indicate something about its theatrical viability.[1] It is indisputable that O'Neill's plays are nearly always more impressive on the stage than on the printed page. I should very much like to see this play done on or off Broadway. If such a play is "impractical" for our theatre, so much the worse for our theatre. The play is the treatment of the most serious playwright our country has produced.

To say this is not to set oneself down as an unqualified O'Neill admirer. O'Neill was a faulty craftsman; he was not a sound thinker. Though he probably read more extensively and profoundly than most of our playwrights, O'Neill could not by any "universal" standard be considered a cultivated man. His view of life is circumscribed; he is often raw, naïve, sentimental and pessimistic in a somewhat adolescent manner.

---

† Reprinted with permission of MacMillan Publishing Company from Harold Clurman *Lies Like Truth: Theatre Reviews and Essays* by Harold Clurman. Pp. 28–33. Copyright © 1958 by Harold Clurman; copyright renewed © 1983 by Juleen Compton.

1. The first production of *Long Day's Journey* took place at the Royal Dramatic theater, Stockholm, February 10, 1956 [*Editor*].

Yet to dwell on these shortcomings as if they negate the value of the man to our stage and to our culture is to confess one's own inadequate and bloodless response to the world we live in. For in a time and place where life is experienced either as a series of mechanistic jerks or sipped in polite doses of borrowed sophistication (when it is not dully recorded in a sort of statistical spiritual bookkeeping), O'Neill not only lived intensely but attempted with perilous honesty to contemplate, absorb and digest the meaning of his life and ours. He possessed an uncompromising devotion to the task he set himself: to present and interpret in stage terms what he had lived through and thought about—a devotion unique in our theatre.

What do we discover in *Long Day's Journey into Night?* Not only the specific sources of O'Neill's suffering: the father, whom he hated and loved, an old-time star actor with the yearning of an artist and the confusion of an ignorant boy ruined by the stage and by the general environment of the gaslight era; the mother, an innocent woman, isolated and bereft of everything but conventional "protection" and finally resorting to the solace of drugs; an older brother whose only rebellion is in blasphemy and alcohol; O'Neill himself, a hypersensitive tubercular boy in quest of a God whose Word builds no true house and achieves no tangible body in the brick desert of the New York to which his father came from the famines of Ireland.

We find O'Neill trying to probe the meaning of all this, making an almost violent effort not only to understand but to forgive—to free himself from resentment, to fight the fate which, as in the Greek plays, seems to burden him unmercifully because of the antecedent crimes of his family heritage.

The family's Catholicism is not so much a faith as a guilt. Because he feels guilt, O'Neill shifts between a self-pity which he despises and a burning blame which he keeps trying in this play (and his whole work) to fight off. The accusation of his own guilt and obsessive desire to purge himself of it through blame nags at him: hence the repetitiousness of phrases and scenes; it is a planned repetitiousness, often wearisome to the reader (or the spectator) but organic to the author.

From this sense of guilt—all his characters suffer it in one form or another—and a corresponding sense that the guilt feeling is in itself a sin or at least a fatal blemish comes a constant alternation of mood. Every character speaks in two voices, two moods—one of rage, the other of apology. This produces a kind of moral schizophrenia which in some of O'Neill's other plays has necessitated an interior monologue and a speech for social use (*Strange Interlude*), or, as in *The Great God Brown* and *Days Without End*, two sets of masks. In this everlasting duality with its equal pressures in several directions lies the brooding power, the emotional grip of O'Neill's work.

There are unforgettable speeches and scenes in *Long Day's Journey*. One of them is the father's confession of how he was destroyed by the success of a romantic melodrama which he felt constrained to play almost throughout his career because it guaranteed him thirty to forty thousand a year. (The triumph and doom of James O'Neill's life was the endless run all over the country of *The Count of Monte-Cristo.*) This is deeply perceptive as well as moving, because it not only touches off the usual case of the artist damaged by commerce, but because O'Neill shows how his immigrant father's fear of poverty led to a concern about money ("stinginess" his family called it) for which his sons hated him and which led to many disasters ostensibly remote from their point of origin. This is a dominant American (O'Neill) theme which finds many symbolic variant expressions in the plays: *Desire Under the Elms, The Great God Brown, Marco Millions.*

The father's confession leads to the boy's (the author's) own confession of what his youthful escapades at sea have meant to him: it is a dream of beatitude, a seeking for God and wholeness—as direct, unabashed and truly soulful as any ever to be written by an American dramatist. To which his father replies, "Yes, there's the *makings* of a poet in you all right," and O'Neill answers, "The *makings* of a poet. . . . I couldn't touch what I tried to tell you just now. I just stammered. That's the best I'll ever do. . . . Well, it will be faithful realism at least."

O'Neill's work is more than realism. And if it is stammering—it is still the most eloquent and significant stammer of the American theatre. We have not yet developed a cultivated speech that is either superior to it or as good.

Directed by José Quintero, *Long Day's Journey into Night* is a play everyone should see and admire. No matter how one views it, it is impressive. It is not only unique among American plays, but in O'Neill's work itself. For it is an unabashedly autobiographical statement, something torn in agonized honesty from the memory and conscience of its author—who appears to have been compelled to set down this testament of his early home life to preserve his sanity. His chief, one might almost say his only, purpose was revelation to himself to himself. There is something moving, even great, in the impulse of the play, and no one can witness it without reverence for the *selflessness* of this extremely personal act.

The result, artistically speaking, is a solid (despite its length), unadorned and arresting piece of realism. What is remarkable about this is that O'Neill, reputedly the archrealist of the American drama, was never wholly a realist; he was largely a romantic—even something of a mystic. He was a romantic struggling to wrest meaning out of the painful data of his life, hope out of the sadness that never ceased to overwhelm him. Yet in this play where he undertook to expose the core and cause of his melancholy—his overpowering, majestic father, his envenomed brother, his shattered, innocent babe of a mother—in this play which he wrote as a release from his torment, as an expiation, as an effort at compassionate understanding and finally to enable himself to forgive, the texture is harder, less evocative, less profound in mood or meaning than in his technically and intellectually more fumbling plays. One leaves *Long Day's Journey* with a sense of stunned awe, but not emotionally transfigured.

One reason for this, I suspect, is that in his determination to be utterly objective—to avoid pitfalls of sentimentality and self-pity—O'Neill, who was neither a thinker nor a sharply observant depicter of character (the portraits in this play are convincing but rudimentary), lost some of the intuitive feeling which informs nearly all his work with a brooding and penetrating power far greater than anything that can be measured by a rational yardstick. O'Neill, the romantic though only half-articulate poet, yielded himself to the fullness of life's turmoil. He could not entirely cope with it; but for all that, it became intensely dramatic and palpitant in his presentation.

O'Neill's formative years, epitomized in the play's long day in 1912, were part of a period when the American experience—no longer a fresh adventure, a healthy exercise in discovery, pluck and epic struggle—hung heavy on the citizens of our big cities and towns. The massive wealth was its raw patches of hangdog poverty, the overfed acquistiveness and the depleted inner energies, the proud muscularity coupled with increasing enervation, went into making that murky brown, dejected yet glamorous gloom which enveloped a giant people. This was the later-day period of America's coming to consciousness, and no one in the theatre ever expressed it nearly as well as O'Neill. But, strangely enough, there is less in this atmosphere in *Long Day's Journey*, which purports to be a forthright document, than in his dramatic inventions, which often range very far from home.

The production of the play may be another cause for my reaction to it. It is a faithful, thoroughly intelligent and professionally knowledgeable production, wholly devoted to the realistic letter of the play. But by being so literal an embodiment of the dramatist's text the production comes to share the play's limitations, whereas it should transcend them. Means might have been found to create from the climate of O'Neill's spirit a greater feeling of shadow and depth out of which the play's figures might emerge with a more poetic and grander stature.

Fredric March and Florence Eldridge, excellent and finely motivated actors though they are, provide rather more characterization than creative interpretation. They excite our interest but tell us little more than what O'Neill has set down verbally. For sheer virtuosity—taking the stage, as professionals say—Jason Robards as the elder brother in the best-focused scene of the production—a drunken midnight exchange with his brother—makes the most vivid theatrical impression. A greater scene—the final confrontation of father and younger son—fails of its full possibilities because the actors (March and Bradford Dillman as the boy) concentrate more on the momentary situation and on the action

of the words than on the over-all inspirational source which gives the
scene its lyric essence and thematic inevitability. For what the play deals
with is not so much the details of one family's misery as the submerged
struggle against the dead weight of material pressures in a world where
the needs of the human soul are clamorous yet barely recognized.

RICHARD B. SEWALL

Long Day's Journey into Night†

What keeps *Long Day's Journey into Night* from "dwindling to a sorrowful tale" is this same capacity for suffering—and for learning from
it—on the part of the four Tyrones, the name O'Neill gives his own
family in this autobiographical play. (They are: James Tyrone, the actor-
father; Mary his wife, far gone in dope; Jamie, the older, wastrel son;
and Edmund, O'Neill himself at twenty-three, the would-be writer and
incipient consumptive.) Each one, during the long day of the play, goes
through a kind of agon, not the lonely ordeal of the hero but inseparable
from the ordeal of the family, so inextricably—and fatefully—are these
four lives woven. No one dominates the scene; there is no Jobian[1] figure
to confront whatever it is that has brought this family to the point of
dissolution. One is reminded of the wrangling Karamazovs; but there is
no Father Zossima to define the evil and send out his Alyosha to do
battle.[2] The fog that thickens during the play is, in one sense, a fitting
symbol: these are the "fog people" (as Edmund calls them, including
himself), individually all but lost in the fog of temperament until, in-
teracting much as had the Karamazovs, in the very torture of their
interaction they have glimpses through the fog to new truth.

The play brings up vividly the question of the involvement of the
tragic artist in his own fictions, a quality in contrast to the so-called
detachment of the satirist or ironist. The closer to modern times, the
more such involvement can be documented. O'Neill made his own
involvement poignantly clear. To his wife Carlotta on their twelfth
wedding anniversary, he wrote:

> Dearest: I give you the original of this play of old sorrow,
> written in tears and blood. A sadly inappropriate gift, it would
> seem, for a day celebrating happiness. But you will understand.
> I mean it as a tribute to your love and tenderness which gave
> me the faith in love that enabled me to face my dead at last

† From Richard B. Sewall, *The Vision of Tragedy*,
third edition, New York, 1990. Copyright Richard
B. Sewall. Reprinted by permission of Richard B.
Sewall.
1. A reference to the long-suffering title character
of the Book of Job in the Bible [*Editor*].

2. In Fedor Dostoevsky's novel *The Brothers Karamazov* (1879–80) the brothers struggle with their
depraved father and themselves. In that struggle
Alyosha is the youngest, a gentle and loving figure
who tries to save his brothers, and Father Zossima
is his sainted religious advisor [*Editor*].

and write this play—write it with deep pity and understanding
and forgiveness for *all* the four haunted Tyrones.

   These twelve years, Beloved One, have been a Journey into
Light—into love. You know my gratitude. And my love!

"To face my dead at last." This confrontation, the "facing," had a
long beginning. (O'Neill was sixty-three when he completed the play.)
It was as surely a quest for meaning as any of the great ones of our
study.[3] The pattern is familiar: out of the welter of experience, out of
the suffering, comes the tragic question, "Why?" In his afflictions, Job
sought meaning: "Teach me and I will hold my tongue, and cause me
to understand wherein I have erred." Lear asked, "Is there any cause in
nature that makes these hard hearts?" And Kalganov, weeping over the
degradation of Dmitri,[4] asks, "What can mankind be after this?" When
O'Neill calls his family the "four haunted Tyrones," he suggests his own
sense of the mystery. Writing the play was the result of his forty-year
attempt to pierce it—to "understand" it, as he wrote to Carlotta, and
"pity" and "forgive." The "tears and blood" suggest the suffering it cost
him.[5]

   Each of the Tyrones, as if in turn, indicates the take-off point of
O'Neill's quest and, had it not been for the play, the end of it—in
fatalism, despair, bitterness. Mary sees them all as prisoners of the past:
"None of us can help the things life has done to us. . . . He [Jamie]
can't help being what the past has made him. Any more than your father
can. Or you [Edmund]. Or I." Edmund would simply deny the problem:
"Who wants to see life as if is, if they can help it? That's what I wanted—
to be alone with myself in another world where truth is untrue and life
can hide from itself." Toward the end, Mary asks a question for them
all: "What is it I'm looking for? I know it's something I lost," and we
see her husband James "trying to shake off his hopeless stupor." "It's no
good, Papa," says Jamie, and quotes Swinburne:

> There is no help, for all things are so,
> And all the world is bitter as a tear.

Or, as Job's wife advised, "Curse God, and die."

   But no one curses God, and no one commits suicide. The very stamina
of these people is awesome as they survive hour after hour (or so it seems)
of the often furious exchange of blame and counterblame. The long day
is very long, reaching far into the night. Edmund's "fog people" hardly
does justice to their emotional capacity—the bursts of temper, the clashes

---

3. That is, in Sewall's study of tragedy. Some of
the "great ones" studied are the Book of Job, Sophocles' *Oedipus the King*, Marlowe's *Dr. Faustus*,
Shakespeare's *King Lear*, and Melville's *Moby
Dick* [Editor].

4. In *The Brothers Karamozov* [Editor].

5. The play has been much discussed in its dramatic, aesthetic, and autobiographical dimen-

sions. I have found most helpful: Doris V. Falk,
Eugene O'Neill and the Tragic Tension (1958);
Travis Bogard, *Contour in Time: The Plays of Eugene O'Neill* (1972); Leonard Chabrowe, *Ritual
and Pathos—The Theater of O'Neill* (1976); Arthur
and Barbara Gelb, *O'Neill* (1960); and Louis Shaeffer, *O'Neill: Son and Playwright* (1968).

of temperament, the excruciating self-revelations, and (most impressive) the love and loyalty that, for all the bickering, keep them from distintegration, as individuals and as a family. If none of the characters in the play achieves the "deep pity and understanding and forgiveness" of the note to Carlotta, they all have moments of redemptive insight. This is not to say that the family (or any member of it) is redeemed. There is no assurance that the next day might be a repetition of this long one; but the play shows, clearly and powerfully, how it might have been. The ultimate perception was O'Neill's: "the faith in love that enabled me to face my dead."

The play opens on an August morning in 1912 with the Tyrones in their New London home near the sea. We are confronted at once with the precariousness of the family situation. As Tyrone and Mary emerge from breakfast, their mood seems happy and loving: Tyrone gives Mary a "playful hug" and calls her "a fine armful." But she is clearly on edge, and she jokes a bit caustically about Tyrone's huge appetite and his inept business dealings. They worry about Edmund's illness and Jamie's failure. When the boys come in, the discords mount, and Tyrone's forced good humor is seen for what it is.

Immediately there is a tiff between Tyrone and Jamie, a prelude to the pattern of encounters to come: blame, counterblame, uneasy truce. It starts with Mary's seemingly innocent remark about Tyrone's snoring; then Jamie's "The Moor, I know his trumpet"; then Tyrone's "If it takes my snoring to make you remember Shakespeare instead of the dope sheet on the ponies, I hope I'll keep on with it." Jamie wants out: "What's all the fuss about? Let's forget it." But one word borrows another: "Yes, forget!" says Tyrone. "Forget everything and face nothing. It's a convenient philosophy if you've no ambition in life except to—." Mary steps in and changes the subject. Truce.

Soon the family is laughing over Edmund's story of old Shaughnessy and his pigs and millionaire Harker's ice pond. But the mood doesn't last. Tyrone suspects the boys, with their "damned Socialist anarchist sentiments," of wanting to get him in trouble with Harker. Mary tries to soothe him. Edmund, in "sudden nervous exasperation," leaves the room; and Mary, "with a strange obstinate set to her face," goes to confer with Bridget the cook. Another truce.

Tyrone and Jamie are left alone, and the stage is set for their first major encounter. The theme, as usual, is guilt. Jamie blames Tyrone for Edmund's illness: he was too stingy to pay for "a real doctor" when Edmund first got sick. Tyrone counters with the terrible accusation that Jamie, out of jealousy, corrupted Edmund to undermine his health. "That's a lie!" Jamie shouts. "I won't stand for that, Papa . . . Oh, for Christ's sake, Papa! Can't you lay off me!" For a moment the two touch bottom: the charges could hardly have been worse. But then something new happens. It is as if both men have been shocked into their senses by what they have said—and shocked into their better natures. Tyrone's thoughts turn to Mary and the bad luck that Edmund's illness should come at a time when her own state is so precarious. His voice "grows husky and trembles a little": "It's damnable she should have this to upset her, just when she needs peace and freedom from worry. She's been so well in the two months since she came home. It's been heaven to me. This home has been a home again. But I needn't tell you, Jamie." The two suddenly see eye to eye. A stage direction makes is explicit: "His son looks at him, for the first time with an understanding sympathy. It is as if suddenly a deep bond of common feeling existed between them in which their antagonisms could be forgotten." Jamie says ("almost gently"): "I've felt the same way, Papa."

But, being what they are (O'Neill seems to be saying), they cannot sustain this mood for long. Within seconds they are quarreling again. Jamie picks up the theme of his mother's illness and blames it on Tyrone: he was too stingy to hire a proper doctor at the time of Edmund's birth. Tyrone's furious "That's a lie!" seems likely to lead to violence except for Mary (again), whose unexpected entrance brings about another truce.

And now Mary herself has her turn. She brings Act I to a close in a flurry of accusations and self-pity. She pours out her heart to Edmund. Everything is Tyrone's fault. He was too stingy to give the family a decent home, with an automobile and nice friends. She is lonely. She is worried about Edmund's health. The family doesn't trust her—they keep spying on her. Edmund's "Mama! Stop it!" is unavailing, and he goes, leaving her alone. As the curtain falls, she is "terribly tense . . . seized by a fit of nervous panic," on the point of another fix. When she reappears in Act II (noon of the same day), "Her eyes are brighter, and there is a peculiar detachment in her voice and manner. . . ." While the others find momentary release in temper and (later) alcohol, she finds it in the detachment of morphine. "The only way,"she tells Edmund, "is to make yourself not care," and it is here that she slips into the fatalism that relieves everyone of blame and puts it all on "Life."

But neither she nor the others can rest long in such an evasion. This is important to the student of tragedy; for suffering we can call tragic is not to be resolved that easily. There is an echo here of the tragic Dostoevskian ethic, so clear with the Karamazovs, that there may be salvation in following one's nature, however violent or however extreme in other ways, to the very end—as Dmitri found "precious metal in the dirt." So it is that violence "becomes" these Tyrones. Mary's combative nature soon reasserts itself, and in the ensuing scenes none of the men escapes. Tyrone, she says, never wanted a home; he should have been a bachelor, with his barrooms and his cheap hotels. Jamie's alcoholism is all his fault, and now he lets the invalid Edmund take a drink: "Do you want to kill him?" she snaps. She turns on Jamie, accusing him of killing her second baby by deliberately exposing him to measles—again, out of jealousy.

Then, alone with Edmund, her favorite, she turns on *him* as the source of all her troubles. It was her illness at his birth that led to the quack doctor who prescribed the morphine. And now it's her worry over his health that has driven her to it again. Suddenly she checks herself, as if shocked by what she has said. She cries ("distractedly"), "But that's no excuse! I'm only trying to explain. It's not an excuse!" ("She hugs him to her—pleadingly.") "Promise me, dear, you won't believe I made you an excuse." But all Edmund can say ("bitterly") is, "What else can I believe?"

And now, in her near-panic, comes her moment of insight and gentleness. She confesses her lies and her guilt. "I don't blame you," she says to Edmund:

> "How could you believe me—when I can't believe myself?
> I've become such a liar. I never lied about anything once upon
> a time. Now I have to lie, especially to myself. I've never
> understood anything about it [her dependence on morphine],
> except that one day long ago I could no longer call my soul
> my own."

Once started, she experiences a tiny epiphany, a vision of a better time to come. It is as if O'Neill, in his quest, were uncovering in his family unsuspected areas of truth (and beauty and goodness). "Lowering her voice to a strange tone of whispered confidence," she pictures for Edmund a time when she might regain her soul, be forgiven, and be believed.

> "But some day, dear, I will find it again—some day when
> you're all well, and I see you healthy and happy and successful,
> and I don't have to feel guilty any more—some day when the
> Blessed Virgin Mary forgives me and gives me back the faith
> in Her love and pity I used to have in my convent days, and
> I can pray to Her again—when She sees no one in the world
> can believe in me even for a moment any more, then She
> will believe in me, and with Her help it will be so easy. I will
> hear myself scream with agony, and at the same time I will
> laugh because I will be so sure of myself."

But this mood doesn't last, either, and like all such moments in the play it is ambivalent. It may have been partly a pose for Edmund's sake. He "remains hopelessly silent," and she concludes curtly, "Of course, you can't believe that, either." Alone a moment later as the scene ends, she is glad the others are gone, glad "to get rid of them." "Then Mother of God," she asks, "why do I feel so lonely?" Pose or no pose, she speaks the plain truth here: she can't get along without her family. Nor can they get along without her.

One simple criterion of tragedy lies in the question, How does our first view of the protagonist (in this case the family) differ from what we see at the end? Has there been a gain, if only minimal, in humanity, self-knowledge, wisdom, insight—all that we have subsumed under the notion of perception? What has been won from "the fine hammered steel of woe"?

When, at the end of Act II, the Tyrones disperse for the afternoon, there seems no good reason, except food and shelter, why they should ever assemble again. Each has said enough, one would think, to make further relations impossible. It is no wonder that when Tyrone and Edmund reappear at dinner time (Act III) they have had a lot to drink. (When Jamie shows up at midnight, in Act IV, he is drunk.) Hearing their voices, Mary says, "Why are they coming back? They don't want to. . . ." And only a few moments later, when the bickering starts all over again, Tyrone says, "Oh, for the love of God! I'm a fool for coming home!" But here they are, together again. As the two men come in, Mary says to herself that she'd "much rather be alone" but in the next breath ("pathetically relieved and eager") adds, "Oh, I'm so glad they've come! I've been so horribly lonely!" What is it at the very end of the play, when the three men sit in silence during Mary's long soliloquy, that gives the scene, as here in this reunion for dinner, a power that goes beyond pathos? How in the last two acts and especially in the final scene does the family transcend itself, leaving us not so much in tears as in awed silence?

The progress, or "journey," of the play is toward a deeper understanding of each other's nature on the part of the four Tyrones. What they go through—what they put themselves through—is hardly heroic suffering. There are no Jobian afflictions, no state is threatened, no fear (except Edmund's illness) for life or limb. What takes place is all *within*— within the confines of the Tyrone living room, within a single day, within the family (Cathleen, the maid, is the only outsider and has no idea of what is going on). The only intrusions from the outside world are the doctor's verdict on Edmund and the sound of the foghorn and the fog itself, which intensifies the fierce concentration of the scene. "It hides you from the world and the world from you," Mary says. The last two acts reiterate the themes already stated—Tyrone's tightfistedness, Mary's addiction, Jamie's jealousy of Edmund, the strange mixture of emotions each member of the family has for the others: pride and shame, love and hate, contempt and admiration. What is new is the degree of understanding each of them achieves. The climax comes in the alcoholic unburdenings of the men and in Mary's dope-induced finale at the end, but not before the old recriminations have gone back and forth in bitterness and (twice) in physical violence. It is as if the truth has had to wait until every other route (and they themselves) has been exhausted. They have had to find out that the endless blame-laying was a dead-end, that there would be no release until they could look within themselves and be honest to what they saw. This is the true within-ness of the play, the true suffering.

It is here that the magnitude of the play—and of the characters—lies.

Nothing would have happened had they not been capable of submitting themselves to each other, of undergoing the agony not only of self-disclosure but of listening to the disclosures of the others. No one walks out and slams the door. They bear it out to the end—and the end is not bitter.

The sequence begins, as we have seen, with Mary's confession to Edmund, who listens in silence. What he learns comes out later as he and his father talk about Mary's condition during their never-finished game of cards at the beginning of Act IV. Edmund stumbles on a major insight:

> "The hardest thing to take [he tells his father] is the blank wall
> she builds around her. Or it's more like a bank of fog in which
> she hides herself. Deliberately, that's the hell of it! You know
> something in her does it deliberately—to get beyond our reach,
> to be rid of us, to forget we're alive! It's as if, in spite of loving
> us, she hated us!"

There is a moment of calm as Tyrone "remonstrates gently": "Now, now, lad. It's not her. It's the damned poison." But the damned poison, Edmund points out ("in bitter accusation") is not her fault: "I know damned well she's not to blame! And I know who is! You are! Your damned stinginess! . . . Jesus, when I think of it I hate your guts!" Then comes more vindictive rage until he, too, near bottom, comes to his senses—and to the same insight he had about his mother: that human beings are capable of loving and hating at the same time. "I didn't mean it, Papa. I'm like Mama, I can't help liking you, in spite of everything." Later in Act IV, after Jamie's shocking confession that it was indeed true that he had intentionally corrupted Edmund, he too finds himself saying, "But don't get the wrong idea, Kid. I love you more that I hate you."

As the card game goes on, we realize that the bottom has not quite been reached. It is not until Edmund, "bursting with anger," his "voice trembling with rage" and "shaken by a fit of coughing," accuses his father of wanting to save money by sending him to a state institution that Tyrone himself is shocked into his better nature. Now, as "his head bows" and "he stares dully at the cards on the table," he talks "without resentment": "A stinking old miser. Well, maybe you're right." And he launches into a long confession in an attempt to explain himself—his poverty-stricken youth in Ireland, the struggle to establish himself in America, his early years in the theater and his "good bad luck" in finding "the big money-maker" (*The Count of Monte Cristo*).[6] The stage directions indicate the mixture of "guilty contrition," "self-contempt," "drunken peevishness," "grim humor," even sentimental nostalgia ("He wipes the tears from his eyes"), and (finally) bitterness: "What the hell

6. This is the play, a version of the Dumas romance, that brought fame and fortune to James O'Neill; but as Arthur and Barbara Gelb point out (p. 48)," . . . it put a strict limitation on his career. It became a trap from which he never escaped and into which Eugene O'Neill was born."

was it I wanted to buy, I wonder, that was worth—Well, no matter. It's a late day for regrets." Edmund is "moved, stares at his father with understanding," and says ("slowly"), I'm glad you've told me this, Papa. I know you a lot better now."

One by one, each member of the family goes through the same harrowing process. Now it's Edmund's turn. "You've just told me some high spots in your memories," he says to his father. "Want to hear mine?" What follows is a long, lyric reminiscence of his life at sea. He recalls two episodes when, "for a second," there was "meaning." The first was on a square rigger bound for Buenos Aires, driving along at fourteen knots under a full moon in the Trades. "I became drunk with the beauty and singing rhythm of it," he says, "and for a moment I lost myself—actually lost my life." He became one with the "white sails and flying spray," he *became* "beauty and rhythm . . . moonlight and the ship and the high dim-starred sky." He felt "peace and unity and wild joy." He "belonged . . . to Life itself! To God, if you want to put it that way." The second moment was on a steamship of the American Line, on lookout in the dawn watch—a "moment of ecstatic freedom . . . the peace, the end of the quest, the last harbor, the joy of belonging to a fulfillment beyond men's lousy, pitiful, greedy fears and hopes and dreams!" In such moments it seems as if a veil were drawn back: "For a second you see—and seeing the secret, are the secret." But the veil drops back again and "you are alone, lost in the fog again, and you stumble on toward nowhere, for no good reason!" At this point, "he grins wryly" by way of ironic comment on his ultimate confession:

> "It was a great mistake, my being born a man. I would have
> been much more successful as a seagull or a fish. As it is, I
> will always be a stranger who never feels at home, who does
> not really want and is not really wanted, who can never belong,
> who must always be a little in love with death!"

Bitter as his conclusion is, he is blaming no one but himself, and his candor brings him and his father to a moment of understanding. Tyrone "stares at him—impressed." "Yes, there's the makings of a poet in you all right." Then, "protesting uneasily": "But that's morbid craziness about not being wanted and loving death." Edmund, perhaps noting the uneasiness of his father's protest, ignores the morbidness and picks up the matter of the poet:

> "The *makings* of a poet. No. . . . I couldn't touch what I tried
> to tell you just now. I just stammered. That's the best I'll ever
> do. I mean, if I live. Well, it will be faithful realism, at least.
> Stammering is the native eloquence of us fog people."

Whether O'Neill actually thought this about himself at age twenty-three, and the way his career belied it, are matters that go beyond the play. What happens in the play is that the moment of harmony between father and son is interupted by Jamie, who comes in drunk. "Get him to bed, Edmund," says Tyrone. "I'll go out on the porch. He has a tongue like an adder when he's drunk. I'd only lose my temper."

The scene that follows is Jamie's. It's his turn now. No great nature is revealed, but there are surprises, like Dmitri's parting words to Alyosha, "Love Ivan!" He is more than the "drunken hulk" his father calls him. His course during the scene is uneven, but it follows the pattern made familiar by the others. From the moment he enters ("Oh, hello, Kid. I'm as drunk as a fiddler's bitch") he is refreshingly honest. He talks frankly but compassionately about his whore, Fat Violet, and, drunk as he is, he is concerned about Edmund: "I know, Kid, it's been a lousy day for you." And then "in vino veritas" (he uses the phrase), it all comes out: his jealousy of Edmund from the first—"Mama's baby and Papa's pet!"; his deliberate attempt to pull Edmund down with him: "Mama and Papa are right. I've been a rotten bad influence. And worst of it is, I did it on purpose"; his love-hate of Edmund; and finally his own explanation, which lays blame on no one but himself: "Can't help it. I hate myself. Got to take revenge. On everyone else. Especially you."

Jamie doesn't repent or promise to reform. He warns Edmund to be on his guard—he'd still stab him in the back "at the first chance I get." He simply tells the truth: "Remember I warned you—for your sake. Give me credit. Greater love hath no man than this, that he saveth his brother from himself." And finally, before sinking into a drunken doze: "Don't die on me. You're all I've got left. God bless you, K. O."

Tyrone, having overheard the last part of the talk, comes in from the porch. "His face is stern and disgusted but at the same time pitying." Looking down on Jamie "with a bitter sadness," he says, "A sweet spectacle for me! My first-born, who I hoped would bear my name in honor and dignity, who showed such brilliant promise!" Edmund, who has hardly noticed Tyrone's entrance, finally breaks his silence: "Keep quiet, can't you, Papa?"

Pity touched with awe is the mood of the final scene. The family has resisted all the forces that would pull it apart. Mary, who has been moving about upstairs for some time and causing anxious remarks from the men, is heard playing the piano, awkwardly, like a schoolgirl. She suddenly appears "in a sky-blue dressing gown," carrying her wedding dress. She is lost in morphine. Jamie's sardonic comment, "The Mad Scene. Enter Ophelia!" infuriates the other two. Edmund slaps him across the mouth, and Tyrone blurts out, "The dirty blackguard! His own mother . . . I'll kick him out in the gutter tomorrow, so help me God." But Jamie's quick admission—"All right, Kid. Had it coming. But I told you how much I'd hoped—" and his sobbing breaks the anger of his father, who pleads, "Jamie, for the love of God, stop it!" It is Mary's quiet, girl-like, detached presence that quiets the men. The rest of the play, save for Jamie's lugubrious quotations from Swinburne, is Mary's. She has, quite literally, the last word.

She moves about the stage like a sleepwalker, talking to herself, ignoring the others. Tyrone, "in anguish," gently takes the wedding dress from her, which she relinquishes "with the shy politeness of a well-bred young girl toward an elderly gentleman who relieves her of a bundle." The men, for all their drinking, are strangely sober. When Mary speaks, "they freeze into silence again, staring at her." Their first reaction, as she proceeds to act out "the mad scene," is hopelessness, and it is here that Jamie says, "It's no good, Papa," and quotes Swinburne. Tyrone gives up: "Oh, we're fools to pay any attention. It's the damned poison. . . . Pass me that bottle, Jamie. And stop reciting that damned morbid poetry. I won't have it in my house."

This turns out to be the last skirmish. They all pour drinks. As they are about to drink, there is an important stage direction: "Tyrone lifts his glass and his sons follow suit mechanically, but before they can drink Mary speaks and they slowly lower their drinks to the table, forgetting them." From here on, the men are under her spell. She "stares dreamily before her. Her face looks extraordinarily youthful and innocent." She reminisces about her days in the convent, about her talk with Mother Elizabeth, "so sweet and good," about praying to the Virgin and finding "peace again because I knew she heard my prayer." The men sit motionless and silent.

There is nothing "great" here, but there is a vision, dope-induced as it is, of the good (and true and beautiful). At least we see what might have been—and recall Alyosha's pastoral charge to the boys at the end of *The Brothers Karamazov*, which, if nothing else, made clear the values missing in that family. Neither Alyosha nor Mary brings about radical change. But when Alyosha talked, the boys stopped quarreling; and when Mary begins her soliloquy, the men put down their drinks and listen. Mary's final sentences end the play in a kind of ironic benediction: "That was in the winter of senior year. Then in the spring something happened to me. Yes, I remember. I fell in love with James Tyrone and was so happy for a time." As the curtain falls, only Tyrone "stirs in his chair."

Such was the situation in the O'Neill family, the play says, in "August, 1912." What "haunted" them? Nothing, surely, like the Curse on the House of Atreus, or a regicide, or the ancestral sins that so haunted Hawthorne. No one killed an albatross or was dismembered by a whale. Perhaps O'Neill's word "haunted" is to be explained mainly by the facts of inherited temperament—the family Irishness, of which he makes a good deal: the bursts of temper, the moodiness, the sudden extremes of emotion, the flamboyance and love of talk, the touch of the visionary in each of them, even Jamie. But temperament isn't all; it doesn't determine everything. O'Neill makes it clear that the fault (Tyrone quotes the passage) is not in their stars. And like all tragic faults (or flaws) it involves the exercise of the will.

Tragedy, to O'Neill, ennobled in art what he called man's "hopeless hopes."[7] If life in 1912 seemed hopeless, something in him—the dream, the vision, the hope, the very Irish vitality that is awesome in the play— kept him going, with the results we all know.[8] There is something here of the hopeless hope that kept young Quentin Compson burrowing into the story of his family in an attempt to understand and perhaps forgive; but we know that in *The Sound and the Fury* Faulkner has his young hero, unable to bear the burden, commit suicide. O'Neill bore it out to the end. He was once reported as saying, "I couldn't ever be negative about life. On that score you've got to decide YES or NO. And I'll always say YES."[9] There was a good deal of the Greek in him, as well as the Irish. "To O'Neill tragedy had the meaning the Greeks gave it, and it was their classic example that he tried to follow. He believed with the Greeks that tragedy always brought exaltation, 'an urge [he once said] toward life and ever more life.' "[1] Tragedy, he said, brought men "to spiritual understandings and released them from the petty greeds of everyday existence." Whatever it was that haunted his family—and him—he found release in his lifelong dedication to the tragic drama, to the dream, he said, that kept man "fighting, willing—living."

7. This and the following remarks by O'Neill on tragedy are quoted in Arthur and Barbara Gelb, *O'Neill*, p. 5.
8. The Gelbs pay this tribute to O'Neill's achievement: "For over a quarter of a century he had battled to lift American drama to the level of art and keep it there, to mold a native, tragic stage literature. The first American to succeed as a writer of theatre tragedy, he had continued shattering Broadway convention and made possible the evolution of an adult theatre in which such playwrights as Thornton Wilder, Tennessee Williams and Arthur Miller could function" (p. 5).
9. *Time*, October 21, 1946. Quoted in Chabrowe, *Ritual and Pathos—The Theater of O'Neill*, p. 198.
1. Arthur and Barbara Gelb, *O'Neill*, p. 5.

Bertolt Brecht
and
Mother Courage and Her Children

BERTOLT BRECHT

"Theatre for Pleasure and Theatre for Instruction"†

The Epic Theatre

Many people imagine that the term 'epic theatre' is self-contradictory, as the epic and dramatic ways of narrating a story are held, following Aristotle, to be basically distinct. The difference between the two forms was never thought simply to lie in the fact that the one is performed by living beings while the other operates via the written word; epic works such as those of Homer and the medieval singers were at the same time theatrical performances, while dramas like Goethe' *Faust* and Byron's *Manfred* are agreed to have been more effective as books.[1] Thus even by Aristotle's definition[2] the difference between the dramatic and epic forms was attributed to their different methods of construction, whose laws were dealt with by two different branches of aesthetics. The method of construction depended on the different way of presenting the work to the public, sometimes via the stage, sometimes through a book; and independently of that there was the 'dramatic element' in epic works and the 'epic element' in dramatic. The bourgeois novel in the last century developed much that was 'dramatic', by which was meant the strong centralization of the story, a momentum that drew the separate parts into a common relationship. A particular passion of utterance, a certain emphasis on the clash of forces are hallmarks of the 'dramatic'. The epic writer Döblin[3] provided an excellent criterion when he said

† Reprinted by permission of Hill and Wang, a division of Farrar, Straus & Giroux, Inc. and Methuen London. Excerpt from *Brecht on Theatre: The Development of an Aesthetic* by Bertolt Brecht, translated by John Willett. Pp. 70–75. Translation copyright © 1964 by John Willett.

1. Johann Wolfgang von Goethe's *Faust* and Lord Byron's *Manfred* (1817) are dramas in verse more often read as poems than staged [*Editor*].
2. In the *Poetics* (c. 350–322 B.C.) [*Editor*].
3. Alfred Döblin (1878–1957), a young writer whom Brecht saw as a colleague in the 1920s and 1930s [*Editor*].

that with an epic work, as opposed to a dramatic, one can as it were take a pair of scissors and cut it into individual pieces, which remain fully capable of life.

This is no place to explain how the opposition of epic and dramatic lost its rigidity after having long been held to be irreconcilable. Let us just point out that the technical advances alone were enough to permit the stage to incorporate an element of narrative in its dramatic productions. The possibility of projections, the greater adaptability of the stage due to mechanization, the film, all completed the theatre's equipment, and did so at a point where the most important transactions between people could no longer be shown simply by personifying the motive forces or subjecting the characters to individual metaphysical powers.

To make these transactions intelligible the environment in which the people lived had to be brought to bear in a big and 'significant' way.

This environment had of course been shown in the existing drama, but only as seen from the central figure's point of view, and not as an independent element. It was defined by the hero's reactions to it. It was seen as a storm can be seen when one sees the ships on a sheet of water unfolding their sails, and the sails filling out. In the epic theatre it was to appear standing on its own.

The stage began to tell a story. The narrator was no longer missing, along with the fourth wall. Not only did the background adopt an attitude to the events on the stage—by big screens recalling other simultaneous events elsewhere, by projecting documents which confirmed or contradicted what the characters said, by concrete and intelligible figures to accompany abstract conversations, by figures and sentences to support mimed transactions whose sense was unclear—but the actors too refrained from going over wholly into their role, remaining detached from the character they were playing and clearly inviting criticism of him.

The spectator was no longer in any way allowed to submit to an experience uncritically (and without practical consequences) by means of simple empathy with the characters in a play. The production took the subject-matter and the incidents shown and put them through a process of alienation: the alienation that is necessary to all understanding. When something seems 'the most obvious thing in the world' it means that any attempt to understand the world has been given up.

What is 'natural' must have the force of what is startling. This is the only way to expose the laws of cause and effect. People's activity must simultaneously be so and be capable of being different.

It was all a great change.

The dramatic theatre's spectator says: Yes, I have felt like that too—Just like me—It's only natural—It'll never change—The sufferings of this man appal me, because they are inescapable—That's great art; it all seems the most obvious thing in the world—I weep when they weep, I laugh when they laugh.

The epic theatre's spectator says: I'd never have thought it—That's

not the way—That's extraordinary, hardly believable—It's got to stop—
The sufferings of this man appal me, because they are unnecessary—
That's great art: nothing obvious in it—I laugh when they weep, I weep
when they laugh.

The Instructive Theatre

The stage began to be instructive.

Oil, inflation, war, social struggles, the family, religion, wheat, the
meat market, all became subjects for theatrical representation. Choruses
enlightened the spectator about facts unknown to him. Films showed a
montage of events from all over the world. Projections added statistical
material. And as the 'background' came to the front of the stage so
people's activity was subjected to criticism. Right and wrong courses of
action were shown. People were shown who knew what they were doing,
and others who did not. The theatre became an affair for philosophers,
but only for such philosophers as wished not just to explain the world
but also to change it. So we had philosophy, and we had instruction.
And where was the amusement in all that? Were they sending us back
to school, teaching us to read and write? Were we supposed to pass
exams, work for diplomas?

Generally there is felt to be a very sharp distinction between learning
and amusing oneself. The first may be useful, but only the second is
pleasant. So we have to defend the epic theatre against the suspicion
that it is a highly disagreeable, humourless, indeed strenuous affair.

Well: all that can be said is that the contrast between learning and
amusing oneself is not laid down by divine rule; it is not one that has
always been and must continue to be.

Undoubtedly there is much that is tedious about the kind of learning
familiar to us from school, from our professional training, etc. But it
must be remembered under what conditions and to what end that takes
place.

It is really a commercial transaction. Knowledge is just a commodity.
It is acquired in order to be resold. All those who have grown out of
going to school have to do their learning virtually in secret, for anyone
who admits that he still has something to learn devalues himself as a
man whose knowledge is inadequate. Moreover the usefulness of learning is very much limited by factors outside the learner's control. There
is unemployment, for instance, against which no knowledge can protect
one. There is the division of labour, which makes generalized knowledge
unnecessary and impossible. Learning is often among the concerns of
those whom no amount of concern will get any forwarder. There is not
much knowledge that leads to power, but plenty of knowledge to which
only power can lead.

Learning has a very different function for different social strata. There
are strata who cannot imagine any improvement in conditions: they find

the conditions good enough for them. Whatever happens to oil they will benefit from it. And: they feel the years beginning to tell. There can't be all that many years more. What is the point of learning a lot now? They have said their final word: a grunt. But there are also strata 'waiting their turn' who are discontented with conditions, have a vast interest in the practical side of learning, want at all costs to find out where they stand, and know that they are lost without learning; these are the best and keenest learners. Similar differences apply to countries and peoples. Thus the pleasure of learning depends on all sorts of things; but none the less there is such a thing as pleasurable learning, cheerful and militant learning.

If there were not such amusement to be had from learning the theatre's whole structure would unfit it for teaching.

Theatre remains theatre even when it is instructive theatre, and in so far as it is good theatre it will amuse.

Theatre and Knowledge

But what has knowledge got to do with art? We know that knowledge can be amusing, but not everything that is amusing belongs in the theatre.

I have often been told, when pointing out the invaluable services that modern knowledge and science, if properly applied, can perform for art and specially for the theatre, that art and knowledge are two estimable but wholly distinct fields of human activity. This is a fearful truism, of course, and it is as well to agree quickly that, like most truisms, it is perfectly true. Art and science work in quite different ways: agreed. But, bad as it may sound, I have to admit that I cannot get along as an artist without the use of one or two sciences. This may well arouse serious doubts as to my artistic capacities. People are used to seeing poets as unique and slightly unnatural beings who reveal with a truly godlike assurance things that other people can only recognize after much sweat and toil. It is naturally distasteful to have to admit that one does not belong to this select band. All the same, it must be admitted. It must at the same time be made clear that the scientific occupations just confessed to are not pardonable side interests, pursued on days off after a good week's work. We all know how Goethe was interested in natural history, Schiller[4] in history: as a kind of hobby, it is charitable to assume. I have no wish promptly to accuse these two of having needed these sciences for their poetic activity; I am not trying to shelter behind them; but I must say that I do need the sciences. I have to admit, however, that I look askance at all sorts of people who I know do not operate on the level of scientific understanding: that is to say, who sing as the birds sing, or as people imagine the birds to sing. I don't mean by that that

4. Like Goethe, Friedrich von Schiller (1759–1805) was a poet and dramatist [Editor].

I would reject a charming poem about the taste of fried fish or the delights of a boating party just because the writer had not studied gastronomy or navigation. But in my view the great and complicated things that go on in the world cannot be adequately recognized by people who do not use every possible aid to understanding.

Let us suppose that great passions or great events have to be shown which influence the fate of nations. The lust for power is nowadays held to be such a passion. Given that a poet 'feels' this lust and wants to have somone strive for power, how is he to show the exceedingly complicated machinery within which the struggle for power nowadays takes place? If his hero is a politician, how do politics work? If he is a business man, how does business work? And yet there are writers who find business and politics nothing like so passionately interesting as the individual's lust for power. How are they to acquire the necessary knowledge? They are scarcely likely to learn enough by going round and keeping their eyes open, though even then it is more than they would get by just rolling their eyes in an exalted frenzy. The foundation of a paper like the *Völkischer Beobachter*[5] or a business like Standard Oil is a pretty complicated affair, and such things cannot be conveyed just like that. One important field for the playwright is psychology. It is taken for granted that a poet, if not an ordinary man, must be able without further instruction to discover the motives that lead a man to commit murder; he must be able to give a picture of a murderer's mental state 'from within himself'. It is taken for granted that one only has to look inside oneself in such a case; and then there's always one's imagination. . . . There are various reasons why I can no longer surrender to this agreeable hope of getting a result quite so simply. I can no longer find in myself all those motives which the press or scientific reports show to have been observed in people. Like the average judge when pronouncing sentence, I cannot without further ado conjure up an adequate picture of a murderer's mental state. Modern psychology, from psychoanalysis to behaviourism, acquaints me with facts that lead me to judge the case quite differently, especially if I bear in mind the findings of sociology and do not overlook economics and history. You will say: but that's getting complicated. I have to answer that it *is* complicated. Even if you let yourself be convinced, and agree with me that a large slice of literature is exceedingly primitive, you may still ask with profound concern: won't an evening in such a theatre be a most alarming affair? The answer to that is: no.

Whatever knowledge is embodied in a piece of poetic writing has to be wholly transmuted into poetry. Its utilization fulfils the very pleasure that the poetic element provokes. If it does not at the same time fulfil that which is fulfilled by the scientific element, none the less in an age of great discoveries and inventions one must have a certain inclination

5. The Nazi party newspaper [*Editor*].

to penetrate deeper into things—a desire to make the world controllable—if one is to be sure of enjoying its poetry.

Is the Epic Theatre Some Kind of 'Moral Institution'?

According to Friedrich Schiller the theatre is supposed to be a moral institution. In making this demand it hardly occurred to Schiller that by moralizing from the stage he might drive the audience out of the theatre. Audiences had no objection to moralizing in his day. It was only later that Friedrich Nietzsche[6] attacked him for blowing a moral trumpet. To Nietzsche any concern with morality was a depressing affair; to Schiller it seemed thoroughly enjoyable. He knew of nothing that could give greater amusement and satisfaction than the propagation of ideas. The bourgeoisie was setting about forming the ideas of the nation.

Putting one's house in order, patting oneself on the back, submitting one's account, is something highly agreeable. But describing the collapse of one's house, having pains in the back, paying one's account, is indeed a depressing affair, and that was how Friedrich Nietzsche saw things a century later. He was poorly disposed towards morality, and thus towards the previous Friedrich too.

The epic theatre was likewise often objected to as moralizing too much. Yet in the epic theatre moral arguments only took second place. Its aim was less to moralize than to observe. That is to say it observed, and then the thick end of the wedge followed: the story's moral. Of course we cannot pretend that we started our observations out of pure passion for observing and without any more practical motive, only to be completely staggered by their results. Undoubtedly there were some painful discrepancies in our environment, circumstances that were barely tolerable, and this not merely on account of moral considerations. It is not only moral considerations that make hunger, cold and oppression hard to bear. Similarly the object of our inquiries was not just to arouse moral objections to such circumstances (even though they could easily be felt—though not by all the audience alike; such objections were seldom for instance felt by those who profited by the circumstances in question) but to discover means for their elimination. We were not in fact speaking in the name of morality but in that of the victims. These truly are two distinct matters, for the victims are often told that they ought to be contented with their lot, for moral reasons. Moralists of this sort see man as existing for morality, not morality for man. At least it should be possible to gather from the above to what degree and in what sense the epic theatre is a moral institution.

6. German philosopher (1844–1900) [Editor].

From A Short Organum for the Theatre†

*   *   *

21

*   *   * What is that productive attitude in face of nature and of society which we children of a scientific age would like to take up pleasurably in our theatre?

22

The attitude is a critical one. Faced with a river, it consists in regulating the river; faced with a fruit tree, in spraying the fruit tree; faced with movement, in constructing vehicles and aeroplanes; faced with society, in turning society upside down. Our representations of human social life are designed for river-dwellers, fruit farmers, builders of vehicles and upturners of society, whom we invite into our theatres and beg not to forget their cheerful occupations while we hand the world over to their minds and hearts, for them to change as they think fit.

23

The theatre can only adopt such a free attitude if it lets itself be carried along by the strongest currents in its society and associates itself with those who are necessarily most impatient to make great alterations there. The bare wish, if nothing else, to evolve an art fit for the times must drive our theatre of the scientific age straight out into the suburbs, where it can stand as it were wide open, at the disposal of those who live hard and produce much, so that they can be fruitfully entertained there with their great problems. They may find it hard to pay for our art, and immediately to grasp the new method of entertainment, and we shall have to learn in many respects what they need and how they need it; but we can be sure of their interest. For these men who seem so far apart from natural science are only apart from it because they are being forcibly kept apart; and before they can get their hands on it they have first to develop and put into effect a new science of society; so that these are the true children of the scientific age, who alone can get the theatre moving if it is to move at all. A theatre which makes productivity its main source of entertainment has also to take it for its theme, and with greater keenness than ever now that man is everywhere hampered by men from self-production: i.e. from maintaining himself, entertaining and being entertained. The theatre has to become geared into reality if

† Reprinted by permission of Hill and Wang, a division of Farrar, Straus and Giroux, Inc. Excerpt from *Brecht on Theatre: The Development of an* *Aesthetic* by Bertolt Brecht, translated by John Willett. Pp. 185–89. Translation copyright © 1964 by John Willett.

it is to be in a position to turn out effective representations of reality, and to be allowed to do so.

24

But this makes it simpler for the theatre to edge as close as possible to the apparatus of education and mass communication. For although we cannot bother it with the raw material of knowledge in all its variety, which would stop it from being enjoyable, it is still free to find enjoyment in teaching and inquiring. It constructs its workable representations of society, which are then in a position to influence society, wholly and entirely as a game: for those who are constructing society it sets out society's experiences, past and present alike, in such a manner that the audience can 'appreciate' the feelings, insights and impulses which are distilled by the wisest, most active and most passionate among us from the events of the day or the century. They must be entertained with the wisdom that comes from the solution of problems, with the anger that is a practical expression of sympathy with the underdog, with the respect due to those who respect humanity, or rather whatever is kind to humanity; in short, with whatever delights those who are producing something.

25

And this also means that the theatre can let its spectators enjoy the particular ethic of their age, which springs from productivity. A theatre which converts the critical approach—i.e. our great productive method—into pleasure finds nothing in the ethical field which it must do and a great deal that it can. Even the wholly anti-social can be a source of enjoyment to society so long as it is presented forcefully and on the grand scale. It then often proves to have considerable powers of understanding and other unusually valuable capacities, applied admittedly to a destructive end. Even the bursting flood of a vast catastrophe can be appreciated in all its majesty by society, if society knows how to master it; then we make it our own.

26

For such an operation as this we can hardly accept the theatre as we see it before us. Let us go into one of these houses and observe the effect which it has on the spectators. Looking about us, we see somewhat motionless figures in a peculiar condition: they seem strenuously to be tensing all their muscles, except where these are flabby and exhausted. They scarcely communicate with each other; their relations are those of a lot of sleepers, though of such as dream restlessly because, as is popularly said of those who have nightmares, they are lying on their backs. True, their eyes are open, but they stare rather than see, just as they listen rather than hear. They look at the stage as if in a trance: an expression which comes from the Middle Ages, the days of witches and priests. Seeing and hearing are activities, and can be pleasant ones, but these people seem relieved of activity and like men to whom something is being done. This detached state, where they seem to be given over to vague but profound sensations, grows deeper the better the work of the actors, and so we, as we do not approve of this situation, should like them to be as bad as possible.

27

As for the world portrayed there, the world from which slices are cut in order to produce these moods and movements of the emotions, its appearance is such, produced from such slight and wretched stuff as a few pieces of cardboard, a little miming, a bit of text, that one has to admire the theatre of folk who, with so feeble a reflection of the real world, can move the feelings of their audience so much more strongly than does the world itself.

28

In any case we should excuse these theatre folk, for the pleasures which they sell for money and fame could not be induced by an exacter representation of the world, not could their inexact renderings be presented in a less magical way. Their capacity to represent people can be seen at work in various instances; it is especially the rogues and the minor figures who reveal their knowledge of humanity and differ one from the other, but the central figures have to be kept general, so that it is easier for the onlooker to identify himself with them, and at all costs each trait of character must be drawn from the narrow field within which everyone can say at once: that is how it is.

For the spectator wants to be put in possession of quite definite sensations, just as a child does when it climbs on to one of the horses on a roundabout: the sensation of pride that it can ride, and has a horse; the pleasure of being carried, and whirled past other children; the adventurous daydreams in which it pursues others or is pursued, etc. In leading the child to experience all this the degree to which its wooden seat resembles a horse counts little, nor does it matter that the ride is confined to a small circle. The one important point for the spectators in these houses is that they should be able to swap a contradictory world for a consistent one, one that they scarcely know for one of which they can dream.

29

That is the sort of theatre which we face in our operations, and so far it has been fully able to transmute our optimistic friends, whom we have

called the children of the scientific era, into a cowed, credulous, hypnotized mass.

30

True, for about half a century they have been able to see rather more
faithful representations of human social life, as well as individual figures
who were in revolt against certain social evils or even against the structure
of society as a whole. They felt interested enough to put up with a
temporary and exceptional restriction of language, plot and spiritual
scope; for the fresh wind of the scientific spirit nearly withered the charms
to which they had grown used. The sacrifice was not especially worth
while. The greater subtlety of the representations subtracted from one
pleasure without satisfying another. The field of human relationships
came within our view, but not within our grasp. Our feelings, having
been aroused in the old (magic) way, were bound themselves to remain
unaltered.

31

For always and everywhere theatres were the amusement centres of a
class which restricted the scientific spirit to the natural field, not daring
to let it loose on the field of human relationships. The tiny proletarian
section of the public, reinforced to a negligible and uncertain extent by
renegade intellectuals, likewise still needed the old kind of entertainment, as a relief from its predetermined way of life.

32

So let us march ahead! Away with all obstacles! Since we seem to have
landed in a battle, let us fight! Have we not seen how disbelief can move
mountains? Is it not enough that we should have found that something
is being kept from us? Before one thing and another there hangs a curtain:
let us draw it up!

33

The theatre as we know it shows the structure of society (represented on
the stage) as incapable of being influenced by society (in the auditorium).
Oedipus,[1] who offended against certain principles underlying the society
of his time, is executed: the gods see to that; they are beyond criticism.
Shakespeare's great solitary figures, bearing on their breast the star of
their fate, carry through with irresistible force their futile and deadly
outbursts; they prepare their own downfall; life, not death, becomes
obscene as they collapse; the catastrophe is beyond criticism. Human

1. The protagonist of Sophocles' tragedy *Oedipus Rex* (c. 430 B.C.), as well as other plays; he unwittingly
kills his father and marries his mother [*Editor*].

sacrifices all round! Barbaric delights! We know that the barbarians have their art. Let us create another.

*   *   *

35

We need a type of theatre which not only releases the feelings, insights and impulses possible within the particular historical field of human relations in which the action takes place, but employs and encourages those thoughts and feelings which help transform the field itself.

36

The field has to be defined in historically relative terms. In other words we must drop our habit of taking the different social structures of past periods, then stripping them of everything that makes them different; so that they all look more or less like our own, which then acquires from this process a certain air of having been there all along, in other words of permanence pure and simple. Instead we must leave them their distinguishing marks and keep their impermanence always before our eyes, so that our own period can be seen to be impermanent too. (It is of course futile to make use of fancy colours and folklore for this, such as our theatres apply precisely in order to emphasize the similarities in human behaviour at different times. We shall indicate the theatrical methods below.)

37

If we ensure that our characters on the stage are moved by social impulses and that these differ according to the period, then we make it harder for our spectator to identify himself with them. He cannot simply feel: that's how I would act, but at most can say: if I had lived under those circumstances. And if we play works dealing with our own time as though they were historical, then perhaps the circumstances under which he himself acts will strike him as equally odd; and this is where the critical attitude begins.

*   *   *

From a Letter to an Actor†

I have been brought to realize that many of my remarks about the theatre are wrongly understood. I realize this above all from those letters and articles which agree with me. I then feel as a mathematician would do

† Reprinted by permission of Hill and Wang, a division of Farrar, Straus and Giroux, Inc. and Methuen London. Excerpt from *Brecht on Thea-* *tre: The Development of an Aesthetic* by Bertolt Brecht, translated by John Willett. Pp. 233–36. Translation copyright © 1964 by John Willett.

if he read: Dear Sir, I am wholly of your opinion that two and two make five. I think that certain remarks are wrongly understood because there were important points which instead of defining I took for granted.

Most of the remarks, if not all, were written as notes to my plays, to allow them to be correctly performed. That gives them a rather dry and practical form, as if a sculptor were writing a matter-of-fact order about the placing of his work: where it should go and on what sort of a base. Those adddressed might have expected something about the spirit in which the work was created. They would find it difficult to get that from the order.

For instance the description of virtuosity. Art of course cannot survive without artistry, and it becomes important to describe 'how it's done'. Especially when the arts have undergone a decade and a half of barbarism, as they have here. But it should not for a moment be thought that this is something to be coldbloodedly practised and learned. Not even speech training, which is something that the bulk of actors badly need, can be done coldbloodedly, in a mechanical way.

Thus the actor must be able to speak clearly, and this is not just a matter of vowels and consonants but also (and primarily) a matter of the meaning. Unless he learns at the same time how to bring out the meaning of his lines he will simply be articulating like a machine and destroying the sense with his 'beautiful speaking voice'. And within clarity there are all kinds of degrees and distinctions. Different social classes have different kinds of clarity: a peasant may speak clearly in comparison with a second peasant, but his clarity will not be the same as that of an engineer. This means that actors learning to speak must always take care to see that their voice is pliant and flexible. They must never lose sight of the way people really talk.

There is also the problem of dialect. Here again technique needs to be linked up with more general considerations. Our theatrical language is based on High German, but over the years it has grown very mannered and stilted, and has developed into a quite special sort of High German which is no longer so flexible as High German everyday speech. There is nothing against the use of 'heightened' language on the stage, that is to say against the theatre's evolving its own stage language. But it must always be lively, varied and capable of further evolution. The people speaks dialect. Dialect is the medium of its most intimate expression. How can our actors portray the people and address it unless they go back to their own dialect, and allow its inflections to permeate the High German of the stage? Another example. The actor must learn how to economize his voice: he must not grow hoarse. But he must also be able to portray a man seized by passion who is speaking or shouting hoarsely. So his exercises have to contain an element of acting. We shall get empty, superficial, formalistic, mechanical acting if in our technical training we forget for a moment that it is the actor's duty to portray living people.

This brings me to your question whether acting is not turned into something purely technical and more or less inhuman by my insistence that the actor oughtn't to be completely transformed into the character portrayed but should, as it were, stand alongside it criticizing and approving. In my view this is not the case. Such an impression must be due to my way of writing, which takes too much for granted. To hell with my way of writing. Of course the stage of a realistic theatre must be peopled by live, three-dimensional, self-contradictory people, with all their passions, unconsidered utterances and actions. The stage is not a hothouse or a zoological museum full of stuffed animals. The actor has to be able to create such people (and if you could attend our productions you would see them; and they succeed in being people because of our principles, not in spite of them!).

There is however a complete fusion of the actor with his role which leads to his making the character seem so natural, so impossible to conceive any other way, that the audience has simply to accept it as it stands, with the result that a completely sterile atmosphere of 'tout comprendre c'est tout pardonner'[1] is engendered, as happened most notably under Naturalism.

We who are concerned to change human as well as ordinary nature must find means of 'shedding light on' the human being at that point where he seems capable of being changed by society's intervention. This means a quite new attitude on the part of the actor, for his art has hitherto been based on the assumption that people are what they are, and will remain so whatever it may cost society or themselves: 'indestructibly human', 'you can't change human nature' and so on. Both emotionally and intellectually he needs to decide his attitude to his scene and his part. The change demanded of the actor is not a cold and mechanical operation: art has nothing cold or mechanical about it, and this change is an artistic one. It cannot take place unless he has real contact with his new audience and a passionate concern for human progress.

So our theatre's significant stage groupings are not just an effect or a 'purely aesthetic' phenomenon, conductive to formal beauty. They are a part of a hugely-conceived theatre for the new social order, and they cannot be achieved without deep understanding and passionate support of the new structure of human relations.

I cannot rewrite all the notes to my plays. Please take these lines as a provisional appendix to them, an attempt to catch up on what had been wrongly assumed.

That leaves me with one thing still to explain: the relatively quiet style of acting which sometimes strikes visitors to the Berliner Ensemble.[2] This has nothing to do with forced objectivity, for the actors adopt an

1. "To understand everything is to forgive everything" [*Editor*].
2. The theatrical company in East Berlin given to

Brecht at the end of World War II by the East German government [*Editor*].

attitude to their parts; and nothing to do with mock-rationalism, for reason never flings itself coldbloodedly into the battle; it is simply due to the fact that plays are no longer subjected to red-hot 'temperamental' acting. True art is stimulated by its material. On those occasions when the recipient thinks he is observing coldness it is just that he has encountered the mastery without which it would not be art at all.[3]

MARTIN ESSLIN

From "The Uses of Commitment"[†]

* * *

Mother Courage was meant as a cautionary tale about the inevitable consequences of battening on war. Anna Fierling, called "Mother Courage," is a camp follower who in her small way helps the prosecution of the Thirty Years' War by providing shoes, ale, and comforts for the soldiers. She was, in Brecht's conception, a negative, villainous character. Those who live by war must pay war its due. So Mother Courage loses her three children. Having sacrificed her family to her commercial instinct, she fails to learn her lesson. She continues her trade, and as the final curtain falls she is seen dragging her cart across the stage to catch up with the advancing army.

Brecht wanted this last scene to arouse the spectator's indignation that such blindness and stupidity were possible. The public was to leave the theatre determined that something positive must be done to stop wars.

But when *Mother Courage* was first performed at the Zurich Schauspielhaus with Therese Giehse, an actress of great power, in the title role, the public's response was quite different: they were moved to tears by the sufferings of a poor woman who, having lost her three children, heroically continued her brave struggle and refused to give in, an embodiment of the eternal virtues of the common people.

Brecht was furious. He rewrote the play to emphasize the villainous side of Mother Courage's character. As he put it in a note to the text of the play in the ninth volume of *Versuche*:[1]

The first performance of *Mother Courage* gave the bourgeois press occasion to talk about a Niobe-tragedy[2] and about the moving endurance of the female animal. Warned by this ex-

3. This letter was written in 1951. The actor addressed has not been identified. This is perhaps the most important of Brecht's modifications of his extreme theoretical position. The doctrines laid down in the "Short Organum" were by all accounts neither discussed nor put into practice in the Berliner Ensemble. Regine Lutz, one of its principal actresses from 1949 on, told me in 1957 that she had never read Brecht's theoretical works.

† From Martin Esslin, *Brecht, The Man and His Work*, Garden City, N.Y., 1961. Pp. 229–33. ©

Martin Esslin. Produced by permission of Curtis Brown, London, on behalf of Martin Esslin.

1. "Experiments." Brecht published fifteen volumes of various writings under this heading [*Editor*].

2. In the Greek story, Niobe was a mother whose children were killed by Apollo and Artemis after she had praised them extravagantly. Zeus turned her into a stone from which tears flowed continuously [*Editor*].

perience, the author has made some alterations for the Berlin performance.[3]

Having underlined the villainy of *Mother Courage*, Brecht himself supervised the Berlin production, in which his own wife, Helene Weigel, also an excellent actress but far less warm and motherly than Therese Giehse and therefore more in line with Brecht's intention, played the title role. The Berlin production was a triumph. But how did the leading Communist critic, Max Schroeder, describe its impact? "Mother Courage," he wrote, "is a humanist saint from the tribe of Niobe and the *mater dolorosa*, who defends the life to which she has given birth with her bared teeth and claws. . . ."[4] Again, hardly anyone had noticed the villainy of Mother Courage, the profiteer who battens on war. Brecht himself admitted this but tried to explain it, not by any failure on his part to make himself clear, but by the obtuseness of the spectators who remained the slaves of long-established habits of emotion:

> Numerous discussions with members of the audience and many notices in the press show that many people regard *Mother Courage* merely as the representative of "the little people," who are "involved" in the war and "who can't do anything about it," who are helplessly at the mercy of events, etc. A deeply ingrained habit induces the audience in the theatre to pick out the more emotional aspects of the characters and to ignore the rest. . . .[5]

The East German authorities also noted the lack of propagandist effect. While *Mother Courage* moved people to tears about the horrors of war, if the play had any lesson at all it was that all soldiers are beasts (and the people of East Berlin automatically thought of Russian soldiers when it came to rape and rapine) and that nevertheless "life goes on" and the little man is eternally resilient. This was not a specifically Communist message, and so it was suggested to Brecht that he might make the end of the play more explicit. Mother Courage might make a little speech drawing a more positively Communist lesson, or she might do something that showed she had at last realized that she would have to become politically active.

If Brecht had really been as cold a rationalist and propagandist as he professed, he could easily have yielded to these demands. In fact, he did nothing of the sort. However willing he had previously been to accept advice and suggestions for alterations from practically any quarter, in this case he refused. With a great display of casuistry he argued that it was *better* propaganda to leave Mother Courage unconverted, untaught, and unteachable.

No doubt Brecht himself was convinced that he was arguing on strictly

3. *Versuche* 9, p. 79.
4. Max Schroeder, "Verflucht sei der Krieg" (1949), reprinted in *Aufbau*, East Berlin, 1957,
no. 1.
5. Brecht, "Der lange Weg in den Krieg," *Theaterarbeit*, p. 230.

logical and rational grounds. Yet his arguments clearly are nothing but the rationalizations of instinctive responses. With the sound instinct of the creative artist Brecht knew that the suggested alterations would simply have spoiled his play. The suggested change did not make sense to his poetic instinct, and so he was unable to accept it. Yet the deeper needs of his personality made it impossible for Brecht to argue on any lines other than strictly rational considerations of political, or propaganda, expediency. The poet deep within him always had to hide behind the Marxist.

*   *   *

RICHARD GILMAN

[Mother Courage and Her Children]†

*   *   *

The full title of the play that is most widely considered to be Brecht's finest achievement is *Mother Courage and Her Children*, the subtitle being "A Chronicle of the Thirty Years' War." That the shortened form of the title—*Mother Courage*—is used in nearly every published text and production and in nearly every critical or scholarly reference is often simply a matter of convenience, but to the unwary it has acted as a source—or confirmation—of the wide misunderstanding to which the play has been subject.

Our habit of identifying almost exclusively with the play's protagonist, to the detriment of the work as a whole, is strengthened when the title is, or includes, a name. The obvious examples are the Greek tragedies, and Shakespeare almost irresistibly. What happens is that the plays then become a kind of invented biography, the *personal story* of Oedipus, the *life of* Hamlet or Lear, instead of the drama of Oedipus at the juncture of human and divine design, Hamlet caught between feeling and fact, Lear in an arena where appetites strike down values. We convert the protagonist into a surrogate self whom we embrace or expel, but who *exists as we might*, and the play into our own possible history, but one narrowed into a single meaning or quality: Hamlet is the indecisive man, Oedipus the reckless one, Macbeth the ambitious, Lear the blind. Tragedy then becomes not the great imaginative map of the world as extremity, disaster, and ennobling awareness but a species of cautionary tale.

This process of reduction to the personal, drama being made into an extended moral or spiritual anecdote, is at work in more recent genres. If instead of being regarded as a cautionary figure, Mother Courage is

† Reprinted by permission of Farrar, Straus and Giroux, Inc. Excerpted from *The Making of Modern Drama* by Richard Gilman. Pp. 223–30. Copyright © 1974 by Richard Gilman.

thought of as an exemplary one, a being who *doesn't die*, the same inability is present to see her in a set of environing circumstances which constitute the true tale, to see her as a locus of meanings and significances having to do with the structure of the world and not with a merely personal fate. By calling his play *Mother Courage and Her Children*, Brecht wished to guard against what we might call the protagonistic fallacy, the notion that a drama (or a novel) is equivalent to its hero's or heroine's fate, which fate ought to be able to be distilled, so to speak, into one or another kind of "value."

Walter Sokel's remark that Brecht doesn't begin with the individual but with the problem applies to all the late major plays but to none with more force than to *Mother Courage* (as, *for convenience*, I shall call it hereafter). In narrative or physical terms, the "problem" is for Mother Courage to get through a long war with her children; in sociological or historical ones, it is the organization of society into structures which promote rapacity and violence; in moral or philosophical ones, it is the internal costs of survival and the relationship of spirit to implacable physical necessity.

To summarize the play's main line of action: Anna Fierling, called Mother Courage (Brecht took her nickname and occupation and the drama's setting, but almost nothing else, from Grimmelshausen's seventeenth-century satirical chronicle),[1] is a sutler who follows the shifting campaigns and battle lines of the Thirty Years' War, selling supplies to one or another of the armies. She is tough, "indomitable," and her steadfast purpose is to preserve her life, for its own sake but that in turn for the sake of her three children, in the midst of unending devastation and death. One by one, however, the children die and the mother is left alone, hitched to her wagon, a survivor in only the narrowest bodily sense.

From the very beginning the ironic perspective is present that will issue in this survival at the cost of everything that has seemed to matter. Mother Courage's own nickname has a grossly ironic origin; as she tells the story, she received it after driving madly through the bombardment of Riga "with fifty loaves of bread in my cart. They were going moldy . . . I was afraid I'd be ruined." Is her virtue therefore founded on a sham? The point Brecht is making is that it is founded on an overwhelming practicality, a business sense that dominates everything she does and that is is seen throughout to be in mortal, insoluble conflict with all other "values," including, in the deepest irony of all, that of life itself.

The deaths of her children all take place as more or less direct results of her making the living that is designed to sustain them. She loses one son to the blandishment of a recruiting officer when she lets him out of her sight in order to make a sale (he will later be killed in the war)

---

1. *The Adventures Simplicissimus* of Hans Jacob von Grimmelshausen (1625–76) [*Editor*].

and the other when she tries to bargain over the ransom demanded of her after he has been captured by enemy soldiers. (Her only means of raising the money is to sell her wagon, which would mean that she could not provide for her other child.) And her mute, defenseless daughter is killed when she is off on business.

In each case there is a further thematic significance, a deepening of the play's vision of personal destiny controlled by ineluctable social forces that have constructed our existences along lines of physical power and that thus force us to betray our most "positive" qualities. In one more irony, Swiss Cheese and Kattrin die in the war for the possession of an attribute that would have been honored in peace, he for his modesty, she for her capacity to love, and Eilif is killed during peacetime for virtues most negotiable in war, his impetuosity and élan.

These particular deaths are the immediate source of the widespread reading of *Mother Courage* as an anti-war play. Less directly, the interpretation rests simply on the play's permeation by images of and references to violence and destruction. Yet it's difficult to see how any sensitive reader or spectator can fail to perceive that if *Mother Courage* arraigns war, it does the same to peace, that, in fact, one of its governing ideas is that war is simply an intensified form of peace, which is a condition possessing its own warlike character. This theme finds expression most directly in Brecht's use of a humor of reversals: "Peace has broken out," a character says, and another speaks of the war as unlikely ever to stop because whenever it "gets in the hole" it has friends to pull it out, so that it can look forward to a "prosperous future."

It may seem reductive or merely witty to say, as Eric Bentley does, that *Mother Courage* is actually a "business play," but the description has much point and is a useful corrective to the notion that it is anything so painless to conceive as an anti-war epic. Its movement and atmosphere incorporate the narrowly conventional meaning of business as "the supplying of commodities" but go beyond this to suggest a world of *quid pro quo*, of ruthlessness (ruth: compassion), and of the triumph of the material. "The business of the United States is business," a famous American once said, and the remark touches on one aspect of Brecht's perception: the human world as institutionalized profit and loss, which in turn of course institutionalizes greed and aggression on the one hand and, literally, "emptiness," deprivation, on the other.

In such a world, values are made material, virtues become a matter of degrees of physical power, and moral being is consequently rendered impotent. Mother Courage is neither a heroine nor a villain (the exquisite balance between the conditions is most splendidly indicated in the scene in which, when she realizes that her captured son is going to die, she murmurs, "I believe—I've haggled too long") since there is no moral dimension in which she can act. She can only try to make a "living"; she cannot choose among values and particularly not an abstract or spiritual value over a material one. Yet she retains the impulse or memory of love, the most spiritual value of all, doggedly attempting to implement it in the face of an institutionalized savagery to which love is not merely superfluous but inimical, and in despite of her own hard-bitten rejection of "sentiment."

She is held in the bitter contradiction by which the attempt to maintain her children in life—to "love" them in the only way she can, materially by providing sustenance—becomes the very principle of their being lost to her. For to make a living is to participate in the world on its warlike terms of profit and loss, and so be mechanically stripped of human substance. She is therefore, in the deepest way of all, deprived of choice, the basis of moral life, and her "courage" becomes in the end, as Joachim Mennemeier has said, "nothing more than the form in which she hides from herself the consciousness of the fruitlessness of all virtues."[2]

Though this is not all it is, the play is an image or dramatic legend of such fruitlessness, and not a tale of stamina in the face of adversity or an inspiring story of how "little" people can survive the depredations of the powerful. As Brecht wrote, his "merchant-mother" is a "great living contradiction who is disfigured and deformed beyond recognition." In her, "antitheses in all their abruptness and incompatibility are united." She is not an image of "the indestructibility of a vital person afflicted by the inequities of war" but almost wholly the opposite: one of the destructibility of humanity within the prevailing system, no matter how tenacious, sinewy, and energetic a particular person might be.

Why then has *Mother Courage* been so widely regarded as precisely the sort of indomitable heroine Brecht was at such pains not to create? Why do audiences identify with her, weep over her misfortunes, and leave the theater full of admiration for her capacity to endure? The usual answer is that she somehow managed to escape Brecht's control, that his own rich humanity won through, transforming what was intended to be a coldly analytic drama into a work of celebration. And this truimph-in-spite-of-himself is then used to cement the argument that Brecht's theories and practices are at variance and, more generally, that drama cannot exist without characters with whom audiences can identify and without having as its purpose an increase of passion or sentiment.

We know that Brecht rewrote several passages in an effort to make Mother Courage less sympathetic than he had discovered audiences found her. This would seem to be damning evidence in the case for the failure of his theories of estrangement and alienation. Yet must we ally ourselves on one or the other side of the controversy? Something subtle and immensely important for an understanding of the changed drama we call "modern" is at work here.

To begin with, that Mother Courage is in some respects an appealing figure is undeniable; she is lusty, sharp-tongued, durable. At least she

2. The quotation is from Franz Norbert Menne-meier's "Mother Courage and Her Children," translated from the German by J. F. Sammons and reprinted by Peter Demetz in *Brecht: A Collection of Critical Essays*, Englewood Cliffs, N.J., 1962, p.145 [*Editor*].

is these things at the outset and even in spasmodic, nearly disembodied movements at the end—like memories of another condition. But to be seduced by these qualities into wishing to embrace Mother Courage as a heroine is to want to embrace air; it is to be blind to the drama itself, wherein she functions less as a biography than as an occasion, a demonstration of how even the wiliest strength will be ground down. If we would allow it, against the pull of our temptation to make dramatic characters into emblems, our consciousness would be aroused to her status as a victim, but more importantly to the fact of victimization in the world, as societies, including our now, have constructed it.

This is not to say that Mother Courage ought not to be appealing; what critical perversity that would be! The point is that her attractive qualities are part of the data of erosion, the substance of what will be lost, as her love is, in the persons of her children. She is exemplary not in being a survivor but in being one at a terrible cost; her virtues thus function dramatically not as attributes to be admired but as annihilated possibilities to be mourned. That she has been seen otherwise is not so much the fault of Brecht as of a certain radical defect in a great many people's experience of drama, a defect that will show itself once more ten years later when Beckett's two tramps will exhibit their nearly historyless condition and critics and theatergoers alike will foolishly struggle to write a history for them.

There is something mean-spirited and obtuse in challenging Brecht to the proving of his theories, which in the first place were never absolutes or even firm doctrines but attempts, dispositions, or perspectives, and beyond that have been immensely valuable in the pointing of directions in which the theater ought to, and has, moved. With the partial exception of the formally didactic plays, Brecht never wished to write a wholly "analytic" drama, and it is a mistake to interpret the notions of alienation, estrangement, and the like as leading to responses of pure cognition, pure rationality.

What he considered indispensable to a modern theater, theater in the age of the authority of science and technology and the depletion of mythical acceptances and beliefs, was a power to cause thought; but thought fused to emotional realities and directed, as its ultimate intention, toward an understanding of how sensuous being is itself destroyed by our wrongly erected lives. Mother Courage's own vitality and implicit sensuality are powerless to declare themselves; and it is this very powerlessness, the silent anguish of her thwarted nature, that is the consciousness we ought to make our own. But we can only do this by being "estranged" from her as a *character*, in order to see her as a battlefield.

Traditionally, drama has been based on nothing so securely as the idea of choice, on the granting of opportunities for characters to elect their destinies, whether trivial or noble, triumphant or disastrous. The fact of consciousness is not essential: the various "blindnesses" of Oedipus, Lear, and Othello do not remove them from a realm in which choice and, therefore, responsibility operate as the central human capacities, the very capacities that most significantly distinguish men from beasts. Drama has largely been the *enactment of choices*, and one reason for the perennial status of *Hamlet* as perhaps the greatest (certainly the least exhaustible) of all plays is the way it moves at the deep center of the mystery of choosing, with its difficulties and pain.

The disappearance of tragedy (which we might describe as the representation of human decisions at their most consequential) as a dramatic mode is due, as much as to anything else, to the erosion of belief in the power of moral or spiritual or existential choice, with a corresponding acceptance of the *chosenness* of our destinies in a secular, technologized, and politically intrusive world. Yet such is our persistence in the habits of our classical and humanist tradition that we suppress such knowledge and are confined in our illusion of freedom by—among other cultural forces—the theater, which has continued to enact moral dramas as though they still had exemplary power, as though we ourselves still had the power of choice.

* * *

Samuel Beckett
and
Happy Days

SAMUEL BECKETT

From Proust†

*   *   *

*   *   * In the closing words of his book[1] he states his position: 'But were I granted time to accomplish my work, I would not fail to stamp it with the seal of that Time, now so forcibly present to my mind, and in it I would describe men, even at the risk of giving them the appearance of monstrous beings, as occupying in Time a much greater place than that so sparingly conceded to them in Space, a place indeed extended beyond measure, because, like giants plunged in the years, they touch at once those periods of their lives—separated by so many days—so far apart in Time.'

Prout's creatures, then, are victims of this predominating condition and circumstance—Time; victims as lower organisms, conscious only of two dimensions and suddenly confronted with the mystery of height, are victims: victims and prisoners. There is no escape from the hours and the days. Neither from to-morrow nor from yesterday. There is no escape from yesterday because yesterday has deformed us, or been deformed by us. The mood is of no importance. Deformation has taken place. Yesterday is not a milestone that has been passed, but a daystone on the beaten track of the years, and irremediably part of us, within us, heavy and dangerous. We are not merely more weary because of yesterday, we are other, no longer what we were before the calamity of yesterday. A calamitous day, but calamitous not necessarily in content. The good or evil disposition of the object has neither reality nor significance. The immediate joys and sorrows of the body and the intelligence

† From *Proust* (1931), New York, 1957. Pp. 2–5; 7–12; 55–57; 59–60. Reprinted by permission of Grove Weidenfeld, a division of Wheatland Corporation. Copyright © 1957 by Samuel Beckett.

1. Marcel Proust's *The Remembrance of Things Past* (1913–27), in seven volumes [*Editor*].

are so many superfoetations. Such as it was, it has been assimilated to
the only world that has reality and significance, the world of our own
latent consciousness, and its cosmography has suffered a dislocation. So
that we are rather in the position of Tantalus,[2] with this difference, that
we allow ourselves to be tantalised. And possibly the perpetuum mobile
of our disillusions is subject to more variety. The aspirations of yesterday
were valid for yesterday's ego, not for to-day's. We are disappointed at
the nullity of what we are pleased to call attainment. But what is attainment? The identification of the subject with the object of his desire.
The subject has died—and perhaps many times—on the way. For subject
B to be disappointed by the banality of an object chosen by subject A
is as illogical as to expect one's hunger to be dissipated by the spectacle
of Uncle eating his dinner. Even suppose that by one of those rare
miracles of coincidence, when the calendar of facts runs parallel to the
calendar of feelings, realisation takes place, that the object of desire (in
the strictest sense of that malady) is achieved by the subject, then the
congruence is so perfect, the time-state of attainment eliminates so
accurately the time-state of aspiration, that the actual seems the inevitable, and, all conscious intellectual effort to reconstitute the invisible
and unthinkable as a reality being fruitless, we are incapable of appreciating our joy by comparing it with our sorrow. Voluntary memory
(Proust repeats it ad nauseam) is of no value as an instrument of evocation, and provides an image as far removed from the real as the myth
of our imagination or the caricature furnished by direct perception.
There is only one real impression and one adequate mode of evocation.
Over neither have we the least control. That reality and that mode will
be discussed in their proper place.

But the poisonous ingenuity of Time in the science of affliction is
not limited to its action on the subject, that action, as has been shown,
resulting in an unceasing modification of his personality, whose permanent reality, if any, can only be apprehended as a retrospective hypothesis. The individual is the seat of a constant process of decantation,
decantation from the vessel containing the fluid of future time, sluggish,
pale and monochrome, to the vessel containing the fluid of past time,
agitated and multicoloured by the phenomena of its hours. Generally
speaking, the former is innocuous, amorphous, without character, without any Borgian virtue.[3] Lazily considered in anticipation and in haze
of our smug will to live, of our pernicious and incurable optimism, it
seems exempt from the bitterness of fatality: in store for us, not in store
in us. On occasions, however, it is capable of supplementing the labours
of its colleague. It is only necessary for its surface to be broken by a

2. Zeus punished Tantalus by making him stand
in water that receded when he tried to drink and
under fruit-laden branches always just out of reach
[Editor].
3. A reference to the Borgia family, the most famous members of which were Cesare (1475–1507)
and Lucrezia (1480–1519). They were notorious
achievers, even villains, in Renaissance Rome
[Editor].

date, by any temporal specification allowing us to measure the days that separate us from a menace—or a promise. * * *

* * *

* * * At the best, all that is realised in Time (all Time produce), whether in Art or Life, can only be possessed successively, by a series of partial annexations—and never integrally and at once. The tragedy of the Marcel-Albertine liaison[4] is the type-tragedy of the human relationship whose failure is preordained. My analysis of that central catastrophe will clarify this too abstract and arbitrary statement of Proust's pessimism. But for every tumour a scalpel and a compress. Memory and Habit are attributes of the Time cancer. They control the most simple Proustian episode, and an understanding of their mechanism must precede any particular analysis of their application. They are the flying buttresses of the temple raised to commemorate the wisdom of the architect that is also the wisdom of all the sages, from Brahma to Leopardi,[5] the wisdom that consists not in the satisfaction but in the ablation of desire:

> 'In noi di cari inganni
> non che la speme, il desiderio è spento.'[6]

The laws of memory are subject to the more general laws of habit. Habit is a compromise effected between the individual and his environment, or between the individual and his own organic eccentricities, the guarantee of a dull inviolability, the lightning-conductor of his existence. Habit is the ballast that chains the dog to his vomit. Breathing is habit. Life is habit. Or rather life is a succession of habits, since the individual is a succession of individuals; the world being a projection of the individual's consciousness (an objectivation of the individuals' will, Schopenhauer[7] would say), the pact must be continually renewed, the letter of safe-conduct brought up to date. The creation of the world did not take place once and for all time, but takes place every day. Habit then is the generic term for the countless treaties concluded between the countless subjects that constitute the individual and their countless correlative objects. The periods of transition that separate consecutive adaptations (because by no expedient of macabre transubstantiation can the grave-sheets serve as swaddling-clothes) represent the perilous zones in the life of the individual, dangerous, precarious, painful, mysterious and fertile, when for a moment the boredom of living is replaced by the suffering of being. * * * The suffering of being: that is, the free play of every faculty. Because the pernicious devotion of habit paralyses our

4. Marcel is the protagonist of Proust's novel; Albertine is his first serious love [Editor].
5. In the Hindu religion Brahma is the absolute primordial essence, or God comprising the Hindu trinity of Brahma, Vishnu, and Shiva. Giacomo Leopardi (1798–1860) was an Italian Romantic poet [Editor].

6. From Leopardi's Canti 27: "Not only hope, but even desire for our cherished illusions is spent" [Editor].
7. Arthur Schopenhauer (1788–1860), German philosopher. His main work, The World as Will and Idea (1818) posits will as the prime moving force in the world [Editor].

attention, drugs those handmaidens of perception whose co-operation is not absolutely essential. Habit is like Françoise, the immortal cook of the Proust household, who knows what has to be done, and will slave all day and all night rather than tolerate any redundant activity in the kitchen. But our current habit of living is as incapable of dealing with the mystery of a strange sky or a strange room, with any circumstance unforeseen in her curriculum, as Françoise of conceiving or realising the full horror of a Duval omelette. [8] Then the atrophied faculties come to the rescue, and the maximum value of our being is restored. But less drastic circumstances may produce this tense and provisional lucidity in the nervous system. Habit may not be dead (or as good as dead, doomed to die) but sleeping. This second and more fugitive experience may or may not be exempt from pain. It does not inaugurate a period of transition. But the first and major mode is inseparable from suffering and anxiety—the suffering of the dying and the jealous anxiety of the ousted. The old ego dies hard. Such as it was, a minister of dulness, it was also an agent of security. When it ceases to perform that second function, when it is opposed by a phenomenon that it cannot reduce to the condition of a comfortable and familiar concept, when, in a word, it betrays its trust as a screen to spare its victim the spectacle of reality, it disappears, and the victim, now an ex-victim, for a moment free, is exposed to that reality—an exposure that has its advantages and its disadvantages. It disappears—with wailing and gnashing of teeth. The moral microcosm cannot forgive the relative immortality of the macrocosm. The whisky bears a grudge against the decanter. The narrator cannot sleep in a strange room, is tortured by a high ceiling, being used to a low ceiling. What is taking place? The old pact is out of date. It contained no clause treating of high ceilings. The habit of friendship for the low ceiling is ineffectual, must die in order that a habit of friendship for the high ceiling may be born. Between this death and that birth, reality, intolerable, absorbed feverishly by his consciousness at the extreme limit of its intensity, by his total consciousness organised to avert the disaster, to create the new habit that will empty the mystery of its threat—and also of its beauty. 'If Habit,' writes Proust, 'is a second nature, it keeps us in ignorance of the first, and is free of its cruelties and its enchantments.' Our first nature, therefore, corresponding, as we shall see later, to a deeper instinct than the mere animal instinct of self-preservation, is laid bare during these periods of abandonment. And its cruelties and enchantments are the cruelties and enchantments of reality. 'Enchantments of reality' has the air of a paradox. But when the object is perceived as particular and unique and not merely the member of a family, when it appears independent of any general notion and detached from the sanity of a cause, isolated and inexplicable in the light of ignorance, then and then only may it be a source of enchantment. Unfortunately

---

8. An omelette prepared in the famous Duval restaurant [*Editor*].

Habit has laid its veto on this form of perception, its action being precisely of the object in the haze of conception—preconception. Normally we are in the position of the tourist (the traditional specification would constitute a pleonasm), whose aesthetic experience consists in a series of identifications and for whom Baedeker[9] is the end rather than the means. Deprived by nature of the faculty of cognition and by upbringing of any acquaintance with the laws of dynamics, a brief inscription immortalises his emotion. The creature of habit turns aside from the object that cannot be made to correspond with one or other of his intellectual prejudices, that resists the propositions of his team of syntheses, organised by Habit on labour-saving principles.

*   *   *

The identification of immediate with past experience, the recurrence of past action or reaction in the present, amounts to a participation between the ideal and the real, imagination and direct apprehension, symbol and substance. Such participation frees the essential reality that is denied to the contemplative as to the active life. What is common to present and past is more essential than either taken separately. Reality, whether approached imaginatively or empirically, remains a surface, hermetic. Imagination, applied—a priori—to what is absent, is exercised in vacuo and cannot tolerate the limits of the real. Nor is any direct and purely experimental contact possible between subject and object, because they are automatically separated by the subject's consciousness of perception, and the object loses its purity and becomes a mere intellectual pretext or motive. But, thanks to this reduplication, the experience is at once imaginative and empirical, at once an evocation and a direct perception, real without being merely actual, ideal without being merely abstract, the ideal real, the essential, the extratemporal. But if this mystical experience communicates an extratemporal essence, it follows that the communicant is for the moment an extratemporal being. Consequently the Proustian solution consists, in so far as it has been examined, in the negation of Time and Death, the negation of Death because the negation of Time. Death is dead because Time is dead. (At this point a brief impertinence, which consists in considering *Le Temps Retrouvé*[1] almost as inappropriate a description of the Proustian solution as *Crime and Punishment* of a masterpiece that contains no allusion to either crime or punishment. Time is not recovered, it is obliterated. Time is recovered, and Death with it, when he leaves the library and joins the guests, perched in precarious decrepitude on the aspiring stilts of the former and preserved from the latter by a miracle of terrified equilibrium. If the title is a good title the scene in the library is an anticlimax.) So now in the exaltation of his brief eternity, having emerged from the darkness of time and habit and passion and intelli-

9. Any of a series of traveler's guidebooks issued by Karl Baedeker (1801–59), a German publisher [*Editor*].

1. The last of the novels comprising Proust's great work. The title means "time recaptured" [*Editor*].

gence, he understands the necessity of art. For in the brightness of art alone can be deciphered the baffled ecstasy that he had known before the inscrutable superficies of a cloud, a triangle, a spire, a flower, a pebble, when the mystery, the essence, the Idea, imprisoned in matter, had solicited the bounty of a subject passing by within the shell of his impurity, and tendered, like Dante his song to the 'ingegni storti e loschi,' at least an incorruptible beauty:

'Ponete mente *almen* com'io son bella.'[2]

And he understands the meaning of Baudelaire's[3] definition of reality as 'the adequate union of subject and object,' and more clearly than ever the grotesque fallacy of a realistic art—'that miserable statement of line and surface,' and the penny-a-line vulgarity of a literature of notations.

*   *   *

In Time creative and destructive Proust discovers himself as an artist: 'I understood the meaning of death, of love and vocation, of the joys of the spirit and the utility of pain.' Allusion has been made to his contempt for the literature that 'describes,' for the realists and naturalists worshipping the offal of experience, prostrate before the epidermis and the swift epilepsy, and content to transcribe the surface, the façade, behind which the Idea is prisoner. Whereas the Proustian procedure is that of Apollo flaying Marsyas[4] and capturing without sentiment the essence, the Phrygian waters. 'Chi non ha la forza di uccidere la realtà non ha la forza di crearla.'[5] But Proust is too much of an affectivist to be satisfied by the intellectual symbolism of a Baudelaire, abstract and discursive. The Baudelaire unity is a unity 'post rem,'[6] a unity abstracted from plurality. His 'correspondence' is determined by a concept, therefore strictly limited and exhausted by its own definition. Proust does not deal in concepts, he pursues the Idea, the concrete. He admires the frescoes of the Paduan Arena[7] because their symbolism is handled as a reality, special, literal and concrete, and is not merely the pictorial transmission of a notion. *   *   *

---

2. Dante's song is for "deformed, shortsighted wits," to whom he has his verse say, "At least consider how fair I am." The line is from the first song of his *Convivio* [*Editor*].
3. Charles Baudelaire (1821–67), French poet [*Editor*].
4. The Phrygian flute player who challenged Apollo to a competition and who, having been beaten, was flayed alive for his presumption [*Editor*].
5. "Whoever lacks the power to destroy reality also lacks the power to create it" [*Editor*].
6. "After the fact" [*Editor*].
7. The interior of the Cappella degli Scrovegni in Padua is decorated with frescoes on various subjects by Giotto [*Editor*].

DANIEL J. ALPAUGH

Negative Definition in Samuel Beckett's *Happy Days*†

If one all-pervading technique can be said to be operating in Samuel Beckett's *Happy Days*, it is the technique of negative definition. Beckett presents his vision of modernity not by showing us what life is but rather by showing us what it is not. As the play begins, we find a man and a woman acting out their drama in a modified Edenistic setting. Instead of the original garden, bountiful and teeming with life, we find a landscape which exhibits a "maximum of simplicity and symmetry".[1] A "blazing" sun beats down mercilessly on a "scorched" earth. Winnie is shocked when she discovers animal life in the form of an "emmet": "Looks like life of some kind!" she cries. (p. 29) [412]. This Eden stands at the very end of the Becketonian time cycle—at that point where an originally energy-charged creation has atrophied to a state of maximum sterility as man and his civilation come to a physical and spiritual dead end. Winnie, who is half buried in a mound of earth, and her husband, Willie, who lives in a hole on the other side of the mound, are aware of the fact that "gravity" isn't what it used to be (p. 33) [414] and that "the earth has lost its atmosphere" (p. 51) [420–21].

In order to develop a flexible and all-inclusive myth of the past, Beckett makes frequent use of the phrase "the old style," using it as a foil by means of which he develops his vision of *comment c'est*.[2] This suggestion of what we might call "the new style" is achieved as much through implicit reference to an ideal past as it is through explicit use of the phrase "the old style." The use of the phrase itself can usually be placed within one or more of the following categories: 1. literary and social. 2. concepts of time. 3. form and content. 4. death.

Ruby Cohn has noted that "the old style" is a reference to Dante's phrase, *"dolce stil nuovo"* (sweet new style), which ushered in the vigorous literature of the Rennaissance,[3] and, indeed, at one point Winnie modifies the phrase to "the sweet old style" (p. 22) [409]. Winnie is almost as good an anthology as Palgrave;[4] she is full of quotations—bits and snatches from Shakespeare, Milton, and Gray. What Beckett emphaizes, however, is the fact that these poets exist only in fragments and that it is very difficult for Winnie to remember more than a few words or phrases. "One loses one's classics," she remarks at one point, after she has had difficulty recalling a verse (p. 57) [423]. But upon second

† Reprinted from *Twentieth Century Literature* 11 (1966): 202–10. With permission of the publishers. Norton Critical Edition pages follow in brackets.
1. Samuel Beckett, *Happy Days* (New York: Grove Press, Inc., 1961), p. 7. All subsequent references will be to this text and will be cited in the body of the study.
2. "How it is" [*Editor*].
3. Ruby Cohn, *Samuel Beckett: The Comic Gamut* (New Brunswick: Rutgers University Press, 1966), p. 233.
4. Francis Turner Palgrave (1824–1897), writer and anthologist best known for his highly successful *Golden Treasury of the Best Songs and Lyrical Poems in the English Language* (1861) [*Editor*].

thought she acknowledges that "a part remains, of one's classics, to help one through the day" (p. 59) [423]. Winnie has lost her classics in the sense that it is impossible for her to share the fundamentally optimistic attitudes which produced them. The part which remains is merely a fragmentary set of lines which Winnie shores against her ruin.

Evidence indicates that Winnie's own personal literary and social heritage is the Victorian period. Beckett focuses on the Victorian period as a means of negatively defining modernity because the Victorians were the last to rationalize the disparity between scientific discoveries and spiritual beliefs and obtain some degree of universal credence for their rationalizations. In this connection we might consider Winnie's first use of the phrase "the old style," when she discovers a bottle of medicine in her bag and tries to read the label:

> Loss of spirits . . . lack of keenness . . . want of appetite . . . infants . . . children . . . adults . . . six level . . . tablespoonfuls daily—(*head up, smile*)—the old style!—(*smile off, head down, reads*)—daily . . . before and after . . . meals . . . instantaneous . . . (*looks closer*) . . . improvement. . . . (p. 13) [406].

The Victorians were notorious for consumption of patent medicines both literally and figuratively speaking. With the impact of new discoveries beginning with Lyell[5] in geology and culminating in Charles Darwin's soul-shaking theory,[6] the Victorians suffered from "loss of spirits," and their literary lions—Tennyson, Browning, Arnold, Carlyle—tried to find some cure-all for man's shattered ego—some substitute religion that could reconcile the discoveries of science, allowing man to retain his soul. Winnie's bottle parodies both the hysterical Victorian attempts and the twentieth century's failure to produce a satisfactory panacea of its own. Winnie downs the bottle with one herioc gulp and hurls it over the mound where we hear the "sound of breaking glass" (p. 14) [406]. The last mainstay against infection has been shattered.

There are many other incidents that point to Winnie's Victorian roots. We might consider her remarks concerning the relativity of perspiration:

> I used to perspire freely. (*Pause.*) Now hardly at all. (*Pause.*) The heat is much greater. (*Pause.*) The perspiration much less. (*Pause.*) That is what I find so wonderful. (*Pause.*) The way man adapts himself. (*Pause.*) To changing conditions. . . . (p. 35) [414–15]

At one point Winnie says that to have her Willy listening to her in the wilderness is "happiness enow," ironically suggesting a contrast between the wilderness of *Happy Days* and that of a great Victorian an-

---

5. Sir Charles Lyell (1797–1875) [*Editor*].
6. Charles Robert Darwin (1809–75), who wrote the classic of evolutionary theory *The Origin of Species* (1859) [*Editor*].

odyne; for even in a deterministic, despair-sown universe, Omar-Fitz-gerald could counter the void with his romantic paraphernalia—"A Jug of Wine, a Loaf of Bread—and Thou / Beside me singing in the Wil-derness".[7] Winnie's wilderness yields less fruit; Willie, her "Thou," only serves to make the Victorian ideals of love and communication seem ridiculous, and, as we shall see later, Winnie is disgusted by sensual pleasure and can sing only with great difficulty.

Willie's roots are even more Victorian than Winnie's, which is only natural since he is ten years her senior. When Willie's head rises into sight, "trickling blood" (p. 14) [406], one is tempted to call to mind Henley's stoical lines, here reduced to the nth degree of absurdity:

> In the fell clutch of circumstance
> I have not winced nor cried aloud
> Under the bludgeonings of chance
> My head is bloody, but unbowed.[8]

And when Willie appears at the end of act two with "striped trousers," "white gloves," and a "Battle of Britain moustache," his roots become obvious (p. 61) [424].

The second use of the phrase "the old style" involves a revolution in time. Although Beckett's use of the phrase is in one sense a reference to Dante, it is at the same time a reference to the change in calculation of the calendar which took place in the eighteenth century, leaving a transition period during which it was necessary to indicate whether one was using the old or new style when calculating dates. If we examine the immediate contexts which inspire Winnie's exclamation "the old style," we shall find the word "day" conscpicuous: "not a day goes by" (p. 18) [407], "the end of the day" (p. 22) [409], "the day is now well advanced" (p. 32) [413], "from this day out" (p. 33) [414], and "day after day" (p. 42) [417] are all phrases containing this word which elicit the phrase "the old style."

We can best understand why Winnie relegates the concept of day to the old style if we compare *Happy Days* with an old-style Victorian play, Browning's *Pippa Passes*. There are many reasons for making this comparison. Both plays concern themselves with loquacious female pro-tagonists. Both trace the activities of their protagonists through the course of a day. Both Pippa and Winnie are in their respective ways singers of song. The differences, however, are more revealing; Pippa rises with the sun in a burst of optimistic energy, rhapsodizing on the sunrise as a dynamic phenomenon:

> Day!
> Faster and more fast,
> O'er night's brim, day boils at last;

7. Edward Fitzgerald, *The Rubaiyat of Omar Khayyam*, in *Poetry of the Victorian Period*, ed. George Woods and Jerome Buckley (Chicago: Scott, Foresman and Co., 1955), p. 417, ll. 45–46.
8. William Ernest Henley, "Invictus," *Ibid.*, p. 789, ll. 5–8.

Boils, pure gold, o'er the cloud-cup's brim
Where spurting and suppressed it lay,
For not a froth-flake touched the rim
Of yonder gap in the solid gray
Of the eastern cloud, an hour away;
But forth one wavelet, then another curled,
Till the whole sunrise, not to be suppressed,
Rose, reddened, and its seething breast
Flickered in bounds, grew gold, then over-flowed the world. [9]

Here the word "day" refers to a meaningful unit of time—an organic, growing thing which bursts into being with a flowering sun, conceived of as a dynamic, life-sustaining force. Pippa, springing out of bed, full of energy, is in tune with her surroundings.

In contrast, Winnie's praise of her day is obviously ironic; for the sun in Winnie's world turns out to be a "blaze of hellish light" which is slowly burning the world to a cinder (p. 11) [405]. Whereas Pippa springs out of bed with the rising sun, Winnie is awakened by the arbitrary ringing of a bell, as mechanical as an alarm clock. She has to order herself to begin her day. The bell, which rings several times during the play, initiates and periodically reinforces Winnie's stream of clichés and fragmentary quotations which can best be thought of as an elaborate Pavlovian response[1] to a mechanical stimulus in contrast to Pippa's spontaneous overflow of powerful emotion.

Pippa and Winnie have diametrically opposed problems in their attempts to cope with their respective days. "O Day, if I squander a wavelet of thee, / A mite of my twelve-hours treasure," cries Pippa.[2] Her holiday takes on a larger meaning, becoming a metaphor for the total amount of life allotted her by God. Her life consists of an organic progression from birth to death, and hers is an attempt to make every minute meaningful. Winnie has quite a different problem: "Sometimes all is over, for the day, all done, all said, all ready for the night, and the day not over, far from over, the night not ready, far, far from ready" (p. 44) [418]. In contrast to the spontaneous, organically oriented Pippa, Winnie has become a mechanical person in a mechanical universe. For Winnie time is a meaningless term; she lives in an everlasting now. Lacking in Winnie's universe is a benevolent deity to stand behind the scenes and endow time with meaning. Winnie speaks of the day as being "well advanced" and immediately relegates her words to "the old style," realizing that there is no God now to advance the day (p. 32) [414].

The Victorians had an especially happy faith in time as an advancing process. Indeed, it was in the Victorian era that the so-called "cult of progress" came to full flower. Somehow, it was believed that man's

9. Robert Browning, *Pippa Passes, ibid.*, 169, 11. 1–12.

1. An automatic response. The phrase refers to the work of Ivan Petrovich Pavlov (1849–1936), a Russian physiologist who demonstrated such responses in a series of famous experiments with dogs [*Editor*].

2. *Ibid.*, p. 169, 11. 13–14.

condition was constantly improving. At the heart of this optimism was a naïve faith in the possibilities of education. Through education all men would one day enjoy the good life. Although the scientific discoveries mentioned earlier had their pessimistic repercussions, to the scientifically oriented mind these initial discoveries about the origin of man were significant portents of the eventual triumph of science, not only over the errors of prejudice and religion, but, ultimately, over the very secrets of existence. Time was to put a damper on Victorian enthusiasm; Winnie, our modern, is disillusioned with education:

> This is what I find so wonderful, that not a day goes by— (*smile*)—to speak in the old style—(*smile off*)—hardly a day, without some addition to one's knowledge however trifling, the addition I mean, provided one takes the pain. . . . And if for some strange reason no further pains are possible. . . . (p. 18) [407]

Education has become both trivial and painful—trivial because man realizes that he will never discover the ultimate answers and painful because each new discovery merely accentuates that bitter truth.

This brings us to Beckett's third use of the phrase "the old style." In this connection a pertinent passage from Beckett's critique of Proust will prove helpful.

> And if you don't understand it, Ladies and Gentlemen, it is because you are too decadent to receive it. You are not satisfied unless form is so strictly divorced from content that you can comprehend the one almost without bothering to read the other. The instinctive skimming and absorption of the scant cream of sense is made possible by what I may call a continuous process of copious intellectual salivation. The form that is independent and arbitrary phenomenon can fulfill no higher function than that of a stimulus for a tertiary or quaternary conditioned reflex of dribbling comprehension.[3]

In *Happy Days* Beckett extends these views on style to create the implicit metaphor of a universe and a way of life in which the sense or meaning has been creamed off, leaving style without sense, form without meaning. The new-style conception of time results, as has already been said, from the loss of a referential deity who can endow the disparate mechanisms of existence with a coherent meaning. With this deity gone only the mechanics remain and man finds himself living on form alone. This is essentially Winnie's predicament. In the face of a complete absence of quality she substitutes a purely quantitative response, trying to convince herself of her own existence by means of an "I talk, therefore I am" hypothesis: "There is so little one can say, one says it all. (*Pause.*)

3. Samuel Beckett, *Proust* (New York: Grove Press, 1957), p. 248.

All one can. (*Pause.*) And no truth in it anywhere (p. 51) [420]." Winnie's use of the phrase "genuine pure" is a fine example of form without meaning. Winnie cannot find the noun which these adjectives modify. Paradoxically, they are finally found to modify "hog's setae," a hog being, as Willie explains, a completely formal, meaningless animal—a "castrated male swine," "reared for slaughter" (p. 47) [419]. Ironically, "filth" is also genuine and pure (p. 19) [408].

There is another way in which Winnie is victimized by the horror of form without meaning. Although she is revolted by sex and by the thought of life and growth, Winnie is unconsciously participating in the mechanics of sex. When Willie takes refuge in his hole in act one the action has a double meaning. Willie is, as Winnie notes, taking shelter from the heat of the sun; he is attempting to return to the womb, longing for the sort of death without dying that Dan Rooney, a Beckett character from the radio play *All That Fall*, desires. There is considerable evidence, however, of underground sexual activity. Notice the suggestive quality of Winnie's advice to Willie as he attempts to crawl into his hole:

> Not head first, stupid, how are you going to turn? (*Pause.*)
> That's it . . . right round . . . now . . . back in. (*Pause.*) Oh
> I know it is not easy, dear, crawling backwards, but it is re-
> warding in the end. (*Pause.*) You have left your vaseline be-
> hind. (*She watches as he crawls back for vaseline.*) The lid!
> (*She watches as he crawls back towards hole. Irritated.*) Not
> head first, I tell you! (*Pause.*) More to the right. (*Pause.*) The
> right, I said. (*Pause. Irritated.*) Keep your tail down, can't you!
> (*Pause.*) Now. (*Pause.*) There! . . . (p. 25) [410]

Here it is ambiguous as to whether these directions are meant to apply to the fetal or coital position. A few pages later, while Willie is still in his hole, Winnie makes these interesting observations:

> The earth is very tight today, can it be I have put on flesh, I
> trust not. (*Pause. Absently, eyes lowered.*) The great heat pos-
> sibly. (*Starts to pat and stroke ground.*) All things expanding,
> some more than others. (*Pause. Patting and stroking.*) Some
> less. (*Pause. Do.*) Oh I can well imagine what is passing
> through your mind, it is not enough to have to listen to the
> woman, now I must look at her as well. . . . (pp 28–29) [412]

To crown this suggestive sequence, an "emmet" soon emerges from the ground with "a little white ball in its arms" which Winnie is unable to recognize but which Willie identifies upon description as an egg. "Formication," he announces. When Winnie responds with the murmur, "God," the word becomes an observation as well as an expletive. The formation of new life has begun through fornication. Although Winnie and Willie both laugh at this manifestation of God's sardonic sense of humor, Winnie is a bit uneasy about Willie's laughter, asking, "Were we perhaps diverted by two quite different things?" (p. 31) [412].

This ridiculously elaborate process, by means of which Willie and Winnie manage to have relations despite overwhelming barriers, emphasizes the impossibility of spontaneous sex in the modern world. Sex has gone underground in this world of the psyche, where, ironically, it still operates as a mechanical reflex which eternalizes the human absurdity. In this respect it is significant that Winnie's first sexual experience occurred "within a toolshed" (p. 16) [407]. Winnie is victimized by the mechanics of sex, and we can almost picture Beckett's malevolent deity "sniggering" at one of his "poorer" jokes (p. 31) [412].

The metaphysical aspect of the new style as form without meaning is evident in the parasol episode. At one point Winnie, searching for some means of filling in her day, decides to put up her parasol as a shade against the sun. After she has held it up a few moments she notes: "Holding up wearies the arm. (*Pause.*) Not if one is going along. (*Pause.*) Only if one is at rest (p. 36) [415]." The Victorians and their predecessors, the Romantics, were "going along," but Winnie has come to a cosmological standstill. Her parasol becomes a striking parody of all cosmologies, all attempts to formulate some metaphysical stance. Dome-shaped, like the sky, but a cheap product of her vanity, absurdly finite in nature, Winnie's parasol is totally ineffectual. Eventually it is set on fire by the brutally real sun, and Winnie tosses it over the mound. She notes significantly, however, that the same thing has happened before and will probably happen again. Man goes from philosophy to philosophy, tossing one away with the left hand while grasping at another with the right. Winnie's parasol hurts her arm; it becomes a very real drawback. Reason tells her "to put the thing down and get on with something else," but there is nothing else to get on with, and, as with the victimized characters in Beckett's radio play, *All That Fall*, the past remains to thwart the present.

It might be worth noting Beckett's careful choice of the word "parasol," which contains the words "par" (by, under) and "sol" (sun). Beckett uses the sun like Ecclesiastes. Everything that occurs, occurs under the sun; our attention is constantly drawn to the sun as the ultimate reality of *Happy Days*. And that reality is the ironic reversal of every optimistic assumption. In a very real sense, *Happy Days* is negatively defined by the opening lines of the Fourth Gospel:

IN THE BEGINNING WAS THE WORD, and the Word was with God, and the Word was God. He was in the beginning with God; all things were made through him, and without him was not anything made that was made. In him was life, and the life was the light of men. The light shines in the darkness, and the darkness has not overcome it.[4]

The Word, once the concrete embodiment of God, charged with ultimate meaning, shrinks by comparison to the mechanical, meaningless words emitted by Winnie. The "light" which "shines in the darkness," creativity opposed to chaos, becomes the "blaze of hellish light" which bobs up "out of dark" in *Happy Days*—the brutal, destructive sun which burns through each and every one of man's pretensions. This light is still equated with God, but the God is evil. Winnie feels that some diabolical eye is fixed on her: "Strange feeling that someone is looking at me. I am clear, then dim, then gone, then dim again, then clear again, and so on, back and forth, in and out of someone's eye (p. 40) [416]." The hypothetical God of *Happy Days* is similar to the diabolical and deceptive God that Descartes postulated and then rejected as unthinkable.

Keeping our knowledge of the old and new styles in mind, we can proceed to examine the seemingly enigmatic ending of *Happy Days*. Before doing this, however, we must consider a fourth aspect of Beckett's negative definition. At one point Winnie considers the possibility of Willie's death and feels the need to relegate this concept to "the old style" (p. 21) [409]. And when Winnie removes the revolver from her bag and places it in sight on the mound so that it becomes a part of the landscape, it inspires a like qualification: "There, that's your home from this day out. (*Smile.*) The old style!" (p. 33) [414]. At other times death is less explicitly linked with the old style, as, for example, when Winnie refers to "the end of the day" or "making ready—for the night" and is consequently reminded of "the old style" (pp. 22, 44) [409, 418].

As in Browning's *Pippa Passes*, Winnie's day is a metaphor for her whole life. Death for Winnie, however, is as novel an idea as life. Having lost the organic, old-style life, she has also lost the triumphant death which crowns such a life, giving it its final meaning. Winnie has neither a past nor a future; her day has neither a beginning nor an end, but is arbitrarily begun and terminated by a bell. And although the revolver in Winnie's bag is always surfacing—although in the second act it is always in sight, it cannot be utilized. It is dying that Beckett emphasizes rather than death. Winnie has two feet in the grave; she is dying in a dying world, and the process continues endlessly.

As the symbolic structure of *Happy Days* becomes clear, we can see a remarkable similarity between the plight of Winnie and the plight of man as described in a sermon by Donne:

> As soon as God set us on work, our very occupation was an Embleme of death; It was to digge the earth; not to digge pitfals for other men, but graves for our selves. Hath any man here

4. *The Holy Bible, Revised Standard Version* (New York: Oxford University Press, 1962), *The Gospel of St. John*, Ch. 1, vv. 1–6.

forgot to day, that yesterday is dead? And the Bell tolls for to day, and will ring out anon; and for as much of every one of us, as appertaines to this day. *Quotidiè morimur, et tamen nos esse aeternos putamus,* sayes S. Hierome; We die every day, and we die all the day long; and because we are not absolutely dead, we call that an eternity, an eternity of dying: And is there comfort in that state? why, that is the state of hell it self, Eternall dying, and not dead.[5]

Beckett carries Donne's figure one step further by literally sinking a woman into the earth and punctuating her "happy days" with a tolling bell. Winnie's state is, as in Donne, one of "Eternall dying," and that state is defined as "the state of hell it self".

Winnie's inability to die is linked with her inability to sing. In this connection we might consider one of Willie's "titbits from Reynolds' News": "His Grace and Most Reverend Father in God Dr. Carolus Hunter dead in tub (p. 15) [406]." Winnie recalls a scene with Hunter, her old beau, "in the back garden of Bourough Green, under the horse beech" (p. 16) [407]. Hunter is implicitly contrasted to the mechanical Mr. Johnson, who kissed Winnie in a toolshed. Indeed, Hunter is a strangely Dionysian figure; he is a high priest and is linked with both nature and love. He has all the attributes of the old-style man. Like Winnie, the Reverend Father is a hunter of song; and what better place to find spontaneous, heartfelt song than in a bathtub? If Hunter dies singing, then he dies with a certain amount of joy and triumph.

Winnie, in contrast to Hunter and to Browning's lyrical Pippa, is unable to burst into spontaneous song. The first act ends with her acknowledgment of defeat in this respect and her consequent substitution of a prayer. In the second act she states her problem in this manner:

> The bell goes for sleep and one has not sung. (*Pause.*) The whole day has flown—(*smile, smile off*)—flown by, quite by, and no song of any class, kind or description. (*Pause.*) There is a problem here. (*Pause.*) One cannot sing . . . just like that, no. (*Pause.*) It bubbles up, for some unknown reason, the time is ill chosen, one chokes it back. (*Pause.*) One says, Now is the time, it is now or never, and one cannot. (*Pause.*) Simply cannot sing. (*Pause.*) Not a note . . . (pp. 56–57) [422–23]

At the end of the second act, however, Winnie orders herself to sing. At this moment Willie emerges from his hermitage behind the mound, "dressed to kill," and his attempts to reach Winnie by climbing the mound on his hands and knees move her to song. Winnie seems to think that Willie is trying to reach her for a kiss, but there is considerable

5. John Donne, "Sermon XV, At Whitehall: lst Friday in Lent. March 8, 1621/2," *Selected Poetry and Selected Prose of John Donne and Complete* *Poetry of William Blake* (New York: Random House, Inc., 1941), p. 375.

ambiguity here. Willie may be coming for a kiss. He may be fulfilling Winnie's first-act wish for him to come live with her and be her love on her side of the mound. On the other hand, Willie may be literally "dressed to kill," and his attempt to climb the mound may be an attempt to get to Brownie, the revolver, in order to put an end to himself or Winnie or both. Hence we are left with a facetious but inevitable question as the curtain falls: Will he? (Willie.) The answer is probably no.

To understand why the answer is no, one must consider the power of Willie's single second-act word, "Win." Through the use of this one word Beckett has added a great irony to the ending of his play. Throughout *Happy Days* Beckett emphasizes the phenomenal lack of communication between Winnie and Willie. They are cut off from each other geographically, sexually, and intellectually. Although Winnie places great importance on Willie's words, it is not actual communication which produces Winnie's "happy days" but rather a fatuous illusion of communication. Willie is merely an object by means of which Winnie convinces herself of her own reality through the reflection of sounds.

Willie is much more of an old-style character than is Winnie. He still possesses flesh, and at one point Beckett is careful to demonstrate that he still has blood in his veins. Although he retreats into the earth as a voluntary means of escape and has difficulty in maintaining an erect position, he has not yet lost his mobility. Willie still retains a certain degree of sexuality, as we have already seen in connection with his underground activities. Willie's use of language is opposed to Winnie's; his extreme economy with words is played off against her prattling volubility. Willie is also a spontaneous singer who gives forth a "burst of hoarse song" in act one (p. 40) [416]; at one point in his past he would have experienced death, we are told, had not Winnie confiscated his revolver. Willie retains a notable strain of Browningesque optimism, reading hopeful advertisements from the newspaper—"Opening for smart youth" and "Wanted bright boy" (p. 48) [419].

Whereas Winnie uses Willie as a means of indulging her own vanity and as a means of self-delusion, Willie is more considerate of Winnie. He answers many of her questions, a definite step towards communication. He is the cause of her "happy days," and at one point Beckett describes his arm as "raised in gesture of giving" (p. 18) [408]. When Willie makes his pathetic struggle to reach Winnie in act two, the novelty of his appearance and the doggedness of his attempt endow him with a certain dramatic urgency. Finally, because he is so sparing with his words, when he manages to eke out a "just audible" "Win," which on face value says little, we can hardly help feeling that some overwhelming, heroic attempt at communication and sympathy with a fellow creature is being made. For these reasons the ending of the play is almost intolerably ironic:

WINNIE: Win! (*Pause.*) Oh this is a happy day, this will have been another happy day! (*Pause.*) After all. (*Pause.*) So far.

Pause. She hums tentatively beginning of song, then sings softly, musical-box tune.

> Though I say not
> What I may not
> Let you hear,
> Yet the swaying
> Dance is saying,
> Love me dear!
> Every touch of fingers
> Tells me what I know,
> Says for you,
> It's true, it's true,
> You love me so!

Pause. Happy expression off. She closes her eyes. Bell rings loudly. She opens her eyes, smiling, to WILLIE, *still on his hands and knees looking up at her. Smile off. They look at each other. Long pause.* (p. 64) [426]

The curtain falls with a man on his knees before a woman, making a mock heroic attempt at communication, sympathy, and love. Everything is set up in Beckett's masterful tableau for a proto-typical Wagnerian *Liebestod*.[6] But although Winnie sings her song—although love, death, and music, the major elements of the *Liebestod*, seem to merge here, the union, obviously a combination of absurdities, remains an ironic impossibility. This final tableau is quintessential Beckett, because, as in *Waiting for Godot*, there is a great sense of urgency and expectation which can never materialize into anything concrete. Beckett sets up this suggestive tableau as a final stroke of negative definition—not to show us what will happen after the curtain falls but rather to show us what can never happen.

Willie's revolutionary action calls for revolutionary behavior on the part of Winnie. Indeed, in the first act she told Willie that she would be "a different woman," if he would come and live with her on her side of the mound (p. 46) [418]. Winnie, however, does not become a different woman; for her this is merely "another happy day". Her additional comment, "so far," indicates that for her Willie's word is merely a sound at a time when sounds have become rare. Willie's action elicits the old meaningles cliché ("Oh this is a happy day") and is thereby reduced to the level of all the other meaningless things that elicited that response.

Winnie cancels the possibility of a *Liebestod*, which requires, above all, an organic union of form and meaning. She sings a song; but instead of a Wagnerian burst of passion we get a cliché-ridden lyric from *The Merry Widow*, mechanically sung—attaining to the level neither of love nor death song. Death remains an impossible solution—something

6. "Love-death." The allusion is to the ecstatic death of the lovers at the end of Wagner's opera *Tristan und Isolde* (1865) [Editor].

which lies forever in sight but which can never be utilized. With the meaningless phrase and the meaningless song, Winnie becomes a victim of the new style. Form seals off meaning just at that moment when meaning becomes possible; and this play, which seems to contain Beckett's happiest ending, actually ends with one of his most devastating commentaries on man's inability to break through habit to perception.

HUGH KENNER

[Happy Days]†

Winnie chattering away, forcing herself through the formulae of cheerful utterance, keeping going, just keeping going, making the day's project out of being happy; Willie grunting, slouching, ignoring her except when much solicited: a day, shall we say, in a shabby-genteel flat where they work hard at being cheerful. It's a curiously *English* play, English in Winnie's tacit assumption that one has a duty not to lapse into gloom; English in the endless struggle to devalue little annoyances, to cherish small mercies; English in the intent façade of garrulity. This is not to say that women everywhere—people everywhere—do not recognize an obligation not to despair. But the unquestioning assumption that the warp and woof of an unfulfilling day consist in maintaining one's cheer is a premise of English gentility as perhaps of no other. Anyone who suspects that Beckett's way of writing is simply to project his own moods should study his portrait of Winnie—no doubt drawn from memories of his London years, a quarter-century before he wrote the play. And the author's affection for Winnie is surely explicit; she is given every opportunity—granted the limited facilities—to be endearing. The actress moreover is given a hundred chances to show what a voice can do, with caresses of inflection, to transform simple words into poetry. Of her parasol:

> I suppose I might—(*takes up parasol*)—yes, I suppose I might
> . . . hoist this thing now. (*Begins to unfurl it. Following
> punctuated by mechanical difficulties overcome.*) One keeps
> putting off—putting up—for fear of putting up—too soon—
> and the day goes by—quite by—without one's having put
> up—at all. (*Parasol now fully open. Turned to her right she
> twirls it idly this way and that.*) Ah yes, so little to say, so
> little to do, and the fear so great, certain days, of finding oneself
> . . . left, with hours still to run, before the bell for sleep, and
> nothing more to say, nothing more to do, that the days go by,

† Reprinted by permission of Farrar, Straus and Giroux, Inc., and Thames and Hudson Ltd. Excerpted from *A Reader's Guide to Samuel Beckett*   by Hugh Kenner. Pp. 147–52. Copyright © 1973 by Thames and Hudson, Ltd.

certain days go by, quite by, the bell goes, and little or nothing said, little or nothing done. (*Raising parasol.*) That is the danger. (*Turning front.*) To be guarded against. (*She gazes front, holding up parasol with right hand. Maximum pause.*)

Of words, and of small duties:

Is not that so, Willie, that even words fail, at times? (*Pause. Back front.*) What is one to do then, until they come again? Brush and comb the hair, if it has not been done, or if there is some doubt, trim the nails if they are in need of trimming, these things tide one over. (*Pause.*) That is what I mean. (*Pause.*) That is all I mean. (*Pause.*) That is what I find so wonderful, that not a day goes by—(*smile*)—to speak in the old style—(*smile off*) without some blessing—(WILLIE *collapses behind slope, his head disappears,* WINNIE *turns towards event*—in disguise.

Of Willie's incompetent locomotion:

Not the crawler you were, poor darling. (*Pause.*) No, not the crawler I gave my heart to. (*Pause.*) The hands and knees, love, try the hands and knees. (*Pause.*) The knees! The knees! (*Pause.*) What a curse, mobility!

It's a splendid virtuoso part, though an immobilized one like Hamm's, and her simple love, largely unrequited, for Willie, lifts the tedium to crescendos of chirpy pathos.

All but the crawling-speech, these speeches might be spoken in any flat on the Edgware Road. But of course they are spoken under conditions never explained, simply taken for granted as so many inconveniences—cockroaches, for instance, defective plumbing, damp, dry rot—are taken for granted. The present condition would appear to be that the earth's rotation has become very slow, hence the days very long and very hot. To speak of days at all is 'to speak in the old style'; she cannot break the habit, but never fails to observe its incongruity. And the earth seems nearly depopulated, though a couple did once come strolling by, she remembers them. And the heat increases. Her parasol, in the play's most spectacular event, takes fire by spontaneous combustion, and she wonders if she herself will not melt in the end, 'Oh, I do not mean necessarily burst into flames, no, just little by little be charred to a black cinder, all this—(*ample gesture of arms*)—visible flesh.' It is as though the flash of a Hydrogen Bomb and its power to incinerate were being lived through in excruciating slow motion.

Or not quite, since we are (as always) on stage, and the first sound is the prompter's bell, and almost her first words—'Begin, Winnie'—are like the words of an actress steeling herself to play the part one more time. (It is an uncomfortable role, we are to reflect, and night after night the woman before us must go through with it, under fierce unchanging artificial lights.) Tomorrow, she reflects, there will be another parasol to put up (though it, too, will burn), and tomorrow the little mirror she breaks on a stone (she breaks it merely to enforce this point) will be intact again in her bag, if the property-master is not negligent. It is a curious effect, the hidden functionaries of the theatre who check the contents of bags and arrange combustible umbrellas being transformed, by a few words, into presiding powers, workers of mysterious miracles; merciful miracles since resources are replenished, merciless since no headway is made, not even headway toward some abyss. Beckett has invoked the repeatability of the play before, the plight of actors trapped in parts, but never so deftly, never with such buoyant pathos. *Happy Days* is like a companion-piece to *Endgame*,[1] with cheer where the latter flaunted cruelty, and renewability where the latter suffered attrition. All the world's a stage, all the world's a Woolworth's; there are always more parasols, more looking-glasses, more words.

For the words are properties also. As parasols are fetched from shops, so words from poets, and it is surprising what resources the poets afford, for cheering one up in the face of the irremediable. 'Fear no more the heat o' the sun', she quotes at one point, when Willie has crawled into the shade; and 'Hail, holy light', as her eyes open on yet another blinding prospect, and as she finishes making up her lips, words Romeo spoke over the inanimate Juliet flit through her head:

> Thou art not conquer'd; beauty's ensign yet
> Is crimson in thy lips and in thy cheeks
> And death's pale flag is not advancèd there.

Winnie's ensign of beauty comes from a tube, and Romeo has his back to her, absorbed in a newspaper, and it is she who speaks, not he, so the scene has to be somewhat transposed:

> (. . . *She pulls down spectacles and resumes lips.* WILLIE *opens newspaper, hands invisible. Tops of yellow sheets appear on either side of his head.* WINNIE *finishes lips, inspects them in mirror held a little further away.*) Ensign crimson. (WILLIE *turns page.* WINNIE *lays down lipstick and mirror, turns towards bag.*) Pale flag.

One enhances one's experience with words one would have been un-qualified to compose, and has for an instant a taste of human grandeur. This is a service writers perform for us, a service less attended to than it might be in schools where the didactic functions of literature nourish the self-esteem of teachers. Poets give us words to say, though they may be imperfectly remembered when we have occasion to say them.

1. An earlier play by Beckett [*Editor*].

What are those exquisite lines? (*Pause.*) Go forget me why
should something o'er that something shadow fling . . . go
forget me . . . why should sorrow . . . brightly smile . . . go
forget me . . . never hear me . . . sweetly smile . . . brightly
sing . . . (*Pause. With a sigh.*) One loses one's classics. (*Pause.*)
Oh not all. (*Pause.*) A part. (*Pause.*) A part remains. (*Pause.*)
That is what I find so wonderful, a part remains, of one's
classics, to help one through the day.

Quotations abound; an inventory would be pointless. For that matter
most of the play (of any play) is quotation, quotation from that epon-
ymous poet the Folk, who have shaped the idiom of which each Winnie
at need avails herself.

The whole day has flown—(*smile, smile off*)—flown by, quite
by, and no song of any class, kind or description. (*Pause.*)
There is a problem here. (*Pause.*) One cannot sing . . . just
like that, no. (*Pause.*) It bubbles up, for some unknown reason,
the time is ill chosen, one chokes it back. (*Pause.*) One says,
Now is the time, it is now or never, and one cannot. (*Pause.*)
Simply cannot sing. (*Pause.*) Not a note.

'Just like that'; 'for some unknown reason'; 'the time is ill chosen';
'not a note'. Not a phrase in this speech but is like these, familiar idiom,
shaped by the imagination of the race, validated (like the familiar quotations in Bartlett) by collective usage. That is Winnie's resource, ultimately, the human community, available to her in speech, its legacy
of speech, though hardly a soul any longer comes this way.

And she sinks; we all do. In the first act she can rummage (like
Malone)[2] through her possessions. In the second she can only look
toward them but not finger them, having sunk further, in fact up to the
neck. This is unexplained. There was a day when she 'was not yet
caught—in this way'—and had the use of her legs; there was the day of
the first kiss, the first ball, the day Willie proposed ('I worship you,
Winnie, be mine. Life's a mockery without Win.') She is caught now,
that is all. It is no more explained than would be an incurable disease.
Willie is caught too, not in a quagmire, but in a defect of locomotion
that compels him to get about only on all fours. (Locomotion, for most
Beckett characters, is so peculiar that we are seldom surprised when one
of them is deprived of it.) He might crawl away, but he does not, which
is a comfort, and perhaps a mute fidelity, unless it bespeaks a lacuna in
his imagination. And when he crawls round at the end, and up her
mound, and gazes into her eyes, or maybe glares ('Don't look at me like
that! Have you gone out of your head, Willie? Out of your poor old
wits, Willie?') it is an open question whether he is moved to reanimate
the past, or has simply made up his mind to use the revolver that lies

2. The protagonist of Beckett's novel *Malone Dies* [*Editor*].

conspicuous before her on the mound. It may even be his intention to use it on her; his tastes are sedentary, his devotion is to the obituaries and the advertisements in *Reynolds' News*, and her talk, talk, talk, it may be, has driven him mad.

Valiant, spunky, imprisoned in habit and in routine, she lives without letting herself know it in a world of little love, and puts amorous construction—to the extent of singing the Merry Widow Waltz—on what for all we know may be a murderous glare. The play, an emptiness filled by indomitable energy, is Beckett's ambiguous celebration of human persistence, which has at many times made it unfashionable to reflect, with Dr Johnson, that there is much in human life to be endured, and little to be enjoyed.

CHARLES R. LYONS

Some Analogies Between the Epic Brecht and the Absurdist Beckett†

Contemporary drama is dominated by two types of dramatic structure: the epic and the absurd. While both of these movements within the *avant-garde* are international and both are fed by complex influences outside of their own literatures, they are, in a sense, primarily German and French movements respectively. The antithetical nature of the epic and the absurd seems clear on a variety of levels—sufficiently clear, surely, to make the title of this paper somewhat surprising: one movement is predominately Marxist and the other largely existential; one assumes the existence of an objective, external reality, and the other sees the subjective consciousness as the only reality; one imitates its concept of reality in loose, episodic structures, frequently representing a wide passage of time, the other functions more as an extended poetic image, concentrating upon a single "psychic moment;" one presents clearly defined social relationships, the other exploits obscurity and density.

These differences are ones we recognize easily, and, to a large degree, they define our sense of the relationship between the epic and the absurd theaters. While the philosophical and formal antitheses have made the playwrights themselves see their work as incompatible, both kinds of structure can satisfy the same audience; and it is not unusual for a critic who celebrates Bertolt Brecht to respond as deeply to Samuel Beckett. In this paper, I would like to explore some of the analogies between the epic and the absurd, using Brecht and Beckett as the prime examples of each of these dramatic forms which, while they seem antithetical, offer analogous satisfactions.

Of course, Brecht's early plays are very similar to the absurdist drama;

† Reprinted from *Comparative Drama* 1.4 (1967–68): 297–304, with the permission of the publishers.

and that relationship has been discussed with some frequency. Interestingly, those works remained strange and obscure until we went back to them after learning how to deal with such plays as *En attendant Godot* and *Fin de partie*.[1] However, in this paper, I am dealing with the analogies which exist between the major Brechtian plays, those written in the controlled and deliberate form of Brecht's Marxist polemic, and the plays of the Theatre of the Absurd.

First of all, in both formal structures, there is a disintegration of the conventional, or Aristotelian, sense of dramatic time in which the temporal sequence of the act imitated determines the order of the play. In his theoretical writings, Brecht argued against what he defined as an Aristotelian structure: one in which the protagonist, the focus of the spectator's identification, suffers an experience whose temporal sequence organizes the play. Rather than having the experience itself determine the structure in an obvious progression of events, Brecht exploited an episodic form in which the progression is delayed by the "interruption" of songs and digressive scenes. The rather complicated structures which Brecht developed are closely unified, but they are unified, thematically, not temporally. Each Brechtian scene is independently coherent, forming an integrity of its own as it clarifies its own theme, like a medieval exemplum, and relates to the major ethical judgment directing the work. Brecht wanted to interfere with the psychological process of identification—the fantasy of self as hero—so that the imagination of the spectator would be free to make an ethical judgment upon the protagonist's act. Act and consequence are known factors, usually, at the beginning of the action, and the rhythm of his plays does not depend upon the suspenseful expectation of the spectator. The exposition of the ethical quality of the event forms the order of scenes. In this perspective, the Brechtian play is a vertical structure, not a horizontal one.

The conventional temporal sequence is also abrogated in the absurdist plays. These works are not imitative of the passage of time in any usual sense. In Beckett's drama, time seems to be one of those futile contracts which one attempts in order to establish relation with another human being; yet time has no more meaning than that which the consciousness invests in it. The nature of Beckett's plays is dynamic, as they imitate the transaction of a consciousness, but each is static in the sense that this transaction has little to do with time itself.

Also, neither the epic nor the absurd dramas assumes the conventional pretense that their action is real. The artifice of the performance is clarified, for example, by both Brecht and Beckett as they remind the spectators that the play itself is an imaginative construct. In *En attendant Godot* the music-hall technique of Vladimir and Estragon make the performance, on one level, a grotesque comic routine. In *Fin de partie*, Hamm refers to the action as a performance; and in *Happy Days*, the

1. The French titles for *Waiting for Godot* and *Endgame*. Both plays were written and produced in French before Beckett translated them into English [*Editor*].

action takes place in front of an obviously "trompe l'oeil" background. In Brecht, the process of alienation, so frequently discussed, illuminates the performance as performance. In Beckett's use of the theatrical image the play itself becomes an obvious metaphor for life itself *as play*, despairing play, but the imaginative implementation of conventional routines to give form to another otherwise formless experience. Here there is the assumption that the real world is no more tangible, no more consistent, no more explicable that the deprived, obscure, and strange world of the play.

Perhaps the serious playwright can no longer make the conventional pretense that the performance is reality. The disintegration of conventional form—the temporal sequence of act and consequence as rational process—occurred in the late 19th and early 20th centuries: the change in dramatic form is marked by the subjective reality of Expressionism in which the scene became the projection of the consciousness of the hero and by the puzzling obscuring of reality in Pirandello. Both Brecht and Beckett are outgrowths of Expressionism in which the distortions of the subjective response of the hero are distributed into the scene itself as a metaphoric representation of his imagination. Those distortions, frequently obvious, blatant and over-simplified, are more subtly contained in Brecht and Beckett in which more complex and ambiguous actions are projected with greater density throughout the whole structure of the play.

We can see the anologies between Brecht and Beckett more clearly by analyzing a particular action which each imitates and comparing the forms of the imitations. We are growing increasingly sensitive to the implications of the term *form*—form as the particular means of ordering human experience in an imaginative imitation. In *Mutter Courage* and *Happy Days* we have examples of an epic and an absurd conception of a similar experience which can illustrate this ordering process. Both Brecht and Beckett have explored the quality of a self-directed isolation in the image of an energetic woman who attempts to maintain herself in a hostile world and suffers the deprivation of all human relationships. Brecht's Anna Fierling, the curious Mutter Courage, chooses her identity as sutler woman. Her commercial identity is the most important aspect of her will as it defines, for her, her very being until she no longer has identity as mother. Beckett's Winnie, from *Happy Days*, longs for the peace of an absolute loneliness but fears, acutely and painfully, that she will lose her consciousness of being in isolation. She seeks identity in that which defines, for her, human life: the trivial processes, the patent phrases—all attenuated, dessicated, and without meaning in her present condition.

Brecht's play is an episodic, quasi-history play (of the Thirty Years' War) which is dominated by the strong figure of Anna Fierling but holds a wide proliferation of characters. Beckett's play is almost an extended monologue in which Winnie, buried up to her breasts and then up to her chin, explores her strange condition. Beckett's play depends upon the immobility of its protagonist; the scene is abstracted into the unspecified mound of sand. Brecht's play ranges from scene to scene in the progress of the war. However, despite these obvious disparities in structure, it is important to recognize the most critical point of analogy between *Mutter Courage* and *Happy Days*: that both plays use the external situation of their protagonists to project actions which explore the crucial relationship between the self and the world, or that which is external to the self.

Mutter Courage lives from the war, feeding on it, and—in turn—it consumes her children (to use Brecht's own metaphors). The playwright condemns her action, using it in the terms of his polemic as a negative in order to clarify the positive. Brecht was repelled by the sentimental interpretations of *Courage* which assumed that Anna Fierling's survival is invested with courage and fortitude and a stoic acceptance of the inhumanity of the human condition. However, neither the sentimental nor the polemic reading does justice to the complexity of Brecht's characterization. The world of *Mutter Courage*, more accurately the human organization of this world, demands *Kapitulation* for survival. In Brecht's vision, compassion is a weakness, an irrationality; it is instinctive behavior which tempts the reason. Each of Anna Fierling's children succumbs to this temptation: Schweizerkas to honesty; Eilif to bravery; and Kattrin to a "terrible compassion" as she acts, suicidally, to save the children of Halle.

Anna Fierling's act, undeniably, is her rational *Kapitulation*. The scene of *Mutter Courage* (in Burke's[2] inclusive sense of economic, social, and philosophical environment) is the war, the business of war, or—in more Brechtian terms—war as business. Anna Fierling's act is her rational submission to the logic and ethic of exploitation, the logic and ethic of the war, which she uses and which, in turn, uses her. Her choice is her rational protection of the self. It is a self-concerned act, and it is a choice which ultimately, denies all bonds which would unite the self to anything beyond it. The family unit of the poem—Anna Fierling, Schweizerkas, Eilif and Kattrin—is a critical image. From one perspective the primary experience of *Mutter Courage* is Anna Fierling's loss of each of her children, her loss of them to the war. However, in a difficult way, Anna Fierling does not passively suffer the loss of her children. In her use of the war, as a means of survival, she denies them. Her loss of them signals her own retreat from those bonds which threaten the self. Each child makes that risk, and—in the hostile world of *Mutter Courage*—is killed.

In *Happy Days* Winnie exists caught between her desire for human contact, exemplified in her efforts to continue her attenuated relationship with Willie, who lives in a hole behind her mound of sand, and her

2. Kenneth Burke (1897–), an American literary critic and theorist [*Editor*].

desire for the peace of complete isolation. However, in the ambivalence of this dense poem, there is a celebration and a fear of that isolation within Winnie's own consciousness. The possibility of absolute isolation terrifies her:

> . . . if only I could bear to be alone, I mean prattle away with not a soul to hear . . . Not that I flatter myself you hear much, no Willie, God forbid . . . Days perhaps when you hear nothing . . . But days too when you answer . . . So that I may say at all times, even when you do not answer and perhaps hear nothing, Something of this is being heard, I am not merely talking to myself, that is in the wilderness, a thing I could never bear to do—for any length of time . . . (whereas if you were to die—(*smile*)—to speak in the old style—or go away and leave me, then what would I do, what *could* I do, all day long, I mean between the bell for waking and the bell for sleep . . . Simply gaze before me with compressed lips . . . Not another word as long as I drew breath, nothing to break the silence of this place.

And yet, the wilderness of this isolation, in which the only resource is the individual consciousness, is also that which is desired by Winnie. Justifying Willie's silence, she says: "One does not appear to be asking a great deal, indeed at times it would seem hardly possible—. . . to ask less—of a fellow creature—to put it mildly—whereas actually—when you think about it—look into your heart—see the other—what he needs—peace—to be left in peace—and then perhaps the moon—all this time—asking for the moon." In the apparently infinite sunlight of Winnie's world—in which there is no night, only the division of activity marked by the bell, the moon becomes the symbol of that which is desired: the dissolution of the present reality: ". . . the happy day to come when flesh melts at so many degrees and the night of the moon has so many hundred hours."

While the result of the abstraction in Brecht and Beckett is very different, the process itself is similar: Anna Fierling's sutler wagon is as much a projection of her being as is the mound in which Winnie is contained. Both define the restrictive identity of the protagonist. However, Beckett's visual imagery is condensed, and, to a degree, static; Brecht presents a more varied visual imagery—an epic panorama of human situations against which the recurrent, insistent act of *Kapitulation* is played. However, that dynamic panorama is scene not action; and the content of the metaphor is analogous to Beckett's visual image. The seemingly endless progress of the war in *Mutter Courage*, the repetitious instances of greed and exploitation and deprivation and killing all project the use of one human being by another. In Beckett's abstraction, the single couple serve: Winnie, using Willie, finding her identity as it is reflected in his response, exploiting his self-concerned memories to aid her in her failing recreations of the past. Their strange and simplified existence—Winnie in her mound and Willie in his hole—contains a sense of futility, use, and exploitation comparable to the expanded and diffuse image of the war in Brecht's play.

In Brecht social relationships are clear-cut and unequivocal; and while the poet in him provided ambiguities which underlie these relationships, the external structure of the plays after *Mann 1st Mann*[3] is clear. In Beckett there is no such thing as a tangible reality or a relationship or identity which has consistent integrity. Consequently, the factors of the scene are not clearly defined. For example: Brecht uses the clearly defined relationship of Anna Fierling and her family to clarify the experience of her isolation from any apprehension of human communion; in Beckett the image of the child is deliberately obscure. Each apparent family structure in Beckett's plays in clouded and equivocal. In *Fin de partie* there is that grimly conceived pair of procreators, Nagg and Nell, Hamm's parents in the ash cans, but the suggestions of a father-son relationship between Hamm and Clov are dim and equivocal. In *Happy Days*, Winnie tells a horrifying story of young Mildred (similar to the story of the threatened child in *Fin de partie*) who was born ("in the old style") and has memories of the womb (with the implication that life is no longer generated in human wombs). Millie, reminiscent of Willie, might be her child; but the obscurity, the tenuousness, the possible fiction of this relationship is more important to the play than anything else. Beckett, of course, confronts an inexplicable reality and affirms its obscurity. Brecht poses the possibility of a better reality in the polemic structure, but, in the poem itself, he responds to a confusing and hostile world.

The ethical perspective of the characters provides the strongest difference between the two forms. Brecht clearly condemns the *Kapitulation* performed by his characters. Yet, regardless of its structural experimentation or manifest content, the Brechtian play holds some form of surrender as its primary action. Consider the insistence upon submission in the Brechtian canon: Baal's aggressive sexuality is described as a surrender to instinct as he succumbs to the "natural" process of consumption;[4] in *Im Dickicht der Staedte*,[5] Shlink surrenders to this natural law of the consumption of one human being by another—discovering that human contact is impossible, he submits to his own destruction in an erotic, homosexual assault; in *Die Massnahme*,[6] Der Junge Genosse attempts to implement his compassion in a concrete and specific realization of his own will, but, recognizing the futility of his action, he submits to his destruction for the good of the Party. In *Leben des Galileo*,[7] the instinctive assertion is associated with the creative sci-

---

3. *Man Equals Man* (1925), an early play by Bertolt Brecht [*Editor*].
4. In the early play *Baal* (1918) [*Editor*].

5. *In the Jungle of Cities* (1923) [*Editor*].
6. *The Measures Taken* (1930) [*Editor*].
7. *The Life of Galileo* (1939) [*Editor*].

entific energy of the villain-hero who, unable to deny his own desires for comfort (nourishment and security), surrenders his freedom and submits to a rational, collective code, the defined authority of the church. In *Mutter Courage*, the energetic movement towards both compassion and individual freedom is seen as self-destructive; Kattrin's compassionate but suicidal assertion is contrasted to Anna Fierling's submission to the collective, rational, and wise. The submission of the self to a power which exists external to the will is insistent, and this awesome force assumes many forms: the forward and inevitable current of the river (one of Brecht's most persistent and arresting metaphors); the wind; the sexual strength of the male; the energy of the horse upon which the Count of Mazzepa is strapped;[8] the whirling force of the planet in orbit; the omnipresence of decay. As I have said before, the negative act in Brecht—in the polemic plays, the submission of *Kapitulation*—exists ostensibly to define the positive; but Brecht presents characters who are victims, and the possibility of the positive seems remote indeed. The sense of human order in the Marxist scheme seems to have given Brecht a sufficient faith in human progress to allow him to accommodate the presence of evil. And yet his poetry demonstrates that the reality of evil within his imagination remained an acute concern, one which Brecht continued to suffer. Man's exploitation of man, through destructive sexual uses and through the uses of power, seems to remain the reality. The "rhetoric of decomposition" persists, and the implicit substructure of Brecht's work, the recurrent myth of submission, the drama of the futile assertion, relates the German poet to the absurdists as he, unconsciously, explores the themes which they develop with greater deliberation.

In developing the concept of the thematic analogies in Brecht and Beckett, it is possible to claim that the work of both dramatists is political. If you define political as that which concerns man's relationship to a community, the quality of his being with other human beings, it is possible to claim that the absurdists share a political concern with Brecht. The Theatre of the Absurd explores man's relationship with man. The result of that explanation is a rehearsal of the futility of such a relationship, and the works decry that futility. Brecht and the absurdists share this sense of futility, and both dramaturgies are forms which contain a confrontation with isolation and the futility of assertion. In both *Mutter Courage* and *Happy Days* the nature of assertion is tested. The explicit polemic of Brecht's play is concerned with the coded compassion of the Marxist ideal; its implicit movement concerns the futility of compassionate gestures. In one sense, Fierling herself makes no assertion. "Das Lied von der Grossen Kapitulation"[9] clarifies that she had already re-

---

8. Although of noble birth, Jan Mazeppa was a page in the court of the king of Poland when he was caught in an intrigue with a Polish countess and lashed to the back of a wild horse by her husband. When the horse fell dead of exhaustion, Mazeppa was released by a cossack and lived to become a prince of the Ukraine [*Editor*].

9. "The Song of the Great Capitulation" [*Editor*].

signed herself. However, the innocence of her children is opposed to her realism, and the futile assertion exists in their acts, their self-destructive compassionate gestures. In *Happy Days* assertion exists in Winnie's attempt to fill the void of her own being with gestures which enact a previous moment. The meaningful assertion would be a rejection of those futile gestures and an acceptance of the wilderness. This tension between assertion and denial is distributed in *Mutter Courage* among the complex of Fierling and her children. In *Happy Days*, that dialectic is contained in the imagination of Winnie herself. This brief essay has suggested some formal and thematic analogies between two plays of Brecht and Beckett. In both of these plays the psychic situation is clarified in a major scenic metaphor; but, even more significantly, in *Mutter Courage* and *Happy Days* the assertion of the self is given a densely ambiguous quality in which the reaching out of the self to another human being is both celebrated and presented as futile, impossible, or self-destructive.

Selected Bibliography

Books and articles excerpted earlier in this volume have not been included in this list.

GENERAL WORKS

Brook, Peter. *The Empty Space*. Hammondsworth, Middlesex, 1979.
Brustein, Robert. *The Theatre of Revolt: An Approach to the Modern Drama*. Boston and Toronto, 1962.
Downer, Alan. *Fifty Years of American Drama*. Chicago, 1951.
Driver, Tom F. *Romantic Quest and Modern Query: A History of the Modern Theatre*. New York, 1970.
Gassner, John. *Form and Idea in Modern Theatre*. New York, 1956.
Jones, Robert Edmond, and Kenneth Macgowan. *Continental Stagecraft*. New York, 1922.
Lahr, John. *Astonish Me: Adventures in Contemporary Theatre*. New York, 1973.
Lamm, Martin. *Modern Drama*. Trans. K. Elliott. Oxford, 1952.
Lumley, Frederick. *Trends in 20th-Century Drama*. Fairlawn, New Jersey, 1956.
Schevill, James. *Breakout! In Search of New Theatrical Environments*. Chicago, 1972.
Valency, Maurice. *The End of the World: An Introduction to Modern Drama*. New York, 1980.

HENRIK IBSEN

Adams, Robert M. "Henrik Ibsen: The Fifty-First Anniversary." *The Hudson Review* 10 (1957) 3: 415–23.
Beyer, Edvard. *Ibsen: The Man and His Work*. New York, 1980.
Downs, Brian W. *Ibsen: The Intellectual Background*. Cambridge, 1946.
Jorgenson, Theodore. *Henrik Ibsen: Life and Drama*. Northfield, Minnesota, 1963.
Kott, Jan. "Ibsen's Deconstruction." *Theater* (Yale) 11 (1980) 2: 37–53.
McCarthy, Mary, "The Will and Testament of Ibsen." *Sights and Spectacles*. London, 1959.
McFarlane, James W. *Ibsen and the Temper of Norwegian Literature*. London, 1960.
Meyer, Michael. *Henrik Ibsen: The Making of the Dramatist*. London, 1967.
———. *Ibsen: A Biography*. New York, 1971.
Mueller, Janel M. "Ibsen's Wild Duck." *Modern Drama* 11 (1969): 347–55.
Northam, John. *Ibsen's Dramatic Method*. London, 1953.
Raphael, Robert. "Illusion and the Self in *The Wild Duck*." *Scandinavian Studies* 35 (1963): 37–42.
States, Bert O. "The Dialectical Drama: Ibsen and His Followers." *Irony and Drama*. Ithaca, New York, 1971.
Tennant, P. F. D. *Ibsen's Dramatic Technique*. Cambridge, 1948.
Wiegand, Hermann J. *The Modern Ibsen: A Reconsideration*. New York, 1925.

ANTON CHEKHOV

Bruford, W. H. *Anton Chekhov*. London, 1957.
Clyman, Toby W. *A Chekhov Companion*. Westport, Connecticut, 1985.
Gorki, Maxim. *Reminiscences of Tolstoy, Chekhov, and Andreyev*. New York, 1921.
Hahn, Beverly. *Chekhov: A Study of the Major Stories and Plays*. Cambridge, 1977.
Hingley, Ronald. *A New Life of Anton Chekhov*. New York, 1976.
Magarshack, David. *Chekhov the Dramatist*. London, 1952.
Melchinger, Siegfried. *Anton Chekhov*. New York, 1972.
Moss, Howard. "Three Sisters." *The Hudson Review* 30 (1977–78): 525–43.
Rayfield, Donald. *Chekhov: The Evolution of His Art*. New York, 1975.

Styan, J. L. *Chekhov in Performance: A Commentary on the Major Plays.* Cambridge, 1973.
World Theater 9 (1960). "Chekhov Centenary Issue."

GEORGE BERNARD SHAW

Bentley, Eric. *Bernard Shaw.* New York, 1947.
Ervine, St. John. *Bernard Shaw; His Life, Works, and Friends.* New York, 1956.
Hardwick, Michael, and Molly. *The Bernard Shaw Companion.* London, 1973.
Henderson, Archibald. *George Bernard Shaw: Man of the Century.* New York, 1956.
Holt, Charles L. "Candida: The Music of Ideas." *Shaw Review* 9 (1966): 2–14.
Hugo, Leon. *Bernard Shaw: Playwright and Preacher.* London, 1971.
Joad, C. E. M. *Shaw.* London, 1949.
Lazenby, Walter. "Love and 'Vitality' in *Candida.*" *Modern Drama* 20 (1977): 1–19.
Matthews, John F. *George Bernard Shaw.* New York, 1969.
Pearson, Hesketh. *G. B. S. A Full-length Portrait.* New York, 1942.
Turco, Alfred. *Shaw's Moral Vision: The Self and Salvation.* Ithaca, New York, 1976.
Whitman, Robert F. *Shaw and the Play of Ideas.* Ithaca, New York, 1977.

AUGUST STRINDBERG

Bandy, Stephen C. "Strindberg's Biblical Sources for *The Ghost Sonata.*" *Scandinavian Studies* 40 (1968): 200–209.
Dahlström, Carl E. W. L. *Strindberg's Dramatic Expressionism.* Ann Arbor, 1930.
Jarvi, Raymond. "Strindberg's *The Ghost Sonata* and Sonata Form." *Mosaic* 5 4 (1972): 69–84.
Johnson, Walter. "Strindberg and the Danse Macabre." *Modern Drama* 3 (1960): 8–15.
Lucas, F. L. *The Drama of Ibsen and Strindberg.* London, 1962.
McGill, V. J. *August Strindberg: The Bedevilled Viking.* London, 1930.
Meyer, Michael. *Strindberg: A Biography.* New York, 1985.
Modern Drama 5 (1962). "Strindberg Issue."
Steene, Brigitta. *The Greatest Fire: A Study of August Strindberg.* Carbondale, Illinois, 1973.
Sprigge, Elizabeth. *The Strange Life of August Strindberg.* New York, 1949.
Sprinchorn, Evert. *Strindberg as Dramatist.* New Haven, 1982.

LUIGI PIRANDELLO

Bentley, Eric. "Father's Day: In Search of Six Characters in Search of an Author." *Drama Review* 13 (Fall 1968) 1: 57–72.
Fioco, Achille. "The Heritage of Pirandello." *World Theatre* 3 (1953) 3:24–30.
Gordon, Jan. "*Sei Personaggi in Cerca d'Autore*: Myth, Ritual, and Pirandello's Anti-Symbolist Theater." *Forum Italicum* 6 (1972): 333–55.
Illiano, Antonio. "Pirandello's *Six Characters in Search of an Author*: A Comedy in the Making." *Italica* 44 (1967): 1–12.
Kennedy, Andrew K. "*Six Characters*: Pirandello's Last Tape." *Modern Drama* 12 (1969): 1–9.
MacClintock, Lander. *The Age of Pirandello.* Bloomington, Indiana, 1951.
Matthaei, Renate. *Luigi Pirandello.* New York, 1973.
Moestrup, Jörn. *The Structural Patterns of Pirandello's Work.* Odense, 1972.
Oliver, Roger W. *Dreams of Passion: The Theater of Luigi Pirandello.* New York, 1979.
Paolucci, Anne. *Pirandello's Theater: The Recovery of the Modern Stage for Dramatic Art.* Carbondale, Illinois, 1974.
Poggioli, Renato. "Pirandello in Retrospect." *Italian Quarterly* 1 (1958) 4: 19–47.
Starkie, Walter. *Luigi Pirandello: 1867–1936.* New York, 1937.

EUGENE O'NEILL

Alexander, Doris. *The Tempering of Eugene O'Neill.* New York, 1962.
Barlow, Judith E. "*Long Day's Journey into Night*: From Early Notes to Finished Play." *Modern Drama* 22 (1979): 19–28.
Bermel, Albert. "The Family as Villain." *Contradictory Characters: An Interpretation of the Modern Theatre.* New York, 1973. 105–21.
Bogard, Travis. *Contour in Time: The Plays of Eugene O'Neill.* New York, 1972.
Bryer, Jackson R. " 'Hell is Other People': *Long Day's Journey into Night.*" *Fifties: Fiction, Poetry, Drama.* Ed. Warren French. Deland, Florida, 1970. 261–70.
Carpenter, Frederic I. *Eugene O'Neill.* New York, 1964.

Falk, Doris V. *Eugene O'Neill and the Tragic Tension*. New Brunswick, New Jersey, 1958.
Gelb, Barbara, and Arthur. *O'Neill*. New York, 1962.
Krutch, Joseph Wood. "O'Neill's Tragic Sense." *American Scholar* 16 (1947): 283–90.
Leech, Clifford. *Eugene O'Neill*. New York, 1963.
Shaeffer, Louis. *O'Neill: Son and Playwright*. Boston, 1968.
———. *O'Neill: Son and Artist*. Boston, 1973.
Tiusanen, Timo. *O'Neill's Scenic Images*. Princeton, New Jersey, 1968.
Winthur, Sophus K. *Eugene O'Neill: A Critical Study*. Rev. ed. New York, 1961.

BERTOLT BRECHT

Barthes, Roland. "Seven Photo Models of Mother Courage." *Tulane Drama Review* 1 (1956): 44–55.
Benjamin, Walter. *Understanding Brecht*. Trans. Anna Bostock. London, 1973.
Blau, Herbert. "Brecht's *Mother Courage*: The Rite of War and the Rhythm of Epic." *Educational Theatre Journal* 9 (1957): 1–10.
Dickson, Keith A. *Towards Utopia: A Study of Brecht*. London, 1978.
Gray, Ronald. *Brecht: The Dramatist*. Cambridge, 1976.
Grossvogel, David I. *Four Playwrights and a Postscript: Brecht, Ionesco, Beckett, Genet*. Ithaca, New York, 1962.
Hecht, Werner. "The Development of Brecht's Theory of Epic Theatre, 1918–1933." *Tulane Drama Review* 6 (1961): 40–97.
Heilman, Robert B. *The Iceman, the Arsonist, and the Troubled Agent: Tragedy and Melodrama on the Modern Stage*. Seattle, 1973.
Hoffmann, C. "Brecht's Humor: Laughter While the Shark Bites." *Germanic Review* 38 (1963): 157–66.
Sokel, Walter H. "Brecht's Concept of Character." *Comparative Drama* 5 (1971): 177–92.
Styan, J. L. *The Dark Comedy: The Development of Modern Comic Tragedy*. Cambridge, 1968. 166–87.
Völker, Klaus. *Brecht: A Biography*. Trans. John Nowell. New York, 1978.
Willett, John. *The Theatre of Bertolt Brecht*. London, 1959.
White, Alfred D. *Bertolt Brecht's Great Plays*. London, 1978.

SAMUEL BECKETT

Brennan, Anthony S. "Winnie's Golden Treasury: The Use of Quotation in *Happy Days*." *Arizona Quarterly* 35 (1979): 205–27.
Coe, Richard. *Samuel Beckett*. New York, 1965.
Collins, P. H. "Proust, Time, and Beckett's *Happy Days*." *French Review* 47 (1974): 105–19.
Friedman, Melvin J. *Samuel Beckett Now: Critical Approaches to His Novels, Poetry, and Plays*. Chicago and London, 1970.
Gontarski, S. E. "Literary Allusions in *Happy Days*." *On Beckett: Essays and Criticism*. New York, 1986. 308–24.
Hayman, Ronald. *Samuel Beckett*. London, 1968.
Kenner, Hugh. *Samuel Beckett: A Critical Study*. New York, 1961.
Lahr, John. "The Language of Silence." *Up Against the Fourth Wall: Essays on Modern Theatre*. New York, 1970. 50–77.